3.50

MAP 2 – PAUL'S TRAVELS (TRIPS 1 AND 2)   **683**

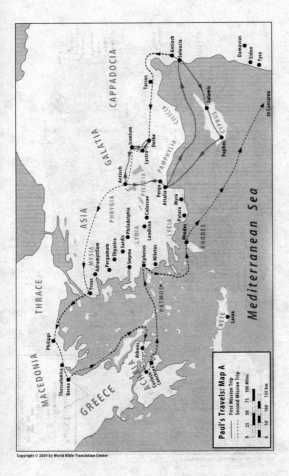

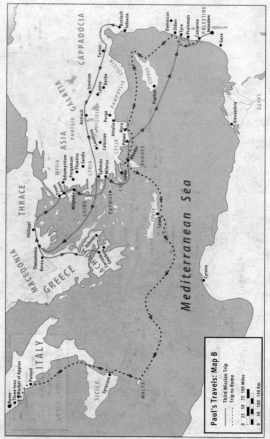

Paul's Travels: Map B
Third Mission Trip
Trip to Rome
0 25 50 75 100 Miles
0 50 100 150 Km

04205

New Testament with Psalms and Proverbs:
Easy-to-Read Version
Revised Edition

Download free electronic copies of
World Bible Translation Center's Bibles
and New Testaments at:

www.wbtc.org

This New Testament with Psalms and Proverbs is from the *Holy Bible: Easy-to Read Version (Revised Edition)*, copyright © 2005 World Bible Translation Center.

This copyrighted material may be quoted up to 1,000 verses without written permission. However, the extent of quotation must not comprise a complete book nor should it amount to more than 50% of the work in which it is quoted. This copyright notice must appear on the title or copyright page:

"Taken from the NEW TESTAMENT WITH PSALMS AND PROVERBS: EASY-TO-READ VERSION (Revised Edition) © 2005 by World Bible Translation Center, Inc. and used by permission."

When quotations from the ERV are used in non-saleable media, such as church bulletins, orders of service, posters, transparencies or similar media, a complete copyright notice is not required, but the initials (ERV) must appear at the end of each quotation.

Requests for permission to use quotations or reprints in excess of 1,000 verses or more than 50% of the work in which they are quoted, or other permission requests, must be directed to and approved in writing by World Bible Translation Center, Inc.

World Bible Translation Center, Inc.
P.O. Box 820648
Fort Worth, Texas 76182-0648
1-888-542-4253

ISBN 1-932438-03-3 (Flex Cover)
ISBN 1-932438-04-1 (Vivella)

New Testament

with

Psalms & Proverbs

Easy-to-Read Version
Translated from the Original Languages

World Bible Translation Center

Old Testament
Abbreviations

New Testament
Contents

39   29

Preface

This special version of the New Testament is for those who want an English translation that accurately expresses the full meaning of the original text in a style that is clear and easy to understand. It is especially helpful to those who have limited experience with English, including children and people who are just learning English. It is designed to help such people overcome or avoid the most common difficulties in reading with understanding.

The writers of Scripture, especially those who produced the New Testament writings, showed by the language style they used that they were interested in good communication. The translators of this English version considered this an important example to follow. So they worked to express the meaning of the Biblical text in a form that would be simple and natural. They used language that, instead of working as a barrier to understanding, would provide a key to unlock the truths of the Scriptures to a large segment of the English-speaking world.

The translation is based directly on the original languages of Scripture. In the case of the New Testament, the source text was that which is found in both the United Bible Societies' *Greek New Testament* (fourth revised edition, 1993) and the Nestle-Aland *Novum Testamentum Graece* (twenty-seventh edition, 1993). For the Old Testament books of Psalms and Proverbs, the translators followed the Hebrew Masoretic Text as it is found in the latest printed edition of *Biblia Hebraica Stuttgartensia* (1984), while referring occasionally to some earlier readings in the Dead Sea Scrolls. In some cases, they also followed the Septuagint (LXX), the Greek translation of the Old Testament, where it has readings that are actually earlier than any known Hebrew manuscript. The occasional variation from these printed editions was guided by reference to the findings of more recent scholarship.

Several special features are used to aid understanding. Brief explanations or synonyms (italicized within parentheses) sometimes follow difficult or ambiguous words in the text. If a word or phrase needs fuller explanation, it is specially marked in one of two ways: (1) If its usage is unique or unusual, it is marked by a letter of the alphabet (^{a}) linking it to a footnote that provides an explanation or important information. Included in such footnotes are references to Scripture quotations and information about alternate readings when significant differences occur in the ancient manuscripts. (2) If it is a word that occurs frequently with the same meaning, its first occurrence in a section is marked with an asterisk (*) indicating that an explanation can be found in a Word List at the end of the book.

In the Old Testament books two different words are translated "Lord." One of these is printed with all capital letters (LORD), as in most modern translations. This represents the Hebrew YHWH, which in some versions has been transliterated into English as "Jehovah" or "YAHWEH." In a few cases, where YHWH is obviously used as the name of God or in place names, it is translated "YAHWEH." When the word "Lord" contains lower case letters, it usually represents part of the Hebrew word *adonai*, which means "my Lord." When it occurs together with YHWH, the combination is usually translated "My Lord GOD." In cases where the speaker does not recognize that the one being addressed is God, *adonai* may be translated "Sir." The same is true in the New Testament for the Greek word *kurios*, which may be translated either "Lord" or "Sir," depending on the context.

Finally, in the Gospels, the first four books of the New Testament, the section headings are often followed by cross references. These identify where the same or similar material is found in one or more of the other Gospels.

Introduction

New Testament is a name that has been used for centuries to describe a group of writings or "books" that make up the second major part of the Bible. So the Bible is actually two collections of books. In fact, the word Bible comes from a Greek word meaning "books." The word translated "testament" was used to mean a "covenant" or "agreement." It refers to God's promise to bless his people. The Old Testament is the collection of writings that relate to the agreement God made with the descendants of Jacob (also called Israel) in the time of Moses. The New Testament is the collection of writings that relate to the agreement God made with all people who believe in Jesus Christ.

The Old Testament writings tell about the great things God did for the people of Israel and his plan for using them to bring his blessings to the whole world. These writings look forward to the coming of a savior or "Messiah" (see "Christ" in the Word List). The New Testament writings continue the Old Testament story. They describe the coming of that savior (Jesus Christ) and the meaning of his coming for all people. The Old Testament is important for understanding the New Testament, since it provides the necessary background. And the New Testament completes the story of salvation that began in the Old Testament.

THE OLD TESTAMENT

The Old Testament writings are a collection of thirty-nine different books produced by many different authors. They were written mainly in Hebrew, the language of ancient Israel. There are a few sections in Aramaic, an international language during the period that some of the later books were written. Portions of the Old Testament were written over 3500 years ago, and more than 1000 years passed between the writing of the first book and the last. In this collection there are books of law, history, prose, songs, poetry, and wise sayings. The books are often divided into three main sections: the Law, the Prophets, and the Holy Writings. The Law includes the first five books, which are also called "The Five Books of Moses." The Prophets and Holy Writings make up the rest of the books, but they are arranged differently in various editions.

The first book, *Genesis*, tells about the beginning of the world as we know it, the first man and woman, and their first sin against God. It tells about the increasing rebellion of people against God's will for them and about the Great Flood and the family God saved through that flood. Most importantly, it tells how God began his plan to establish a perfect spiritual "kingdom" where anyone who chooses can enjoy all the blessings God originally intended for the people he created. He began by choosing a man named Abraham, whose descendants would become the people God would use to bring about his plan.

THE STORY OF ABRAHAM

God made an agreement with Abraham, a great man of faith. In that agreement God promised to make Abraham the father of a great nation and to give him and his descendants the land of Canaan. Abraham was circumcised to show that he had accepted the agreement, and circumcision became the proof of the agreement between God and his people. Abraham did not know how God would do what he had promised but trusted him to make it happen. This pleased God very much.

God told Abraham to leave his home in Mesopotamia and led him to Canaan (later called the land of Israel, which was approximately the same geographical area known today as Palestine). In his old age Abraham had a son named Isaac, who had a son named Jacob. Jacob (Israel) had twelve sons and a daughter. This family became the nation of Israel, but it never forgot its tribal origin. It continued to refer to itself as the twelve tribes of Israel—descendants of the twelve sons of Jacob: Reuben, Simeon, Levi, Judah, Dan, Naphtali, Gad, Asher, Issachar, Zebulun, Joseph, and Benjamin. The three main ancestors—Abraham, Isaac, and Jacob (Israel)—are known as the "fathers" or "patriarchs" of Israel.

Abraham was also a "father" of another kind. Many times in ancient Israel, God called certain people to speak for him. These special people, or prophets, were God's representatives to the rest of his people. Through the prophets God gave the people of Israel promises, warnings, laws, teachings, lessons drawn from past experiences, and lessons based on future events. Abraham "the Hebrew" is the first prophet mentioned in the Scriptures.

ISRAEL SET FREE FROM SLAVERY

The family of Jacob (Israel) grew to include about 70 of his direct descendants. One of his sons, Joseph, became a high official in Egypt. Times were hard, so Jacob and his family moved to Egypt, where there was plenty of food and life was easier. This tribe of Hebrews grew to be a small nation, and Pharaoh (the title or name of the king of Egypt) made them serve as slaves. The book of Exodus tells about how finally, after 400 years, God used the prophet Moses to free the people of Israel from slavery in Egypt and take them back to Palestine. The price for freedom was high, but the Egyptians were the ones who had to pay. Pharaoh and all the families of Egypt lost their firstborn sons before the king finally agreed to let the people go free. The firstborn had to die so that the people could be set free—and the people of Israel later remembered this in many ways in their worship and sacrifices.

The people of Israel were ready for their trip to freedom. They had dressed for the escape from Egypt. Each family killed and roasted a lamb. They put the blood from the lamb on their doorposts as a special sign to God. They hurriedly baked bread without yeast and ate their meal. That night the Angel of the Lord went through the land. If the blood of the lamb was not on the doorposts, the firstborn of that family died. The people of Israel were set free. But as the Israelite slaves were about to leave Egypt, Pharaoh changed his mind. He sent his army to catch them and bring them back, but God saved his people. He divided the Red Sea, making a path through it to lead his people to freedom on the other side. Then he released the waters to destroy the army of Egypt that was following behind them. After that, at a mountain in the Sinai desert on the Arabian Peninsula, God made a special agreement with his people.

THE LAW OF MOSES

God's rescue of the people of Israel and his agreement with them at Sinai set this nation apart from all others. This agreement contained promises and laws for the people of Israel, all intended to prepare them to understand God's justice and goodness. A part of this agreement, known as the Ten Commandments, was written by God on two stone tablets and given to the people. These commands contain the basic principles for the kind of life God wanted the people of Israel to live, including their duty to God, family, and others.

The Ten Commandments and the rest of the rules and teachings given at Mount Sinai became known as "the Law of Moses" or simply "the Law." Many times these terms are used to refer to the first five books of the Scriptures and often to the entire Old Testament.

Besides the Ten Commandments and other rules of conduct, the Law of Moses contains rules about priests, sacrifices, worship, and holy days. These rules are found in the book of Leviticus. According to the Law of Moses, all priests and their helpers came from the tribe of Levi. These helpers were called "Levites." The most important priest was called the high priest.

The Law of Moses included instructions for building the Holy Tent (traditionally known as the "Tabernacle") or Meeting Tent, the place where the people of Israel went to worship God. It also has instructions for making all the things to be used in their worship. This prepared the Israelites for the building of the Temple, the holy building in Jerusalem on Mount Zion, where the people would later go to worship God. The rules about sacrifices and worship forced the people to see that they sinned against each other and against God. But they also gave the people a way to be forgiven and to be reunited with one another and with God. These sacrifices were symbolic, preparing the way for a better understanding of the sacrifice God was planning to give for all the people of the world.

The Law of Moses also contained instructions for celebrating a number of holy days or festivals. Each festival had its own special meaning. Some festivals were happy occasions to celebrate special times of the year, such as the harvest festivals of First Fruits, Shabuoth (Pentecost or the Festival of Weeks), and Succoth (the Festival of Shelters).

Other festivals were for remembering the wonderful things God had done for his people. Passover was this kind of holy day. Each family relived the escape from Egypt, gathering in their homes to remember this part of Israel's history and to sing songs of praise to God. A lamb was slaughtered and the meal prepared. Each cup of wine and piece of food reminded the people of the things God had done to save them from a life of pain and sadness.

One holy day, in particular, was very serious. Every year, on the Day of Atonement, the people had to remember the many wrong things they had done to others and to God. This was a day of sadness, and the people did not eat. But on that day the high priest offered special sacrifices to 'cover over' or atone for their sins.

The agreement between God and Israel was very important to the writers of the Old Testament. Almost all of the books of the Prophets and Holy Writings are based on the fact that the nation of Israel, and every citizen of Israel, had made a very special agreement with their God. They called it the "Agreement of the Lord" or simply "the Agreement." Their books of history interpret events in light of the Agreement: If the individual or nation was faithful to God and the Agreement, then God rewarded them. If the people abandoned the Agreement, then God punished them. God sent his prophets to remind the people of their agreement with him. The poets of Israel sang of the wonderful things God did for his obedient people, and they mourned the pain and punishments that came to those who disobeyed. These writers based their concepts of right and wrong on the teaching of the Agreement. And when innocent people suffered, the poets struggled to understand why.

THE KINGDOM OF ISRAEL

The story of ancient Israel is the story of people who were always leaving God, God rescuing the people, the people turning back to God and eventually leaving him again. This cycle began almost as soon as the people had accepted God's Agreement, and it was repeated again and again. At Mount

Sinai the people of Israel agreed to follow God, and then they rebelled and were forced to wander 40 years in the desert. Finally, Moses' helper, Joshua, led the people into the promised land. Then came the battles to gain control of the different areas and to settle the first parts of what later came to be known as the land of Israel. For the first few centuries after this settlement, the people were governed by local leaders called judges.

Eventually, the people wanted a king. The first king God appointed for them was Saul. But Saul did not obey God, so God chose a shepherd boy named David to be the new king. The prophet Samuel came and poured oil on his head, anointing him king of Israel. God promised David that the future kings of Israel would be his descendants from the tribe of Judah. David conquered the city of Jerusalem and made it his capital and the future site of the Temple. He organized the priests, prophets, song writers, musicians, and singers for the Temple worship. David even wrote many of the songs (or psalms) himself, but God did not let him build the Temple.

When David was old and about to die, with God's blessing he made his son Solomon king of Israel. David warned his son to always follow God and obey the Agreement. As king, Solomon built the Temple in Jerusalem that David had planned, and he expanded Israel's borders. At this time Israel was at the high point of its power. Solomon became famous, and Israel became strong.

JUDAH AND ISRAEL—THE DIVIDED KINGDOM

At Solomon's death there was disagreement and a struggle among the people, and the nation was divided. The northern ten tribes called themselves Israel. The southern tribes called themselves Judah. (The modern term "Jew" comes from this name.) Judah remained loyal to the Agreement, and David's family continued ruling in Jerusalem for several hundred years. In the northern kingdom (Israel) numerous kings and dynasties came and went, because the people did not follow the Agreement. The kings of Israel had several capital cities at various times, the last of which was Samaria. In order to strengthen their hold on the people, the kings of Israel changed the way to worship God. They chose new priests and built two new temples—one at Dan (on the northern border of Israel) and the other at Bethel (along Israel's border with Judah). There were many wars between Israel and Judah.

During this time of civil war and troubles, God sent many prophets to Judah and Israel. Some of the prophets were priests; others were farmers. Some were advisors to kings; others lived a much simpler life. Some of the prophets wrote their teachings or prophecies; many others did not. But all the prophets spoke for justice, fairness, and the need to depend on God for help.

Many prophets warned that the people would be defeated and scattered if they did not turn back to God. Some prophets saw visions of future glories as well as future punishments. Many of them looked forward to the time when a new king would come to rule the kingdom. Some saw this king as a descendant of David who would lead the people of God into a new Golden Age. Some spoke of this king as ruling forever over an eternal kingdom. Others saw him as a servant who would suffer many things in order to bring his people back to God. But all of them saw him as the Messiah, the one anointed (chosen) by God to bring in a new age.

THE DESTRUCTION OF ISRAEL AND JUDAH

The people of Israel did not listen to God's warnings. So in 722/721 B.C. Samaria fell to the invading Assyrians. The people of Israel were taken from their homes and scattered throughout the Assyrian empire, lost forever to their brothers and sisters in Judah. Then the Assyrians brought in foreigners to settle the land of Israel again. These people were taught about the religion of Judah and Israel, and many of them tried to follow the Agreement. These people came to be known as the Samaritans. The Assyrians tried to invade Judah. Many cities fell to the invaders, but God saved Jerusalem. The defeated king of Assyria returned to his homeland, and there he was murdered by two of his sons. So Judah was saved.

For a while the people of Judah changed. They began to obey God, but only for a short time. They, too, were finally defeated and scattered. The nation of Babylon rose to power and invaded Judah. At first they took only a few important people away as captives. But a few years later, in 587/586 B.C., they returned to destroy Jerusalem and the Temple. Some of the people escaped to Egypt, but most of them were taken as slaves to Babylon. Again God sent prophets to the people, and they began to listen. It seems that the destruction of the Temple and Jerusalem and the time of exile in Babylon brought about a real change in the people. The prophets spoke more and more about the new king and his kingdom. One of the prophets, Jeremiah, even spoke of a new agreement. This agreement would not be written on tablets of stone but would be in the hearts of God's people.

THE RETURN TO PALESTINE

Meanwhile, Cyrus came to power over the Medo-Persian empire and conquered Babylon. Cyrus allowed people to return to their homelands. So, after 70 years of exile, many of the people of Judah went back home. The people tried to rebuild their nation, but Judah remained small and weak. The people rebuilt the Temple, although it was not as beautiful as the one Solomon had built. Many of the people truly turned to God and began studying the Law, the writings of the prophets, and the other holy writings. Many men became scribes (or experts in the Law), who made copies of the Scriptures. Eventually, these men organized schools for studying the Scriptures. The people began meeting together on the Sabbath (Saturday) to study, pray, and worship God together. In their synagogues (meeting places) they studied the Scriptures, and many people began looking for the Messiah to come.

In the West, Alexander the Great gained control of Greece and soon conquered the world. He spread the Greek language as well as the customs and culture of Greece to many parts of the world. When he died, his kingdom was divided. Soon another empire grew and gained control of a large part of the known world, including Palestine, where the people of Judah lived.

The new rulers, the Romans, were often cruel and harsh, and the Jewish people were proud and defiant. In these troubled times there were many Jews who were looking for the Messiah to come in their own lifetime. They wanted to be ruled only by God and the Messiah that God had promised to send them. They did not understand that God planned to save the world through the Messiah. They thought that God's plan was to save the Jews from the world! Some were content to wait for God to send his Messiah. Others thought that they should "help" God establish his new kingdom by making sure that the law of Moses was observed and that the Temple, the land, and the Jewish people were kept pure. In order to make this happen, they were willing to suffer, to die, or to kill anyone, foreigners or other Jews, who threatened these goals. Such Jews eventually came to be known as "Zealots."

THE JEWISH RELIGIOUS GROUPS

By the first century B.C., the Law of Moses had become extremely important to the Jews. They had studied and argued over the Law. The people understood the Law in different ways, but many Jews were ready to die for that Law. There were three major religious groups among the Jews, and there were scribes in each group.

The Sadducees

One of the groups was called the Sadducees. This name probably comes from the name Zadok, the high priest in King David's time. Many of the priests and the people in authority were Sadducees. These men accepted only the Law (the five books of Moses) as their authority in religious matters. The Law of Moses taught many things about the priests and sacrifices, but it did not teach about life after death. So the Sadducees did not believe that people would ever be raised from death.

The Pharisees

Another group was called the Pharisees. This name comes from a Hebrew word meaning "to interpret (explain)" or "to separate." These men tried to teach or interpret the Law of Moses to the common people. The Pharisees believed that there was an oral tradition going back to Moses' time. They believed that people of each generation could interpret the Law in a way that would allow it to meet the needs of that generation. This meant that the Pharisees could accept not only the Law of Moses as their authority, but also the Prophets, the Holy Writings, and even their own traditions. These men tried very hard to follow the Law and their traditions. So they were very careful about what they ate and what they touched. They were careful about washing their hands and bathing. They also believed that people would be raised from death, because they understood many of the prophets to say that would happen.

The Essenes

The third major group was the Essenes. Many of the priests in Jerusalem did not live the way God wanted them to. Also, the Romans had appointed many of the high priests, and some of these men were not qualified according to the Law of Moses. Because of this, the Essenes did not think the worship and sacrifices were being done properly in the Jerusalem Temple. So they moved out into the Judean desert to live. They formed their own community, where only other Essenes could come and live. They fasted, prayed, and waited for God to send the Messiah to purify the Temple and the priesthood. Many scholars believe that the Essenes were connected in some way with the Qumran Community and the many ancient writings (including the Dead Sea Scrolls) found at Qumran and other places in that area of the Judean desert.

THE NEW TESTAMENT

God had begun his plan. He had chosen a special nation. He had made an agreement with those people that would prepare them to understand his justice and his goodness. Through prophets and poets he had revealed his plan to bless the world by establishing a perfect spiritual "kingdom" based on a new and better agreement. This plan would begin with the coming of the promised Messiah. The prophets had spoken of his coming in great detail. They had told where the Messiah would be born, the type of person he would be, and the work he would have to do. It was now time for the Messiah to come and begin the new agreement.

The writings of the New Testament describe how God's new agreement was revealed and put into effect by Jesus, who was the Christ (meaning "the Anointed One," the Messiah). They teach that this agreement was to be for all people. And they tell how people in the first century responded to God's kind offer of love and became a part of the new agreement. Many things that were part of the first agreement are given new meaning under the new agreement, especially ideas related to Israelite worship, such as temple, priesthood, and sacrifice. These writings give instructions to God's people about how to live in this world. They also describe the blessings that God promises his people for a full and meaningful life here and for life with him after death.

The New Testament writings include twenty-seven different "books" by at least eight different writers. All of them wrote in Greek, which was widely spoken in the first-century world. More than half of the total writing was done by four apostles, men chosen by Jesus to be his special representatives or helpers. Three of these, Matthew, John, and Peter, were among the twelve closest followers of Jesus during his life on earth. The fourth, Paul, was chosen as an apostle later by Jesus through a miraculous appearance.

The first four books, called "Gospels," are separate accounts of the life and death of Jesus Christ. Generally, these books emphasize Jesus' teaching, the purpose of his appearance on earth, and the special significance of his death, rather than just the historical facts of his life. This is especially true of the fourth book, the Gospel of John. The first three Gospels are very similar in content. In fact, much of the material in one is found in one or both of the others. Each writer, however, may be writing to a different audience and seems to have a slightly different goal in view.

The four Gospels are followed by Acts, a history of the events following the death of Jesus. It describes how God's offer of love to all people was announced throughout the world by Jesus' followers. It tells how the proclaiming of this "gospel" or "Good News" resulted in the conversion of thousands of people throughout Palestine and the Roman world to faith in Jesus Christ. The book of Acts was written by a medical doctor named Luke, an eyewitness of much that he recorded. Luke was also the author of the third Gospel. His two books make a logical unit with Acts being the natural sequel to his account of the life of Jesus.

Following Acts, there is a collection of letters written to individuals or groups of believers in Christ. These letters were sent from leaders in the faith, such as Paul and Peter, two of Jesus' apostles. These letters were written to help the people of that time deal with problems they were facing. They serve to inform, correct, teach, and encourage not only those people but all who become followers of Jesus in regard to their faith, their life together, and their life in the world.

The final book of the New Testament, Revelation, is very different from all the others, although its purpose is similar to that of other letters to churches. Most of it is written in a fantasy-like style using symbolic images, many from the Old Testament.

Its central aim is to encourage followers of Christ, assuring them of victory over evil.

THE BOOKS OF THE NEW TESTAMENT

The following additional information on each of the New Testament books should be helpful in preparation for reading each book:

Matthew. Matthew is the name of one of Jesus' twelve closest followers. Matthew was a Jewish tax collector when Jesus chose him as one of his apostles. Matthew's writing shows the influence of his Jewish background and interests. He seems especially interested in the fulfillment of Old Testament prophecies in the life of Jesus. He really centers his book, however, around the teaching of Jesus.

Mark. John Mark was a young companion to some of the apostles. Mark's style of writing is brief and full of action. Unlike Matthew and Luke, he shows very little interest in Jesus' teachings. Mark apparently aimed his writing at the Roman, non-Jewish mind and centers on the actions of Jesus that prove him to be the Son of God. Mark seems mainly interested in people knowing that Jesus came to earth for the purpose of saving them from the consequences of sin.

Luke. This is one of two books written by a traveling companion of the apostle Paul. Luke was a well-educated medical doctor and a talented writer. He seems familiar with Mark's Gospel and much of the material in the Gospel of Matthew, but he chooses to include mainly the parts that would be attractive and understandable to his non-Jewish audience. More than the other Gospel writers, he seems interested in an orderly account of Jesus' life as a historical reality. Emphasis, however, is not on the events in Jesus' life, but on Jesus himself as a loving, caring person who taught people the real meaning of life and who reached out to the needs of all people with power to help and save.

John. This Gospel is very different from the first three. This is seen immediately from the beautiful but profound introduction. John introduces much material that is not found in the other Gospels. His main interest is in proving Jesus to be the Messiah (Christ), the divine Son of God and savior of the world.

Acts. This book, written by Luke, takes up where his first book ends. It begins with Jesus' instructions to his followers to go throughout the world announcing the "Good News," a message about God's love for all people. Jesus wanted them to tell what they now knew about his divine mission to save people from the consequences of their wrongdoing. Luke traces the exciting fulfillment of this assignment, centering on the activities of two main characters, Peter and Paul. He shows how the movement that began shortly after the death and resurrection of Jesus spread rapidly from a small beginning in Jerusalem into the surrounding regions of Judea and Samaria, and eventually to the farthest areas of the Roman empire.

The next group of New Testament writings consists of the Letters of Paul. The apostle Paul (originally named Saul) was a well-educated Jew from Tarsus in Cilicia (Southeast Turkey). Educated in Jerusalem, he was a leader among the Pharisees, and he was violently opposed to the movement made up of followers of Jesus Christ. Jesus appeared to him in a vision, however, and changed the whole direction of his life. About ten years later, he began traveling all over the Roman world to proclaim the message about Christ. During this period he wrote many letters to churches (groups of believers in Christ) and to individuals. Thirteen of these letters are included in the New Testament.

Paul's letter to the **Romans** is the longest and fullest of all his letters. Most of his letters are to groups of believers in cities where he had pioneered in teaching people about Christ and forming churches. However, when he wrote this letter to "Christ followers" living in Rome, he had never been there. He was in Greece about 57 A.D., and not being able to travel on to Rome as he had wanted, he wrote his teaching in this letter. Besides dealing with a number of other issues, he includes a carefully-written presentation of the fundamental truths regarding faith in Jesus.

The letters of **1 Corinthians** and **2 Corinthians** are two of several that Paul wrote to the believers in Corinth, a city in southern Greece. In the first of these two letters, Paul deals with some problems that had developed among the believers there and answers questions that some of them had sent to him. Among the many subjects Paul covers are unity, marriage, sexual sin, divorce, and Jewish customs. Of particular interest is chapter 13, Paul's famous writing on love, which he sees as the solution to their problems. The second letter follows up on the Corinthians' response to the first letter.

Paul's letter to the **Galatians** deals with a problem of a different kind among the believers in Galatia. Paul had proclaimed the message about Christ there and had formed some churches. Then a group of Jewish teachers went there and taught some ideas that were very different from the true teaching of Christ. The problem was a crucial one, because it involved the basis for a person's good relationship with God. Being unable to travel to Galatia at the time, Paul strongly confronted the problem in this letter. Like his letter to the Romans, it also includes a presentation of the basics of faith in Jesus, but for a different reason.

Paul wrote the letter to the **Ephesians** while he was in prison, but it is not certain where or when. The theme of this letter is God's plan to bring all people together under the rule of Christ. Paul encourages believers to live their lives in harmony with each other and with complete commitment to God's purpose for them.

Paul's letter to the **Philippians** was also written from prison, probably from Rome. Paul was facing many troubles at the time, but he trusted God, and this letter is full of confidence and joy. Paul wrote to encourage the believers in Philippi and to thank them for some financial help they had sent to him.

Paul wrote the letter to the **Colossians** to confront some false teachings that were troubling the church in Colossae, a city in Asia Minor (modern Turkey). Parts of this letter are similar to the letter to the Ephesians. Paul gives some practical lessons for living the way a follower of Christ should.

The letters of **1 Thessalonians** and **2 Thessalonians** were probably among the first of Paul's letters. On Paul's first trip to Macedonia (northern Greece), he told the people of Thessalonica the message about Christ. Many people believed, but Paul had to leave after a short time. Paul wrote to encourage the people in their new faith. He also discusses some things the people did not understand, especially concerning Christ's expected return. The second letter continues this discussion.

The letters of **1 Timothy**, **2 Timothy**, and **Titus** were written toward the end of Paul's life to two of his close companions. Paul had left Timothy in Ephesus and Titus in Crete to help with some problems about the organization and function of the churches there. Apparently Timothy and Titus were to help the churches in these places prepare for independent leadership and operation. In the first letter to Timothy and the letter to Titus, Paul gives some guidelines for the selection of leaders as well as instructions for dealing with various problems and situations. The second letter to Timothy, written from prison as Paul faced what he felt was the end of his life, is very personal. The letter is full of advice and encouragement as he urges Timothy to follow his own example of faith, courage, and endurance.

Philemon is a short letter written by Paul at the same time he wrote the letter to the Colossians. Philemon, a believer in Colossae, was the master of a runaway slave Onesimus, who had become a follower of Christ through Paul's influence. The letter is Paul's appeal to Philemon to forgive Onesimus and welcome him back.

In addition to the letters of Paul, there are eight letters written by other followers of Jesus. The author of **Hebrews** is unknown, but it is clear that is was written to Jewish believers in Christ. They were in danger of being pulled away from their belief in Jesus. This letter was written to encourage and strengthen the faith of these believers. The writer emphasizes the superiority of Jesus Christ over all other beings and persons. He teaches that the eternal priesthood of Jesus Christ and the "better agreement" are superior to the Old Testament priesthood and the "first agreement." The writer closes by encouraging the people to trust in God and to live for Him.

The word "practical" is almost always used in describing the letter of **James**, "a servant" of God and Jesus. Some people think this is one of Jesus' brothers. The Jewish background of James is clear as he teaches about fairness and justice, helping the poor, friendship with the world, wisdom, self-control, trials and temptations, doing and hearing, and faith and works. He also encourages people to pray and be patient.

The letters of **1 Peter** and **2 Peter** were written by the apostle Peter to followers of Christ who were living in many different places. Peter teaches such believers about their living hope and their real home in heaven. Because of the hard times they are facing, Peter assures them that God has not forgotten them. They will be better because of their suffering. He reminds them that God has blessed them and has forgiven their sins through Jesus Christ. They should respond by living right. In his second letter the apostle confronts false teachers. He teaches about true knowledge and the second coming of Christ.

The letters of **1 John**, **2 John**, and **3 John** were written by the apostle John. John's letters of love assure the believers that God will always accept them. John teaches that people show their love to God by loving the people around them and by doing the things God wants them to do. The second and third letters appeal to Christ's followers to love one another, and they warn against false teachers and ungodly behavior.

The writer of the letter **Jude** is a brother of James and probably a brother of Jesus. This letter encourages faithfulness and speaks out against troublemakers and false teachers.

The **Revelation** of the apostle John begins with words of criticism, encouragement, and instruction addressed to groups of believers in seven different cities of Asia Minor (modern Turkey). But it continues with a picture of spiritual warfare that is of interest to all followers of Christ. It uses highly figurative language as it tells of visions seen by the author. Many of the figures and images are from the Old Testament and can best be understood by comparing them to Old Testament writings. This last book of the New Testament writings assures believers of ultimate victory over the forces of evil through the power of God and Jesus Christ, their leader and helper.

THE OLD TESTAMENT BOOKS OF PSALMS AND PROVERBS

The book of **Psalms** is a collection of songs and poetic prayers written by many different people over a period of hundreds of years. Most of them are addressed to God, although some are about God or about people and their relationship to God. Some express the feelings of a single person, while others speak for all of God's people. Many of these hymns were used by the people of Israel in their meetings for worship or by individuals for praise and prayer.

The Psalms were often quoted by Jesus as Scripture and were used by his followers as fitting expressions of their faith and devotion to God. They were the first songbook for believers in Christ.

The book of **Proverbs** is a collection of wise sayings from the time of Solomon, who wrote most of them. Solomon was the third king of Israel about a thousand years before the time of the New Testament writings. These proverbs are short sayings written in poetic form, making them enjoyable to read and easy to remember. Like many of the letters to believers in the New Testament, these proverbs teach God's people how to live right. They provide godly advice about practical matters to help people make wise choices and enjoy happier lives.

THE BIBLE AND TODAY'S READER

Today's reader of the Bible should keep in mind that these books were written thousands of years ago for people who lived in cultures very different from ours today. Many of the historical accounts, illustrations, and references they contain can only be understood with some knowledge of the time and culture in which the writers lived. Generally, however, the writings focus on principles that are universally true. For example, Jesus told a story about a man sowing grain in a field that had different types of soil conditions. Those exact conditions may be unfamiliar to a person today, but the lesson Jesus draws from the example is appropriate for people in any time or place.

The modern reader may find the world of the Bible somewhat strange. The customs, the attitudes, and the way people talk may be quite unfamiliar. It is only reasonable to judge these things by their experience and ideals, not by today's standards. It is also important to note that the Bible was not written as a book of science. It was written mainly to describe historical events and present the significance of those events in ways that relate to all people. Its teachings present universal truths that are beyond the realm of science. It remains relevant even in our own time, because it deals with people's basic spiritual needs, which never change.

If you read the Bible with an open mind, you can expect to receive many benefits. You will gain knowledge about the history and culture of the ancient world. You will learn about the life and teachings of Jesus Christ and what it means to be his follower. You will gain basic spiritual insights and learn practical lessons for living a dynamic and joy-filled life. You will find answers to life's most difficult questions. There are, therefore, many good reasons for reading this book, and if you read it with a sincere and receptive spirit, you may well discover God's purpose for your life.

Matthew

The Family History of Jesus
(Lk. 3:23b–38)

1 ¹This is the family history of Jesus Christ. He came from the family of David* and Abraham.*

² Abraham was the father of Isaac.
   Isaac was the father of Jacob.*
   Jacob was the father of Judah and his brothers.
³ Judah was the father of Perez and Zerah. (Their mother was Tamar.)
   Perez was the father of Hezron.
   Hezron was the father of Ram.
⁴ Ram was the father of Amminadab.
   Amminadab was the father of Nahshon.
   Nahshon was the father of Salmon.
⁵ Salmon was the father of Boaz. (His mother was Rahab.)
   Boaz was the father of Obed. (His mother was Ruth.)
   Obed was the father of Jesse.
⁶ Jesse was the father of King David.
   David was the father of Solomon. (His mother had been Uriah's wife.)
⁷ Solomon was the father of Rehoboam.
   Rehoboam was the father of Abijah.
   Abijah was the father of Asa.
⁸ Asa was the father of Jehoshaphat.
   Jehoshaphat was the father of Jehoram.
   Jehoram was the father of Uzziah.
⁹ Uzziah was the father of Jotham.
   Jotham was the father of Ahaz.
   Ahaz was the father of Hezekiah.
¹⁰ Hezekiah was the father of Manasseh.
   Manasseh was the father of Amon.
   Amon was the father of Josiah.
¹¹ Josiah was the grandfather of Jehoiachin*ᵃ* and his brothers who lived during the time that the people were taken away to Babylon.
¹² After they were taken to Babylon:
   Jehoiachin was the father of Shealtiel.
   Shealtiel was the grandfather of Zerubbabel.

*ᵃ**1:11** Jehoiachin Literally, "Jechoniah," another name for Jehoiachin.*

13 Zerubbabel was the father of Abiud.
   Abiud was the father of Eliakim.
   Eliakim was the father of Azor.
14 Azor was the father of Zadok.
   Zadok was the father of Achim.
   Achim was the father of Eliud.
15 Eliud was the father of Eleazar.
   Eleazar was the father of Matthan.
   Matthan was the father of Jacob.
16 Jacob was the father of Joseph.
   Joseph was the husband of Mary,
   and Mary was the mother of Jesus,
   who is called the Christ.*

17So there were fourteen generations from Abraham to David. There were also fourteen generations from David until the people were taken away to Babylon. And there were fourteen more from the time the people were taken to Babylon until Christ was born.

The Birth of Jesus Christ
(Lk. 2:1–7)

18This is how the birth of Jesus Christ happened. His mother Mary was engaged to marry Joseph. But before they married, he learned that she was expecting a baby. (She was pregnant by the power of the Holy Spirit.*) 19Mary's husband, Joseph, was a good man. He did not want to cause her public disgrace, so he planned to divorce her secretly.

20But after Joseph thought about this, an angel from the Lord came to him in a dream. The angel said, "Joseph, son of David,* don't be afraid to accept Mary to be your wife. The baby inside her is from the Holy Spirit. 21She will give birth to a son. You will name him Jesus.*a Give him that name because he will save his people from their sins."

22All this happened to make clear the full meaning of what the Lord said through the prophet*: 23"The virgin* will be pregnant and will give birth to a son. They will name him Immanuel."*b (Immanuel means "God with us.")

24When Joseph woke up, he did what the Lord's angel told him to do. He married Mary. 25But Joseph did not have sexual relations with her until her son was born. And he named him Jesus.

Wise Men Come to Visit Jesus

2 1Jesus was born in the town of Bethlehem in Judea during the time when Herod* was king. After Jesus was born, some wise men* from the east came to Jerusalem. 2They asked

---

a1:21 Jesus The name Jesus means "the Lord (Yahweh) saves." *b1:23* Quote from Isa. 7:14.

people, "Where is the child that has been born to be the king of the Jews? We saw the star that shows he was born. We saw it rise in the sky in the east and have come to worship him."

³When King Herod heard about this, it upset him as well as everyone else in Jerusalem. ⁴Herod called a meeting of all the leading Jewish priests* and teachers of the law. He asked them where the Christ* would be born. ⁵They answered, "In the town of Bethlehem in Judea, just as the prophet* wrote:

⁶ 'Bethlehem, in the land of Judah,
　　you are important among the rulers of Judah.
　Yes, a ruler will come from you,
　　and that ruler will lead Israel, my people.'"　　　*Micah 5:2*

⁷Then Herod had a private meeting with the wise men from the east. He learned from them the exact time they first saw the star. ⁸Then he sent them to Bethlehem. He said, "Go and look carefully for the child. When you find him, come tell me. Then I can go worship him too."

⁹After the wise men heard the king, they left. They saw the same star they had seen in the east, and they followed it. The star went before them until it stopped above the place where the child was. ¹⁰They were very happy and excited to see the star.

¹¹The wise men came to the house where the child was with his mother Mary. They bowed down and worshiped him. Then they opened the boxes of gifts they had brought for him. They gave him treasures of gold, frankincense,* and myrrh.* ¹²But God warned the wise men in a dream not to go back to Herod. So they went home to their own country a different way.

Jesus' Parents Take Him to Egypt

¹³After the wise men* left, an angel from the Lord came to Joseph in a dream. The angel said, "Get up! Take the child with his mother and escape to Egypt. Herod* wants to kill the child and will soon start looking for him. Stay in Egypt until I tell you to come back."

¹⁴So Joseph got ready and left for Egypt with the child and the mother. They left during the night. ¹⁵Joseph stayed in Egypt until Herod died. This gave full meaning to what the Lord said through the prophet*: "I called my son to come out of Egypt."ᵃ

Herod Kills the Baby Boys in Bethlehem

¹⁶Herod* saw that the wise men* had fooled him, and he was very angry. So he gave an order to kill all the baby boys in Bethlehem and the whole area around Bethlehem. Herod had learned from the wise men the time the baby was born. It was now two years from that time. So he said to kill all the boys

ᵃ**2:15** Quote from Hos. 11:1.

who were two years old and younger. [17]This gave full meaning to what God said through the prophet* Jeremiah:

[18]"A sound was heard in Ramah—
    bitter crying and great sadness.
  Rachel cries for her children,
    and she cannot be comforted,
      because her children are gone."

                                                    Jeremiah 31:15

Joseph and Mary Return From Egypt

[19]While Joseph was in Egypt, Herod* died. An angel from the Lord came to Joseph in a dream [20]and said, "Get up! Take the child with his mother and go to Israel. Those who were trying to kill the child are now dead."

[21]So Joseph took the child and the mother and went to Israel. [22]But he heard that Archelaus was now king in Judea. Archelaus became king when his father Herod died. So Joseph was afraid to go there. Then, after being warned in a dream, he went away to the area of Galilee. [23]He went to a town called Nazareth and lived there. This gave full meaning to what God said through the prophets.* God said the Christ* would be called a Nazarene.*[a]*

John Prepares the Way for Jesus
(Mk. 1:1–8; Lk. 3:1–9, 15–17; Jn. 1:19–28)

3 [1]When it was the right time, John the Baptizer* began telling people a message from God. This was out in the desert area of Judea. [2]John said, "Change your hearts and lives, because God's kingdom* is coming soon." [3]John is the one Isaiah the prophet* was talking about when he said,

"There is someone shouting in the desert:
  'Prepare the way for the Lord.
  Make the road straight for him.'"   *Isaiah 40:3*

[4]John's clothes were made from camel's hair, and he had a leather belt around his waist. For food, he ate locusts* and wild honey. [5]People came to John from Jerusalem and the rest of Judea and from all the areas along the Jordan River. [6]They confessed the bad things they had done, and John baptized* them in the Jordan.

[7]Many Pharisees* and Sadducees* came to the place where John was baptizing people. When John saw them, he said, "You are all snakes! Who warned you to run away from the punishment that God is about to send? [8]Change your hearts! And show by the way you live that you have changed. [9]I know what you are thinking. You want to say, 'but Abraham* is our

---

[a] **2:23** *Nazarene* A person from the city of Nazareth. This name sounds like the Hebrew word for "branch." So Matthew may be referring to the promise of a "branch" of David's family. See Isa. 11:1.

father!' That means nothing. I tell you, God could make children for Abraham from these rocks. ¹⁰The ax is now ready to cut down the trees.ᵃ Every tree that does not produce good fruit will be cut down and thrown into the fire.

¹¹"I baptize you with water to show that you changed your hearts and lives. But there is someone coming later who is able to do more than I can. I am not good enough to be the slave who takes off his sandals. He will baptize you with the Holy Spirit* and with fire. ¹²He will come ready to clean the grain.ᵇ He will separate the good grain from the straw, and he will put the good part into his barn. Then he will burn the useless part with a fire that cannot be stopped."

Jesus Is Baptized by John
(Mk. 1:9–11; Lk. 3:21–22)

¹³Then Jesus came from Galilee to the Jordan River. He came to John, wanting John to baptize* him. ¹⁴But John tried to find a way to say no. He said, "Why do you come to me to be baptized? I should be baptized by you!"

¹⁵Jesus answered, "Let it be this way for now. We should do whatever God says is right." Then John agreed.

¹⁶So Jesus was baptized. As soon as he came up out of the water, the sky opened, and he saw God's Spirit coming down on him like a dove. ¹⁷A voice from heaven said, "This is my Son, the one I love. I am very pleased with him."

The Temptation of Jesus
(Mk. 1:12–13; Lk. 4:1–13)

4 ¹Then the Spirit* led Jesus into the desert. He was taken there to be tempted by the devil. ²Jesus ate nothing for 40 days and nights. After this, he was very hungry. ³The devilᶜ came to tempt him and said, "If you are the Son of God, tell these rocks to become bread."

⁴Jesus answered him, "The Scriptures* say,

'It is not just bread that keeps people alive.
    Their lives depend on what God says.'"   *Deuteronomy 8:3*

⁵Then the devil led Jesus to the holy* city of Jerusalem and put him on a high place at the edge of the Temple* area. ⁶He said to Jesus, "If you are the Son of God, jump off, because the Scriptures say,

'God will command his angels to help you,
    and their hands will catch you,
    so that you will not hit your foot on a rock.'"   *Psalm 91:11–12*

ᵃ3:10 *trees* The people who don't obey God. They are like "trees" that will be cut down. ᵇ3:12 *clean the grain* Meaning that Jesus will separate the good people from those who are bad. ᶜ4:3 *The devil* Literally, "The tempter."

[7]Jesus answered, "The Scriptures also say,

'You must not test the Lord your God.'"   *Deuteronomy 6:16*

[8]Then the devil led Jesus to the top of a very high mountain and showed him all the kingdoms of the world and all the wonderful things in them. [9]The devil said, "If you will bow down and worship me, I will give you all these things."

[10]Jesus said to him, "Get away from me, Satan*! The Scriptures say,

'You must worship the Lord your God.
    Serve only him!'"   *Deuteronomy 6:13*

[11]So the devil left him. Then some angels came to Jesus and helped him.

Jesus Begins His Work in Galilee
(Mk. 1:14–15; Lk. 4:14–15)

[12]Jesus heard that John was put in prison, so he went back to Galilee. [13]But he did not stay in Nazareth. He went to live in Capernaum,* a town near Lake Galilee in the area near Zebulun and Naphtali. [14]He did this to give full meaning to what the prophet* Isaiah said,

[15]"Listen, land of Zebulun and land of Naphtali,
    lands by the road that goes to the sea,
        the area past the Jordan River—
    Galilee, where those from other nations live.
[16] The people who live in spiritual darkness
    have seen a great light.
The light has shined for those
    who live in the land that is as dark as a grave."

Isaiah 9:1–2

[17]From that time Jesus began to tell people his message: "Change your hearts and lives, because God's kingdom* is coming soon."

Jesus Chooses Some Followers
(Mk. 1:16–20; Lk. 5:1–11)

[18]As Jesus was walking by Lake Galilee, he saw two brothers, Simon (called Peter) and Simon's brother Andrew. These brothers were fishermen, and they were fishing in the lake with a net. [19]Jesus said to them, "Come, follow me, and I will make you a different kind of fishermen. You will bring in people, not fish." [20]Simon and Andrew immediately left their nets and followed him.

[21]Jesus continued walking by Lake Galilee. He saw two other brothers, James and John, the sons of Zebedee. They were in a boat with their father Zebedee. They were preparing their nets to catch fish. Jesus told the brothers to come with him. [22]So

they immediately left the boat and their father, and they followed Jesus.

Jesus Teaches and Heals the People
(Lk. 6:17–19)

²³Jesus went everywhere in the country of Galilee. He taught in the synagogues* and told the Good News about God's kingdom.ᵃ And he healed all the people's diseases and sicknesses. ²⁴The news about Jesus spread all over Syria, and people brought to him all those who were sick. They were suffering from different kinds of diseases and pain. Some had demons* inside them, some suffered from seizures, and some were paralyzed. Jesus healed them all. ²⁵Large crowds followed him—people from Galilee, the Ten Towns,* Jerusalem, Judea, and the area across the Jordan River.

Jesus Teaches the People
(Lk. 6:20–23)

5 ¹When Jesus saw the crowds of people there, he went up on a hill and sat down. His followers came and sat next to him. ²Then Jesus began teaching the people. He said,

³ "What great blessings there are for those who know
    they are spiritually in need.ᵇ
  God's kingdom* belongs to them.
⁴ What great blessings there are for those who are sad now.
  God will comfort them.
⁵ What great blessings there are for those who are humble.
  They will be given the land God promised.ᶜ
⁶ What great blessings there are for those who want
    to do right more than anything else.ᵈ
  God will fully satisfy them.
⁷ What great blessings there are for those who show
    mercy to others.
  Mercy will be given to them.
⁸ What great blessings there are for those whose thoughts
    are pure.
  They will be with God.
⁹ What great blessings there are for those who work
    to bring peace.
  God will call them his sons and daughters.
¹⁰ What great blessings there are for those who suffer
    persecution for doing what is right.
  God's kingdom belongs to them.

ᵃ**4:23** *God's kingdom* Literally, "the kingdom." See "God's kingdom" in the Word List. ᵇ**5:3** *those … in need* Literally, "the poor in spirit." ᶜ**5:5** *They will … promised* This is the meaning of these words in Ps. 37:11. Here, they probably refer to a spiritual "promised land," but they can also mean "The earth will belong to them." ᵈ**5:6** *want … more than anything else* Literally, "hunger and thirst for righteousness."

¹¹"People will insult you and hurt you. They will lie and say all kinds of evil things about you because you follow me. But when they do that, know that God will bless you. ¹²Be happy about it. Be very glad because you have a great reward waiting for you in heaven. People did these same bad things to the prophets* who lived before you.

You Are Like Salt and Light
(Mk. 9:50; Lk. 14:34–35)

¹³"You are the salt of the earth. But if the salt loses its taste, it cannot be made salty again. Salt is useless if it loses its salty taste. It will be thrown out where people will just walk on it.

¹⁴"You are the light that shines for the world to see. You are like a city built on a hill that cannot be hidden. ¹⁵People don't hide a lamp under a bowl. They put it on a lampstand. Then the light shines for everyone in the house. ¹⁶In the same way, you should be a light for other people. Live so that they will see the good things you do and praise your Father in heaven.

Jesus and the Old Testament Writings

¹⁷"Don't think that I have come to destroy the law of Moses* or the teaching of the prophets.* I have come not to destroy their teachings but to give full meaning to them. ¹⁸I assure you that nothing will disappear from the law until heaven and earth are gone. The law will not lose even the smallest letter or the smallest part of a letter until it has all been done.

¹⁹"A person should obey every command in the law, even one that does not seem important. Whoever refuses to obey any command and teaches others not to obey it will be the least important in God's kingdom.* But whoever obeys the law and teaches others to obey it will be great in God's kingdom. ²⁰I tell you that you must do better than the teachers of the law and the Pharisees.* If you are not better people than they are, you will not enter God's kingdom.

Jesus Teaches About Anger

²¹"You have heard that it was said to our people long ago, 'You must not murder anyone.ᵃ Any person who commits murder will be judged.' ²²But I tell you, don't be angry with anyone. If you are angry with others, you will be judged. And if you insult someone, you will be judged by the high court. And if you call someone a fool, you will be in danger of the fire of hell.

²³"So, what if you are offering your gift at the altar* and remember that someone has something against you? ²⁴Leave your gift there and go make peace with that person. Then come and offer your gift.

ᵃ**5:21** Quote from Ex. 20:13; Deut. 5:17.

25"If anyone wants to take you to court, make friends with them quickly. Try to do that before you get to the court. If you don't, they might hand you over to the judge. And the judge will hand you over to a guard, who will throw you into jail. 26I assure you that you will not leave there until you have paid everything you owe.

Jesus Teaches About Sexual Sin

27"You have heard that it was said, 'You must not commit adultery.'*ª 28But I tell you that if a man looks at a woman and wants to sin sexually with her, he has already committed that sin with her in his mind. 29If your right eye makes you sin, take it out and throw it away. It is better to lose one part of your body than to have your whole body thrown into hell. 30If your right hand makes you sin, cut it off and throw it away. It is better to lose one part of your body than for your whole body to go into hell.

Jesus Teaches About Divorce
(Mt. 19:9; Mk. 10:11–12; Lk. 16:18)

31"It was also said, 'Any man who divorces his wife must give her a written notice of divorce.'b 32But I tell you that any man who divorces his wife, except for the problem of sexual sin, is causing his wife to be guilty of adultery.* And whoever marries a divorced woman is guilty of adultery.

Jesus Teaches About Making Promises

33"You have heard that it was said to our people long ago, 'When you make a vow,* you must not break your promise. Keep the vows that you make to the Lord.'c 34But I tell you, when you make a promise, don't try to make it stronger with a vow. Don't make a vow using the name of heaven, because heaven is God's throne. 35Don't make a vow using the name of the earth, because the earth belongs to him.d Don't make a vow using the name of Jerusalem, because it also belongs to him, the great King. 36And don't even say that your own head is proof that you will keep your promise. You cannot make one hair on your head white or black. 37Say only 'yes' if you mean 'yes,' and say only 'no' if you mean 'no.' If you say more than that, it is from the Evil One.*

Jesus Teaches About Fighting Back
(Lk. 6:29–30)

38"You have heard that it was said, 'An eye for an eye, and a tooth for a tooth.'e 39But I tell you, don't fight back against someone who is mean to you. If someone hits you on the right cheek, let them hit the other cheek too. 40If someone

---

ª**5:27** Quote from Ex. 20:14; Deut. 5:18.   b**5:31** Quote from Deut. 24:1.   c**5:33** See Lev. 19:12; Num. 30:2; Deut. 23:21.   d**5:35** *the earth . . . him* Literally, "it is the footstool of his feet."   e**5:38** Quote from Ex. 21:24; Lev. 24:20.

wants to sue you in court and take your shirt, let them have your coat too. 41If a soldier forces you to walk with him one mile,*a* go with him two. 42Give to anyone who asks you for something. Don't refuse to give to anyone who wants to borrow from you.

Love Your Enemies
(Lk. 6:27–28, 32–36)

43"You have heard that it was said, 'Love your neighbor,*b* and hate your enemy.' 44But I tell you, love your enemies. Pray for those who treat you badly. 45If you do this, you will be children who are truly like your Father in heaven. He lets the sun rise for all people, whether they are good or bad. He sends rain to those who do right and to those who do wrong. 46If you love only those who love you, why should you get a reward for that? Even the tax collectors* do that. 47And if you are nice only to your friends, you are no better than anyone else. Even the people who don't know God are nice to their friends. 48What I am saying is that you must be perfect, just as your Father in heaven is perfect.

Jesus Teaches About Giving

6 1"Be careful! When you do something good, don't do it in front of others so that they will see you. If you do that, you will have no reward from your Father in heaven.

2"When you give to those who are poor, don't announce that you are giving. Don't be like the hypocrites.* When they are in the synagogues* and on the streets, they blow trumpets before they give so that people will see them. They want everyone to praise them. The truth is, that's all the reward they will get. 3So when you give to the poor, don't let anyone know what you are doing.*c* 4Your giving should be done in private. Your Father can see what is done in private, and he will reward you.

Jesus Teaches About Prayer
(Lk. 11:2–4)

5"When you pray, don't be like the hypocrites.* They love to stand in the synagogues* and on the street corners and pray loudly. They want people to see them. The truth is, that's all the reward they will get. 6But when you pray, you should go into your room and close the door. Then pray to your Father. He is there in that private place. He can see what is done in private, and he will reward you.

7"And when you pray, don't be like the people who don't know God. They say the same things again and again. They think that if they say it enough, their god will hear them.

---

*a***5:41** *one mile* Literally, "one *milion,*" about 1,5 km.   *b***5:43** Quote from Lev. 19:18.
*c***6:3** *don't . . . doing* Literally, "don't let your left hand know what your right hand is doing."

⁸Don't be like them. Your Father knows what you need before you ask him. ⁹So this is how you should pray:

'Our Father in heaven,
  we pray that your name will always be kept holy.*
10 We pray that your kingdom* will come,
    that what you want will be done here on earth,
      the same as in heaven.
11 Give us the food we need for each day.
12 Forgive our sins,
    just as we have forgiven those who did wrong to us.
13 Don't let us be tempted,
    but save us from the Evil One.'*ᵃ

¹⁴Yes, if you forgive others for the wrongs they do to you, then your Father in heaven will also forgive your wrongs. ¹⁵But if you don't forgive others, then your Father in heaven will not forgive the wrongs you do.

Jesus Teaches About Fasting

¹⁶"When you fast,* don't make yourselves look sad like the hypocrites.* They put a look of suffering on their faces so that people will see they are fasting. The truth is, that's all the reward they will get. ¹⁷So when you fast, wash your face and make yourself look nice. ¹⁸Then no one will know you are fasting, except your Father, who is with you even in private. He can see what is done in private, and he will reward you.

You Cannot Serve Two Masters
(Lk. 12:33–34; 11:34–36; 16:13)

¹⁹"Don't save treasures for yourselves here on earth. Moths and rust will destroy them. And thieves can break into your house and steal them. ²⁰Instead, save your treasures in heaven, where they cannot be destroyed by moths or rust and where thieves cannot break in and steal them. ²¹Your heart will be where your treasure is.

²²"The only source of light for the body is the eye. If you look at people and want to help them, you will be full of light.* ²³But if you look at people in a selfish way, you will be full of darkness.* And if the only light you have is really darkness, you have the worst kind of darkness.ᵇ

²⁴"You cannot serve two masters at the same time. You will hate one and love the other, or you will be loyal to one and not care about the other. You cannot serve God and Moneyᶜ at the same time.

ᵃ**6:13** Some Greek copies add: "For the kingdom and the power and the glory belong to you for ever and ever. Amen." ᵇ**6:23** Literally, "²²The lamp of the body is the eye. So, if your eye is pure, your whole body will be full of light. ²³But if your eye is evil, your whole body will be dark. So, if the light in you is darkness, how much is the darkness." ᶜ**6:24** *Money* Or, *mamona*, an Aramaic word meaning "wealth."

Put God's Kingdom First
(Lk. 12:22–34)

²⁵"So I tell you, don't worry about the things you need to live—what you will eat, drink or wear. Life is more important than food, and the body is more important than what you put on it. ²⁶Look at the birds. They don't plant, harvest, or save food in barns, but your heavenly Father feeds them. Don't you know you are worth much more than they are? ²⁷You cannot add any time to your life by worrying about it.

²⁸"And why do you worry about clothes? Look at the wildflowers in the field. See how they grow. They don't work or make clothes for themselves. ²⁹But I tell you that even Solomon, the great and rich king, was not dressed as beautifully as one of these flowers. ³⁰If God makes what grows in the field so beautiful, what do you think he will do for you? It's just grass—one day it's alive, and the next day someone throws it into a fire. But God cares enough to make it beautiful. Surely he will do much more for you. Your faith is so small!

³¹"Don't worry and say, 'What will we eat?' or 'What will we drink?' or 'What will we wear?' ³²That's what those people who don't know God are always thinking about. Don't worry, because your Father in heaven knows that you need all these things. ³³What you should want most is God's kingdom* and doing what he wants you to do. Then he will give you all these other things you need. ³⁴So don't worry about tomorrow. Each day has enough trouble of its own. Tomorrow will have its own worries.

Be Careful About Criticizing Others
(Lk. 6:37–38, 41–42)

7¹"Don't judge others, and God will not judge you. ²If you judge others, you will be judged in the same way you judge them. God will treat you just as you treat others.

³"Why do you notice the small piece of dust that is in your friend's eye, but you don't notice the big piece of wood that is in your own? ⁴Why do you say to your friend, 'Let me take that piece of dust out of your eye'? Look at yourself first! You still have that big piece of wood in your own eye. ⁵What a hypocrite* you are! First, take the wood out of your own eye. Then you will see clearly to take the dust out of your friend's eye.

⁶"Don't give something that is holy* to dogs. They will only turn and hurt you. And don't throw your pearls to pigs. They will only step on them.

Ask God for What You Need
(Lk. 11:9–13)

⁷"Continue to ask, and God will give to you. Continue to search, and you will find. Continue to knock, and the door will open for you. ⁸Yes, whoever continues to ask will receive.

Whoever continues to look will find. And whoever continues to knock will have the door opened for them.

⁹"Do any of you have a son? If he asked for bread, would you give him a rock? ¹⁰Or if he asked for a fish, would you give him a snake? Of course not! ¹¹Even you bad people know how to give good things to your children. So surely your heavenly Father will give good things to those who ask him.

A Very Important Rule

¹²"Do for others what you would want them to do for you. This is the meaning of the law of Moses* and the teaching of the prophets.*

The Way to Heaven and the Way to Hell
(Lk. 13:24)

¹³"You can enter true life only through the narrow gate. The gate to hell is very wide, and there is plenty of room on the road that leads there. Many people go that way. ¹⁴But the gate that opens the way to true life is narrow. And the road that leads there is hard to follow. Only a few people find it.

What People Do Shows What They Are
(Lk. 6:43-44; 13:25-27)

¹⁵"Be careful of false prophets.* They come to you and look gentle like sheep. But they are really dangerous like wolves. ¹⁶You will know these people because of what they do. Good things don't come from bad people, just as grapes don't come from thornbushes, and figs don't come from thorny weeds. ¹⁷In the same way, every good tree produces good fruit, and bad trees produce bad fruit. ¹⁸A good tree cannot produce bad fruit, and a bad tree cannot produce good fruit. ¹⁹Every tree that does not produce good fruit is cut down and thrown into the fire. ²⁰You will know these false people by what they do.ᵃ

²¹"Not everyone who says that I am their Lord will enter God's kingdom.* The only people who will enter are those who do what my Father in heaven wants. ²²On the last day many people will say to me, 'You are our Lord! We spoke for you. And for you we forced out demons* and did many miracles.' ²³Then I will tell those people clearly, 'Get away from me, you people who do wrong. I never knew you.'

Two Kinds of People
(Lk. 6:47-49)

²⁴"Whoever hears these teachings of mine and obeys them is like a wise man who built his house on rock. ²⁵It rained hard, and the floods came. The winds blew and beat against that house. But it did not fall because it was built on rock.

ᵃ **7:20** *by what they do* Literally, "by their fruits."

²⁶"Whoever hears these teachings of mine and does not obey them is like a foolish man who built his house on sand. ²⁷It rained hard, the floods came, the winds blew and beat against that house. And it fell with a loud crash."

²⁸When Jesus finished speaking, the people were amazed at his teaching. ²⁹He did not teach like their teachers of the law. He taught like someone who has authority.

Jesus Heals a Sick Man
(Mk. 1:40–45; Lk. 5:12–16)

8 ¹Jesus came down from the hill, and a large crowd followed him. ²Then a man sick with leprosy* came to him. The man bowed down before Jesus and said, "Lord, you have the power to heal me if you want."

³Jesus touched the man. He said, "I want to heal you. Be healed!" Immediately the man was healed from his leprosy. ⁴Then Jesus said to him, "Don't tell anyone about what happened. Go and show yourself to the priest.ᵃ And offer the gift that Moses* commanded for people who are made well. This will show everyone that you are healed."

Jesus Heals an Officer's Servant
(Lk. 7:1–10; Jn. 4:43–54)

⁵Jesus went to the city of Capernaum. When he entered the city, an army officer* came to him and begged for help. ⁶The officer said, "Lord, my servant is very sick at home in bed. He can't move his body and has much pain."

⁷Jesus said to the officer, "I will go and heal him."

⁸The officer answered, "Lord, I am not good enough for you to come into my house. You need only to give the order, and my servant will be healed. ⁹I know this, because I understand authority. There are people who have authority over me, and I have soldiers under my authority. I tell one soldier, 'Go,' and he goes. I tell another soldier, 'Come,' and he comes. I say to my servant, 'Do this,' and my servant obeys me."

¹⁰When Jesus heard this, he was amazed. He said to those who were with him, "The truth is, this man has more faith than anyone I have found, even in Israel.* ¹¹Many people will come from the east and from the west. These people will sit and eat with Abraham,* Isaac,* and Jacob* in God's kingdom.* ¹²And those who should have the kingdom will be thrown out. They will be thrown outside into the darkness, where people will cry and grind their teeth with pain."

¹³Then Jesus said to the officer, "Go home. Your servant will be healed the way you believed he would." Right then his servant was healed.

ᵃ8:4 show yourself to the priest The law of Moses said a priest must decide when a person with leprosy was well.

Jesus Heals Many People
(Mk. 1:29–34; Lk. 4:38–41)

[14]Jesus went to Peter's house. He saw that Peter's mother-in-law was in bed with a high fever. [15]He touched her hand, and the fever left her. Then she stood up and began to serve him.

[16]That evening people brought to Jesus many people who had demons* inside them. He spoke and the demons left the people. He healed all those who were sick. [17]So Jesus made clear the full meaning of what Isaiah the prophet* said,

> "He took away our diseases
>   and carried away our sicknesses."   *Isaiah 53:4*

Following Jesus
(Lk. 9:57–62)

[18]When Jesus saw the crowd around him, he told his followers to go to the other side of the lake. [19]Then a teacher of the law came to him and said, "Teacher, I will follow you any place you go."

[20]Jesus said to him, "The foxes have holes to live in. The birds have nests. But the Son of Man* has no place to rest."

[21]Another of Jesus' followers said to him, "Lord, I will follow you too, but let me go and bury my father first."

[22]But Jesus said to him, "Follow me, and let those who are dead bury their own dead."

Jesus' Followers See His Power
(Mk. 4:35–41; Lk. 8:22–25)

[23]Jesus got into a boat, and his followers went with him. [24]After the boat left the shore, a very bad storm began on the lake. The waves covered the boat. But Jesus was sleeping. [25]The followers went to him and woke him. They said, "Lord, save us! We will drown!"

[26]Jesus answered, "Why are you afraid? You don't have enough faith." Then he stood up and gave a command to the wind and the water. The wind stopped, and the lake became very calm.

[27]The men were amazed. They said, "What kind of man is this? Even the wind and the water obey him!"

Jesus Sends Demons Out of Two Men
(Mk. 5:1–20; Lk. 8:26–39)

[28]Jesus arrived at the other side of the lake in the country of the Gadarene[a] people. There, two men who had demons* inside them came to him. They lived in the burial caves and were so dangerous that no one could use the road by those caves. [29]They came to Jesus and shouted, "What do you want

a 8:28 Gadarene From Gadara, an area southeast of Lake Galilee.

with us, Son of God? Did you come here to punish us before the right time?"

³⁰Near that place there was a large herd of pigs feeding. ³¹The demons begged Jesus, "If you make us leave these men, please send us into that herd of pigs."

³²Jesus said to them, "Go!" So the demons left those men and went into the pigs. Then the whole herd of pigs ran down the hill into the lake, and all were drowned. ³³The men who had the work of caring for the pigs ran away. They went into town and told the people everything that happened, especially about the men who had the demons. ³⁴Then the whole town went out to see Jesus. When the people saw him, they begged him to leave their area.

Jesus Heals a Crippled Man
(Mk. 2:1–12; Lk. 5:17–26)

9 ¹Jesus got into a boat and went back across the lake to his own town. ²Some people brought to him a man who was paralyzed and was lying on a mat. Jesus saw that these people had much faith. So he said to the paralyzed man, "Young man, you'll be glad to hear this. Your sins are forgiven."

³Some of the teachers of the law heard what Jesus said. They said to themselves, "What an insult to God for this man to say that!"

⁴Jesus knew what they were thinking. So he said, "Why are you thinking such evil thoughts? ⁵⁻⁶The Son of Man* has power on earth to forgive sins. But how can I prove this to you? Maybe you are thinking it was easy for me to say, 'Your sins are forgiven.' There's no proof that it really happened. But what if I say to the man, 'Stand up and walk'? Then you will be able to see that I really have this power." So Jesus said to the paralyzed man, "Stand up. Take your mat and go home."

⁷The man stood up and went home. ⁸The people saw this and they were amazed. They praised God for letting someone have such power.

Matthew (Levi) Follows Jesus
(Mk. 2:13–17; Lk. 5:27–32)

⁹When Jesus was leaving, he saw a man named Matthew sitting at the place for collecting taxes. Jesus said to him, "Follow me." So he got up and followed Jesus.

¹⁰Jesus ate dinner at Matthew's house. Many tax collectors* and others with bad reputations came and ate with him and his followers. ¹¹The Pharisees* saw that Jesus was eating with these people. They asked his followers, "Why does your teacher eat with tax collectors and other sinners?"

¹²Jesus heard them say this. So he said to them, "It is the sick people who need a doctor, not those who are healthy. ¹³You need to go and learn what this Scripture means: 'I don't want

animal sacrifices; I want you to show kindness to people.'*a* I did not come to invite good people. I came to invite sinners."

Jesus Is Not Like Other Religious Leaders
(Mk. 2:18–22; Lk. 5:33–39)

¹⁴Then the followers of John* came to Jesus and said, "We and the Pharisees* fast* often, but your followers don't ever fast. Why?"

¹⁵Jesus answered, "At a wedding the friends of the bridegroom* are not sad while he is with them. They cannot fast then. But the time will come when the bridegroom will be taken from them. Then they will fast.

¹⁶"When someone sews a patch over a hole in an old coat, they never use a piece of cloth that has not already been shrunk. If they do, the patch will shrink and pull away from the coat. Then the hole will be worse. ¹⁷Also, people never pour new wine into old wineskins.* They would break, the wine would spill out, and the wineskins would be ruined. People always put new wine into new wineskins, which won't break, and the wine stays good."

Jesus Gives Life to a Dead Girl and Heals a Sick Woman
(Mk. 5:21–43; Lk. 8:40–56)

¹⁸While Jesus was still talking, a leader of the synagogue* came to him. The leader bowed down before him and said, "My daughter has just died. But if you will come and touch her with your hand, she will live again."

¹⁹So Jesus and his followers went with the man.

²⁰On the way, there was a woman who had been bleeding for twelve years. She came close behind Jesus and touched the bottom of his coat. ²¹She was thinking, "If I can touch his coat, I will be healed."

²²Jesus turned and saw the woman. He said, "Be happy, dear woman. You are made well because you believed." Then the woman was healed.

²³Jesus continued going with the Jewish leader and went into the leader's house. He saw people there who make music for funerals. And he saw a crowd of people crying loudly. ²⁴Jesus said, "Go away. The girl is not dead. She is only sleeping." But the people laughed at him. ²⁵After the people were put out of the house, Jesus went into the girl's room. He held the girl's hand, and the girl stood up. ²⁶The news about this spread all around the area.

Jesus Heals More People

²⁷As Jesus was going away from there, two blind men followed him. They said loudly, "Show kindness to us, Son of David.*"

a 9:13 Quote from Hos. 6:6.

²⁸Jesus went inside, and the blind men went with him. He asked them, "Do you believe that I am able to make you see again?" They answered, "Yes, Lord, we believe."

²⁹Then Jesus touched their eyes and said, "You believe that I can make you see again, so it will happen." ³⁰Then the men were able to see. Jesus gave them a strong warning. He said, "Don't tell anyone about this." ³¹But they left and spread the news about Jesus all around that area.

³²As these two men were leaving, some people brought another man to Jesus. This man could not talk because he had a demon* inside him. ³³Jesus forced the demon out, and the man was able to talk. The people were amazed and said, "We have never seen anything like this in Israel."

³⁴But the Pharisees* said, "The ruler of demons is the one that gives him power to force demons out."

Jesus Feels Sorry for the People

³⁵Jesus traveled through all the towns and villages. He taught in their synagogues* and told people the Good News about God's kingdom.ᵃ He healed all kinds of diseases and sicknesses. ³⁶Jesus saw the many people and felt sorry for them because they were worried and helpless—like sheep without a shepherd to lead them. ³⁷Jesus said to his followers, "There is such a big harvest of people to bring in. But there are only a few workers to help harvest them. ³⁸God owns the harvest. Ask him to send more workers to help gather his harvest."

Jesus Sends His Apostles on a Mission
(Mk. 3:13–19; 6:7–13; Lk. 6:12–16; 9:1–6)

10 ¹Jesus called his twelve followers together. He gave them power over evil spirits and power to heal every kind of disease and sickness. ²These are the names of the twelve apostles*:

Simon (also called Peter),
Andrew, the brother of Peter,
James, the son of Zebedee,
John, the brother of James,
³ Philip,
Bartholomew,
Thomas,
Matthew, the tax collector,*
James, the son of Alphaeus,
Thaddaeus,
⁴ Simon, the Zealot,ᵇ
Judas Iscariot (the one who handed Jesus over to his enemies).

ᵃ **9:35** *God's kingdom* Literally, "the kingdom." See "God's kingdom" in the Word List.
ᵇ **10:4** *Zealot* Literally, "*Cananaean,*" an Aramaic word meaning "Zealot" or "Enthusiast." See "Zealot" in the Word List.

[5]Jesus sent the twelve men out with these instructions: "Don't go to the non-Jewish people. And don't go into any town where the Samaritans* live. [6]But go to the people of Israel.* They are like sheep that are lost. [7]When you go, tell them this: 'God's kingdom* is coming soon.' [8]Heal the sick. Bring the dead back to life. Heal the people who have leprosy.* And force demons* out of people. I give you these powers freely, so help others freely. [9]Don't carry any money with you— gold or silver or copper. [10]Don't carry a bag. Take only the clothes and sandals you are wearing. And don't take a walking stick. A worker should be given what he needs.

[11]"When you enter a city or town, find some worthy person there and stay in his home until you leave. [12]When you enter that home, say, 'Peace be with you.' [13]If the people in that home welcome you, they are worthy of your peace. May they have the peace you wished for them. But if they don't welcome you, they are not worthy of your peace. Take back the peace you wished for them. [14]And if the people in a home or a town refuse to welcome you or listen to you, then leave that place and shake the dust off your feet.[a] [15]I can assure you that on the judgment day it will be worse for that town than for the people of Sodom* and Gomorrah.*

Jesus Warns About Troubles
(Mk. 13:9–13; Lk. 21:12–17)

[16]"Listen! I am sending you, and you will be like sheep among wolves. So be smart like snakes. But also be like doves and don't hurt anyone. [17]Be careful! There are people who will arrest you and take you to be judged. They will whip you in their synagogues.* [18]You will be taken to stand before governors and kings. People will do this to you because you follow me. You will tell about me to those kings and governors and to the non-Jewish people. [19]When you are arrested, don't worry about what to say or how you should say it. At that time you will be given the words to say. [20]It will not really be you speaking; the Spirit of your Father will be speaking through you.

[21]"Brothers will turn against their own brothers and hand them over to be killed. Fathers will hand over their own children to be killed. Children will fight against their own parents and will have them killed. [22]Everyone will hate you because you follow me. But the one who remains faithful to the end will be saved. [23]When you are treated badly in one city, go to another city. I promise you that you will not finish going to all the cities of Israel before the Son of Man* comes again.

[24]"Students are not better than their teacher. Servants are not better than their master. [25]Students should be happy to be

---

a **10:14** *shake the dust off your feet* A warning. It would show that they were finished talking to these people.

treated the same as their teacher. And servants should be happy to be treated the same as their master. If those people call them 'the ruler of demons,' and I am the head of the family,^a then it is even more certain that they will insult you, the members of the family!

Fear God, Not People
(Lk. 12:2–7)

²⁶"So don't be afraid of those people. Everything that is hidden will be shown. Everything that is secret will be made known. ²⁷I tell you all this secretly,^b but I want you to tell it publicly.^c Whatever I tell you privately,^d you should shout for everyone to hear.^e

²⁸"Don't be afraid of people. They can kill the body, but they cannot kill the soul. The only one you should fear is God, who can destroy both the body and the soul in hell. ²⁹When birds are sold, two small birds cost only a penny. But not even one of those little birds can die without your Father knowing it. ³⁰God even knows how many hairs are on your head. ³¹So don't be afraid. You are worth more than a whole flock of birds.

Don't Be Ashamed of Your Faith
(Lk. 12:8–9)

³²"If you stand before others and are willing to say you believe in me, then I will tell my Father in heaven that you belong to me. ³³But if you stand before others and say you do not believe in me, then I will tell my Father in heaven that you do not belong to me.

Following Jesus May Bring You Trouble
(Lk. 12:51–53; 14:26–27)

³⁴"Do not think that I have come to bring peace to the earth. I did not come to bring peace. I came to bring trouble.^f ³⁵I have come to make this happen:

'A son will turn against his father.
A daughter will turn against her mother.
A daughter-in-law will turn against her mother-in-law.
³⁶ Even members of your own family will be your enemies.'

Micah 7:6

³⁷"Those who love their father or mother more than they love me are not worthy of me. And those who love their son or daughter more than they love me are not worthy of me. ³⁸Those who will not accept the cross* that is given to them when they follow me are not worthy of me. ³⁹Those who try to

---

^a**10:25** *call me … family* Literally, "call the head of the household *Beelzebul*." See verse 9:34. ^b**10:27** *secretly* Literally, "in the dark." ^c**10:27** *publicly* Literally, "in the light." ^d**10:27** *privately* Literally, "in the ear." ^e**10:27** *for everyone to hear* Literally, "on the housetops." ^f**10:34** *trouble* Literally, "a sword."

keep the life they have will lose it. But those who give up their life for me will find true life.

God Will Bless Those Who Welcome You
(Mk. 9:41)

40"Whoever accepts you also accepts me. And whoever accepts me accepts the one who sent me. 41Whoever accepts a prophet* because he is a prophet will get the same reward a prophet gets. And whoever accepts a godly person just because that person is godly will get the same reward a godly person gets. 42Whoever helps one of these little ones because they are my followers will definitely get a reward, even if they only give them a cup of cold water."

John Sends Men to Ask Jesus a Question
(Lk. 7:18–35)

11 1When Jesus finished these instructions for his twelve followers, he left there. He went to the towns in Galilee to teach the people and tell them God's message.

2When John was in prison, he heard about the things that were happening—things the Christ* would do. So he sent some of his followers to Jesus. 3They asked Jesus, "Are you the one we have been expecting, or should we wait for someone else?"

4Jesus answered, "Go tell John what you have heard and seen: 5The blind can see. The crippled can walk. People with leprosy* are healed. The deaf can hear. The dead are brought back to life. And the Good News* is being told to the poor. 6What great blessings there are for those who don't have a problem accepting me."

7When John's followers left, Jesus began talking to the people about John. He said, "What did you people go out to the desert to see? Someone who is weak, like a stem of grass*a* blowing in the wind? 8Really, what did you expect to see? Someone dressed in fine clothes? Of course not. People who wear fine clothes are all in king's palaces. 9So what did you go out to see? A prophet*? Yes, John is a prophet. But I tell you, he is more than that. 10This Scripture* was written about him:

'Listen! I will send my messenger ahead of you.
    He will prepare the way for you.'   *Malachi 3:1*

11"The truth is that John the Baptizer* is greater than anyone who has ever come into this world. But even the least important person in God's kingdom* is greater than John. 12Since the time John the Baptizer came until now, God's kingdom has been going forward strongly.*b* People have been trying to take control of the kingdom by force. 13Before John came, the law of Moses*

---

*a*11:7 *stem of grass* Literally, "reed." *b*11:12 *has been ... strongly* Or, "has suffered violence."

and all the prophets told about the things that would happen. [14]And if you believe what they said, then John is Elijah.[a] He is the one they said would come. [15]You people who hear me, listen!

[16]"What can I say about the people who live today? What are they like? The people today are like children sitting in the marketplace. One group of children calls to the other group,

[17] 'We played flute music for you,
    but you did not dance;
we sang a funeral song,
    but you were not sad.'

[18]Why do I say people are like that? Because John came, not eating like other people or drinking wine, and people say, 'He has a demon* inside him.' [19]The Son of Man* came eating and drinking, and people say, 'Look at him! He eats too much and drinks too much wine. He's a friend of tax collectors* and other bad people.' But wisdom is shown to be right by what it does."

Jesus Warns People Who Refuse to Believe
(Lk. 10:13–15)

[20]Then Jesus criticized the cities where he did most of his miracles.* He criticized these cities because the people there did not change their lives and stop sinning. [21]Jesus said, "It will be bad for you Chorazin*! It will be bad for you Bethsaida*! I did many miracles in you. If these same miracles had happened in Tyre* and Sidon,* the people there would have changed their lives a long time ago. They would have worn sackcloth* and put ashes on themselves to show that they were sorry for their sins. [22]But I tell you, on the day of judgment it will be worse for you than for Tyre and Sidon.

[23]"And you, Capernaum,* will you be lifted up to heaven? No! You will be thrown down to the place of death. I did many miracles in you. If these same miracles had happened in Sodom,* the people there would have stopped sinning, and it would still be a city today. [24]But I tell you, it will be worse for you in the day of judgment than for Sodom."

Jesus Offers Rest to His People
(Lk. 10:21–22)

[25]Then Jesus said, "I praise you, Father, Lord of heaven and earth. I am thankful that you have hidden these things from those who are so wise and so smart. But you have shown them to people who are like little children. [26]Yes, Father, you did this because it's what you really wanted to do.

[27]"My Father has given me everything. No one knows the Son—only the Father knows the Son. And no one knows the

---

[a]**11:14** *Elijah* See Mal. 4:5–6.

Father—only the Son knows the Father. And the only people who will know about the Father are those the Son chooses to tell.

[28]"Come to me all of you who are tired from the heavy burden you have been forced to carry. I will give you rest. [29]Accept my teaching.[a] Learn from me. I am gentle and humble in spirit. And you will be able to get some rest. [30]Yes, the teaching that I ask you to accept is easy. The load I give you to carry is light."

Jesus Is Lord Over the Sabbath Day
(Mk. 2:23–28; Lk. 6:1–5)

12 [1]About that same time, Jesus was walking through the fields of grain on a Sabbath* day. His followers were with him, and they were hungry. So they began to pick the grain and eat it. [2]The Pharisees* saw this. They said to Jesus, "Look! Your followers are doing something that is against the law to do on the Sabbath day."

[3]Jesus said to them, "You have read what David* did when he and those with him were hungry. [4]David went into God's house. He and those with him ate the bread that was offered to God. It was against the law for David or those with him to eat that bread. Only the priests were allowed to eat it. [5]And you have read in the law of Moses* that on every Sabbath day the priests at the Temple* break the law about the Sabbath day. But they are not wrong for doing that. [6]I tell you that there is something here that is greater than the Temple. [7]The Scriptures* say, 'I don't want animal sacrifices; I want you to show kindness to people.'[b] You don't really know what that means. If you understood it, you would not judge those who have done nothing wrong.

[8]"The Son of Man* is Lord over the Sabbath day."

Jesus Heals a Man on the Sabbath Day
(Mk. 3:1–6; Lk. 6:6–11)

[9]Jesus went from there to their synagogue.* [10]In the synagogue there was a man with a crippled hand. Some Jews there were looking for a reason to accuse Jesus of doing wrong. So they asked him, "Is it right to heal on the Sabbath* day?"[c]

[11]Jesus answered, "If any of you has a sheep and it falls into a ditch on the Sabbath day, you will take the sheep and help it out of the ditch. [12]Surely a man is more important than a sheep. So it is right to do good on the Sabbath day."

[13]Then Jesus said to the man with the crippled hand, "Hold out your hand." The man held out his hand, and it became well again, the same as the other hand. [14]But the Pharisees* left and made plans to kill Jesus.

---

[a]**11:29** *Accept my teaching* Literally, "Take my yoke upon you." A yoke was put on the neck of a work animal for pulling a load. It was a Jewish symbol for the law. See Acts 15:10; Gal. 5:1. [b]**12:7** Quote from Hos. 6:6. [c]**12:10** *"Is it right ... day"* It was against Jewish law to work on the Sabbath day.

Jesus Is God's Chosen Servant

[15]Jesus knew what the Pharisees* were planning. So he left that place, and many people followed him. He healed all who were sick, [16]but he warned them not to tell others who he was. [17]This was to give full meaning to what Isaiah the prophet* said when he spoke for God,

[18]"Here is my servant,
　　the one I have chosen.
He is the one I love,
　　and I am very pleased with him.
I will fill him with my Spirit,*
　　and he will judge the nations fairly.
[19] He will not argue or shout;
　　people will not hear his voice in the streets.
[20] He will not break off even a bent stem of grass.[a]
　　He will not put out even the weakest flame.
　　He will not quit until he makes fair judgment victorious.
[21] All people will hope in him."

Isaiah 42:1–4

Jesus' Power Is From God
(Mk. 3:20–30; Lk. 11:14–23; 12:10)

[22]Then some people brought a man to Jesus. This man was blind and could not talk, because he had a demon* inside him. Jesus healed the man, and he could talk and see. [23]All the people were amazed. They said, "Maybe this man is the Son of David*!"

[24]When the Pharisees* heard this, they said, "This man uses the power of Satan[b] to force demons out of people. Satan is the ruler of demons."

[25]Jesus knew what the Pharisees were thinking. So he said to them, "Every kingdom that fights against itself will be destroyed. And every city or family that is divided against itself will not survive. [26]So if Satan* forces out his own demons,[c] then he is fighting against himself, and his kingdom will not survive. [27]You say that I use the power of Satan to force out demons. If that is true, then what power do your people use when they force out demons? So your own people will prove that you are wrong. [28]But I use the power of God's Spirit to force out demons, and this shows that God's kingdom* has come to you. [29]Whoever wants to enter a strong man's house and steal his things must first tie him up. Then they can steal the things from his house. [30]Whoever is not with me is against me. And anyone who does not work with me is working against me.

[31]"So I tell you, people can be forgiven for every sinful thing they do and for every bad thing they say against God. But

---

[a]12:20 stem of grass Literally, "reed." [b]12:24 Satan Literally, "Beelzebul" (the devil). Also in verse 27. [c]12:26 if Satan … demons Literally, "if Satan forces out Satan."

anyone who speaks against the Holy Spirit* will not be forgiven. ³²You can even speak against the Son of Man* and be forgiven. But anyone who speaks against the Holy Spirit will never be forgiven—not now or in the future.

What You Do Shows What You Are
(Lk. 6:43–45)

³³"If you want good fruit, you must make the tree good. If your tree is not good, it will have bad fruit. A tree is known by the kind of fruit it produces. ³⁴You snakes! You are so evil. How can you say anything good? What you say with your mouths comes from what fills your hearts. ³⁵Those who are good have good things saved in their heart. That's why they say good things. But those who are evil have hearts full of evil, and that's why they say things that are evil. ³⁶I tell you that everyone will have to answer for all the careless things they have said. This will happen on the day of judgment. ³⁷Your words will be used to judge you. What you have said will show whether you are right or whether you are guilty."

Some People Doubt Jesus' Authority
(Mk. 8:11–12; Lk. 11:29–32)

³⁸Then some of the Pharisees* and teachers of the law answered Jesus. They said, "Teacher, we want to see you do a miracle* as a sign from God."

³⁹Jesus answered, "Evil and sinful people are the ones who want to see a miracle as a sign. But no miracle will be done to prove anything to them. The only sign will be the miracle that happened to the prophet* Jonah.ᵃ ⁴⁰Jonah was in the stomach of the big fish for three days and three nights. In the same way, the Son of Man* will be in the grave three days and three nights. ⁴¹On the judgment day, you people who live now will be compared with the people from Nineveh,ᵇ and they will be witnesses who show how guilty you are. Why do I say this? Because when Jonah preached to those people, they changed their lives. And you are listening to someone greater than Jonah, but you refuse to change!

⁴²"On the judgment day, you people who live now will also be compared with the Queen of the South,ᶜ and she will be a witness who shows how guilty you are. I say this because she traveled from far, far away to listen to Solomon's wise teaching. And I tell you that someone greater than Solomon is right here, but you won't listen!

ᵃ**12:39** *Jonah* The story of Jonah is found in the Old Testament book of Jonah. ᵇ**12:41** *Nineveh* City where Jonah preached. See Jonah 3. ᶜ**12:42** *Queen of the South* Or, "Queen of Sheba." She traveled about 1000 miles (1600 km) to learn God's wisdom from Solomon. See 1 Kings 10:1–13.

The Danger of Emptiness
(Lk. 11:24–26)

⁴³"When an evil spirit comes out of a person, it travels through dry places looking for a place to rest, but it finds none. ⁴⁴So it says, 'I will go back to the home I left.' When it comes back, it finds that home still empty. It is all neat and clean. ⁴⁵Then the evil spirit goes out and brings seven other spirits more evil than itself. They all go and live there, and that person has even more trouble than before. It is the same way with the evil people who live today."

Jesus' Followers Are His True Family
(Mk. 3:31–35; Lk. 8:19–21)

⁴⁶While Jesus was talking to the people, his mother and brothers stood outside. They wanted to talk to him. ⁴⁷Someone told him, "Your mother and brothers are waiting for you outside. They want to talk to you."

⁴⁸Jesus answered, "Who is my mother? Who are my brothers?" ⁴⁹Then he pointed to his followers and said, "See! These people are my mother and my brothers. ⁵⁰My true brother and sister and mother is anyone who does what my Father in heaven wants."

A Story About a Farmer Sowing Seed
(Mk. 4:1–9; Lk. 8:4–8)

13 ¹That same day Jesus went out of the house and sat by the lake. ²A large crowd gathered around him. So he got into a boat and sat down. All the people stayed on the shore. ³Then Jesus used stories to teach them many things. He told them this story:

"A farmer went out to sow seed. ⁴While he was scattering the seed, some of it fell by the road. The birds came and ate all that seed. ⁵Other seed fell on rocky ground, where there was not enough dirt. It grew very fast there, because the soil was not deep. ⁶But when the sun rose, it burned the plants. The plants died because they did not have deep roots. ⁷Some other seed fell among thorny weeds. The weeds grew and stopped the good plants from growing. ⁸But some of the seed fell on good ground. There it grew and made grain. Some plants made 100 times more grain, some 60 times more, and some 30 times more. ⁹You people who hear me, listen!"

Why Jesus Used Stories to Teach
(Mk. 4:10–12; Lk. 8:9–10)

¹⁰The followers came to Jesus and asked, "Why do you use these stories to teach the people?"

¹¹Jesus answered, "Only you can know the secret truths about God's kingdom.* Those other people cannot know these secret truths. ¹²The people who have some understanding will

be given more. And they will have even more than they need. But those who do not have much understanding will lose even the little understanding that they have. ¹³This is why I use these stories to teach the people: They see, but they don't really see. They hear, but they don't really hear or understand. ¹⁴So they show that what Isaiah said about them is true:

'You people will listen and you will hear,
  but you will not understand.
You people will look and you will see,
  but you will not understand what you see.
¹⁵ Yes, the minds of these people are now closed.
    They have ears, but they don't listen.
    They have eyes, but they refuse to see.
  If their minds were not closed,
    they might see with their eyes;
    they might hear with their ears;
    they might understand with their minds.
  Then they might turn back to me and be healed.'

Isaiah 6:9-10

¹⁶But God has blessed you. You understand what you see with your eyes. And you understand what you hear with your ears. ¹⁷I can assure you, many prophets* and godly people wanted to see what you now see. But they did not see it. And many prophets and godly people wanted to hear what you now hear. But they did not hear it.

Jesus Explains the Story About Seed
(Mk. 4:13–20; Lk. 8:11–15)

¹⁸"So listen to the meaning of that story about the farmer:

¹⁹"What about the seed that fell by the path? That is like the people who hear the teaching about God's kingdom*a* but do not understand it. The Evil One* comes and takes away what was planted in their hearts.

²⁰"And what about the seed that fell on rocky ground? That is like the people who hear the teaching and quickly and gladly accept it. ²¹But they do not let the teaching go deep into their lives. They keep it only a short time. As soon as trouble or persecution* comes because of the teaching they accepted, they give up.

²²"And what about the seed that fell among the thorny weeds? That is like the people who hear the teaching but let worries about this life and love for money stop it from growing. So it does not produce a crop*b* in their lives.

²³"But what about the seed that fell on the good ground? That is like the people who hear the teaching and understand it. They

---

a **13:19** *God's kingdom* Literally, "the kingdom." Also in verse 38. See "God's kingdom" in the Word List. *b* **13:22** *produce a crop* Meaning to do the good things God wants his people to do.

grow and produce a good crop, sometimes 100 times more, sometimes 60 times more, and sometimes 30 times more."

A Story About Wheat and Weeds

24Then Jesus used another story to teach them. Jesus said, "God's kingdom* is like a man who planted good seed in his field. 25That night, while everyone was asleep, the man's enemy came and planted weeds among the wheat and then left. 26Later, the wheat grew, and heads of grain grew on the plants. But at the same time the weeds also grew. 27Then the man's servants came to him and said, 'You planted good seed in your field. Where did the weeds come from?'

28"The man answered, 'An enemy planted weeds.'

"The servants asked, 'Do you want us to go and pull up the weeds?'

29"He answered, 'No, because when you pull up the weeds, you might also pull up the wheat. 30Let the weeds and the wheat grow together until the harvest time. At the harvest time I will tell the workers this: First, gather the weeds and tie them together to be burned. Then gather the wheat and bring it to my barn.'"

What Is God's Kingdom Like?
(Mk. 4:30–34; Lk. 13:18–21)

31Then Jesus told the people another story: "God's kingdom* is like a mustard seed that a man plants in his field. 32It is one of the smallest of all seeds. But when it grows, it is one of the largest garden plants. It becomes a tree big enough for the birds to come and make nests in its branches."

33Then Jesus told them another story: "God's kingdom is like yeast that a woman mixes into a big bowl of flour to make bread. The yeast makes all the dough rise."

34Jesus used stories to tell all these things to the people. He always used stories to teach them. 35This was to make clear the full meaning of what the prophet* said,

"I will speak using stories;
    I will tell things that have been secrets
        since the world was made."   *Psalm 78:2*

Jesus Explains a Hard Story

36Then Jesus left the people and went into the house. His followers came to him and said, "Explain to us the meaning of the story about the weeds in the field."

37He answered, "The man who planted the good seed in the field is the Son of Man.* 38The field is the world. The good seed are the people in God's kingdom.* The weeds are the people who belong to the Evil One.* 39And the enemy who planted the bad seed is the devil. The harvest is the end of time. And the workers who gather are God's angels.

40"The weeds are pulled up and burned in the fire. It will be the same at the end of time. 41The Son of Man will send his angels, and they will find the people who cause sin and all those who do evil. The angels will take those people out of his kingdom.* 42They will throw them into the place of fire. There the people will be crying and grinding their teeth with pain. 43Then the godly people will shine like the sun. They will be in the kingdom of their Father. You people who hear me, listen!

Stories About a Treasure and a Pearl

44"God's kingdom* is like a treasure hidden in a field. One day a man found the treasure. He hid it again and was so happy that he went and sold everything he owned and bought the field.

45"Also, God's kingdom is like a merchant* looking for fine pearls. 46One day he found a very fine pearl. He went and sold everything he had to buy it.

A Story About a Fishing Net

47"Also, God's kingdom* is like a net that was put into the lake. The net caught many different kinds of fish. 48It was full, so the fishermen pulled it to the shore. They sat down and put all the good fish in baskets. Then they threw away the bad fish. 49It will be the same at the end of time. The angels will come and separate the evil people from the godly people. 50They will throw the evil people into the place of fire. There the people will cry and grind their teeth with pain."

51Then Jesus asked his followers, "Do you understand all these things?"

They said, "Yes, we understand."

52Then Jesus said to the followers, "So every teacher of the law who has learned about God's kingdom has some new things to teach. He is like the owner of a house. He has new things and old things saved in that house. And he brings out the new with the old."

Jesus Goes to His Hometown
(Mk. 6:1–6; Lk. 4:16–30)

53When Jesus finished teaching with these stories, he left there. 54He went to the town where he grew up. He taught the people in the synagogue,* and they were amazed. They said, "Where did this man get such wisdom and this power to do miracles*? 55Isn't he just the son of the carpenter we know? Isn't his mother's name Mary, and aren't his brothers James, Joseph, Simon, and Judas? 56And don't all his sisters still live here in town? How is he able to do these things?" 57So they had a problem accepting him.

But Jesus said to them, "People everywhere give honor to a prophet,* but in his own town or in his own home a prophet does not get any honor." [58]Jesus did not do many miracles there, because the people did not believe in him.

Herod Thinks Jesus Is John the Baptizer
(Mk. 6:14–29; Lk. 9:7–9)

14 [1]About that time, Herod,* the ruler of Galilee, heard what the people were saying about Jesus. [2]So he said to his servants, "This man is really John the Baptizer.* He must have risen from death, and that is why he can do these miracles.*"

How John the Baptizer Was Killed

[3]Before this time, Herod* had arrested John.* He had him chained and put in prison. He arrested John because of Herodias, the wife of Philip, Herod's brother. [4]John had told him, "It is not right for you to be married to Herodias." [5]Herod wanted to kill him, but he was afraid of the people. They believed that John was a prophet.*

[6]On Herod's birthday, the daughter of Herodias danced for him and his group. Herod was very pleased with her. [7]So he promised that he would give her anything she wanted. [8]Herodias told her daughter what to ask for. So she said to Herod, "Give me the head of John the Baptizer* here on this plate."

[9]King Herod was very sad. But he had promised to give the daughter anything she wanted. And the people eating with Herod had heard his promise. So he ordered what she asked to be done. [10]He sent men to the prison, where they cut off John's head. [11]And the men brought John's head on a plate and gave it to the girl. Then she took the head to her mother, Herodias. [12]John's followers came and got his body and buried it. Then they went and told Jesus what happened.

Jesus Feeds More Than 5000
(Mk. 6:30–44; Lk. 9:10–17; Jn. 6:1–14)

[13]When Jesus heard what happened to John,* he left in a boat. He went alone to a place where no one lived. But the people heard that Jesus had left. So they left their towns and followed him. They went by land to the same place he went. [14]When Jesus got out of the boat, he saw a large crowd of people. He felt sorry for them, and he healed the ones who were sick.

[15]Late that afternoon, the followers came to Jesus and said, "No one lives in this place. And it is already late. Send the people away so they can go to the towns and buy food for themselves."

[16]Jesus said, "The people don't need to go away. You give them some food to eat."

[17]The followers answered, "But we have only five loaves of bread and two fish."

¹⁸Jesus said, "Bring the bread and the fish to me." ¹⁹Then he told the people to sit down on the grass. He took the five loaves of bread and the two fish. He looked into the sky and thanked God for the food. Then he broke the bread into pieces, which he gave to the followers, and they gave the food to the people. ²⁰Everyone ate until they were full. When they finished eating, the followers filled twelve baskets with the pieces of food that were not eaten. ²¹There were about 5000 men there who ate. There were also women and children who ate.

Jesus Walks on Water
(Mk. 6:45–52; Jn. 6:16–21)

²²Then Jesus made the followers get into the boat. He told them to go to the other side of the lake. He said he would come later. He stayed there to tell everyone they could go home. ²³After Jesus said goodbye to the people, he went up into the hills by himself to pray. It was late, and he was there alone. ²⁴By this time the boat was already a long way from shore. Since the wind was blowing against it, the boat was having trouble because of the waves.

²⁵Between three and six o'clock in the morning, Jesus' followers were still in the boat. Jesus came to them. He was walking on the water. ²⁶When they saw him walking on the water, it scared them. "It's a ghost!" they said, screaming in fear.

²⁷But Jesus quickly spoke to them. He said, "Don't worry! It's me! Don't be afraid."

²⁸Peter said, "Lord, if that is really you, tell me to come to you on the water."

²⁹Jesus said, "Come, Peter."

Then Peter left the boat and walked on the water to Jesus. ³⁰But while Peter was walking on the water, he saw the wind and the waves. He was afraid and began sinking into the water. He shouted, "Lord, save me!"

³¹Then Jesus caught Peter with his hand. He said, "Your faith is small. Why did you doubt?"

³²After Peter and Jesus were in the boat, the wind stopped. ³³Then the followers in the boat worshiped Jesus and said, "You really are the Son of God."

Jesus Heals Many Sick People
(Mk. 6:53–56)

³⁴After they crossed the lake, they came to the shore at Gennesaret. ³⁵Some men there saw Jesus and knew who he was. So they sent word to the other people throughout that area that Jesus had come. The people brought all their sick people to him. ³⁶They begged Jesus to let them only touch the edge of his coat to be healed. And all the sick people who touched his coat were healed.

God's Law and Human Traditions
(Mk. 7:1–23)

15 ¹Then some Pharisees* and teachers of the law came to Jesus. They came from Jerusalem and asked him, ²"Why do your followers not obey the traditions we have from our great leaders who lived long ago? Your followers don't wash their hands before they eat!"

³Jesus answered, "And why do you refuse to obey God's command so that you can follow those traditions you have? ⁴God said, 'You must respect your father and mother.'ᵃ And God also said, 'Whoever says anything bad to their father or mother must be killed.'ᵇ ⁵But you teach that a person can say to their father or mother, 'I have something I could use to help you. But I will not use it for you. I will give it to God.' ⁶You are teaching them not to respect their father. So you are teaching that it is not important to do what God said. You think it is more important to follow those traditions you have. ⁷You are hypocrites*! Isaiah was right when he spoke for God about you:

⁸ 'These people say they honor me,
     but they don't really make me
         an important part of their lives.
⁹ Their worship of me is for nothing.
     The things they teach are only rules
         that people have made.'"

Isaiah 29:13

¹⁰Jesus called the people to him. He said, "Listen and understand what I am saying. ¹¹It is not what people put in their mouth that makes them wrong.ᶜ It is what comes out of their mouth that makes them wrong."

¹²Then the followers came to Jesus and asked, "Do you know that the Pharisees are upset about what you said?"

¹³Jesus answered, "Every plant that my Father in heaven has not planted will be pulled up by the roots. ¹⁴Stay away from the Pharisees. They lead the people, but they are like blind men leading other blind men. And if a blind man leads another blind man, both of them will fall into a ditch."

¹⁵Peter said, "Explain to us what you said earlier to the people."

¹⁶Jesus said, "Do you still have trouble understanding? ¹⁷Surely you know that all the food that enters the mouth goes into the stomach. Then it goes out of the body. ¹⁸But the bad things people say with their mouth come from the way they think. And that's what can make people wrong. ¹⁹All these bad things begin in the mind: evil thoughts, murder, adultery,* sexual sins, stealing, lying, and insulting people. ²⁰These are the

---

ᵃ**15:4** Quote from Ex. 20:12; Deut. 5:16. ᵇ**15:4** Quote from Ex. 21:17. ᶜ**15:11** *wrong* Literally, "unclean" or "not pure," meaning unacceptable to God. Also in verse 18.

things that make people wrong. Eating without washing their hands will never make people unacceptable to God."

Jesus Helps a Non-Jewish Woman
(Mk. 7:24–30)

²¹Jesus went from there to the area of Tyre and Sidon. ²²A Canaanite woman from that area came out and began shouting, "Lord, Son of David,* please help me! My daughter has a demon* inside her, and she is suffering very much."

²³But Jesus did not answer her. So the followers came to him and said, "Tell her to go away. She keeps crying out and will not leave us alone."

²⁴Jesus answered, "God sent me only to the lost people*a* of Israel.*"

²⁵Then the woman came over to Jesus and bowed before him. She said, "Lord, help me!"

²⁶He answered her with this saying: "It is not right to take the children's bread and give it to the dogs."

²⁷The woman said, "Yes, Lord, but even the dogs eat the pieces of food that fall from their master's table."

²⁸Then Jesus answered, "Woman, you have great faith! You will get what you asked for." And right then the woman's daughter was healed.

Jesus Heals Many People

²⁹Then Jesus went from there to the shore of Lake Galilee. He went up on a hill and sat down.

³⁰A large crowd of people came to him. They brought many other sick people and put them before him. There were people who could not walk, people who were blind, crippled, or deaf, and many others. Jesus healed them all. ³¹People were amazed when they saw that those who could not speak were now able to speak. Crippled people were made strong. Those who could not walk were now able to walk. The blind were able to see. Everyone thanked the God of Israel* for this.

Jesus Feeds More Than 4000
(Mk. 8:1–10)

³²Jesus called his followers to him and said, "I feel sorry for these people. They have been with me three days, and now they have nothing to eat. I don't want to send them away hungry. They might faint while going home."

³³The followers asked Jesus, "Where can we get enough bread to feed all these people? We are a long way from any town."

³⁴Jesus asked, "How many loaves of bread do you have?"

They answered, "We have seven loaves of bread and a few small fish."

a **15:24** *people* Literally, "sheep."

³⁵Jesus told the people to sit on the ground. ³⁶He took the seven loaves of bread and the fish. Then he gave thanks to God for the food. He broke the bread into pieces, which he gave to the followers, and they gave the food to the people. ³⁷All the people ate until they were full. After this, the followers filled seven baskets with the pieces of food that were not eaten. ³⁸There were about 4000 men there who ate. There were also some women and children. ³⁹After they all ate, Jesus told the people they could go home. He got into the boat and went to the area of Magadan.

Some People Doubt Jesus' Authority
(Mk. 8:11–13; Lk. 12:54–56)

16 ¹The Pharisees* and Sadducees* came to Jesus. They wanted to test him. So they asked him to show them a miracle* as a sign from God.

²Jesus answered, "When you people see the sunset, you know what the weather will be. If the sky is red, you say we will have good weather. ³And in the morning, if the sky is dark and red, you say that it will be a rainy day. These are signs of the weather. You see these signs in the sky and know what they mean. In the same way, you see the things that are happening now. These are also signs, but you don't know their meaning. ⁴It is the evil and sinful people who want to see a miracle as a sign from God. But no miracle will be done to prove anything to them. The only sign will be the miracle that happened to Jonah.ᵃ" Then Jesus went away from there.

Jesus' Followers Misunderstand Him
(Mk. 8:14–21)

⁵Jesus and his followers went across the lake. But the followers forgot to bring bread. ⁶Jesus said to the followers, "Be careful! Guard against the yeast* of the Pharisees* and the Sadducees.*"

⁷The followers discussed the meaning of this. They said, "Did Jesus say this because we forgot to bring bread?"

⁸Jesus knew that they were talking about this. So he asked them, "Why are you talking about not having bread? Your faith is small. ⁹Do you still not understand? Remember the five loaves of bread that fed the 5000 people and the many baskets you filled with the bread that was left? ¹⁰And remember the seven loaves of bread that fed the 4000 people and the many baskets you filled then? ¹¹So why don't you understand that I was not talking to you about bread? I am telling you to be careful and guard against the yeast of the Pharisees and the Sadducees."

ᵃ **16:4** *Jonah* A prophet in the Old Testament. After three days in a big fish he came out alive, just as Jesus would come out from the tomb on the third day.

¹²Then the followers understood what Jesus meant. He was not telling them to guard against the yeast used in bread. He was telling them to guard against the teaching of the Pharisees and the Sadducees.

Peter Says Jesus Is the Christ
(Mk. 8:27–30; Lk. 9:18–21)

¹³Jesus went to the area of Caesarea Philippi. He said to his followers, "Who do people say I am*ᵃ*?"

¹⁴They answered, "Some people say you are John the Baptizer.* Others say you are Elijah.* And some say you are Jeremiah* or one of the prophets.*"

¹⁵Then Jesus said to his followers, "And who do you say I am?"

¹⁶Simon Peter answered, "You are the Christ,* the Son of the living God."

¹⁷Jesus answered, "You are blessed, Simon son of Jonah. No one taught you that. My Father in heaven showed you who I am. ¹⁸So I tell you, you are Peter.*ᵇ* And I will build my church* on this rock. The power of death*ᶜ* will not be able to defeat my church. ¹⁹I will give you the keys to God's kingdom.* When you speak judgment here on earth, that judgment will be God's judgment. When you promise forgiveness here on earth, that forgiveness will be God's forgiveness."*ᵈ*

²⁰Then Jesus warned his followers not to tell anyone he was the Christ.

Jesus Says He Must Die
(Mk. 8:31–9:1; Lk. 9:22–27)

²¹From that time Jesus began telling his followers that he must go to Jerusalem. He explained that the older Jewish leaders, the leading priests, and the teachers of the law would make him suffer many things. And he told his followers that he must be killed. Then, on the third day, he would be raised from death.

²²Peter took Jesus away from the other followers to talk to him alone. He began to criticize him. He said, "God save you from these sufferings, Lord! That will never happen to you!"

²³Then Jesus said to Peter, "Get away from me, Satan*ᵉ*! You are not helping me! You don't care about the same things God does. You care only about things that people think are important."

²⁴Then Jesus said to his followers, "Whoever wants to be my follower must say no to themselves and what they want to do. They must accept the cross* that is given to them and follow me.

*ᵃ***16:13** *I am* Literally, "the Son of Man is." *ᵇ***16:18** *Peter* The Greek name "Peter," like the Aramaic name "Cephas," means "rock." *ᶜ***16:18** *power of death* Literally, "gates of Hades." *ᵈ***16:19** *When you speak … God's forgiveness* Literally, "Whatever you bind on earth will have been bound in heaven, and whatever you loose on earth will have been loosed in heaven." *ᵉ***16:23** *Satan* Name for the devil meaning "the enemy." Jesus means that Peter was talking like Satan.

25Those who try to keep the life they have will lose it. But those who give up their life for me will save it. 26It is worth nothing for you to have the whole world if you yourself are lost. You could never pay enough to buy back your life. 27The Son of Man* will come again with his Father's glory* and with his angels. And he will reward everyone for what they have done. 28Believe me when I say that there are some people standing here who will see the Son of Man coming with his kingdom before they die."

Jesus Is Seen With Moses and Elijah
(Mk. 9:2–13; Lk. 9:28–36)

17 1Six days later, Jesus took Peter, James, and John the brother of James and went up on a high mountain. They were all alone there. 2While these followers watched him, Jesus was changed. His face became bright like the sun, and his clothes became white as light. 3Then two men were there, talking with him. They were Moses* and Elijah.*

4Peter said to Jesus, "Lord, it is good that we are here. If you want, I will put three tents here—one for you, one for Moses, and one for Elijah."

5While Peter was talking, a bright cloud came over them. A voice came from the cloud and said, "This is my Son, the one I love. I am very pleased with him. Obey him!"

6The followers with Jesus heard this voice. They were very afraid, so they fell to the ground. 7But Jesus came to them and touched them. He said, "Stand up. Don't be afraid." 8The followers looked up, and they saw that Jesus was now alone.

9As Jesus and the followers were coming down the mountain, he gave them this command: "Don't tell anyone about what you saw on the mountain. Wait until the Son of Man* has been raised from death. Then you can tell people about what you saw."

10The followers asked Jesus, "Why do the teachers of the law say that Elijah must come*a* before the Christ* comes?"

11Jesus answered, "They are right to say Elijah is coming. And it is true that Elijah will make all things the way they should be. 12But I tell you, Elijah has already come. People did not know who he was, and they treated him badly, doing whatever they wanted to do. It is the same with the Son of Man. Those same people will make the Son of Man suffer." 13Then the followers understood that when Jesus said Elijah, he was really talking about John the Baptizer.*

Jesus Frees a Boy From an Evil Spirit
(Mk. 9:14–29; Lk. 9:37–43a)

14Jesus and the followers went back to the people. A man came to Jesus and bowed before him. 15The man said, "Lord, be kind to my son. He suffers so much from the seizures he

a **17:10 Elijah must come** See Mal. 4:5–6.

has. He often falls into the fire or into the water. ¹⁶I brought him to your followers, but they could not heal him."

¹⁷Jesus answered, "You people today have no faith. Your lives are so wrong! How long must I stay with you? How long must I continue to be patient with you? Bring the boy here." ¹⁸Jesus gave a strong command to the demon* inside the boy. The demon came out of the boy, and the boy was healed.

¹⁹Then the followers came to Jesus alone. They said, "We tried to force the demon out of the boy, but we could not. Why were we not able to make the demon go out?"

²⁰Jesus answered, "You were not able to make the demon go out, because your faith is too small. Believe me when I tell you, if your faith is only as big as a mustard* seed you can say to this mountain, 'Move from here to there,' and it will move. You will be able to do anything." ²¹ᵃ

Jesus Talks About His Death
(Mk. 9:30–32; Lk. 9:43b–45)

²²Later, the followers met together in Galilee. Jesus said to them, "The Son of Man* will be handed over to the control of other men, ²³who will kill him. But on the third day he will be raised from death." The followers were very sad to hear that Jesus would be killed.

Jesus Teaches About Paying Taxes

²⁴Jesus and his followers went to Capernaum.* There the men who collect the two-drachma Temple* tax came to Peter and asked, "Does your teacher pay the Temple tax?"

²⁵Peter answered, "Yes, he does."

Peter went into the house where Jesus was. Before Peter could speak, Jesus said to him, "The kings on the earth get different kinds of taxes from people. But who are those who pay the taxes? Are they the king's children? Or do other people pay the taxes? What do you think?"

²⁶Peter answered, "The other people pay the taxes."

Jesus said, "Then the children of the king don't have to pay taxes. ²⁷But we don't want to upset these tax collectors. So do this: Go to the lake and fish. After you catch the first fish, open its mouth. Inside its mouth you will find a four-drachma coin. Take that coin and give it to the tax collectors.* That will pay the tax for you and me."

Who Is the Greatest?
(Mk. 9:33–37; Lk. 9:46–48)

18 ¹About that time the followers came to Jesus and asked, "Who is the greatest in God's kingdom*?"

ᵃ**17:21** Some Greek copies add verse 21: "But that kind of spirit comes out only with prayer and fasting."

²Jesus called a little child to come to him. He stood the child in front of the followers. ³Then he said, "The truth is, you must change your thinking and become like little children. If you don't do this, you will never enter God's kingdom. ⁴The greatest person in God's kingdom is the one who makes himself humble like this child.

⁵"Whoever accepts a little child like this in my name is accepting me.

Jesus Warns About Causes of Sin
(Mk. 9:42–48; Lk. 17:1–2)

⁶"If one of these little children believes in me, and someone causes that child to sin, it will be very bad for that person. It would be better for them to have a millstone* tied around their neck and be drowned in the deep sea. ⁷I feel sorry for the people in the world because of the things that make people sin. These things must happen, but it will be very bad for anyone who causes them to happen.

⁸"If your hand or your foot makes you sin, cut it off and throw it away. It is better for you to lose part of your body and have eternal life than to have two hands and two feet and be thrown into the fire that burns forever. ⁹If your eye makes you sin, take it out and throw it away. It is better for you to have only one eye and have eternal life than to have two eyes and be thrown into the fire of hell.

Jesus Uses a Story About a Lost Sheep
(Lk. 15:3–7)

¹⁰"Be careful. Don't think these little children are not important. I tell you that these children have angels in heaven. And those angels are always with my Father in heaven. ¹¹ᵃ

¹²"If a man has 100 sheep, but one of the sheep is lost, what will he do? He will leave the other 99 sheep on the hill and go look for the lost sheep. Right? ¹³And if he finds the lost sheep, he is happier about that one sheep than about the 99 sheep that were never lost. I can assure you, ¹⁴in the same way your Father in heaven does not want any of these little children to be lost.

When Someone Hurts You
(Lk. 17:3)

¹⁵"If your brother or sister in God's family does something wrong, go and tell them what they did wrong. Do this when you are alone with them. If they listen to you, then you have helped them to be your brother or sister again. ¹⁶But if they refuse to listen, go to them again and take one or two people with you. Then there will be two or three people who will be able to tell all that happened.ᵇ ¹⁷If they refuse to listen to them,

ᵃ**18:11** Some Greek copies add verse 11: "The Son of Man came to save lost people." See Lk. 19:10.   ᵇ**18:16** Then … happened See Deut. 19:15.

then tell the church.* And if they refuse to listen to the church, treat them as you would treat someone who does not know God or who is a tax collector.*

¹⁸"I can assure you that when you speak judgment here on earth, it will be God's judgment. And when you promise forgiveness here on earth, it will be God's forgiveness.ᵃ ¹⁹To say it another way, if two of you on earth agree on anything you pray for, my Father in heaven will do what you ask. ²⁰Yes, if two or three people are together believing in me, I am there with them."

A Story About Forgiveness

²¹Then Peter came to Jesus and asked, "Lord, when someoneᵇ won't stop doing wrong to me, how many times must I forgive them? Seven times?"

²²Jesus answered, "I tell you, you must forgive them more than seven times. You must continue to forgive them even if they do wrong to you seventy-seven times.ᶜ"

²³"So God's kingdom* is like a king who decided to collect the money his servants owed him. ²⁴The king began to collect his money. One servant owed him several thousand poundsᵈ of silver. ²⁵He was not able to pay the money to his master, the king. So the master ordered that he and everything he owned be sold, even his wife and children. The money would be used to pay the king what the servant owed.

²⁶"But the servant fell on his knees and begged, 'Be patient with me. I will pay you everything I owe.' ²⁷The master felt sorry for him. So he told the servant he did not have to pay. He let him go free.

²⁸"Later, that same servant found another servant who owed him a hundred silver coins.* He grabbed him around the neck and said, 'Pay me the money you owe me!'

²⁹"The other servant fell on his knees and begged him, 'Be patient with me. I will pay you everything I owe.'

³⁰"But the first servant refused to be patient. He told the judge that the other servant owed him money, and that servant was put in jail until he could pay everything he owed. ³¹All the other servants saw what happened. They felt very sorry for the man. So they went and told their master everything that happened.

³²"Then the master called his servant in and said, 'You evil servant. You begged me to forgive your debt, and I said you did not have to pay anything! ³³So you should have given that other

---

ᵃ**18:18** *when you speak ... God's forgiveness* Literally, "whatever you bind on earth will have been bound in heaven, and whatever you loose on earth will have been loosed in heaven." ᵇ**18:21** *someone* Literally, "my brother." ᶜ**18:22** *seventy-seven times* Or, "seventy times seven," a very large number, meaning there should be no limit to forgiveness. ᵈ**18:24** *several thousand pounds* Literally, "10,000 *talanta*" or "talents." A talent was about 27 to 36 kg (60 to 80 pounds) of gold, silver, or copper coins.

man who serves with you the same mercy I gave you.' ³⁴The master was very angry, so he put the servant in jail to be punished. And he had to stay in jail until he could pay everything he owed.

³⁵"This king did the same as my heavenly Father will do to you. You must forgive your brother or sister with all your heart, or my heavenly Father will not forgive you."

Jesus Teaches About Divorce
(Mk. 10:1–12)

19 ¹After Jesus said all these things, he left Galilee. He went into the area of Judea on the other side of the Jordan River. ²Many people followed him. Jesus healed the sick people there.

³Some Pharisees* came to Jesus. They tried to make him say something wrong. They asked him, "Is it right for a man to divorce his wife for any reason he chooses?"

⁴Jesus answered, "Surely you have read this in the Scriptures*: When God made the world, 'he made people male and female.'ᵃ ⁵And God said, 'That is why a man will leave his father and mother and be joined to his wife. And the two people will become one.'ᵇ ⁶So they are no longer two, but one. God has joined them together, so no one should separate them."

⁷The Pharisees asked, "Then why did Moses* give a command allowing a man to divorce his wife by writing a certificate of divorceᶜ?"

⁸Jesus answered, "Moses allowed you to divorce your wives because you refused to accept God's teaching. But divorce was not allowed in the beginning. ⁹I tell you that whoever divorces his wife, except for the problem of sexual sin, and marries another woman is guilty of adultery.'"

¹⁰The followers said to Jesus, "If that is the only reason a man can divorce his wife, it is better not to marry."

¹¹He answered, "This statement is true for some, but not for everyone—only for those who have been given this gift. ¹²There are different reasons why some men don't marry.ᵈ Some were born without the ability to produce children. Others were made that way later in life. And others have given up marriage because of God's kingdom.* This is for anyone who is able to accept it.

Jesus Welcomes Children
(Mk. 10:13–16; Lk. 18:15–17)

¹³Then the people brought their little children to Jesus so that he could lay his hands on them to bless them and pray for them. When the followers saw this, they told the people to stop

---

ᵃ**19:4** Quote from Gen. 1:27; 5:2.   ᵇ**19:5** Quote from Gen. 2:24.   ᶜ**19:7** *a command … certificate of divorce* See Deut. 24:1.   ᵈ**19:12** *some men don't marry* Literally, "there are eunuchs."

bringing their children to him. ¹⁴But Jesus said, "Let the little children come to me. Don't stop them, because God's kingdom* belongs to people who are like these children." ¹⁵After Jesus blessed the children, he left there.

A Rich Man Refuses to Follow Jesus
(Mk. 10:17–31; Lk. 18:18–30)

¹⁶A man came to Jesus and asked, "Teacher, what good thing must I do to have eternal life?"

¹⁷Jesus answered, "Why do you ask me about what is good? Only God is good. But if you want to have eternal life, obey the law's commands."

¹⁸The man asked, "Which ones?"

Jesus answered, "'You must not murder anyone, you must not commit adultery,* you must not steal, you must not tell lies about others, ¹⁹you must respect your father and mother,'ᵃ and 'love your neighborᵇ the same as you love yourself.'ᶜ"

²⁰The young man said, "I have obeyed all these commands. What else do I need?"

²¹Jesus answered, "If you want to be perfect, then go and sell all that you own. Give the money to the poor, and you will have riches in heaven. Then come and follow me!"

²²But when the young man heard Jesus tell him to give away his money, he was sad. He didn't want to do this, because he was very rich. So he left.

²³Then Jesus said to his followers, "The truth is, it will be very hard for a rich person to enter God's kingdom.* ²⁴Yes, I tell you, it is easier for a camel to go through the eye of a needle than for a rich person to enter God's kingdom."

²⁵The followers were amazed to hear this. They asked, "Then who can be saved?"

²⁶Jesus looked at them and said, "This is something that people cannot do. But God can do anything."

²⁷Peter said to him, "We left everything we had and followed you. So what will we have?"

²⁸Jesus said to them, "When the time of the new world comes, the Son of Man* will sit on his great and glorious throne. And I can promise that you who followed me will sit on twelve thrones, and you will judge the twelve tribes of Israel.ᵈ ²⁹Everyone who has left houses, brothers, sisters, father, mother, children, or farms to follow me will get much more than they left. And they will have eternal life. ³⁰Many people who have the highest place in life now will have the lowest place in the future. And many people who have the lowest place now will have the highest place in the future.

ᵃ**19:19** Quote from Ex. 20:12–16; Deut. 5:16–20. ᵇ**19:19** *your neighbor* Or, "others." Jesus' teaching in Lk. 10:25–37 makes clear that this includes anyone in need. ᶜ**19:19** Quote from Lev. 19:18. ᵈ**19:28** *Israel* First, Israel was the people descended from Jacob (see "Israel" in the Word List), but the name is also used in Scripture to mean all of God's people.

Jesus Uses a Story About Farm Workers

20 ¹"God's kingdom* is like a man who owned some land. One morning, the man went out very early to hire some people to work in his vineyard.* ²He agreed to pay the workers one silver coin* for working that day. Then he sent them into the vineyard to work.

³"About nine o'clock the man went to the marketplace and saw some other people standing there. They were doing nothing. ⁴So he said to them, 'If you go and work in my field, I will pay you what your work is worth.' ⁵So they went to work in the vineyard.

"The man went out again about twelve o'clock and again at three o'clock. Both times he hired some others to work in his vineyard. ⁶About five o'clock the man went to the marketplace again. He saw some other people standing there. He asked them, 'Why did you stand here all day doing nothing?'

⁷"They said, 'No one gave us a job.'

"The man said to them, 'Then you can go and work in my vineyard.'

⁸"At the end of the day, the owner of the field said to the boss of all the workers, 'Call the workers and pay them all. Start by paying the last people I hired. Then pay all of them, ending with the ones I hired first.'

⁹"The workers who were hired at five o'clock came to get their pay. Each worker got one silver coin. ¹⁰Then the workers who were hired first came to get their pay. They thought they would be paid more than the others. But each one of them also received one silver coin. ¹¹When they got their silver coin, they complained to the man who owned the land. ¹²They said, 'Those people were hired last and worked only one hour. But you paid them the same as us. And we worked hard all day in the hot sun.'

¹³"But the man who owned the field said to one of them, 'Friend, I am being fair with you. You agreed to work for one silver coin. Right? ¹⁴So take your pay and go. I want to give the man who was hired last the same pay I gave you. ¹⁵I can do what I want with my own money. Why would you be mad at me for being good to someone?'

¹⁶"So those who have the last place now will have the first place in the future. And those who have the first place now will have the last place in the future."

Jesus Talks Again About His Death
(Mk. 10:32–34; Lk. 18:31–34)

¹⁷Jesus was going to Jerusalem. His twelve followers were with him. While they were walking, he gathered the followers together and spoke to them privately. He said to them, ¹⁸"We are going to Jerusalem. The Son of Man* will be handed over to the leading priests and the teachers of the law, and they will

say he must die. ¹⁹They will hand him over to the foreigners, who will laugh at him and beat him with whips, and then they will kill him on a cross. But on the third day after his death, he will be raised to life again."

A Mother Asks a Special Favor
(Mk. 10:35–45)

²⁰Then Zebedee's wife came to Jesus and brought her sons. She bowed before Jesus and asked him to do something for her.

²¹Jesus said, "What do you want?"

She said, "Promise that one of my sons will sit at your right side in your kingdom and the other at your left."

²²So Jesus said to the sons, "You don't understand what you are asking. Can you drink from the cup[a] that I must drink from?"

The sons answered, "Yes, we can!"

²³Jesus said to them, "It is true that you will drink from the cup that I drink from. But it is not for me to say who will sit at my right or my left. My Father has decided who will do that. He has prepared those places for them."

²⁴The other ten followers heard this and were angry with the two brothers. ²⁵So Jesus called the followers together. He said, "You know that the rulers of the non-Jewish people love to show their power over the people. And their important leaders love to use all their authority over the people. ²⁶But it should not be that way with you. Whoever wants to be your leader must be your servant. ²⁷Whoever wants to be first must serve the rest of you like a slave. ²⁸Do as I did: The Son of Man* did not come for people to serve him. He came to serve others and to give his life to save many people."

Jesus Heals Two Blind Men
(Mk. 10:46–52; Lk. 18:35–43)

²⁹When Jesus and his followers were leaving Jericho, a large crowd followed him. ³⁰There were two blind men sitting by the road. They heard that Jesus was coming by. So they shouted, "Lord, Son of David,* please help us!"

³¹The people there criticized the blind men and told them to be quiet. But they shouted more and more, "Lord, Son of David, please help us!"

³²Jesus stopped and said to them, "What do you want me to do for you?"

³³They answered, "Lord, we want to be able to see."

³⁴Jesus felt sorry for the blind men. He touched their eyes, and immediately they were able to see. Then they became followers of Jesus.

---

[a] **20:22 cup** A symbol of suffering. Jesus used the idea of drinking from a cup to mean accepting the suffering he would face in the terrible events that were soon to come. Also in verse 23.

Jesus Enters Jerusalem Like a King
(Mk. 11:1–11; Lk. 19:28–38; Jn. 12:12–19)

21 ¹Jesus and his followers were coming closer to Jerusalem. But first they stopped at Bethphage at the hill called the Mount of Olives.* From there Jesus sent two of his followers into town. ²He said to them, "Go to the town you can see there. When you enter it, you will find a donkey with her colt. Untie them both, and bring them to me. ³If anyone asks you why you are taking the donkeys, tell them, 'The Master needs them. He will send them back soon.'"

⁴This showed the full meaning of what the prophet* said,

⁵"Tell the city of Zion,
   'Now your king is coming to you.
He is humble and riding on a donkey.
   He is riding on a young donkey,
     born from a work animal.'"

                               Zechariah 9:9

⁶The followers went and did what Jesus told them to do. ⁷They brought the mother donkey and the young donkey to him. They covered the donkeys with their coats, and Jesus sat on them. ⁸On the way to Jerusalem many people spread their coats on the road for Jesus. Others cut branches from the trees and spread them on the road. ⁹Some of the people were walking ahead of Jesus. Others were walking behind him. They all shouted,

   "Praise*ᵃ* to the Son of David*!
   'Welcome! God bless the one who comes
     in the name of the Lord!'

                               Psalm 118:25–26

   Praise to God in heaven!"

¹⁰Then Jesus went into Jerusalem. All the people in the city were confused. They asked, "Who is this man?"
¹¹The crowds following Jesus answered, "This is Jesus. He is the prophet from the town of Nazareth in Galilee."

Jesus Goes to the Temple
(Mk. 11:15–19; Lk. 19:45–48; Jn. 2:13–22)

¹²Jesus went into the Temple* area. He threw out all those who were selling and buying things there. He turned over the tables that belonged to those who were exchanging different kinds of money. And he turned over the benches of those who were selling doves. ¹³Jesus said to them, "The Scriptures* say, 'My house will be called a house of prayer.'*ᵇ* But you are changing God's house into a 'hiding place for thieves.'*ᶜ*"

---

*ᵃ***21:9** *Praise* Literally, *"Hosanna,"* a Hebrew word used in praying to God for help. Here, it was probably a shout of celebration used in praising God or his Messiah. Also in the last line of this verse and in verse 15. *ᵇ***21:13** Quote from Isa. 56:7. *ᶜ***21:13** Quote from Jer. 7:11.

¹⁴Some blind people and some who were crippled came to Jesus in the Temple area. Jesus healed them. ¹⁵The leading priests and the teachers of the law saw the wonderful things he was doing. And they saw the children praising him in the Temple area. The children were saying, "Praise to the Son of David.*" All this made the priests and the teachers of the law angry.

¹⁶They asked Jesus, "Do you hear what these children are saying?"

He answered, "Yes. The Scriptures say, 'You have taught children and babies to give praise.'ᵃ Have you not read that Scripture?"

¹⁷Then Jesus left them and went out of the city to Bethany, where he spent the night.

Jesus Shows the Power of Faith
(Mk. 11:12–14, 20–24)

¹⁸Early the next morning, Jesus was going back to the city. He was very hungry. ¹⁹He saw a fig tree beside the road and went to get a fig from it. But there were no figs on the tree. There were only leaves. So Jesus said to the tree, "You will never again produce fruit!" The tree immediately dried up and died.

²⁰When the followers saw this, they were very surprised. They asked, "How did the fig tree dry up and die so quickly?"

²¹Jesus answered, "The truth is, if you have faith and no doubts, you will be able to do the same as I did to this tree. And you will be able to do more. You will be able to say to this mountain, 'Go, mountain, fall into the sea.' And if you have faith, it will happen. ²²If you believe, you will get anything you ask for in prayer."

Jewish Leaders Doubt Jesus' Authority
(Mk. 11:27–33; Lk. 20:1–8)

²³Jesus went into the Temple* area. While Jesus was teaching there, the leading priests and the older leaders of the people came to him. They said, "Tell us! What authority do you have to do these things you are doing? Who gave you this authority?"

²⁴Jesus answered, "I will ask you a question too. If you answer me, then I will tell you what authority I have to do these things. ²⁵Tell me: When John baptized* people, did his authority come from God or was it only from other people?"

The priests and the Jewish leaders talked about Jesus' question. They said to each other, "If we answer, 'John's baptism was from God,' then he will say, 'Then why didn't you believe John?' ²⁶But we can't say John's baptism was from someone else. We are afraid of the people, because they all believe John was a prophet.*"

ᵃ **21:16** Quote from Ps. 8:2 (Greek version).

²⁷So they told Jesus, "We don't know the answer."

Jesus said, "Then I will not tell you who gave me the authority to do these things.

Jesus Uses a Story About Two Sons

²⁸"Tell me what you think about this: There was a man who had two sons. He went to the first son and said, 'Son, go and work today in the vineyard.'"

²⁹"The son answered, 'I will not go.' But later he decided he should go, and he went.

³⁰"Then the father went to the other son and said, 'Son, go and work today in the vineyard.' He answered, 'Yes, sir, I will go and work.' But he did not go.

³¹"Which of the two sons obeyed his father?"

The Jewish leaders answered, "The first son."

Jesus said to them, "The truth is, you are worse than the tax collectors* and the prostitutes. In fact, they will enter God's kingdom* before you enter. ³²John came showing you the right way to live, and you did not believe him. But the tax collectors and prostitutes believed John. You saw that happening, but you would not change. You still refused to believe him.

God Sends His Son
(Mk. 12:1–12; Lk. 20:9–19)

³³"Listen to this story: There was a man who owned a vineyard.* He put a wall around the field and dug a hole for a winepress.* Then he built a tower. He leased the land to some farmers and then left on a trip. ³⁴Later, it was time for the grapes to be picked. So the man sent his servants to the farmers to get his share of the grapes.

³⁵"But the farmers grabbed the servants and beat one. They killed another one and then stoned to death a third servant. ³⁶So the man sent some other servants to the farmers. He sent more servants than he sent the first time. But the farmers did the same thing to them that they did the first time. ³⁷So the man decided to send his son to the farmers. He said, 'The farmers will respect my son.'

³⁸"But when the farmers saw the son, they said to each other, 'This is the owner's son. This vineyard will be his. If we kill him, it will be ours.' ³⁹So the farmers took the son, threw him out of the vineyard, and killed him.

⁴⁰"So what will the owner of the vineyard do to these farmers when he comes?"

⁴¹The Jewish priests and leaders said, "He will surely kill those evil men. Then he will lease the land to other farmers, who will give him his share of the crop at harvest time."

⁴²Jesus said to them, "Surely you have read this in the Scriptures*:

'The stone that the builders refused to accept
　　became the cornerstone.*
The Lord did this, and it is wonderful to us.'

Psalm 118:22–23

⁴³"So I tell you that God's kingdom* will be taken away from you. It will be given to people who do what God wants in his kingdom. ⁴⁴Whoever falls on this stone will be broken. And it will crush anyone it falls on."^a

⁴⁵The leading priests and the Pharisees* heard these stories that Jesus told. They knew that Jesus was talking about them. ⁴⁶They wanted to find a way to arrest Jesus. But they were afraid to do anything, because the people believed that Jesus was a prophet.*

A Story About People Invited to a Dinner
(Lk. 14:15–24)

22¹Jesus used some more stories to teach the people. He said, ²"God's kingdom* is like a king who prepared a wedding feast for his son. ³He invited some people to the feast. When it was ready, the king sent his servants to tell the people to come. But they refused to come to the king's feast.

⁴"Then the king sent some more servants. He said to them, 'I have already invited the people. So tell them that my feast is ready. I have killed my best bulls and calves to be eaten. Everything is ready. Come to the wedding feast.'

⁵"But when the servants told the people to come, they refused to listen. They all went to do other things. One went to work in his field, and another went to his business. ⁶Some of the other people grabbed the servants, beat them, and killed them. ⁷The king was very angry. He sent his army to kill those who murdered his servants. And the army burned their city.

⁸"After that, the king said to his servants, 'The wedding feast is ready. I invited those people, but they were not good enough to come to my feast. ⁹So go to the street corners and invite everyone you see. Tell them to come to my feast.' ¹⁰So the servants went into the streets. They gathered everyone they could find. They brought good people and bad people to the place where the wedding feast was ready. And the place was filled with guests.

¹¹"When the king came in to meet the guests, he saw a man there who was not dressed in the right clothes for a wedding. ¹²The king said, 'Friend, how were you allowed to come in here? You are not wearing the right clothes.' But the man said nothing. ¹³So the king told some servants, 'Tie this man's hands and feet. Throw him out into the darkness, where people are crying and grinding their teeth with pain.'

¹⁴"Yes, many people are invited. But only a few are chosen."

^a**21:44** Some Greek copies do not have verse 44.

The Jewish Leaders Try to Trick Jesus
(Mk. 12:13–17; Lk. 20:20–26)

¹⁵Then the Pharisees* left the place where Jesus was teaching. They made plans to catch him saying something wrong. ¹⁶They sent some men to Jesus. They were some of their own followers and some from the group called Herodians.* They said, "Teacher, we know you are an honest man. We know you teach the truth about God's way. You are not afraid of what others think about you. All people are the same to you. ¹⁷So tell us what you think. Is it right to pay taxes to Caesar* or not?"

¹⁸But Jesus knew that these men were trying to trick him. So he said, "You hypocrites*! Why are you trying to catch me saying something wrong? ¹⁹Show me a coin used for paying the tax." They showed Jesus a silver coin.* ²⁰Then he asked, "Whose picture is on the coin? And whose name is written on the coin?"

²¹They answered, "It is Caesar's picture and Caesar's name."

Then Jesus said to them, "Give to Caesar what belongs to Caesar, and give to God what belongs to God."

²²When they heard what Jesus said, they were amazed. They left him and went away.

Some Sadducees Try to Trick Jesus
(Mk. 12:18–27; Lk. 20:27–40)

²³That same day some Sadducees* came to Jesus. (Sadducees believe that no one will rise from death.) The Sadducees asked Jesus a question. ²⁴They said, "Teacher, Moses* told us that if a married man dies and had no children, his brother must marry the woman. Then they will have children for the dead brother.ᵃ ²⁵There were seven brothers among us. The first brother married but died. He had no children. So his brother married the woman. ²⁶Then the second brother also died. The same thing happened to the third brother and all the other brothers. ²⁷The woman was the last to die. ²⁸But all seven men had married her. So when people rise from death, whose wife will she be?"

²⁹Jesus answered, "You are so wrong! You don't know what the Scriptures* say. And you don't know anything about God's power. ³⁰At the time when people rise from death, there will be no marriage. People will not be married to each other. Everyone will be like the angels in heaven. ³¹Surely you have read what God said to you about people rising from death. ³²God said, 'I am the God of Abraham,* the God of Isaac,* and the God of Jacob.'*ᵇ So they were not still dead, because he is the God only of living people."

³³When the people heard this, they were amazed at Jesus' teaching.

ᵃ**22:24** *if . . . dead brother* See Deut. 25:5, 6.   ᵇ**22:32** Quote from Ex. 3:6.

Which Command Is the Most Important?
(Mk. 12:28–34; Lk. 10:25–28)

³⁴The Pharisees* learned that Jesus had made the Sadducees* look so foolish that they stopped trying to argue with him. So the Pharisees had a meeting. ³⁵Then one of them, an expert in the law of Moses,* asked Jesus a question to test him. ³⁶He said, "Teacher, which command in the law is the most important?"

³⁷Jesus answered, "'Love the Lord your God with all your heart, all your soul, and all your mind.'ᵃ ³⁸This is the first and most important command. ³⁹And the second command is like the first: 'Love your neighborᵇ the same as you love yourself.'ᶜ ⁴⁰All of the law and the writings of the prophets* take their meaning from these two commands."

Is the Christ David's Son or David's Lord?
(Mk. 12:35–37; Lk. 20:41–44)

⁴¹So while the Pharisees* were together, Jesus asked them a question. ⁴²He said, "What do you think about the Christ*? Whose son is he?"

The Pharisees answered, "The Christ is the Son of David.*"

⁴³Jesus said to them, "Then why did David call him 'Lord'? David was speaking by the power of the Spirit.* He said,

⁴⁴ 'The Lord God said to my Lord:
Sit by me at my right side,
and I will put your enemies under your control.'ᵈ

Psalm 110:1

⁴⁵David calls the Christ 'Lord.' So how can he be David's son?" ⁴⁶None of the Pharisees could answer Jesus' question. And after that day, no one was brave enough to ask him any more questions.

Jesus Criticizes the Religious Leaders
(Mk. 12:38–40; Lk. 11:37–52; 20:45–47)

23 ¹Then Jesus spoke to the people and to his followers. He said, ²"The teachers of the law and the Pharisees* have the authority to tell you what the law of Moses* says. ³So you should obey them. Do everything they tell you to do. But their lives are not good examples for you to follow. They tell you to do things, but they don't do those things themselves. ⁴They make strict rules that are hard for people to obey. They try to force others to obey all their rules. But they themselves will not try to follow any of those rules.

⁵"The only reason they do what they do is for other people to see them. They make the little Scripture* boxesᵉ they wear

---

ᵃ**22:37** Quote from Deut. 6:5. ᵇ**22:39** *your neighbor* Or, "others." Jesus' teaching in Lk. 10:25–37 makes clear that this includes anyone in need. ᶜ**22:39** Quote from Lev. 19:18. ᵈ**22:44** *control* Literally, "feet." ᵉ**23:5** *little Scripture boxes* Small leather boxes containing four important Scriptures. Some Jews tied these to the forehead and left arm to show that they were very religious.

bigger and bigger. And they make the tassels on their prayer clothes long enough for people to notice them. [6]These men love to have the places of honor at banquets and the most important seats in the synagogues.* [7]They love for people to show respect to them in the marketplaces and to call them 'Teacher.'

[8]"But you must not be called 'Teacher.' You are all equal as brothers and sisters. You have only one Teacher. [9]And don't call anyone on earth 'Father.' You have one Father. He is in heaven. [10]And you should not be called 'Master.' You have only one Master, the Christ.* [11]Whoever serves you like a servant is the greatest among you. [12]People who think they are better than others will be made humble. But people who humble themselves will be made great.

[13]"It will be bad for you teachers of the law and you Pharisees! You are hypocrites*! You close the way for people to enter God's kingdom.* You yourselves don't enter, and you stop those who are trying to enter. [14]*a*

[15]"It will be bad for you teachers of the law and you Pharisees! You are hypocrites. You travel across the seas and across different countries to find one person who will follow your ways. When you find that person, you make him worse than you are. And you are so bad that you belong in hell!

[16]"It will be bad for you teachers of the law and you Pharisees! You guide the people, but you are blind. You say, 'If anyone uses the name of the Temple* to make a promise, that means nothing. But anyone who uses the gold that is in the Temple to make a promise must keep that promise.' [17]You are blind fools! Can't you see that the Temple is greater than the gold on it? It's the Temple that makes the gold holy*!

[18]"And you say, 'If anyone uses the altar* to make a promise, that means nothing. But anyone who uses the gift on the altar to make a promise must keep that promise.' [19]You are blind! Can't you see that the altar is greater than any gift on it? It's the altar that makes the gift holy! [20]Whoever uses the altar to make a promise is really using the altar and everything on the altar. [21]And anyone who uses the Temple to make a promise is really using the Temple and God, who lives in it. [22]Whoever uses heaven to make a promise is using God's throne and the one who is seated on it.

[23]"It will be bad for you teachers of the law and you Pharisees! You are hypocrites! You give God a tenth of everything you own—even your mint, dill, and cumin.*b* But you don't obey the really important teachings of the law—being fair, showing mercy, and being faithful. These are the things you should do. And you

---

*a***23:14** Some Greek copies add verse 14: "It will be bad for you, teachers of the law and you Pharisees. You are hypocrites. You cheat widows and take their homes. Then you make long prayers so that people can see you. So you will have a worse punishment." See Mk. 12:40; Lk. 20:47. *b***23:23** mint, dill, cumin Small plants grown in gardens and used for spices. Only very religious people would be careful enough to give a tenth of these plants.

should also continue to do those other things. [24]You guide the people, but you are blind! Think about a man picking a little fly out of his drink and then swallowing a camel! You are like that.[a]

[25]"It will be bad for you teachers of the law and you Pharisees. You are hypocrites! You wash clean the outside of your cups and dishes. But inside they are full of what you got by cheating others and pleasing yourselves. [26]Pharisees, you are blind! First make the inside of the cup clean and good. Then the outside of the cup will also be clean.

[27]"It will be bad for you teachers of the law and you Pharisees! You are hypocrites! You are like tombs* that are painted white. Outside they look fine, but inside they are full of dead people's bones and all kinds of filth. [28]It is the same with you. People look at you and think you are godly. But on the inside you are full of hypocrisy* and evil.

[29]"It will be bad for you teachers of the law and you Pharisees! You are hypocrites! You build tombs for the prophets.* And you show honor to the graves of the godly people who were killed. [30]And you say, 'If we had lived during the time of our ancestors,* we would not have helped them kill these prophets.' [31]So you give proof that you are descendants of those who killed the prophets. [32]And you will finish the sin that your ancestors started!

[33]"You are snakes! You are from a family of poisonous snakes! You will not escape God. You will all be judged guilty and go to hell! [34]So I tell you this: I send to you prophets and teachers who are wise and know the Scriptures. You will kill some of them. You will hang some of them on crosses. You will beat some of them in your synagogues. You will chase them from town to town.

[35]"So you will be guilty for the death of all the good people who have been killed on earth. You will be guilty for the killing of that godly man Abel.[b] And you will be guilty for the killing of Zechariah[c] son of Berachiah. He was killed between the Temple and the altar. You will be guilty for the killing of all the good people who lived between the time of Abel and the time of Zechariah. [36]Believe me when I say that all of these things will happen to you people who are living now.

Jesus Warns the People of Jerusalem
(Lk. 13:34–35)

[37]"O Jerusalem, Jerusalem! You kill the prophets.* You stone to death those that God has sent to you. Many, many times I wanted to help your people. I wanted to gather them together like a hen gathers her chicks under her wings. But you did not let me. [38]Now your house will be left completely empty. [39]I tell

---

[a]**23:24** *You are like that* Meaning "You worry about the smallest mistakes but commit the biggest sin." [b]**23:35** *Abel* In the Hebrew Old Testament, the first person to be murdered. [c]**23:35** *Zechariah* In the Hebrew Old Testament, the last person to be murdered.

you, you will not see me again until that time when you will say, 'Welcome! God bless the one who comes in the name of the Lord.'[a]"

Jesus Warns About the Future
(Mk. 13:1–31; Lk. 21:5–33)

24 [1]Jesus left the Temple* area and was walking away. But his followers came to him to show him the Temple's buildings. [2]He asked them, "Are you looking at these buildings? The fact is, they will be destroyed. Every stone will be thrown down to the ground. Not one stone will be left on another."

[3]Later, Jesus was sitting at a place on the Mount of Olives.* The followers came to be alone with him. They said, "Tell us when these things will happen. And what will happen to prepare us for your coming and the end of time?"

[4]Jesus answered, "Be careful! Don't let anyone fool you. [5]Many people will come and use my name. They will say, 'I am the Christ.'*' And they will fool many people. [6]You will hear about wars that are being fought. And you will hear stories about other wars beginning. But don't be afraid. These things must happen before the end comes. [7]Nations will fight against other nations. Kingdoms will fight against other kingdoms. There will be times when there is no food for people to eat. And there will be earthquakes in different places. [8]These things are only the beginning of troubles, like the first pains of a woman giving birth.

[9]"Then you will be arrested and handed over to be punished and killed. People all over the world will hate you because you believe in me. [10]During that time many believers will lose their faith. They will turn against each other and hate each other. [11]Many false prophets* will come. They will cause many people to believe wrong things. [12]There will be more and more evil in the world. So most believers will stop showing love. [13]But the one who remains faithful to the end will be saved. [14]The Good News about God's kingdom[b] will be told in the whole world. It will be told to every nation. Then the end will come.

[15]"Daniel the prophet* spoke about 'the terrible thing that causes destruction.'[c] You will see this terrible thing standing in the holy place." (You who read this should understand what it means.) [16]"The people in Judea at that time should run away to the mountains. [17]They should run away without wasting time to stop for anything. If they are on the roof of their house, they must not go down to get anything out of the house. [18]If they are in the field, they must not go back to get a coat.

[19]"During that time it will be hard for women who are pregnant or have small babies! [20]Pray that it will not be winter or a

---

[a]23:39 Quote from Ps. 118:26. [b]24:14 God's kingdom Literally, "the kingdom." See "God's kingdom" in the Word List. [c]24:15 'the terrible thing … destruction' See Dan. 9:27; 12:11 (also Dan. 11:31).

Sabbath* day when these things happen and you have to run away, [21]because it will be a time of great trouble. There will be more trouble than has ever happened since the beginning of the world. And nothing as bad as that will ever happen again.

[22]"But God has decided to make that terrible time short. If it were not made short, no one would continue living. But God will make that time short to help the people he has chosen.

[23]"Someone might say to you at that time, 'Look, there is the Christ!' Or someone else might say, 'There he is!' But don't believe them. [24]False Christs and false prophets will come and do great miracles and wonders,[a] trying to fool the people God has chosen, if that is possible. [25]Now I have warned you about this before it happens.

[26]"Someone might tell you, 'The Christ is there in the desert!' But don't go into the desert to look for him. Someone else might say, 'There is the Christ in that room!' But don't believe it. [27]When the Son of Man* comes, everyone will see him. It will be like lightning flashing in the sky that can be seen everywhere. [28]It's like looking for a dead body: You will find it where the vultures* are gathering above.

[29]"Right after the trouble of those days, this will happen:

'The sun will become dark,
    and the moon will not give light.
The stars will fall from the sky,
    and everything in the sky will be changed.'[b]

[30]"Then there will be something in the sky that shows the Son of Man is coming. All the people of the world will cry. Everyone will see the Son of Man coming on the clouds in the sky. He will come with power and great glory.* [31]He will use a loud trumpet to send his angels all around the earth. They will gather his chosen people from every part of the earth.

[32]"The fig tree teaches us a lesson: When its branches become green and soft, and new leaves begin to grow, then you know that summer is near. [33]In the same way, when you see all these things happening, you will know that the time[c] is near, ready to come. [34]I assure you that all these things will happen while some of the people of this time are still living. [35]The whole world, earth and sky, will be destroyed, but my words will last forever.

Only God Knows When the Time Will Be
(Mk. 13:32–37; Lk. 17:26–30, 34–36)

[36]"No one knows when that day or time will be. The Son and the angels in heaven don't know when it will be. Only the Father knows.

---

[a]**24:24** *miracles and wonders* Here, amazing acts done by Satan's power.   [b]**24:29** See Isa. 13:10, 34:4.   [c]**24:33** *time* The time Jesus has been talking about when something important will happen. See Lk. 21:31, where Jesus says that this is the time for God's kingdom to come.

[37] "When the Son of Man* comes, it will be the same as what happened during Noah's time. [38] In those days before the flood, people were eating and drinking, marrying and giving their children to be married right up to the day Noah entered the boat. [39] They knew nothing about what was happening until the flood came and destroyed them all.

"It will be the same when the Son of Man comes. [40] Two men will be working together in the field. One will be taken and the other will be left. [41] Two women will be grinding grain with a mill.* One will be taken and the other will be left.

[42] "So always be ready. You don't know the day your Lord will come. [43] Obviously, a homeowner who knew what time a thief was planning to come would be ready and not let the thief break in. [44] So you also must be ready. The Son of Man will come at a time when you don't expect him.

Good Servants and Bad Servants
(Lk. 12:41–48)

[45] "Who is the wise and trusted servant? The master trusts one servant to give the other servants their food at the right time. Who is the one the master trusts to do that work? [46] When the master comes and finds that servant doing the work he gave him, what a great day it will be for that servant. [47] I can tell you without a doubt, the master will choose that servant to take care of everything he owns.

[48] But what will happen if that servant is evil and thinks his master will not come back soon? [49] He will begin to beat the other servants. He will eat and drink with others who are drunk. [50] Then the master will come when the servant is not ready, at a time when the servant is not expecting him. [51] Then the master will punish that servant. He will send him away to be with the hypocrites,* where people will cry and grind their teeth with pain.

A Story About Ten Girls

25 [1] "At that time God's kingdom* will be like ten girls who went to wait for the bridegroom.* They took their lamps with them. [2] Five of the girls were foolish, and five were wise. [3] The foolish girls took their lamps with them, but they did not take extra oil for the lamps. [4] The wise girls took their lamps and more oil in jars. [5] When the bridegroom was very late, the girls could not keep their eyes open, and they all fell asleep.

[6] "At midnight someone announced, 'The bridegroom is coming! Come and meet him!'

[7] "Then all the girls woke up. They made their lamps ready. [8] But the foolish girls said to the wise girls, 'Give us some of your oil. The oil in our lamps is all gone.'

[9] "The wise girls answered, 'No! The oil we have might not be enough for all of us. But go to those who sell oil and buy some for yourselves.'

¹⁰"So the foolish girls went to buy oil. While they were gone, the bridegroom came. The girls who were ready went in with the bridegroom to the wedding feast. Then the door was closed and locked.

¹¹"Later, the other girls came. They said, 'Sir, sir! Open the door to let us in.'

¹²"But the bridegroom answered, 'Certainly not! I don't even know you.'

¹³"So always be ready. You don't know the day or the time when the Son of Man* will come.

A Story About Three Servants
(Lk. 19:11–27)

¹⁴"At that time God's kingdom* will also be like a man leaving home to travel to another place for a visit. Before he left, he talked with his servants. He told his servants to take care of his things while he was gone. ¹⁵He decided how much each servant would be able to care for. The man gave one servant five bags of money.ᵃ He gave another servant two bags. And he gave a third servant one bag. Then he left. ¹⁶The servant who got five bags went quickly to invest the money. Those five bags of money earned five more. ¹⁷It was the same with the servant who had two bags. That servant invested the money and earned two more. ¹⁸But the servant who got one bag of money went away and dug a hole in the ground. Then he hid his master's money in the hole.

¹⁹"After a long time the master came home. He asked the servants what they did with his money. ²⁰The servant who got five bags brought that amount and five more bags of money to the master. The servant said, 'Master, you trusted me to care for five bags of money. So I used them to earn five more.'

²¹"The master answered, 'You did right. You are a good servant who can be trusted. You did well with that small amount of money. So I will let you care for much greater things. Come and share my happiness with me.'

²²"Then the servant who got two bags of money came to the master. The servant said, 'Master, you gave me two bags of money to care for. So I used your two bags to earn two more.'

²³"The master answered, 'You did right. You are a good servant who can be trusted. You did well with a small amount of money. So I will let you care for much greater things. Come and share my happiness with me.'

²⁴"Then the servant who got one bag of money came to the master. The servant said, 'Master, I knew you were a very hard man. You harvest what you did not plant. You gather crops where you did not put any seed. ²⁵So I was afraid. I went and

---

ᵃ**25:15** *bags of money* Literally, *"talanton"* or *"talent,"* about 27 to 36 kg (60 to 80 pounds) of gold, silver, or copper coins. Also in verses 20, 22, 24, 28.

hid your money in the ground. Here is the one bag of money you gave me.'

²⁶"The master answered, 'You are a bad and lazy servant! You say you knew that I harvest what I did not plant and that I gather crops where I did not put any seed. ²⁷So you should have put my money in the bank. Then, when I came home, I would get my money back. And I would also get the interest that my money earned.'

²⁸"So the master told his other servants, 'Take the one bag of money from that servant and give it to the servant who has ten bags. ²⁹Everyone who uses what they have will get more. They will have much more than they need. But people who do not use what they have will have everything taken away from them.' ³⁰Then the master said, 'Throw that useless servant outside into the darkness, where people will cry and grind their teeth with pain.'

The Son of Man Will Judge All People

³¹"The Son of Man* will come again with divine greatness,* and all his angels will come with him. He will sit as king on his great and glorious throne. ³²All the people of the world will be gathered before him. Then he will separate everyone into two groups. It will be like a shepherd separating his sheep from his goats. ³³He will put the sheep on his right and the goats on his left.

³⁴"Then the king will say to the godly people on his right, 'Come, my Father has great blessings for you. The kingdom* he promised is now yours. It has been prepared for you since the world was made. ³⁵It is yours because when I was hungry, you gave me food to eat. When I was thirsty, you gave me something to drink. When I had no place to stay, you welcomed me into your home. ³⁶When I was without clothes, you gave me something to wear. When I was sick, you cared for me. When I was in prison, you came to visit me.'

³⁷"Then the godly people will answer, 'Lord, when did we see you hungry and give you food? When did we see you thirsty and give you something to drink? ³⁸When did we see you with no place to stay and welcome you into our home? When did we see you without clothes and give you something to wear? ³⁹When did we see you sick or in prison and care for you?'

⁴⁰"Then the king will answer, 'The truth is, anything you did for any of my people here,^a you also did for me.'

⁴¹"Then the king will say to the evil people on his left, 'Get away from me. God has already decided that you will be punished. Go into the fire that burns forever—the fire that was prepared for the devil and his angels. ⁴²You must go away because

^a**25:40** *any of my people here* Literally, "one of the least of these brothers of mine." Also in verse 45.

when I was hungry, you gave me nothing to eat. When I was thirsty, you gave me nothing to drink. ⁴³When I had no place to stay, you did not welcome me into your home. When I was without clothes, you gave me nothing to wear. When I was sick and in prison, you did not care for me.'

⁴⁴"Then those people will answer, 'Lord, when did we see you hungry or thirsty? When did we see you without a place to stay? Or when did we see you without clothes or sick or in prison? When did we see any of this and not help you?'

⁴⁵"The king will answer, 'The truth is, anything you refused to do for any of my people here, you refused to do for me.'

⁴⁶"Then these evil people will go away to be punished forever. But the godly people will go and enjoy eternal life."

The Jewish Leaders Plan to Kill Jesus
(Mk. 14:1–2; Lk. 22:1–2; Jn. 11:45–53)

26 ¹After Jesus finished saying all these things, he said to his followers, ²"You know that the day after tomorrow is Passover.* On that day the Son of Man* will be handed over to his enemies to be killed on a cross."

³Then the leading priests and the older Jewish leaders had a meeting at the palace where the high priest* lived. The high priest's name was Caiaphas. ⁴In the meeting they tried to find a way to arrest and kill Jesus without anyone knowing what they were doing. They planned to arrest Jesus and kill him. ⁵They said, "We cannot arrest Jesus during Passover. We don't want the people to become angry and cause a riot."

A Woman Does Something Special
(Mk. 14:3–9; Jn. 12:1–8)

⁶Jesus was in Bethany at the house of Simon the leper.* ⁷While he was there, a woman came to him. She had an alabaster* jar filled with expensive perfume. She poured the perfume on Jesus' head while he was eating.

⁸The followers saw the woman do this and were upset at her. They said, "Why waste that perfume? ⁹It could be sold for a lot of money, and the money could be given to those who are poor."

¹⁰But Jesus knew what happened. He said, "Why are you bothering this woman? She did a very good thing for me. ¹¹You will always have the poor with you.ᵃ But you will not always have me. ¹²This woman poured perfume on my body. She did this to prepare me for burial after I die. ¹³The Good News* will be told to people all over the world. And I can assure you that everywhere the Good News is told, the story of what this woman did will also be told, and people will remember her."

ᵃ**26:11** *You will . . . with you* See Deut. 15:11.

Judas Agrees to Help Jesus' Enemies
(Mk. 14:10–11; Lk. 22:3–6)

¹⁴Then one of the twelve followers went to talk to the leading priests. This was the follower named Judas Iscariot. ¹⁵He said, "I will hand Jesus over to you. What will you pay me for doing this?" The priests gave him 30 silver coins. ¹⁶After that, Judas waited for the best time to hand Jesus over to them.

The Passover Meal
(Mk. 14:12–21; Lk. 22:7–14, 21–23; Jn. 13:21–30)

¹⁷On the first day of the Festival of Unleavened Bread,* the followers came to Jesus. They said, "We will prepare everything for you to eat the Passover* meal. Where do you want us to have the meal?"

¹⁸Jesus answered, "Go into the city. Go to a man I know. Tell him that the Teacher says, 'The chosen time is near. I will have the Passover meal with my followers at your house.'" ¹⁹They obeyed and did what Jesus told them to do. They prepared the Passover meal.

²⁰In the evening Jesus was at the table with the twelve followers. ²¹They were all eating. Then Jesus said, "Believe me when I say that one of you twelve here will hand me over to my enemies."

²²The followers were very sad to hear this. Each one said, "Lord, surely I am not the one!"

²³Jesus answered, "One who has dipped his bread in the same bowl with me will be the one to hand me over. ²⁴The Son of Man* will suffer what the Scriptures* say will happen to him. But it will be very bad for the one who hands over the Son of Man to be killed. It would be better for him if he had never been born."

²⁵Then Judas, the very one who would hand him over, said to Jesus, "Teacher, surely I am not the one you are talking about, am I?"

Jesus answered, "Yes, it is you."

The Lord's Supper
(Mk. 14:22–26; Lk. 22:15–20; 1 Cor. 11:23–25)

²⁶While they were eating, Jesus took some bread and thanked God for it. He broke off some pieces, gave them to his followers and said, "Take this bread and eat it. It is my body."

²⁷Then he took a cup of wine, thanked God for it, and gave it to them. He said, "Each one of you drink some of it. ²⁸This wine is my blood, which will be poured out to forgive the sins of many and begin the new agreement* from God to his people. ²⁹I want you to know, I will not drink this wine again until that day when we are together in my Father's kingdom* and the wine is new. Then I will drink it again with you."

³⁰They all sang a song and then went out to the Mount of Olives.*

Jesus Says His Followers Will Leave Him
(Mk. 14:27–31; Lk. 22:31–34; Jn. 13:36–38)

³¹Jesus told the followers, "Tonight you will all lose your faith in me. The Scriptures* say,

> 'I will kill the shepherd,
>   and the sheep will run away.'   *Zechariah 13:7*

³²But after I am killed, I will rise from death. Then I will go into Galilee. I will be there before you go there."

³³Peter answered, "All the other followers may lose their faith in you. But my faith will never be shaken."

³⁴Jesus answered, "The truth is, tonight you will say you don't know me. You will deny me three times before the rooster crows."

³⁵But Peter answered, "I will never say I don't know you! I will even die with you!" And all the other followers said the same thing.

Jesus Prays Alone
(Mk. 14:32–42; Lk. 22:39–46)

³⁶Then Jesus went with his followers to a place called Gethsemane. He said to them, "Sit here while I go there and pray." ³⁷He told Peter and the two sons of Zebedee to come with him. Then he began to be very sad and troubled. ³⁸Jesus said to Peter and the two sons of Zebedee, "My heart is so heavy with grief, I feel as if I am dying. Wait here and stay awake with me."

³⁹Then Jesus went on a little farther away from them. He fell to the ground and prayed, "My Father, if it is possible, don't make me drink from this cup.*ᵃ* But do what you want, not what I want." ⁴⁰Then he went back to his followers and found them sleeping. He said to Peter, "Could you men not stay awake with me for one hour? ⁴¹Stay awake and pray for strength against temptation. Your spirit wants to do what is right, but your body is weak."

⁴²Then Jesus went away a second time and prayed, "My Father, if I must do this*ᵇ* and it is not possible for me to escape it, then I pray that what you want will be done."

⁴³Then he went back to the followers. Again he found them sleeping. They could not stay awake. ⁴⁴So he left them and went away one more time and prayed. This third time he prayed, he said the same thing.

⁴⁵Then Jesus went back to the followers and said, "Are you still sleeping and resting? The time has come for the Son of Man* to be handed over to the control of sinful men. ⁴⁶Stand up! We must go. Here comes the one who will hand me over."

---

*ᵃ***26:39** *cup* A symbol of suffering. Jesus used the idea of drinking from a cup to mean accepting the suffering he would face in the terrible events that were soon to come.
*ᵇ***26:42** *do this* Literally, "drink this," referring to the "cup," the symbol of suffering in verse 39.

Jesus Is Arrested
(Mk. 14:43–50; Lk. 22:47–53; Jn. 18:3–12)

47While Jesus was still speaking, Judas, one of the twelve apostles* came there. He had a big crowd of people with him, all carrying swords and clubs. They had been sent from the leading priests and the older leaders of the people. 48Judas[a] planned to do something to show them which one was Jesus. He said, "The one I kiss will be Jesus. Arrest him." 49So he went to Jesus and said, "Hello, Teacher!" Then Judas kissed him.

50Jesus answered, "Friend, do the thing you came to do."

Then the men came and grabbed Jesus and arrested him. 51When that happened, one of the followers with Jesus grabbed his sword and pulled it out. He swung it at the servant of the high priest* and cut off his ear.

52Jesus said to the man, "Put your sword back in its place. People who use swords will be killed with swords. 53Surely you know I could ask my Father and he would give me more than twelve armies of angels. 54But it must happen this way to show the truth of what the Scriptures* said."

55Then Jesus said to the crowd, "Why do you come to get me with swords and clubs as if I were a criminal. Every day I sat in the Temple* area teaching. You did not arrest me there. 56But all these things have happened to show the full meaning of what the prophets* wrote." Then all of Jesus' followers left him and ran away.

Jesus Before the Jewish Leaders
(Mk. 14:53–65; Lk. 22:54–55, 63–71; Jn. 18:13–14, 19–24)

57The men who arrested Jesus led him to the house of Caiaphas the high priest.* The teachers of the law and the older Jewish leaders were gathered there. 58Peter followed Jesus but stayed back at a distance. He followed him to the yard of the high priest's house. Peter went in and sat with the guards. He wanted to see what would happen to Jesus.

59The leading priests and the high council tried to find something against Jesus so that they could kill him. They tried to find people to lie and say that Jesus had done wrong. 60Many people came and told lies about him. But the council could find no real reason to kill him. Then two people came 61and said, "This man[b] said, 'I can destroy the Temple* of God and build it again in three days.'"

62Then the high priest stood up and said to Jesus, "Don't you have anything to say about these charges against you? Are they telling the truth?" 63But Jesus said nothing.

Again the high priest said to Jesus, "You are now under oath. I command you by the power of the living God to tell us the truth. Tell us, are you the Christ,* the Son of God?"

[a]**26:48** *Judas* Literally, "the one who handed him over." [b]**26:61** *this man* That is, Jesus. His enemies avoided saying his name.

⁶⁴Jesus answered, "Yes, that's right. But I tell you, in the future you will see the Son of Man* sitting at the right side of God. And you will see the Son of Man coming on the clouds of heaven."

⁶⁵When the high priest heard this, he tore his clothes in anger. He said, "This man has said things that insult God! We don't need any more witnesses. You all heard his insulting words. ⁶⁶What do you think?"

The Jewish leaders answered, "He is guilty, and he must die."

⁶⁷Then some there spit in Jesus' face, and they hit him with their fists. Others slapped him. ⁶⁸They said, "Show us that you are a prophet,ᵃ Christ! Tell us who hit you!"

Peter Is Afraid to Say He Knows Jesus
(Mk. 14:66–72; Lk. 22:56–62; Jn. 18:15–18, 25–27)

⁶⁹While Peter was sitting outside in the yard, a servant girl came up to him. She said, "You were with Jesus, that man from Galilee."

⁷⁰But Peter told everyone there that this was not true. "I don't know what you are talking about," he said.

⁷¹Then he left the yard. At the gate another girl saw him and said to the people there, "This man was with Jesus of Nazareth."

⁷²Again, Peter said he was never with Jesus. He said, "I swear to God I don't know the man!"

⁷³A short time later those standing there went to Peter and said, "We know you are one of them. It's clear from the way you talk."

⁷⁴Then Peter began to curse. He said, "I swear to God, I don't know the man!" As soon as he said this, a rooster crowed. ⁷⁵Then he remembered what Jesus had told him: "Before the rooster crows, you will say three times that you don't know me." Then Peter went outside and cried bitterly.

Jesus Is Taken to Governor Pilate
(Mk. 15:1; Lk. 23:1–2; Jn. 18:28–32)

27 ¹Early the next morning, all the leading priests and older leaders of the people met and decided to kill Jesus. ²They tied him, led him away, and handed him over to Pilate, the governor.

Judas Kills Himself
(Acts 1:18–19)

³Judas saw that they had decided to kill Jesus. He was the one who had handed him over. When he saw what happened, he was very sorry for what he had done. So he took the 30 silver coins back to the priests and the older leaders. ⁴Judas said, "I sinned. I handed over to you an innocent man to be killed."

The Jewish leaders answered, "We don't care! That's a problem for you, not us."

ᵃ 26:68 prophet A prophet often knows things that are hidden to other people.

⁵So Judas threw the money into the Temple.* Then he went out from there and hanged himself.

⁶The leading priests picked up the silver coins in the Temple. They said, "Our law does not allow us to keep this money with the Temple money, because this money has paid for a man's death." ⁷So they decided to use the money to buy a field called Potter's Field. This field would be a place to bury people who died while visiting in Jerusalem. ⁸That is why that field is still called the Field of Blood. ⁹This showed the full meaning of what Jeremiah the prophet* said,

> "They took 30 silver coins. That was how much the Jewish people decided to pay for his life. ¹⁰They used those 30 silver coins to buy the potter's field, like the Lord commanded me."ᵃ

Governor Pilate Questions Jesus
(Mk. 15:2-5; Lk. 23:3-5; Jn. 18:33-38)

¹¹Jesus stood before Pilate the governor, who asked him, "Are you the king of the Jews?"

Jesus answered, "Yes, that's right."

¹²Then, when the leading priests and the older Jewish leaders made their accusations against Jesus, he said nothing.

¹³So Pilate said to him, "Don't you hear all these charges they are making against you? Why don't you answer?"

¹⁴But Jesus did not say anything, and this really surprised the governor.

Pilate Tries but Fails to Free Jesus
(Mk. 15:6-15; Lk. 23:13-25; Jn. 18:39-19:16)

¹⁵Every year at Passover* time the governor would free one prisoner—whichever one the people wanted him to free. ¹⁶At that time there was a man in prison who was known to be very bad. His name was Barabbas.ᵇ

¹⁷When a crowd gathered, Pilate said to them, "I will free one man for you. Which one do you want me to free: Barabbas or Jesus who is called the Christ*?" ¹⁸Pilate knew that they had handed Jesus over to him because they were jealous of him.

¹⁹While Pilate was sitting there in the place for judging, his wife sent a message to him. It said, "Don't do anything with that man. He is not guilty. Last night I had a dream about him, and it troubled me very much."

²⁰But the leading priests and older Jewish leaders told the people to ask for Barabbas to be set free and for Jesus to be killed.

²¹Pilate said, "I have Barabbas and Jesus. Which one do you want me to set free for you?"

The people answered, "Barabbas!"

ᵃ**27:10** *"They took … me"* See Zech. 11:12-13; Jer. 32:6-9.   ᵇ**27:16** *Barabbas* In some Greek copies the name is Jesus Barabbas.

²²Pilate asked, "So what should I do with Jesus, the one called the Christ?"

All the people said, "Kill him on a cross!"

²³Pilate asked, "Why do you want me to kill him? What wrong has he done?"

But they shouted louder, "Kill him on a cross!"

²⁴Pilate saw that there was nothing he could do to make the people change. In fact, it looked as if there would be a riot. So he took some water and washed his hands*a* in front of them all. He said, "I am not guilty of this man's death. You are the ones who are doing it!"

²⁵The people answered, "We will take full responsibility for his death. You can blame us and even our children!"

²⁶Then Pilate freed Barabbas. And he told some soldiers to beat Jesus with whips. Then he handed him over to the soldiers to be killed on a cross.

Pilate's Soldiers Make Fun of Jesus
(Mk. 15:16-20; Jn. 19:2-3)

²⁷Then Pilate's soldiers took Jesus into the governor's palace. All the soldiers gathered around him. ²⁸They took off Jesus' clothes and put a red robe on him. ²⁹Then they made a crown from thorny branches and put it on his head, and they put a stick in his right hand. Then they bowed before him, making fun of him. They said, "We salute you, king of the Jews!" ³⁰They spit on him. Then they took his stick and kept hitting him on the head with it. ³¹After they finished making fun of him, the soldiers took off the robe and put his own clothes on him again. Then they led him away to be killed on a cross.

Jesus Is Nailed to a Cross
(Mk. 15:21-32; Lk. 23:26-39; Jn. 19:17-19)

³²The soldiers were going out of the city with Jesus. They saw a man from Cyrene named Simon, and they forced him to carry Jesus' cross. ³³They came to the place called Golgotha. (Golgotha means "The Place of the Skull.") ³⁴There the soldiers gave Jesus some wine mixed with gall.*b* But when he tasted it, he refused to drink it.

³⁵The soldiers nailed Jesus to a cross. Then they threw dice to divide his clothes between them. ³⁶The soldiers stayed there to guard him. ³⁷They put a sign above his head with the charge against him written on it: "THIS IS JESUS, THE KING OF THE JEWS."

³⁸Two criminals were nailed to crosses beside Jesus—one on the right and the other on the left. ³⁹People walked by and shouted insults at Jesus. They shook their heads ⁴⁰and said, "You said you could destroy the Temple* and build it again in

---

a27:24 washed his hands Pilate did this as a sign to show that he wanted no part in what the people did.   *b27:34 gall* Probably used as a drug to relieve pain.

three days. So save yourself! Come down from that cross if you really are the Son of God!"

⁴¹The leading priests, the teachers of the law, and the older Jewish leaders were also there. They made fun of Jesus the same as the other people did. ⁴²They said, "He saved others, but he can't save himself! People say he is the king of Israel.* If he is the king, he should come down now from the cross. Then we will believe in him. ⁴³He trusted God. So let God save him now, if God really wants him. He himself said, 'I am the Son of God.'" ⁴⁴And in the same way, the criminals on the crosses beside Jesus also insulted him.

Jesus Dies
(Mk. 15:33–41; Lk. 23:44–49; Jn. 19:28–30)

⁴⁵At noon the whole country became dark. The darkness continued for three hours. ⁴⁶About three o'clock Jesus cried with a loud voice, *"Eli, Eli, lema sabachthani?"* This means "My God, my God, why have you left me alone?"ª

⁴⁷Some of the people standing there heard this. They said, "He is calling Elijah."ᵇ

⁴⁸Quickly, one of them ran and got a sponge. He filled the sponge with sour wine and tied the sponge to a stick. Then he used the stick to give the sponge to Jesus to get a drink from it. ⁴⁹But the others said, "Don't bother him. We want to see if Elijah will come to save him."

⁵⁰Again Jesus cried with a loud voice. Then he died.ᶜ

⁵¹When Jesus died, the curtain* in the Temple* was torn into two pieces. The tear started at the top and tore all the way to the bottom. Also, the earth shook and rocks were broken. ⁵²The graves opened, and many of God's people who had died were raised from death. ⁵³They came out of the graves. And after Jesus was raised from death, they went into the holy city, and many people saw them.

⁵⁴The army officer* and the soldiers guarding Jesus saw this earthquake and everything that happened. They were very afraid and said, "He really was the Son of God!"

⁵⁵Many women were standing away from the cross, watching. These were the women who had followed Jesus from Galilee to care for him. ⁵⁶Mary Magdalene, Mary the mother of James and Joseph, and the mother of James and Johnᵈ were there.

Jesus Is Buried
(Mk. 15:42–47; Lk. 23:50–56; Jn. 19:38–42)

⁵⁷That evening a rich man named Joseph came to Jerusalem. He was a follower of Jesus from the town of Arimathea. ⁵⁸He

ª**27:46** Quote from Ps. 22:1. ᵇ**27:47** *"He is calling Elijah"* The word for "My God" (*Eli* in Hebrew or *Eloi* in Aramaic) sounded to the people like the name of Elijah, a famous man who spoke for God about 850 B.C. ᶜ**27:50** *died* Literally, "let his spirit leave." ᵈ**27:56** *James and John* Literally, "the sons of Zebedee."

went to Pilate and asked to have Jesus' body. Pilate gave orders for the soldiers to give Jesus' body to him. 59Then Joseph took the body and wrapped it in a new linen cloth. 60He put Jesus' body in a new tomb* that he had dug in a wall of rock. Then he closed the tomb by rolling a very large stone to cover the entrance. After he did this, he went away. 61Mary Magdalene and the other woman named Mary were sitting near the tomb.

The Tomb of Jesus Is Guarded

62That day was the day called Preparation day.* The next day, the leading priests and the Pharisees* went to Pilate. 63They said, "Sir, we remember that while that liar was still alive he said, 'I will rise from death in three days.' 64So give the order for the tomb* to be guarded well for three days. His followers might come and try to steal the body. Then they could tell everyone that he has risen from death. That lie will be even worse than what they said about him before."

65Pilate said, "Take some soldiers and go guard the tomb the best way you know." 66So they all went to the tomb and made it safe from thieves. They did this by sealing the stone in the entrance and putting soldiers there to guard it.

News That Jesus Has Risen From Death
(Mk. 16:1–8; Lk. 24:1–12; Jn. 20:1–10)

28 1The day after the Sabbath* day was the first day of the week. That day at dawn Mary Magdalene and the other woman named Mary went to look at the tomb.*

2Suddenly an angel of the Lord came from the sky, and there was a huge earthquake. The angel went to the tomb and rolled the stone away from the entrance. Then he sat on top of the stone. 3The angel was shining as bright as lightning. His clothes were as white as snow. 4The soldiers guarding the tomb were very afraid of the angel. They shook with fear and then became like dead men.

5The angel said to the women, "Don't be afraid. I know you are looking for Jesus, the one who was killed on the cross. 6But he is not here. He has risen from death, as he said he would. Come and see the place where his body was. 7And go quickly and tell his followers, 'Jesus has risen from death. He is going into Galilee and will be there before you. You will see him there.'" Then the angel said, "Now I have told you."

8So the women left the tomb quickly. They were afraid, but they were also very happy. They ran to tell his followers what happened. 9Suddenly, Jesus was there in front of them. He said, "Hello!" The women went to him and, holding on to his feet, worshiped him. 10Then Jesus said to them, "Don't be afraid. Go tell my followers[a] to go to Galilee. They will see me there."

---

a **28:10** followers Literally, "brothers."

Report to the Jewish Leaders

¹¹The women went to tell the followers. At the same time, some of the soldiers who were guarding the tomb* went into the city. They went to tell the leading priests everything that happened. ¹²Then the priests met with the older Jewish leaders and made a plan. They paid the soldiers a lot of money ¹³and said to them, "Tell the people that Jesus' followers came during the night and stole the body while you were sleeping. ¹⁴If the governor hears about this, we will talk to him and keep you out of trouble." ¹⁵So the soldiers kept the money and obeyed the priests. And that story is still spread among the Jews even today.

Jesus Talks to His Followers
(Mk. 16:14–18; Lk. 24:36–49; Jn. 20:19–23; Acts 1:6–8)

¹⁶The eleven followers went to Galilee, to the mountain where Jesus told them to go. ¹⁷On the mountain the followers saw Jesus. They worshiped him. But some of the followers did not believe that it was really Jesus. ¹⁸So he came to them and said, "All authority in heaven and on earth is given to me. ¹⁹So go and make followers of all people in the world. Baptize* them in the name of the Father and the Son and the Holy Spirit.* ²⁰Teach them to obey everything that I have told you. You can be sure that I will be with you always. I will continue with you until the end of time."

Mark

John Prepares the Way for Jesus
(Mt. 3:1–12; Lk. 3:1–9, 15–17; Jn. 1:19–28)

1 ¹The Good News* about Jesus Christ, the Son of God,ᵃ begins
²with what the prophet* Isaiah said would happen. He wrote:

"Listen! I will send my messenger ahead of you.
 He will prepare the way for you."   *Malachi 3:1*

³"There is someone shouting in the desert:
 'Prepare the way for the Lord.
 Make his paths straight.'"   *Isaiah 40:3*

⁴So John the Baptizer* came and was baptizing* people in
the desert area. He told them to be baptized to show that they
wanted to change their lives, and then their sins would be forgiven. ⁵All the people from Judea, including everyone from
Jerusalem, came out to John. They confessed the bad things
they had done, and he baptized them in the Jordan River.

⁶John wore clothes made from camel's hair and a leather belt
around his waist. He ate locusts* and wild honey.

⁷This is what John told the people: "There is someone
coming later who is able to do more than I can. I am not good
enough to be the slave who stoops down to untie his sandals. ⁸I
baptize you with water, but the one who is coming will baptize
you with the Holy Spirit.*"

Jesus Is Baptized by John
(Mt. 3:13–17; Lk. 3:21–22)

⁹About that time Jesus came from the town of Nazareth in
Galilee to the place where John was. John baptized* Jesus in
the Jordan River. ¹⁰As Jesus was coming up out of the water, he
saw the sky torn open. The Spirit* came down on him like a
dove. ¹¹A voice came from heaven and said, "You are my Son,
the one I love. I am very pleased with you."

Jesus Goes Away to Be Tempted
(Mt. 4:1–11; Lk. 4:1–13)

¹²Then the Spirit* sent Jesus into the desert alone. ¹³He was
there for 40 days, being tempted by Satan.* During this time

ᵃ**1:1** *the Son of God* Some Greek copies do not have these words.

he was out among the wild animals. Then angels came and helped him.

Jesus Begins His Work in Galilee
(Mt. 4:12–17; Lk. 4:14–15)

14After John was put in prison, Jesus went into Galilee and told people the Good News* from God. 15He said, "The right time is now here. God's kingdom* is near. Change your hearts and lives, and believe the Good News!"

Jesus Chooses Some Followers
(Mt. 4:18–22; Lk. 5:1–11)

16Jesus was walking by Lake Galilee. He saw Simon*a* and his brother, Andrew. These two men were fishermen, and they were throwing a net into the lake to catch fish. 17Jesus said to them, "Come, follow me, and I will make you a different kind of fishermen. You will bring in people, not fish." 18So they immediately left their nets and followed Jesus.

19Jesus continued walking by Lake Galilee. He saw two more brothers, James and John, the sons of Zebedee. They were in their boat, preparing their nets to catch fish. 20Their father Zebedee and the men who worked for him were in the boat with the brothers. When Jesus saw the brothers, he told them to come. They left their father and followed Jesus.

Jesus Frees a Man From an Evil Spirit
(Lk. 4:31–37)

21Jesus and his followers went to Capernaum.* On the Sabbath* day, Jesus went into the synagogue* and taught the people. 22They were amazed at his teaching. He did not teach like their teachers of the law. He taught like someone with authority. 23While Jesus was in the synagogue, a man was there who had an evil spirit inside him. The man shouted, 24"Jesus of Nazareth! What do you want with us? Did you come to destroy us? I know who you are—God's Holy One!"

25Jesus, his voice full of warning, said, "Be quiet, and come out of him!" 26The evil spirit made the man shake. Then the spirit made a loud noise and came out of him.

27The people were amazed. They asked each other, "What is happening here? This man is teaching something new, and he teaches with authority! He even commands evil spirits, and they obey him." 28So the news about Jesus spread quickly everywhere in the area of Galilee.

Jesus Heals Many People
(Mt. 8:14–17; Lk. 4:38–41)

29Jesus and the followers left the synagogue.* They all went with James and John to the home of Simon and Andrew.

a1:16 Simon Simon's other name was Peter. Also in verses 29, 36.

³⁰Simon's mother-in-law was very sick. She was in bed and had a fever. The people there told Jesus about her. ³¹So he went to her bed. Jesus held her hand and helped her stand up. The fever left her, and she was healed. Then she began serving them.

³²That night, after the sun went down, the people brought to Jesus many who were sick. They also brought those who had demons* inside them. ³³Everyone in the town gathered at the door of that house. ³⁴Jesus healed many of those who had different kinds of sicknesses. He also forced many demons out of people. But he would not allow the demons to speak, because they knew who he was.ᵃ

Jesus Goes to Other Towns
(Lk. 4:42–44)

³⁵The next morning Jesus woke up very early. He left the house while it was still dark and went to a place where he could be alone and pray. ³⁶Later, Simon and his friends went to look for Jesus. ³⁷They found him and said, "Everyone is looking for you!"

³⁸Jesus answered, "We should go to another place. We can go to other towns around here, and I can tell God's message to those people too. That is why I came." ³⁹So Jesus traveled everywhere in Galilee. He spoke in the synagogues,* and he forced demons* out of people.

Jesus Heals a Sick Man
(Mt. 8:1–4; Lk. 5:12–16)

⁴⁰A man who had leprosy* came to Jesus. The man bowed on his knees and begged him, "You have the power to heal me if you want."

⁴¹Jesus felt sorry for the man. So he touched him and said, "I want to heal you. Be healed!" ⁴²Immediately the leprosy disappeared, and the man was healed.

⁴³Jesus told the man to go, but he gave him a strong warning: ⁴⁴"Don't tell anyone about what I did for you. But go and show yourself to the priest. And offer a gift to God because you have been healed. Offer the gift that Moses* commanded.ᵇ This will show everyone that you are healed." ⁴⁵The man left there and told everyone he saw that Jesus had healed him. So the news about Jesus spread. And that is why he could not enter a town if people saw him. He stayed in places where people did not live. But people came from all the towns to the places where he was.

Jesus Heals a Crippled Man
(Mt. 9:1–8; Lk. 5:17–26)

2 ¹A few days later, Jesus came back to Capernaum.* The news spread that he was back home. ²A large crowd gathered to hear him speak. The house was so full that there was

---

ᵃ **1:34** *who he was* Meaning that the demons knew that Jesus was the Christ, the Son of God.
ᵇ **1:44** *Moses commanded* See Lev. 14:1–32.

no place to stand, not even outside the door. While Jesus was teaching, ³some people brought a paralyzed man to see him. He was being carried by four of them. ⁴But they could not get the man inside to Jesus because the house was so full of people. So they went to the roof above Jesus and made a hole in it. Then they lowered the mat with the paralyzed man on it. ⁵When Jesus saw how much faith they had, he said to the paralyzed man, "Young man, your sins are forgiven."

⁶Some of the teachers of the law were sitting there. They saw what Jesus did, and they said to themselves, ⁷"Why does this man say things like that? What an insult to God! No one but God can forgive sins."

⁸Jesus knew immediately what these teachers of the law were thinking. So he said to them, "Why do you have these questions in your minds? ⁹⁻¹⁰The Son of Man* has power on earth to forgive sins. But how can I prove this to you? Maybe you are thinking it was easy for me to say to the crippled man, 'Your sins are forgiven.' There's no proof it really happened. But what if I say to the man, 'Stand up. Take your mat and walk'? Then you will be able to see if I really have this power or not." So Jesus said to the paralyzed man, ¹¹"I tell you, stand up. Take your mat and go home."

¹²Immediately the paralyzed man stood up. He picked up his mat and walked out of the room. Everyone could see him. They were amazed and praised God. They said, "This is the most amazing thing we have ever seen!"

Levi (Matthew) Follows Jesus
(Mt. 9:9–13; Lk. 5:27–32)

¹³Jesus went to the lake again, and many people followed him there. So Jesus taught them. ¹⁴He was walking beside the lake, and he saw a man named Levi, son of Alphaeus. Levi was sitting at his place for collecting taxes. Jesus said to him, "Follow me." Then Levi stood up and followed Jesus.

¹⁵Later that day, Jesus and his followers ate at Levi's house. There were also many tax collectors* and others with bad reputations eating with them. (There were many of these people who followed Jesus.) ¹⁶When some teachers of the law who were Pharisees* saw Jesus eating with such bad people, they asked his followers, "Why does he eat with tax collectors and sinners?"

¹⁷When Jesus heard this, he said to them, "It is the sick people who need a doctor, not those who are healthy. I did not come to invite good people. I came to invite sinners."

Jesus Is Not Like Other Religious Leaders
(Mt. 9:14–17; Lk. 5:33–39)

¹⁸The followers of John* and the Pharisees* were fasting.* Some people came to Jesus and said, "John's followers fast,

and the followers of the Pharisees fast. But your followers don't fast. Why?"

¹⁹Jesus answered, "At a wedding the friends of the bridegroom* are not sad while he is with them. They cannot fast while the bridegroom is still there. ²⁰But the time will come when the bridegroom will be taken from them. Then they will fast.

²¹"When someone sews a patch over a hole in an old coat, they never use a piece of cloth that is not yet shrunk. If they do, the patch will shrink and pull away from the coat. Then the hole will be worse. ²²Also, no one ever pours new wine into old wineskins.* The wine would break them, and the wine would be ruined along with the wineskins. You always put new wine into new wineskins."

Jesus Is Lord Over the Sabbath Day
(Mt. 12:1–8; Lk. 6:1–5)

²³On the Sabbath* day, Jesus and his followers were walking through some grain fields. The followers picked some grain to eat. ²⁴Some Pharisees* said to Jesus, "Why are your followers doing this? It is against the law to pick grain on the Sabbath."

²⁵Jesus answered, "You have read what David* did when he and the people with him were hungry and needed food. ²⁶It was during the time of Abiathar the high priest.* David went into God's house and ate the bread that was offered to God. And the law of Moses* says that only priests can eat that bread. David also gave some of the bread to the people with him."

²⁷Then Jesus said to the Pharisees, "The Sabbath day was made to help people. People were not made to be ruled by the Sabbath. ²⁸So the Son of Man* is Lord of every day, even the Sabbath."

Jesus Heals a Man on the Sabbath Day
(Mt. 12:9–14; Lk. 6:6–11)

3 ¹Another time Jesus went into the synagogue.* In the synagogue there was a man with a crippled hand. ²Some Jews there were watching Jesus closely. They were waiting to see if he would heal the man on a Sabbath* day. They wanted to see Jesus do something wrong so that they could accuse him. ³Jesus said to the man with the crippled hand, "Stand up here so that everyone can see you."

⁴Then Jesus asked the people, "Which is the right thing to do on the Sabbath day: to do good or to do evil? Is it right to save a life or to destroy one?" The people said nothing to answer him.

⁵Jesus looked at the people. He was angry, but he felt very sad because they were so stubborn. He said to the man, "Hold out your hand." The man held out his hand, and it was healed. ⁶Then the Pharisees* left and made plans with the Herodians* about a way to kill Jesus.

Many Follow Jesus

[7]Jesus went away with his followers to the lake. A large crowd of people from Galilee followed them. [8]Many also came from Judea, from Jerusalem, from Idumea, from the area across the Jordan River, and from the area around Tyre and Sidon. These people came because they heard about all that Jesus was doing.

[9]Jesus saw how many people there were, so he told his followers to get a small boat and make it ready for him. He wanted the boat so that the crowds of people could not push against him. [10]He had healed many of them, so all the sick people were pushing toward him to touch him. [11]Some people had evil spirits inside them. When the evil spirits saw Jesus, they bowed before him and shouted, "You are the Son of God!" [12]But Jesus gave the spirits a strong warning not to tell anyone who he was.

Jesus Chooses His Twelve Apostles
(Mt. 10:1-4; Lk. 6:12-16)

[13]Then Jesus went up on a hill and invited those he wanted to go with him. So they joined him there. [14]And he chose twelve men and called them apostles.* He wanted these twelve men to be with him, and he wanted to send them to other places to tell people God's message. [15]He also wanted them to have the power to force demons* out of people. [16]These are the names of the twelve men Jesus chose:

Simon (the one Jesus named Peter),

[17] James and his brother John, the sons of Zebedee (the ones Jesus named Boanerges, which means "Sons of Thunder"),

[18] Andrew,
Philip,
Bartholomew,
Matthew,
Thomas,
James, the son of Alphaeus,
Thaddaeus,
Simon, the Zealot,[a]

[19] Judas Iscariot (the one who handed Jesus over to his enemies).

Jesus' Power Is From God
(Mt. 12:22-32; Lk. 11:14-23; 12:10)

[20]Then Jesus went home, but again a large crowd gathered there. There were so many people that he and his followers could not eat. [21]His family heard about all these things. They went to get him because people said he was crazy.

[22]And the teachers of the law from Jerusalem said, "Satan[b] is living inside him! He uses power from the ruler of demons* to force demons out of people."

[a]**3:18** *Zealot* Literally, "Cananaean," an Aramaic word meaning "Zealot" or "Enthusiast." See "Zealot" in the Word List.　[b]**3:22** *Satan* Literally, "Beelzebul" (the devil).

²³So Jesus called them together and talked to them using some stories. He said, "Satan* will not force his own demons out of people. ²⁴A kingdom that fights against itself will not survive. ²⁵And a family that is divided will not survive. ²⁶If Satan is against himself and is fighting against his own people, he will not survive. That would be the end of Satan.

²⁷"Whoever wants to enter a strong man's house and steal his things must first tie him up. Then they can steal the things from his house.

²⁸"I want you to know that people can be forgiven for all the sinful things they do. They can even be forgiven for the bad things they say against God. ²⁹But anyone who speaks against the Holy Spirit* will never be forgiven. They will always be guilty of that sin."

³⁰Jesus said this because the teachers of the law had accused him of having an evil spirit inside him.

Jesus' Followers Are His True Family
(Mt. 12:46–50; Lk. 8:19–21)

³¹Then Jesus' mother and brothers came. They stood outside and sent someone in to tell him to come out. ³²Many people were sitting around Jesus. They said to him, "Your mother and brothers are waiting for you outside."

³³Jesus asked, "Who is my mother? Who are my brothers?" ³⁴Then he looked at the people sitting around him and said, "These people are my mother and my brothers! ³⁵My true brother and sister and mother are those who do what God wants."

A Story About a Farmer Sowing Seed
(Mt. 13:1–9; Lk. 8:4–8)

4 ¹Another time Jesus began teaching by the lake, and a large crowd gathered around him. He got into a boat so that he could sit and teach from the lake. All the people stayed on the shore near the water. ²Jesus used stories to teach them many things. One of his lessons included this story:

³"Listen! A farmer went out to sow seed. ⁴While he was scattering the seed, some of it fell by the road. The birds came and ate all that seed. ⁵Other seed fell on rocky ground, where there was not enough dirt. It grew quickly there because the soil was not deep. ⁶But then the sun rose and the plants were burned. They died because they did not have deep roots. ⁷Some other seed fell among thorny weeds. The weeds grew and stopped the good plants from growing. So they did not make grain. ⁸But some of the seed fell on good ground. There it began to grow, and it made grain. Some plants made 30 times more grain, some 60 times more, and some 100 times more."

⁹Then Jesus said, "You people who hear me, listen!"

Why Jesus Used Stories to Teach
(Mt. 13:10–17; Lk. 8:9–10)

¹⁰Later, Jesus was away from the people. The twelve apostles* and his other followers asked him about the stories.

¹¹Jesus said, "Only you can know the secret truth about God's kingdom.* But to those other people I tell everything by using stories. ¹²I do this so that,

'They will look and look but never really see;
    they will listen and listen but never understand.
If they saw and understood, they might change
    and be forgiven.'"

                                                Isaiah 6:9–10

Jesus Explains the Story About Seed
(Mt. 13:18–23; Lk. 8:11–15)

¹³Then Jesus said to the followers, "Do you understand this story? If you don't, how will you understand any story? ¹⁴The farmer is like someone who plants God's teaching in people. ¹⁵Sometimes the teaching falls on the path. That is like some people who hear the teaching of God. As soon as they hear it, Satan* comes and takes away the teaching that was planted in them.

¹⁶"Other people are like the seed planted on rocky ground. They hear the teaching, and they quickly and gladly accept it. ¹⁷But they don't allow it to go deep into their lives. They keep it only a short time. As soon as trouble or persecution* comes because of the teaching they accepted, they give up.

¹⁸"Others are like the seed planted among the thorny weeds. They hear the teaching, ¹⁹but their lives become full of other things: the worries of this life, the love of money, and everything else they want. This keeps the teaching from growing, and it does not produce a crop*ᵃ in their lives.

²⁰"And others are like the seed planted on the good ground. They hear the teaching and accept it. Then they grow and produce a good crop—sometimes 30 times more, sometimes 60 times more, and sometimes 100 times more."

Use the Understanding You Have
(Lk. 8:16–18)

²¹Then Jesus said to them, "You don't take a lamp and hide it under a bowl or a bed, do you? Of course not. You put it on a lampstand. ²²Everything that is hidden will be made clear. Every secret thing will be made known. ²³You people who hear me, listen! ²⁴Think carefully about what you are hearing. God will know how much to give you by how much you understand now. But he will give you more than you deserve. ²⁵The people who have some understanding will receive more. But those who do not have much will lose even the small amount they have."

ᵃ4:19 produce a crop Meaning to do the good things God wants his people to do.

Jesus Uses a Story About Seed

²⁶Then Jesus said, "God's kingdom* is like a man who plants seed in the ground. ²⁷The seed begins to grow. It grows night and day. It doesn't matter whether the man is sleeping or awake, the seed still grows. He doesn't know how it happens. ²⁸Without any help the ground produces grain. First the plant grows, then the head, and then all the grain in the head. ²⁹When the grain is ready, the man cuts it. This is the harvest time."

What Is God's Kingdom Like?
(Mt. 13:31–32, 34–35; Lk. 13:18–19)

³⁰Then Jesus said, "What can I use to show you what God's kingdom* is like? What story can I use to explain it? ³¹God's kingdom is like a mustard seed, which is smaller than any other seed on earth that you can plant. ³²But when you plant it, it grows and becomes the largest of all the plants in your garden. It has branches that are very big. The wild birds can come and make nests there and be protected from the sun."

³³Jesus used many stories like these to teach the people. He taught them all they could understand. ³⁴He always used stories to teach them. But when he was alone with his followers, Jesus explained everything to them.

Jesus' Followers See His Power
(Mt. 8:23–27; Lk. 8:22–25)

³⁵That day, at evening, Jesus said to his followers, "Come with me across the lake." ³⁶So they left the crowd behind and went with Jesus in the boat he was already in. There were also other boats that went with them. ³⁷A very bad wind came up on the lake. The waves were coming over the sides and into the boat, and it was almost full of water. ³⁸Jesus was inside the boat, sleeping with his head on a pillow. The followers went and woke him. They said, "Teacher, don't you care about us? We are going to drown!"

³⁹Jesus stood up and gave a command to the wind and the water. He said, "Quiet! Be still!" Then the wind stopped, and the lake became calm.

⁴⁰He said to his followers, "Why are you afraid? Do you still have no faith?"

⁴¹They were very afraid and asked each other, "What kind of man is this? Even the wind and the water obey him!"

Jesus Frees a Man From Evil Spirits
(Mt. 8:28–34; Lk. 8:26–39)

5 ¹Jesus and his followers went across the lake to the area where the Gerasene people lived. ²When Jesus got out of the boat, a man came to him from the caves where the dead are buried. This man had an evil spirit inside him. ³He lived in the burial caves. No one could keep him tied up, even

with chains. [4]Many times people had put chains on his hands and feet, but he broke the chains. No one was strong enough to control him. [5]Day and night he stayed around the burial caves and on the hills. He would scream and cut himself with rocks.

[6]While Jesus was still far away, the man saw him. He ran to Jesus and bowed down before him. [7-8]As Jesus was saying, "You evil spirit, come out of this man," the man shouted loudly, "What do you want with me, Jesus, Son of the Most High God? I beg you in God's name not to punish me!"

[9]Then Jesus asked the man, "What is your name?"

The man answered, "My name is Legion,[a] because there are many spirits inside me." [10]The spirits inside the man begged Jesus again and again not to send them out of that area.

[11]A large herd of pigs was eating on a hill near there. [12]The evil spirits begged Jesus, "Send us to the pigs. Let us go into them." [13]So Jesus allowed them to do this. The evil spirits left the man and went into the pigs. Then the herd of pigs ran down the hill and into the lake. They were all drowned. There were about 2000 pigs in that herd.

[14]The men who had the work of caring for the pigs ran away. They ran to the town and to the farms and told everyone what happened. The people went out to see. [15]They came to Jesus, and they saw the man who had the many evil spirits. He was sitting down and was wearing clothes. He was in his right mind again. When they saw this, they were afraid. [16]Those who had seen what Jesus did told the others what happened to the man who had the demons* living in him. And they also told about the pigs. [17]Then the people began to beg Jesus to leave their area.

[18]Jesus was preparing to leave in the boat. The man who was freed from the demons begged to go with him. [19]But Jesus did not allow the man to go. He said, "Go home to your family and friends. Tell them about all that the Lord did for you. Tell them how the Lord was good to you."

[20]So the man left and told the people in the Ten Towns* about the great things Jesus did for him. Everyone was amazed.

Jesus Gives Life to a Dead Girl and Heals a Sick Woman
(Mt. 9:18–26; Lk. 8:40–56)

[21]Jesus went back to the other side of the lake in the boat. There, a large crowd of people gathered around him on the shore. [22]A leader of the synagogue* came. His name was Jairus. He saw Jesus and bowed down before him. [23]He begged Jesus again and again, saying, "My little daughter is dying. Please come and lay your hands on her. Then she will be healed and will live."

[24]So Jesus went with Jairus. Many people followed Jesus. They were pushing very close around him.

---

[a]5:9 Legion This name means very many. A legion was about 6000 men in the Roman army.

²⁵There among the people was a woman who had been bleeding for the past twelve years. ²⁶She had suffered very much. Many doctors had tried to help her, and all the money she had was spent, but she was not improving. In fact, her sickness was getting worse.

²⁷The woman heard about Jesus, so she followed him with the other people and touched his coat. ²⁸She thought, "If I can just touch his clothes, that will be enough to heal me." ²⁹As soon as she touched his coat, her bleeding stopped. She felt that her body was healed from all the suffering. ³⁰Jesus immediately felt power go out from him, so he stopped and turned around. "Who touched my clothes?" he asked.

³¹The followers said to Jesus, "There are so many people pushing against you. But you ask, 'Who touched me?'"

³²But Jesus continued looking for the one who touched him. ³³The woman knew that she was healed, so she came and bowed at Jesus' feet. She was shaking with fear. She told Jesus the whole story. ³⁴He said to her, "Dear woman, you are made well because you believed. Go in peace. You will not suffer anymore."

³⁵While Jesus was still there speaking, some men came from the house of Jairus, the synagogue leader. They said, "Your daughter is dead. There is no need to bother the Teacher."

³⁶But Jesus did not care what the men said. He said to the synagogue leader, "Don't be afraid; just believe."

³⁷Jesus let only Peter, James, and John the brother of James go with him. ³⁸They went to the synagogue leader's house, where Jesus saw many people crying loudly. There was a lot of confusion. ³⁹He entered the house and said, "Why are you people crying and making so much noise? This child is not dead. She is only sleeping." ⁴⁰But everyone laughed at him.

Jesus told the people to leave the house. Then he went into the room where the child was. He brought the child's father and mother and his three followers into the room with him. ⁴¹Then Jesus held the girl's hand and said to her, *"Talitha, koum!"* (This means "Little girl, I tell you to stand up!") ⁴²The girl immediately stood up and began walking. (She was twelve years old.) The father and mother and the followers were amazed. ⁴³Jesus gave the father and mother very strict orders not to tell people about this. Then he told them to give the girl some food to eat.

Jesus Goes to His Hometown
(Mt. 13:53–58; Lk. 4:16–30)

6 ¹Jesus left and went back to his hometown. His followers went with him. ²On the Sabbath* day Jesus taught in the synagogue,* and many people heard him. They were amazed and said, "Where did this man get this teaching? How did he get such wisdom? Who gave it to him? And where did he get the power to do miracles*? ³Isn't he just the carpenter we know—Mary's son, the brother of James, Joses, Judas, and Simon? And don't his sisters still live here in town?" So they had a problem accepting him.

⁴Then Jesus said to them, "People everywhere give honor to a prophet,* except in his own town, with his own people, or in his home." ⁵Jesus was not able to do any miracles there except the healing of some sick people by laying his hands on them. ⁶He was surprised that the people there had no faith. Then he went to other villages in that area and taught.

Jesus Sends His Apostles on a Mission
(Mt. 10:1, 5–15; Lk. 9:1–6)

⁷Jesus called his twelve apostles* together. He sent them out in groups of two and gave them power over evil spirits. ⁸This is what he told them: "Take nothing for your trip except a stick for walking. Take no bread, no bag, and no money. ⁹You can wear sandals, but don't take extra clothes. ¹⁰When you enter a house, stay there until you leave that town. ¹¹If any town refuses to accept you or refuses to listen to you, then leave that town and shake the dust off your feet*ᵃ as a warning to them."

¹²The apostles left and went to other places. They talked to the people and told them to change their hearts and lives. ¹³They forced many demons* out of people and put olive oil onᵇ many who were sick and healed them.

Herod Thinks Jesus Is John the Baptizer
(Mt. 14:1–12; Lk. 9:7–9)

¹⁴King Herod* heard about Jesus, because Jesus was now famous. Some people said, "He is John the Baptizer.* He must have risen from death, and that is why he can do these miracles.*"

¹⁵Other people said, "He is Elijah.*"

And others said, "He is a prophet.* He is like the prophets who lived long ago."

¹⁶Herod heard these things about Jesus. He said, "I killed John by cutting off his head. Now he has been raised from death!"

How John the Baptizer Was Killed

¹⁷Herod* himself had ordered his soldiers to arrest John and put him in prison. Herod did this to please his wife Herodias. She had been married to Herod's brother Philip, but then Herod married her. ¹⁸John told Herod, "It is not right for you to be married to your brother's wife." ¹⁹So Herodias hated John. She wanted him dead, but she was not able to persuade Herod to

---

ᵃ**6:11** *shake the dust off your feet* A warning. It would show that they were finished talking to these people. ᵇ**6:13** *put olive oil on* Olive oil was used like a medicine.

kill him. [20]Herod was afraid to kill John, because he knew that he was a good and holy* man. So he protected him. He liked listening to John, although what John said left him with so many questions.

[21]Then the right time came for Herodias to cause John's death. It happened on Herod's birthday. Herod gave a dinner party for the most important government leaders, the commanders of his army, and the most important people in Galilee. [22]The daughter of Herodias came to the party and danced. When she danced, Herod and the people eating with him were very pleased.

So King Herod said to the girl, "I will give you anything you want." [23]He promised her, "Anything you ask for I will give to you—even half of my kingdom."

[24]The girl went to her mother and asked, "What should I ask King Herod to give me?"

Her mother answered, "Ask for the head of John the Baptizer.*"

[25]So right then the girl went back in to the king. She said to him, "Please give me the head of John the Baptizer. Bring it to me now on a plate."

[26]King Herod was very sad, but he didn't want to break the promise he had made to her in front of his guests. [27]So he sent a soldier to cut off John's head and bring it to him. The soldier went and cut off John's head in the prison. [28]He brought the head back on a plate and gave it to the girl, and the girl gave it to her mother. [29]John's followers heard about what happened, so they came and got John's body and put it in a tomb.*

Jesus Feeds More Than 5000
(Mt. 14:13-21; Lk. 9:10-17; Jn. 6:1-14)

[30]The apostles* Jesus sent out came back to him. They gathered around him and told him about all they had done and taught. [31]Jesus and his followers were in a very busy place. There were so many people that he and his followers did not even have time to eat. He said to them, "Come with me. We will go to a quiet place to be alone. There we will get some rest."

[32]So Jesus and his followers went away alone. They went in a boat to a place where no one lived. [33]But many people saw them leave and knew who they were. So people from every town ran to the place where they were going and got there before Jesus. [34]As Jesus stepped out of the boat, they saw a large crowd waiting. He felt sorry for them, because they were like sheep without a shepherd to care for them. So he taught the people many things.

[35]It was now very late in the day. Jesus' followers came to him and said, "No one lives around here, and it is already very late. [36]So send the people away. They need to go to the farms and towns around here to buy some food to eat."

[37]But Jesus answered, "You give them some food to eat."

They said to Jesus, "We can't buy enough bread to feed all these people. We would all have to work a month to earn enough to buy that much bread!"

[38]Jesus asked them, "How many loaves of bread do you have now? Go and see."

They counted their loaves of bread. They came to Jesus and said, "We have five loaves of bread and two fish."

[39]Then Jesus said to them, "Tell everyone to sit in groups on the green grass." [40]So all the people sat in groups. There were about 50 or 100 people in each group.

[41]Jesus took the five loaves and two fish. He looked up to the sky and thanked God for the food. Then he broke the bread into pieces, which he gave to his followers to distribute to the people. Then he divided the two fish among everyone there.

[42]They all ate until they were full. [43]After they finished eating, the followers filled twelve baskets with the pieces of bread and fish that were left. [44]There were about 5000 men there who ate.

Jesus Walks on Water
(Mt. 14:22–33; Jn. 6:16–21)

[45]Then Jesus told the followers to get into the boat. He told them to go to the other side of the lake to Bethsaida. He said he would come later. He stayed there to tell everyone they could go home. [46]After he said goodbye to them, he went up into the hills to pray.

[47]That night, the boat was still in the middle of the lake. Jesus was alone on the land. [48]He saw the boat far away on the lake. And he saw the followers working hard to row the boat. The wind was blowing against them. Sometime between three and six o'clock in the morning, Jesus went out to the boat, walking on the water. He continued walking until he was almost past the boat. [49]But the followers saw Jesus walking on the water. They thought he was a ghost, and they started screaming. [50]It scared them all to see him. But he spoke to them and said, "Don't worry! It's me! Don't be afraid." [51]When he got into the boat with the followers, the wind stopped. The followers were completely amazed. [52]They could not believe what happened. It was like the miracle he did with the bread. They still didn't understand what that meant.

Jesus Heals Many Sick People
(Mt. 14:34–36)

[53]Jesus and his followers went across the lake and came to shore at Gennesaret. They tied the boat there. [54]When they were out of the boat, the people there saw Jesus. They knew who he was, [55]so they ran to tell others throughout that area. They brought sick people on mats to every place Jesus went. [56]Jesus went into towns, cities, and farms around that area. And

every place he went, the people brought sick people to the marketplaces. They begged him to let them touch any part of his coat. And all those who touched him were healed.

God's Law and Human Traditions
(Mt. 15:1–20)

7 ¹Some Pharisees* and some teachers of the law came from Jerusalem and gathered around Jesus. ²They saw that some of his followers ate food with hands that were not clean, meaning that they did not wash their hands in a special way. ³The Pharisees and all the other Jews never eat before washing their hands in this special way. They do this to follow the traditions they have from their great leaders who lived long ago. ⁴And when these Jews buy something in the market, they never eat it until they wash it in a special way. They also follow other rules from their people who lived before them. They follow rules like the washing of cups, pitchers, and pots.ᵃ

⁵The Pharisees and teachers of the law said to Jesus, "Your followers don't follow the traditions we have from our great leaders who lived long ago. They eat their food with hands that are not clean. Why do they do this?"

⁶Jesus answered, "You are all hypocrites.* Isaiah was right when he wrote these words from God about you:

> 'These people say they honor me,
>   but they don't really make me
>   an important part of their lives.
> ⁷ Their worship of me is for nothing.
>   The things they teach are only rules
>   that people have made.'
>   *Isaiah 29:13*

⁸You have stopped following God's commands, preferring instead the man-made rules you got from others."

⁹Then he said, "You show great skill in avoiding the commands of God so that you can follow your own teachings! ¹⁰Moses* said, 'You must respect your father and mother.'ᵇ He also said, 'Whoever says anything bad to their father or mother must be killed.'ᶜ ¹¹But you teach that people can say to their father or mother, 'I have something I could use to help you, but I will not use it for you. I will give it to God.' ¹²You are telling people that they do not have to do anything for their father or mother. ¹³So you are teaching that it is not important to do what God said. You think it is more important to follow those traditions you have, which you pass on to others. And you do many things like that."

¹⁴Jesus called the people to him again. He said, "Everyone should listen to me and understand what I am saying. ¹⁵There

---

ᵃ**7:4** *pots* Some Greek copies add "and couches."   ᵇ**7:10** Quote from Ex. 20:12; Deut. 5:16.   ᶜ**7:10** Quote from Ex. 21:17.

is nothing people can put in their mouth that will make them wrong.[a] People are made wrong by what comes from inside them." 16b

17Then Jesus left the people and went into the house. The followers asked Jesus about what he had told the people. 18He said, "Do you still have trouble understanding? Surely you know that nothing that enters the mouth from the outside can make people unacceptable to God. 19Food does not go into a person's mind. It goes into the stomach. Then it goes out of the body." (When Jesus said this, he meant there is no food that is wrong for people to eat.)

20And Jesus said, "The things that make people wrong are the things that come from the inside. 21All these bad things begin inside a person, in the mind: bad thoughts, sexual sins, stealing, murder, 22adultery,* greed, doing bad things to people, lying, doing things that are morally wrong, jealousy, insulting people, proud talking, and foolish living. 23These evil things come from inside a person. And these are the things that make people unacceptable to God."

Jesus Helps a Non-Jewish Woman
(Mt. 15:21–28)

24Jesus went from there to the area around Tyre. He did not want the people in that area to know he was there, so he went into a house. But he could not stay hidden. 25A woman heard that he was there. Her little daughter had an evil spirit inside her. So the woman came to Jesus and bowed down near his feet. 26She was not a Jew. She was born in Phoenicia, an area in Syria. She begged Jesus to force the demon* out of her daughter.

27Jesus told the woman, "It is not right to take the children's bread and give it to the dogs. First let the children eat all they want."

28She answered, "That is true, Lord. But the dogs under the table can eat the pieces of food that the children don't eat."

29Then he told her, "That is a very good answer. You may go. The demon has left your daughter."

30The woman went home and found her daughter lying on the bed. The demon was gone.

Jesus Heals a Deaf Man

31Then Jesus left the area around Tyre and went through Sidon. On his way to Lake Galilee he went through the area of the Ten Towns.* 32While he was there, some people brought a man to him who was deaf and could not talk clearly. The people begged Jesus to put his hand on the man to heal him.

---

a7:15 wrong Literally, "unclean" or "not pure," meaning unacceptable to God. Also in verse 20.   b7:16 Some Greek copies add verse 16: "You people who hear me, listen!"

³³Jesus led the man away from the people to be alone with him. He put his fingers in the man's ears. Then he spit on a finger and put it on the man's tongue. ³⁴Jesus looked up to the sky and with a loud sigh he said, *"Ephphatha!"* (This means "Open!") ³⁵As soon as Jesus did this, the man was able to hear. He was able to use his tongue, and he began to speak clearly.

³⁶Jesus told the people not to tell anyone about this. But the more he told them not to say anything, the more people they told. ³⁷They were all completely amazed. They said, "Look at what he has done. It's all good. He makes deaf people able to hear and gives a new voice to people who could not talk."

Jesus Feeds More Than 4000
(Mt. 15:32–39)

8 ¹Another time there were many people with Jesus. The people had nothing to eat. So he called his followers to him and said, ²"I feel sorry for these people. They have been with me for three days, and now they have nothing to eat. ³I should not send them home hungry. If they leave without eating, they will faint on the way home. Some of them live a long way from here."

⁴Jesus' followers answered, "But we are far away from any towns. Where can we get enough bread to feed all these people?"

⁵Then Jesus asked them, "How many loaves of bread do you have?"

They answered, "We have seven loaves of bread."

⁶Jesus told the people to sit on the ground. Then he took the seven loaves and gave thanks to God. He broke the bread into pieces and gave them to his followers. He told them to give the bread to the people, and they did as he said. ⁷The followers also had a few small fish. Jesus gave thanks for the fish and told them to give the fish to the people.

⁸They all ate until they were full. Then the followers filled seven baskets with the pieces of food that were left. ⁹There were about 4000 men who ate. After they ate, Jesus told them to go home. ¹⁰Then he went in a boat with his followers to the area of Dalmanutha.

Some People Doubt Jesus' Authority
(Mt. 16:1–4; Lk. 11:16, 29)

¹¹The Pharisees* came to Jesus and asked him questions. They wanted to test him. So they asked him to do a miracle* as a sign from God. ¹²Jesus sighed deeply and said, "Why do you people ask to see a miracle as a sign? I want you to know that no miracle will be done to prove anything to you." ¹³Then Jesus left them and went in the boat to the other side of the lake.

Jesus' Followers Misunderstand Him
(Mt. 16:5–12)

[14]The followers had only one loaf of bread with them in the boat. They forgot to bring more bread. [15]Jesus warned them, "Be careful! Guard against the yeast* of the Pharisees* and the yeast of Herod.*"

[16]The followers discussed the meaning of this. They said, "He said this because we have no bread."

[17]Jesus knew that the followers were talking about this. So he asked them, "Why are you talking about having no bread? Do you still not see or understand? Are you not able to understand? [18]Do you have eyes that can't see? Do you have ears that can't hear? Remember what I did before, when we did not have enough bread? [19]I divided five loaves of bread for 5000 people. Remember how many baskets you filled with pieces of food that were not eaten?"

The followers answered, "We filled twelve baskets."

[20]"And when I divided seven loaves of bread for 4000 people, how many baskets did you fill with leftover pieces that were not eaten?"

They answered, "We filled seven baskets."

[21]Then he said to them, "You remember these things I did, but you still don't understand?"

Jesus Heals a Blind Man in Bethsaida

[22]Jesus and his followers came to Bethsaida. Some people brought a blind man to him and begged him to touch the man. [23]So Jesus held the blind man's hand and led him out of the village. Then he spit on the man's eyes. He laid his hands on him and asked, "Can you see now?"

[24]The man looked up and said, "Yes, I see people. They look like trees walking around."

[25]Again Jesus laid his hands on the man's eyes, and the man opened them wide. His eyes were healed, and he was able to see everything clearly. [26]Jesus told him to go home. He said, "Don't go into the town."

Peter Says Jesus Is the Christ
(Mt. 16:13–20; Lk. 9:18–21)

[27]Jesus and his followers went to the towns in the area of Caesarea Philippi. While they were traveling, Jesus asked the followers, "Who do people say I am?"

[28]They answered, "Some people say you are John the Baptizer.* Others say you are Elijah.* And others say you are one of the prophets.*"

[29]Then Jesus asked, "Who do you say I am?"

Peter answered, "You are the Christ.*"

[30]Jesus told the followers, "Don't tell anyone who I am."

Jesus Says He Must Die
(Mt. 16:21–28; Lk. 9:22–27)

[31]Then Jesus began to teach his followers that the Son of Man* must suffer many things. He taught that the Son of Man would not be accepted by the older Jewish leaders, the leading priests, and the teachers of the law. He said that the Son of Man must be killed and then rise from death after three days. [32]Jesus told them everything that would happen. He did not keep anything secret.

Peter took Jesus away from the other followers to talk to him alone. Peter criticized him for saying these things. [33]But Jesus turned and looked at his followers. Then he criticized Peter. He said to Peter, "Get away from me, Satan*! You don't care about the same things God does. You care only about things that people think are important."

[34]Then Jesus called the people to him. His followers were also there. He said, "Whoever wants to be my follower must say no to themselves and what they want to do. They must accept the cross* that is given to them and follow me. [35]Those who try to save the life they have will lose it. But those who give up their life for me and for the Good News* about me will save it. [36]It is worth nothing for you to have the whole world if you yourself are lost. [37]You could never pay enough to buy back your life. [38]People today are so sinful. They have not been faithful to God. As you live among them, don't be ashamed of me and my teaching. If that happens, I[b] will be ashamed of you when I come with the glory* of my Father and the holy* angels."

9 [1]Then Jesus said, "Believe me when I say that some of you people standing here will see God's kingdom* come with power before you die."

Jesus Is Seen With Moses and Elijah
(Mt. 17:1–13; Lk. 9:28–36)

[2]Six days later, Jesus took Peter, James, and John and went up on a high mountain. They were all alone there. While these followers watched him, Jesus was changed. [3]His clothes became shining white—whiter than anyone on earth could make them. [4]Then two men were there talking with Jesus. They were Elijah* and Moses.*

[5]Peter said to Jesus, "Teacher, it is good that we are here. We will put three tents here—one for you, one for Moses, and one for Elijah." [6]Peter did not know what to say, because he and the other two followers were so afraid.

[7]Then a cloud came and covered them. A voice came from the cloud and said, "This is my Son, the one I love. Obey him!"

---

*a*8:33 *Satan* Name for the devil meaning "the enemy." Jesus means that Peter was talking like Satan. *b*8:38 *I* Literally, "the Son of Man" (Jesus).

⁸The followers looked, but they saw only Jesus there alone with them.

⁹As Jesus and the followers were walking back down the mountain, he gave them these instructions: "Don't tell anyone about what you saw on the mountain. Wait until after the Son of Man* rises from death. Then you can tell people what you saw."

¹⁰So the followers waited to say anything about what they saw. But they discussed among themselves what Jesus meant about rising from death. ¹¹They asked him, "Why do the teachers of the law say that Elijah must come*ᵃ* first?"

¹²Jesus answered, "They are right to say that Elijah must come first. Elijah makes all things the way they should be. But why do the Scriptures* say that the Son of Man will suffer much and that people will think he is worth nothing? ¹³I tell you that Elijah has already come. And people did to him all the bad things they wanted to do. The Scriptures said this would happen to him."

Jesus Frees a Boy From an Evil Spirit
(Mt. 17:14–20; Lk. 9:37–43a)

¹⁴Then Jesus, Peter, James, and John went to the other followers. They saw many people around them. The teachers of the law were arguing with the followers. ¹⁵When the people saw Jesus, they were very surprised and ran to welcome him.

¹⁶Jesus asked, "What are you arguing about with the teachers of the law?"

¹⁷A man answered, "Teacher, I brought my son to you. He is controlled by an evil spirit that keeps him from talking. ¹⁸The spirit attacks him and throws him on the ground. He foams at the mouth, grinds his teeth, and becomes very stiff. I asked your followers to force the evil spirit out, but they could not."

¹⁹Jesus answered, "You people today don't believe! How long must I stay with you? How long must I be patient with you? Bring the boy to me!"

²⁰So the followers brought the boy to Jesus. When the evil spirit saw Jesus, it attacked the boy. The boy fell down and rolled on the ground. He was foaming at the mouth.

²¹Jesus asked the boy's father, "How long has this been happening to him?"

The father answered, "Since he was very young. ²²The spirit often throws him into a fire or into water to kill him. If you can do anything, please have pity on us and help us."

²³Jesus said to the father, "Why did you say 'if you can'? All things are possible for the one who believes."

²⁴Immediately the father shouted, "I do believe. Help me to believe more!"

²⁵Jesus saw that all the people were running there to see what was happening. So he spoke to the evil spirit. He said,

---

ᵃ9:11 *Elijah must come* See Mal. 4:5–6.

"You evil spirit that makes this boy deaf and stops him from talking—I command you to come out of him and never enter him again!"

²⁶The evil spirit screamed. It caused the boy to fall on the ground again, and then it came out. The boy looked as if he was dead. Many people said, "He is dead!" ²⁷But Jesus took hold of his hand and helped him stand up.

²⁸Then Jesus went into the house. His followers were alone with him there. They said, "Why weren't we able to force that evil spirit out?"

²⁹Jesus answered, "That kind of spirit can be forced out only with prayer.ᵃ"

Jesus Talks About His Death
(Mt. 17:22–23; Lk. 9:43b–45)

³⁰Then Jesus and his followers left there and went through Galilee. Jesus did not want the people to know where they were. ³¹He wanted to teach his followers alone. He said to them, "The Son of Man* will be handed over to the control of other men, who will kill him. After three days, he will rise from death." ³²But the followers did not understand what he meant, and they were afraid to ask him.

Who Is the Greatest?
(Mt. 18:1–5; Lk. 9:46–48)

³³Jesus and his followers went to Capernaum.* They went into a house, and Jesus said to them, "I heard you arguing on the way here today. What were you arguing about?" ³⁴But the followers did not answer, because their argument on the road was about which one of them was the greatest.

³⁵Jesus sat down and called the twelve apostles* to him. He said, "Whoever wants to be the most important must make others more important than themselves. They must serve everyone else."

³⁶Then Jesus took a small child and stood the child in front of the followers. He held the child in his arms and said, ³⁷"Whoever accepts children like these in my name is accepting me. And anyone who accepts me is also accepting the one who sent me."

Whoever Is Not Against Us Is For Us
(Lk. 9:49–50)

³⁸Then John said, "Teacher, we saw a man using your name to force demons* out of someone. He is not one of us. So we told him to stop, because he does not belong to our group."

³⁹Jesus said, "Don't stop him. Whoever uses my name to do powerful things will not soon say bad things about me. ⁴⁰Whoever is not against us is with us. ⁴¹I can assure you that

ᵃ**9:29 prayer** Some Greek copies have "prayer and fasting."

anyone who helps you by giving you a drink of water because you belong to the Christ* will definitely get a reward.

Jesus Warns About Causes of Sin
(Mt. 18:6–9; Lk. 17:1–2)

⁴²"If one of these little children believes in me, and someone causes that child to sin, it will be very bad for that person. It would be better for them to have a millstone* tied around their neck and be drowned in the sea. ⁴³If your hand makes you sin, cut it off. It is better for you to lose part of your body and have eternal life than to have two hands and go to hell. There the fire never stops. ⁴⁴ᵃ ⁴⁵If your foot makes you sin, cut it off. It is better for you to lose part of your body and have eternal life than to have two feet and be thrown into hell. ⁴⁶ᵇ ⁴⁷If your eye makes you sin, take it out. It is better for you to have only one eye and enter God's kingdom* than to have two eyes and be thrown into hell. ⁴⁸The worms that eat the people in hell never die. The fire there is never stopped.

⁴⁹"Everyone will be salted with fire.ᶜ

⁵⁰"Salt is good. But if it loses its salty taste, you can't make it good again. So, don't lose that good quality of salt you have. And live in peace with each other."

Jesus Teaches About Divorce
(Mt. 19:1–12)

10 ¹Then Jesus left there and went into the area of Judea and across the Jordan River. Again, many people came to him, and Jesus taught them as he always did.

²Some Pharisees* came to Jesus and tried to make him say something wrong. They asked him, "Is it right for a man to divorce his wife?"

³Jesus answered, "What did Moses* command you to do?"

⁴The Pharisees said, "Moses allowed a man to divorce his wife by writing a certificate of divorce."ᵈ

⁵Jesus said, "Moses wrote that command for you because you refused to accept God's teaching. ⁶But when God made the world, 'he made people male and female.'ᵉ ⁷'That is why a man will leave his father and mother and be joined to his wife. ⁸And the two people will become one.'ᶠ So they are no longer two, but one. ⁹God has joined them together, so no one should separate them."

¹⁰Later, when the followers and Jesus were in the house, they asked him again about the question of divorce. ¹¹He said,

---

ᵃ9:44 Some Greek copies add verse 44, which is the same as verse 48. ᵇ9:46 Some Greek copies add verse 46, which is the same as verse 48. ᶜ9:49 Some Greek copies add, "and every sacrifice will be salted with salt." In the Old Testament salt was put on sacrifices. This verse could mean that Jesus' followers will be tested by suffering and that they must offer themselves to God as sacrifices. ᵈ10:4 "Moses ... certificate of divorce" See Deut. 24:1. ᵉ10:6 Quote from Gen. 1:27; 5:2. ᶠ10:8 Quote from Gen. 2:24.

"Whoever divorces his wife and marries another woman has sinned against his wife. He is guilty of adultery.* [12]And the woman who divorces her husband and marries another man is also guilty of adultery."

Jesus Welcomes Children
(Mt. 19:13–15; Lk. 18:15–17)

[13]People brought their small children to Jesus, so that he could lay his hands on them to bless them. But the followers told the people to stop bringing their children to him. [14]Jesus saw what happened. He did not like his followers telling the children not to come. So he said to them, "Let the little children come to me. Don't stop them, because God's kingdom* belongs to people who are like these little children. [15]The truth is, you must accept God's kingdom like a little child accepts things, or you will never enter it." [16]Then Jesus held the children in his arms. He laid his hands on them and blessed them.

A Rich Man Refuses to Follow Jesus
(Mt. 19:16–30; Lk. 18:18–30)

[17]Jesus started to leave, but a man ran to him and bowed down on his knees before him. The man asked, "Good Teacher, what must I do to get the life that never ends?"

[18]Jesus answered, "Why do you call me good? Only God is good. [19]And you know his commands: 'You must not murder anyone, you must not commit adultery,* you must not steal, you must not lie, you must not cheat, you must respect your father and mother ....'[a]"

[20]The man said, "Teacher, I have obeyed all these commands since I was a boy."

[21]Jesus looked at the man in a way that showed how much he cared for him. He said, "There is still one thing you need to do. Go and sell everything you have. Give the money to those who are poor, and you will have riches in heaven. Then come and follow me."

[22]The man was upset when Jesus told him to give away his money. He didn't want to do this, because he was very rich. So he went away sad.

[23]Then Jesus looked at his followers and said to them, "It will be very hard for a rich person to enter God's kingdom*!"

[24]The followers were amazed at what Jesus said. But he said again, "My children, it is very hard to enter God's kingdom! [25]It is easier for a camel to go through the eye of a needle than for a rich person to enter God's kingdom!"

[26]The followers were even more amazed and said to each other, "Then who can be saved?"

[a]**10:19** Quote from Ex. 20:12–16; Deut. 5:16–20.

27Jesus looked at them and said, "That is something people cannot do, but God can. He can do anything."

28Peter said to Jesus, "We left everything to follow you!"

29Jesus said, "I can promise that everyone who has left their home, brothers, sisters, mother, father, children, or farm for me and for the Good News* about me 30will get a hundred times more than they left. Here in this world they will get more homes, brothers, sisters, mothers, children, and farms. And with these things they will have persecutions.* But in the world that is coming they will also get the reward of eternal life. 31Many people who have the highest place now will have the lowest place in the future. And the people who have the lowest place now will have the highest place then."

Jesus Talks Again About His Death
(Mt. 20:17–19; Lk. 18:31–34)

32Jesus and those with him were on their way to Jerusalem. He was at the front of the group. His followers were wondering what was happening, and the people who followed behind them were feeling afraid. Jesus gathered the twelve apostles* again and talked with them alone. He told them what would happen in Jerusalem. 33He said, "We are going to Jerusalem. The Son of Man* will be handed over to the leading priests and teachers of the law. They will say that he must die and will hand him over to the foreigners, 34who will laugh at him and spit on him. They will beat him with whips and kill him. But on the third day after his death, he will rise to life again."

James and John Ask for a Favor
(Mt. 20:20–28)

35Then James and John, sons of Zebedee, came to Jesus and said, "Teacher, we want to ask you to do something for us."

36Jesus asked, "What do you want me to do for you?"

37The sons answered, "Let us share the great honor you will have as king. Let one of us sit at your right side and the other at your left."

38Jesus said, "You don't understand what you are asking. Can you drink from the cup^a that I must drink from? Can you be baptized with the same baptism^b that I must go through?"

39The sons answered, "Yes, we can!"

Jesus said to the sons; "It is true that you will drink from the cup that I drink from. And you will be baptized with the same baptism that I must go through. 40But it is not for me to say

---

^{a}10:38 cup A symbol of suffering. Jesus used the idea of drinking from a cup to mean accepting the suffering he would face in the terrible events that were soon to come. Also in verse 39. ^{b}10:38 baptized with the same baptism Baptism, which usually means to be immersed in water, has a special meaning here—being immersed or "buried" in troubles. Also in verse 39.

who will sit at my right or my left. God has prepared those places for the ones he chooses."

⁴¹When the other ten followers heard this, they were angry with James and John. ⁴²Jesus called all the followers together. He said, "The non-Jewish people have men they call rulers. You know that those rulers love to show their power over the people. And their important leaders love to use all their authority over the people. ⁴³But it should not be that way with you. Whoever wants to be your leader must be your servant. ⁴⁴Whoever wants to be first must serve the rest of you like a slave. ⁴⁵Follow my example: Even the Son of Man* did not come for people to serve him. He came to serve others and to give his life to save many people."

Jesus Heals a Blind Man
(Mt. 20:29–34; Lk. 18:35–43)

⁴⁶Then they came to the town of Jericho. When Jesus left there with his followers, a large crowd was with them. A blind man named Bartimaeus (meaning, "son of Timaeus") was sitting by the road. He was always begging for money. ⁴⁷He heard that Jesus from Nazareth was walking by. So he began shouting, "Jesus, Son of David,* please help me!"

⁴⁸Many people criticized the blind man and told him to be quiet. But he shouted more and more, "Son of David, please help me!"

⁴⁹Jesus stopped and said, "Tell him to come here."

So they called the blind man and said, "You can be happy now. Stand up! Jesus is calling you." ⁵⁰The blind man stood up quickly. He left his coat there and went to Jesus.

⁵¹Jesus asked the man, "What do you want me to do for you?"

He answered, "Teacher, I want to see again."

⁵²Jesus said, "Go. You are healed because you believed." Immediately the man was able to see again. He followed Jesus down the road.

Jesus Enters Jerusalem Like a King
(Mt. 21:1–11; Lk. 19:28–40; Jn. 12:12–19)

11 ¹Jesus and his followers were coming closer to Jerusalem. They came to the towns of Bethphage and Bethany at the Mount of Olives.* There Jesus sent two of his followers to do something. ²He said to them, "Go to the town you can see there. When you enter it, you will find a young donkey that no one has ever ridden. Untie it and bring it here to me. ³If anyone asks you why you are taking the donkey, tell them, 'The Master needs it. He will send it back soon.'"

⁴The followers went into the town. They found a young donkey tied in the street near the door of a house, and they untied it. ⁵Some people were standing there and saw this. They asked, "What are you doing? Why are you untying that

donkey?" ⁶The followers answered the way Jesus told them, and the people let them take the donkey.

⁷The followers brought the donkey to Jesus. They put their coats on it, and Jesus sat on it. ⁸Many people spread their coats on the road for Jesus. Others cut branches in the fields and spread the branches on the road. ⁹Some of them were walking ahead of Jesus. Others were walking behind him. Everyone shouted,

"'Praise[a] Him!'
'Welcome! God bless the one who comes
in the name of the Lord!'   *Psalm 118:25–26*

¹⁰"God bless the kingdom of our father David.*
That kingdom is coming!
Praise to God in heaven!"

¹¹Jesus entered Jerusalem and went to the Temple.* He looked at everything in the Temple area, but it was already late. So he went to Bethany with the twelve apostles.*

Jesus Says a Fig Tree Will Die
(Mt. 21:18–19)

¹²The next day, Jesus was leaving Bethany. He was hungry. ¹³He saw a fig tree with leaves. So he went to the tree to see if it had any figs growing on it. But he found no figs on the tree. There were only leaves, because it was not the right time for figs to grow. ¹⁴So Jesus said to the tree, "People will never eat fruit from you again." His followers heard him say this.

Jesus Goes to the Temple
(Mt. 21:12–17; Lk. 19:45–48; Jn. 2:13–22)

¹⁵Jesus went to Jerusalem and entered the Temple* area. He began driving out the people who were buying and selling things there. He turned over the tables that belonged to those who were exchanging different kinds of money. And he turned over the benches of those who were selling doves. ¹⁶He refused to allow anyone to carry things through the Temple area. ¹⁷Then Jesus began teaching the people and said, "It is written in the Scriptures,* 'My house will be called a house of prayer for all people.'[b] But you are changing God's house into a 'hiding place for thieves.'[c]"

¹⁸When the leading priests and the teachers of the law heard what Jesus said, they began trying to find a way to kill him. They were afraid of him because all the people were amazed at his teaching. ¹⁹That night Jesus and his followers left the city.

---

[a]**11:9** *Praise* Literally, *"Hosanna,"* a Hebrew word used in praying to God for help. Here, it was probably a shout of celebration used in praising God or his Messiah. Also in verse 10.
[b]**11:17** Quote from Isa. 56:7.   [c]**11:17** Quote from Jer. 7:11.

Jesus Shows the Power of Faith
(Mt. 21:20–22)

²⁰The next morning Jesus was walking with his followers. They saw the fig tree that he spoke to the day before. The tree was dry and dead, even the roots. ²¹Peter remembered the tree and said to Jesus, "Teacher, look! Yesterday, you told that fig tree to die. Now it is dry and dead!"

²²Jesus answered, "Have faith in God. ²³The truth is, you can say to this mountain, 'Go, mountain, fall into the sea.' And if you have no doubts in your mind and believe that what you say will happen, then God will do it for you. ²⁴So I tell you to ask for what you want in prayer. And if you believe that you have received those things, then they will be yours. ²⁵When you are praying, and you remember that you are angry with another person about something, then forgive that person. Forgive them so that your Father in heaven will also forgive your sins." ²⁶ᵃ

Jewish Leaders Doubt Jesus' Authority
(Mt. 21:23–27; Lk. 20:1–8)

²⁷Jesus and his followers went again to Jerusalem. Jesus was walking in the Temple* area. The leading priests, the teachers of the law, and the older Jewish leaders came to him. ²⁸They said, "Tell us! What authority do you have to do these things? Who gave you this authority?"

²⁹Jesus answered, "I will ask you a question. You answer my question. Then I will tell you whose authority I use to do these things. ³⁰Tell me: When John baptized* people, did his authority come from God or was it only from other people? Answer me."

³¹These Jewish leaders talked about Jesus' question. They said to each other, "If we answer, 'John's baptism was from God,' then he will say, 'Then why didn't you believe John?' ³²But we can't say that John's baptism was from someone else." (These leaders were afraid of the people, because the people believed that John was a prophet.*)

³³So the leaders answered Jesus, "We don't know the answer." Jesus said, "Then I will not tell you who gave me the authority to do these things."

God Sends His Son
(Mt. 21:33–46; Lk. 20:9–19)

12 ¹Jesus used stories to teach the people. He said, "A man planted a vineyard.* He put a wall around the field and dug a hole for a winepress.* Then he built a tower. He leased the land to some farmers and left for a trip.

²"Later, it was time for the grapes to be picked. So the man sent a servant to the farmers to get his share of the grapes. ³But

---

ᵃ**11:26** Some early Greek copies add verse 26: "But if you don't forgive others, then your Father in heaven will not forgive your sins."

the farmers grabbed the servant and beat him. They sent him away with nothing. 4Then the man sent another servant to the farmers. They hit this servant on the head, showing no respect for him. 5So the man sent another servant. The farmers killed this servant. The man sent many other servants to the farmers. The farmers beat some of them and killed the others.

6"The man had only one person left to send to the farmers. It was his son. He loved his son, but he decided to send him. He said, 'The farmers will respect my son.'

7"But the farmers said to each other, 'This is the owner's son, and this vineyard will be his. If we kill him, it will be ours.' 8So they took the son, threw him out of the vineyard, and killed him.

9"So what will the man who owns the vineyard do? He will go and kill those farmers. Then he will lease the land to others. 10Surely you have read this in the Scriptures*:

'The stone that the builders refused to accept
　　became the cornerstone.*
11　The Lord did this, and it is wonderful to us.'"

Psalm 118:22–23

12When these Jewish leaders heard this story, they knew it was about them. They wanted to find a way to arrest Jesus, but they were afraid of the people. So they left him and went away.

The Jewish Leaders Try to Trick Jesus
(Mt. 22:15–22; Lk. 20:20–26)

13Later, the Jewish leaders sent some Pharisees* and some men from the group called Herodians* to Jesus. They wanted to catch him saying something wrong. 14They went to Jesus and said, "Teacher, we know that you are an honest man. You are not afraid of what others think about you. All people are the same to you. And you teach the truth about God's way. Tell us, is it right to pay taxes to Caesar*? Should we pay them or not?"

15But Jesus knew that these men were really trying to trick him. He said, "Why are you trying to catch me saying something wrong? Bring me a silver coin.* Let me see it." 16They gave Jesus a coin and he asked, "Whose picture is on the coin? And whose name is written on it?" They answered, "It is Caesar's picture and Caesar's name."

17Then Jesus said to them, "Give to Caesar what belongs to Caesar, and give to God what belongs to God." The men were amazed at what Jesus said.

Some Sadducees Try to Trick Jesus
(Mt. 22:23–33; Lk. 20:27–40)

18Then some Sadducees* came to Jesus. (Sadducees believe that no one will rise from death.) They asked him a question:

[19]"Teacher, Moses* wrote that if a married man dies and had no children, his brother must marry the woman. Then they will have children for the dead brother.[a] [20]There were seven brothers. The first brother married but died. He had no children. [21]So the second brother married the woman. But he also died and had no children. The same thing happened with the third brother. [22]All seven brothers married the woman and died. None of the brothers had any children with her. And she was the last to die. [23]But all seven brothers had married her. So at the time when people rise from death, whose wife will she be?"

[24]Jesus answered, "How could you be so wrong? It's because you don't know what the Scriptures* say. And you don't know anything about God's power. [25]When people rise from death, there will be no marriage. People will not be married to each other. All people will be like angels in heaven. [26]Surely you have read what God said about people rising from death. In the book where Moses wrote about the burning bush,[b] it says that God told Moses this: 'I am the God of Abraham,* the God of Isaac,* and the God of Jacob.'*[c] [27]So they were not still dead, because he is the God only of living people. You Sadducees are so wrong!"

Which Command Is the Most Important?
(Mt. 22:34–40; Lk. 10:25–28)

[28]One of the teachers of the law came to Jesus. He heard Jesus arguing with the Sadducees* and the Pharisees.* He saw that Jesus gave good answers to their questions. So he asked him, "Which of the commands is the most important?"

[29]Jesus answered, "The most important command is this: 'People of Israel,* listen! The Lord our God is the only Lord. [30]Love the Lord your God with all your heart, all your soul, all your mind, and all your strength.'[d] [31]The second most important command is this: 'Love your neighbor[e] the same as you love yourself.'[f] These two commands are the most important."

[32]The man answered, "That was a good answer, Teacher. You are right in saying that God is the only Lord and that there is no other God. [33]And you must love God with all your heart, all your mind, and all your strength. And you must love others the same as you love yourself. These commands are more important than all the animals and sacrifices we offer to God."

[34]Jesus saw that the man answered him wisely. So he said to him, "You are close to God's kingdom.*" And after that time, no one was brave enough to ask Jesus any more questions.

---

[a]**12:19** if … dead brother See Deut. 25:5, 6.   [b]**12:26** burning bush See Ex. 3:1–12.   [c]**12:26** Quote from Ex. 3:6.   [d]**12:30** Quote from Deut. 6:4–5.   [e]**12:31** your neighbor Or, "others." Jesus' teaching in Lk. 10:25–37 makes clear that this includes anyone in need.   [f]**12:31** Quote from Lev. 19:18.

Is the Christ David's Son or David's Lord?
(Mt. 22:41–46; Lk. 20:41–44)

[35]Jesus was teaching in the Temple* area. He asked, "Why do the teachers of the law say that the Christ* is the son of David*? [36]With the help of the Holy Spirit,* David himself says,

'The Lord God said to my Lord:
  Sit by me at my right side,
    and I will put your enemies under your control.[a]'

Psalm 110:1

[37]David himself calls the Christ 'Lord.' So how can the Christ be David's son?" Many people listened to Jesus and were very pleased.

Jesus Criticizes the Teachers of the Law
(Mt. 23:1–36; Lk. 20:45–47)

[38]Jesus continued teaching. He said, "Be careful of the teachers of the law. They like to walk around wearing clothes that look important. And they love for people to show respect to them in the marketplaces. [39]They love to have the most important seats in the synagogues* and the places of honor at banquets. [40]But they cheat widows and take their homes. Then they try to make themselves look good by saying long prayers. God will punish them very much."

True Giving
(Lk. 21:1–4)

[41]Jesus sat near the Temple* collection box[b] and watched as people put money into it. Many rich people put in a lot of money. [42]Then a poor widow came and put in two very small copper coins, worth less than a penny.

[43]Jesus called his followers to him and said, "This poor widow put in only two small coins. But the truth is, she gave more than all those rich people. [44]They have plenty, and they gave only what they did not need. This woman is very poor, but she gave all she had. It was money she needed to live on."

Jesus Warns About the Future
(Mt. 24:1–44; Lk. 21:5–33)

13 [1]Jesus was leaving the Temple* area. One of his followers said to him, "Teacher, look how big those stones are! What beautiful buildings!"

[2]Jesus said, "Do you see these great buildings? They will all be destroyed. Every stone will be thrown down to the ground. Not one stone will be left on another."

[3]Later, Jesus was sitting at a place on the Mount of Olives.* He was alone with Peter, James, John, and Andrew. They could

---

[a]**12:36** *control* Literally, "feet." [b]**12:41** *collection box* A special box in the Jewish place for worship where people put their gifts to God.

all see the Temple, and they said to Jesus, [4]"Tell us when these things will happen. And what will show us it is time for them to happen?"

[5]Jesus said to them, "Be careful! Don't let anyone fool you. [6]Many people will come and use my name. They will say, 'I am the one' and will fool many people. [7]You will hear about wars that are being fought. And you will hear stories about other wars beginning. But don't be afraid. These things must happen before the end comes. [8]Nations will fight against other nations. Kingdoms will fight against other kingdoms. There will be times when there is no food for people to eat. And there will be earthquakes in different places. These things are only the beginning of troubles, like the first pains of a woman giving birth.

[9]"You must be careful! There are people who will arrest you and take you to be judged for being my followers. They will beat you in their synagogues.* You will be forced to stand before kings and governors. You will tell them about me. [10]Before the end comes, the Good News* must be told to all people. [11]Even when you are arrested and put on trial, don't worry about what you will say. Say whatever God tells you at the time. It will not really be you speaking. It will be the Holy Spirit.*

[12]"Brothers will turn against their own brothers and hand them over to be killed. Fathers will hand over their own children to be killed. Children will fight against their own parents and have them killed. [13]All people will hate you because you follow me. But those who remain faithful to the end will be saved.

[14]"You will see 'the terrible thing that causes destruction.'[a] You will see this thing standing in the place where it should not be." (Reader, I trust you understand what this means.) "Everyone in Judea at that time should run away to the mountains. [15]They should run away without wasting time to stop for anything. If someone is on the roof of their house, they must not go down to take things out of the house. [16]If someone is in the field, they must not go back to get a coat.

[17]"During that time it will be hard for women who are pregnant or have small babies. [18]Pray that these things will not happen in winter, [19]because those days will be full of trouble. There will be more trouble than has ever happened since the beginning, when God made the world. And nothing that bad will ever happen again. [20]But the Lord has decided to make that terrible time short. If it were not made short, no one could survive. But the Lord will make that time short to help the special people he has chosen.

[21]"Someone might say to you at that time, 'Look, there is the Christ*!' Or another person might say, 'There he is!' But don't believe them. [22]False Christs and false prophets* will come and do miracles and wonders,[b] trying to fool the people God has

---

[a]13:14 'the terrible thing ... destruction' See Dan. 9:27; 12:11 (also Dan. 11:31).
[b]13:22 miracles and wonders Here, amazing acts done by Satan's power.

chosen, if that is possible. ²³So be careful. Now I have warned you about all this before it happens.

²⁴"During the days following that time of trouble,

'The sun will become dark,
    and the moon will not give light.
²⁵ The stars will fall from the sky,
    and everything in the sky will be changed.'ᵃ

²⁶"Then people will see the Son of Man* coming in the clouds with great power and glory.* ²⁷He will send his angels all around the earth. They will gather his chosen people from every part of the earth.

²⁸"The fig tree teaches us a lesson: When its branches become green and soft, and new leaves begin to grow, then you know that summer is near. ²⁹In the same way, when you see all these things happening, you will know that the timeᵇ is near, ready to come. ³⁰I assure you that all these things will happen while some of the people of this time are still living. ³¹The whole world, earth and sky, will be destroyed, but my words will last forever.

³²"No one knows when that day or time will be. The Son and the angels in heaven don't know when that day or time will be. Only the Father knows. ³³Be careful! Always be ready. You don't know when that time will be.

³⁴"It's like a man who goes on a trip and leaves his house in the care of his servants. He gives each one a special job to do. He tells the servant guarding the door to always be ready. And this is what I am telling you now. ³⁵You must always be ready. You don't know when the owner of the house will come back. He might come in the afternoon, or at midnight, or in the early morning, or when the sun rises. ³⁶If you are always ready, he will not find you sleeping, even if he comes back earlier than expected. ³⁷I tell you this, and I say it to everyone: 'Be ready!'"

The Jewish Leaders Plan to Kill Jesus
(Mt. 26:1–5; Lk. 22:1–2; Jn. 11:45–53)

14 ¹It was now only two days before the Passover* and the Festival of Unleavened Bread.* The leading priests and teachers of the law were trying to find a way to arrest Jesus without the people seeing it. Then they could kill him. ²They said, "But we cannot arrest Jesus during the festival. We don't want the people to be angry and cause a riot."

A Woman Does Something Special
(Mt. 26:6–13; Jn. 12:1–8)

³Jesus was in Bethany at the house of Simon the leper.* While he was eating there, a woman came to him. She had an

---

ᵃ**13:25** See Isa. 13:10, 34:4.   ᵇ**13:29** *time* The time Jesus has been talking about when something important will happen. See Lk. 21:31, where Jesus says that this is the time for God's kingdom to come.

alabaster* jar filled with expensive perfume made of pure nard.* She opened the jar and poured the perfume on Jesus' head.

⁴Some of the followers there saw this. They were upset and complained to each other. They said, "Why waste that perfume? ⁵It was worth a full year's pay.ᵃ It could have been sold and the money given to those who are poor." And they told the woman what a bad thing she had done.

⁶Jesus said, "Leave her alone. Why are you giving her such trouble? She did a very good thing for me. ⁷You will always have the poor with you,ᵇ and you can help them any time you want. But you will not always have me. ⁸This woman did the only thing she could do for me. She poured perfume on my body before I die to prepare it for burial. ⁹The Good News* will be told to people all over the world. And I can assure you that everywhere the Good News is told, the story of what this woman did will also be told, and people will remember her."

Judas Agrees to Help Jesus' Enemies
(Mt. 26:14–16; Lk. 22:3–6)

¹⁰Then Judas Iscariot, one of the twelve apostles,* went to talk to the leading priests about handing Jesus over to them. ¹¹They were very happy about this, and they promised to pay him. So he waited for the best time to hand Jesus over to them.

The Passover Meal
(Mt. 26:17–25; Lk. 22:7–14, 21–23; Jn. 13:21–30)

¹²It was now the first day of the Festival of Unleavened Bread*—the day the lambs were killed for the Passover.* Jesus' followers came to him and said, "We will go and prepare everything for you to eat the Passover meal. Where do you want us to have the meal?"

¹³Jesus sent two of his followers into the city. He said to them, "Go into the city. You will see a man carrying a jar of water. He will come to you. Follow him. ¹⁴He will go into a house. Tell the owner of the house, 'The Teacher asks that you show us the room where he and his followers can eat the Passover meal.' ¹⁵The owner will show you a large room upstairs that is ready for us. Prepare the meal for us there."

¹⁶So the followers left and went into the city. Everything happened the way Jesus said. So the followers prepared the Passover meal.

¹⁷In the evening, Jesus went to that house with the twelve apostles.* ¹⁸While they were all at the table eating, he said, "Believe me when I say that one of you will hand me over to my enemies—one of you eating with me now."

¹⁹The followers were very sad to hear this. Each one said to Jesus, "Surely I am not the one!"

ᵃ**14:5** *a full year's pay* Literally, "300 *denarii* (silver coins)." One coin, a Roman *denarius*, was the average pay for one day's work. ᵇ**14:7** *You will ... with you* See Deut. 15:11.

²⁰Jesus answered, "It is one of you twelve—one who is dipping his bread in the same bowl with me. ²¹The Son of Man* will suffer what the Scriptures* say will happen to him. But it will be very bad for the one who hands over the Son of Man to be killed. It would be better for him if he had never been born."

The Lord's Supper
(Mt. 26:26–30; Lk. 22:15–20; 1 Cor. 11:23–25)

²²While they were eating, Jesus took some bread and thanked God for it. He broke off some pieces, gave them to his followers and said, "Take and eat this bread. It is my body."

²³Then he took a cup of wine, thanked God for it, and gave it to them. They all drank from the cup. ²⁴Then he said, "This wine is my blood, which will be poured out for many to begin the new agreement* from God to his people. ²⁵I want you to know, I will not drink this wine again until that day when I drink it in God's kingdom* and the wine is new."

²⁶They all sang a song and then went out to the Mount of Olives.*

Jesus Says His Followers Will Leave Him
(Mt. 26:31–35; Lk. 22:31–34; Jn. 13:36–38)

²⁷Then Jesus told the followers, "You will all lose your faith. The Scriptures* say,

'I will kill the shepherd,
  and the sheep will run away.'   *Zechariah 13:7*

²⁸But after I am killed, I will rise from death. Then I will go to Galilee. I will be there before you come."

²⁹Peter said, "All the other followers may lose their faith. But my faith will never be shaken."

³⁰Jesus answered, "The truth is, tonight you will say you don't know me. You will say it three times before the rooster crows twice."

³¹But Peter strongly protested, "I will never say I don't know you! I will even die with you!" And all the other followers said the same thing.

Jesus Prays Alone
(Mt. 26:36–46; Lk. 22:39–46)

³²Jesus and his followers went to a place named Gethsemane. He said to them, "Sit here while I pray." ³³But he told Peter, James, and John to come with him. He began to be very distressed and troubled, ³⁴and he said to them, "My heart is so heavy with grief, I feel as if I am dying. Wait here and stay awake."

³⁵Jesus went on a little farther away from them, fell to the ground, and prayed. He asked that, if possible, he would not

have this time of suffering. [36]He said, "*Abba*,[a] Father! You can do all things. Don't make me drink from this cup.[b] But do what you want, not what I want."

[37]Then he went back to his followers and found them sleeping. He said to Peter, "Simon, why are you sleeping? Could you not stay awake with me for one hour? [38]Stay awake and pray for strength against temptation. Your spirit wants to do what is right, but your body is weak."

[39]Again Jesus went away and prayed the same thing. [40]Then he went back to the followers and again found them sleeping. They could not stay awake. They did not know what they should say to him.

[41]After Jesus prayed a third time, he went back to his followers. He said to them, "Are you still sleeping and resting? That's enough! The time has come for the Son of Man* to be handed over to the control of sinful men. [42]Stand up! We must go. Here comes the man who is handing me over to them."

Jesus Is Arrested
(Mt. 26:47–56; Lk. 22:47–53; Jn. 18:3–12)

[43]While Jesus was still speaking, Judas, one of the twelve apostles,* came there. He had a big crowd of people with him, all carrying swords and clubs. They had been sent from the leading priests, the teachers of the law, and the older Jewish leaders.

[44]Judas[c] planned to do something to show them which one was Jesus. He said, "The one I kiss will be Jesus. Arrest him and guard him while you lead him away." [45]So Judas went over to Jesus and said, "Teacher!" Then he kissed him. [46]The men grabbed Jesus and arrested him. [47]One of the followers standing near Jesus grabbed his sword and pulled it out. He swung it at the servant of the high priest* and cut off his ear.

[48]Then Jesus said, "Why do you come to get me with swords and clubs as if I were a criminal? [49]Every day I was with you teaching in the Temple* area. You did not arrest me there. But all these things have happened to show the full meaning of what the Scriptures* said." [50]Then all of Jesus' followers left him and ran away.

[51]One of those following Jesus was a young man wearing only a linen cloth. When the people tried to grab him, [52]he left the cloth in their hands and ran away naked.

Jesus Before the Jewish Leaders
(Mt. 26:57–68; Lk. 22:54–55, 63–71; Jn. 18:13–14, 19–24)

[53]Those who arrested Jesus led him to the house of the high priest.* All the leading priests, the older Jewish leaders, and the

---

[a]**14:36** *Abba* An Aramaic word that was used by Jewish children as a name for their fathers.
[b]**14:36** *cup* A symbol of suffering. Jesus used the idea of drinking from a cup to mean accepting the suffering he would face in the terrible events that were soon to come.
[c]**14:44** *Judas* Literally, "the one who handed him over."

teachers of the law were gathered there. ⁵⁴Peter followed Jesus but stayed back at a distance. He followed him to the yard of the high priest's house. He went into the yard and sat there with the guards, warming himself by their fire.

⁵⁵The leading priests and the whole high council tried to find something that Jesus had done wrong so they could kill him. But the council could find no proof that would allow them to kill Jesus. ⁵⁶Many people came and told lies against Jesus, but they all said different things. None of them agreed.

⁵⁷Then some others stood up and told more lies against Jesus. They said, ⁵⁸"We heard this man*a* say, 'I will destroy this Temple* built by human hands. And three days later, I will build another Temple not made by human hands.'" ⁵⁹But also what these people said did not agree.

⁶⁰Then the high priest stood up before everyone and said to Jesus, "These people said things against you. Do you have something to say about their charges? Are they telling the truth?" ⁶¹But Jesus said nothing to answer him.

The high priest asked Jesus another question: "Are you the Christ,* the Son of the blessed God?"

⁶²Jesus answered, "Yes, I am the Son of God. And in the future you will see the Son of Man* sitting at the right side of God All-Powerful. And you will see the Son of Man coming on the clouds of heaven."

⁶³When the high priest heard this, he tore his clothes in anger. He said, "We don't need any more witnesses! ⁶⁴You all heard these insults to God. What do you think?"

Everyone agreed that Jesus was guilty and must be killed. ⁶⁵Some of the people there spit at him. They covered his eyes and hit him with their fists. They said, "Be a prophet*b* and tell us who hit you!" Then the guards led Jesus away and beat him.

Peter Is Afraid to Say He Knows Jesus
(Mt. 26:69–75; Lk. 22:56–62; Jn. 18:15–18, 25–27)

⁶⁶While Peter was still in the yard, a servant girl of the high priest* came there. ⁶⁷She saw him warming himself by the fire. She looked closely at him and said, "You were with Jesus, that man from Nazareth."

⁶⁸But Peter said this was not true. "That makes no sense," he said. "I don't know what you are talking about!" Then he left and went to the entrance of the yard, and a rooster crowed.*c*

⁶⁹When the servant girl saw him there, she began saying again to the people standing around, "This man is one of them." ⁷⁰Again Peter said it was not true.

A short time later, the people standing there said, "We know you are one of them, because you are from Galilee."

a14:58 this man That is, Jesus. His enemies avoided saying his name. *b14:65 prophet* A prophet often knows things that are hidden from other people. *c14:68* Some Greek copies do not have "and a rooster crowed."

⁷¹Then Peter began to curse. He said, "I swear to God, I don't know this man you are talking about!"

⁷²As soon as Peter said this, the rooster crowed the second time. Then he remembered what Jesus had told him: "Before the rooster crows twice, you will say three times that you don't know me." Then Peter began to cry.

Governor Pilate Questions Jesus
(Mt. 27:1–2, 11–14; Lk. 23:1–5; Jn. 18:28–38)

15 ¹Very early in the morning, the leading priests, the older Jewish leaders, the teachers of the law, and the whole high council decided what to do with Jesus. They tied him, led him away, and handed him over to governor Pilate.*

²Pilate asked Jesus, "Are you the king of the Jews?"

Jesus answered, "Yes, that is right."

³The leading priests accused Jesus of many things. ⁴So Pilate asked Jesus another question. He said, "You can see that these people are accusing you of many things. Why don't you answer?"

⁵But Jesus still did not answer, and this really surprised Pilate.

Pilate Tries but Fails to Free Jesus
(Mt. 27:15–31; Lk. 23:13–25; Jn. 18:39–19:16)

⁶Every year at the Passover* time the governor would free one prisoner—whichever one the people wanted. ⁷There was a man in prison at that time named Barabbas. He and the rebels with him had been put in prison for committing murder during a riot.

⁸The people came to Pilate and asked him to free a prisoner as he always did. ⁹Pilate asked them, "Do you want me to free the king of the Jews?" ¹⁰Pilate knew that the leading priests had handed Jesus over to him because they were jealous of him. ¹¹But the leading priests persuaded the people to ask Pilate to free Barabbas, not Jesus.

¹²Pilate asked the people again, "So what should I do with this man you call the king of the Jews?"

¹³The people shouted, "Kill him on a cross!"

¹⁴Pilate asked, "Why? What wrong has he done?"

But the people shouted louder and louder, "Kill him on a cross!"

¹⁵Pilate wanted to please the people, so he freed Barabbas for them. And he told the soldiers to beat Jesus with whips. Then he handed him over to the soldiers to be killed on a cross.

¹⁶Pilate's soldiers took Jesus into the governor's palace (called the Praetorium). They called all the other soldiers together. ¹⁷They put a purple robe on Jesus, made a crown from thorny branches, and put it on his head. ¹⁸Then they began shouting, "Welcome, king of the Jews!" ¹⁹They kept on beating his head with a stick and spitting on him. Then they bowed down on their knees and pretended to honor him as a king. ²⁰After they

finished making fun of him, they took off the purple robe and put his own clothes on him again. Then they led him out of the palace to be killed on a cross.

Jesus Is Nailed to a Cross
(Mt. 27:32–44; Lk. 23:26–39; Jn. 19:17–19)

²¹There was a man from Cyrene named Simon walking into the city from the fields. He was the father of Alexander and Rufus. The soldiers forced him to carry Jesus' cross. ²²They led Jesus to the place called Golgotha. (Golgotha means "The Place of the Skull.") ²³There they gave him some wine mixed with myrrh,* but he refused to drink it. ²⁴The soldiers nailed Jesus to a cross. Then they divided his clothes among themselves, throwing dice to see who would get what.

²⁵It was nine o'clock in the morning when they nailed Jesus to the cross. ²⁶There was a sign with the charge against him written on it. It said, "THE KING OF THE JEWS." ²⁷They also nailed two criminals to crosses beside Jesus—one on the right and the other on the left. ²⁸ᵃ

²⁹People walked by and said bad things to Jesus. They shook their heads and said, "You said you could destroy the Temple* and build it again in three days. ³⁰So save yourself! Come down from that cross!"

³¹The leading priests and the teachers of the law were also there. They made fun of Jesus the same as the other people did. They said to each other, "He saved others, but he can't save himself! ³²If he is really the Christ,* the king of Israel,* he should come down from the cross now. When we see this, then we will believe in him." The criminals on the crosses beside Jesus also said bad things to him.

Jesus Dies
(Mt. 27:45–56; Lk. 23:44–49; Jn. 19:28–30)

³³At noon the whole country became dark. This darkness continued until three o'clock. ³⁴At three o'clock Jesus cried with a loud voice, *"Eloi, Eloi, lama sabachthani."* This means "My God, my God, why have you left me alone?"ᵇ

³⁵Some of the people standing there heard this. They said, "Listen! He is calling Elijah."ᶜ

³⁶One man there ran and got a sponge. He filled the sponge with sour wine and tied it to a stick. Then he used the stick to give the sponge to Jesus to get a drink from it. The man said, "We should wait now and see if Elijah will come to take him down from the cross."

³⁷Then Jesus cried with a loud voice and died.

ᵃ**15:28** Some Greek copies add verse 28: "And this showed the full meaning of the Scripture that says, 'They put him with criminals.'" ᵇ**15:34** Quote from Ps. 22:1. ᶜ**15:35** *He is calling Elijah* The word for "My God" (*Eli* in Hebrew or *Eloi* in Aramaic) sounded to the people like the name of Elijah, a famous man who spoke for God about 850 B.C.

38When Jesus died, the curtain* in the Temple* was torn into two pieces. The tear started at the top and tore all the way to the bottom. 39The army officer* who was standing there in front of the cross saw what happened when Jesus died. The officer said, "This man really was the Son of God!"

40Some women were standing away from the cross, watching. Among these women were Mary Magdalene, Salome, and Mary the mother of James and Joses. (James was her youngest son.) 41These were the women who had followed Jesus in Galilee and cared for him. Many other women who had come with Jesus to Jerusalem were also there.

Jesus Is Buried
(Mt. 27:57–61; Lk. 23:50–56; Jn. 19:38–42)

42This day was called Preparation day. (That means the day before the Sabbath* day.) It was becoming dark. 43A man named Joseph from Arimathea was brave enough to go to Pilate and ask for Jesus' body. Joseph was an important member of the high council. He was one of the people who wanted God's kingdom* to come.

44Pilate was surprised to hear that Jesus was already dead. So he called for the army officer* in charge and asked him if Jesus was already dead. 45When Pilate heard it from the officer, he told Joseph he could have the body. 46Joseph bought some linen cloth. He took the body from the cross, wrapped it in the linen, and put the body in a tomb* that was dug in a wall of rock. Then he closed the tomb by rolling a large stone to cover the entrance. 47Mary Magdalene and Mary the mother of Joses saw the place where Jesus was put.

News That Jesus Has Risen From Death
(Mt. 28:1–8; Lk. 24:1–12; Jn. 20:1–10)

16 1The next day after the Sabbath* day, Mary Magdalene, Salome, and Mary the mother of James bought some sweet-smelling spices to put on Jesus' body. 2Very early on that day, the first day of the week, the women were going to the tomb.* It was very early after sunrise. 3The women said to each other, "There is a large stone covering the entrance of the tomb. Who will move the stone for us?"

4Then the women looked and saw that the stone was moved. The stone was very large, but it was moved away from the entrance. 5The women walked into the tomb and saw a young man there wearing a white robe. He was sitting on the right side of the tomb. The women were afraid.

6But the man said, "Don't be afraid. You are looking for Jesus from Nazareth, the one who was killed on a cross. He has risen from death! He is not here. Look, here is the place they put him when he was dead. 7Now go and tell his followers. And be sure to tell Peter. Tell them, 'Jesus is going into Galilee and will be there before you come. You will see him there, as he told you before.'"

[8]The women were very afraid and confused. They left the tomb and ran away. They did not tell about what happened, because they were afraid.[a]

Some Followers See Jesus
(Mt. 28:9–10; Jn. 20:11–18; Lk. 24:13–35)

[9]Jesus rose from death early on the first day of the week. He showed himself first to Mary Magdalene. One time in the past Jesus had forced seven demons* out of Mary. [10]After Mary saw Jesus, she went and told his followers. They were very sad and were crying. [11]But Mary told them that Jesus was alive. She said that she had seen Jesus, but they did not believe her.

[12]Later, Jesus showed himself to two followers while they were walking in the country. But Jesus did not look the same as before he was killed. [13]These followers went back to the other followers and told them what happened. Again, the followers did not believe them.

Jesus Talks to His Followers
(Mt. 28:16–20; Lk. 24:36–49; Jn. 20:19–23; Acts 1:6–8)

[14]Later, Jesus showed himself to the eleven followers while they were eating. He criticized them because they had so little faith. They were stubborn and refused to believe the people who said Jesus had risen from death.

[15]He said to them, "Go everywhere in the world. Tell the Good News* to everyone. [16]Whoever believes and is baptized* will be saved. But those who do not believe will be judged guilty. [17]And the people who believe will be able to do these things as proof: They will use my name to force demons* out of people. They will speak in languages they never learned. [18]If they pick up snakes or drink any poison, they will not be hurt. They will lay their hands on sick people, and they will get well."

Jesus Goes Back to Heaven
(Lk. 24:50–53; Acts 1:9–11)

[19]After the Lord Jesus said these things to his followers, he was carried up into heaven. There, Jesus sat at the right side of God. [20]The followers went everywhere in the world telling people the Good News,* and the Lord helped them. By giving them power to do miracles* the Lord proved that their message was true.

---

[a]**16:8** Some of the oldest Greek copies end the book here. A few later copies have this shorter ending: "But they soon gave all the instructions to Peter and those with him. After that, Jesus himself sent them out from east to west with the holy message that will never change—that people can be saved forever."

Luke

Luke Writes About the Life of Jesus

1 ¹Most Honorable Theophilus:

Many others have tried to give a report of the things that happened among us to complete God's plan. ²What they have written agrees with what we learned from the people who saw those events from the beginning. They also served God by telling people his message. ³I studied it all carefully from the beginning. Then I decided to write it down for you in an organized way. ⁴I did this so that you can be sure that what you have been taught is true.

Zechariah and Elizabeth

⁵During the time when Herod* ruled Judea, there was a priest named Zechariah. He belonged to Abijah's group.ᵃ His wife came from the family of Aaron. Her name was Elizabeth. ⁶Zechariah and Elizabeth were both good people who pleased God. They did everything the Lord commanded, always following his instructions completely. ⁷But they had no children. Elizabeth could not have a baby, and both of them were very old.

⁸Zechariah was serving as a priest before God for his group. It was his group's time to serve. ⁹The priests always chose one priest to offer the incense,* and Zechariah was the one chosen this time. So he went into the Temple* of the Lord to offer the incense. ¹⁰There was a large crowd outside praying at the time the incense was offered.

¹¹Then, on the right side of the incense table an angel of the Lord came and stood before Zechariah. ¹²When he saw the angel, Zechariah was upset and very afraid. ¹³But the angel said to him, "Zechariah, don't be afraid. Your prayer has been heard by God. Your wife Elizabeth will give birth to a baby boy, and you will name him John. ¹⁴You will be very happy, and many others will share your joy over his birth. ¹⁵He will be a great man for the Lord. He will never drink wine or liquor. Even before he is born, he will be filled with the Holy Spirit.*

¹⁶"John will help many people of Israel* return to the Lord their God. ¹⁷John himself will go ahead of the Lord and make people ready for his coming. He will be powerful like Elijah* and will have the same spirit. He will make peace between

---

ᵃ **1:5** *Abijah's group* Jewish priests were divided into 24 groups. See 1 Chron. 24.

fathers and their children. He will cause people who are not obeying God to change and start thinking the way they should."

¹⁸Zechariah said to the angel, "How can I know that what you say is true? I am an old man, and my wife is also old."

¹⁹The angel answered him, "I am Gabriel, the one who always stands ready before God. He sent me to talk to you and to tell you this good news. ²⁰Now, listen! You will not be able to talk until the day when these things happen. You will lose your speech because you did not believe what I told you. But everything I said will really happen."

²¹Outside, the people were still waiting for Zechariah. They were surprised that he was staying so long in the Temple. ²²Then Zechariah came outside, but he could not speak to them. So the people knew that he had seen a vision* inside the Temple. He was not able to speak, so he could only make signs to the people. ²³When his time of service was finished, he went home.

²⁴Later, Zechariah's wife Elizabeth became pregnant. So she did not go out of her house for five months. She said, ²⁵"Look what the Lord has done for me! He decided to help me. Now people will stop thinking there is something wrong with me."

The Virgin Mary

²⁶⁻²⁷During Elizabeth's sixth month of pregnancy, God sent the angel Gabriel to a virgin* girl who lived in Nazareth, a town in Galilee. She was engaged to marry a man named Joseph from the family of David.* Her name was Mary. ²⁸The angel came to her and said, "Greetings! The Lord is with you; you are very special to him."

²⁹But Mary was very confused about what the angel said. She wondered, "What does this mean?"

³⁰The angel said to her, "Don't be afraid, Mary, because God is very pleased with you. ³¹Listen! You will become pregnant and have a baby boy. You will name him Jesus. ³²He will be great. People will call him the Son of the Most High God, and the Lord God will make him king like his ancestor David. ³³He will rule over the people of Jacob* forever; his kingdom will never end."

³⁴Mary said to the angel, "How will this happen? I am still a virgin."

³⁵The angel said to Mary, "The Holy Spirit* will come to you, and the power of the Most High God will cover you. The baby will be holy and will be called the Son of God. ³⁶And here's something else: Your relative Elizabeth is pregnant. She is very old, but she is going to have a son. Everyone thought she could not have a baby, but she has been pregnant now for six months. ³⁷God can do anything!"

³⁸Mary said, "I am the servant of the Lord God. Let this thing you have said happen to me!" Then the angel went away.

Mary Visits Zechariah and Elizabeth

[39] Mary got up and went quickly to a town in the hill country of Judea. [40] She went into Zechariah's house and greeted Elizabeth. [41] When Elizabeth heard Mary's greeting, the unborn baby inside her jumped, and she was filled with the Holy Spirit.*

[42] In a loud voice she said to Mary, "God has blessed you more than any other woman. And God has blessed the baby you will have. [43] You are the mother of my Lord, and you have come to me! Why has something so good happened to me? [44] When I heard your voice, the baby inside me jumped with joy. [45] What a great blessing is yours because you believed what the Lord said to you! You believed this would happen."

Mary Praises God

[46] Then Mary said,

[47] "I praise the Lord with all my heart.
     I am very happy because God is my Savior.
[48] I am not important,
     but he has shown his care for me, his lowly servant.
   From now until the end of time,
     people will remember how much God blessed me.
[49] Yes, the Powerful One has done great things for me.
     His name is very holy.
[50] He always gives mercy to those who worship him.
[51] He reached out his arm and showed his power.
   He scattered those who are proud and think great things
     about themselves.
[52] He brought down rulers from their thrones
     and raised up the humble people.
[53] He filled the hungry with good things,
     but he sent the rich away with nothing.
[54] God has helped Israel—the people he chose to serve him.
   He did not forget his promise to give us his mercy.
[55] He has done what he promised to our ancestors,*
     to Abraham* and his children forever."

[56] Mary stayed with Elizabeth for about three months and then went home.

The Birth of John

[57] When it was time for Elizabeth to give birth, she had a boy. [58] Her neighbors and relatives heard that the Lord was very good to her, and they were happy for her.

[59] When the baby was eight days old, they came to circumcise* him. They wanted to name him Zechariah because this was his father's name. [60] But his mother said, "No, he will be named John."

⁶¹The people said to Elizabeth, "But no one in your family has that name." ⁶²Then they made signs to his father, "What would you like to name him?"

⁶³Zechariah asked for something to write on. Then he wrote, "His name is John." Everyone was surprised. ⁶⁴Then Zechariah could talk again, and he began praising God. ⁶⁵And all their neighbors were afraid. In all the hill country of Judea people continued talking about these things. ⁶⁶Everyone who heard about these things wondered about them. They thought, "What will this child be?" They could see that the Lord was with him.

Zechariah Praises God

⁶⁷Then Zechariah, John's father, was filled with the Holy Spirit* and told the people a message from God:

⁶⁸"Praise to the Lord God of Israel.*
　　He has come to help his people
　　　and has given them freedom.
⁶⁹ He has given us a powerful Savior
　　　from the family of his servant David.*
⁷⁰ This is what he promised
　　　through his holy* prophets* long ago.
⁷¹ He will save us from our enemies
　　　and from the power of all those who hate us.
⁷² God said he would show mercy to our fathers,*
　　　and he remembered his holy agreement.*
⁷³ This was the promise he made to our father Abraham,*
⁷⁴ 　a promise to free us from the power of our enemies,
　　　so that we could serve him without fear
⁷⁵ 　in a way that is holy and right for as long as we live.

⁷⁶"Now you, little boy, will be called a prophet
　　　of the Most High God.
　　You will go first before the Lord to prepare the way for him.
⁷⁷ You will make his people understand
　　　that they will be saved by having their sins forgiven.

⁷⁸"With the loving mercy of our God,
　　a new day*ᵃ* from heaven will shine on us.
⁷⁹ It will bring light to those who live in darkness,
　　　in the fear of death.
　　It will guide us into the way that brings peace."

⁸⁰And so the little boy John grew up and became stronger in spirit. Then he lived in areas away from other people until the time when he came out to tell God's message to the people of Israel.

---

*ᵃ*1:78 new day Literally, "dawn," used here as a symbol, probably meaning the Lord's Messiah.

The Birth of Jesus Christ
(Mt. 1:18–25)

2 1It was about that same time that Augustus Caesar* sent out an order to all people in the countries that were under Roman rule. The order said that everyone's name must be put on a list. 2This was the first counting of all the people while Quirinius was governor of Syria. 3Everyone traveled to their own hometowns to have their name put on the list.

4So Joseph left Nazareth, a town in Galilee, and went to the town of Bethlehem in Judea. It was known as the town of David.* Joseph went there because he was from the family of David. 5Joseph registered with Mary because she was engaged to marry him. (She was now pregnant.) 6While Joseph and Mary were in Bethlehem, the time came for her to have the baby. 7She gave birth to her first son. She wrapped him up well and laid him in a box where cattle are fed. She put him there because the guest room was full.

Some Shepherds Hear About Jesus

8That night, some shepherds were out in the fields near Bethlehem watching their sheep. 9An angel of the Lord appeared to them, and the glory* of the Lord was shining around them. The shepherds were very afraid. 10The angel said to them, "Don't be afraid. I have some very good news for you—news that will make everyone happy. 11Today your Savior was born in David's town. He is Christ,* the Lord. 12This is how you will know him: You will find a baby wrapped in pieces of cloth and lying in a feeding box."

13Then a huge army of angels from heaven joined the first angel, and they were all praising God, saying,

14"Praise God in heaven,
     and on earth let there be peace
          to the people who please him."

15The angels left the shepherds and went back to heaven. The shepherds said to each other, "What a great event this is that the Lord has told us about. Let's go to Bethlehem and see it."

16So they went running and found Mary and Joseph. And there was the baby, lying in the feeding box. 17When they saw the baby, they told what the angels said about this child. 18Everyone was surprised when they heard what the shepherds told them. 19Mary continued to think about these things, trying to understand them. 20The shepherds went back to their sheep, praising God and thanking him for everything they had seen and heard. It was just as the angel had told them.

21When the baby was eight days old, he was circumcised,* and he was named Jesus. This name was given by the angel before the baby began to grow inside Mary.

Jesus Is Presented in the Temple

[22]The time came for Mary and Joseph to do the things the law of Moses* taught about being made pure.[a] They brought Jesus to Jerusalem so that they could present him to the Lord. [23]It is written in the law of the Lord: "When a mother's first baby is a boy, he shall be called 'special for the Lord.'"[b] [24]The law of the Lord also says that people must give a sacrifice*: "You must sacrifice two doves or two young pigeons."[c] So Joseph and Mary went to Jerusalem to do this.

Simeon Sees Jesus

[25]A man named Simeon lived in Jerusalem. He was a good man who was devoted to God. He was waiting for the time when God would come to help Israel.* The Holy Spirit* was with him. [26]The Holy Spirit told him that he would not die before he saw the Christ* from the Lord. [27]The Spirit led Simeon to the Temple.* So he was there when Mary and Joseph brought the baby Jesus to do what the Jewish law said they must do. [28]Simeon took the baby in his arms and thanked God:

[29]"Now, Lord, you can let me, your servant,
        die in peace as you said.
[30] I have seen with my own eyes how you
        will save your people.
[31]   Now all people can see your plan.
[32] He is a light to show your way to the other nations.
        And he will bring honor to your people Israel."

[33]Jesus' father and mother were amazed at what Simeon said about him. [34]Then Simeon blessed them and said to Mary, "Many Jews will fall and many will rise because of this boy. He will be a sign from God that some will not accept. [35]So the secret thoughts of many will be made known. And the things that happen will be painful for you—like a sword cutting through your heart."

Anna Sees Jesus

[36]Anna, a prophetess,* was there at the Temple.* She was from the family of Phanuel in the tribe of Asher. She was now very old. She had lived with her husband seven years [37]before he died and left her alone. She was now 84 years old. Anna was always at the Temple; she never left. She worshiped God by fasting* and praying day and night.

[38]Anna was there when Joseph and Mary came to the Temple. She praised God and talked about Jesus to all those who were waiting for God to free Jerusalem.

*a*2:22 *pure* The law of Moses said that 40 days after a Jewish woman gave birth to a baby, she must be made ritually clean by a ceremony at the Temple. See Lev. 12:2–8. *b*2:23 *"When ... 'special for the Lord'"* See Ex. 13:2, 12. *c*2:24 Quote from Lev. 12:8.

Joseph and Mary Return Home

³⁹Joseph and Mary finished doing all the things that the law of the Lord commanded. Then they went home to Nazareth, their own town in Galilee. ⁴⁰The little boy Jesus was developing into a mature young man, full of wisdom. God was blessing him.

Jesus as a Boy

⁴¹Every year Jesus' parents went to Jerusalem for the Passover* festival. ⁴²When Jesus was twelve years old, they went to the festival as usual. ⁴³When the festival was over, they went home, but Jesus stayed in Jerusalem. His parents did not know about it. ⁴⁴They traveled for a whole day thinking that Jesus was with them in the group. They began looking for him among their family and close friends, ⁴⁵but they did not find him. So they went back to Jerusalem to look for him there.

⁴⁶After three days they found him. Jesus was sitting in the Temple* area with the religious teachers, listening and asking them questions. ⁴⁷Everyone who heard him was amazed at his understanding and wise answers. ⁴⁸When his parents saw him, they wondered how this was possible. And his mother said, "Son, why did you do this to us? Your father and I were very worried about you. We have been looking for you."

⁴⁹Jesus said to them, "Why did you have to look for me? You should have known that I must be where my Father's work is.ᵃ" ⁵⁰But they did not understand the meaning of what he said to them.

⁵¹Jesus went with them to Nazareth and obeyed them. His mother was still thinking about all these things. ⁵²As Jesus grew taller, he continued to grow in wisdom. God was pleased with him and so were the people who knew him.

John Prepares the Way for Jesus
(Mt. 3:1–12; Mk. 1:1–8; Jn. 1:19–28)

3 ¹It was the 15ᵗʰ year of the rule of Tiberius Caesar.* These men were under Caesar:

> Pontius Pilate, the governor of Judea;
> Herod,* the ruler of Galilee;
> Philip, Herod's brother, the ruler of Iturea and Trachonitis;
> Lysanias, the ruler of Abilene.

²Annas and Caiaphas were the high priests.* During this time, John, the son of Zechariah, was living in the desert and received a message from God. ³So he went through the whole area around the Jordan River and told the people God's message. He told them to be baptized* to show that they wanted to change their lives, and then their sins would be forgiven. ⁴This is like the words written in the book of Isaiah the prophet*:

ᵃ **2:49** *where ... work is* Or, "in my Father's house."

"There is someone shouting in the desert:
'Prepare the way for the Lord.
  Make the path straight for him.
⁵ Every valley will be filled,
  and every mountain and hill will be made flat.
Roads with turns will be made straight,
  and rough roads will be made smooth.
⁶ Then everyone will see how God will save his people!'"

Isaiah 40:3–5

⁷Crowds of people came to be baptized by John. But he said to them, "You are all snakes! Who warned you to run away from God's anger that is coming? ⁸Change your hearts! And show by your lives that you have changed. I know what you are about to say—'but Abraham* is our father!' That means nothing. I tell you that God can make children for Abraham from these rocks! ⁹The ax is now ready to cut down the trees.ᵃ Every tree that does not produce good fruit will be cut down and thrown into the fire."

¹⁰The people asked John, "What should we do?"

¹¹He answered, "If you have two shirts, share with someone who does not have one. If you have food, share that too."

¹²Even the tax collectors* came to John. They wanted to be baptized. They said to him, "Teacher, what should we do?"

¹³He told them, "Don't take more taxes from people than you have been ordered to collect."

¹⁴The soldiers asked him, "What about us? What should we do?"

He said to them, "Don't use force or lies to make people give you money. Be happy with the pay you get."

¹⁵Everyone was hoping for the Christ* to come, and they wondered about John. They thought, "Maybe he is the Christ."

¹⁶John's answer to this was, "I baptize you in water, but there is someone coming later who is able to do more than I can. I am not good enough to be the slave who unties his sandals. He will baptize you with the Holy Spirit* and with fire. ¹⁷He will come ready to clean the grain.ᵇ He will separate the good grain from the straw, and he will put the good part into his barn. Then he will burn the useless part with a fire that cannot be stopped."

¹⁸John said many other things like this to encourage the people to change, and he told them the Good News.*

How John's Work Later Ended

¹⁹John criticized Herod* the ruler for what he had done with Herodias, the wife of Herod's brother, as well as for all the other bad things he had done. ²⁰So Herod added another bad thing to all his other wrongs: He put John in jail.

ᵃ3:9 *trees* Meaning the people who don't obey God. They are like "trees" that will be cut down. ᵇ3:17 *clean the grain* Meaning that Jesus will separate the good people from those who are bad.

Jesus Is Baptized by John
(Mt. 3:13–17; Mk. 1:9–11)

²¹When all the people were being baptized,* Jesus came and was baptized too. And while he was praying, the sky opened, ²²and the Holy Spirit* came down on him. The Spirit looked like a real dove. Then a voice came from heaven and said, "You are my Son, the one I love. I am very pleased with you."

The Family History of Joseph
(Mt. 1:1–17)

²³When Jesus began to teach, he was about 30 years old. People thought that Jesus was Joseph's son.

Joseph was the son of Eli.
24 Eli was the son of Matthat.
Matthat was the son of Levi.
Levi was the son of Melchi.
Melchi was the son of Jannai.
Jannai was the son of Joseph.
25 Joseph was the son of Mattathias.
Mattathias was the son of Amos.
Amos was the son of Nahum.
Nahum was the son of Esli.
Esli was the son of Naggai.
26 Naggai was the son of Maath.
Maath was the son of Mattathias.
Mattathias was the son of Semein.
Semein was the son of Josech.
Josech was the son of Joda.
27 Joda was the son of Joanan.
Joanan was the son of Rhesa.
Rhesa was the son of Zerubbabel.
Zerubbabel was the son of Shealtiel.
Shealtiel was the son of Neri.
28 Neri was the son of Melchi.
Melchi was the son of Addi.
Addi was the son of Cosam.
Cosam was the son of Elmadam.
Elmadam was the son of Er.
29 Er was the son of Joshua.
Joshua was the son of Eliezer.
Eliezer was the son of Jorim.
Jorim was the son of Matthat.
Matthat was the son of Levi.
30 Levi was the son of Simeon.
Simeon was the son of Judah.
Judah was the son of Joseph.
Joseph was the son of Jonam.
Jonam was the son of Eliakim.

³¹ Eliakim was the son of Melea.
Melea was the son of Menna.
Menna was the son of Mattatha.
Mattatha was the son of Nathan.
Nathan was the son of David.
³² David was the son of Jesse.
Jesse was the son of Obed.
Obed was the son of Boaz.
Boaz was the son of Salmon.
Salmon was the son of Nahshon.
³³ Nahshon was the son of Amminadab.
Amminadab was the son of Admin.
Admin was the son of Arni.
Arni was the son of Hezron.
Hezron was the son of Perez.
Perez was the son of Judah.
³⁴ Judah was the son of Jacob.
Jacob was the son of Isaac.
Isaac was the son of Abraham.
Abraham was the son of Terah.
Terah was the son of Nahor.
³⁵ Nahor was the son of Serug.
Serug was the son of Reu.
Reu was the son of Peleg.
Peleg was the son of Eber.
Eber was the son of Shelah.
³⁶ Shelah was the son of Cainan.
Cainan was the son of Arphaxad.
Arphaxad was the son of Shem.
Shem was the son of Noah.
Noah was the son of Lamech.
³⁷ Lamech was the son of Methuselah.
Methuselah was the son of Enoch.
Enoch was the son of Jared.
Jared was the son of Mahalaleel.
Mahalaleel was the son of Cainan.
³⁸ Cainan was the son of Enos.
Enos was the son of Seth.
Seth was the son of Adam.
Adam was the son of God.

Jesus Is Tempted by the Devil
(Mt. 4:1–11; Mk. 1:12–13)

4 ¹Jesus returned from the Jordan River. He was full of the
Holy Spirit.* And the Spirit led him into the desert. ²There
the devil tempted Jesus for 40 days. Jesus ate nothing during
this time, and when it was finished, he was very hungry.

³The devil said to him, "If you are the Son of God, tell this
rock to become bread."

⁴Jesus answered, "The Scriptures* say,

'It is not just food that keeps people alive.'" *Deuteronomy 8:3*

⁵Then the devil took Jesus and in a moment of time showed him all the kingdoms of the world. ⁶The devil said to him, "I will make you king over all these places. You will have power over them, and you will get all the glory.* It has all been given to me. I can give it to anyone I want. ⁷I will give it all to you, if you will only worship me."

⁸Jesus answered, "The Scriptures say,

'You must worship the Lord your God.
    Serve only him.'"
                                                   Deuteronomy 6:13

⁹Then the devil led Jesus to Jerusalem and put him on a high place at the edge of the Temple* area. He said to him, "If you are the Son of God, jump off! ¹⁰The Scriptures say,

'God will command his angels to take care of you.'
                                                   Psalm 91:11

¹¹It is also written,

'Their hands will catch you
    so that you will not hit your foot on a rock.'" *Psalm 91:12*

¹²Jesus answered, "But the Scriptures also say,

'You must not test the Lord your God.'" *Deuteronomy 6:16*

¹³The devil finished tempting Jesus in every way and went away to wait until a better time.

Jesus Begins His Work in Galilee
(Mt. 4:12–17; Mk. 1:14–15)

¹⁴Jesus went back to Galilee with the power of the Spirit.* Stories about him spread all over the area around Galilee. ¹⁵He began to teach in the synagogues,* and everyone praised him.

Jesus Goes to His Hometown
(Mt. 13:53–58; Mk. 6:1–6)

¹⁶Jesus traveled to Nazareth, the town where he grew up. On the Sabbath* day he went to the synagogue* as he always did. He stood up to read. ¹⁷The book of Isaiah the prophet* was given to him. He opened the book and found the place where this is written:

¹⁸"The Spirit of the Lord is on me.
    He has chosen me to tell good news to the poor.
    He sent me to tell prisoners that they are free
        and to tell the blind that they can see again.
    He sent me to free those who have been treated badly
¹⁹   and to announce that the time has come for the Lord
        to show his kindness." *Isaiah 61:1–2*

²⁰Jesus closed the book, gave it back to the helper, and sat down. As everyone in the synagogue watched him closely, ²¹he began to speak to them. He said, "While you heard me reading these words just now, they were coming true!"

²²Everyone there said good things about Jesus. They were amazed to hear him speak such wonderful words. They said, "How is this possible? Isn't he Joseph's son?"

²³Jesus said to them, "I know you will tell me the old saying: 'Doctor, heal yourself.' You want to say, 'We heard about the things you did in Capernaum.* Do those same things here in your own hometown!'" ²⁴Then he said, "The truth is, a prophet is not accepted in his own hometown.

²⁵⁻²⁶"During the time of Elijah* it did not rain in Israel for three and a half years. There was no food anywhere in the whole country. There were many widows in Israel during that time. But the fact is, Elijah was sent to none of those widows in Israel. He was sent only to a widow in Zarephath, a town in Sidon.

²⁷"And there were many people with leprosy* living in Israel during the time of the prophet Elisha.* But none of them were healed; the only one was Naaman. And he was from the country of Syria, not Israel."

²⁸When the people in the synagogue heard this, they were very angry. ²⁹They got up and forced Jesus to go out of town. Their town was built on a hill. They took Jesus to the edge of the hill to throw him off. ³⁰But he walked through the middle of the crowd and went away.

Jesus Frees a Man From an Evil Spirit
(Mk. 1:21–28)

³¹Jesus went to Capernaum, a city in Galilee. On the Sabbath* day he taught the people. ³²They were amazed at his teaching because he spoke with authority.

³³In the synagogue* there was a man who had an evil spirit from the devil inside him. The man shouted with a loud voice, ³⁴"Jesus of Nazareth! What do you want with us? Did you come here to destroy us? I know who you are—God's Holy One!" ³⁵But Jesus warned the evil spirit to stop. He said, "Be quiet! Come out of the man!" The evil spirit threw the man down on the ground in front of everyone. Then the evil spirit left the man and did not hurt him.

³⁶The people were amazed. They said to each other, "What does this mean? With authority and power he commands evil spirits and they come out." ³⁷And so the news about Jesus spread to every place in the whole area.

Jesus Heals Peter's Mother-in-Law
(Mt. 8:14–17; Mk. 1:29–34)

³⁸Jesus left the synagogue* and went to Simon'sᵃ house. Simon's mother-in-law was very sick. She had a high fever.

ᵃ 4:38 Simon Simon's other name was Peter. Also in 5:3, 4, 5, 10.

They asked Jesus to do something to help her. ³⁹He stood very close to her and ordered the sickness to go away. The sickness left her, and she got up and began serving them.

Jesus Heals Many Others

⁴⁰When the sun went down, the people brought their sick friends to Jesus. They had many different kinds of sicknesses. Jesus laid his hands on each sick person and healed them all. ⁴¹Demons* came out of many people. The demons shouted, "You are the Son of God." But Jesus gave a strong command for the demons not to speak, because they knew he was the Christ.*

Jesus Goes to Other Towns
(Mk. 1:35–39)

⁴²The next day Jesus went to a place to be alone. The people looked for him. When they found him, they tried to stop him from leaving. ⁴³But he said to them, "I must tell the Good News* about God's kingdom* to other towns too. This is why I was sent."

⁴⁴Then Jesus told the Good News in the synagogues* in Judea.

Jesus Chooses Some Followers
(Mt. 4:18–22; Mk. 1:16–20)

5 ¹As Jesus stood beside Lake Galilee,ᵃ a crowd of people pushed to get closer to him and to hear the teachings of God. ²Jesus saw two boats at the shore of the lake. The fishermen were washing their nets. ³Jesus got into the boat that belonged to Simon. He asked Simon to push off a little from the shore. Then he sat down in the boat and taught the people on the shore.

⁴When Jesus finished speaking, he said to Simon, "Take the boat into the deep water. If all of you will put your nets into the water, you will catch some fish."

⁵Simon answered, "Master, we worked hard all night trying to catch fish and caught nothing. But you say I should put the nets into the water, so I will." ⁶The fishermen put their nets into the water. Their nets were filled with so many fish that they began to break. ⁷They called to their friends in the other boat to come and help them. The friends came, and both boats were filled so full of fish that they were almost sinking.

⁸⁻⁹The fishermen were all amazed at the many fish they caught. When Simon Peter saw this, he bowed down before Jesus and said, "Go away from me, Lord. I am a sinful man!" ¹⁰James and John, the sons of Zebedee, were amazed too. (James and John worked together with Simon.)

Jesus said to Simon, "Don't be afraid. From now on your work will be to bring in people, not fish!"

ᵃ **5:1** *Galilee* Literally, "Gennesaret."

¹¹The men brought their boats to the shore. They left everything and followed Jesus.

Jesus Heals a Sick Man
(Mt. 8:1–4; Mk. 1:40–45)

¹²One time Jesus was in a town where a very sick man lived. This man was covered with leprosy.* When the man saw Jesus, he bowed before Jesus and begged him, "Lord, you have the power to heal me if you want."

¹³Jesus said, "I want to heal you. Be healed!" Then he touched the man, and immediately the leprosy disappeared. ¹⁴Then Jesus said, "Don't tell anyone about what happened. But go show yourself to the priest.*ᵃ And offer a gift to God for your healing as Moses* commanded. This will show people that you are healed."

¹⁵But the news about Jesus spread more and more. Many people came to hear him and to be healed of their sicknesses. ¹⁶Jesus often went away to other places to be alone so that he could pray.

Jesus Heals a Crippled Man
(Mt. 9:1–8; Mk. 2:1–12)

¹⁷One day Jesus was teaching the people. The Pharisees* and teachers of the law were sitting there too. They had come from every town in Galilee and Judea and from Jerusalem. The Lord was giving Jesus the power to heal people. ¹⁸There was a man who was paralyzed, and some other men were carrying him on a mat. They tried to bring him and put him down before Jesus. ¹⁹But there were so many people that they could not find a way to Jesus. So they went up on the roof and lowered the crippled man down through a hole in the ceiling. They lowered the mat into the room so that the crippled man was lying before Jesus. ²⁰Jesus saw how much faith they had and said to the sick man, "Friend, your sins are forgiven."

²¹The Jewish teachers of the law and the Pharisees thought to themselves, "Who is this man who dares to say such things? What an insult to God! No one but God can forgive sins."

²²But Jesus knew what they were thinking and said, "Why do you have these questions in your minds? ²³⁻²⁴The Son of Man* has power on earth to forgive sins. But how can I prove this to you? Maybe you are thinking it was easy for me to say, 'Your sins are forgiven.' There's no proof that it really happened. But what if I say to the man, 'Stand up and walk'? Then you will be able to see that I really have this power." So Jesus said to the paralyzed man, "I tell you, stand up! Take your mat and go home!"

²⁵The man immediately stood up in front of everyone. He picked up his mat and walked home, praising God. ²⁶Everyone

---

ᵃ**5:14** *show yourself to the priest* The law of Moses said a priest must decide when a person with leprosy was well.

was completely amazed and began to praise God. They were filled with great respect for God's power. They said, "Today we saw amazing things!"

Levi (Matthew) Follows Jesus
(Mt. 9:9-13; Mk. 2:13-17)

27After this Jesus went out and saw a tax collector* sitting at his place for collecting taxes. His name was Levi. Jesus said to him, "Follow me!" 28Levi got up, left everything, and followed Jesus.

29Then Levi gave a big dinner at his house for Jesus. At the table there were many tax collectors and some other people too. 30But the Pharisees* and those who taught the law for the Pharisees began to complain to the followers of Jesus, "Why do you eat and drink with tax collectors and other sinners?"

31Jesus answered them, "It is the sick people who need a doctor, not those who are healthy. 32I have not come to ask good people to change. I have come to ask sinners to change the way they live."

Jesus Is Not Like Other Religious Leaders
(Mt. 9:14-17; Mk. 2:18-22)

33They said to Jesus, "John's followers often fast* and pray, the same as the followers of the Pharisees.* But your followers eat and drink all the time."

34Jesus said to them, "At a wedding you can't ask the friends of the bridegroom* to be sad and fast while he is still with them. 35But the time will come when the groom will be taken away from them. Then his friends will fast."

36Jesus told them this story: "No one takes cloth off a new coat to cover a hole in an old coat. That would ruin the new coat, and the cloth from the new coat would not be the same as the old cloth. 37Also, no one ever pours new wine into old wineskins.* The new wine would break them. The wine would spill out, and the wineskins would be ruined. 38You always put new wine into new wineskins. 39No one who drinks old wine wants new wine. They say, 'The old wine is just fine.'"

Jesus Is Lord Over the Sabbath Day
(Mt. 12:1-8; Mk. 2:23-28)

6 1One time on a Sabbath* day, Jesus was walking through some grain fields. His followers picked the grain, rubbed it in their hands, and ate it. 2Some Pharisees* said, "Why are you doing that? It is against the law of Moses* to do that on the Sabbath day."

3Jesus answered, "You have read about what David* did when he and the people with him were hungry. 4David went into God's house. He took the bread that was offered to God and ate it. And he gave some of the bread to the people with him. This was against the law of Moses, which says that only the priests can eat that bread." ⁵Then Jesus said to the Pharisees, "The Son of Man* is Lord over the Sabbath day."

Jesus Heals a Man on the Sabbath Day
(Mt. 12:9-14; Mk. 3:1-6)

⁶On another Sabbath* day Jesus went into the synagogue* and taught the people. A man with a crippled right hand was there. ⁷The teachers of the law and the Pharisees* were watching Jesus closely. They were waiting to see if he would heal on the Sabbath day. They wanted to see him do something wrong so that they could accuse him. ⁸But Jesus knew what they were thinking. He said to the man with the crippled hand, "Get up and stand here where everyone can see." The man got up and stood there. ⁹Then Jesus said to them, "I ask you, which is the right thing to do on the Sabbath day: to do good or to do evil? Is it right to save a life or to destroy one?"

¹⁰Jesus looked around at all of them, then said to the man, "Hold out your hand." The man held out his hand, and it was healed. ¹¹The Pharisees and the teachers of the law got so mad they couldn't think straight. They talked to each other about what they could do to Jesus.

Jesus Chooses His Twelve Apostles
(Mt. 10:1-4; Mk. 3:13-19)

¹²A few days later, Jesus went out to a mountain to pray. He stayed there all night praying to God. ¹³The next morning he called his followers. He chose twelve of them and called them apostles.* These are the ones he chose:

¹⁴ Simon (Jesus named him Peter),
   Andrew, brother of Peter,
   James,
   John,
   Philip,
   Bartholomew,
¹⁵ Matthew,
   Thomas,
   James, the son of Alphaeus,
   Simon, called the Zealot,*
¹⁶ Judas, the son of James,
   Judas Iscariot (the one who turned against Jesus).

Jesus Teaches and Heals the People
(Mt. 4:23-25; 5:1-12)

¹⁷Jesus and the apostles* came down from the mountain. Jesus stood on a flat place. A large crowd of his followers was there. Also, there were many people from all around Judea, Jerusalem, and the seacoast cities of Tyre* and Sidon.* ¹⁸They

all came to hear Jesus teach and to be healed of their sicknesses. He healed the people who were troubled by evil spirits. [19]Everyone was trying to touch him, because power was coming out from him. Jesus healed them all.

[20]Jesus looked at his followers and said,

"What great blessings there are for you who are poor.
God's kingdom* belongs to you.
[21] What great blessings there are for you who are hungry now.
You will be filled.
What great blessings there are for you who are crying now.
You will be happy and laughing.

[22]"People will hate you because you belong to the Son of Man.* They will make you leave their group. They will insult you. They will think it is wrong even to say your name. When these things happen, know that God will bless you. [23]You can be happy then and jump for joy, because you have a great reward in heaven. The ancestors* of those people did the same things to the prophets.*

[24]"But how bad it will be for you rich people,
because you had your easy life.
[25] How bad it will be for you people who are full now,
because you will be hungry.
How bad it will be for you people who are laughing now,
because you will be sad and cry.

[26]"How bad it is when everyone says nothing but good about you. Just look at the false prophets.* Their ancestors always said good things about them.

Love Your Enemies
(Mt. 5:38–48; 7:12a)

[27]"I say to you people who are listening to me, love your enemies. Do good to those who hate you. [28]Ask God to bless the people who ask for bad things to happen to you. Pray for the people who are mean to you. [29]If someone hits you on the side of your face, let them hit the other side too. If someone takes your coat, don't stop them from taking your shirt too. [30]Give to everyone who asks you for something. When someone takes something that is yours, don't ask for it back. [31]Do for others what you want them to do for you.

[32]"If you love only those who love you, should you get any special praise for doing that? No, even sinners love those who love them! [33]If you do good only to those who do good to you, should you get any special praise for doing that? No, even sinners do that! [34]If you lend things to people, always expecting to get something back, should you get any special praise for that? No, even sinners lend to other sinners so that they can get back the same amount!

[35]"I'm telling you to love your enemies and do good to them. Lend to people without expecting to get anything back. If you do this, you will have a great reward. You will be children of the Most High God. That's because God is good even to the people who are full of sin and not thankful. [36]Give love and mercy the same as your Father gives love and mercy.

Be Careful About Criticizing Others
(Mt. 7:1–5)

[37]"Don't judge others, and you will not be judged. Don't condemn others, and you will not be condemned. Forgive others, and you will be forgiven. [38]Give to others, and you will receive. You will be given much. It will be poured into your hands—more than you can hold. You will be given so much that it will spill into your lap. The way you give to others is the way God will give to you."

[39]Jesus told them this story: "Can a blind man lead another blind man? No. Both of them will fall into a ditch. [40]Students are not better than their teacher. But when they have been fully taught, they will be like their teacher.

[41]"Why do you notice the small piece of dust that is in your friend's eye, but you don't see the big piece of wood that is in your own eye? [42]You say to your friend, 'Let me get that little piece of dust out of your eye.' Why do you say this? Can't you see that big piece of wood in your own eye? You are a hypocrite.* First, take the wood out of your own eye. Then you will see clearly to get the dust out of your friend's eye.

Only Good Trees Produce Good Fruit
(Mt. 7:17–20; 12:34b–35)

[43]"A good tree does not produce bad fruit. And a bad tree does not produce good fruit. [44]Every tree is known by the kind of fruit it produces. You won't find figs on thorny weeds. And you can't pick grapes from thornbushes! [45]Good people have good things saved in their hearts. That's why they say good things. But those who are evil have hearts full of evil, and that's why they say things that are evil. What people say with their mouths comes from what fills their hearts.

Two Kinds of People
(Mt. 7:24–27)

[46]"Why do you call me, 'Lord, Lord,' but you don't do what I say? [47]The people who come to me, who listen to my teachings and obey them—I will show you what they are like: [48]They are like a man building a house. He digs deep and builds his house on rock. The floods come, and the water crashes against the house. But the flood cannot move the house, because it was built well.

49"But the people who hear my words and do not obey are like a man who builds a house without preparing a foundation. When the floods come, the house falls down easily and is completely destroyed."

Jesus Heals an Officer's Servant
(Mt. 8:5–13; Jn. 4:43–54)

7 ¹Jesus finished saying all these things to the people. Then he went into Capernaum.* ²In Capernaum there was an army officer.* He had a servant who was very sick; he was near death. The officer loved the servant very much. ³When he heard about Jesus, he sent some older Jewish leaders to him. He wanted the men to ask Jesus to come and save the life of his servant. ⁴The men went to Jesus. They begged Jesus to help the officer. They said, "This officer is worthy to have your help. ⁵He loves our people and he built the synagogue* for us."

⁶So Jesus went with them. He was coming near the officer's house when the officer sent friends to say, "Lord, you don't need to do anything special for me. I am not good enough for you to come into my house. ⁷That is why I did not come to you myself. You need only to give the order, and my servant will be healed. ⁸I know this because I am a man under the authority of other men. And I have soldiers under my authority. I tell one soldier, 'Go,' and he goes. And I tell another soldier, 'Come,' and he comes. And I say to my servant, 'Do this,' and my servant obeys me."

⁹When Jesus heard this, he was amazed. He turned to the people following him and said, "I tell you, this is the most faith I have seen anywhere, even in Israel.*"

¹⁰The group that was sent to Jesus went back to the house. There they found that the servant was healed.

Jesus Brings a Woman's Son Back to Life

¹¹The next day Jesus and his followers went to a town called Nain. A big crowd was traveling with them. ¹²When Jesus came near the town gate, he saw some people carrying a dead body. It was the only son of a woman who was a widow. Walking with her were many other people from the town. ¹³When the Lord saw the woman, he felt very sorry for her and said, "Don't cry." ¹⁴He walked to the open coffin and touched it. The men who were carrying the coffin stopped. Jesus spoke to the dead son: "Young man, I tell you, get up!" ¹⁵Then the boy sat up and began to talk, and Jesus gave him back to his mother.

¹⁶Everyone was filled with fear. They began praising God and said, "A great prophet* is here with us!" and "God is taking care of his people."

¹⁷This news about Jesus spread all over Judea and to all the other places around there.

John Sends Men to Ask Jesus a Question
(Mt. 11:2–19)

¹⁸John's followers told him about all these things. John called for two of his followers. ¹⁹He sent them to the Lord to ask, "Are you the one we heard was coming, or should we wait for someone else?"

²⁰So the men came to Jesus. They said, "John the Baptizer* sent us to you with this question: 'Are you the one who is coming, or should we wait for someone else?'"

²¹Right then Jesus healed many people of their sicknesses and diseases. He healed those who had evil spirits and made many who were blind able to see again. ²²Then he said to John's followers, "Go tell John what you have seen and heard: The blind can see. The crippled can walk. People with leprosy* are healed. The deaf can hear. The dead are brought back to life. And the Good News* is being told to the poor. ²³What great blessings there are for those who don't have a problem accepting me."

²⁴When John's followers left, Jesus began talking to the people about John: "What did you people go out into the desert to see? Someone who is weak, like a stem of grass*ᵃ blowing in the wind? ²⁵Really, what did you expect to see? Someone dressed in fine clothes? Of course not. People who wear fancy clothes and live in luxury are all in kings' palaces. ²⁶So what did you go out to see? A prophet*? Yes, John is a prophet. But I tell you, he is more than that. ²⁷This Scripture* was written about him:

'Listen! I will send my messenger ahead of you.
    He will prepare the way for you.'
                                                    Malachi 3:1

²⁸I tell you, no one ever born is greater than John. But even the least important person in God's kingdom* is greater than John."

²⁹(When the people heard this, they all agreed that God's teaching was good. Even the tax collectors* agreed. These were the people who were baptized* by John. ³⁰But the Pharisees* and experts in the law refused to accept God's plan for themselves; they did not let John baptize them.)

³¹"What shall I say about the people of this time? What can I compare them to? What are they like? ³²They are like children sitting in the marketplace. One group of children calls to the other children and says,

'We played flute music for you,
    but you did not dance;
we sang a sad song,
    but you did not cry.'

³³John the Baptizer came and did not eat the usual food or drink wine. And you say, 'He has a demon* inside him.' ³⁴The Son of Man* came eating and drinking. And you say, 'Look at

ᵃ**7:24 stem of grass** Literally, "reed."

him! He eats too much and drinks too much wine! He is a friend of the tax collectors and other bad people!' 35But wisdom is shown to be right by those who accept it."

Simon the Pharisee

36One of the Pharisees* asked Jesus to eat with him. Jesus went into the Pharisee's house and took a place at the table.

37There was a sinful woman in that town. She knew that Jesus was eating at the Pharisee's house. So the woman brought some expensive perfume in an alabaster* jar. 38She stood at Jesus' feet, crying. Then she began to wash his feet with her tears. She dried his feet with her hair. She kissed his feet many times and rubbed them with the perfume.

39When the Pharisee who asked Jesus to come to his house saw this, he thought to himself, "If this man were a prophet,a he would know that the woman who is touching him is a sinner!"

40In response, Jesus said to the Pharisee, "Simon, I have something to say to you."

Simon said, "Let me hear it, Teacher."

41Jesus said, "There were two men. Both men owed money to the same banker. One man owed him 500 silver coins.* The other man owed him 50 silver coins. 42The men had no money, so they could not pay their debt. But the banker told the men that they did not have to pay him. Which one of those two men will love him more?"

43Simon answered, "I think it would be the one who owed him the most money."

Jesus said to him, "You are right." 44Then he turned to the woman and said to Simon, "Do you see this woman? When I came into your house, you gave me no water for my feet. But she washed my feet with her tears and dried my feet with her hair. 45You did not greet me with a kiss, but she has been kissing my feet since I came in. 46You did not honor me with oil for my head, but she rubbed my feet with her sweet-smelling oil. 47I tell you that her many sins are forgiven. This is clear, because she showed great love. People who are forgiven only a little will love only a little."

48Then Jesus said to her, "Your sins are forgiven."

49The people sitting at the table began to think to themselves, "Who does this man think he is? How can he forgive sins?"

50Jesus said to the woman, "Because you believed, you are saved from your sins. Go in peace."

The Group With Jesus

8 1The next day, Jesus traveled through some cities and small towns. Jesus told the people a message from God, the Good News about God's kingdom.* The twelve apostles* were with

---

a7:39 *prophet* A prophet often knows things that are hidden to other people.

him. [2]There were also some women with him. Jesus had healed these women of sicknesses and evil spirits. One of them was Mary, who was called Magdalene. Seven demons had come out of her. [3]Also with these women were Joanna, the wife of Chuza (the manager of Herod's* property), Suzanna, and many other women. These women used their own money to help Jesus and his apostles.

A Story About a Farmer Sowing Seed
(Mt. 13:1–17; Mk. 4:1–12)

[4]A large crowd came together. People came to Jesus from every town, and he told them this story:

[5]"A farmer went out to sow seed. While he was scattering the seed, some of it fell beside the road. People walked on the seed, and the birds ate it all. [6]Other seed fell on rock. It began to grow but then died because it had no water. [7]Some other seed fell among thorny weeds. This seed grew, but later the weeds stopped the plants from growing. [8]The rest of the seed fell on good ground. This seed grew and made 100 times more grain."

Jesus finished the story. Then he called out, "You people who hear me, listen!"

[9]Jesus' followers asked him, "What does this story mean?"

[10]He said, "You have been chosen to know the secret truths about God's kingdom.* But I use stories to speak to other people. I do this so that,

'They will look,
　　but they will not see,
and they will listen,
　　but they will not understand.'

　　　　　　　　　　　　　　　　　Isaiah 6:9

Jesus Explains the Story About Seed
(Mt. 13:18–23; Mk. 4:13–20)

[11]"This is what the story means: The seed is God's teaching. [12]Some people are like the seed that fell beside the path. They hear God's teaching, but then the devil comes and causes them to stop thinking about it. This keeps them from believing it and being saved. [13]Others are like the seed that fell on rock. That is like the people who hear God's teaching and gladly accept it. But they don't have deep roots. They believe for a while. But when trouble comes, they turn away from God.

[14]"What about the seed that fell among the thorny weeds? That is like the people who hear God's teaching, but they let the worries, riches, and pleasures of this life stop them from growing. So they never produce a crop.[a] [15]And what about the seed that fell on the good ground? That is like the people who hear God's teaching with a good, honest heart. They obey it and patiently produce a good crop.

*a*8:14 produce a crop Meaning to do the good things God wants his people to do.

Use the Understanding You Have
(Mk. 4:21–25)

16"No one lights a lamp and then covers it with a bowl or hides it under a bed. Instead, they put the lamp on a lampstand so that the people who come in will have enough light to see. 17Everything that is hidden will become clear. Every secret thing will be made known, and everyone will see it. 18So think carefully about what you are hearing. The people who have some understanding will receive more. But those who do not have understanding will lose even what they think they have."

Jesus' Followers Are His True Family
(Mt. 12:46–50; Mk. 3:31–35)

19Jesus' mother and brothers came to visit him. But they could not get close to him, because there were so many people. 20Someone said to Jesus, "Your mother and your brothers are standing outside. They want to see you."

21Jesus answered them, "My mother and my brothers are those who listen to God's teaching and obey it."

Jesus' Followers See His Power
(Mt. 8:23–27; Mk. 4:35–41)

22One day Jesus and his followers got into a boat. He said to them, "Come with me across the lake." And so they started across. 23While they were sailing, Jesus slept. A big storm blew across the lake, and the boat began to fill with water. They were in danger. 24The followers went to Jesus and woke him. They said, "Master! Master! We will drown!"

Jesus got up. He gave a command to the wind and the waves. The wind stopped, and the lake became calm. 25He said to his followers, "Where is your faith?"

They were afraid and amazed. They said to each other, "What kind of man is this? He commands the wind and the water, and they obey him."

Jesus Frees a Man From Evil Spirits
(Mt. 8:28–34; Mk. 5:1–20)

26Jesus and his followers sailed on across the lake. They sailed to the area where the Gerasene people live, across from Galilee. 27When Jesus got out of the boat, a man from that town came to him. This man had demons* inside him. For a long time he had worn no clothes. He did not live in a house but in the caves where the dead are buried.

28-29The demon inside the man had often seized him, and he had been put in jail with his hands and feet in chains. But he would always break the chains. The demon inside him would force him to go out to the places where no one lived. Jesus commanded the evil spirit to come out of the man. When the man saw Jesus, he fell down before him, shouting with a loud voice, "What do you want with me, Jesus, Son of the Most High God? Please, don't punish me!"

³⁰Jesus asked him, "What is your name?"

The man answered, "Legion."ᵃ (He said his name was "Legion" because many demons had gone into him.) ³¹The demons begged Jesus not to send them into the bottomless pit.ᵇ ³²On that hill there was a big herd of pigs eating. The demons begged Jesus to allow them to go into the pigs. So he allowed them to do this. ³³Then the demons came out of the man and went into the pigs. The herd of pigs ran down the hill into the lake, and all were drowned.

³⁴The men who were caring for the pigs ran away and told the story in the fields and in the town. ³⁵People went out to see what had happened. They came to Jesus and found the man sitting there at the feet of Jesus. The man had clothes on and was in his right mind again; the demons were gone. This made the people afraid. ³⁶The men who saw these things happen told the others all about how Jesus made the man well. ³⁷All those who lived in the area around Gerasa asked Jesus to go away because they were afraid.

So Jesus got into the boat to go back to Galilee. ³⁸The man he had healed begged to go with him. But Jesus sent him away, saying, ³⁹"Go back home and tell people what God did for you."

So the man went all over town telling what Jesus had done for him.

Jesus Gives Life to a Dead Girl and Heals a Sick Woman
(Mt. 9:18–26; Mk. 5:21–43)

⁴⁰When Jesus went back to Galilee, the people welcomed him. Everyone was waiting for him. ⁴¹⁻⁴²A man named Jairus came to him. He was a leader of the synagogue.* He had only one daughter. She was twelve years old, and she was dying. So Jairus bowed down at the feet of Jesus and begged him to come to his house.

While Jesus was going to Jairus' house, the people crowded all around him. ⁴³A woman was there who had been bleeding for twelve years. She had spent all her money on doctors,ᶜ but no doctor was able to heal her. ⁴⁴The woman came behind Jesus and touched the bottom of his coat. At that moment, her bleeding stopped. ⁴⁵Then Jesus said, "Who touched me?"

They all said they had not touched him. And Peter said, "Master, people are all around you, pushing against you."

⁴⁶But Jesus said, "Someone touched me. I felt power go out from me." ⁴⁷When the woman saw that she could not hide, she came forward, shaking. She bowed down before Jesus. While

---

ᵃ**8:30** *"Legion"* This name means very many. A legion was about 6000 men in the Roman army. ᵇ**8:31** *bottomless pit* Literally, "the abyss," something like a deep hole where evil spirits are kept. ᶜ**8:43** *She had spent ... doctors* Some Greek copies do not have these words.

everyone listened, she told why she touched him. Then she said that she was healed immediately when she touched him. 48Jesus said to her, "My daughter, you are made well because you believed. Go in peace."

49While Jesus was still speaking, someone came from the house of the synagogue leader and said, "Your daughter has died! Don't bother the Teacher anymore."

50Jesus heard this and said to Jairus, "Don't be afraid! Just believe and your daughter will be well."

51Jesus went to the house. He let only Peter, John, James, and the girl's father and mother go inside with him. 52Everyone was crying and feeling sad because the girl was dead. But Jesus said, "Don't cry. She is not dead. She is only sleeping."

53The people laughed at him, because they knew that the girl was dead. 54But Jesus held her hand and called to her, "Little girl, stand up!" 55Her spirit came back into her, and she stood up immediately. Jesus said, "Give her something to eat." 56The girl's parents were amazed. He told them not to tell anyone about what happened.

Jesus Sends His Apostles on a Mission
(Mt. 10:5–15; Mk. 6:7–13)

9 1Jesus called his twelve apostles* together. He gave them power to heal sicknesses and power to force demons* out of people. 2He sent them to tell about God's kingdom* and to heal the sick. 3He said to them, "When you travel, don't take a walking stick. Also, don't carry a bag, food, or money. Take for your trip only the clothes you are wearing. 4When you go into a house, stay there until it is time to leave. 5If the people in the town will not welcome you, go outside the town and shake the dust off your feet*a* as a warning to them."

6So the apostles went out. They traveled through all the towns. They told the Good News* and healed people everywhere.

Herod Is Confused About Jesus
(Mt. 14:1–12; Mk. 6:14–29)

7Herod* the ruler heard about all these things that were happening. He was confused because some people said, "John the Baptizer has risen from death." 8Others said, "Elijah* has come to us." And some others said, "One of the prophets* from long ago has risen from death." 9Herod said, "I cut off John's head. So who is this man I hear these things about?" Herod continued trying to see Jesus.

---

a9:5 shake the dust off your feet A warning. It would show that they were finished talking to these people.

Jesus Feeds More Than 5000
(Mt. 14:13–21; Mk. 6:30–44; Jn. 6:1–14)

¹⁰When the apostles* came back, they told Jesus what they had done on their trip. Then he took them away to a town called Bethsaida. There, he and his apostles could be alone together. ¹¹But the people learned where Jesus went and followed him. He welcomed them and talked with them about God's kingdom.* He healed the people who were sick.

¹²Late in the afternoon, the twelve apostles came to Jesus and said, "No one lives in this place. Send the people away. They need to find food and places to sleep in the farms and towns around here."

¹³But Jesus said to the apostles, "You give them something to eat."

They said, "We have only five loaves of bread and two fish. Do you want us to go buy food for all these people? There are too many! ¹⁴(There were about 5000 men there.)

Jesus said to his followers, "Tell the people to sit in groups of about 50 people."

¹⁵So the followers did this and everyone sat down. ¹⁶Then Jesus took the five loaves of bread and two fish. He looked up into the sky and thanked God for the food. Then he broke it into pieces, which he gave to the followers to give to the people. ¹⁷They all ate until they were full. And there was a lot of food left. Twelve baskets were filled with the pieces of food that were not eaten.

Peter Says Jesus Is the Christ
(Mt. 16:13–19; Mk. 8:27–29)

¹⁸One time Jesus was praying alone. His followers came together there, and he asked them, "Who do the people say I am?"

¹⁹They answered, "Some people say you are John the Baptizer. Others say you are Elijah.* And some people say you are one of the prophets* from long ago that has come back to life."

²⁰Then Jesus said to his followers, "And who do you say I am?"

Peter answered, "You are the Christ* from God."

²¹Jesus warned them not to tell anyone.

Jesus Says He Must Die
(Mt. 16:21–28; Mk. 8:30–9:1)

²²Then Jesus said, "The Son of Man* must suffer many things. He will be rejected by the older Jewish leaders, the leading priests, and teachers of the law. And he will be killed. But after three days he will be raised from death."

²³Jesus continued to say to all of them, "Whoever wants to be my follower must say no to themselves and what they want to do. They must accept the cross* that is given to them every

day and follow me. ²⁴Those who try to keep the life they have will lose it. But those who give up their life for me will save it. ²⁵It is worth nothing for you to have the whole world if you yourself are destroyed or lost. ²⁶Don't be ashamed of me and my teaching. If that happens, I*ᵃ* will be ashamed of you when I come with my divine greatness* and that of the Father and the holy angels. ²⁷Believe me when I say that some of you people standing here will see God's kingdom* before you die."

Jesus Is Seen With Moses and Elijah
(Mt. 17:1–8; Mk. 9:2–8)

²⁸About eight days after Jesus said these things, he took Peter, John, and James and went up on a mountain to pray. ²⁹While Jesus was praying, his face began to change. His clothes became shining white. ³⁰Then two men were there, talking with him. They were Moses* and Elijah.* ³¹They also looked bright and glorious. They were talking with Jesus about his death that would happen in Jerusalem. ³²Peter and the others were asleep. But they woke up and saw the glory* of Jesus. They also saw the two men who were standing with him. ³³When Moses and Elijah were leaving, Peter said, "Master, it is good that we are here. We will put three tents here—one for you, one for Moses, and one for Elijah." (He did not know what he was saying.)

³⁴While Peter was saying these things, a cloud came all around them. Peter, John, and James were afraid when the cloud covered them. ³⁵A voice came from the cloud and said, "This is my Son. He is the one I have chosen. Obey him."

³⁶When the voice stopped, only Jesus was there. Peter, John, and James said nothing. And for a long time after that they told no one about what they had seen.

Jesus Frees a Boy From an Evil Spirit
(Mt. 17:14–18; Mk. 9:14–27)

³⁷The next day, Jesus, Peter, John, and James came down from the mountain. A large group of people met Jesus. ³⁸A man in the group shouted to him, "Teacher, please come and look at my son. He is the only child I have. ³⁹An evil spirit comes into him, and then he shouts. He loses control of himself and foams at the mouth. The evil spirit continues to hurt him and almost never leaves him. ⁴⁰I begged your followers to make the evil spirit leave my son, but they could not do it."

⁴¹Jesus answered, "You people today have no faith. Your lives are all wrong. How long must I be with you and be patient with you?" Then Jesus said to the man, "Bring your son here."

⁴²While the boy was coming, the demon* threw the boy to the ground. The boy lost control of himself. But Jesus gave a

*ᵃ*9:26 / Literally, "the Son of Man" (Jesus).

strong command to the evil spirit. Then the boy was healed, and Jesus gave him back to his father. [43]All the people were amazed at the great power of God.

Jesus Talks About His Death
(Mt. 17:22–23; Mk. 9:30–32)

The people were still amazed about all the things Jesus did. He said to his followers, [44]"Don't forget what I will tell you now: The Son of Man* will soon be handed over to the control of other men." [45]But the followers did not understand what he meant. The meaning was hidden from them so that they could not understand it. But they were afraid to ask Jesus about what he said.

Who Is the Greatest?
(Mt. 18:1–5; Mk. 9:33–37)

[46]Jesus' followers began to have an argument about which one of them was the greatest. [47]Jesus knew what they were thinking, so he took a little child and stood the child beside him. [48]Then he said to the followers, "Whoever accepts a little child like this in my name is accepting me. And anyone who accepts me is also accepting the one who sent me. The one among you who is the most humble—this is the one who is great."

Whoever Is Not Against You Is for You
(Mk. 9:38–40)

[49]John answered, "Master, we saw someone using your name to force demons* out of people. We told him to stop because he does not belong to our group."

[50]Jesus said to him, "Don't stop him. Whoever is not against you is for you."

A Samaritan Town

[51]The time was coming near when Jesus would leave and go back to heaven. He decided to go to Jerusalem. [52]He sent some men ahead of him. They went into a town in Samaria to make everything ready for him. [53]But the people there would not welcome Jesus because he was going toward Jerusalem. [54]James and John, the followers of Jesus, saw this. They said, "Lord, do you want us to call fire down from heaven and destroy those people?"[a]

[55]But Jesus turned and criticized them for saying this.[b] [56]Then he and his followers went to another town.

---

[a]9:54 Some Greek copies add "like Elijah did?" [b]9:55 Some Greek copies add "And he said, 'You don't know what kind of spirit you belong to. [56]The Son of Man did not come to destroy people's lives but to save them.'"

Following Jesus
(Mt. 8:19–22)

57They were all traveling along the road. Someone said to Jesus, "I will follow you anywhere you go."

58He answered, "The foxes have holes to live in. The birds have nests. But the Son of Man* has no place where he can rest his head."

59Jesus said to another man, "Follow me!"

But the man said, "Lord, let me go and bury my father first."

60But Jesus said to him, "Let the people who are dead bury their own dead. You must go and tell about God's kingdom.*"

61Another man said, "I will follow you, Lord, but first let me go and say goodbye to my family."

62Jesus said, "Anyone who begins to plow a field but looks back is not prepared for God's kingdom."

Jesus Sends the 72 Men

10 1After this, the Lord chose 72*a* more followers. He sent them out in groups of two. He sent them ahead of him into every town and place where he planned to go. 2He said to them, "There is such a big harvest of people to bring in. But there are only a few workers to help harvest them. God owns the harvest. Ask him to send more workers to help bring in his harvest.

3"You can go now. But listen! I am sending you, and you will be like sheep among wolves. 4Don't carry any money, a bag, or sandals. Don't stop to talk with people on the road. 5Before you go into a house, say, 'Peace be with this home.' 6If the people living there love peace, your blessing of peace will stay with them. But if not, your blessing of peace will come back to you. 7Stay in the peace-loving house. Eat and drink what the people there give you. A worker should be given his pay. Don't leave that house to stay in another house.

8"If you go into a town and the people welcome you, eat the food they give you. 9Heal the sick people who live there, and tell them, 'God's kingdom* is coming to you soon!'

10"But if you go into a town, and the people don't welcome you, then go out into the streets of that town and say, 11'Even the dirt from your town that sticks to our feet we wipe off against you. But remember that God's kingdom is coming soon.' 12I tell you, on the judgment day it will be worse for the people of that town than for the people of Sodom.*

Jesus Warns People Who Refuse to Believe
(Mt. 11:20–24)

13"It will be bad for you, Chorazin*! It will be bad for you, Bethsaida*! I did many miracles* in you. If those same miracles

*a***10:1** 72 Some Greek copies say 70. Also in verse 17.

had happened in Tyre* and Sidon,* then the people in those cities would have changed their lives and stopped sinning a long time ago. They would have worn sackcloth* and sat in ashes to show that they were sorry for their sins. ¹⁴But on the judgment day it will be worse for you than for Tyre and Sidon. ¹⁵And you, Capernaum,* will you be lifted up to heaven? No, you will be thrown down to the place of death!

¹⁶"When anyone listens to you my followers, they are really listening to me. But when anyone refuses to accept you, they are really refusing to accept me. And when anyone refuses to accept me, they are refusing to accept the one who sent me."

Satan Falls

¹⁷When the 72 followers came back from their trip, they were very happy. They said, "Lord, even the demons* obeyed us when we used your name!"

¹⁸Jesus said to them, "I saw Satan* falling like lightning from the sky. ¹⁹He is the enemy, but know that I have given you more power than he has. I have given you power to crush his snakes and scorpions under your feet. Nothing will hurt you. ²⁰Yes, even the spirits obey you. And you can be happy, not because you have this power, but because your names are written in heaven."

Jesus Prays to the Father
(Mt. 11:25–27; 13:16–17)

²¹Then the Holy Spirit* made Jesus feel very happy. Jesus said, "I praise you, Father, Lord of heaven and earth. I am thankful that you have hidden these things from those who are so wise and so smart. But you have shown them to people who are like little children. Yes, Father, you did this because it's what you really wanted to do.

²²"My Father has given me all things. No one knows who the Son is—only the Father knows. And only the Son knows who the Father is. The only people who will know about the Father are those the Son chooses to tell."

²³Then Jesus turned to his followers. They were there alone with him. He said, "What a blessing it is for you to see what you now see! ²⁴I tell you, many prophets* and kings wanted to see what you now see, but they could not. And they wanted to hear what you now hear, but they could not."

A Story About the Good Samaritan

²⁵Then an expert in the law stood up to test Jesus. He said, "Teacher, what must I do to get eternal life?"

²⁶Jesus said to him, "What is written in the law? What do you understand from it?"

²⁷The man answered, "'Love the Lord your God with all your heart, all your soul, all your strength, and all your mind.'ᵃ Also, 'Love your neighbor the same as you love yourself.'ᵇ"

²⁸Jesus said, "Your answer is right. Do this and you will have eternal life."

²⁹But the man wanted to show that the way he was living was right. So he said to Jesus, "But who is my neighbor?"

³⁰To answer this question, Jesus said, "A man was going down the road from Jerusalem to Jericho. Some robbers surrounded him, tore off his clothes, and beat him. Then they left him lying there on the ground almost dead.

³¹"It happened that a Jewish priest was going down that road. When he saw the man, he did not stop to help him. He walked away. ³²Next, a Levite* came near. He saw the hurt man, but he went around him. He would not stop to help him either. He just walked away.

³³"Then a Samaritan* man traveled down that road. He came to the place where the hurt man was lying. He saw the man and felt very sorry for him. ³⁴The Samaritan went to him and poured olive oil and wineᶜ on his wounds. Then he covered the man's wounds with cloth. The Samaritan had a donkey. He put the hurt man on his donkey, and he took him to an inn. There he cared for him. ³⁵The next day, the Samaritan took out two silver coins* and gave them to the man who worked at the inn. He said, 'Take care of this hurt man. If you spend more money on him, I will pay it back to you when I come again.'"

³⁶Then Jesus said, "Which one of these three men do you think was really a neighbor to the man who was hurt by the robbers?"

³⁷The teacher of the law answered, "The one who helped him."

Jesus said, "Then you go and do the same."

Mary and Martha

³⁸While Jesus and his followers were traveling, he went into a town, and a woman named Martha let him stay at her house. ³⁹She had a sister named Mary. Mary was sitting at Jesus' feet and listening to him teach. ⁴⁰But her sister Martha was busy doing all the work that had to be done. Martha went in and said, "Lord, don't you care that my sister has left me to do all the work by myself? Tell her to help me!"

⁴¹But the Lord answered her, "Martha, Martha, you are getting worried and upset about too many things. ⁴²Only one thing is important. Mary has made the right choice, and it will never be taken away from her."

ᵃ**10:27** Quote from Deut. 6:5.   ᵇ**10:27** Quote from Lev. 19:18.   ᶜ**10:34** *olive oil and wine* These were used like medicine to soften and clean wounds.

Jesus Teaches About Prayer
(Mt. 6:9–15)

11 ¹One time Jesus was out praying, and when he finished, one of his followers said to him, "John* taught his followers how to pray. Lord, teach us how to pray too."

²Jesus said to the followers, "This is how you should pray:

'Father, we pray that your name will always be kept holy.
   We pray that your kingdom* will come.
³ Give us the food we need for each day.
⁴ Forgive our sins,
   just as we forgive everyone who has done wrong to us.
And don't let us be tempted.'"

Ask God for What You Need
(Mt. 7:7–11)

⁵⁻⁶Then Jesus said to them, "Suppose one of you went to your friend's house very late at night and said to him, 'A friend of mine has come into town to visit me. But I have nothing for him to eat. Please give me three loaves of bread.' ⁷Your friend inside the house answers, 'Go away! Don't bother me! The door is already locked. My children and I are in bed. I cannot get up and give you the bread now.' ⁸I tell you, maybe friendship is not enough to make him get up to give you the bread. But he will surely get up to give you what you need if you continue to ask. ⁹So I tell you, continue to ask, and God will give to you. Continue to search, and you will find. Continue to knock, and the door will open for you. ¹⁰Yes, whoever continues to ask will receive. Whoever continues to look will find. And whoever continues to knock will have the door opened for them. ¹¹Do any of you have a son? What would you do if your son asked you for a fish? Would any father give him a snake? ¹²Or, if he asked for an egg, would you give him a scorpion? Of course not! ¹³Even you who are bad know how to give good things to your children. So surely your heavenly Father knows how to give the Holy Spirit* to the people who ask him."

Jesus' Power Is From God
(Mt. 12:22–30; Mk. 3:20–27)

¹⁴One time Jesus was sending a demon* out of a man who could not talk. When the demon came out, the man was able to speak. The crowds were amazed. ¹⁵But some of the people said, "He uses the power of Satan*ᵃ* to force demons out of people. Satan is the ruler of demons."

¹⁶Some others there wanted to test Jesus. They asked him to do a miracle as a sign from God. ¹⁷But he knew what they were thinking. So he said to them, "Every kingdom that fights against itself will be destroyed. And a family that fights against

---

*ᵃ*11:15 Satan Literally, "Beelzebul" (the devil). Also in verses 18 and 19.

itself will break apart. ¹⁸So if Satan* is fighting against himself, how will his kingdom survive? You say that I use the power of Satan to force out demons. ¹⁹But if I use Satan's power to force out demons, then what power do your people use when they force out demons? So your own people will prove that you are wrong. ²⁰But I use the power of God to force out demons. This shows that God's kingdom* has come to you.

²¹"When a strong man with many weapons guards his own house, the things in his house are safe. ²²But suppose a stronger man comes and defeats him. The stronger man will take away the weapons that the first man trusted to keep his house safe. Then the stronger man will do what he wants with the other man's things.

²³"Whoever is not with me is against me. And anyone who does not work with me is working against me.

The Danger of Emptiness
(Mt. 12:43–45)

²⁴"When an evil spirit comes out of someone, it travels through dry places, looking for a place to rest. But it finds no place to rest. So it says, 'I will go back to the home I left.' ²⁵When it comes back, it finds that home all neat and clean. ²⁶Then the evil spirit goes out and brings back seven other spirits more evil than itself. They all go and live there, and that person has even more trouble than before."

The People God Blesses

²⁷As Jesus was saying these things, a woman with the people there called out to him, "What a great blessing God gave your mother, because she gave birth to you and fed you!"

²⁸But Jesus said, "The people who hear the teaching of God and obey it—they are the ones who have God's blessing."

Some People Doubt Jesus' Authority
(Mt. 12:38–42; Mk. 8:12)

²⁹The crowd grew larger and larger. Jesus said, "The people who live today are evil. They ask for a miracle* as a sign from God. But no miracle will be done to prove anything to them. The only sign will be the miracle that happened to Jonah.ᵃ ³⁰Jonah was a sign for those who lived in Nineveh.ᵇ It is the same with the Son of Man.* He will be a sign for the people of this time.

³¹"On the judgment day, you people who live now will be compared with the Queen of the South,ᶜ and she will be a witness who shows how guilty you are. Why do I say this?

ᵃ**11:29** *Jonah* A prophet in the Old Testament. After three days in a big fish he came out alive, just as Jesus would come out from the tomb on the third day. ᵇ**11:30** *Nineveh* City where Jonah preached. See Jonah 3. ᶜ**11:31** *Queen of the South* Or, "Queen of Sheba." She traveled about 1000 miles (1600 km) to learn God's wisdom from Solomon. See 1 Kings 10:1–13.

Because she traveled from far, far away to listen to Solomon's wise teaching. And I tell you that someone[a] greater than Solomon is right here, but you won't listen!

³²"On the judgment day, you people who live now will also be compared with the people from Nineveh, and they will be witnesses who show how guilty you are. I say this because when Jonah preached to those people, they changed their hearts and lives. And you are listening to someone greater than Jonah, but you refuse to change!

Be a Light for the World
(Mt. 5:15; 6:22-23)

³³"No one takes a light and puts it under a bowl or hides it. Instead, they put it on a lampstand so that the people who come in can see. ³⁴The only source of light for the body is the eye. When you look at people and want to help them, you are full of light. But when you look at people in a selfish way, you are full of darkness.[b] ³⁵So be careful! Don't let the light in you become darkness. ³⁶If you are full of light, and there is no part of you that is dark, then you will be all bright, as though you have the light of a lamp shining on you."

Jesus Criticizes the Religious Leaders
(Mt. 23:1-36; Mk. 12:38-40; Lk. 20:45-47)

³⁷After Jesus had finished speaking, a Pharisee* asked Jesus to eat with him. So he went and took a place at the table. ³⁸But the Pharisee was surprised when he saw that Jesus did not wash his hands[c] first before the meal. ³⁹The Lord said to him, "The washing you Pharisees do is like cleaning only the outside of a cup or a dish. But what is inside you? You want only to cheat and hurt people. ⁴⁰You are foolish! The same one who made what is outside also made what is inside. ⁴¹So pay attention to what is inside. Give to the people who need help. Then you will be fully clean.

⁴²"But it will be bad for you Pharisees! You give God a tenth of everything you have—even your mint, your rue, and every other little plant in your garden. But you forget to be fair to others and to love God. These are the things you should do. And you should also continue to do those other things.

⁴³"It will be bad for you Pharisees because you love to have the most important seats in the synagogues.* And you love for people to show respect to you in the marketplaces. ⁴⁴It will be bad for you, because you are like hidden graves. People walk on them without knowing it."

---

[a]11:31 someone Literally, "something." Also in verse 32. [b]11:34 Literally, "The lamp of the body is your eye. When your eye is pure, your whole body is full of light. But if it is evil, your body is dark." [c]11:38 wash his hands Washing the hands was a Jewish religious custom that the Pharisees thought was very important.

⁴⁵One of the experts in the law said to Jesus, "Teacher, when you say these things about the Pharisees, you are criticizing our group too."

⁴⁶Jesus answered, "It will be bad for you, you experts in the law! You make strict rules that are very hard for people to obey.ᵃ You try to force others to obey your rules. But you yourselves don't even try to follow any of those rules. ⁴⁷It will be bad for you, because you build tombs* for the prophets.* But these are the same prophets your ancestors* killed! ⁴⁸And now you show all people that you agree with what your ancestors did. They killed the prophets, and you build tombs for the prophets! ⁴⁹This is why God in his wisdom said, 'I will send prophets and apostlesᵇ to them. Some of my prophets and apostles will be killed by evil men. Others will be treated badly.'

⁵⁰"So you people who live now will be punished for the deaths of all the prophets who were killed since the beginning of the world. ⁵¹You will be punished for the killing of Abel.ᶜ And you will be punished for the killing of Zechariah,ᵈ who was killed between the altar* and the Temple.* Yes, I tell you that you people will be punished for them all.

⁵²"It will be bad for you, you experts in the law! You have taken away the key to learning about God. You yourselves would not learn, and you stopped others from learning too."

⁵³When Jesus went out, the teachers of the law and the Pharisees began to give him much trouble. They tried to make him answer questions about many things. ⁵⁴They were trying to find a way to catch Jesus saying something wrong.

Don't Be Like the Pharisees

12 ¹Many thousands of people came together. There were so many people that they were stepping on each other. Before Jesus spoke to the people, he said to his followers, "Be careful of the yeast* of the Pharisees.* I mean that they are hypocrites.* ²Everything that is hidden will be shown, and everything that is secret will be made known. ³What you say in the dark will be told in the light. And what you whisper in a private room will be shouted from the top of the house."

Fear Only God
(Mt. 10:28–31)

⁴Then Jesus said to the people, "I tell you, my friends, don't be afraid of people. They can kill the body, but after that they can do nothing more to hurt you. ⁵I will show you the

---

ᵃ**11:46** *You make ... obey* Literally, "You put heavy burdens on people that are hard for them to carry." ᵇ**11:49** *prophets and apostles* People chosen by God to tell his Good News to the world. ᶜ**11:51** *Abel* In the Hebrew Old Testament, the first person to be murdered. ᵈ**11:51** *Zechariah* In the Hebrew Old Testament, the last person to be murdered.

one to fear. You should fear God, who has the power to kill you and also to throw you into hell. Yes, he is the one you should fear.

6"When birds are sold, five small birds cost only two pennies. But God does not forget any of them. 7Yes, God even knows how many hairs you have on your head. Don't be afraid. You are worth much more than many birds.

Don't Be Ashamed of Your Faith
(Mt. 10:32-33; 12:32; 10:19-20)

8"I tell you, if you stand before others and are willing to say you believe in me, then I[a] will say that you belong to me. I will say this in the presence of God's angels. 9But if you stand before others and say you do not believe in me, then I will say that you do not belong to me. I will say this in the presence of God's angels.

10"Whoever says something against the Son of Man* can be forgiven. But whoever speaks against the Holy Spirit* will not be forgiven.

11"When men bring you into the synagogues* before the leaders and other important men, don't worry about what you will say. 12The Holy Spirit will teach you at that time what you should say."

Jesus Warns Against Selfishness

13One of the men in the crowd said to Jesus, "Teacher, our father just died and left some things for us. Tell my brother to share them with me."

14But Jesus said to him, "Who said I should be your judge or decide how to divide your father's things between you two?" 15Then Jesus said to them, "Be careful and guard against all kinds of greed. People do not get life from the many things they own."

16Then Jesus used this story: "There was a rich man who had some land. His land grew a very good crop of food. 17He thought to himself, 'What will I do? I have no place to keep all my crops.'

18"Then he said, 'I know what I will do. I will tear down my barns and build bigger barns! I will put all my wheat and good things together in my new barns. 19Then I can say to myself, I have many good things stored. I have saved enough for many years. Rest, eat, drink, and enjoy life!'

20"But God said to that man, 'Foolish man! Tonight you will die. So what about the things you prepared for yourself? Who will get those things now?'

21"This is how it will be for anyone who saves things only for himself. To God that person is not rich."

---

[a]12:8 / Literally, "the Son of Man" (Jesus).

Put God's Kingdom First
(Mt. 6:25–34; 19–21)

²²Jesus said to his followers, "So I tell you, don't worry about the things you need to live—what you will eat or what you will wear. ²³Life is more important than food, and the body is more important than what you put on it. ²⁴Look at the birds. They don't plant, harvest, or save food in houses or barns, but God feeds them. And you are worth much more than crows. ²⁵None of you can add any time to your life by worrying about it. ²⁶And if you can't do the little things, why worry about the big things?

²⁷"Think about how the wildflowers grow. They don't work or make clothes for themselves. But I tell you that even Solomon, the great and rich king, was not dressed as beautifully as one of these flowers. ²⁸If God makes what grows in the field so beautiful, what do you think he will do for you? That's just grass—one day it's alive, and the next day someone throws it into a fire. But God cares enough to make it beautiful. Surely he will do so much more for you. Your faith is so small!

²⁹"So don't always think about what you will eat or what you will drink. Don't worry about it. ³⁰That's what all those people who don't know God are always thinking about. But your Father knows that you need these things. ³¹What you should be thinking about is God's kingdom.* Then he will give you all these other things you need.

Don't Trust in Money

³²"Don't fear, little flock. Your Father wants to share his kingdom with you. ³³Sell the things you have and give that money to those who need it. This is the only way you can keep your riches from being lost. You will be storing treasure in heaven that lasts forever. Thieves can't steal that treasure, and moths can't destroy it. ³⁴Your heart will be where your treasure is.

Always Be Ready
(Mt. 24:42–44)

³⁵"Be ready! Be fully dressed and have your lights shining. ³⁶Be like servants who are waiting for their master to come home from a wedding party. The master comes and knocks, and the servants immediately open the door for him. ³⁷When their master sees that they are ready and waiting for him, it will be a great day for those servants. I can tell you without a doubt, the master will get himself ready to serve a meal and tell the servants to sit down. Then he will serve them. ³⁸Those servants might have to wait until midnight or later for their master. But they will be glad they did when he comes in and finds them still waiting.

³⁹"Remember this: If the owner of the house knew what time a thief was coming, he would not allow the thief to enter his house. ⁴⁰So you also must be ready, because the Son of Man* will come at a time when you don't expect him!"

Who Is the Trusted Servant?
(Mt. 24:45–51)

⁴¹Peter said, "Lord, did you tell this story for us or for all people?"

⁴²The Lord said, "Who is the wise and trusted servant? The master trusts one servant to give the other servants their food at the right time. Who is the servant that the master trusts to do that work? ⁴³When the master comes and finds him doing the work he gave him, what a great day it will be for that servant! ⁴⁴I can tell you without a doubt, the master will choose that servant to take care of everything he owns.

⁴⁵"But what will happen if that servant is evil and thinks his master will not come back soon? He will begin to beat the other servants, men and women. He will eat and drink until he has had too much. ⁴⁶Then the master will come when the servant is not ready, at a time when the servant is not expecting him. Then the master will punish that servant and send him away to be with the other people who don't obey.

⁴⁷"That servant knew what his master wanted him to do. But he did not make himself ready or try to do what his master wanted. So that servant will be punished very much! ⁴⁸But what about the servant who does not know what his master wants? He also does things that deserve punishment. But he will get less punishment than the servant who knew what he should do. Whoever has been given much will be responsible for much. Much more will be expected from the one who has been given more."

Following Jesus May Bring You Trouble
(Mt. 10:34–36)

⁴⁹Jesus continued speaking: "I came to bring fire to the world. I wish it were already burning! ⁵⁰There is a kind of baptism[a] that I must suffer through. I feel very troubled until it is finished. ⁵¹Do you think I came to give peace to the world? No, I came to divide the world! ⁵²From now on, a family of five will be divided, three against two, and two against three.

⁵³ A father and son will be divided:
> The son will turn against his father.
> The father will turn against his son.
A mother and her daughter will be divided:
> The daughter will turn against her mother.
> The mother will turn against her daughter.
A mother-in-law and her daughter-in-law will be divided:
> The daughter-in-law will turn against her mother-in-law.
> The mother-in-law will turn against her daughter-in-law."

---

[a]**12:50 baptism** This word, which usually means to be immersed in water, has a special meaning here—being covered or "buried" in troubles.

Understanding the Times
(Mt. 16:2–3)

⁵⁴Then Jesus said to the people, "When you see clouds growing bigger in the west, you say, 'A rainstorm is coming.' And soon it begins to rain. ⁵⁵When you feel the wind begin to blow from the south, you say, 'It will be a hot day.' And you are right. ⁵⁶You hypocrites*! You can understand the weather. Why don't you understand what is happening now?

Settle Your Problems
(Mt. 5:25–26)

⁵⁷"Why can't you decide for yourselves what is right? ⁵⁸Suppose someone is suing you, and you are both going to court. Try hard to settle it on the way. If you don't settle it, you may have to go before the judge. And the judge will hand you over to the officer, who will throw you into jail. ⁵⁹I tell you, you will not get out of there until you have paid every cent you owe."

Change Your Hearts

13 ¹Some people there with Jesus at that time told him about what had happened to some worshipers from Galilee. Pilate* had them killed. Their blood was mixed with the blood of the animals they had brought for sacrificing.* ²Jesus answered, "Do you think this happened to those people because they were more sinful than all other people from Galilee? ³No, they were not. But if you don't decide now to change your lives, you will all be destroyed like those people! ⁴And what about those 18 people who died when the tower of Siloam fell on them? Do you think they were more sinful than everyone else in Jerusalem? ⁵They were not. But I tell you if you don't decide now to change your lives, you will all be destroyed too!"

The Useless Tree

⁶Jesus told this story: "A man had a fig tree. He planted it in his garden. He came looking for some fruit on it, but he found none. ⁷He had a servant who took care of his garden. So he said to his servant, 'I have been looking for fruit on this tree for three years, but I never find any. Cut it down! Why should it waste the ground?' ⁸But the servant answered, 'Master, let the tree have one more year to produce fruit. Let me dig up the dirt around it and fertilize it. ⁹Maybe the tree will have fruit on it next year. If it still does not produce, then you can cut it down.'"

Jesus Heals a Woman on the Sabbath

¹⁰Jesus taught in one of the synagogues* on the Sabbath* day. ¹¹A woman was there who had a spirit inside her. It had made

the woman crippled for 18 years. Her back was always bent; she could not stand up straight. ¹²When Jesus saw her, he called to her, "Woman, you have been made free from your sickness!" ¹³He laid his hands on her, and immediately she was able to stand up straight. She began praising God.

¹⁴The synagogue leader was angry because Jesus healed on the Sabbath day. He said to the people, "There are six days for work. So come to be healed on one of those days. Don't come for healing on the Sabbath day."

¹⁵The Lord answered, "You people are hypocrites*! All of you untie your work animals and lead them to drink water every day—even on the Sabbath day. ¹⁶This woman that I healed is our Jewish sister.ᵃ But Satan* has held her for 18 years. Surely it is not wrong for her to be made free from her sickness on a Sabbath day!" ¹⁷When Jesus said this, all those who were criticizing him felt ashamed of themselves. And all the people were happy for the wonderful things he was doing.

What Is God's Kingdom Like?
(Mt. 13:31–33; Mk. 4:30–32)

¹⁸Then Jesus said, "What is God's kingdom* like? What can I compare it to? ¹⁹God's kingdom is like the seed of the mustard* plant. Someone plants this seed in their garden. The seed grows and becomes a tree, and the birds build nests on its branches."

²⁰Jesus said again, "What can I compare God's kingdom with? ²¹It is like yeast that a woman mixes into a big bowl of flour to make bread. The yeast makes all the dough rise."

The Narrow Door
(Mt. 7:13–14, 21–23)

²²Jesus was teaching in every town and village. He continued to travel toward Jerusalem. ²³Someone said to him, "Lord, how many people will be saved? Only a few?"

Jesus said, ²⁴"The door to heaven is narrow. Try hard to enter it. Many people will want to enter there, but they will not be able to go in. ²⁵If a man locks the door of his house, you can stand outside and knock on the door, but he won't open it. You can say, 'Sir, open the door for us.' But he will answer, 'I don't know you. Where did you come from?' ²⁶Then you will say, 'We ate and drank with you. You taught in the streets of our town.' ²⁷Then he will say to you, 'I don't know you. Where did you come from? Get away from me! You are all people who do wrong!'

²⁸"You will see Abraham,* Isaac,* Jacob,* and all the prophets* in God's kingdom.* But you will be left outside. There you will cry and grind your teeth with pain. ²⁹People will

ᵃ 13:16 *Jewish sister* Literally, "daughter of Abraham."

come from the east, west, north, and south. They will sit down at the table in God's kingdom. ³⁰People who have the lowest place in life now will have the highest place in God's kingdom. And people who have the highest place now will have the lowest place in God's kingdom."

Jesus Will Die in Jerusalem
(Mt. 23:37–39)

³¹Just then some Pharisees* came to Jesus and said, "Go away from here and hide. Herod* wants to kill you!"

³²Jesus said to them, "Go tell that fox,ᵃ 'Today and tomorrow I am forcing demons* out of people and finishing my work of healing. Then, the next day, the work will be finished.' ³³After that, I must go, because all prophets* should die in Jerusalem.

³⁴"Jerusalem, Jerusalem! You kill the prophets. You stone to death the people God has sent to you. How many times I wanted to help your people. I wanted to gather them together as a hen gathers her chicks under her wings. But you did not let me. ³⁵Now your home will be left completely empty. I tell you, you will not see me again until that time when you will say, 'Welcome! God bless the one who comes in the name of the Lord.'ᵇ"

Is It Right to Heal on the Sabbath Day?

14 ¹On a Sabbath* day, Jesus went to the home of a leading Pharisee* to eat with him. The people there were all watching him very closely. ²A man with a bad diseaseᶜ was there in front of him. ³Jesus said to the Pharisees and experts in the law, "Is it right or wrong to heal on the Sabbath day?" ⁴But they would not answer his question. So he took the man and healed him. Then he sent the man away. ⁵Jesus said to the Pharisees and teachers of the law, "If your son or work animal falls into a well on the Sabbath day, you know you would pull him out immediately." ⁶The Pharisees and teachers of the law could say nothing against what he said.

Don't Make Yourself Important

⁷Then Jesus noticed that some of the guests were choosing the best places to sit. So he told this story: ⁸"When someone invites you to a wedding, don't sit in the most important seat. They may have invited someone more important than you. ⁹And if you are sitting in the most important seat, they will come to you and say, 'Give this man your seat!' Then you will have to move down to the last place and be embarrassed.

ᵃ**13:32** *fox* Jesus means that Herod is clever and sly like a fox.   ᵇ**13:35** Quote from Ps. 118:26.   ᶜ**14:2** *disease* The man had dropsy, a sickness that causes the body to swell larger and larger.

¹⁰"So when someone invites you, go sit in the seat that is not important. Then they will come to you and say, 'Friend, move up here to this better place!' What an honor this will be for you in front of all the other guests. ¹¹Everyone who makes themselves important will be made humble. But everyone who makes themselves humble will be made important."

You Will Be Rewarded

¹²Then Jesus said to the Pharisee* who had invited him, "When you give a lunch or a dinner, don't invite only your friends, brothers, relatives, and rich neighbors. At another time they will pay you back by inviting you to eat with them. ¹³Instead, when you give a feast, invite the poor, the crippled, and the blind. ¹⁴Then you will have great blessings, because these people cannot pay you back. They have nothing. But God will reward you at the time when all godly people rise from death."

A Story About People Invited to a Dinner
(Mt. 22:1–10)

¹⁵One of the men sitting at the table with Jesus heard these things. The man said to him, "What a great blessing it will be for anyone to eat a meal in God's kingdom*!"

¹⁶Jesus said to him, "A man gave a big dinner. He invited many people. ¹⁷When it was time to eat, he sent his servant to tell the guests, 'Come. The food is ready.' ¹⁸But all the guests said they could not come. Each one made an excuse. The first one said, 'I have just bought a field, so I must go look at it. Please excuse me.' ¹⁹Another man said, 'I have just bought five pairs of work animals; I must go and try them out. Please excuse me.' ²⁰A third man said, 'I just got married; I can't come.'

²¹"So the servant returned and told his master what happened. The master was angry. He said, 'Hurry! Go into the streets and alleys of the town. Bring me the poor, the crippled, the blind, and the lame.'

²²"Later, the servant said to him, 'Master, I did what you told me to do, but we still have places for more people.' ²³The master said to the servant, 'Go out to the highways and country roads. Tell the people there to come. I want my house to be full! ²⁴None of those people I invited first will get to eat any of this food.'"

Decide if You Can Follow Me
(Mt. 10:37–38)

²⁵Many people were traveling with Jesus. He said to them, ²⁶"If you come to me but will not leave your family, you cannot be my follower. You must love me more than your father, mother, wife, children, brothers, and sisters—even more than

your own life! 27Whoever will not carry the cross* that is given to them when they follow me cannot be my follower.

28"If you wanted to build a building, you would first sit down and decide how much it would cost. You must see if you have enough money to finish the job. 29If you don't do that, you might begin the work, but you would not be able to finish. And if you could not finish it, everyone would laugh at you. 30They would say, 'This man began to build, but he was not able to finish.'

31"If a king is going to fight against another king, first he will sit down and plan. If he has only 10,000 men, he will try to decide if he is able to defeat the other king who has 20,000 men. 32If he thinks he cannot defeat the other king, he will send some men to ask for peace while that king's army is still far away.

33"It is the same for each of you. You must leave everything you have to follow me. If not, you cannot be my follower.

Don't Lose Your Influence
(Mt. 5:13; Mk. 9:50)

34"Salt is a good thing. But if the salt loses its salty taste, you can't make it salty again. 35It is worth nothing. You can't even use it as dirt or dung. People just throw it away.

"You people who hear me, listen!"

Joy in Heaven
(Mt. 18:12–14)

15 1Many tax collectors* and sinners came to listen to Jesus. 2Then the Pharisees* and the teachers of the law began to complain, "Look, this man*a* welcomes sinners and even eats with them!"

3Then Jesus told them this story: 4"Suppose one of you has 100 sheep, but one of them gets lost. What will you do? You will leave the other 99 sheep there in the field and go out and look for the lost one. You will continue to search for it until you find it. 5And when you find it, you will be very happy. You will carry it 6home, to your friends and neighbors and say to them, 'Be happy with me because I found my lost sheep!' 7In the same way, I tell you, heaven is a happy place when one sinner decides to change. There is more joy for that one sinner than for 99 good people who don't need to change.

8"Suppose a woman has ten silver coins,*b* but she loses one of them. She will take a light and clean the house. She will look carefully for the coin until she finds it. 9And when she finds it, she will call her friends and neighbors and say to them,

*a*15:2 *this man* That is, Jesus. His enemies avoided saying his name.   *b*15:8 *silver coins* Each coin, a Greek *drachma*, was worth the average pay for one day's work.

'Be happy with me because I have found the coin that I lost!' ¹⁰In the same way, it's a happy time for the angels of God when one sinner decides to change."

Story About Two Sons

¹¹Then Jesus said, "There was a man who had two sons. ¹²The younger son said to his father, 'Give me now the part of your property that I am supposed to receive someday.' So the father divided his wealth between his two sons.

¹³"A few days later the younger son gathered up all that he had and left. He traveled far away to another country, and there he wasted his money living like a fool. ¹⁴After he spent everything he had, there was a terrible famine throughout the country. He was hungry and needed money. ¹⁵So he went and got a job with one of the people who lived there. The man sent him into the fields to feed pigs. ¹⁶He was so hungry that he wanted to eat the food the pigs were eating. But no one gave him anything.

¹⁷"The son realized that he had been very foolish. He thought, 'All my father's hired workers have plenty of food. But here I am, almost dead because I have nothing to eat. ¹⁸I will leave and go to my father. I will say to him: Father, I have sinned against God and have done wrong to you. ¹⁹I am no longer worthy to be called your son. But let me be like one of your hired workers.' ²⁰So he left and went to his father.

The Younger Son Returns

"While the son was still a long way off, his father saw him coming and felt sorry for him. So he ran to him and hugged and kissed him. ²¹The son said, 'Father, I have sinned against God and have done wrong to you. I am no longer worthy to be called your son.'

²²"But the father said to his servants, 'Hurry! Bring the best clothes and put them on him. Also, put a ring on his finger and good sandals on his feet. ²³And bring our best calf and kill it so that we can celebrate with plenty to eat. ²⁴My son was dead, but now he is alive again! He was lost, but now he is found!' So they began to have a party.

The Older Son Complains

²⁵"The older son had been out in the field. When he came near the house, he heard the sound of music and dancing. ²⁶So he called to one of the servant boys and asked, 'What does all this mean?' ²⁷The boy said, 'Your brother has come back, and your father killed the best calf to eat. He is happy because he has his son back safe and sound.'

²⁸"The older son was angry and would not go in to the party. So his father went out and begged him to come in. ²⁹But he said to his father, 'Look, for all these years I have

worked like a slave for you. I have always done what you told me to do, and you never gave me even a young goat for a party with my friends. ³⁰But then this son of yours comes home after wasting your money on prostitutes, and you kill the best calf for him!'

³¹"His father said to him, 'Oh, my son, you are always with me, and everything I have is yours. ³²But this was a day to be happy and celebrate. Your brother was dead, but now he is alive. He was lost, but now he is found.'"

True Wealth

16 ¹Jesus said to his followers, "Once there was a rich man. He hired a manager to take care of his business. Later, he learned that his manager was cheating him. ²So he called the manager in and said to him, 'I have heard bad things about you. Give me a report of what you have done with my money. You can't be my manager anymore.'

³"So, the manager thought to himself, 'What will I do? My master is taking my job away from me. I am not strong enough to dig ditches. I am too proud to beg. ⁴I know what I will do! I will do something to make friends, so that when I lose my job, they will welcome me into their homes.'

⁵"So the manager called in each person who owed the master some money. He asked the first one, 'How much do you owe my master?' ⁶He answered, 'I owe him 800 gallons*ᵃ* of olive oil.' The manager said to him, 'Here is your bill. Hurry! Sit down and make the bill less. Write 400 gallons.'

⁷"Then the manager asked another one, 'How much do you owe my master?' He answered, 'I owe him 1000 bushels*ᵇ* of wheat.' Then the manager said to him, 'Here is your bill; you can make it less. Write 800 bushels.'

⁸"Later, the master told the dishonest manager that he had done a smart thing. Yes, worldly people are smarter in their business with each other than spiritual people are.

⁹"I tell you, use the worldly things you have now to make 'friends' for later. Then, when those things are gone, you will be welcomed into a home that lasts forever. ¹⁰Whoever can be trusted with small things can also be trusted with big things. Whoever is dishonest in little things will be dishonest in big things too. ¹¹If you cannot be trusted with worldly riches, you will not be trusted with the true riches. ¹²And if you cannot be trusted with the things that belong to someone else, you will not be given anything of your own.

¹³"You cannot serve two masters at the same time. You will hate one master and love the other. Or you will be loyal to one

---

*ᵃ***16:6** *gallons* Literally, "100 *batous*." A *batos* was about 34 liters.   *ᵇ***16:7** *bushels* Literally, "*korous.*" A *koros* was about 393 liters.

and not care about the other. You cannot serve God and Money[a] at the same time."

God's Law Cannot Be Changed
(Mt. 11:12-13)

14The Pharisees* were listening to all these things. They criticized Jesus because they all loved money. 15Jesus said to them, "You make yourselves look good in front of people. But God knows what is really in your hearts. What people think is important is worth nothing to God.

16"Before John the Baptizer* came, people were taught the law of Moses* and the writings of the prophets.* But since the time of John, the Good News* about God's kingdom* is being told. And everyone is trying hard to get into it. 17But even the smallest part of a letter in the law cannot be changed. It would be easier for heaven and earth to pass away.

Divorce and Remarriage

18"Any man who divorces his wife and marries another woman is guilty of adultery.* And the man who marries a divorced woman is also guilty of adultery."

The Rich Man and Lazarus

19Jesus said, "There was a rich man who always dressed in the finest clothes. He was so rich that he was able to enjoy all the best things every day. 20There was also a very poor man named Lazarus. Lazarus' body was covered with sores. He was often put by the rich man's gate. 21Lazarus wanted only to eat the scraps of food left on the floor under the rich man's table. And the dogs came and licked his sores.

22"Later, Lazarus died. The angels took him and placed him in the arms of Abraham.* The rich man also died and was buried. 23He was sent to the place of death[b] and was in great pain. He saw Abraham far away with Lazarus in his arms. 24He called, 'Father Abraham, have mercy on me! Send Lazarus to me so that he can dip his finger in water and cool my tongue. I am suffering in this fire!'

25"But Abraham said, 'My child, remember when you lived? You had all the good things in life. But Lazarus had nothing but problems. Now he is comforted here, and you are suffering. 26Also, there is a big pit between you and us. No one can cross over to help you, and no one can come here from there.'

27"The rich man said, 'Then please, father Abraham, send Lazarus to my father's house on earth. 28I have five brothers. He could warn my brothers so that they will not come to this place of pain.'

a16:13 Money Or, mamona, an Aramaic word meaning "wealth." b16:23 place of death Literally, "Hades."

²⁹"But Abraham said, 'They have the law of Moses* and the writings of the prophets* to read; let them learn from that.'

³⁰"The rich man said, 'No, father Abraham! But if someone came to them from the dead, then they would decide to change their lives.'

³¹"But Abraham said to him, 'If your brothers won't listen to Moses and the prophets, they won't listen to someone who comes back from the dead.'"

Sin and Forgiveness
(Mt. 18:6–7, 21–22; Mk. 9:42)

17 ¹Jesus said to his followers, "Things will surely happen that will make people sin. But it will be very bad for anyone who makes this happen. ²It will be very bad for anyone who makes one of these little children sin. It would be better for them to have a millstone* tied around their neck and be drowned in the sea. ³So be careful!

"If your brother or sister in God's family does something wrong, warn them. If they are sorry for what they did, forgive them. ⁴Even if they do something wrong to you seven times in one day, but they say they are sorry each time, you should forgive them."

How Big Is Your Faith?

⁵The apostles* said to the Lord, "Give us more faith!"

⁶The Lord said, "If your faith is as big as a mustard* seed, you can say to this mulberry tree, 'Dig yourself up and plant yourself in the ocean!' And the tree will obey you.

Be Good Servants

⁷"Suppose one of you has a servant who has been working in the field, plowing or caring for the sheep. When he comes in from work, what would you say to him? Would you say, 'Come in, sit down and eat'? ⁸Of course not! You would say to your servant, 'Prepare something for me to eat. Then get ready and serve me. When I finish eating and drinking, then you can eat.' ⁹The servant should not get any special thanks for doing his job. He is only doing what his master told him to do. ¹⁰It is the same with you. When you finish doing all that you are told to do, you should say, 'We are not worthy of any special thanks. We have only done the work we should do.'"

Be Thankful

¹¹Jesus was traveling to Jerusalem. He went from Galilee to Samaria. ¹²He came into a small town, and ten men met him there. They did not come close to him, because they all had leprosy.* ¹³But the men shouted, "Jesus! Master! Please help us!"

¹⁴When Jesus saw the men, he said, "Go and show yourselves to the priests."[a]

While the ten men were going to the priests, they were healed. ¹⁵When one of them saw that he was healed, he went back to Jesus. He praised God loudly. ¹⁶He bowed down at Jesus' feet and thanked him. (He was a Samaritan.[*]) ¹⁷Jesus said, "Ten men were healed; where are the other nine? ¹⁸This man is not even one of our people. Is he the only one who came back to give praise to God?" ¹⁹Then Jesus said to the man, "Stand up! You can go. You were healed because you believed."

The Coming of God's Kingdom
(Mt. 24:23–28, 37–41)

²⁰Some of the Pharisees[*] asked Jesus, "When will God's kingdom[*] come?"

Jesus answered, "God's kingdom is coming, but not in a way that you can see it. ²¹People will not say, 'Look, God's kingdom is here!' Or, 'There it is!' No, God's kingdom is here with you.[b]"

²²Then Jesus said to his followers, "The time will come when you will want very much to see one of the days of the Son of Man,[*] but you will not be able to. ²³People will say to you, 'Look, there it is!' or 'Look, here it is!' Stay where you are; don't go away and search.

When Jesus Comes Again

²⁴"When the Son of Man[*] comes again, you will know it. On that day he will shine like lightning flashes across the sky. ²⁵But first, the Son of Man must suffer many things. The people of today will refuse to accept him.

²⁶"When the Son of Man comes again, it will be the same as it was when Noah lived. ²⁷People were eating, drinking, and getting married even on the day when Noah entered the boat. Then the flood came and killed them all.

²⁸"It will be the same as during the time of Lot, when God destroyed Sodom.[*] Those people were eating, drinking, buying, selling, planting, and building houses for themselves. ²⁹They were doing these things even on the day when Lot left town. Then fire and sulfur rained down from the sky and killed them all. ³⁰This is exactly how it will be when the Son of Man comes again.

³¹"On that day if a man is on his roof, he will not have time to go inside and get his things. If a man is in the field, he cannot go back home. ³²Remember what happened to Lot's wife[c]!

ᵃ17:14 show yourselves to the priests The law of Moses said a priest must decide when a person with leprosy was well. ᵇ17:21 here with you Or, "inside you." ᶜ17:32 Lot's wife The story about Lot's wife is found in Gen. 19:15–17, 26.

³³"Those who try to keep the life they have will lose it. But those who give up their life will save it. ³⁴That night there may be two people sleeping in one room. One will be taken and the other will be left. ³⁵There may be two women working together. One will be taken and the other will be left." ³⁶ᵃ

³⁷The followers asked Jesus, "Where will this be, Lord?"

Jesus answered, "It's like looking for a dead body—you will find it where the vultures* are gathering above."

God Will Answer His People

18 ¹Then Jesus taught the followers that they should always pray and never lose hope. He used this story to teach them: ²"Once there was a judge in a town. He did not care about God. He also did not care what people thought about him. ³In that same town there was a woman whose husband had died. She came many times to this judge and said, 'There is a man who is doing bad things to me. Give me my rights!' ⁴But the judge did not want to help the woman. After a long time, the judge thought to himself, 'I don't care about God. And I don't care about what people think. ⁵But this woman is bothering me. If I give her what she wants, then she will leave me alone. But if I don't give her what she wants, she will bother me until I am sick.'"

⁶The Lord said, "Listen, there is meaning in what the bad judge said. ⁷God's people shout to him night and day, and he will always give them what is right. He will not be slow to answer them. ⁸I tell you, God will help his people quickly. But when the Son of Man* comes again, will he find people on earth who believe in him?"

Being Right With God

⁹There were some people who thought they were very good and looked down on everyone else. Jesus used this story to teach them: ¹⁰"One time there was a Pharisee* and a tax collector.* One day they both went to the Temple* to pray. ¹¹The Pharisee stood alone, away from the tax collector. When the Pharisee prayed, he said, 'O God, I thank you that I am not as bad as other people. I am not like men who steal, cheat, or commit adultery.* I thank you that I am better than this tax collector. ¹²I fast* twice a week, and I give a tenth of everything I get!'

¹⁴"The tax collector stood alone too. But when he prayed, he would not even look up to heaven. He felt very humble before God. He said, 'O God, have mercy on me. I am a sinner!' ¹⁴I tell you, when this man finished his prayer and went home, he

---

ᵃ**17:36** A few Greek copies add verse 36: "Two men will be in the same field. One man will be taken, but the other man will be left behind."

was right with God. But the Pharisee, who felt that he was better than others, was not right with God. People who make themselves important will be made humble. But those who make themselves humble will be made important."

Jesus Welcomes Children
(Mt. 19:13–15; Mk. 10:13–16)

[15]Some people brought their small children to Jesus so that he could lay his hands on them to bless them. But when the followers saw this, they told the people not to do this. [16]But Jesus called the little children to him and said to his followers, "Let the little children come to me. Don't stop them, because God's kingdom* belongs to people who are like these little children. [17]The truth is, you must accept God's kingdom like a little child accepts things, or you will never enter it."

A Rich Man Refuses to Follow Jesus
(Mt. 19:16–30; Mk. 10:17–31)

[18]A religious leader asked Jesus, "Good Teacher, what must I do to get eternal life?"

[19]Jesus said to him, "Why do you call me good? Only God is good. [20]And you know his commands: 'You must not commit adultery,* you must not murder anyone, you must not steal, you must not tell lies about others, you must respect your father and mother ....'[a]"

[21]But the leader said, "I have obeyed all these commands since I was a boy."

[22]When Jesus heard this, he said to the leader, "But there is still one thing you need to do. Sell everything you have and give the money to those who are poor. You will have riches in heaven. Then come and follow me." [23]But when the man heard Jesus tell him to give away his money, he was sad. He didn't want to do this, because he was very rich.

[24]When Jesus saw that the man was sad, he said, "It will be very hard for rich people to enter God's kingdom.* [25]It is easier for a camel to go through the eye of a needle than for a rich person to enter God's kingdom."

Who Can Be Saved?

[26]When the people heard this, they said, "Then who can be saved?"

[27]Jesus answered, "God can do things that are not possible for people to do."

[28]Peter said, "Look, we left everything we had and followed you."

[29]Jesus said, "I can promise that everyone who has left their home, wife, brothers, parents, or children for God's kingdom*

[a]18:20 Quote from Ex. 20:12–16; Deut. 5:16–20.

30will get much more than they left. They will get many times more in this life. And in the world that is coming they will get the reward of eternal life."

Jesus Talks Again About His Death
(Mt. 20:17–19; Mk. 10:32–34)

31Then Jesus talked to the twelve apostles* alone. He said to them, "Listen, we are going to Jerusalem. Everything that God told the prophets* to write about the Son of Man* will happen. 32He will be handed over to the foreigners, who will laugh at him, insult him, and spit on him. 33They will beat him with whips and then kill him. But on the third day after his death, he will rise to life again." 34The apostles tried to understand this, but they could not; the meaning was hidden from them.

Jesus Heals a Blind Man
(Mt. 20:29–34; Mk. 10:46–52)

35Jesus came near the city of Jericho. There was a blind man sitting beside the road. He was begging people for money. 36When he heard the people coming down the road, he asked, "What is happening?"

37They told him, "Jesus, the one from Nazareth, is coming here."

38The blind man was excited and said, "Jesus, Son of David,* please help me!"

39The people who were in front, leading the group, criticized the blind man. They told him to be quiet. But he shouted more and more, "Son of David, please help me!"

40Jesus stopped there and said, "Bring that man to me!" When he came close, Jesus asked him, 41"What do you want me to do for you?"

He said, "Lord, I want to see again."

42Jesus said to him, "You can see now. You are healed because you believed."

43Then the man was able to see. He followed Jesus, thanking God. Everyone who saw this praised God for what happened.

Zacchaeus

19 1Jesus was going through the city of Jericho. 2In Jericho there was a man named Zacchaeus. He was a wealthy, very important tax collector.* 3He wanted to see who Jesus was. There were many others who wanted to see Jesus too. Zacchaeus was too short to see above the people. 4So he ran to a place where he knew Jesus would come. Then he climbed a sycamore tree so he could see him.

5When Jesus came to where Zacchaeus was, he looked up and saw him in the tree. Jesus said, "Zacchaeus, hurry! Come down! I must stay at your house today."

⁶Zacchaeus hurried and came down. He was happy to have Jesus in his house. ⁷Everyone saw this. They began to complain, "Look at the kind of man Jesus is staying with. Zacchaeus is a sinner!"

⁸Zacchaeus said to the Lord, "I want to do good. I will give half of my money to the poor. If I have cheated anyone, I will pay them back four times more."

⁹Jesus said, "Today is the day for this family to be saved from sin. Yes, even this tax collector is one of God's chosen people.ᵃ ¹⁰The Son of Man* came to find lost people and save them."

Use What God Gives You
(Mt. 25:14–30)

¹¹Jesus traveled closer to Jerusalem. Some of the people thought that God's kingdom* would come soon. ¹²Jesus knew the people thought this, so he told them this story: "A very important man was preparing to go to a country far away to be made a king. Then the man planned to return home and rule his people. ¹³So he called ten of his servants together. He gave a bag of moneyᵇ to each servant. He said, 'Do business with this money until I come back.' ¹⁴But the people in the kingdom hated the man. They sent a group to follow him to the other country. There they said, 'We don't want this man to be our king.'

¹⁵"But the man was made king. When he came home, he said, 'Call those servants who have my money. I want to know how much more money they earned with it.' ¹⁶The first servant came and said, 'Sir, I earned ten bags of money with the one bag you gave me.' ¹⁷The king said to him, 'That's great! You are a good servant. I see that I can trust you with small things. So now I will let you rule over ten of my cities.'

¹⁸"The second servant said, 'Sir, with your one bag of money I earned five bags.' ¹⁹The king said to this servant, 'You can rule over five cities.'

²⁰"Then another servant came in and said to the king, 'Sir, here is your bag of money. I wrapped it in a piece of cloth and hid it. ²¹I was afraid of you because you are a hard man. You even take money that you didn't earn and gather food that you didn't grow.'

²²"Then the king said to him, 'What a bad servant you are! I will use your own words to condemn you. You said that I am a hard man. You said that I even take money that I didn't earn and gather food that I didn't grow. ²³If that is true, you should have put my money in the bank. Then, when I came back, my money would have earned some interest.' ²⁴Then the king said to the

---

ᵃ **19:9** *one of God's chosen people* Literally, "a son of Abraham."   ᵇ **19:13** *bag of money* One bag of money was a Greek *mina,* enough to pay a person for working three months. Also in verses 16, 18, 20, 24, 25.

men who were watching, 'Take the bag of money away from this servant and give it to the servant who earned ten bags of money.'

25"The men said to the king, 'But sir, that servant already has ten bags of money.'

26"The king said, 'People who use what they have will get more. But those who do not use what they have will have everything taken away from them. 27Now where are my enemies? Where are the people who did not want me to be king? Bring my enemies here and kill them. I will watch them die.'"

Jesus Enters Jerusalem Like a King
(Mt. 21:1–11; Mk. 11:1–11; Jn. 12:12–19)

28After Jesus said these things, he continued traveling toward Jerusalem. 29He came near Bethphage and Bethany, towns near the hill called the Mount of Olives.* He sent out two of his followers. 30He said, "Go into the town you can see there. When you enter the town, you will find a young donkey tied there that no one has ever ridden. Untie it, and bring it here to me. 31If anyone asks you why you are taking the donkey, you should say, 'The Master needs it.'"

32The two followers went into town. They found the donkey exactly like Jesus told them. 33They untied it, but its owners came out. They said to the followers, "Why are you untying our donkey?"

34The followers answered, "The Master needs it." 35So the followers brought the donkey to Jesus. They put their coats on its back. Then they put Jesus on the donkey. 36He rode along the road toward Jerusalem. The followers spread their coats on the road before him.

37Jesus was coming close to Jerusalem. He was already near the bottom of the Mount of Olives. The whole group of followers was happy. They were very excited and praised God. They thanked God for all the powerful things they had seen. 38They said,

> "'Welcome! God bless the king who comes
>   in the name of the Lord.'   *Psalm 118:26*
>
> Peace in heaven and glory* to God!"

39Some of the Pharisees* said to Jesus, "Teacher, tell your followers not to say these things."

40But Jesus answered, "I tell you, if my followers didn't say them, these stones would shout them."

Jesus Cries for Jerusalem

41Jesus came near Jerusalem. Looking at the city, he began to cry for it 42and said, "I wish you knew today what would bring you peace. But it is hidden from you now. 43A time is coming when your enemies will build a wall around you and hold you in on all sides. ⁴⁴They will destroy you and all your people. Not one stone of your buildings will stay on top of another. All this will happen because you did not know the time when God came to save you."

Jesus Goes to the Temple
(Mt. 21:12–17; Mk. 11:15–19; Jn. 2:13–22)

⁴⁵Jesus went into the Temple* area. He began to throw out the people who were selling things there. ⁴⁶He said, "The Scriptures* say, 'My house will be a house of prayer.'*ᵃ* But you have changed it into a 'hiding place for thieves.'*ᵇ*

⁴⁷Jesus taught the people in the Temple area every day. The leading priests, the teachers of the law, and some of the leaders of the people wanted to kill him. ⁴⁸But they did not know how they could do it, because everyone was listening to him. The people were very interested in what Jesus said.

Jewish Leaders Doubt Jesus' Authority
(Mt. 21:23–27; Mk. 11:27–33)

20 ¹One day Jesus was in the Temple* area teaching the people. He was telling them the Good News.* The leading priests, teachers of the law, and older Jewish leaders came to talk to Jesus. ²They said, "Tell us what authority you have to do these things. Who gave you this authority?"

³Jesus answered, "I will ask you a question too. Tell me: ⁴When John* baptized* people, did his authority come from God or was it only from other people?"

⁵The priests, the teachers of the law, and the Jewish leaders all talked about this. They said to each other, "If we answer, 'John's baptism was from God,' then he will say, 'Then why did you not believe John?' ⁶But if we say that John's baptism was from someone else, the people will stone us to death. They all believe that John was a prophet.*" ⁷So they answered, "We don't know the answer."

⁸So Jesus said to them, "Then I will not tell you who gave me the authority to do these things."

God Sends His Son
(Mt 21:33–46; Mk. 12:1–12)

⁹Then Jesus told the people this story: "A man planted a vineyard.* He leased the land to some farmers. Then he went away for a long time. ¹⁰Later, it was time for the grapes to be picked. So the man sent a servant to those farmers so that they would give him his share of the grapes. But they beat the servant and sent him away with nothing. ¹¹So the man sent another servant. They beat this servant too and showed no respect for him. They sent the servant away with nothing. ¹²So

---

*ᵃ***19:46** Quote from Isa. 56:7.   *ᵇ***19:46** Quote from Jer. 7:11.

the man sent a third servant to the farmers. They hurt this servant badly and threw him out.

¹³"The owner of the vineyard said, 'What will I do now? I will send my son. I love my son very much. Maybe the farmers will respect my son.' ¹⁴When the farmers saw the son, they said to each other, 'This is the owner's son. This vineyard will be his. If we kill him, it will be ours.' ¹⁵So the farmers threw the son out of the vineyard and killed him.

"What will the owner of the vineyard do? ¹⁶He will come and kill those farmers. Then he will lease the land to some other farmers."

When the people heard this story, they said, "This should never happen!" ¹⁷But Jesus looked into their eyes and said, "Then what does this verse mean:

'The stone that the builders refused to accept
    became the cornerstone*'?   *Psalm 118:22*

¹⁸Everyone who falls on that stone will be broken. If that stone falls on you, it will crush you!"

¹⁹The teachers of the law and the leading priests heard this story that Jesus told. They knew it was about them. So they wanted to arrest Jesus right then, but they were afraid of what the people would do.

The Jewish Leaders Try to Trick Jesus
(Mt. 22:15–22; Mk. 12:13–17)

²⁰So the Jewish leaders waited for the right time to get Jesus. They sent some men to him, who pretended to be sincere. They wanted to find something wrong with what Jesus said. (If they found something wrong, then they could hand him over to the governor, who had the authority to arrest him.) ²¹So the men said to Jesus, "Teacher, we know that what you say and teach is true. It doesn't matter who is listening—you teach the same to all people. You always teach the truth about God's way. ²²Tell us, is it right for us to pay taxes to Caesar* or not?"

²³But Jesus knew that these men were trying to trick him. He said to them, ²⁴"Show me a silver coin.* Whose name and picture are on it?"

They said, "Caesar's."

²⁵He said to them, "Then give to Caesar what belongs to Caesar, and give to God what belongs to God."

²⁶The men were amazed at his wise answer. They could say nothing. They were not able to trick Jesus there in front of the people. He said nothing they could use against him.

Some Sadducees Try to Trick Jesus
(Mt. 22:23–33; Mk. 12:18–27)

²⁷Some Sadducees* came to Jesus. (Sadducees believe that people will not rise from death.) They asked him, ²⁸"Teacher,

Moses* wrote that if a married man dies and had no children, his brother must marry his widow. Then they will have children for the dead brother.*ᵃ ²⁹One time there were seven brothers. The first brother married a woman but died. He had no children. ³⁰Then the second brother married the woman, and he died. ³¹And the third brother married the woman, and he died. The same thing happened with all the other brothers. They all died and had no children. ³²The woman was the last to die. ³³But all seven brothers married her. So when people rise from death, whose wife will this woman be?"

³⁴Jesus said to the Sadducees, "On earth, people marry each other. ³⁵Some people will be worthy to be raised from death and live again after this life. In that life they will not marry. ³⁶In that life people are like angels and cannot die. They are children of God, because they have been raised from death. ³⁷Moses clearly showed that people are raised from death. When Moses wrote about the burning bush,ᵇ he said that the Lord is 'the God of Abraham,* the God of Isaac,* and the God of Jacob.'*ᶜ ³⁸So they were not still dead, because he is the God only of living people. Yes, to God they are all still living."

³⁹Some of the teachers of the law said, "Teacher, your answer was very good." ⁴⁰No one was brave enough to ask him another question.

Is the Christ David's Son or David's Lord?
(Mt. 22:41–46; Mk. 12:35–37)

⁴¹Then Jesus said, "Why do people say that the Christ* is the Son of David*? ⁴²In the book of Psalms, David* himself says,

'The Lord God said to my Lord:
  Sit by me at my right side,
⁴³   and I will put your enemies under your power.'ᵈ

Psalm 110:1

⁴⁴David calls the Christ 'Lord.' So how can the Christ also be David's son?"

Warning Against the Teachers of the Law
(Mt. 23:1–36; Mk. 12:38–40; Lk. 11:37–54)

⁴⁵While all the people were listening to Jesus, he said to his followers, ⁴⁶"Be careful of the teachers of the law. They like to walk around wearing clothes that look important. And they love for people to show respect to them in the marketplaces. They love to have the most important seats in the synagogues* and the places of honor at banquets. ⁴⁷But they cheat widows

ᵃ20:28 *if ... dead brother* See Deut. 25:5, 6. ᵇ20:37 *burning bush* See Ex. 3:1–12.
ᶜ20:37 *'the God of ... Jacob'* Words taken from Ex. 3:6. ᵈ20:43 *and I ... power* Literally, "until I make your enemies a footstool for your feet."

and take their homes. Then they try to make themselves look good by saying long prayers. God will punish them very much."

True Giving
(Mk. 12:41–44)

21 ¹Jesus looked up and saw some rich people putting their gifts to God into the Temple* collection box.ᵃ ²Then he saw a poor widow put two small copper coins into the box. ³He said, "This poor widow gave only two small coins. But the truth is, she gave more than all those rich people. ⁴They have plenty, and they gave only what they did not need. This woman is very poor, but she gave all she had to live on."

Jesus Warns About the Future
(Mt. 24:1–14; Mk. 13:1–13)

⁵Some of the followers were talking about the Temple.* They said, "This is a beautiful Temple, built with the best stones. Look at the many good gifts that have been offered to God."

⁶But Jesus said, "The time will come when all that you see here will be destroyed. Every stone of these buildings will be thrown down to the ground. Not one stone will be left on another."

⁷Some followers asked Jesus, "Teacher, when will these things happen? What will show us that it is time for these things to happen?"

⁸Jesus said, "Be careful! Don't be fooled. Many people will come using my name. They will say, 'I am the Christ*' and 'The right time has come!' But don't follow them. ⁹When you hear about wars and riots, don't be afraid. These things must happen first. Then the end will come later."

¹⁰Then Jesus said to them, "Nations will fight against other nations. Kingdoms will fight against other kingdoms. ¹¹There will be great earthquakes, sicknesses, and other bad things in many places. In some places there will be no food for the people to eat. Terrible things will happen, and amazing things will come from heaven to warn people.

¹²"But before all these things happen, people will arrest you and do bad things to you. They will judge you in their synagogues* and put you in jail. You will be forced to stand before kings and governors. They will do all these things to you because you follow me. ¹³But this will give you an opportunity to tell about me. ¹⁴Decide now not to worry about what you will say. ¹⁵I will give you the wisdom to say things that none of your enemies can answer. ¹⁶Even your parents, brothers, relatives, and friends will turn against you. They will have some of you killed.

ᵃ21:1 collection box A special box in the Jewish place for worship where people put their gifts to God.

[17]Everyone will hate you because you follow me. [18]But none of these things can really harm you. [19]You will save yourselves by continuing strong in your faith through all these things.

The Destruction of Jerusalem
(Mt. 24:15-21; Mk. 13:14-19)

[20]"You will see armies all around Jerusalem. Then you will know that the time for its destruction has come. [21]The people in Judea at that time should run away to the mountains. The people in Jerusalem must leave quickly. If you are near the city, don't go in! [22]The prophets* wrote many things about the time when God will punish his people. The time I am talking about is when all these things must happen. [23]During that time, it will be hard for women who are pregnant or have small babies, because very bad times will come to this land. God will be angry with these people. [24]Some of the people will be killed by soldiers. Others will be made prisoners and taken to all the different countries. The holy city of Jerusalem will be under the control of foreigners until their time is completed.

Don't Fear
(Mt. 24:29-31; Mk. 13:24-27)

[25]"Amazing things will happen to the sun, moon, and stars. And people all over the earth will be upset and confused by the noise of the sea and its crashing waves. [26]They will be afraid and worried about what will happen to the world. Everything in the sky will be changed. [27]Then people will see the Son of Man* coming in a cloud with power and great glory.* [28]When these things begin to happen, stand up tall and don't be afraid. Know that it is almost time for God to free you!"

My Words Will Live Forever
(Mt. 24:32-35; Mk. 13:28-31)

[29]Then Jesus told this story: "Look at all the trees. The fig tree is a good example. [30]When it turns green, you know that summer is near. [31]In the same way, when you see all these things happening, you will know that God's kingdom* is coming very soon.

[32]"I assure you that all these things will happen while some of the people of this time are still living. [33]The whole world, earth and sky, will be destroyed, but my words will last forever.

Be Ready All the Time

[34]"Be careful not to spend your time having parties and getting drunk or worrying about this life. If you do that, you won't be able to think straight, and the end might come when you are not ready. [35]It will come as a surprise to everyone on earth. [36]So be ready all the time. Pray that you will be able to get

through all these things that will happen and stand safe before the Son of Man.'"

37During the day Jesus taught the people in the Temple* area. At night he went out of the city and stayed all night on the Mount of Olives.* 38Every morning all the people got up early to go listen to Jesus at the Temple.

The Jewish Leaders Plan to Kill Jesus
(Mt. 26:1–5, 14–16; Mk. 14:1–2, 10–11; Jn. 11:45–53)

22 1It was almost time for the Jewish Festival of Unleavened Bread,* called the Passover.* 2The leading priests and teachers of the law wanted to kill Jesus. But they were trying to find a quiet way to do it, because they were afraid of what the people would do.

Judas Agrees to Help Jesus' Enemies
(Mt. 26:14–16; Mk. 14:10–11)

3One of Jesus' twelve apostles* was named Judas Iscariot. Satan* entered him, 4and he went and talked with the leading priests and some of the soldiers who guarded the Temple.* He talked to them about a way to hand Jesus over to them. 5The priests were very happy about this. They promised to give Judas money for doing this. 6He agreed. Then he waited for the best time to hand him over to them. He wanted to do it when no one was around to see it.

The Passover Meal
(Mt. 26:17–25; Mk. 14:12–21; Jn. 13:21–30)

7The Day of Unleavened Bread*a* came. This was the day when the Jews always killed the lambs for the Passover.* 8Jesus said to Peter and John, "Go and prepare the Passover meal for us to eat."

9They said to him, "Where do you want us to prepare the meal?"

He said to them, 10"When you go into the city, you will see a man carrying a jar of water. Follow him. He will go into a house. 11Tell the owner of the house, 'The Teacher asks that you please show us the room where he and his followers can eat the Passover meal.' 12Then the owner will show you a large room upstairs that is ready for us. Prepare the meal there."

13So Peter and John left. Everything happened the way Jesus said. So they prepared the Passover meal.

The Lord's Supper
(Mt. 26:26–30; Mk. 14:22–26; 1 Cor. 11:23–25)

14The time came for them to eat the Passover* meal. Jesus and the apostles* were together at the table. 15Jesus said to them, "I wanted very much to eat this Passover meal with you

a22:7 Day of Unleavened Bread Same as Passover.

before I die. [16]I will never eat another Passover meal until it is given its full meaning in God's kingdom."

[17]Then Jesus took a cup of wine. He gave thanks to God for it and said, "Take this cup and give it to everyone here. [18]I will never drink wine again until God's kingdom comes."

[19]Then he took some bread and thanked God for it. He broke off some pieces, gave them to the apostles and said, "This bread is my body that I am giving for you. Eat this to remember me." [20]In the same way, after supper, Jesus took the cup of wine and said, "This wine represents the new agreement* from God to his people. It will begin when my blood is poured out for you."[a]

Who Will Turn Against Jesus?

[21]Jesus said, "But here on this table is the hand of the one who will hand me over to my enemies. [22]The Son of Man* will do what God has planned. But it will be very bad for the one who hands over the Son of Man to be killed."

[23]Then the apostles* asked each other, "Which one of us would do that?"

Be Like a Servant

[24]Later, the apostles* began to argue about which one of them was the most important. [25]But Jesus said to them, "The kings of the world rule over their people, and those who have authority over others want to be called 'the great providers for the people.' [26]But you must not be like that. The one with the most authority among you should act as if he is the least important. The one who leads should be like one who serves. [27]Who is more important: the one serving or the one sitting at the table being served? Everyone thinks it's the one being served, right? But I have been with you as the one who serves.

[28]"You men have stayed with me through many struggles. [29]So I give you authority to rule with me in the kingdom the Father has given me. [30]You will eat and drink at my table in that kingdom. You will sit on thrones and judge the twelve tribes of Israel.[b]

Peter Will Be Tested and Fail
(Mt. 26:31-35; Mk. 14:27-31; Jn. 13:36-38)

[31]"Satan* has asked to test you men like a farmer tests his wheat. O Simon, Simon,[c] [32]I have prayed that you will not lose your faith! Help your brothers be stronger when you come back to me."

[33]But Peter said to Jesus, "Lord, I am ready to go to jail with you. I will even die with you!"

---

[a]22:20 A few Greek copies do not have Jesus' words in the last part of verse 19 and all of verse 20. [b]22:30 Israel First, Israel was the people descended from Jacob (see "Israel" in the Word List), but the name is also used in Scripture to mean all of God's people. [c]22:31 Simon Simon's other name was Peter.

³⁴But Jesus said, "Peter, before the rooster crows tomorrow morning, you will say you don't know me. You will say this three times."

Be Ready for Trouble

³⁵Then Jesus said to the apostles,* "Remember when I sent you out without money, a bag, or sandals? Did you need anything?"

The apostles said, "No."

³⁶Jesus said to them, "But now if you have money or a bag, carry that with you. If you don't have a sword, sell your coat and buy one. ³⁷The Scriptures* say,

'People said he was a criminal.'   *Isaiah 53:12*

This Scripture must happen. It was written about me, and it is happening now."

³⁸The followers said, "Look, Lord, here are two swords."

Jesus said to them, "That's enough."ᵃ

Jesus Prays Alone
(Mt. 26:36–46; Mk. 14:32–42)

³⁹⁻⁴⁰Jesus left the city and went to the Mount of Olives.* His followers went with him. (He went there often.) He said to his followers, "Pray for strength against temptation."

⁴¹Then Jesus went about 50 steps away from them. He knelt down and prayed, ⁴²"Father, if you are willing, please don't make me drink from this cup.ᵇ But do what you want, not what I want." ⁴³Then an angel from heaven came to help him. ⁴⁴Jesus was full of pain; he struggled hard in prayer. Sweat dripped from his face like drops of blood falling to the ground.ᶜ ⁴⁵When he finished praying, he went to his followers. He found them asleep, worn out from their grieving. ⁴⁶Jesus said to them, "Why are you sleeping? Get up and pray for strength against temptation."

Jesus Is Arrested
(Mt. 26:47–56; Mk. 14:43–50; Jn. 18:3–11)

⁴⁷While Jesus was speaking, a crowd came up. It was led by Judas, one of the twelve apostles.* He came over to Jesus to kiss him.

⁴⁸But Jesus said to him, "Judas, are you using the kiss of friendship to hand over the Son of Man* to his enemies?" ⁴⁹The followers of Jesus were standing there too. They saw what was happening and said to Jesus, "Lord, should we use our swords?" ⁵⁰And one of them did use his sword. He cut off the right ear of the servant of the high priest.*

ᵃ**22:38** *"That's enough"* Or, "Enough of that!" meaning, "Don't talk anymore about such things." ᵇ**22:42** *cup* A symbol of suffering. Jesus used the idea of drinking from a cup to mean accepting the suffering he would face in the terrible events that were soon to come. ᶜ**22:44** Some Greek copies do not have verses 43 and 44.

⁵¹Jesus said, "Stop!" Then he touched the servant's ear and healed him.

⁵²Jesus spoke to the group that came to arrest him. They were the leading priests, the older Jewish leaders, and the Jewish soldiers. He said to them, "Why did you come out here with swords and clubs? Do you think I am a criminal? ⁵³I was with you every day in the Temple* area. Why didn't you try to arrest me there? But this is your time—the time when darkness rules."

Peter Is Afraid to Say He Knows Jesus
(Mt. 26:57–58, 69–75; Mk. 14:53–54, 66–72; Jn. 18:12–18, 25–27)

⁵⁴They arrested Jesus and took him away to the house of the high priest.* Peter followed Jesus but stayed back at a distance. ⁵⁵The soldiers started a fire in the middle of the yard and sat together. Peter sat with them. ⁵⁶A servant girl saw him sitting there. She could see because of the light from the fire. She looked closely at Peter's face. Then she said, "This man was also with Jesus."

⁵⁷But Peter said this was not true. He said, "Lady, I don't know him." ⁵⁸A short time later, someone else saw Peter and said, "You are also one of them."

But Peter said, "Man, I am not!"

⁵⁹About an hour later, another man said, "It's true. I'm sure this man was with him, because he is from Galilee."

⁶⁰But Peter said, "Man, I don't know what you are talking about!"

Immediately, while he was still speaking, a rooster crowed. ⁶¹Then the Lord turned and looked into Peter's eyes. And Peter remembered what the Lord had said, "Before the rooster crows in the morning, you will say three times that you don't know me." ⁶²Then Peter went outside and cried bitterly.

The Guards Treat Jesus Badly
(Mt. 26:67–68; Mk. 14:65)

⁶³The men guarding Jesus made fun of him and beat him. ⁶⁴They covered his eyes so that he could not see them. Then they hit him and said, "Be a prophet*a* and tell us who hit you!" ⁶⁵And they shouted all kinds of insults at him.

Jesus Before the Jewish Leaders
(Mt. 26:59–66; Mk. 14:55–64; Jn. 18:19–24)

⁶⁶The next morning, the older leaders of the people, the leading priests, and the teachers of the law came together. They led Jesus away to their high council. ⁶⁷They said, "If you are the Christ,* then tell us that you are."

Jesus said to them, "If I tell you I am the Christ, you will not believe me. ⁶⁸And if I ask you, you will not answer. ⁶⁹But

a **22:64** *prophet* A prophet often knows things that are hidden to other people.

beginning now, the Son of Man* will sit at the right side of God All-Powerful.'"

⁷⁰They all said, "Then are you the Son of God?" Jesus said to them, "You are right in saying that I am."

⁷¹They said, "Why do we need witnesses now? We all heard what he said!"

Governor Pilate Questions Jesus
(Mt. 27:1–2, 11–14; Mk. 15:1–5; Jn. 18:28–38)

23 ¹Then the whole group stood up and led Jesus away to Pilate.* ²They began to accuse Jesus and said to Pilate, "We caught this man trying to change the thinking of our people. He says we should not pay taxes to Caesar.* He calls himself the Christ,* a king."

³Pilate asked Jesus, "Are you the king of the Jews?"

Jesus answered, "Yes, what you say is true."

⁴Pilate said to the leading priests and the people, "I find nothing wrong with this man."

⁵But they kept on saying, "His teaching is causing trouble all over Judea. He began in Galilee, and now he is here!"

Pilate Sends Jesus to Herod

⁶Pilate heard this and asked if Jesus was from Galilee. ⁷He learned that Jesus was under Herod's* authority. Herod was in Jerusalem at that time, so Pilate sent Jesus to him.

⁸When Herod saw Jesus, he was very happy. He had heard all about him and had wanted to meet him for a long time. Herod wanted to see a miracle,* so he was hoping that Jesus would do one. ⁹He asked him many questions, but Jesus said nothing. ¹⁰The leading priests and teachers of the law were standing there shouting things against Jesus. ¹¹Then Herod and his soldiers laughed at him. They made fun of him by dressing him in clothes like kings wear. Then Herod sent him back to Pilate. ¹²In the past Pilate and Herod had always been enemies. But on that day they became friends.

Pilate Tries but Fails to Free Jesus
(Mt. 27:15–26; Mk. 15:6–15; Jn. 18:39–19:16)

¹³Pilate called all the people together with the leading priests and the Jewish leaders. ¹⁴He said to them, "You brought this man to me. You said he was trying to change the people. But I judged him before you all and have not found him guilty of the things you say he has done. ¹⁵Herod* didn't find him guilty either. He sent him back to us. Look, he has done nothing bad enough for the death penalty. ¹⁶So, after I punish him a little, I will let him go free." ¹⁷ᵃ

ᵃ**23:17** A few Greek copies add verse 17: "Every year at the Passover festival, Pilate had to release one prisoner to the people."

¹⁸But they all shouted, "Kill him! Let Barabbas go free!" ¹⁹(Barabbas was a man who was in jail for starting a riot in the city and for murder.)

²⁰Pilate wanted to let Jesus go free. So again Pilate told them that he would let him go. ²¹But they shouted again, "Kill him! Kill him on a cross!"

²²A third time Pilate said to the people, "Why? What wrong has he done? He is not guilty. I can find no reason to kill him. So I will let him go free after I punish him a little."

²³But the people continued to shout. They demanded that Jesus be killed on a cross. Their shouting got so loud that ²⁴Pilate decided to give them what they wanted. ²⁵They wanted Barabbas to go free—the one who was in jail for starting a riot and for murder. Pilate let Barabbas go free. And he handed Jesus over to be killed. This is what the people wanted.

Jesus Is Nailed to a Cross
(Mt. 27:32–44; Mk. 15:21–32; Jn. 19:17–19)

²⁶The soldiers led Jesus away. At that same time there was a man from Cyrene named Simon coming into the city from the fields. The soldiers forced him to carry Jesus' cross and walk behind him.

²⁷A large crowd followed Jesus. Some of the women were sad and crying. They felt sorry for him. ²⁸But Jesus turned and said to the women, "Women of Jerusalem, don't cry for me. Cry for yourselves and for your children too. ²⁹The time is coming when people will say, 'The women who cannot have babies are the ones God has blessed. It's really a blessing that they have no children to care for.' ³⁰Then the people will say to the mountains, 'Fall on us!' They will say to the hills, 'Cover us!'ᵃ ³¹If this can happen to someone who is good, what will happen to those who are guilty?ᵇ"

³²There were also two criminals led out with Jesus to be killed. ³³They were led to a place called "The Skull." There the soldiers nailed Jesus to the cross. They also nailed the criminals to crosses beside Jesus—one on the right and the other on the left.

³⁴Jesus said, "Father, forgive them. They don't know what they are doing."ᶜ

The soldiers threw dice to divide Jesus' clothes between them. ³⁵The people stood there watching everything. The Jewish leaders laughed at Jesus. They said, "If he is God's Chosen One, the Christ,* then let him save himself. He saved others, didn't he?"

³⁶Even the soldiers laughed at Jesus and made fun of him. They came and offered him some sour wine. ³⁷They said, "If you

---

ᵃ**23:30** Quote from Hos. 10:8. ᵇ**23:31** If this can happen ... guilty Literally, "If they do these things in the green tree, what will happen in the dry?" ᶜ**23:34** Jesus said, "Father ... doing" Some early copies of Luke do not have these words.

are the king of the Jews, save yourself!" 38(At the top of the cross these words were written: "THIS IS THE KING OF THE JEWS.")

39One of the criminals hanging there began to shout insults at Jesus: "Aren't you the Christ? Then save yourself, and save us too!"

40But the other criminal stopped him. He said, "You should fear God. All of us will die soon. 41You and I are guilty. We deserve to die because we did wrong. But this man has done nothing wrong." 42Then he said, "Jesus, remember me when you begin ruling as king!"

43Then Jesus said to him, "I promise you, today you will be with me in paradise.*"

Jesus Dies
(Mt. 27:45–56; Mk. 15:33–41; Jn. 19:28–30)

44It was about noon, but it turned dark throughout the land until three o'clock in the afternoon, 45because the sun stopped shining. The curtain* in the Temple* was torn into two pieces. 46Jesus shouted, "Father, I put my life in your hands!"*a* After Jesus said this, he died.

47The army officer* there saw what happened. He praised God, saying, "I know this man was a good man!"

48Many people had come out of the city to see all this. When they saw it, they felt very sorry and left. 49The people who were close friends of Jesus were there. Also, there were some women who had followed Jesus from Galilee. They all stood far away from the cross and watched these things.

Jesus Is Buried
(Mt. 27:57–61; Mk. 15:42–47; Jn. 19:38–42)

50-51A man named Joseph was there from the Jewish town of Arimathea. He was a good man, who lived the way God wanted. He was waiting for God's kingdom* to come. Joseph was a member of the Jewish council. But he did not agree when the other Jewish leaders decided to kill Jesus. 52He went to Pilate and asked for the body of Jesus. 53He took the body down from the cross and wrapped it in cloth. Then he put it in a tomb* that was dug in a wall of rock. This tomb had never been used before. 54It was late on Preparation day.* When the sun went down, the Sabbath* day would begin.

55The women who had come from Galilee with Jesus followed Joseph. They saw the tomb. Inside they saw where he put Jesus' body. 56Then they left to prepare some sweet-smelling spices to put on the body.

On the Sabbath day they rested, as commanded in the law of Moses.*

---

a23:46 "I put … hands" Literally, "I put my spirit in your hands." Quote from Ps. 31:5.

News That Jesus Has Risen From Death
(Mt. 28:1–10; Mk. 16:1–8; Jn. 20:1–10)

24 ¹Very early Sunday morning, the women came to the tomb* where Jesus' body was laid. They brought the sweet-smelling spices they had prepared. ²They saw that the heavy stone that covered the entrance had been rolled away. ³They went in, but they did not find the body of the Lord Jesus. ⁴They did not understand this. While they were wondering about it, two men in shining clothes stood beside them. ⁵The women were very afraid. They bowed down with their faces to the ground. The men said to them, "Why are you looking for a living person here? This is a place for dead people. ⁶Jesus is not here. He has risen from death. Do you remember what he said in Galilee? ⁷He said the Son of Man* must be handed over to the control of sinful men, be killed on a cross, and rise from death on the third day." ⁸Then the women remembered what Jesus had said.

⁹The women left the tomb and went to the eleven apostles* and the other followers. They told them everything that happened at the tomb. ¹⁰These women were Mary Magdalene, Joanna, Mary, the mother of James, and some others. They told the apostles everything that happened. ¹¹But the apostles did not believe what they said. It sounded like nonsense. ¹²But Peter got up and ran to the tomb to see. He looked in, but he saw only the cloth that Jesus' body had been wrapped in. It was just lying there. Peter went away to be alone, wondering what had happened.*a*

On The Road to Emmaus
(Mk. 16:12–13)

¹³That same day two of Jesus' followers were going to a town named Emmaus. It is about seven miles*b* from Jerusalem. ¹⁴They were talking about everything that had happened. ¹⁵While they were talking, discussing these things, Jesus himself came near and walked with them. ¹⁶(But the two men were not allowed to recognize Jesus.) ¹⁷He asked them, "What's this I hear you discussing with each other as you walk?"

The two men stopped, their faces looking very sad. ¹⁸The one named Cleopas said, "You must be the only person in Jerusalem who doesn't know what has just happened there."

¹⁹Jesus said, "What are you talking about?"

They said, "It's about Jesus, the one from Nazareth. To God and to all the people he was a great prophet.* He said and did many powerful things. ²⁰But our leaders and the leading priests handed him over to be judged and killed. They nailed him to a

---

*a*24:12 A few Greek copies do not have this verse.   *b*24:13 *seven miles* Literally, "seven stadious," almost 12 km.

cross. ²¹We were hoping that he would be the one to free Israel.* But then all this happened.

"And now something else: It has been three days since he was killed, ²²but today some of our women told us an amazing thing. Early this morning they went to the tomb* where the body of Jesus was laid. ²³But they did not find his body there. They came and told us they had seen some angels in a vision.* The angels told them Jesus was alive! ²⁴So some of our group went to the tomb too. It was just like the women said. They saw the tomb, but they did not see Jesus."

²⁵Then Jesus said to the two men, "You are foolish and slow to realize what is true. You should believe everything the prophets said. ²⁶The prophets said the Christ* must suffer these things before he begins his time of glory.*" ²⁷Then he began to explain everything that had been written about himself in the Scriptures.* He started with the books of Moses* and then he talked about what the prophets had said about him.

²⁸They came near the town of Emmaus, and Jesus acted as if he did not plan to stop there. ²⁹But they wanted him to stay. They begged him, "Stay with us. It's almost night. There's hardly any daylight left." So he went in to stay with them.

³⁰Joining them at the supper table, Jesus took some bread and gave thanks. Then he broke some off and gave it to them. ³¹Just then the men were allowed to recognize him. But when they saw who he was, he disappeared. ³²They said to each other, "When he talked to us on the road, it felt like a fire burning in us. How exciting it was when he explained to us the true meaning of the Scriptures!"

³³So the two men got up then and went back to Jerusalem. There they found the followers of Jesus meeting together. The eleven apostles* and the people with them ³⁴said, "The Lord really has risen from death! He showed himself to Simon."

³⁵Then the two men told what had happened on the road. They talked about how they recognized Jesus when he shared the bread with them.

Jesus Appears to His Followers
(Mt. 28:16–20; Mk. 16:14–18; Jn. 20:19–23; Acts 1:6–8)

³⁶While the two men were saying these things to the other followers, Jesus himself came and stood among them. He said to them, "Peace be with you."

³⁷This surprised the followers. They were afraid. They thought they were seeing a ghost. ³⁸But Jesus said, "Why are you troubled? Why do you doubt what you see? ³⁹Look at my hands and my feet. It's really me. Touch me. You can see that I have a living body; a ghost does not have a body like this."

⁴⁰After Jesus told them this, he showed them his hands and his feet. ⁴¹The followers were amazed and very, very happy to see that Jesus was alive. They still could not believe what they

saw. He said to them, "Do you have any food here?" ⁴²They gave him a piece of cooked fish. ⁴³While the followers watched, he took the fish and ate it.

⁴⁴Jesus said to them, "Remember when I was with you before? I said that everything written about me must happen— everything written in the law of Moses,* the books of the prophets,* and the Psalms."

⁴⁵Then Jesus helped the followers understand these Scriptures* about him. ⁴⁶Jesus said to them, "It is written that the Christ* would be killed and rise from death on the third day. ⁴⁷⁻⁴⁸You saw these things happen—you are witnesses. You must go and tell people that they must change and turn to God, which will bring them his forgiveness. You must start from Jerusalem and tell this message in my name to the people of all nations. ⁴⁹Remember that I will send you the one my Father promised. Stay in the city until you are given that power from heaven."

Jesus Goes Back to Heaven
(Mk. 16:19–20; Acts 1:9–11)

⁵⁰Jesus led his followers out of Jerusalem almost to Bethany. He raised his hands and blessed his followers. ⁵¹While he was blessing them, he was separated from them and carried into heaven. ⁵²They worshiped him and went back to Jerusalem very happy. ⁵³They stayed at the Temple* all the time, praising God.

John

Christ Comes to the World

1 ¹Before the world began, the Word*ᵃ* was there. The Word was with God, and the Word was God. ²He was there with God in the beginning. ³Everything was made through him, and nothing was made without him. ⁴In him there was life, and that life was a light for the people of the world. ⁵The light*ᵇ* shines in the darkness,* and the darkness has not defeated*ᶜ* it.

⁶There was a man named John,* who was sent by God. ⁷He came to tell people about the light. Through him all people could hear about the light and believe. ⁸John was not the light. But he came to tell people about the light. ⁹The true light was coming into the world. This is the true light that gives light to all people.

¹⁰The Word was already in the world. The world was made through him, but the world did not know him. ¹¹He came to the world that was his own. And his own people did not accept him. ¹²But some people did accept him. They believed in him, and he gave them the right to become children of God. ¹³They became God's children, but not in the way babies are usually born. It was not because of any human desire or plan. They were born from God himself.

¹⁴The Word became a man and lived among us. We saw his divine greatness*—the greatness that belongs to the only Son of the Father. The Word was full of grace* and truth. ¹⁵John told people about him. He said, "This is the one I was talking about when I said, 'The one who is coming after me is greater than I am, because he was living before I was even born.'"

¹⁶Yes, the Word was full of grace and truth, and from him we all received one blessing after another.*ᵈ* ¹⁷That is, the law was given to us through Moses,* but grace and truth came through Jesus Christ. ¹⁸No one has ever seen God. The only Son is the one who has shown us what God is like. He is himself God and is very close to the Father.*ᵉ*

---

*ᵃ*1:1 *Word* The Greek word is *"logos,"* meaning any kind of communication. It could be translated "message." Here, it means Christ—the way God told the world about himself. Also in verses 10, 14, 16. *ᵇ*1:5 *light* Meaning Christ, the Word, who brought to the world understanding about God. Also in verse 7. *ᶜ*1:5 *defeated* Or, "understood." *ᵈ*1:16 *one blessing after another* Literally, "grace in place of grace." *ᵉ*1:18 *The only Son ... Father* Or, more literally, "The only God, who is very close to the Father, has shown us what he is like." Some other Greek copies say, "The only Son is very close to the Father and has shown us what he is like."

John Tells About the Christ
(Mt. 3:1–12; Mk. 1:1–8; Lk. 3:1–9, 15–17)

¹⁹The Jewish leaders in Jerusalem sent some priests and Levites* to John* to ask him, "Who are you?" He told them the truth. ²⁰Without any hesitation he said openly and plainly, "I am not the Christ.*"

²¹They asked him, "Then who are you? Are you Elijah*?"

He answered, "No, I am not Elijah."

They asked, "Are you the Prophet*ᵃ?"

He answered, "No, I am not the Prophet."

²²Then they said, "Who are you? Tell us about yourself. Give us an answer to tell the people who sent us. What do you say about yourself?"

²³John told them the words of the prophet* Isaiah:

"I am the voice of someone shouting in the desert:
  'Make a straight road ready for the Lord.'"   *Isaiah 40:3*

²⁴These Jews were sent from the Pharisees.* ²⁵They said to John, "You say you are not the Christ. You say you are not Elijah or the Prophet. Then why do you baptize* people?"

²⁶John answered, "I baptize people with water. But there is someone here with you that you don't know. ²⁷He is the one who is coming later. I am not good enough to be the slave who unties the strings on his sandals."

²⁸These things all happened at Bethany on the other side of the Jordan River. This is where John was baptizing people.

Jesus, the Lamb of God

²⁹The next day John saw Jesus coming toward him and said, "Look, the Lamb* of God! He takes away the sins of the world! ³⁰This is the one I was talking about when I said, 'There is a man coming after me who is greater than I am, because he was living even before I was born.' ³¹I did not know who he was. But I came baptizing people with water so that Israel* could know that Jesus is the Christ.*"

³²⁻³³Then John said, "I also did not know who the Christ was. But the one who sent me to baptize* with water told me, 'You will see the Spirit* come down and rest on a man. He is the one who will baptize with the Holy Spirit.' I have seen this happen. I saw the Spirit come down from heaven like a dove and rest on this man. ³⁴So this is what I tell people: 'He is the Son of God.'"

The First Followers of Jesus

³⁵The next day John was there again and had two of his followers with him. ³⁶He saw Jesus walking by and said, "Look, the Lamb* of God!"

ᵃ**1:21** *Prophet* They probably meant the prophet that God told Moses he would send. See Deut. 18:15–19. Also in verse 24.

³⁷The two followers heard him say this, so they followed Jesus. ³⁸Jesus turned and saw the two men following him. He asked, "What do you want?"

They said, "*Rabbi*, where are you staying?" ("*Rabbi*" means "Teacher.")

³⁹He answered, "Come with me and you will see." So the two men went with him. They saw the place where he was staying, and they stayed there with him that day. It was about four o'clock.

⁴⁰These men followed Jesus after they had heard about him from John. One of them was Andrew, the brother of Simon Peter. ⁴¹The first thing Andrew did was to go and find his brother Simon. Andrew said to him, "We have found the Messiah." ("Messiah" means "Christ.*")

⁴²Then Andrew brought Simon to Jesus. Jesus looked at him and said, "You are Simon, the son of John. You will be called Cephas." ("Cephas" means "Peter.ᵃ")

⁴³The next day Jesus decided to go to Galilee. He met Philip and said to him, "Follow me." ⁴⁴Philip was from the town of Bethsaida, the same as Andrew and Peter. ⁴⁵Philip found Nathanael and told him, "We have found the man that Moses* wrote about in the law. The prophets* wrote about him too. He is Jesus, the son of Joseph. He is from Nazareth."

⁴⁶But Nathanael said to Philip, "Nazareth! Can anything good come from Nazareth?"

Philip answered, "Come and see."

⁴⁷Jesus saw Nathanael coming toward him and said, "This man coming is a true Israelite,* one you can trust.ᵇ"

⁴⁸Nathanael asked, "How do you know me?"

Jesus answered, "I saw you when you were under the fig tree, before Philip told you about me."

⁴⁹Then Nathanael said, "Teacher, you are the Son of God. You are the King of Israel.*"

⁵⁰Jesus said to him, "Do you believe this just because I said I saw you under the fig tree? You will see much greater things than that!" ⁵¹Then he said, "Believe me when I say that you will all see heaven open. You will see 'angels of God going up and coming down'ᶜ on the Son of Man.*"

The Wedding at Cana

2 ¹Two days later there was a wedding in the town of Cana in Galilee, and Jesus' mother was there. ²Jesus and his followers were also invited. ³At the wedding there was not enough wine, so Jesus' mother said to him, "They have no more wine."

ᵃ**1:42** *Peter* The Greek name "Peter," like the Aramaic name "Cephas," means "rock."
ᵇ**1:47** *you can trust* Literally, "in whom is no deceit." In the Old Testament, Israel's other name, Jacob, is explained with words that mean "deceit" or "trickery," for which he was well-known. See Gen. 27:35, 36. ᶜ**1:51** Quote from Gen. 28:12.

⁴Jesus answered, "Dear woman, why are you telling me this? It is not yet time for me to begin my work."

⁵His mother said to the servants, "Do what he tells you."

⁶There were six large stone waterpots there that were used by the Jews in their washing ceremonies.ᵃ Each one held about 20 or 30 gallons.ᵇ

⁷Jesus said to the servants, "Fill the waterpots with water." So they filled them to the top.

⁸Then he said to them, "Now dip out some water and take it to the man in charge of the feast."

So they did what he said. ⁹Then the man in charge tasted it, but the water had become wine. He did not know where the wine had come from, but the servants who brought the water knew. He called the bridegroom* ¹⁰and said to him, "People always serve the best wine first. Later, when the guests are drunk, they serve the cheaper wine. But you have saved the best wine until now."

¹¹This was the first of all the miraculous signs* Jesus did. He did it in the town of Cana in Galilee. By this he showed his divine greatness,* and his followers believed in him.

¹²Then Jesus went to the town of Capernaum.* His mother and brothers and his followers went with him. They all stayed there a few days.

Jesus at the Temple
(Mt. 21:12–13; Mk. 11:15–17; Lk. 19:45–46)

¹³It was almost time for the Jewish Passover,* so Jesus went to Jerusalem. ¹⁴There in the Temple* area he saw men selling cattle, sheep, and doves. He saw others sitting at tables, exchanging and trading people's money. ¹⁵Jesus made a whip with some pieces of rope. Then he forced all these men and the sheep and cattle to leave the Temple area. He turned over the tables of the money traders and scattered their money. ¹⁶Then he said to those who were selling pigeons, "Take these things out of here! Don't make my Father's house a place for buying and selling!"

¹⁷When this happened, his followers remembered what was written in the Scriptures*:

"My strong devotion to your Temple will destroy me."

Psalm 69:9

¹⁸Some Jews said to Jesus, "Show us a miracle* as a sign from God. Prove that you have the right to do these things."

¹⁹Jesus answered, "Destroy this temple and I will build it again in three days."

ᵃ**2:6** *washing ceremonies* The Jews had religious rules about washing in special ways before eating, before worshiping in the Temple, and at other special times. ᵇ**2:6** *20 or 30 gallons* Literally, "2 or 3 *metretas*," about 80 to 120 liters.

²⁰They answered, "People worked 46 years to build this Temple! Do you really believe you can build it again in three days?"

²¹But the temple Jesus meant was his own body. ²²After he was raised from death, his followers remembered that he had said this. So they believed the Scriptures, and they believed the words Jesus said.

²³Jesus was in Jerusalem for the Passover festival. Many people believed in him because they saw the miraculous signs* he did. ²⁴But Jesus did not trust them, because he knew how all people think. ²⁵He did not need anyone to tell him what a person was like. He already knew.

Jesus and Nicodemus

3 ¹There was a man named Nicodemus, one of the Pharisees.* He was an important Jewish leader. ²One night he came to Jesus and said, "Teacher, we know that you are a teacher sent from God. No one can do these miraculous signs* that you do unless they have God's help."

³Jesus answered, "I assure you, everyone must be born again. Anyone who is not born again cannot be in God's kingdom.*"

⁴Nicodemus said, "How can a man who is already old be born again? Can he go back into his mother's womb and be born a second time?"

⁵Jesus answered, "Believe me when I say that everyone must be born from water and the Spirit.* Anyone who is not born from water and the Spirit cannot enter God's kingdom. ⁶The only life people get from their human parents is physical. But the new life that the Spirit gives a person is spiritual. ⁷Don't be surprised that I told you, 'You must be born again.' ⁸The wind blows wherever it wants to. You hear it, but you don't know where it is coming from or where it is going. It is the same with everyone who is born from the Spirit."

⁹Nicodemus asked, "How is all this possible?"

¹⁰Jesus said, "You are an important teacher of Israel,* and you still don't understand these things? ¹¹The truth is, we talk about what we know. We tell about what we have seen. But you people don't accept what we tell you. ¹²I have told you about things here on earth, but you do not believe me. So I'm sure you will not believe me if I tell you about heavenly things! ¹³The only one who has ever gone up to heaven is the one who came down from heaven—the Son of Man.*

¹⁴"Moses lifted up the snake in the desert.ᵃ It is the same with the Son of Man. He must be lifted up too. ¹⁵Then everyone who believes in him can have eternal life."ᵇ

ᵃ3:14 **Moses lifted … desert** When God's people were dying from snake bites, God told Moses to put a brass snake on a pole for them to look at and be healed. See Num. 21:4–9.
ᵇ3:15 Some scholars think that this quotation of Jesus' words continues in verses 16–21.

¹⁶Yes, God loved the world so much that he gave his only Son, so that everyone who believes in him would not be lost but have eternal life. ¹⁷God sent his Son into the world. He did not send him to judge the world guilty, but to save the world through him. ¹⁸People who believe in God's Son are not judged guilty. But people who do not believe are already judged, because they have not believed in God's only Son. ¹⁹They are judged by this fact: The light[a] has come into the world. But they did not want light. They wanted darkness,* because they were doing evil things. ²⁰Everyone who does evil hates the light. They will not come to the light, because the light will show all the bad things they have done. ²¹But anyone who follows the true way comes to the light. Then the light will show that whatever they have done was done through God.

Jesus and John the Baptizer

²²After this, Jesus and his followers went into the area of Judea. There he stayed with his followers and baptized* people. ²³John was also baptizing people in Aenon, a place near Salim with plenty of water. People were going there to be baptized. ²⁴This was before John was put in prison.

²⁵Some of John's followers had an argument with another Jew about religious washing.[b] ²⁶Then they came to John and said, "Teacher, remember the man who was with you on the other side of the Jordan River? He is the one you were telling everyone about. He is also baptizing people, and many are going to him."

²⁷John answered, "A person can receive only what God gives. ²⁸You yourselves heard me say, 'I am not the Christ.* I am only the one God sent to prepare the way for him.' ²⁹The bride always belongs to the bridegroom.* The friend who helps the bridegroom just waits and listens. He is happy just to hear the bridegroom talk. That's how I feel now. I am so happy that he is here. ³⁰He must become more and more important, and I must become less important.

The One Who Comes From Heaven

³¹"The one who comes from above is greater than all others. The one who is from the earth belongs to the earth. He talks about things that are on the earth. But the one who comes from heaven is greater than all others. ³²He tells what he has seen and heard, but people don't accept what he says. ³³Whoever accepts what he says has given proof that God speaks the truth. ³⁴God sent him, and he tells people what God says. God gives him the Spirit* fully. ³⁵The Father loves the Son and has given

---

[a]3:19 *light* This means Christ, the Word, who brought to the world understanding about God. [b]3:25 *religious washing* The Jews had religious rules about washing in special ways before eating, before worshiping in the Temple, and at other special times.

him power over everything. [36]Whoever believes in the Son has eternal life. But those who do not obey the Son will never have that life. They cannot get away from God's anger."

Jesus Talks to a Woman in Samaria

4 [1]Jesus learned that the Pharisees* had heard the report that he was making and baptizing* more followers than John. [2](But really, Jesus himself did not baptize anyone; his followers baptized people for him.) [3]So he left Judea and went back to Galilee. [4]On the way to Galilee he had to go through the country of Samaria.

[5]In Samaria Jesus came to the town called Sychar, which is near the field that Jacob gave to his son Joseph. [6]Jacob's well was there. Jesus was tired from his long trip, so he sat down beside the well. It was about noon. [7]A Samaritan* woman came to the well to get some water, and Jesus said to her, "Please give me a drink." [8]This happened while his followers were in town buying some food.

[9]The woman answered, "I am surprised that you ask me for a drink! You are a Jew and I am a Samaritan woman!" (Jews are not friends with Samaritans.[a])

[10]Jesus answered, "You don't know what God can give you. And you don't know who I am, the one who asked you for a drink. If you knew, you would have asked me, and I would have given you living water."

[11]The woman said, "Sir, where will you get that living water? The well is very deep, and you have nothing to get water with. [12]Are you greater than Jacob* our father? He is the one who gave us this well. He drank from it himself, and his sons and all his animals drank from it too."

[13]Jesus answered, "Everyone who drinks this water will be thirsty again. [14]But anyone who drinks the water I give will never be thirsty again. The water I give people will be like a spring flowing inside them. It will bring them eternal life."

[15]The woman said to Jesus, "Sir, give me this water. Then I will never be thirsty again and won't have to come back here to get more water."

[16]Jesus told her, "Go get your husband and come back."

[17]The woman answered, "But I have no husband."

Jesus said to her, "You are right to say you have no husband. [18]That's because, although you have had five husbands, the man you live with now is not your husband. That much was the truth."

[19]The woman said, "Sir, I can see that you are a prophet.[b] [20]Our fathers worshiped on this mountain. But you Jews say that Jerusalem is the place where people must worship."

---

[a]4:9 Jews are not friends with Samaritans Or, "Jews don't use things that Samaritans have used." [b]4:19 prophet A prophet often knows things that are hidden to other people.

²¹Jesus said, "Believe me, woman! The time is coming when you will not have to be in Jerusalem or on this mountain to worship the Father. ²²You Samaritans worship something you don't understand. We Jews understand what we worship, since salvation comes from the Jews. ²³But the time is coming when the true worshipers will worship the Father in spirit and truth. In fact, that time is now here. And these are the kind of people the Father wants to be his worshipers. ²⁴God is spirit. So the people who worship him must worship in spirit and truth."

²⁵The woman said, "I know that the Messiah is coming." (Messiah is the one called Christ.*) "When he comes, he will explain everything to us."

²⁶Then Jesus said, "He is talking to you now—I'm the Messiah."

²⁷Just then Jesus' followers came back from town. They were surprised because they saw Jesus talking with a woman. But none of them asked, "What do you want?" or "Why are you talking with her?"

²⁸Then the woman left her water jar and went back to town. She told the people there, ²⁹"A man told me everything I have ever done. Come see him. Maybe he is the Christ." ³⁰So the people left the town and went to see Jesus.

³¹While the woman was in town, Jesus' followers were begging him, "Teacher, eat something!"

³²But Jesus answered, "I have food to eat that you know nothing about."

³³So the followers asked themselves, "Did someone already bring him some food?"

³⁴Jesus said, "My food is to do what the one who sent me wants me to do. My food is to finish the work that he gave me to do. ³⁵When you plant, you always say, 'Four more months to wait before we gather the grain.' But I tell you, open your eyes, and look at the fields. They are ready for harvesting now. ³⁶Even now, the people who harvest the crop are being paid. They are gathering crops for eternal life. So now the people who plant can be happy together with those who harvest. ³⁷It is true when we say, 'One person plants, but another person harvests the crop.' ³⁸I sent you to harvest a crop that you did not work for. Others did the work, and you get the profit from their work."

³⁹Many of the Samaritan people in that town believed in Jesus. They believed because of what the woman had told them about him. She had told them, "He told me everything I have ever done." ⁴⁰The Samaritans went to Jesus. They begged him to stay with them. So he stayed there two days. ⁴¹Many more people believed because of the things he said.

⁴²The people said to the woman, "First we believed in Jesus because of what you told us. But now we believe because we heard him ourselves. We know now that he really is the one who will save the world."

Jesus Heals an Official's Son
(Mt. 8:5–13; Lk. 7:1–10)

⁴³Two days later Jesus left and went to Galilee. ⁴⁴(Jesus had said before that a prophet* is not respected in his own country.) ⁴⁵When he arrived in Galilee, the people there welcomed him. They had been at the Passover* festival in Jerusalem and had seen everything he did there.

⁴⁶Jesus went to visit Cana in Galilee again. Cana is where he had changed the water into wine. One of the king's important officials lived in the city of Capernaum.* This man's son was sick. ⁴⁷The man heard that Jesus had come from Judea and was now in Galilee. So he went to Jesus and begged him to come to Capernaum and heal his son, who was almost dead. ⁴⁸Jesus said to him, "You people must see miraculous signs* and wonders* before you will believe in me."

⁴⁹The king's official said, "Sir, come before my little son dies."

⁵⁰Jesus answered, "Go. Your son will live."

The man believed what Jesus told him and went home. ⁵¹On the way home the man's servants came and met him. They said, "Your son is well."

⁵²The man asked, "What time did my son begin to get well?"

They answered, "It was about one o'clock yesterday when the fever left him."

⁵³The father knew that one o'clock was the same time that Jesus had said, "Your son will live." So the man and everyone in his house believed in Jesus.

⁵⁴That was the second miraculous sign that Jesus did after coming from Judea to Galilee.

Jesus Heals a Man at a Pool

5 ¹Later, Jesus went to Jerusalem for a special Jewish festival. ²In Jerusalem there is a pool with five covered porches. In Aramaic* it is called Bethzatha.ᵃ This pool is near the Sheep Gate. ³Many sick people were lying on the porches beside the pool. Some of them were blind, some were crippled, and some were paralyzed.ᵇ ⁴ᶜ ⁵One of the men lying there had been sick for 38 years. ⁶Jesus saw him lying there and knew that he had been sick for a very long time. So he asked him, "Do you want to be well?"

⁷The sick man answered, "Sir, there is no one to help me get into the water when it starts moving. I try to be the first one into the water. But when I try, someone else always goes in before I can."

ᵃ5:2 *Bethzatha* Also called Bethsaida or Bethesda, a pool of water north of the Temple in Jerusalem. ᵇ5:3 At the end of verse 3 some Greek copies add "and they waited for the water to move." ᶜ5:4 A few later copies add verse 4: "Sometimes an angel of the Lord came down to the pool and shook the water. After the angel did this, the first person to go into the pool was healed from any sickness he had."

⁸Then Jesus said, "Stand up! Pick up your mat and walk." ⁹Immediately the man was well. He picked up his mat and started walking.

The day all this happened was a Sabbath* day. ¹⁰So some Jews said to the man who had been healed, "Today is the Sabbath. It is against our law for you to carry your mat on the Sabbath day."

¹¹But he answered, "The man who made me well told me, 'Pick up your mat and walk.'"

¹²They asked him, "Who is the man who told you to pick up your mat and walk?"

¹³But the man who had been healed did not know who it was. There were many people there, and Jesus had left.

¹⁴Later, Jesus found the man at the Temple* and said to him, "See, you are well now. But stop sinning or something worse may happen to you!"

¹⁵Then the man left and went back to the Jews who questioned him. He told them that Jesus was the one who made him well.

¹⁶Jesus was doing all this on the Sabbath day. So these Jews began trying to make him stop. ¹⁷But he said to them, "My Father never stops working, and so I work too."

¹⁸This made them try harder to kill him. They said, "First this man was breaking the law about the Sabbath day. Then he said that God is his Father! He is making himself equal with God!"

Jesus Has God's Authority

¹⁹But Jesus answered, "I assure you that the Son can do nothing alone. He does only what he sees his Father doing. The Son does the same things that the Father does. ²⁰The Father loves the Son and shows him everything he does. This man was healed. But the Father will show the Son greater things than this to do. Then you will all be amazed. ²¹The Father raises the dead and gives them life. In the same way, the Son gives life to those he wants to.

²²"Also, the Father judges no one. He has given the Son power to do all the judging. ²³God did this so that all people will respect the Son the same as they respect the Father. Anyone who does not respect the Son does not respect the Father. He is the one who sent the Son.

²⁴"I assure you, anyone who hears what I say and believes in the one who sent me has eternal life. They will not be judged guilty. They have already left death and have entered into life. ²⁵Believe me, an important time is coming. That time is already here. People who are dead will hear the voice of the Son of God. And those who listen will live. ²⁶Life comes from the Father himself. So the Father has also allowed the Son to give life. ²⁷And the Father has given him the power to judge all people because he is the Son of Man.*

²⁸"Don't be surprised at this. A time is coming when all people who are dead and in their graves will hear his voice. ²⁹Then they will come out of their graves. Those who did good in this life will rise and have eternal life. But those who did evil will rise to be judged guilty.

³⁰"I can do nothing alone. I judge only the way I am told. And my judgment is right, because I am not trying to please myself. I want only to please the one who sent me.

Jesus Says More to the Jewish Leaders

³¹"If I tell people about myself, they cannot be sure that what I say is true. ³²But there is someone else who tells people about me, and I know that what he says about me is true.

³³"You sent men to John,* and he told you what is true. ³⁴I don't need anyone to tell people about me, but I remind you of what John said so that you can be saved. ³⁵John was like a lamp that burned and gave light, and you were happy to enjoy his light for a while.

³⁶"But I have a proof about myself that is greater than anything John said. The things I do are my proof. These are what my Father gave me to do. They show that the Father sent me. ³⁷And the Father who sent me has given proof about me himself. But you have never heard his voice. You have never seen what he looks like. ³⁸The Father's teaching does not live in you, because you don't believe in the one the Father sent. ³⁹You carefully study the Scriptures.* You think that they give you eternal life. These same Scriptures tell about me! ⁴⁰But you refuse to come to me to have that life.

⁴¹"I don't want praise from you or any other human. ⁴²But I know you—I know that you have no love for God. ⁴³I have come from my Father and speak for him, but you don't accept me. But when other people come speaking only for themselves, you accept them. ⁴⁴You like to have praise from each other. But you never try to get the praise that comes from the only God. So how can you believe? ⁴⁵Don't think that I will be the one to stand before the Father and accuse you. Moses* is the one to accuse you. And he is the one you hoped would save you. ⁴⁶If you really believed Moses, you would believe me, because he wrote about me. ⁴⁷But you don't believe what he wrote, so you can't believe what I say."

Jesus Feeds More Than 5000
(Mt. 14:13–21; Mk. 6:30–44; Lk. 9:10–17)

6 ¹Later, Jesus went across Lake Galilee (also known as Lake Tiberias). ²A great crowd of people followed him because they saw the miraculous signs* he did in healing the sick. ³Jesus went up on the side of the hill and sat there with his followers. ⁴It was almost the time for the Jewish Passover* festival.

⁵Jesus looked up and saw a crowd of people coming toward him. He said to Philip, "Where can we buy enough bread for all these people to eat?" ⁶He asked Philip this question to test him. Jesus already knew what he planned to do.

⁷Philip answered, "We would all have to work a month to buy enough bread for each person here to have only a little piece!"

⁸Another follower there was Andrew, the brother of Simon Peter. Andrew said, ⁹"Here is a boy with five loaves of barley bread and two little fish. But that is not enough for so many people."

¹⁰Jesus said, "Tell everyone to sit down." This was a place with a lot of grass, and about 5000 men sat down there. ¹¹Jesus took the loaves of bread and gave thanks for them. Then he gave them to the people who were waiting to eat. He did the same with the fish. He gave them as much as they wanted.

¹²They all had plenty to eat. When they finished, Jesus said to his followers, "Gather the pieces of fish and bread that were not eaten. Don't waste anything." ¹³So they gathered up the pieces that were left. The people had started eating with only five loaves of barley bread. But the followers filled twelve large baskets with the pieces of food that were left.

¹⁴The people saw this miraculous sign that Jesus did and said, "He must be the Prophet[a] who is coming into the world."

¹⁵Jesus knew that the people planned to come get him and make him their king. So he left and went into the hills alone.

Jesus Walks on Water
(Mt. 14:22–27; Mk. 6:45–52)

¹⁶That evening Jesus' followers went down to the lake. ¹⁷It was dark now, and Jesus had not yet come back to them. They got into a boat and started going across the lake to Capernaum. ¹⁸The wind was blowing very hard. The waves on the lake were becoming bigger. ¹⁹They rowed the boat about three or four miles.[b] Then they saw Jesus. He was walking on the water, coming to the boat. They were afraid. ²⁰But he said to them, "Don't be afraid. It's me." ²¹When he said this, they were glad to take him into the boat. And then the boat reached the shore at the place they wanted to go.

The People Look for Jesus

²²The next day came. Some people had stayed on the other side of the lake. They knew that Jesus did not go with his followers in the boat. They knew that the followers had left in the boat alone. And they knew it was the only boat that was there. ²³But then some boats from Tiberias came and landed near the place where the people had eaten the day before. This was

---

[a] 6:14 Prophet They probably meant the prophet that God told Moses he would send. See Deut. 18:15–19. [b] 6:19 three or four miles Literally, "25 or 30 stadia," about 5 or 6 km.

where they had eaten the bread after the Lord gave thanks. ²⁴The people saw that Jesus and his followers were not there now. So they got into the boats and went to Capernaum* to find Jesus.

Jesus, the Bread of Life

²⁵The people found Jesus on the other side of the lake. They asked him, "Teacher, when did you come here?"

²⁶He answered, "Why are you looking for me? Is it because you saw miraculous signs*? The truth is, you are looking for me because you ate the bread and were satisfied. ²⁷But earthly food spoils and ruins. So don't work to get that kind of food. But work to get the food that stays good and gives you eternal life. The Son of Man* will give you that food. He is the only one qualified by God the Father to give it to you."

²⁸The people asked Jesus, "What does God want us to do?"

²⁹Jesus answered, "The work God wants you to do is this: to believe in the one he sent."

³⁰So the people asked, "What miraculous sign will you do for us? If we can see you do a miracle, then we will believe you. What will you do? ³¹Our ancestors* were given manna* to eat in the desert. As the Scriptures* say, 'He gave them bread from heaven to eat.'ᵃ"

³²Jesus said, "I can assure you that Moses* was not the one who gave your people bread from heaven. But my Father gives you the true bread from heaven. ³³God's bread is the one who comes down from heaven and gives life to the world."

³⁴The people said, "Sir, from now on give us bread like that."

³⁵Then Jesus said, "I am the bread that gives life. No one who comes to me will ever be hungry. No one who believes in me will ever be thirsty. ³⁶I told you before that you have seen me, and still you don't believe. ³⁷The Father gives me my people. Every one of them will come to me. I will always accept them. ³⁸I came down from heaven to do what God wants, not what I want. ³⁹I must not lose anyone God has given me. But I must raise them up on the last day. This is what the one who sent me wants me to do. ⁴⁰Everyone who sees the Son and believes in him has eternal life. I will raise them up on the last day. This is what my Father wants."

⁴¹Some Jews began to complain about Jesus because he said, "I am the bread that comes down from heaven." ⁴²They said, "This is Jesus. We know his father and mother. He is only Joseph's son. How can he say, 'I came down from heaven'?"

⁴³But Jesus said, "Stop complaining to each other. ⁴⁴The Father is the one who sent me, and he is the one who brings people to me. I will raise them up on the last day. Anyone the Father does not bring to me cannot come to me. ⁴⁵It is written

ᵃ6:31 Quote from Ps. 78:24.

in the prophets*: 'God will teach all the people.'[a] People listen to the Father and learn from him. They are the ones who come to me. 46I don't mean that there is anyone who has seen the Father. The only one who has ever seen the Father is the one who came from God. He has seen the Father.

47"I can assure you that anyone who believes has eternal life. 48I am the bread that gives life. 49Your ancestors ate the manna God gave them in the desert, but it didn't keep them from dying. 50Here is the bread that comes down from heaven. Whoever eats this bread will never die. 51I am the living bread that came down from heaven. Whoever eats this bread will live forever. This bread is my body. I will give my body so that the people in the world can have life."

52Then the Jews began to argue among themselves. They said, "How can this man give us his body to eat?"

53Jesus said, "Believe me when I say that you must eat the body of the Son of Man, and you must drink his blood. If you don't do this, you have no real life. 54Those who eat my body and drink my blood have eternal life. I will raise them up on the last day. 55My body is true food, and my blood is true drink. 56Those who eat my body and drink my blood live in me, and I live in them.

57"The Father sent me. He lives, and I live because of him. So everyone who eats me will live because of me. 58I am not like the bread that your ancestors ate. They ate that bread, but they still died. I am the bread that came down from heaven. Whoever eats this bread will live forever."

59Jesus said all this while he was teaching in the synagogue* in the city of Capernaum.*

Many Followers Leave Jesus

60When Jesus' followers heard this, many of them said, "This teaching is hard. Who can accept it?"

61Jesus already knew that his followers were complaining about this. So he said, "Is this teaching a problem for you? 62Then what will you think when you see the Son of Man* going up to where he came from? 63It is the Spirit* that gives life. The body is of no value for that. But the things I have told you are from the Spirit, so they give life. 64But some of you don't believe." (Jesus knew the people who did not believe. He knew this from the beginning. And he knew the one who would hand him over to his enemies.) 65Jesus said, "That is why I said, 'Anyone the Father does not help to come to me cannot come.'"

66After Jesus said these things, many of his followers left and stopped following him.

67Jesus asked the twelve apostles,* "Do you want to leave too?"

a6:45 Quote from Isa. 54:13.

⁶⁸Simon Peter answered him, "Lord, where would we go? You have the words that give eternal life. ⁶⁹We believe in you. We know that you are the Holy One from God."

⁷⁰Then Jesus answered, "I chose all twelve of you. But one of you is a devil." ⁷¹He was talking about Judas, the son of Simon Iscariot. Judas was one of the twelve apostles, but later he would hand Jesus over to his enemies.

Jesus and His Brothers

7 ¹After this, Jesus traveled around the country of Galilee. He did not want to travel in Judea, because the Jewish leaders there wanted to kill him. ²It was time for the Jewish Festival of Shelters.* ³So his brothers said to him, "You should leave here and go to the festival in Judea. Then your followers there can see the miracles* you do. ⁴If you want to be well-known, you must not hide what you do. So show yourself to the world. Let them see these things you do." ⁵Jesus' brothers said this because even they did not believe in him.

⁶Jesus said to them, "The right time for me has not yet come, but any time is right for you to go. ⁷The world cannot hate you. But the world hates me, because I tell the people in the world that they do evil things. ⁸So you go to the festival. I will not go now, because the right time for me has not yet come." ⁹After Jesus said this, he stayed in Galilee.

¹⁰So his brothers left to go to the festival. After they left, Jesus went too, but he did not let people see him. ¹¹At the festival the Jewish leaders were looking for him. They said, "Where is that man?"

¹²There was a large group of people there. Many of them were talking secretly to each other about Jesus. Some people said, "He is a good man." But others said, "No, he fools the people." ¹³But no one was brave enough to talk about him openly. They were afraid of the Jewish leaders.

Jesus Teaches in Jerusalem

¹⁴When the festival was about half finished, Jesus went to the Temple* area and began to teach. ¹⁵The Jews were amazed and said, "This man has never studied in school. How did he learn so much?"

¹⁶Jesus answered, "What I teach is not my own. My teaching comes from the one who sent me. ¹⁷People who really want to do what God wants will know that my teaching comes from God. They will know that this teaching is not my own. ¹⁸If I taught my own ideas, I would just be trying to get honor for myself. But if I am trying to bring honor to the one who sent me, I can be trusted. Anyone doing that is not going to lie. ¹⁹Moses* gave you the law,* right? But you don't obey that law. If you do, then why are you trying to kill me?"

²⁰The people answered, "A demon* is making you crazy! We are not trying to kill you."

²¹Jesus said to them, "I did one miracle* on a Sabbath* day, and you were all surprised. ²²But you obey the law Moses gave you about circumcision*—and sometimes you do it on a Sabbath day. (Really, Moses is not the one who gave you circumcision. It came from our ancestors* who lived before Moses.) Yes, you often circumcise baby boys on a Sabbath day. ²³This shows that someone can be circumcised on a Sabbath day to obey the law of Moses. So why are you angry with me for healing a person's whole body on the Sabbath day? ²⁴Stop judging by the way things look. Be fair and judge by what is really right."

The People Wonder if Jesus Is the Christ

²⁵Then some of the people who lived in Jerusalem said, "This is the man they are trying to kill. ²⁶But he is teaching where everyone can see and hear him. And no one is trying to stop him from teaching. Maybe the leaders have decided that he really is the Christ.* ²⁷But when the real Christ comes, no one will know where he comes from. And we know where this man's home is."

²⁸Jesus was still teaching in the Temple* area when he said loudly, "Do you really know me and where I am from? I am here, but not by my own decision. I was sent by one who is very real. But you don't know him. ²⁹I know him because I am from him. He is the one who sent me."

³⁰When Jesus said this, the people tried to grab him. But no one was able even to touch him, because the right time for him had not yet come. ³¹But many of the people believed in Jesus. They said, "We are waiting for the Christ to come. When he comes, will he do more miraculous signs* than this man has done?"

The Jewish Leaders Try to Arrest Jesus

³²The Pharisees* heard what the people were saying about Jesus. So the leading priests and the Pharisees sent some Temple* police to arrest him. ³³Then Jesus said, "I will be with you a little while longer. Then I will go back to the one who sent me. ³⁴You will look for me, but you will not find me. And you cannot come where I am."

³⁵These Jews said to each other, "Where will this man go that we cannot find him? Will he go to the Greek cities where our people live? Will he teach the Greek people there? ³⁶He says, 'You will look for me, but you will not find me.' He also says, 'You cannot come where I am.' What does this mean?"

Jesus Talks About the Holy Spirit

³⁷The last day of the festival came. It was the most important day. On that day Jesus stood up and said with a loud

voice, "Whoever is thirsty may come to me and drink. [38]If anyone believes in me, rivers of living water will flow out from their heart. That is what the Scriptures* say." [39]Jesus was talking about the Spirit.* The Spirit had not yet been given to people, because Jesus had not yet been raised to glory.* But later, those who believed in Jesus would receive the Spirit.

The People Argue About Jesus

[40]The people heard these things that Jesus said. Some of them said, "This man really is the Prophet.[a]"

[41]Other people said, "He is the Christ.*"

And others said, "The Christ* will not come from Galilee. [42]The Scriptures* say that he will come from the family of David.* And they say that he will come from Bethlehem, the town where David lived." [43]So the people did not agree with each other about Jesus. [44]Some of the people wanted to arrest him. But no one tried to do it.

The Jewish Leaders Refuse to Believe

[45]The Temple* police went back to the leading priests and the Pharisees.* The priests and the Pharisees asked, "Why didn't you bring Jesus?"

[46]The Temple police answered, "We have never heard anyone say such amazing things!"

[47]The Pharisees answered, "So he has fooled you too! [48]You don't see any of the leaders or any of us Pharisees believing in him, do you? [49]But those people out there know nothing about the law.* They are under God's curse!"

[50]But Nicodemus was there in that group. He was the one who had gone to see Jesus before.[b] He said, [51]"Our law will not let us judge anyone without first hearing them and finding out what they have done."

[52]The Jewish leaders answered, "You must be from Galilee too! Study the Scriptures.* You will find nothing about a prophet[c] coming from Galilee." [53]Then they all left and went home.

The Woman Caught in Adultery

8 [1]Jesus went to the Mount of Olives.* [2]Early in the morning he went back to the Temple* area. The people all came to him, and he sat and taught them.

[3]The teachers of the law and the Pharisees* brought a woman they had caught in bed with a man who was not her husband. They forced her to stand in front of the people. [4]They

---

*a*7:40 *Prophet* They probably meant the prophet that God told Moses he would send. See Deut. 18:15–19. *b*7:50 *He was the one ... before* The story about Nicodemus going and talking to Jesus is in Jn. 3:1–21. *c*7:52 *a prophet* Two early Greek copies have "the Prophet," which would mean the "prophet like Moses" mentioned in Deut. 18:15. In Acts 3:22 and 7:37 this is understood to be the Messiah, as in verse 40 above.

said to Jesus, "Teacher, this woman was caught in the act of adultery.* ⁵The law of Moses* commands us to stone to death any such woman. What do you say we should do?"

⁶They were saying this to trick Jesus. They wanted to catch him saying something wrong so that they could have a charge against him. But Jesus stooped down and started writing on the ground with his finger. ⁷The Jewish leaders continued to ask him their question. So he stood up and said, "Anyone here who has never sinned should throw the first stone at her." ⁸Then Jesus stooped down again and wrote on the ground.

⁹When they heard this, they began to leave one by one. The older men left first, and then the others. Jesus was left alone with the woman standing there in front of him. ¹⁰He looked up again and said to her, "Where did they all go? Did no one judge you guilty?"

¹¹She answered, "No one, sir."

Then Jesus said, "I don't judge you either. You can go now, but don't sin again."ᵃ

Jesus Is the Light of the World

¹²Later, Jesus talked to the people again. He said, "I am the light of the world. Whoever follows me will never live in darkness.* They will have the light that gives life."

¹³But the Pharisees* said to Jesus, "When you talk about yourself, you are the only one to say that these things are true. So we cannot accept what you say."

¹⁴Jesus answered, "Yes, I am saying these things about myself. But people can believe what I say, because I know where I came from. And I know where I am going. But you don't know where I came from or where I am going. ¹⁵You judge the way people judge other people. I don't judge anyone. ¹⁶But if I judge, my judging is true, because when I judge I am not alone. The Father who sent me is with me. ¹⁷Your own law says that when two witnesses say the same thing, you must accept what they say. ¹⁸I am one of the witnesses who speaks about myself. And the Father who sent me is my other witness."

¹⁹The people asked, "Where is your father?"

Jesus answered, "You don't know me or my Father. But if you knew me, you would know my Father too." ²⁰Jesus said these things while he was teaching in the Temple* area, near the room where the Temple offerings were kept. But no one arrested him, because the right time for him had not yet come.

Some Jews Don't Understand Jesus

²¹Again, Jesus said to the people, "I will leave you. You will look for me, but you will die in your sin. You cannot come where I am going."

ᵃ8:11 The oldest and best Greek copies do not have verses 7:53–8:11. Other copies have this section in different places.

²²So the Jewish leaders asked themselves, "Will he kill himself? Is that why he said, 'You cannot come where I am going'?"

²³But Jesus said to them, "You people are from here below, but I am from above. You belong to this world, but I don't belong to this world. ²⁴I told you that you would die in your sins. Yes, if you don't believe that I AM,ª you will die in your sins."

²⁵They asked, "Then who are you?"

Jesus answered, "I am what I have told you from the beginning. ²⁶I have much more I could say to judge you. But I tell people only what I have heard from the one who sent me, and he speaks the truth."

²⁷They did not understand who he was talking about. He was telling them about the Father. ²⁸So he said to them, "You will lift up the Son of Man.* Then you will know that I AM. You will know that these things I do are not by my own authority. You will know that I say only what the Father has taught me. ²⁹The one who sent me is with me. I always do what pleases him. So he has not left me alone." ³⁰While he was saying these things, many people believed in him.

Jesus Talks About Freedom From Sin

³¹So Jesus said to the Jews who believed in him, "If you continue to accept and obey my teaching, you are really my followers. ³²You will know the truth, and the truth will make you free."

³³They answered, "We are Abraham's* descendants. And we have never been slaves. So why do you say that we will be free?"

³⁴Jesus said, "The truth is, everyone who sins is a slave—a slave to sin. ³⁵A slave does not stay with a family forever. But a son belongs to the family forever. ³⁶So if the Son makes you free, you are really free. ³⁷I know you are Abraham's descendants. But you want to kill me, because you don't want to accept my teaching. ³⁸I am telling you what my Father has shown me. But you do what your father has told you."

³⁹They said, "Our father is Abraham."

Jesus said, "If you were really Abraham's descendants, you would do what Abraham did. ⁴⁰I am someone who has told you the truth I heard from God. But you are trying to kill me. Abraham did nothing like that. ⁴¹So you are doing what your own father did."

But they said, "We are not like children who never knew who their father was. God is our Father. He is the only Father we have."

⁴²Jesus said to them, "If God were really your Father, you would love me. I came from God, and now I am here. I did not come by my own authority. God sent me. ⁴³You don't understand these things I say, because you cannot accept my

---

ª**8:24** *I AM* This is like the name of God used in the Old Testament. See Isa. 41:4; 43:10; Ex. 3:14. However, it can also mean "I am he (the Christ)." Also in verse 28.

teaching. ⁴⁴Your father is the devil. You belong to him. You want to do what he wants. He was a murderer from the beginning. He was always against the truth. There is no truth in him. He is like the lies he tells. Yes, the devil is a liar. He is the father of lies.

⁴⁵"I am telling you the truth, and that's why you don't believe me. ⁴⁶Can any of you prove that I am guilty of sin? If I tell the truth, why don't you believe me? ⁴⁷Whoever belongs to God accepts what he says. But you don't accept what God says, because you don't belong to God."

Jesus Talks About Himself and Abraham

⁴⁸The Jews there answered, "We say you are a Samaritan.* We say a demon* is making you crazy! Are we not right when we say this?"

⁴⁹Jesus answered, "I have no demon in me. I give honor to my Father, but you give no honor to me. ⁵⁰I am not trying to get honor for myself. There is one who wants this honor for me. He is the judge. ⁵¹I promise you, whoever continues to obey my teaching will never die."

⁵²The Jews said to Jesus, "Now we know that you have a demon in you! Even Abraham* and the prophets* died. But you say, 'Whoever obeys my teaching will never die.' ⁵³Do you think you are greater than our father Abraham? He died, and so did the prophets. Who do you think you are?"

⁵⁴Jesus answered, "If I give honor to myself, that honor is worth nothing. The one who gives me honor is my Father. And you say that he is your God. ⁵⁵But you don't really know him. I know him. If I said I did not know him, I would be a liar like you. But I do know him, and I obey what he says. ⁵⁶Your father* Abraham was very happy that he would see the day when I came. He saw that day and was happy."

⁵⁷The Jews said to Jesus, "What? How can you say you have seen Abraham? You are not even 50 years old!"

⁵⁸Jesus answered, "The fact is, before Abraham was born, I AM.^a" ⁵⁹When he said this, they picked up stones to throw at him. But Jesus hid, and then he left the Temple* area.

Jesus Heals a Man Born Blind

9 ¹While Jesus was walking, he saw a man who had been blind since the time he was born. ²Jesus' followers asked him, "Teacher, why was this man born blind? Whose sin made it happen? Was it his own sin or that of his parents?"

³Jesus answered, "It was not any sin of this man or his parents that caused him to be blind. He was born blind so that he could be used to show what great things God can do. ⁴While it

---

^a8:58 *I AM* This is like the name of God used in the Old Testament. See Isa. 41:4; 43:10; Ex. 3:14. However, it can also mean "I am he (the Christ)."

is daytime, we must continue doing the work of the one who sent me. The night is coming, and no one can work at night. ⁵While I am in the world, I am the light of the world."

⁶After Jesus said this, he spit on the dirt, made some mud and put it on the man's eyes. ⁷Jesus told him, "Go and wash in Siloam pool." (Siloam means "Sent.") So the man went to the pool, washed and came back. He was now able to see.

⁸His neighbors and some others who had seen him begging said, "Look! Is this the same man who always sits and begs?"

⁹Some people said, "Yes! He is the one." But others said, "No, he can't be the same man. He only looks like him."

So the man himself said, "I am that same man."

¹⁰They asked, "What happened? How did you get your sight?"

¹¹He answered, "The man they call Jesus made some mud and put it on my eyes. Then he told me to go to Siloam and wash. So I went there and washed. And then I could see."

¹²They asked him, "Where is this man?"

He answered, "I don't know."

Some Pharisees Have Questions

¹³Then the people brought the man to the Pharisees.* ¹⁴The day Jesus had made mud and healed the man's eyes was a Sabbath* day. ¹⁵So the Pharisees asked the man, "How did you get your sight?"

He answered, "He put mud on my eyes. I washed, and now I can see."

¹⁶Some of the Pharisees said, "That man does not obey the law about the Sabbath day. So he is not from God."

Others said, "But someone who is a sinner cannot do these miraculous signs.*" So they could not agree with each other.

¹⁷They asked the man again, "Since it was your eyes he healed, what do you say about him?"

He answered, "He is a prophet.*"

¹⁸The Jewish leaders still did not believe that this really happened to the man—that he was blind and was now healed. But later they sent for his parents. ¹⁹They asked them, "Is this your son? You say he was born blind. So how can he see?"

²⁰His parents answered, "We know that this man is our son. And we know that he was born blind. ²¹But we don't know why he can see now. We don't know who healed his eyes. Ask him. He is old enough to answer for himself." ²²They said this because they were afraid of the Jewish leaders. The leaders had already decided that they would punish anyone who said Jesus was the Christ.* They would stop them from coming to the synagogue.* ²³That is why his parents said, "He is old enough. Ask him."

²⁴So the Jewish leaders called the man who had been blind. They told him to come in again. They said, "You should honor God by telling the truth. We know that this man is a sinner."

²⁵The man answered, "I don't know if he is a sinner. But I do know this: I was blind, and now I can see."

²⁶They asked, "What did he do to you? How did he heal your eyes?"

²⁷He answered, "I have already told you that. But you would not listen to me. Why do you want to hear it again? Do you want to be his followers too?"

²⁸At this they shouted insults at him and said, "You are his follower, not us! We are followers of Moses.* ²⁹We know that God spoke to Moses. But we don't even know where this man comes from!"

³⁰The man answered, "This is really strange! You don't know where he comes from, but he healed my eyes. ³¹We all know that God does not listen to sinners, but he will listen to anyone who worships and obeys him. ³²This is the first time we have ever heard of anyone healing the eyes of someone born blind. ³³This man must be from God. If he were not from God, he could not do anything like this."

³⁴The Jewish leaders answered, "You were born full of sin! Are you trying to teach us?" And they told the man to get out of the synagogue and to stay out.

Spiritual Blindness

³⁵When Jesus heard that they had forced the man to leave, he found him and asked him, "Do you believe in the Son of Man*?"

³⁶The man said, "Tell me who he is, sir, so I can believe in him."

³⁷Jesus said to him, "You have already seen him. The Son of Man is the one talking with you now."

³⁸The man answered, "Yes, I believe, Lord!" Then he bowed and worshiped Jesus.

³⁹Jesus said, "I came into this world so that the world could be judged. I came so that people who are blind*a* could see. And I came so that people who think they see would become blind."

⁴⁰Some of the Pharisees* were near Jesus. They heard him say this. They asked, "What? Are you saying that we are blind too?"

⁴¹Jesus said, "If you were really blind, you would not be guilty of sin. But you say that you see, so you are still guilty."

The Shepherd and His Sheep

10 ¹Jesus said, "It is certainly true that when a man enters the sheep pen, he should use the gate. If he climbs in some other way, he is a robber. He is trying to steal the sheep. ²But the man who takes care of the sheep enters through the gate. He is the shepherd. ³The man who guards the gate opens the gate for the shepherd. And the sheep listen to the voice of

---

a 9:39 people who are blind Jesus is talking about people who are spiritually blind (without understanding), not physically blind.

the shepherd. He calls his own sheep, using their names, and he leads them out. [4]He brings all of his sheep out. Then he goes ahead of them and leads them. The sheep follow him, because they know his voice. [5]But sheep will never follow someone they don't know. They will run away from him, because they don't know his voice."

[6]Jesus told the people this story, but they did not understand what it meant.

Jesus Is the Good Shepherd

[7]So Jesus said again, "I assure you, I am the gate for the sheep. [8]All those who came before me were thieves and robbers. The sheep did not listen to them. [9]I am the gate. Whoever enters through me will be saved. They will be able to come in and go out. They will find everything they need. [10]A thief comes to steal, kill, and destroy. But I came to give life—life that is full and good.

[11]"I am the good shepherd, and the good shepherd gives his life for the sheep. [12]The worker who is paid to keep the sheep is different from the shepherd. The paid worker does not own the sheep. So when he sees a wolf coming, he runs away and leaves the sheep alone. Then the wolf attacks the sheep and scatters them. [13]The man runs away because he is only a paid worker. He does not really care for the sheep.

[14-15]"I am the shepherd who cares for the sheep. I know my sheep just as the Father knows me. And my sheep know me just as I know the Father. I give my life for these sheep. [16]I have other sheep too. They are not in this flock here. I must lead them also. They will listen to my voice. In the future there will be one flock and one shepherd.[a] [17]The Father loves me because I give my life. I give my life so that I can get it back again. [18]No one takes my life away from me. I give my own life freely. I have the right to give my life, and I have the right to get it back again. This is what the Father told me."

[19]Again the Jews were divided over what Jesus was saying. [20]Many of them said, "A demon* has come into him and made him crazy. Why listen to him?"

[21]But others said, "These aren't the words of someone controlled by a demon. A demon cannot heal the eyes of a blind man."

The Jewish Leaders Against Jesus

[22]It was winter, and the time came for the Festival of Dedication[b] at Jerusalem. [23]Jesus was in the Temple* area at Solomon's Porch.* [24]The Jewish leaders gathered around him.

---

[a]**10:16** *I have other sheep … shepherd* Jesus means he has followers who are not Jews. See Jn. 11:52.   [b]**10:22** *Festival of Dedication* Hanukkah, a special week in December, when the Jewish people celebrated the rebuilding of the Jerusalem Temple in 165/164 B.C.

They said, "How long will you make us wonder about you? If you are the Christ,* then tell us clearly."

²⁵Jesus answered, "I told you already, but you did not believe. I do miracles* in my Father's name. These miracles show who I am. ²⁶But you do not believe, because you are not my sheep. ²⁷My sheep listen to my voice. I know them, and they follow me. ²⁸I give my sheep eternal life. They will never die, and no one can take them out of my hand. ²⁹My Father is the one who gave them to me, and he is greater than all.ᵃ No one can steal my sheep out of his hand. ³⁰The Father and I are one."

³¹Again the Jews there picked up stones to kill Jesus. ³²But he said to them, "The many wonderful things you have seen me do are from the Father. Which of these good things are you killing me for?"

³³They answered, "We are not killing you for any good thing you did. But you say things that insult God. You are only a man, but you say you are the same as God! That is why we are trying to kill you!"

³⁴Jesus answered, "It is written in your law that God said, 'I said you are gods.'ᵇ ³⁵This Scripture* called those people gods—the people who received God's message. And Scripture is always true. ³⁶So why do you accuse me of insulting God for saying, 'I am God's Son'? I am the one God chose and sent into the world. ³⁷If I don't do what my Father does, then don't believe what I say. ³⁸But if I do what my Father does, you should believe in what I do. You might not believe in me, but you should believe in the things I do. Then you will know and understand that the Father is in me and I am in the Father."

³⁹They tried to get Jesus again, but he escaped from them.

⁴⁰Then he went back across the Jordan River to the place where John* began his work of baptizing* people. Jesus stayed there, ⁴¹and many people came to him. They said, "John never did any miraculous signs,* but everything John said about this man is true." ⁴²And many people there believed in Jesus.

The Death of Lazarus

11 ¹There was a man named Lazarus who was sick. He lived in the town of Bethany, where Mary and her sister Martha lived. ²(Mary is the same woman who later put perfume on the Lord and wiped his feet with her hair.) Mary's brother was Lazarus, the man who was now sick. ³So Mary and Martha sent someone to tell Jesus, "Lord, your dear friend Lazarus is sick."

⁴When Jesus heard this he said, "The end of this sickness will not be death. No, this sickness is for the glory* of God. This has happened to bring glory to the Son of God." ⁵Jesus loved Martha and her sister and Lazarus. ⁶So when he heard

---

ᵃ**10:29** he ... than all Some Greek copies have "They are greater than all." ᵇ**10:34** Quote from Ps. 82:6.

that Lazarus was sick, he stayed where he was two more days [7]and then said to his followers, "We should go back to Judea."

[8]They answered, "But Teacher, those Jews there tried to stone you to death. That was only a short time ago. Now you want to go back there?"

[9]Jesus answered, "There are twelve hours of light in the day. Whoever walks in the day will not stumble and fall because they can see with the light from the sun.[a] [10]But whoever walks at night will stumble because there is no light."

[11]Then Jesus said, "Our friend Lazarus is now sleeping, but I am going there to wake him."

[12]The followers answered, "But Lord, if he can sleep, he will get well." [13]They thought Jesus meant that Lazarus was literally sleeping, but he really meant that Lazarus was dead.

[14]So then Jesus said plainly, "Lazarus is dead. [15]And I am glad I was not there. I am happy for you because now you will believe in me. We will go to him now."

[16]Then Thomas, the one called "Twin," said to the other followers, "We will go too. We will die there with Jesus."

Jesus in Bethany

[17]Jesus arrived in Bethany and found that Lazarus had already been dead and in the tomb* for four days. [18]Bethany was about two miles[b] from Jerusalem. [19]Many Jews had come to see Martha and Mary. They came to comfort them about their brother Lazarus.

[20]When Martha heard that Jesus was coming, she went out to greet him. But Mary stayed home. [21]Martha said to Jesus, "Lord, if you had been here, my brother would not have died. [22]But I know that even now God will give you anything you ask."

[23]Jesus said, "Your brother will rise and be alive again."

[24]Martha answered, "I know that he will rise to live again at the time of the resurrection* on the last day."

[25]Jesus said to her, "I am the resurrection. I am life. Everyone who believes in me will have life, even if they die. [26]And everyone who lives and believes in me will never really die. Martha, do you believe this?"

[27]Martha answered, "Yes, Lord. I believe that you are the Christ,* the Son of God. You are the one who was coming to the world."

Jesus Cries

[28]After Martha said these things, she went back to her sister Mary. She talked to Mary alone and said, "The Teacher is here. He is asking for you." [29]When Mary heard this, she stood up and went quickly to Jesus. [30]He had not yet come into the village.

---

[a]**11:9** *from the sun* Literally, "of this world." [b]**11:18** *two miles* Literally, "15 stadia," almost 3 km.

He was still at the place where Martha met him. ³¹The Jews who were in the house comforting Mary saw her get up and leave quickly. They thought she was going to the tomb* to cry there. So they followed her. ³²Mary went to the place where Jesus was. When she saw him, she bowed at his feet and said, "Lord, if you had been here, my brother would not have died."

³³When Jesus saw Mary crying and the people with her crying too, he was very upset and deeply troubled. ³⁴He asked, "Where did you put him?"

They said, "Lord, come and see."

³⁵Jesus cried.

³⁶And the Jews said, "Look! He loved Lazarus very much!"

³⁷But some of them said, "Jesus healed the eyes of the blind man. Why didn't he help Lazarus and stop him from dying?"

Jesus Raises Lazarus From Death

³⁸Again feeling very upset, Jesus came to the tomb.* It was a cave with a large stone covering the entrance. ³⁹He said, "Move the stone away."

Martha said, "But Lord, it has been four days since Lazarus died. There will be a bad smell." Martha was the sister of the dead man.

⁴⁰Then Jesus said to her, "Remember what I told you? I said that if you believed, you would see God's divine greatness.*"

⁴¹So they moved the stone away from the entrance. Then Jesus looked up and said, "Father, I thank you that you heard me. ⁴²I know that you always hear me. But I said these things because of the people here around me. I want them to believe that you sent me." ⁴³After Jesus said this he called in a loud voice, "Lazarus, come out!" ⁴⁴The dead man came out. His hands and feet were wrapped with pieces of cloth. He had a handkerchief covering his face.

Jesus said to the people, "Take the cloth off of him and let him go."

The Jewish Leaders Plan to Kill Jesus
(Mt. 26:1–5; Mk. 14:1–2; Lk. 22:1–2)

⁴⁵There were many Jews who came to visit Mary. When they saw what Jesus did, many of them believed in him. ⁴⁶But some of them went to the Pharisees* and told them what Jesus did. ⁴⁷Then the leading priests and Pharisees called a meeting of the high council. They said, "What should we do? This man is doing many miraculous signs.* ⁴⁸If we let him continue doing these things, everyone will believe in him. Then the Romans will come and take away our Temple* and our nation."

⁴⁹One of the men there was Caiaphas. He was the high priest* that year. He said, "You people know nothing! ⁵⁰It is better for one man to die for the people than for the whole nation to be destroyed. But you don't realize this."

⁵¹Caiaphas did not think of this himself. As that year's high priest, he was really prophesying* that Jesus would die for the Jewish people. ⁵²Yes, he would die for the Jewish people. But he would also die for God's other children scattered all over the world. He would die to bring them all together and make them one people.

⁵³That day the Jewish leaders began planning to kill Jesus. ⁵⁴So Jesus stopped traveling around openly among the Jews. He went away to a town called Ephraim in an area near the desert. He stayed there with his followers.

⁵⁵It was almost time for the Jewish Passover* festival. Many people from the country went to Jerusalem before the Passover. They went to do the special things to make themselves pure for the festival. ⁵⁶The people looked for Jesus. They stood in the Temple area and asked each other, "Is he coming to the festival? What do you think?" ⁵⁷But the leading priests and the Pharisees had given a special order about Jesus. They said that anyone who knew where he was must tell them so that they could arrest him.

Jesus in Bethany With His Friends
(Mt. 26:6–13; Mk. 14:3–9)

12 ¹Six days before the Passover* festival, Jesus went to Bethany. That is where Lazarus lived, the man Jesus raised from death. ²There they had a dinner for Jesus. Martha served the food, and Lazarus was one of the people eating with Jesus. ³Mary brought in a pint*ᵃ* of expensive perfume made of pure nard.* She poured the perfume on Jesus' feet. Then she wiped his feet with her hair. And the sweet smell from the perfume filled the whole house.

⁴Judas Iscariot, one of Jesus' followers, was there—the one who would later hand Jesus over to his enemies. Judas said, ⁵"That perfume was worth a full year's pay.*ᵇ* It should have been sold, and the money should have been given to the poor people." ⁶But Judas did not really care about the poor. He said this because he was a thief. He was the one who kept the money box for the group of followers. And he often stole money from the box.

⁷Jesus answered, "Don't stop her. It was right for her to save this perfume for today—the day for me to be prepared for burial. ⁸You will always have those who are poor with you.*ᶜ* But you will not always have me."

The Plot Against Lazarus

⁹Many of the Jews heard that Jesus was in Bethany, so they went there to see him. They also went there to see Lazarus, the one Jesus raised from death. ¹⁰So the leading priests made

---

*ᵃ***12:3** pint Literally, *litra* or a Roman pound, equal to 327 grams (11.5 ounces). *ᵇ***12:5** *a full year's pay* Literally, "300 *denarii* (silver coins)." One coin, a Roman *denarius*, was the average pay for one day's work. *ᶜ***12:8** *You will … with you* See Deut. 15:11.

plans to kill Lazarus too. ¹¹Because of him, many Jews were leaving them and believing in Jesus. That is why they wanted to kill Lazarus too.

Jesus Enters Jerusalem Like a King
(Mt. 21:1–11; Mk. 11:1–11; Lk. 19:28–40)

¹²The next day the people in Jerusalem heard that Jesus was coming there. These were the crowds of people who had come to the Passover* festival. ¹³They took branches of palm trees and went out to meet Jesus. They shouted,

"'Praise*ᵃ* Him!'
'Welcome! God bless the one who comes
in the name of the Lord!'   *Psalm 118:25–26*

God bless the King of Israel!"

¹⁴Jesus found a donkey and rode on it, as the Scriptures* say,

¹⁵"Do not be afraid, city of Zion*ᵇ*!
Look! Your king is coming.
He is riding on a young donkey."   *Zechariah 9:9*

¹⁶The followers of Jesus did not understand at that time what was happening. But after he was raised to glory,* they understood that this was written about him. Then they remembered that they had done these things for him.

¹⁷There were many people with Jesus when he raised Lazarus from death and told him to come out of the tomb.* Now they were telling others about what Jesus did. ¹⁸That's why so many people went out to meet him—because they had heard about this miraculous sign* he did. ¹⁹So the Pharisees* said to each other, "Look! Our plan is not working. The people are all following him!"

Jesus Talks About Life and Death

²⁰There were some Greeks* there too. These were some of the people who went to Jerusalem to worship at the Passover* festival. ²¹They went to Philip, who was from Bethsaida in Galilee. They said, "Sir, we want to meet Jesus." ²²Philip went and told Andrew. Then Andrew and Philip went and told Jesus.

²³Jesus said to them, "The time has come for the Son of Man* to receive his glory.* ²⁴It is a fact that a grain of wheat must fall to the ground and die before it can grow and produce much more wheat. If it never dies, it will never be more than a single seed. ²⁵Those who love the life they have now will lose it. But those who are willing to give up their life in this world will keep it. They will have eternal life. ²⁶Whoever serves me

*ᵃ*12:13 *Praise* Literally, *"Hosanna,"* a Hebrew word used in praying to God for help. Here, it was probably a shout of celebration used in praising God or his Messiah.   *ᵇ*12:15 *city of Zion* Literally, "daughter of Zion," meaning Jerusalem.

must follow me. My servants must be with me everywhere I am. My Father will give honor to anyone who serves me.

Jesus Talks About His Death

27"Now I am very troubled. What should I say? Should I say, 'Father save me from this time of suffering'? No, I came to this time so that I could suffer. 28Father, do what will bring you glory*!"

Then a voice came from heaven, "I have already brought glory to myself. I will do it again."

29The people standing there heard the voice. They said it was thunder.

But others said, "An angel spoke to him!"

30Jesus said, "That voice was for you and not for me. 31Now is the time for the world to be judged. Now the ruler of this world* will be thrown out. 32I will be lifted up*a* from the earth. When that happens, I will draw all people to myself." 33Jesus said this to show how he would die.

34The people said, "But our law says that the Christ* will live forever. So why do you say, 'The Son of Man* must be lifted up'? Who is this 'Son of Man'?"

35Then Jesus said, "The light*b* will be with you for only a short time more. So walk while you have the light. Then the darkness* will not catch you. People who walk in the darkness don't know where they are going. 36So put your trust in the light while you still have it. Then you will be children of light." When Jesus finished saying these things, he went away to a place where the people could not find him.

Some Jews Refuse to Believe in Jesus

37The people saw all these miraculous signs* Jesus did, but they still did not believe in him. 38This was to give full meaning to what Isaiah the prophet* said,

"Lord, who believed what we told them?
Who has seen the Lord's power?"   *Isaiah 53:1*

39This is why the people could not believe. Because Isaiah also said,

40"God made the people blind.
He closed their minds.
He did this so that they will not see with their eyes
    and understand with their minds.
He did it so that they would not turn and be healed."

                                        Isaiah 6:10

---

*a*12:32 *lifted up* Meaning to be nailed to a cross and "lifted up" on it to die. It may also have a second meaning: to be "lifted up" from death to heaven. Also in verse 34. *b*12:35 *light* This means Christ, as in Jn. 1:5–9. Also, it is a symbol of goodness and truth, qualities associated with Christ and his kingdom.

[41]Isaiah said this because he saw Jesus' divine greatness.* So he spoke about him.

[42]But many people believed in Jesus. Even many of the Jewish leaders believed in him, but they were afraid of the Pharisees,* so they did not say openly that they believed. They were afraid they would be ordered to stay out of the synagogue.* [43]They loved praise from people more than praise from God.

Jesus' Teaching Will Judge People

[44]Then Jesus said loudly, "Everyone who believes in me is really believing in the one who sent me. [45]Everyone who sees me is really seeing the one who sent me. [46]I came into this world as a light. I came so that everyone who believes in me would not stay in darkness.

[47]"I did not come into the world to judge people. I came to save the people in the world. So I am not the one who judges those who hear my teaching and do not obey. [48]But there is a judge for all those who refuse to believe in me and do not accept what I say. The message I have spoken will judge them on the last day. [49]That is because what I taught was not from myself. The Father who sent me told me what to say and what to teach. [50]And I know that whatever he says to do will bring eternal life. So the things I say are exactly what the Father told me to say."

Jesus Washes His Followers' Feet

13 [1]It was almost time for the Jewish Passover* festival. Jesus knew that the time had come for him to leave this world and go back to the Father. Jesus had always loved the people in the world who were his. Now was the time he showed them his love the most.

[2]Jesus and his followers were at the evening meal. The devil had already persuaded Judas Iscariot to hand Jesus over to his enemies. (Judas was the son of Simon.) [3]The Father had given Jesus power over everything. Jesus knew this. He also knew that he had come from God. And he knew that he was going back to God. [4]So while they were eating, Jesus stood up and took off his robe. He got a towel and wrapped it around his waist. [5]Then he poured water into a bowl and began to wash the followers' feet.[a] He dried their feet with the towel that was wrapped around his waist.

[6]He came to Simon Peter. But Peter said to him, "Lord, you should not wash my feet."

[7]Jesus answered, "You don't know what I am doing now. But later you will understand."

[8]Peter said, "No! You will never wash my feet."

---

[a]13:5 wash ... feet A social custom of the first century, because people wore open sandals on very dusty roads. It was a humble duty, usually done by a servant. Also in verses 6–14.

Jesus answered, "If I don't wash your feet, you are not one of my people."

⁹Simon Peter said, "Lord, after you wash my feet, wash my hands and my head too!"

¹⁰Jesus said, "After a person has a bath, his whole body is clean. He needs only to wash his feet. And you are clean, but not all of you." ¹¹Jesus knew who would hand him over to his enemies. That is why he said, "Not all of you are clean."

¹²When Jesus finished washing their feet, he put on his clothes and went back to the table. He asked, "Do you understand what I did for you? ¹³You call me 'Teacher.' And you call me 'Lord.' And this is right, because that is what I am. ¹⁴I am your Lord and Teacher. But I washed your feet. So you also should wash each other's feet. ¹⁵I did this as an example for you. So you should serve each other just as I served you. ¹⁶Believe me, servants are not greater than their master. Those who are sent to do something are not greater than the one who sent them. ¹⁷If you know these things, you will be happy if you do them.

¹⁸"I am not talking about all of you. I know the people I have chosen. But what the Scriptures* say must happen: 'The man who shared my food has turned against me.'ᵃ ¹⁹I am telling you this now before it happens. Then when it happens, you will believe that I AM.ᵇ ²⁰I assure you, whoever accepts the person I send also accepts me. And whoever accepts me also accepts the one who sent me."

Jesus Tells Who Will Turn Against Him
(Mt. 26:20–25; Mk. 14:17–21; Lk. 22:21–23)

²¹After Jesus said these things, he felt very troubled. He said openly, "Believe me when I say that one of you will hand me over to my enemies."

²²His followers all looked at each other. They did not understand who Jesus was talking about. ²³One of the followers was next to Jesus and was leaning close to him. This was the one Jesus loved very much. ²⁴Simon Peter made signs to this follower to ask Jesus who he was talking about.

²⁵That follower leaned closer to Jesus and asked, "Lord, who is it?"

²⁶Jesus answered him, "I will dip this bread into the dish. The man I give it to is the one." So Jesus took a piece of bread, dipped it, and gave it to Judas Iscariot, the son of Simon. ²⁷When Judas took the bread, Satan* entered him. Jesus said to Judas, "What you will do—do it quickly!" ²⁸No one at the table understood why Jesus said this to Judas. ²⁹Since Judas was the one in charge of the money, some of them thought that Jesus meant for

ᵃ13:18 *has turned against me'* Literally, "has lifted up his heel against me." Quote from Ps. 41:9. ᵇ13:19 *I AM* This is like the name of God used in the Old Testament. See Isa. 41:4; 43:10; Ex. 3:14. However, it can also mean "I am he *(the Christ)*."

him to go and buy some things they needed for the feast. Or they thought that Jesus wanted him to go give something to the poor.

³⁰Judas ate the bread Jesus gave him. Then he immediately went out. It was night.

Jesus Talks About His Death

³¹When Judas was gone, Jesus said, "Now is the time for the Son of Man* to receive his glory.* And God will receive glory through him. ³²If God receives glory through him, he will give glory to the Son through himself. And that will happen very soon."

³³Jesus said, "My children, I will be with you only a short time more. You will look for me, but I tell you now what I told the Jewish leaders: Where I am going you cannot come.

³⁴"I give you a new command: Love each other. You must love each other just as I loved you. ³⁵All people will know that you are my followers if you love each other."

Jesus Says Peter Will Deny Him
(Mt. 26:31–35; Mk. 14:27–31; Lk. 22:31–34)

³⁶Simon Peter asked Jesus, "Lord, where are you going?"

Jesus answered, "Where I am going you cannot follow now. But you will follow later."

³⁷Peter asked, "Lord, why can't I follow you now? I am ready to die for you!"

³⁸Jesus answered, "Will you really give your life for me? The truth is, before the rooster crows, you will say three times that you don't know me."

Jesus Comforts His Followers

14 ¹Jesus said, "Don't be troubled. Trust in God, and trust in me. ²There are many rooms in my Father's house. I would not tell you this if it were not true. I am going there to prepare a place for you. ³After I go and prepare a place for you, I will come back. Then I will take you with me, so that you can be where I am. ⁴You know the way to the place where I am going."

⁵Thomas said, "Lord, we don't know where you are going, so how can we know the way?"

⁶Jesus answered, "I am the way, the truth, and the life. The only way to the Father is through me. ⁷If you really knew me, you would know my Father too. But now you know the Father. You have seen him."

⁸Philip said to him, "Lord, show us the Father. That is all we need."

⁹Jesus answered, "Philip, I have been with you for a long time. So you should know me. Anyone who has seen me has seen the Father too. So why do you say, 'Show us the Father'? ¹⁰Don't you believe that I am in the Father and the Father is in me? The things I have told you don't come from me. The

Father lives in me, and he is doing his own work. ¹¹Believe me when I say that I am in the Father and the Father is in me. Or believe because of the miracles* I have done.

¹²"I can assure you that whoever believes in me will do the same things I have done. And they will do even greater things than I have done, because I am going to the Father. ¹³And if you ask for anything in my name, I will do it for you. Then the Father's glory* will be shown through the Son. ¹⁴If you ask me for anything in my name, I will do it.

The Promise of the Holy Spirit

¹⁵"If you love me, you will do what I command. ¹⁶I will ask the Father, and he will give you another Helper*a* to be with you forever. ¹⁷The Helper is the Spirit of truth.*b* The people of the world cannot accept him, because they don't see him or know him. But you know him. He lives with you, and he will be in you.

¹⁸"I will not leave you all alone like children without parents. I will come back to you. ¹⁹In a very short time the people in the world will not see me anymore. But you will see me. You will live because I live. ²⁰On that day you will know that I am in the Father. You will know that you are in me and I am in you. ²¹Those who really love me are the ones who not only know my commands but also obey them. My Father will love such people, and I will love them. I will show myself to them."

²²Then Judas (not Judas Iscariot) said, "But Lord, why do you plan to show yourself to us, but not to the world?"

²³Jesus answered, "All who love me will obey my teaching. My Father will love them. My Father and I will come to them and live with them. ²⁴But anyone who does not love me does not obey my teaching. This teaching that you hear is not really mine. It is from my Father who sent me.

²⁵"I have told you all these things while I am with you. ²⁶But the Helper will teach you everything and cause you to remember all that I told you. This Helper is the Holy Spirit* that the Father will send in my name.

²⁷"I leave you peace. It is my own peace I give you. I give you peace in a different way than the world does. So don't be troubled. Don't be afraid. ²⁸You heard me say to you, 'I am leaving, but I will come back to you.' If you loved me, you would be happy that I am going back to the Father, because the Father is greater than I am. ²⁹I have told you this now, before it happens. Then when it happens, you will believe.

³⁰"I will not talk with you much longer. The ruler of this world* is coming. He has no power over me. ³¹But the world

a **14:16** *Helper* Or, "Comforter," the Holy Spirit. Also in verse 26. *b* **14:17** *Spirit of truth* The Holy Spirit. It was his work to help Jesus' followers understand God's truth. See Jn. 16:13.

must know that I love the Father. So I do exactly what the Father told me to do.

"Come now, let's go."

Jesus Is Like a Vine

15 [1]Jesus said, "I am the true vine, and my Father is the gardener. [2]He cuts off every branch[a] of mine that does not produce fruit.[b] He also trims every branch that produces fruit to prepare it to produce even more. [3]You have already been prepared to produce more fruit by the teaching I have given you. [4]Stay joined to me and I will stay joined to you. No branch can produce fruit alone. It must stay connected to the vine. It is the same with you. You cannot produce fruit alone. You must stay joined to me.

[5]"I am the vine, and you are the branches. If you stay joined to me and I to you, you will produce plenty of fruit. But separated from me you won't be able to do anything. [6]If you don't stay joined to me, you will be like a branch that has been thrown out and has dried up. All the dead branches like that are gathered up, thrown into the fire and burned. [7]Stay joined together with me, and follow my teachings. If you do this, you can ask for anything you want, and it will be given to you. [8]I want you to produce much fruit and show that you are my followers. This will bring glory* to my Father.

[9]"I have loved you as the Father has loved me. Now continue in my love. [10]I have obeyed my Father's commands, and he continues to love me. In the same way, if you obey my commands, I will continue to love you. [11]I have told you these things so that you can have the true happiness that I have. I want you to be completely happy. [12]This is what I command you: Love each other as I have loved you. [13]The greatest love people can show is to die for their friends. [14]You are my friends if you do what I tell you to do. [15]I no longer call you servants, because servants don't know what their master is doing. But now I call you friends, because I have told you everything that my Father told me.

[16]"You did not choose me. I chose you. And I gave you this work: to go and produce fruit—fruit that will last. Then the Father will give you anything you ask for in my name. [17]This is my command: Love each other.

Jesus Warns His Followers

[18]"If the world hates you, remember that they hated me first. [19]If you belonged to the world, the world would love you as it loves its own people. But I have chosen you to be different from those in the world. So you don't belong to the world, and that is why the world hates you.

---

[a]15:2 *branch* The "branches" are Jesus' followers. See verse 5.   [b]15:2 *produce fruit* Meaning the way Jesus' followers must live to show they belong to him. See verses 7–10.

²⁰"Remember the lesson I told you: Servants are not greater than their master. If people treated me badly, they will treat you badly too. And if they obeyed my teaching, they will obey yours too. ²¹They will do to you whatever they did to me, because you belong to me. They don't know the one who sent me. ²²If I had not come and spoken to the people of the world, they would not be guilty of sin. But now I have spoken to them. So they have no excuse for their sin.

²³"Whoever hates me also hates my Father. ²⁴I did things among the people of the world that no one else has ever done. If I had not done those things, they would not be guilty of sin. But they have seen what I did, and still they hate me and my Father. ²⁵But this happened to make clear the full meaning of what is written in their law: 'They hated me for no reason.'ᵃ

²⁶"I will send you the Helperᵇ from the Father. The Helper is the Spirit of truthᶜ who comes from the Father. When he comes, he will tell about me. ²⁷And you will tell people about me too, because you have been with me from the beginning.

16 ¹"I have told you all this so that you won't lose your faith when you face troubles. ²People will tell you to leave their synagogues* and never come back. In fact, the time will come when they will think that killing you would be doing service for God. ³They will do this because they have not known the Father, and they have not known me. ⁴I have told you all this now to prepare you. So when the time comes for these things to happen, you will remember that I warned you.

The Work of the Holy Spirit

"I did not tell you these things at the beginning, because I was with you then. ⁵Now I am going back to the one who sent me. And none of you asks me, 'Where are you going?' ⁶But you are filled with sadness because I have told you all this. ⁷Let me assure you, it is better for you that I go away. I say this because when I go away I will send the Helper to you. But if I did not go, the Helper would not come.

⁸"When the Helper comes, he will show the people of the world how wrong they are about sin, about being right with God, and about judgment. ⁹He will prove that they are guilty of sin, because they don't believe in me. ¹⁰He will show them how wrong they are about how to be right with God. The Helper will do this, because I am going to the Father. You will not see me then. ¹¹And he will show them how wrong their judgment is, because their leaderᵈ has already been condemned.

ᵃ**15:25** *'They hated me for no reason'* These words could be from Ps. 35:19 or Ps. 69:4.
ᵇ**15:26** *Helper* Or, "Comforter," the Holy Spirit. Also in 16:7, 8. ᶜ**15:26** *Spirit of truth* The Holy Spirit. It was his work to help Jesus' followers understand God's truth. See Jn. 16:13.
ᵈ**16:11** *their leader* Literally, "the ruler of this world." See "Satan" in the Word List.

¹²"I have so much more to tell you, but it is too much for you to accept now. ¹³But when the Spirit* of truth comes, he will lead you into all truth. He will not speak his own words. He will speak only what he hears and will tell you what will happen in the future. ¹⁴The Spirit of truth will bring glory* to me by telling you what he receives from me. ¹⁵All that the Father has is mine. That is why I said that the Spirit will tell you what he receives from me.

Sadness Will Change to Happiness

¹⁶"After a short time you won't see me. Then after another short time you will see me again."

¹⁷Some of the followers said to each other, "What does he mean when he says, 'After a short time you won't see me. Then after another short time you will see me again'? And what does he mean when he says, 'Because I am going to the Father'?" ¹⁸They also asked, "What does he mean by 'a short time'? We don't understand what he is saying."

¹⁹Jesus saw that the followers wanted to ask him about this. So he said to them, "Are you asking each other what I meant when I said, 'After a short time you won't see me. Then after another short time you will see me again'? ²⁰The truth is, you will cry and be sad, but the world will be happy. You will be sad, but then your sadness will change to happiness.

²¹"When a woman gives birth to a baby, she has pain, because her time has come. But when her baby is born, she forgets the pain. She forgets because she is so happy that a child has been born into the world. ²²It is the same with you. Now you are sad, but I will see you again, and you will be happy. You will have a joy that no one can take away. ²³In that day you will not have to ask me about anything. And I assure you, my Father will give you anything you ask him for in my name. ²⁴You have never asked for anything in this way before. But ask in my name, and you will receive. And you will have the fullest joy possible.

Victory Over the World

²⁵"I have told you these things, using words that hide the meaning. But the time will come when I will not use words like that to tell you things. I will speak to you in plain words about the Father. ²⁶Then you will be able to ask the Father for things in my name. I'm not saying that I will have to ask the Father for you. ²⁷The Father himself loves you because you have loved me. And he loves you because you have believed that I came from God. ²⁸I came from the Father into the world. Now I am leaving the world and going back to the Father."

²⁹Then his followers said, "You are already speaking plainly to us. You are not using words that hide the meaning. ³⁰We can see now that you know all things. You answer our questions

even before we ask them. This makes us believe that you came from God."

[31]Jesus said, "So now you believe? [32]Listen to me. A time is coming when you will be scattered, each to his own home. In fact, that time is already here. You will leave me, and I will be alone. But I am never really alone, because the Father is with me.

[33]"I have told you these things so that you can have peace in me. In this world you will have troubles. But be brave! I have defeated the world!"

Jesus Prays for Himself and His Followers

17 [1]After Jesus said these things, he looked toward heaven and prayed, "Father, the time has come. Give glory* to your Son so that the Son can give glory to you. [2]You gave the Son power over all people so that he could give eternal life to all those you have given to him. [3]And this is eternal life: that people can know you, the only true God, and that they can know Jesus Christ, the one you sent. [4]I finished the work you gave me to do. I brought you glory on earth. [5]And now, Father, give me glory with you. Give me the glory I had with you before the world was made.

[6]"You gave me some people from the world. I have shown them what you are like. They belonged to you, and you gave them to me. They have obeyed your teaching. [7]Now they know that everything I have came from you. [8]I told them the words you gave me, and they accepted them. They realized the fact that I came from you and believed that you sent me. [9]I pray for them now. I am not praying for the people in the world. But I am praying for these people you gave me, because they are yours. [10]All I have is yours, and all you have is mine. And my glory is seen in them.

[11]"Now I am coming to you. I will not stay in the world, but these followers of mine are still in the world. Holy Father, keep them safe by the power of your name—the name you gave me. Then they will be one, just as you and I are one. [12]While I was with them, I kept them safe by the power of your name—the name you gave me. I protected them. And only one of them was lost—the one who was sure to be lost. This was to show the truth of what the Scriptures* said would happen.

[13]"I am coming to you now. But I pray these things while I am still in the world. I say all this so that these followers can have the true happiness that I have. I want them to be completely happy. [14]I have given them your teaching. And the world has hated them, because they don't belong to the world, just as I don't belong to the world.

[15]"I am not asking you to take them out of the world. But I am asking that you keep them safe from the Evil One.* [16]They don't belong to the world, just as I don't belong to the world. [17]Make them ready for your service through your truth. Your

teaching is truth. [18]I have sent them into the world, just as you sent me into the world. [19]I am making myself completely ready to serve you. I do this for them, so that they also might be fully qualified for your service.

[20]"I pray not only for these followers but also for those who will believe in me because of their teaching. [21]Father, I pray that all who believe in me can be one. You are in me and I am in you. I pray that they can also be one in us. Then the world will believe that you sent me. [22]I have given them the glory that you gave me. I gave them this glory so that they can be one, just as you and I are one. [23]I will be in them, and you will be in me. So they will be completely one. Then the world will know that you sent me and that you loved them just as you loved me.

[24]"Father, I want these people you have given me to be with me in every place I am. I want them to see my glory—the glory you gave me because you loved me before the world was made. [25]Father, you are the one who always does what is right. The world does not know you, but I know you, and these followers of mine know that you sent me. [26]I showed them what you are like, and I will show them again. Then they will have the same love that you have for me, and I will live in them."

Jesus Is Arrested
(Mt. 26:47–56; Mk. 14:43–50; Lk. 22:47–53)

18 [1]When Jesus finished praying, he left with his followers and went across the Kidron Valley. He went into a garden there, his followers still with him.

[2]Judas, the one responsible for handing Jesus over, knew where this place was. He knew because Jesus often met there with his followers. [3]So Judas led a group of soldiers to the garden, along with some guards from the leading priests and the Pharisees.* They were carrying torches, lanterns, and weapons.

[4]Jesus already knew everything that would happen to him. So he went out and asked them, "Who are you looking for?"

[5]They answered, "Jesus from Nazareth."

He said, "I am Jesus."[a] (Judas, the one responsible for handing Jesus over, was standing there with them.) [6]When Jesus said, "I am Jesus," the men moved back and fell to the ground.

[7]He asked them again, "Who are you looking for?"

They said, "Jesus from Nazareth."

[8]Jesus said, "I told you that I am Jesus. So if you are looking for me, let these other men go free." [9]This was to show the truth of what Jesus said earlier: "I have not lost anyone you gave me."

[10]Simon Peter had a sword, which he pulled out and struck the servant of the high priest,* cutting off his right ear. (The servant's name was Malchus.) [11]Jesus said to Peter, "Put your

---

[a]**18:5** *"I am Jesus"* Literally, "I am," which could have the same meaning here that it has in 8:24, 28, 58; 13:19. Also in verse 8.

sword back in its place! I must drink from the cup*a* the Father has given me."

Jesus Is Brought Before Annas
(Mt. 26:57–58; Mk. 14:53–54; Lk. 22:54)

¹²Then the soldiers with their commander and the Jewish guards arrested Jesus. They tied him ¹³and brought him to Annas, the father-in-law of Caiaphas. Caiaphas was the high priest* that year. ¹⁴He was also the one who had told the other Jewish leaders that it would be better if one man died for all the people.

Peter Lies About Knowing Jesus
(Mt. 26:69–70; Mk. 14:66–68; Lk. 22:55–57)

¹⁵Simon Peter and another one of Jesus' followers went with Jesus. This follower knew the high priest.* So he went with Jesus into the yard of the high priest's house. ¹⁶But Peter waited outside near the door. The follower who knew the high priest came back outside and spoke to the gatekeeper. Then he brought Peter inside. ¹⁷The girl at the gate said to Peter, "Are you also one of the followers of that man?"

Peter answered, "No, I am not!"

¹⁸It was cold, so the servants and guards had built a fire. They were standing around it, warming themselves, and Peter was standing with them.

The High Priest Questions Jesus
(Mt. 26:59–66; Mk. 14:55–64; Lk. 22:66–71)

¹⁹The high priest* asked Jesus questions about his followers and what he taught them. ²⁰Jesus answered, "I have always spoken openly to all people. I always taught in the synagogues* and in the Temple* area. All the Jews come together there. I never said anything in secret. ²¹So why do you question me? Ask the people who heard my teaching. They know what I said."

²²When Jesus said this, one of the guards standing there hit him. The guard said, "You should not talk to the high priest like that!"

²³Jesus answered, "If I said something wrong, tell everyone here what was wrong. But if what I said is right, then why do you hit me?"

²⁴So Annas sent Jesus to Caiaphas the high priest. He was still tied.

Peter Lies Again
(Mt. 26:71–75; Mk. 14:69–72; Lk. 22:58–62)

²⁵Simon Peter was standing at the fire, keeping himself warm. The other people said to Peter, "Aren't you one of the followers of that man?"

---

a **18:11** cup A symbol of suffering. Jesus used the idea of drinking from a cup to mean accepting the suffering he would face in the terrible events that were soon to come.

Peter denied it. He said, "No, I am not."

²⁶One of the servants of the high priest* was there. He was a relative of the man whose ear Peter had cut off. The servant said, "I think I saw you with him in the garden!"

²⁷But again Peter said, "No, I was not with him!" As soon as he said this, a rooster crowed.

Jesus Is Brought Before Pilate
(Mt. 27:1–2, 11–31; Mk. 15:1–20; Lk. 23:1–25)

²⁸Then the guards took Jesus from Caiaphas' house to the Roman governor's palace. It was early in the morning. The Jews there would not go inside the palace. They did not want to make themselves unclean,ᵃ because they wanted to eat the Passover* meal. ²⁹So Pilate went outside to them and asked, "What do you say this man has done wrong?"

³⁰They answered, "He is a bad man. That is why we brought him to you."

³¹Pilate said to them, "You take him yourselves and judge him by your own law."

The Jewish leaders answered, "But your law does not allow us to punish anyone by killing them." ³²(This was to show the truth of what Jesus said about how he would die.)

³³Then Pilate went back inside the palace. He called for Jesus and asked him, "Are you the king of the Jews?"

³⁴Jesus said, "Is that your own question, or did other people tell you about me?"

³⁵Pilate said, "I'm not a Jew! It was your own people and their leading priests who brought you before me. What have you done wrong?"

³⁶Jesus said, "My kingdom does not belong to this world. If it did, my servants would fight so that I would not be handed over to the Jewish leaders. No, my kingdom is not an earthly one."

³⁷Pilate said, "So you are a king."

Jesus answered, "You are right to say that I am a king. I was born for this: to tell people about the truth. That is why I came into the world. And everyone who belongs to the truth listens to me."

³⁸Pilate said, "What is truth?" Then he went out to the Jewish leaders again and said to them, "I can find nothing against this man. ³⁹But it is one of your customs for me to free one prisoner to you at the time of the Passover. Do you want me to free this 'king of the Jews'?"

⁴⁰They shouted back, "No, not him! Let Barabbas go free!" (Barabbas was a rebel.)

19 ¹Then Pilate ordered that Jesus be taken away and whipped. ²The soldiers made a crown from thorny

---

ᵃ**18:28** *unclean* Going into a non-Jewish place would ruin the special cleansing the Jews did to make themselves fit for worship. See Jn. 11:55.

branches and put it on his head. Then they put a purple robe around him. ³They kept coming up to him and saying, "Hail to the king of the Jews!" And they hit him in the face.

⁴Again Pilate came out and said to the Jewish leaders, "Look! I am bringing Jesus out to you. I want you to know that I find nothing I can charge him with." ⁵Then Jesus came out wearing the crown of thorns and the purple robe. Pilate said to the Jews, "Here is the man!"

⁶When the leading priests and the Jewish guards saw Jesus they shouted, "Kill him on a cross! Kill him on a cross!"

But Pilate answered, "You take him and nail him to a cross yourselves. I find nothing I can charge him with."

⁷The Jewish leaders answered, "We have a law that says he must die, because he said he is the Son of God."

⁸When Pilate heard this, he was more afraid. ⁹So he went back inside the palace and asked Jesus, "Where are you from?" But Jesus did not answer him. ¹⁰Pilate said, "You refuse to speak to me? Remember, I have the power to make you free or to kill you on a cross."

¹¹Jesus answered, "The only power you have over me is the power given to you by God. So the one who handed me over to you is guilty of a greater sin."

¹²After this, Pilate tried to let Jesus go free. But the Jewish leaders shouted, "Anyone who makes himself a king is against Caesar.* So if you let this man go free, that means you are not Caesar's friend."

¹³When Pilate heard this, he brought Jesus out to the place called "The Stone Pavement." (In Aramaic* the name is "Gabbatha.") Pilate sat down on the judge's seat there. ¹⁴It was now almost noon on Preparation day* of Passover week. Pilate said to the Jews, "Here is your king!"

¹⁵They shouted, "Take him away! Take him away! Kill him on a cross!"

Pilate asked them, "Do you want me to kill your king on a cross?"

The leading priests answered, "The only king we have is Caesar!"

¹⁶So Pilate handed Jesus over to them to be killed on a cross.

Jesus Is Nailed to a Cross
(Mt. 27:32–44; Mk. 15:21–32; Lk. 23:26–39)

The soldiers took Jesus. ¹⁷He carried his own cross to a place called "The Place of the Skull." (In Aramaic* the name of this place is "Golgotha.") ¹⁸There they nailed Jesus to the cross. They also nailed two other men to crosses. They put them on each side of Jesus with him in the middle.

¹⁹Pilate told them to write a sign and put it on the cross. The sign said, "JESUS OF NAZARETH, THE KING OF THE JEWS." ²⁰The sign was written in Aramaic, in Latin, and in Greek. Many of

the Jews read this sign, because the place where Jesus was nailed to the cross was near the city.

²¹The leading Jewish priests said to Pilate, "Don't write, 'The King of the Jews.' But write, 'This man said, I am the King of the Jews.'"

²²Pilate answered, "I will not change what I have written."

²³After the soldiers nailed Jesus to the cross, they took his clothes and divided them into four parts. Each soldier got one part. They also took his tunic.* It was all one piece of cloth woven from top to bottom. ²⁴So the soldiers said to each other, "We should not tear this into parts. Let's throw lots* to see who will get it." This happened to make clear the full meaning of what the Scriptures* say,

"They divided my clothes among them,
      and they threw lots for what I was wearing."   *Psalm 22:18*

So the soldiers did this.

²⁵Jesus' mother stood near his cross. Her sister was also standing there with Mary the wife of Clopas, and Mary Magdalene. ²⁶Jesus saw his mother. He also saw the follower he loved very much standing there. He said to his mother, "Dear woman, here is your son." ²⁷Then he said to the follower, "Here is your mother." So after that, this follower took Jesus' mother to live in his home.

Jesus Dies
(Mt. 27:45–56; Mk. 15:33–41; Lk. 23:44–49)

²⁸Later, Jesus knew that everything had been done. To make the Scriptures* come true he said, "I am thirsty."ᵃ ²⁹There was a jar full of sour wine there, so the soldiers soaked a sponge in it. They put the sponge on a branch of a hyssop plant and lifted it to Jesus' mouth. ³⁰When he tasted the wine, he said, "It is finished." Then he bowed his head and died.

³¹This day was Preparation day.* The next day was a special Sabbath* day. The Jewish leaders did not want the bodies to stay on the cross on the Sabbath day. So they asked Pilate to order that the legs of the men be broken. And they asked that the bodies be taken down from the crosses. ³²So the soldiers came and broke the legsᵇ of the two men on the crosses beside Jesus. ³³But when the soldiers came close to Jesus, they saw that he was already dead. So they did not break his legs.

³⁴But one of the soldiers stuck his spear into Jesus' side. Immediately blood and water came out. ³⁵(The one who saw this happen has told about it. He told about it so that you also can believe. The things he says are true. He knows that he tells the truth.) ³⁶These things happened to give full meaning to the

---

ᵃ19:28 *"I am thirsty"* See Ps. 22:15; 69:21.   ᵇ19:32 *broke the legs* The legs were broken to make those on the crosses die more quickly.

Scriptures that said, "None of his bones will be broken"[a] [37]and "People will look at the one they stabbed."[b]

Jesus Is Buried
(Mt. 27:57–61; Mk. 15:42–47; Lk. 23:50–56)

[38]Later, a man named Joseph from Arimathea asked Pilate for the body of Jesus. (Joseph was a follower of Jesus, but he did not tell anyone, because he was afraid of the Jewish leaders.) Pilate said Joseph could take Jesus' body, so he came and took it away.

[39]Nicodemus went with Joseph. He was the man who had come to Jesus before and talked to him at night. He brought about 100 pounds[c] of spices—a mixture of myrrh* and aloes.* [40]These two men took Jesus' body and wrapped it in pieces of linen cloth with the spices. (This is how the Jews bury people.) [41]In the place where Jesus was killed on the cross, there was a garden. In the garden there was a new tomb.* No one had ever been buried there before. [42]The men put Jesus in that tomb because it was near, and the Jews were preparing to start their Sabbath* day.

News That Jesus Has Risen From Death
(Mt. 28:1–10; Mk. 16:1–8; Lk. 24:1–12)

20 [1]Early on Sunday morning, while it was still dark, Mary Magdalene went to the tomb.* She saw that the large stone was moved away from the entrance. [2]So she ran to Simon Peter and the other follower (the one Jesus loved very much). She said, "They have taken the Lord out of the tomb, and we don't know where they put him."

[3]So Peter and the other follower started going to the tomb. [4]They were both running, but the other follower ran faster than Peter and reached the tomb first. [5]He bent down and looked in. He saw the pieces of linen cloth lying there, but he did not go in.

[6]Then Simon Peter finally reached the tomb and went in. He saw the pieces of linen lying there. [7]He also saw the cloth that had been around Jesus' head. It was folded up and laid in a different place from the pieces of linen. [8]Then the other follower went in—the one who had reached the tomb first. He saw what had happened and believed. [9](These followers did not yet understand from the Scriptures* that Jesus must rise from death.)

Jesus Appears to Mary Magdalene
(Mk. 16:9–11)

[10]Then the followers went back home. [11]But Mary stood outside the tomb,* crying. While she was crying, she bent down and looked inside the tomb. [12]She saw two angels dressed in white

[a]19:36 Quote from Ps. 34:20. The idea is from Ex. 12:46; Num. 9:12. [b]19:37 Quote from Zech. 12:10. [c]19:39 100 pounds Literally, 100 litras or Roman pounds, equal to 32.7 kg (72 pounds).

sitting where Jesus' body had been. One was sitting where the head had been; the other was sitting where the feet had been.

[13]The angels asked Mary, "Woman, why are you crying?"

Mary answered, "They took away the body of my Lord, and I don't know where they put him." [14]When Mary said this, she turned around and saw Jesus standing there. But she did not know that it was Jesus.

[15]He asked her, "Woman, why are you crying? Who are you looking for?"

She thought that this was the man who takes care of the garden. So she said to him, "Did you take him away, sir? Tell me where you put him. I will go and get him."

[16]Jesus said to her, "Mary."

She turned toward him and said in Aramaic,* *"Rabboni."* (This means "Teacher.")

[17]Jesus said to her, "You don't need to hold on to me! I have not yet gone back up to the Father. But go to my followers[a] and tell them this: 'I am going back to my Father and your Father. I am going back to my God and your God.'"

[18]Mary Magdalene went to the followers and told them, "I saw the Lord!" And she told them what he had said to her.

Jesus Appears to His Followers
(Mt. 28:16–20; Mk. 16:14–18; Lk. 24:36–49)

[19]The day was Sunday, and that same evening the followers were together. They had the doors locked because they were afraid of the Jewish leaders. Suddenly, Jesus was standing there among them. He said, "Peace be with you!" [20]As soon as he said this, he showed them his hands and his side. When the followers saw the Lord, they were very happy.

[21]Then Jesus said again, "Peace be with you. It was the Father who sent me, and I am now sending you in the same way." [22]Then he breathed on them and said, "Receive the Holy Spirit.* [23]If you forgive the sins of anyone, their sins are forgiven. If there is anyone whose sins you don't forgive, their sins are not forgiven."

Jesus Appears to Thomas

[24]Thomas (called Didymus) was one of the twelve, but he was not with the other followers when Jesus came. [25]They told him, "We saw the Lord." Thomas said, "That's hard to believe. I will have to see the nail holes in his hands, put my finger where the nails were, and put my hand into his side. Only then will I believe it."

[26]A week later the followers were in the house again, and Thomas was with them. The doors were locked, but Jesus came and stood among them. He said, "Peace be with you!" [27]Then

---

[a]**20:17** *followers* Literally, "brothers."

he said to Thomas, "Put your finger here. Look at my hands. Put your hand here in my side. Stop doubting and believe."

²⁸Thomas said to Jesus, "My Lord and my God!"

²⁹Jesus said to him, "You believe because you see me. What great blessings there are for the people who believe without seeing me!"

Why John Wrote This Book

³⁰Jesus did many other miraculous signs* that his followers saw, which are not written in this book. ³¹But these are written so that you can believe that Jesus is the Christ,* the Son of God. Then, by believing, you can have life through his name.

Jesus Appears to Seven Followers

21 ¹Later, Jesus showed himself again to his followers by Lake Galilee.ᵃ This is how it happened: ²Some of the followers were together—Simon Peter, Thomas (called Didymus), Nathanael from Cana in Galilee, the two sons of Zebedee, and two other followers. ³Simon Peter said, "I am going out to fish."

The other followers said, "We will go with you." So all of them went out and got into the boat. They fished that night but caught nothing.

⁴Early the next morning Jesus stood on the shore. But the followers did not know it was Jesus. ⁵Then he said to them, "Friends, have you caught any fish?"

They answered, "No."

⁶He said, "Throw your net into the water on the right side of your boat. You will find some fish there." So they did this. They caught so many fish that they could not pull the net back into the boat.

⁷The follower Jesus loved very much said to Peter, "That man is the Lord!" When Peter heard him say it was the Lord, he wrapped his coat around himself. (He had taken his clothes off to work.) Then he jumped into the water. ⁸The other followers went to shore in the boat. They pulled the net full of fish. They were not very far from shore, only about 100 yards. ⁹When they stepped out of the boat and onto the shore, they saw a fire of hot coals. There were fish on the fire and some bread there too. ¹⁰Then Jesus said, "Bring some of the fish that you caught."

¹¹Simon Peter got into the boat and pulled the net to the shore. It was full of big fish—153 of them! But even with that many fish, the net did not tear. ¹²Jesus said to them, "Come and eat." None of the followers would ask him, "Who are you?" They knew he was the Lord. ¹³Jesus walked over to get the bread and gave it to them. He also gave them the fish.

¹⁴This was now the third time Jesus showed himself to his followers after he was raised from death.

ᵃ**21:1** *Lake Galilee* Literally, "Lake of Tiberias," another name for Lake Galilee. See Jn. 6:1.

Jesus Talks to Peter

¹⁵When they finished eating, Jesus said to Simon Peter, "Simon, son of John, do you love me more than these other men love me?"

Peter answered, "Yes, Lord, you know that I love you."

Then Jesus said to him, "Take care of my lambs.ᵃ"

¹⁶Again Jesus said to him, "Simon, son of John, do you love me?"

Peter answered, "Yes, Lord, you know that I love you."

Then Jesus said, "Take care of my sheep."

¹⁷A third time Jesus said, "Simon, son of John, do you love me?"

Peter was sad because Jesus asked him three times, "Do you love me?" He said, "Lord, you know everything. You know that I love you!"

Jesus said to him, "Take care of my sheep. ¹⁸The truth is, when you were young, you tied your own belt and went where you wanted. But when you are old, you will put out your hands, and someone else will tie your belt. They will lead you where you don't want to go." ¹⁹(Jesus said this to show how Peter would die to give glory* to God.) Then he said to Peter, "Follow me!"

²⁰Peter turned and saw the follower Jesus loved very much walking behind them. (This was the follower who had leaned against Jesus at the supper and said, "Lord, who is it that will hand you over?") ²¹When Peter saw him behind them he asked Jesus, "Lord, what about him?"

²²Jesus answered, "Maybe I want him to live until I come. That should not matter to you. You follow me!"

²³So a story spread among the followers of Jesus. They were saying that this follower would not die. But Jesus did not say he would not die. He only said, "Maybe I want him to live until I come. That should not matter to you."

²⁴That follower is the one who is telling these things. He is the one who has now written them all down. We know that what he says is true.

²⁵There are many other things that Jesus did. If every one of them were written down, I think the whole world would not be big enough for all the books that would be written.

ᵃ21:15 *lambs* Jesus uses this word and the word "sheep" in verses 16 and 17 to mean his followers, as in Jn. 10.

Acts

Luke Writes Another Book

1 [1]Dear Theophilus,
The first book I wrote was about everything Jesus did and taught from the beginning [2]until the day he was carried up into heaven. Before he went, he talked to the apostles* he had chosen. With the help of the Holy Spirit,* he told them what they should do. [3]This was after his death, but he showed them that he was alive, proving it to them in many ways. The apostles saw Jesus many times during the 40 days after he was raised from death. He spoke to them about God's kingdom.* [4]One time when Jesus was eating with them, he told them not to leave Jerusalem. He said, "Wait here until you receive what the Father promised to send. Remember, I told you about it before. [5]John baptized* people with water, but in a few days you will be baptized with the Holy Spirit."

Jesus Is Carried Up Into Heaven

[6]The apostles* were all together. They asked Jesus, "Lord, is this the time for you to give the people of Israel* their kingdom again?"

[7]Jesus said to them, "The Father is the only one who has the authority to decide dates and times. They are not for you to know. [8]But the Holy Spirit* will come on you and give you power. You will be my witnesses. You will tell people everywhere about me—in Jerusalem, in the rest of Judea, in Samaria, and in every part of the world."

[9]After Jesus said this, he was lifted up into the sky. While they were watching, he went into a cloud, and they could not see him. [10]They were staring into the sky where he had gone. Suddenly two men wearing white clothes were standing beside them. [11]They said, "Men from Galilee, why are you standing here looking into the sky? You saw Jesus carried away from you into heaven. He will come back in the same way you saw him go."

A New Apostle Is Chosen

[12]Then the apostles* went back to Jerusalem from the Mount of Olives. (This mountain is about a half mile from Jerusalem.) [13]When they entered the city, they went to the

upstairs room where they were staying. These are the ones who were there:

Peter,
John,
James,
Andrew,
Philip,
Thomas,
Bartholomew,
Matthew,
James (the son of Alphaeus),
Simon, the Zealot,*
and Judas (the son of James).

¹⁴The apostles were all together. They were constantly praying with the same purpose. Some women, Mary the mother of Jesus, and his brothers were there with the apostles.

¹⁵After a few days there was a meeting of the believers.* (There were about 120 of them.) Peter stood up and said, ¹⁶⁻¹⁷"Brothers and sisters, in the Scriptures* the Holy Spirit* said through David* that something must happen. He was talking about Judas, one of our own group. Judas served together with us. The Spirit said that Judas would lead men to arrest Jesus."

¹⁸(Judas was paid money for doing this. His money was used to buy him a field. But he fell on his head, his body broke open, and all his intestines poured out. ¹⁹And all the people of Jerusalem learned about this. That is why they named that field Akeldama, which in their language means "field of blood.")

²⁰Peter said, "In the book of Psalms, this is written about Judas:

'People should not go near his land;
    no one should live there.'   *Psalm 69:25*

And it is also written:

'Let another man have his work.'   *Psalm 109:8*

²¹⁻²²"So now another man must join us and be a witness of Jesus' resurrection.* He must be one of those men who were part of our group during all the time the Lord Jesus was with us. He must have been with us from the time John was baptizing* people until the day when Jesus was carried up from us into heaven."

²³They put two men before the group. One was Joseph Barsabbas. He was also called Justus. The other man was Matthias. ²⁴⁻²⁵They prayed, "Lord, you know the minds of all people. Show us which one of these two men you choose to do this work. Judas turned away from it and went where he belongs. Lord, show us which man should take his place as an apostle!" ²⁶Then they used lots* to choose one of the two men.

The lots showed that Matthias was the one the Lord wanted. So he became an apostle with the other eleven.

The Coming of the Holy Spirit

2 ¹When the day of Pentecost* came, they were all together in one place. ²Suddenly a noise came from heaven. It sounded like a strong wind blowing. This noise filled the whole house where they were sitting. ³They saw something that looked like flames of fire. The flames were separated and stood over each person there. ⁴They were all filled with the Holy Spirit,* and they began to speak different languages. The Holy Spirit was giving them the power to do this.

⁵There were some godly Jewish men in Jerusalem at this time. They were from every country in the world. ⁶A large group of these men came together because they heard the noise. They were surprised because, as the apostles* were speaking, every person heard in their own language.

⁷They were all amazed at this. They did not understand how the apostles could do this. They said, "Look! These men we hear speaking are all from Galilee.ᵃ ⁸But we hear them in our own languages. How is this possible? We are from all these different places: ⁹Parthia, Media, Elam, Mesopotamia, Judea, Cappadocia, Pontus, Asia,* ¹⁰Phrygia, Pamphylia, Egypt, the areas of Libya near the city of Cyrene, Rome, ¹¹Crete, and Arabia. Some of us were born Jews, and others have changed their religion to worship God like Jews. We are from these different countries, but we can hear these men in our own languages! We can all understand the great things they are saying about God."

¹²The people were all amazed and confused. They asked each other, "What is happening?" ¹³But others were laughing at the apostles, saying they were drunk from too much wine.

Peter Speaks to the People

¹⁴Then Peter stood up with the other eleven apostles.* He spoke loudly so that all the people could hear. He said, "My Jewish brothers and all of you who live in Jerusalem, listen to me. I will tell you something you need to know. Listen carefully. ¹⁵These men are not drunk as you think; it's only nine o'clock in the morning. ¹⁶But Joel the prophet* wrote about what you see happening here today. This is what he wrote:

¹⁷ 'God says:
    In the last days I will pour out my Spirit* on all people.
      Your sons and daughters will prophesy.*
      Your young men will see visions.*
      Your old men will have special dreams.
¹⁸ In those days I will pour out my Spirit on my servants,
      men and women, and they will prophesy.

ᵃ2:7 from Galilee The people thought men from Galilee could speak only their own language.

¹⁹ I will work wonders* in the sky above.
   I will cause miraculous signs* on the earth below.
   There will be blood, fire, and thick smoke.
²⁰ The sun will be changed into darkness,
   and the moon will become red like blood.
   Then the great and glorious day of the Lord will come.
²¹ And everyone who trusts in the Lord*ᵃ* will be saved.'

Joel 2:28–32

²²"My fellow Israelites,* listen to these words: Jesus from Nazareth was a very special man. God clearly showed this to you. He proved it by the miracles,* wonders, and miraculous signs he did through Jesus. You all saw these things, so you know this is true. ²³Jesus was handed over to you, and you killed him. With the help of evil men, you nailed him to a cross. But God knew all this would happen. It was his plan—a plan he made long ago. ²⁴Jesus suffered the pain of death, but God made him free. He raised him from death. There was no way for death to hold him. ²⁵David* said this about him:

'I saw the Lord before me always;
   he is at my right side to keep me safe.
²⁶ So my heart is happy,
   and the words I speak are words of joy.
   Yes, even my body will live with hope,
²⁷   because you will not leave me in the place of death.*ᵇ*
   You will not let the body of your Holy One rot in the grave.
²⁸ You taught me how to live.
   You will come close to me and give me great joy.'

Psalm 16:8–11

²⁹"My brothers, I can tell you for sure about David, our great ancestor. He died, was buried, and his tomb* is still here with us today. ³⁰He was a prophet and knew something that God had said. God had promised David that someone from his own family would sit on David's throne as king.*ᶜ* ³¹David knew this before it happened. That is why he said this about that future king:

'He was not left in the place of death.
   His body did not rot in the grave.'

David was talking about the Christ* rising from death. ³²So Jesus is the one God raised from death. We are all witnesses of this. We saw him. ³³Jesus was lifted up to heaven. Now he is with God, at God's right side. The Father has given the Holy Spirit to him, as he promised. So Jesus has now poured out that Spirit. This is what you see and hear. ³⁴David was not the one who was lifted up to heaven. David himself said,

---

*ᵃ*2:21 *who trusts in the Lord* Literally, "who calls on the name of the Lord," meaning to show faith in him by worshiping him or praying to him for help. *ᵇ*2:27 *place of death* Literally, "Hades." Also in verse 31. *ᶜ*2:30 *God had promised ... as king* See 2 Sam. 7:12, 13 and Ps. 132:11.

'The Lord God said to my Lord:

Sit at my right side,

³⁵   until I put your enemies under your power.ᵃ'   *Psalm 110:1*

³⁶"So, all the Jewish people should know this for certain: God has made Jesus to be Lord and Christ. He is the man you nailed to the cross!"

³⁷When the people heard this, they felt very, very sorry. They asked Peter and the other apostles, "Brothers, what should we do?"

³⁸Peter said to them, "Change your hearts and lives and be baptized,* each one of you, in the name of Jesus Christ. Then God will forgive your sins, and you will receive the gift of the Holy Spirit. ³⁹This promise is for you. It is also for your children and for the people who are far away. It is for everyone the Lord our God calls to himself."

⁴⁰Peter warned them with many other words; he begged them, "Save yourselves from the evil of the people who live now!" ⁴¹Then those who accepted what Peter said were baptized. On that day about 3000 people were added to the group of believers.

The Believers Share

⁴²The believers spent their time listening to the teaching of the apostles.* They shared everything with each other. They ateᵇ together and prayed together. ⁴³Many wonders* and miraculous signs* were happening through the apostles, and everyone felt great respect for God. ⁴⁴All the believers stayed together and shared everything. ⁴⁵They sold their land and the things they owned. Then they divided the money and gave it to those who needed it. ⁴⁶The believers shared a common purpose, and every day they spent much of their time together in the Temple* area. They also ate together in their homes. They were happy to share their food and ate with joyful hearts. ⁴⁷The believers praised God and were respected by all the people. More and more people were being saved every day, and the Lord was adding them to their group.

Peter Heals a Crippled Man

3 ¹One day Peter and John went to the Temple* area. It was three o'clock in the afternoon, which was the time for the daily Temple prayer service. ²As they were entering the Temple area, a man was there who had been crippled all his life. He was being carried by some friends who brought him to the Temple every day. They put him by one of the gates outside the Temple. It was called Beautiful Gate. There he begged for money from

---

ᵃ**2:35** *until I put … power* Literally, "until I make your enemies a footstool for your feet."
ᵇ**2:42** *ate* Literally, "broke bread." This may mean a meal or the Lord's Supper, the special meal Jesus told his followers to eat to remember him. Also in verse 46. See Lk. 22:14–20.

the people going to the Temple. ³That day he saw Peter and John going into the Temple area. He asked them for money.

⁴Peter and John looked at the crippled man and said, "Look at us!" ⁵He looked at them; he thought they would give him some money. ⁶But Peter said, "I don't have any silver or gold, but I do have something else I can give you. By the power of Jesus Christ from Nazareth—stand up and walk!"

⁷Then Peter took the man's right hand and lifted him up. Immediately his feet and legs became strong. ⁸He jumped up, stood on his feet, and began to walk. He went into the Temple area with them. He was walking and jumping and praising God. ⁹⁻¹⁰All the people recognized him. They knew he was the crippled man who always sat by the Beautiful Gate to beg for money. Now they saw this same man walking and praising God. They were amazed. They did not understand how this could happen.

Peter Speaks to the People

¹¹The man was holding on to Peter and John. All the people were amazed. They ran to Peter and John at Solomon's Porch.*

¹²When Peter saw this, he said to the people, "My Jewish brothers, why are you surprised at this? You are looking at us as if it was our power that made this man walk. Do you think this was done because we are good? ¹³No, God did it! He is the God of Abraham,* the God of Isaac,* and the God of Jacob.* He is the God of all our fathers.* He gave glory* to Jesus, his special servant. But you handed him over to be killed. Pilate decided to let him go free. But you told Pilate you did not want him. ¹⁴Jesus was holy* and good, but you said you did not want him. You told Pilate to give you a murdererᵃ instead of Jesus. ¹⁵And so you killed the one who gives life! But God raised him from death. We are witnesses of this—we saw it with our own eyes.

¹⁶"This crippled man was healed because we trusted in Jesus. It was Jesus' power that made him well. You can see this man, and you know him. He was made completely well because of faith in Jesus. You all saw it happen!

¹⁷"My brothers, I know that what you did to Jesus was done because you did not understand what you were doing. And your leaders did not understand any more than you did. ¹⁸But God said these things would happen. Through the prophets* he said that his Christ* would suffer and die. I have told you how God made this happen. ¹⁹So you must change your hearts and lives. Come back to God, and he will forgive your sins. ²⁰Then the Lord will give you times of spiritual rest. He will send you Jesus, the one he chose to be the Christ.

²¹"But Jesus must stay in heaven until the time when all things will be made right again. God told about this time when

ᵃ**3:14** *murderer* Barabbas, the man the Jews chose to let go free instead of Jesus. See Lk. 23:18.

he spoke long ago through his holy prophets. ²²Moses* said, 'The Lord your God will give you a prophet. That prophet will come from among your own people. He will be like me. You must obey everything he tells you. ²³And anyone who refuses to obey that prophet will die, separated from God's people.'*a*

²⁴"Samuel, and all the other prophets who spoke for God after Samuel, said that this time would come. ²⁵And what those prophets talked about is for you, their descendants. You have received the agreement that God made with your fathers. God said to your father Abraham, 'Every nation on earth will be blessed through your descendants.'*b* ²⁶God has sent his special servant Jesus. He sent him to you first. He sent him to bless you by causing each of you to turn away from your evil ways."

The Apostles and the Jewish High Council

4 ¹While Peter and John were speaking to the people, some Jewish leaders came up to them. There were some priests, the captain of the soldiers that guarded the Temple,* and some Sadducees.* ²They were upset because of what Peter and John were teaching the people. By telling people about Jesus, the apostles* were teaching that people will rise from death. ³The Jewish leaders arrested Peter and John and put them in jail. It was already night, so they kept them in jail until the next day. ⁴But many of the people who heard the apostles believed what they said. There were now about 5000 men in the group of believers.

⁵The next day the Jewish rulers, the older Jewish leaders, and the teachers of the law met in Jerusalem. ⁶Annas the high priest,* Caiaphas, John, and Alexander were there. Everyone from the high priest's family was there. ⁷They made Peter and John stand before all the people. They asked them over and over, "How did you make this crippled man well? What power did you use? By whose authority did you do this?"

⁸Then Peter was filled with the Holy Spirit* and said to them, "Rulers of the people and you older leaders, ⁹are you questioning us today about what we did to help this crippled man? Are you asking us what made him well? ¹⁰We want all of you and all the Jewish people to know that this man was made well by the power of Jesus Christ from Nazareth. You nailed Jesus to a cross, but God raised him from death. This man was crippled, but he is now well. He is able to stand here before you because of the power of Jesus! ¹¹Jesus is

'the stone*c* that you builders thought was not important.
    But this stone has become the cornerstone.'* *Psalm 118:22*

¹²Jesus is the only one who can save people. His name is the only power in the world that has been given to save anyone. We must be saved through him!"

a 3:22–23 Quote from Deut. 18:15, 19. *b* 3:25 Quote from Gen. 22:18; 26:24. *c* 4:11 *stone* A picture or symbol meaning Jesus.

¹³The Jewish leaders understood that Peter and John had no special training or education. But they also saw that they were not afraid to speak. So the leaders were amazed. They also realized that Peter and John had been with Jesus. ¹⁴They saw the crippled man standing there beside the apostles. They saw that he was healed, so they could say nothing against the apostles.

¹⁵The Jewish leaders told them to leave the council meeting. Then the leaders talked to each other about what they should do. ¹⁶They said, "What shall we do with these men? Everyone in Jerusalem knows about the miracle* they did as a sign from God. It's too obvious. We can't say it didn't happen. ¹⁷But we must make them afraid to talk to anyone again about that man. Then this problem will not spread among the people."

¹⁸So the Jewish leaders called Peter and John in again. They told the apostles not to say anything or to teach anything in the name of Jesus. ¹⁹But Peter and John answered them, "What do you think is right? What would God want? Should we obey you or God? ²⁰We cannot be quiet. We must tell people about what we have seen and heard."

²¹⁻²²The Jewish leaders could not find a way to punish the apostles, because all the people were praising God for what had been done. (This miracle was a sign from God. The man who was healed was more than 40 years old.) So the Jewish leaders warned the apostles again and let them go free.

Peter and John Return to the Believers

²³Peter and John left the meeting of Jewish leaders and went to their own group. They told the group everything that the leading priests and the older Jewish leaders had said to them. ²⁴When the believers heard this, they all prayed to God with one purpose. They said, "Master, you are the one who made the sky, the earth, the sea, and everything in the world. ²⁵Our ancestor David* was your servant. With the help of the Holy Spirit* he wrote these words:

'Why are the nations shouting?
Why are the people planning such useless things?

²⁶ The kings of the earth prepare themselves to fight,
     and the rulers all come together against the Lord
         and against his Christ.*'

                                          Psalm 2:1–2

²⁷"That's what actually happened when Herod,* Pontius Pilate, the other nations, and the Jewish people all came together against Jesus here in Jerusalem. He is your holy* Servant, the one you made to be the Christ. ²⁸These people who came together against Jesus made your plan happen. It was done because of your power and your will. ²⁹And now, Lord, listen to what they are saying. They are trying to make us afraid. We are

your servants. Help us to say what you want us to say without fear. [30]Help us to be brave by showing us your power. Make sick people well. Cause miraculous signs* and wonders* to happen by the authority[a] of Jesus, your holy servant."

[31]After the believers prayed, the place where they were meeting shook. They were all filled with the Holy Spirit, and they continued to speak God's message* without fear.

The Believers Share

[32]The whole group of believers was united in their thinking and in what they wanted. None of them said that the things they had were their own. Instead, they shared everything. [33]With great power the apostles* were making it known to everyone that the Lord Jesus was raised from death. And God blessed all the believers very much. [34]None of them could say they needed anything. Everyone who owned fields or houses sold them. They brought the money they got [35]and gave it to the apostles. Then everyone was given whatever they needed.

[36]One of the believers was named Joseph. The apostles called him Barnabas. (This name means "one who encourages others.") He was a Levite* born in Cyprus. [37]Joseph sold a field he owned. He brought the money and gave it to the apostles.

Ananias and Sapphira

5 [1]There was a man named Ananias. His wife's name was Sapphira. Ananias sold some land he had, [2]but he gave only part of the money to the apostles.* He secretly kept some of the money for himself. His wife knew this, and she agreed with it.

[3]Peter said, "Ananias, why did you let Satan* fill your mind with such an idea? You kept part of the money for yourself and lied about it to the Holy Spirit.* [4]Before you sold the field, it belonged to you, right? And even after you sold it, you could have used the money any way you wanted. How could you even think of doing such a thing? You lied to God, not to us!"

[5-6]When Ananias heard this, he fell down and died. Some young men came and wrapped his body. They carried it out and buried it. And everyone who heard about this was filled with fear.

[7]About three hours later his wife came in. Sapphira did not know about what had happened to her husband. [8]Peter said to her, "Tell me how much money you got for your field. Was it this much?"

Sapphira answered, "Yes, that was all we got for the field."

[9]Peter said to her, "Why did you and your husband agree to test the Spirit of the Lord? Listen! Do you hear those footsteps? The men who buried your husband are at the door.

---

[a] **4:30** *authority* Literally, "name."

They will carry you out in the same way." ¹⁰At that moment Sapphira fell down by his feet and died. The young men came in and saw that she was dead. They carried her out and buried her beside her husband. ¹¹The whole group of believers*a* and all the other people who heard about this were filled with fear.

Proofs From God

¹²The apostles* were given the power to do many miraculous signs* and wonders* among the people. They were together in Solomon's Porch,* and they all had the same purpose. ¹³None of the other people dared to stand with the apostles, but everyone was saying wonderful things about them. ¹⁴More and more people believed in the Lord, and many men and women were added to the group of believers. ¹⁵So the people brought those who were sick into the streets and put them on little beds and mats. They were hoping that Peter's shadow might fall on them as he walked by. ¹⁶People came from all the towns around Jerusalem. They brought those who were sick or troubled by evil spirits. All of them were healed.

The Apostles Are Arrested

¹⁷The high priest* and all his friends (a group called the Sadducees*) became very jealous. ¹⁸They grabbed the apostles* and put them in jail. ¹⁹But during the night, an angel of the Lord opened the doors of the jail. The angel led the apostles outside and said, ²⁰"Go and stand in the Temple* area. Tell the people everything about this new life." ²¹When the apostles heard this, they did what they were told. They went into the Temple area about sunrise and began to teach the people.

The high priest and his friends came together and called a meeting of the high council and all the older Jewish leaders. They sent some men to the jail to bring the apostles to them. ²²When the men went to the jail, they could not find the apostles there. So they went back and told the Jewish leaders about this. ²³They said, "The jail was closed and locked. The guards were standing at the doors. But when we opened the doors, the jail was empty!" ²⁴The captain of the Temple guards and the leading priests heard this. They were confused and wondered what it all meant.

²⁵Then another man came and told them, "Listen! The men you put in jail are standing in the Temple area teaching the people." ²⁶The captain and his men went out and brought the apostles back. But the soldiers did not use force, because they were afraid of the people. They were afraid the people would stone them to death.

a **5:11** *group of believers* Literally, "church."

²⁷The soldiers brought the apostles in and made them stand before the council. The high priest questioned them. ²⁸He said, "We told you never again to teach as followers of that man. But look at what you have done! You have filled Jerusalem with your teaching. And you are trying to blame us for his death."

²⁹Peter and the other apostles answered, "We must obey God, not you! ³⁰You killed Jesus by nailing him to a cross. But God, the same God our fathers* had, raised Jesus up from death. ³¹Jesus is the one God honored by giving him a place at his right side. He made him our Leader and Savior. God did this to give all the people of Israel* the opportunity to change and turn to God to have their sins forgiven. ³²We saw all these things happen, and we can say that they are true. The Holy Spirit* also shows that these things are true. God has given this Spirit to all those who obey him."

³³When the council members heard this, they became very angry. They began to plan a way to kill the apostles. ³⁴But one member of the council, a Pharisee* named Gamaliel, stood up. He was a teacher of the law, and all the people respected him. He told the men to make the apostles leave the meeting for a few minutes. ³⁵Then he said to them, "Men of Israel, be careful of what you are planning to do to these men. ³⁶Remember when Theudas appeared? He said he was an important man, and about 400 men joined him. But he was killed, and all who followed him were scattered and ran away. They were not able to do anything. ³⁷Later, during the time of the census, a man named Judas came from Galilee. A lot of people joined his group, but he was also killed, and all his followers were scattered. ³⁸And so now I tell you, stay away from these men. Leave them alone. If their plan is something they thought up, it will fail. ³⁹But if it is from God, you will not be able to stop them. You might even be fighting against God himself!"

The Jewish leaders agreed with what Gamaliel said. ⁴⁰They called the apostles in again. They beat them and told them not to talk to people about Jesus again. Then they let them go free. ⁴¹The apostles left the council meeting. They were happy because they were given the honor of suffering dishonor for Jesus. ⁴²The apostles did not stop teaching the people. They continued to tell the Good News*—that Jesus is the Christ.* They did this every day in the Temple area and in people's homes.

Seven Men Chosen for a Special Work

6 ¹More and more people were becoming followers of Jesus. But during this same time, the Greek-speaking followers began to complain against the other Jewish followers. They said that their widows were not getting their share of what the followers received every day. ²The twelve apostles* called the whole group of followers together.

The apostles said to them, "It would not be right for us to give up our work of teaching God's word in order to be in charge of getting food to people. ³So, brothers and sisters, choose seven of your men who have a good reputation. They must be full of wisdom and the Spirit.* We will give them this work to do. ⁴Then we can use all our time to pray and to teach the word of God."

⁵The whole group liked the idea. So they chose these seven men: Stephen (a man with great faith and full of the Holy Spirit), Philip,ᵃ Prochorus, Nicanor, Timon, Parmenas, and Nicolaus (a man from Antioch who had become a Jew). ⁶Then they put these men before the apostles, who prayed and laid their hands onᵇ them.

⁷The word of God was reaching more and more people. The group of followers in Jerusalem became larger and larger. Even a big group of Jewish priests believed and obeyed.

Some Jews Against Stephen

⁸Stephen received a great blessing. God gave him power to do great wonders* and miraculous signs* among the people. ⁹But some of the Jews there were from the synagogue* of Free Men,* as it was called. The group included Jews from Cyrene, Alexandria, Cilicia, and Asia.* They started arguing with Stephen. ¹⁰But the Spirit* was helping him speak with wisdom. His words were so strong that these Jews could not argue with him.

¹¹So they told some men to say, "We heard Stephen say bad things against Moses* and against God!" ¹²By doing this, these Jews upset the people, the older Jewish leaders, and the teachers of the law. They became so angry that they came and grabbed Stephen and took him to a meeting of the high council.

¹³The Jews brought some men into the meeting to tell lies about Stephen. These men said, "This man is always saying things against this holy place and against the law of Moses. ¹⁴We heard him say that Jesus from Nazareth will destroy this place and change what Moses told us to do." ¹⁵Everyone there in the council meeting was staring at Stephen. They saw that his face looked like the face of an angel.

Stephen's Speech

7 ¹The high priest* said to Stephen, "Is all this true?" ²Stephen answered, "My Jewish fathers and brothers, listen to me. Our great and glorious God appeared to Abraham, our ancestor,* when he was in Mesopotamia. This was before he lived in Haran. ³God said to him, 'Leave your country and your people, and go to the country I will show you.'ᶜ

ᵃ6:5 Philip Not the apostle named Philip. ᵇ6:6 laid their hands on This act was a way of asking God to bless people in a special way—here, to give them power for a special work. ᶜ7:3 Quote from Gen. 12:1.

[4]"So Abraham left the country of Chaldea.[a] He went to live in Haran. After his father died, God sent him to this place, where you live now. [5]But God did not give Abraham any of this land, not even a foot of it. But God promised that in the future he would give Abraham this land for himself and for his children. (This was before Abraham had any children.)

[6]"This is what God said to him: 'Your descendants will live in another country. They will be strangers. The people there will make them slaves and do bad things to them for 400 years. [7]But I will punish the nation that made them slaves.'[b] And God also said, 'After those things happen, your people will come out of that country. Then they will worship me here in this place.'[c]

[8]"God made an agreement with Abraham; the sign for this agreement was circumcision.* And so when Abraham had a son, he circumcised him when he was eight days old. His son's name was Isaac. Isaac also circumcised his son Jacob. And Jacob did the same for his sons who became the twelve great ancestors of our people.

[9]"These ancestors of ours became jealous of their brother Joseph and sold him to be a slave in Egypt. But God was with him [10]and saved him from all his troubles. Pharaoh was the king of Egypt then. He liked Joseph and respected him because of the wisdom God gave him. Pharaoh gave Joseph the job of being a governor of Egypt. He even let him rule over all the people in Pharaoh's house. [11]But all the land of Egypt and of Canaan became dry. It became so dry that food could not grow, and the people suffered very much. Our people could not find anything to eat.

[12]"But Jacob heard that there was food in Egypt. So he sent our people there. (This was their first trip to Egypt.) [13]Then they went there a second time. This time Joseph told his brothers who he was. And Pharaoh learned about Joseph's family. [14]Then Joseph sent some men to invite Jacob, his father, to come to Egypt. He also invited all his relatives, a total of 75 people. [15]So Jacob went down to Egypt. He and our other ancestors lived there until they died. [16]Later, their bodies were moved to Shechem, where they were put in a tomb.* (It was the same tomb that Abraham had bought in Shechem from the sons of Hamor. He paid them with silver.)

[17]"The number of our people in Egypt grew. There were more and more of our people there. (The promise that God made to Abraham was soon to come true.) [18]Then a different king began to rule Egypt, one who knew nothing about Joseph. [19]This king tricked our people. He treated them badly, making them leave their children outside to die.

[20]"This was the time when Moses* was born. He was a very beautiful child, and for three months his parents took care of

[a]**7:4** *Chaldea* Or, "Babylonia," a land in the southern part of Mesopotamia. See verse 2.
[b]**7:7** Quote from Gen. 15:13–14. [c]**7:7** Quote from Gen. 15:14; Ex. 3:12.

him at home. [21]When they put him outside, Pharaoh's daughter took him. She raised him as her own son. [22]The Egyptians taught Moses everything they knew. He was powerful in all he said and did.

[23]"When Moses was about 40 years old, he decided to visit his own people, the people of Israel.* [24]He saw one of them being mistreated by an Egyptian, so he defended him. Moses hit the Egyptian to pay him back for hurting the man. He hit him so hard that it killed him. [25]Moses thought that his people would understand that God was using him to save them. But they did not understand.

[26]"The next day, Moses saw two of his own people fighting. He tried to make peace between them. He said, 'Men, you are brothers! Why are you trying to hurt each other?' [27]The man who was hurting the other one pushed Moses away and said to him, 'Did anyone say you could be our ruler and judge? [28]Will you kill me just as you killed that Egyptian yesterday?'[a] [29]When Moses heard him say this, he left Egypt. He went to live in the land of Midian, where he was a stranger. During the time he lived there, he had two sons.

[30]"Forty years later Moses was in the desert near Mount Sinai. An angel appeared to him in the flame of a burning bush. [31]When Moses saw this, he was amazed. He went near to look closer at it. He heard a voice; it was the Lord's. [32]The Lord said, 'I am the same God your ancestors had—the God of Abraham,* the God of Isaac,* and the God of Jacob.'*[b] Moses began to shake with fear. He was afraid to look at the bush.

[33]"The Lord said to him, 'Take off your sandals, because the place where you are now standing is holy ground. [34]I have seen my people suffer much in Egypt. I have heard my people crying and have come down to save them. Come now, Moses, I am sending you back to Egypt.'[c]

[35]"This Moses was the one his people said they did not want. They said, 'Did anyone say you could be our ruler and judge?'[d] But he is the one God sent to be a ruler and savior. God sent him with the help of an angel, the one Moses saw in the burning bush. [36]So Moses led the people out of Egypt. He worked wonders* and miraculous signs* in Egypt, at the Red Sea, and then in the desert for 40 years.

[37]"This is the same Moses who said these words to the people of Israel: 'God will give you a prophet.* That prophet will come from among your own people. He will be like me.'[e] [38]This same Moses was with the gathering of God's people in the desert. He was with the angel who spoke to him at Mount Sinai, and he was with our ancestors. He received life-giving words from God to give to us.

[a]**7:28** Quote from Ex. 2:14.   [b]**7:32** Quote from Ex. 3:6.   [c]**7:34** Quote from Ex. 3:5–10.
[d]**7:35** Quote from Ex. 2:14.   [e]**7:37** Quote from Deut. 18:15.

39"But our ancestors did not want to obey Moses. They rejected him. They wanted to go back to Egypt again. 40They said to Aaron, 'Moses led us out of the country of Egypt. But we don't know what has happened to him. So make some gods to go before us and lead us.'ª 41So the people made an idol that looked like a calf. Then they brought sacrifices to it. They were very happy with what they had made with their own hands. 42But God turned against them and let them continue worshiping the army of false gods in the sky. This is what God says in the book that contains what the prophets wrote:

'People of Israel, you did not bring me blood offerings
      and sacrifices* in the desert for 40 years;
43 You carried with you the tent for worshiping Moloch
      and the image of the star of your god Rephan.
   These were the idols you made to worship.
   So I will send you away beyond Babylon.'   *Amos 5:25–27*

44"The Holy Tentᵇ was with our ancestors in the desert. God told Moses how to make this tent. He made it like the plan that God showed him. 45Later, Joshua led our ancestors to capture the lands of the other nations. Our people went in and God made the other people go out. When our people went into this new land, they took with them this same tent. Our people received this tent from their fathers, and our people kept it until the time of David.* 46God was very pleased with David. He asked God to let him build a Temple* for the people of Jacob.ᶜ 47But Solomon was the one who built the Temple.

48"But the Most High God does not live in houses built by human hands. This is what the prophetᵈ writes:

49 'The Lord says,
   Heaven is my throne.
      The earth is a place to rest my feet.
   What kind of house can you build for me?
      Do I need a place to rest?
50 Remember, I made all these things!'"   *Isaiah 66:1–2*

51Then Stephen said, "You stubborn leaders! You refuse to give your hearts to God or even listen to him. You are always against what the Holy Spirit* wants you to do. That's how your ancestors were, and you are just like them! 52They persecuted* every prophet who ever lived. They even killed those who long ago said that the Righteous One would come. And now you have turned against that Righteous One and killed him. 53You are the people who received God's law, which he gave you through his angels. But you don't obey it!"

ª7:40 Quote from Ex. 32:1. ᵇ7:44 *Holy Tent* Literally, "Tent of the Testimony," See "Holy Tent" in the Word List. ᶜ7:46 *for the people of Jacob* Some Greek copies have "for the God of Jacob." ᵈ7:48 *prophet* Isaiah, who spoke for God about 740–700 B.C.

Stephen Is Killed

⁵⁴When those in the council meeting heard this, they became very angry. They were so mad they were grinding their teeth at him. ⁵⁵But Stephen was full of the Holy Spirit.* He looked up into heaven and saw the glory* of God. And he saw Jesus standing at God's right side. ⁵⁶Stephen said, "Look! I see heaven open. And I see the Son of Man* standing at God's right side."

⁵⁷Everyone there started shouting loudly, covering their ears with their hands. Together they all ran at Stephen. ⁵⁸They took him out of the city and began throwing stones at him. The men who told lies against Stephen gave their coats to a young man named Saul. ⁵⁹As they were throwing the stones at him, Stephen was praying. He said, "Lord Jesus, receive my spirit!" ⁶⁰He fell on his knees and shouted, "Lord, don't blame them for this sin!" These were his last words before he died.

8 ¹⁻³Saul agreed that the killing of Stephen was a good thing. Some godly men buried Stephen and cried loudly for him.

Trouble for the Believers

On that day the Jews began to persecute* the church* in Jerusalem, making them suffer very much. Saul was also trying to destroy the group. He went into their houses, dragged out men and women, and put them in jail. All the believers left Jerusalem. Only the apostles* stayed. The believers went to different places in Judea and Samaria. ⁴They were scattered everywhere, and in every place they went, they told people the Good News.*

Philip Tells the Good News in Samaria

⁵Philip*ᵃ* went to the city of Samaria and told people about the Christ.* ⁶The people there heard Philip and saw the miraculous signs* he was doing. They all listened carefully to what he said. ⁷Many of these people had evil spirits inside them, but Philip made the evil spirits leave them. The spirits made a lot of noise as they came out. There were also many weak and crippled people there. Philip made these people well too. ⁸What a happy day this was for that city!

⁹Now there was a man named Simon who lived in that city. Before Philip came there, Simon had been doing magic and amazing all the people of Samaria. He bragged and called himself a great man. ¹⁰All the people—the least important and the most important—believed what he said. They said, "This man has the power of God that is called 'the Great Power.'" ¹¹Simon amazed the people with his magic for so long that the people became his followers. ¹²But Philip told the people the Good News* about God's kingdom* and the power of Jesus Christ. Men and women believed Philip and were baptized.* ¹³Simon himself also believed, and after he was baptized, he stayed

ᵃ8:5 Philip Not the apostle named Philip.

close to Philip. When he saw the miraculous signs* and powerful things Philip did, he was amazed.

¹⁴The apostles* in Jerusalem heard that the people of Samaria had accepted the word of God. So they sent Peter and John to the people in Samaria. ¹⁵When Peter and John arrived, they prayed for the Samaritan believers to receive the Holy Spirit.* ¹⁶These people had been baptized in the name of the Lord Jesus, but the Holy Spirit had not yet come down on any of them. This is why Peter and John prayed. ¹⁷When the two apostles laid their hands on*ᵃ* the people, they received the Holy Spirit.

¹⁸Simon saw that the Spirit was given to people when the apostles laid their hands on them. So he offered the apostles money. ¹⁹He said, "Give me this power so that when I lay my hands on someone, they will receive the Holy Spirit."

²⁰Peter said to Simon, "You and your money should both be destroyed because you thought you could buy God's gift with money. ²¹You cannot share with us in this work. Your heart is not right before God. ²²Change your heart! Turn away from these evil thoughts and pray to the Lord. Maybe he will forgive you. ²³I see that you are full of bitter jealousy and cannot stop yourself from doing wrong."

²⁴Simon answered, "Both of you pray to the Lord for me, so that what you have said will not happen to me."

²⁵Then the two apostles told the people what they had seen Jesus do. They told them the message* of the Lord. Then they went back to Jerusalem. On the way, they went through many Samaritan towns and told people the Good News.

Philip Teaches a Man From Ethiopia

²⁶An angel of the Lord spoke to Philip. The angel said, "Get ready and go south on the road that leads down to Gaza from Jerusalem—the road that goes through the desert."

²⁷So Philip got ready and went. On the road he saw a man from Ethiopia. He was a eunuch* and an important officer in the service of Candace, the queen of the Ethiopians. He was responsible for taking care of all her money. This man had gone to Jerusalem to worship. ²⁸Now he was on his way home. He was sitting in his chariot* reading from the book of Isaiah the prophet.*

²⁹The Spirit* said to Philip, "Go to that chariot and stay near it." ³⁰So he went toward the chariot, and he heard the man reading from Isaiah the prophet. Philip asked him, "Do you understand what you are reading?"

³¹The man answered, "How can I understand? I need someone to explain it to me." Then he invited Philip to climb

---

*ᵃ*8:17 *laid their hands on* This act was a way of asking God to bless people in a special way—here, to give them power through his Spirit.

in and sit with him. ³²The part of the Scriptures* that he was reading was this:

"He was like a sheep being led to the butcher.
He was like a lamb that makes no sound
   as its wool is being cut off.
He said nothing.
³³ He was shamed, and all his rights were taken away.
His life on earth has ended.
   So there will be no story about his descendants."

Isaiah 53:7–8

³⁴The officer said to Philip, "Please, tell me, who is the prophet talking about? Is he talking about himself or about someone else?" ³⁵Philip began to speak. He started with this same Scripture and told the man the Good News* about Jesus.

³⁶While they were traveling down the road, they came to some water. The officer said, "Look, here is water! What is stopping me from being baptized*?" ³⁷ᵃ ³⁸Then the officer ordered the chariot to stop. Both Philip and the officer went down into the water, and Philip baptized him. ³⁹When they came up out of the water, the Spirit of the Lord took Philip away; the officer never saw him again. The officer continued on his way home. He was very happy. ⁴⁰But Philip appeared in a city called Azotus. He was going to the city of Caesarea. He told people the Good News in all the towns on the way from Azotus to Caesarea.

Saul Becomes a Follower of Jesus

9 ¹In Jerusalem Saul was still trying to scare the followers of the Lord, even saying he would kill them. He went to the high priest* ²and asked him to write letters to the synagogues* in the city of Damascus. Saul wanted the high priest to give him the authority to find people in Damascus who were followers of the Way.* If he found any believers there, men or women, he would arrest them and bring them back to Jerusalem.

³So Saul went to Damascus. When he came near the city, a very bright light from heaven suddenly shined around him. ⁴He fell to the ground and heard a voice saying to him, "Saul, Saul! Why are you persecuting* me?"

⁵Saul said, "Who are you, Lord?"

The voice answered, "I am Jesus, the one you are persecuting. ⁶Get up now and go into the city. Someone there will tell you what you must do."

⁷The men traveling with Saul just stood there, unable to speak. They heard the voice, but they saw no one. ⁸Saul got up from the ground and opened his eyes, but he could not see. So the men with him held his hand and led him into Damascus. ⁹For three days Saul could not see; he did not eat or drink.

ᵃ8:37 Some late copies of Acts add verse 37: "Philip answered, 'If you believe with all your heart, you can.' The officer said, 'I believe that Jesus Christ is the Son of God.'"

[10]There was a follower of Jesus in Damascus named Ananias. In a vision* the Lord said to him, "Ananias!"

Ananias answered, "Here I am, Lord."

[11]The Lord said to him, "Get up and go to the street called Straight Street. Find the house of Judas[a] and ask for a man named Saul from the city of Tarsus. He is there now, praying. [12]He has seen a vision in which a man named Ananias came and laid his hands on[b] him so that he could see again."

[13]But Ananias answered, "Lord, many people have told me about this man. They told me about the many bad things he did to your holy people* in Jerusalem. [14]Now he has come here to Damascus. The leading priests have given him the power to arrest all people who trust in you.[c]"

[15]But the Lord Jesus said to Ananias, "Go! I have chosen Saul for an important work. He must tell about me to other nations and their rulers and to the Jewish people. [16]I will show him all that he must suffer for me."

[17]So Ananias left and went to the house of Judas. He laid his hands on Saul and said, "Saul, my brother, the Lord Jesus sent me. He is the one you saw on the road when you came here. He sent me so that you can see again and also be filled with the Holy Spirit.*" [18]Immediately, something that looked like fish scales fell off Saul's eyes. He was able to see! Then he got up and was baptized.* [19]After he ate, he began to feel strong again.

Saul Begins to Tell About Jesus

Saul stayed with the followers of Jesus in Damascus for a few days. [20]Soon he began to go to the synagogues* and tell people about Jesus. He told the people, "Jesus is the Son of God!"

[21]All the people who heard Saul were amazed. They said, "This is the same man who was in Jerusalem trying to destroy the people who trust in Jesus[d]! And that's why he has come here—to arrest the followers of Jesus and take them back to the leading priests."

[22]But Saul became more and more powerful in proving that Jesus is the Christ.* His proofs were so strong that the Jews who lived in Damascus could not argue with him.

Saul Escapes From Some Jews

[23]After many days, some Jews made plans to kill Saul. [24]They were watching the city gates day and night. They wanted to kill Saul, but he learned about their plan. [25]One night some followers that Saul had taught helped him leave the city. They

---

*a*9:11 *Judas* This is not either of the apostles named Judas. *b*9:12 *laid his hands on* This act was a way of asking God to bless people in a special way—here, to give Saul sight and the Holy Spirit. Also in verse 17. *c*9:14 *who trust in you* Literally, "who call on your name," meaning to show faith in Jesus by worshiping him or praying to him for help. *d*9:21 *who trust in Jesus* Literally, "who call on this name."

put him in a basket and lowered it down through a hole in the city wall.

Saul in Jerusalem

²⁶Then Saul went to Jerusalem. He tried to join the group of followers, but they were all afraid of him. They did not believe that he was really a follower of Jesus. ²⁷But Barnabas accepted Saul and took him to the apostles.* He told them how Saul had seen the Lord on the road and how the Lord had spoken to Saul. Then he told them how boldly Saul had spoken for the Lord in Damascus.

²⁸And so Saul stayed with the followers and went all around Jerusalem speaking boldly for the Lord. ²⁹He often had arguments with the Greek-speaking Jews, who began making plans to kill him. ³⁰When the believers* learned about this, they took Saul to Caesarea, and from there they sent him to the city of Tarsus.

³¹The church* in Judea, Galilee, and Samaria had a time of peace. With the help of the Holy Spirit,* the groups of believers became stronger and showed their respect for the Lord by the way they lived. So the church everywhere grew in numbers.

Peter in Lydda and Joppa

³²Peter was traveling through all the areas around Jerusalem, and he stopped to visit the believers^a who lived in Lydda. ³³There he met a man named Aeneas, who was paralyzed and had not been able to get out of bed for the past eight years. ³⁴Peter said to him, "Aeneas, Jesus Christ heals you. Get up and make your bed!" He stood up immediately. ³⁵All the people living in Lydda and on the plain of Sharon saw him, and they decided to follow the Lord.

³⁶In the city of Joppa there was a follower of Jesus named Tabitha. (Her Greek name, Dorcas, means "a deer.") She was always doing good things for people and giving money to those in need. ³⁷While Peter was in Lydda, Tabitha became sick and died. They washed her body and put it in an upstairs room. ³⁸The followers in Joppa heard that Peter was in Lydda, which was not far away. So they sent two men, who begged him, "Hurry, please come quickly!"

³⁹Peter got ready and went with them. When he arrived, they took him to the upstairs room. All the widows stood around him. They were crying and showing him the coats and other clothes that Tabitha had made during her time with them. ⁴⁰Peter sent all the people out of the room. He knelt down and prayed. Then he turned to Tabitha's body and said, "Tabitha, stand up!" She opened her eyes. When she saw Peter, she sat up. ⁴¹He gave her his hand and helped her stand up.

---

^a 9:32 believers Literally, "holy ones," a name for people who believe in Jesus. Also in verse 41.

Then he called the believers and the widows into the room. He showed them Tabitha; she was alive!

⁴²People everywhere in Joppa learned about this, and many believed in the Lord. ⁴³Peter stayed in Joppa for many days at the home of a man named Simon, who was a leatherworker.*

Peter and Cornelius

10 ¹In the city of Caesarea there was a man named Cornelius, a Roman army officer* in what was called the Italian Unit. ²He was a religious man. He and all the others who lived in his house were worshipers of the true God. He gave much of his money to help the Jewish poor people and always prayed to God. ³One afternoon about three o'clock, Cornelius had a vision.* He clearly saw an angel from God coming to him and saying, "Cornelius!"

⁴Staring at the angel and feeling afraid, Cornelius said, "What do you want, sir?"

The angel said to him, "God has heard your prayers and has seen your gifts to the poor. He remembers you and all you have done. ⁵Send some men now to the city of Joppa to get a man named Simon, who is also called Peter. ⁶He is staying with someone also named Simon, a leatherworker* who has a house beside the sea." ⁷The angel who spoke to Cornelius left. Then Cornelius called two of his servants and a soldier. The soldier was a religious man, one of his close helpers. ⁸Cornelius explained everything to these three men and sent them to Joppa.

⁹The next day they were coming near Joppa about noon, when Peter was going up to the roof to pray. ¹⁰He was hungry and wanted to eat. But while they were preparing the food for Peter to eat, he had a vision. ¹¹He saw something coming down through the open sky. It looked like a big sheet being lowered to the ground by its four corners. ¹²In it were all kinds of animals, reptiles, and birds. ¹³Then a voice said to him, "Get up, Peter; kill anything here and eat it."

¹⁴But Peter said, "I can't do that, Lord! I have never eaten anything that is not pure or fit to be used for food."

¹⁵But the voice said to him again, "God has made these things pure. Don't say they are unfit to eat." ¹⁶This happened three times. Then the whole thing was taken back up into heaven. ¹⁷Peter wondered what this vision meant.

The men Cornelius sent had found Simon's house. They were standing at the door. ¹⁸They asked, "Is Simon Peter staying here?"

¹⁹While Peter was still thinking about the vision, the Spirit* said to him, "Listen, three men are looking for you. ²⁰Get up and go downstairs. Go with these men without wondering if it's all right, because I sent them." ²¹So Peter went downstairs and said to them, "I think I'm the man you are looking for. Why did you come here?"

²²The men said, "A holy* angel told Cornelius to invite you to his house. He is an army officer. He is a good man, one who worships God, and all the Jewish people respect him. The angel told him to invite you to his house so that he can listen to what you have to say." ²³Peter asked the men to come in and stay for the night.

The next day Peter got ready and went away with the three men. Some of the believers* from Joppa went with him. ²⁴The next day they came to the city of Caesarea. Cornelius was waiting for them and had already gathered his relatives and close friends at his house.

²⁵When Peter entered the house, Cornelius met him. He fell down at Peter's feet and worshiped him. ²⁶But Peter told him to get up. Peter said, "Stand up! I am only a man like you." ²⁷Peter continued talking with Cornelius. Then Peter went inside and saw a large group of people gathered there.

²⁸Peter said to the people, "You understand that it is against our law for a Jew to associate with or visit anyone who is not a Jew. But God has shown me that I should not consider anyone unfit or say they are not pure. ²⁹That's why I didn't argue when your men asked me to come here. Now, please tell me why you sent for me."

³⁰Cornelius said, "Four days ago, I was praying in my house. It was at this same time—three o'clock in the afternoon. Suddenly there was someone standing before me wearing bright, shiny clothes. ³¹He said, 'Cornelius, God has heard your prayer and has seen your gifts to the poor. He remembers you and all you have done. ³²So send some men to the city of Joppa and ask Simon Peter to come. He is staying with another man named Simon, a leatherworker who has a house beside the sea.' ³³So I sent for you immediately. It was very good of you to come here. Now we are all here before God to hear everything the Lord has commanded you to tell us."

Peter Speaks in the House of Cornelius

³⁴Peter began to speak: "I really understand now that God does not consider some people to be better than others. ³⁵He accepts anyone who worships him and does what is right. It is not important what nation they come from. ³⁶God has spoken to the Jewish people. He sent them the Good News* that peace has come through Jesus Christ, the Lord of all people.

³⁷"You know what has happened all over Judea. It began in Galilee after John* told the people they needed to be baptized.* ³⁸You know about Jesus from Nazareth. God made him the Christ* by giving him the Holy Spirit* and power. Jesus went everywhere doing good for people. He healed those who were ruled by the devil, showing that God was with him.

³⁹"We saw all that Jesus did in Judea and in Jerusalem. But he was killed. They put him on a cross made of wood. ⁴⁰But on

the third day after his death, God raised him to life and let him be seen openly. ⁴¹He was not seen by everyone, but only by us, the ones God had already chosen to be witnesses. We ate and drank with him after he was raised from death.

⁴²"Jesus told us to go and speak to the people. He told us to tell them that he is the one God chose to be the Judge of all who are living and all who have died. ⁴³Everyone who believes in Jesus will have their sins forgiven through his name. All the prophets* agree that this is true."

The Spirit Comes to Non-Jewish People

⁴⁴While Peter was still speaking these words, the Holy Spirit* came down on all those who were listening to his speech. ⁴⁵The Jewish believers who came with Peter were amazed that the Holy Spirit had been poured out as a gift also to people who were not Jews. ⁴⁶They heard them speaking different languages and praising God. Then Peter said, ⁴⁷"How can anyone object to these people being baptized* in water? They have received the Holy Spirit the same as we did!" ⁴⁸So Peter told them to baptize Cornelius and his relatives and friends in the name of Jesus Christ. Then they asked Peter to stay with them for a few days.

Peter Returns to Jerusalem

11 ¹The apostles* and the believers* in Judea heard that non-Jewish people had accepted God's teaching too. ²But when Peter came to Jerusalem, some Jewish believers*ᵃ argued with him. ³They said, "You went into the homes of people who are not Jews and are not circumcised,* and you even ate with them!"

⁴So Peter explained the whole story to them. ⁵He said, "I was in the city of Joppa. While I was praying, I had a vision.* I saw something coming down from heaven. It looked like a big sheet being lowered to the ground by its four corners. It came down close to me, ⁶and I looked inside. I saw all kinds of animals, including wild ones, as well as reptiles and birds. ⁷I heard a voice say to me, 'Get up, Peter. Kill anything here and eat it!'

⁸"But I said, 'I can't do that, Lord! I have never eaten anything that is not pure or fit to be used for food.'

⁹"But the voice from heaven answered again, 'God has made these things pure. Don't say they are unfit to eat!'

¹⁰"This happened three times. Then the whole thing was taken back into heaven. ¹¹Suddenly there were three men standing outside the house where I was staying. They had been sent from Caesarea to get me. ¹²The Spirit* told me to go with them without wondering if it was all right. These six

---

ᵃ**11:2** *Jewish believers* Literally, "those of circumcision." This may mean Jews who thought all followers of Christ must be circumcised and obey the law of Moses. See Gal. 2:12.

brothers here also went with me, and we went to the house of Cornelius. [13]He told us about the angel he had seen standing in his house. The angel said, 'Send some men to Joppa to get Simon, the one who is also called Peter. [14]He will speak to you, and what he tells you will save you and everyone living in your house.'

[15]"After I began speaking, the Holy Spirit came on them just as he came on us at the beginning.[a] [16]Then I remembered the words of the Lord Jesus: 'John baptized* people in water, but you will be baptized in the Holy Spirit.' [17]God gave these people the same gift he gave us who believed in the Lord Jesus Christ. So how could I object to what God wanted to do?"

[18]When the Jewish believers heard this, they stopped arguing. They praised God and said, "So God is also allowing the non-Jewish people to change their hearts and have the life he gives!"

The Good News Comes to Antioch

[19]The believers were scattered by the persecution[b] that began when Stephen was killed. Some of them went as far as Phoenicia, Cyprus, and Antioch. They told the Good News* in these places, but only to Jews. [20]Some of these believers were men from Cyprus and Cyrene. When these men came to Antioch, they began speaking to people who were not Jews.[c] They told them the Good News about the Lord Jesus. [21]The Lord was helping these men, and a large number of people believed and decided to follow the Lord.

[22]The church* in Jerusalem heard about these new believers in Antioch. So the believers in Jerusalem sent Barnabas to Antioch. [23-24]Barnabas was a good man, full of the Holy Spirit* and faith. When he went to Antioch and saw how God had blessed the believers there, he was very happy. He encouraged them all, saying, "Always be faithful to the Lord. Serve him with all your heart." Many more people became followers of the Lord.

[25]Then Barnabas went to the city of Tarsus to look for Saul. [26]When he found him, he brought him to Antioch. They stayed there a whole year. Every time the church came together, Barnabas and Saul met with them and taught many people. It was in Antioch that the followers were called "Christ followers" for the first time.

[27]About that same time some prophets* went from Jerusalem to Antioch. [28]One of them, named Agabus, stood up

---

[a]11:15 beginning The beginning of the church on the day of Pentecost. See Acts 2.
[b]11:19 persecution A time when the Jewish leaders in Jerusalem were punishing people who believed in Christ. See Acts 8:1–4. [c]11:20 people who were not Jews Literally, "Hellenists," meaning people who have been influenced by Greek culture. Some Greek copies have "Greeks."

and spoke with the help of the Spirit. He said, "A very bad time is coming to the whole world. There will be no food for people to eat." (This time of famine happened when Claudius was emperor.*) 29The Lord's followers decided that they would each send as much as they could to help their brothers and sisters who lived in Judea. 30They gathered the money and gave it to Barnabas and Saul, who took it to the elders* in Judea.

Herod Agrippa Hurts the Church

12 1During this same time, King Herod* began to persecute* some of the people who were part of the church.* 2He ordered James, the brother of John, to be killed with a sword. 3Herod saw that the Jews liked this, so he decided to arrest Peter too. (This happened during the Festival of Unleavened Bread.*) 4He arrested Peter and put him in jail, where he was guarded by a group of 16 soldiers. Herod planned to bring Peter before the people, but he wanted to wait until after the Passover festival. 5So Peter was kept in jail, but the church was constantly praying to God for him.

Peter Leaves the Jail

6One night, Peter, bound with two chains, was sleeping between two of the soldiers. More soldiers were guarding the door of the jail. Herod* was planning to bring Peter out before the people the next day. 7Suddenly an angel of the Lord was standing there, and the room was filled with light. The angel tapped Peter on the side and woke him up. The angel said, "Hurry, get up!" The chains fell off Peter's hands. 8The angel said, "Get dressed and put on your sandals." Peter did as he was told. Then the angel said, "Put on your coat and follow me."

9So the angel went out and Peter followed. He did not know if the angel was really doing this. He thought he might be seeing a vision.* 10Peter and the angel went past the first guard and the second guard. Then they came to the iron gate that separated them from the city. The gate opened for them by itself. After they went through the gate and walked about a block, the angel suddenly left.

11Peter realized then what had happened. He thought, "Now I know that the Lord really sent his angel to me. He rescued me from Herod and from all the bad things the Jewish leaders were planning to do to me."

12When Peter realized this, he went to the home of Mary, the mother of John, who was also called Mark. Many people were gathered there and were praying. 13Peter knocked on the outside door. A servant girl named Rhoda came to answer it. 14She recognized Peter's voice, and she was very happy. She even forgot to open the door. She ran inside and told the group, "Peter is at the door!" 15The believers said to her, "You are crazy!" But she continued to say that it was true. So they said, "It must be Peter's angel."

¹⁶But Peter continued to knock. When the believers opened the door, they saw him. They were amazed. ¹⁷Peter made a sign with his hand to tell them to be quiet. He explained to them how the Lord led him out of the jail. He said, "Tell James and the other brothers what happened." Then he left and went to another place.

¹⁸The next day the soldiers were very upset. They wondered what happened to Peter. ¹⁹Herod looked everywhere for him but could not find him. So he questioned the guards and then ordered that they be killed.

The Death of Herod Agrippa

Later, Herod* moved from Judea. He went to the city of Caesarea and stayed there a while. ²⁰Herod was very angry with the people from the cities of Tyre and Sidon. But these cities needed food from his country, so a group of them came to ask him for peace. They were able to get Blastus, the king's personal servant, on their side.

²¹Herod decided on a day to meet with them. On that day he was wearing a beautiful royal robe. He sat on his throne and made a speech to the people. ²²The people shouted, "This is the voice of a god, not a man!" ²³Herod did not give the glory* to God. So an angel of the Lord caused him to get sick. He was eaten by worms inside him, and he died.

²⁴The message* of God was spreading, reaching more and more people.

²⁵After Barnabas and Saul finished their work in Jerusalem, they returned to Antioch, taking John Mark with them.

Barnabas and Saul Given a Special Work

13 ¹In the church* at Antioch there were some prophets* and teachers. They were Barnabas, Simeon (also called Niger), Lucius (from the city of Cyrene), Manaen (who had grown up with King Herod*ᵃ), and Saul. ²These men were all serving the Lord and fasting* when the Holy Spirit* said to them, "Appoint Barnabas and Saul to do a special work for me. They are the ones I have chosen to do it."

³So the church fasted and prayed. They laid their hands onᵇ Barnabas and Saul and sent them out.

Barnabas and Saul in Cyprus

⁴Barnabas and Saul were sent out by the Holy Spirit.* They went to the city of Seleucia. Then they sailed from there to the island of Cyprus. ⁵When Barnabas and Saul came to the city of

---

ᵃ 13:1 *King Herod* Literally, "Herod the tetrarch." See "Herod Agrippa I" in the Word List.
ᵇ 13:3 *laid their hands on* This act was a way of asking God to bless people in a special way—here, to give them power for a special work.

Salamis, they told the message* of God in the Jewish synagogues.* (John Mark was with them to help.)

⁶They went across the whole island to the city of Paphos. There they met a Jewish man named Barjesus who did magic. He was a false prophet.* ⁷He always stayed close to Sergius Paulus, who was the governor and a very smart man. He invited Barnabas and Saul to come visit him, because he wanted to hear the message of God. ⁸But the magician Elymas (as Barjesus was called in Greek) spoke against them, trying to stop the governor from believing in Jesus. ⁹But Saul (also known as Paul), filled with the Holy Spirit, looked hard at Elymas ¹⁰and said, "You son of the devil, full of lies and all kinds of evil tricks! You are an enemy of everything that is right. Will you never stop trying to change the Lord's truths into lies? ¹¹Now the Lord will touch you and you will be blind. For a time you will not be able to see anything—not even the light from the sun."

Then everything became dark for Elymas. He walked around lost. He was trying to find someone to lead him by the hand. ¹²When the governor saw this, he believed. He was amazed at the teaching about the Lord.

Paul and Barnabas Go to Antioch in Pisidia

¹³Paul and the people with him sailed away from Paphos. They came to Perga, a city in Pamphylia. There John Mark left them and returned to Jerusalem. ¹⁴They continued their trip from Perga and went to Antioch, a city near Pisidia.

On the Sabbath* day they went into the Jewish synagogue* and sat down. ¹⁵The law of Moses* and the writings of the prophets* were read. Then the leaders of the synagogue sent a message to Paul and Barnabas: "Brothers, if you have something to say that will help the people here, please speak."

¹⁶Paul stood up, raised his hand to get their attention, and said, "My Jewish brothers and you other people who also worship the true God, please listen to me! ¹⁷The God of Israel* chose our ancestors.* And during the time our people lived in Egypt as foreigners, he made them great. Then he brought them out of that country with great power. ¹⁸And he was patient with them for 40 years in the desert. ¹⁹God destroyed seven nations in the land of Canaan and gave their land to his people. ²⁰All this happened in about 450 years.

"After this, God gave our people judges until the time of Samuel* the prophet. ²¹Then the people asked for a king. God gave them Saul, the son of Kish. Saul was from the tribe of Benjamin. He was king for 40 years. ²²After God took Saul away, God made David* their king. This is what God said about David: 'David, the son of Jesse, is the kind of person who does what pleases me. He will do everything I want him to do.'

²³"As he promised, God has brought one of David's descendants to Israel to be their Savior. That descendant is Jesus. ²⁴Before

he came, John* told all the Jewish people what they should do. He told them to be baptized* to show they wanted to change their lives. 25When John was finishing his work, he said, 'Who do you think I am? I am not the Christ.* He is coming later, and I am not worthy to be the slave who unties his sandals.'

26"My brothers, sons in the family of Abraham,* and you other people who also worship the true God, listen! The news about this salvation has been sent to us. 27The Jews living in Jerusalem and their leaders did not realize that Jesus was the Savior. The words the prophets wrote about him were read every Sabbath day, but they did not understand. They condemned Jesus. When they did this, they made the words of the prophets come true. 28They could not find any real reason why Jesus should die, but they asked Pilate to kill him.

29"These Jews did all the bad things that the Scriptures* said would happen to Jesus. Then they took Jesus down from the cross and put him in a tomb.* 30But God raised him up from death! 31After this, for many days, those who had gone with Jesus from Galilee to Jerusalem saw him. They are now his witnesses to our people.

32"We tell you the Good News* about the promise God made to our ancestors. 33We are their descendants, and God has made this promise come true for us. God did this by raising Jesus from death. We also read about this in Psalm 2:

> 'You are my Son.
>> Today I have become your Father.'   *Psalm 2:7*

34God raised Jesus from death. Jesus will never go back to the grave and become dust. So God said,

> 'I will give you the true and holy promises
>> that I made to David.'   *Isaiah 55:3*

35But in another Psalm it says,

> 'You will not let your Holy One rot in the grave.'   *Psalm 16:10*

36David did God's will during the time he lived. Then he died and was buried like all his ancestors. And his body did rot in the grave! 37But the one God raised from death did not rot in the grave. 38-39Brothers, understand what we are telling you. You can have forgiveness of your sins through this Jesus. The law of Moses could not free you from your sins. But you can be made right with God if you believe in Jesus. 40So be careful! Don't let what the prophets said happen to you:

41 'Listen, you people who doubt!
> You can wonder, but then go away and die;
> because during your time,
>> I will do something that you will not believe.
> You will not believe it, even if someone explains it to you!'"
    Habakkuk 1:5

⁴²As Paul and Barnabas were leaving the synagogue, the people asked them to come again on the next Sabbath day and tell them more about these things. ⁴³After the meeting, many of the people followed Paul and Barnabas, including many Jews and people who had changed their religion to be like Jews and worship the true God. Paul and Barnabas encouraged them to continue trusting in God's grace.*

⁴⁴On the next Sabbath day, almost all the people in the city came together to hear the word of the Lord. ⁴⁵When the Jews there saw all these people, they became very jealous. Shouting insults, they argued against everything Paul said. ⁴⁶But Paul and Barnabas spoke very boldly. They said, "We had to tell God's message* to you Jews first, but you refuse to listen. You have made it clear that you are not worthy of having eternal life. So we will now go to those who are not Jews. ⁴⁷This is what the Lord told us to do:

'I have made you a light for other nations,
    to show the way of salvation to people all over the world.'"
                                                            Isaiah 49:6

⁴⁸When the non-Jewish people heard Paul say this, they were happy. They gave honor to the message of the Lord, and many of them believed it. These were the ones chosen to have eternal life.

⁴⁹And so the message of the Lord was being told throughout the whole country. ⁵⁰But the Jews there caused some of the important religious women and the leaders of the city to be angry and turn against Paul and Barnabas and throw them out of town. ⁵¹So Paul and Barnabas shook the dust off their feet.ᵃ Then they went to the city of Iconium. ⁵²But the Lord's followers in Antioch were happy and filled with the Holy Spirit.*

Paul and Barnabas in Iconium

14 ¹Paul and Barnabas went to the city of Iconium and entered the Jewish synagogue.* (This is what they did in every city.) They spoke to the people there. They spoke so well that many Jews and Greeks believed what they said. ²But some of the Jews did not believe. They said things that caused the non-Jewish people to be angry and turn against the Lord's followers.

³So Paul and Barnabas stayed in Iconium a long time, and they spoke bravely for the Lord. They told the people about God's grace.* The Lord proved that what they said was true by causing miraculous signs* and wonders* to be done through them. ⁴But some of the people in the city agreed with the Jews who did not believe Paul and Barnabas. Others followed the apostles. So the city was divided.

ᵃ**13:51** *shook the dust off their feet* A warning. It showed they were finished talking to these people.

⁵Some of the Jews there, as well as their leaders and some of the non-Jewish people, were determined to hurt Paul and Barnabas. They wanted to stone them to death. ⁶When Paul and Barnabas learned about this, they left the city. They went to Lystra and Derbe, cities in Lycaonia, and to the surrounding areas. ⁷They told the Good News* there too.

Paul in Lystra and Derbe

⁸In Lystra there was a man who had something wrong with his feet. He had been born crippled and had never walked. ⁹He was sitting and listening to Paul speak. Paul looked straight at him and saw that the man believed God could heal him. ¹⁰So Paul shouted, "Stand up on your feet!" The man jumped up and began walking around.

¹¹When the people saw what Paul did, they shouted in their own Lycaonian language. They said, "The gods have come down to us in the form of humans!" ¹²The people began to call Barnabas "Zeus,*" and they called Paul "Hermes,*" because he was the main speaker. ¹³The temple of Zeus was near the city. The priest of this temple brought some bulls and flowers to the city gates. The priest and the people wanted to offer a sacrifice to Paul and Barnabas.

¹⁴But when the apostles,* Barnabas and Paul, understood what the people were doing, they tore their own clothes.ᵃ Then they ran in among the people and shouted to them: ¹⁵"Men, why are you doing this? We are not gods. We are human just like you. We came to tell you the Good News.* We are telling you to turn away from these worthless things. Turn to the true living God, the one who made the sky, the earth, the sea, and everything that is in them. ¹⁶In the past God let all the nations do what they wanted. ¹⁷But God was always there doing the good things that prove he is real. He gives you rain from heaven and good harvests at the right times. He gives you plenty of food and fills your hearts with joy."

¹⁸Even after saying all this, Paul and Barnabas still could hardly stop the people from offering sacrifices to them.

¹⁹Then some Jews came from Antioch and Iconium and persuaded the people to turn against Paul. So they threw stones at him and dragged him out of the town. They thought they had killed him. ²⁰But when the followers of Jesus gathered around him, he got up and went back into the town. The next day he and Barnabas left and went to the city of Derbe.

The Return to Antioch in Syria

²¹They also told the Good News* in the city of Derbe, and many people became followers of Jesus. Then Paul and

---

ᵃ14:14 tore ... clothes This showed they were very upset.

Barnabas returned to the cities of Lystra, Iconium, and Antioch. [22]In those cities they strengthened the commitment of the followers and encouraged them to continue in the faith. They told them, "We must suffer many things on our way into God's kingdom.*" [23]They also chose elders* for each church* and stopped eating for a period of time to pray for them. These elders were men who had put their trust in the Lord Jesus, so Paul and Barnabas put them in his care.

[24]Paul and Barnabas went through the country of Pisidia. Then they came to the country of Pamphylia. [25]They told people the message* of God in the city of Perga, and then they went down to the city of Attalia. [26]And from there they sailed away to Antioch in Syria. This is the city where the believers had put them into God's care and sent them to do this work. Now they had finished it.

[27]When they arrived, they gathered the church together and told them about all that God had done with them. They said, "God opened a door so that the non-Jewish people could also believe!" [28]And they stayed there a long time with the Lord's followers.

The Meeting at Jerusalem

15 [1]Then some men came to Antioch from Judea and began teaching the non-Jewish believers: "You cannot be saved if you are not circumcised* as Moses* taught us." [2]Paul and Barnabas were against this teaching and argued with these men about it. So the group decided to send Paul, Barnabas, and some others to Jerusalem to talk more about this with the apostles* and elders.*

[3]The church* helped them get ready to leave on their trip. The men went through the countries of Phoenicia and Samaria, where they told all about how the non-Jewish people had turned to the true God. This made all the believers very happy. [4]When the men arrived in Jerusalem, the apostles, the elders, and the whole church welcomed them. Paul, Barnabas, and the others told about all that God had done with them. [5]Some of the believers in Jerusalem had belonged to the Pharisees.* They stood up and said, "The non-Jewish believers must be circumcised. We must tell them to obey the law of Moses!"

[6]Then the apostles and the elders gathered to study this problem. [7]After a long debate, Peter stood up and said to them, "My brothers, I am sure you remember what happened in the early days. God chose me from among you to tell the Good News* to those who are not Jewish. It was from me that they heard the Good News and believed. [8]God knows everyone, even their thoughts, and he accepted these non-Jewish people. He showed this to us by giving them the Holy Spirit* the same as he did to us. [9]To God, those people are not different from us.

When they believed, God made their hearts pure. [10]So now, why are you putting a heavy burden[a] around the necks of the non-Jewish followers? Are you trying to make God angry? We and our fathers* were not able to carry that burden. [11]No, we believe that we and these people will be saved the same way—by the grace* of the Lord Jesus."

[12]Then the whole group became quiet. They listened while Paul and Barnabas told about all the miraculous signs* and wonders* that God had done through them among the non-Jewish people. [13]When they finished speaking, James said, "My brothers, listen to me. [14]Simon Peter has told us how God showed his love for the non-Jewish people. For the first time God accepted them and made them his people. [15]The words of the prophets* agree with this too:

[16] 'I will return after this.
    I will build David's* house again.
    It has fallen down.
  I will build again the parts of his house that have been
        pulled down.
    I will make his house new.

[17] Then the rest of the world will look for the Lord God—
    all those of other nations who are my people too.
  The Lord said this.
    And he is the one who does all these things.'

Amos 9:11-12

[18] 'All this has been known from the beginning of time.'[b]

[19]"So I think we should not bother those who have turned to God from among the non-Jewish people. [20]Instead, we should write a letter to them and tell them:

Don't eat food that has been given to idols.*
  (This makes the food unclean.)
Don't be involved in sexual sin.
Don't eat meat from animals that have been strangled
  or any meat that still has the blood in it.

[21]They should not do any of these things, because there are still men in every city who teach the law of Moses. The words of Moses have been read in the synagogue* every Sabbath* day for many years."

The Letter to the Non-Jewish Believers

[22]The apostles,* the elders,* and the whole church* wanted to send some men with Paul and Barnabas to Antioch. The group decided to choose some of their own men. They chose Judas (also called Barsabbas) and Silas, men who were

---

*a*15:10 burden The Jewish law. Some of the Jews tried to make the non-Jewish believers follow this law.   *b*15:18 See Isa. 45:21.

respected by the believers.* ²³The group sent the letter with these men. The letter said:

From the apostles and elders, your brothers.
To all the non-Jewish brothers in the city of Antioch and in the countries of Syria and Cilicia.

Dear Brothers:

²⁴We have heard that some men have come to you from our group. What they said troubled and upset you. But we did not tell them to do this. ²⁵We have all agreed to choose some men and send them to you. They will be with our dear friends, Barnabas and Paul. ²⁶Barnabas and Paul have given their lives to serve our Lord Jesus Christ. ²⁷So we have sent Judas and Silas with them. They will tell you the same things. ²⁸We agree with the Holy Spirit* that you should have no more burdens, except for these necessary things:

²⁹ Don't eat food that has been given to idols.*
Don't eat meat from animals that have been strangled
or any meat that still has the blood in it.
Don't be involved in sexual sin.

If you stay away from these, you will do well.
We say goodbye now.

³⁰So Paul, Barnabas, Judas, and Silas left Jerusalem and went to Antioch. There they gathered the group of believers together and gave them the letter. ³¹When the believers read it, they were happy. The letter comforted them. ³²Judas and Silas, who were also prophets,* said many things to encourage the believers and make them stronger in their faith. ³³After Judas and Silas stayed there for a while, they left. They received a blessing of peace from the believers. Then they went back to those who had sent them. ³⁴ᵃ

³⁵But Paul and Barnabas stayed in Antioch. They and many others taught the believers and told other people the Good News* about the Lord.

Paul and Barnabas Separate

³⁶A few days later, Paul said to Barnabas, "We should go back to all the towns where we told people the message* of the Lord. We should visit our brothers and sisters in God's family there to see how they are doing."

³⁷Barnabas wanted to bring John Mark with them too. ³⁸But on their first trip John Mark did not continue with them in the work. He had left them at Pamphylia. So Paul did not think it was a good idea to take him this time. ³⁹Paul and Barnabas had a big argument about this. It was so bad that they separated

ᵃ**15:34** Some Greek copies add verse 34: "But Silas decided to remain there."

and went different ways. Barnabas sailed to Cyprus and took Mark with him.

⁴⁰Paul chose Silas to go with him. The believers* in Antioch put Paul into the Lord's care and sent him out. ⁴¹Paul and Silas went through the countries of Syria and Cilicia, helping the churches* grow stronger.

Timothy Goes With Paul and Silas

16 ¹Paul went to the city of Derbe and then to Lystra, where a follower of Jesus named Timothy lived. Timothy's mother was a Jewish believer, but his father was a Greek. ²The believers* in the cities of Lystra and Iconium had only good things to say about him. ³Paul wanted Timothy to travel with him, but all the Jews living in that area knew that his father was a Greek. So Paul circumcised* Timothy to please the Jews.

⁴Then Paul and those with him traveled through other cities. They gave the believers the rules and decisions from the apostles* and elders* in Jerusalem. They told them to obey these rules. ⁵So the churches* were becoming stronger in the faith and were growing bigger every day.

Paul Is Called to Macedonia

⁶Paul and those with him went through the areas of Phrygia and Galatia because the Holy Spirit* did not allow them to tell the Good News* in the province of Asia.* ⁷When they reached the border of Mysia, they tried to go on into Bithynia, but the Spirit of Jesus did not let them go there. ⁸So they passed by Mysia and went to the city of Troas.

⁹That night Paul saw a vision.* In it, a man from Macedonia* came to Paul. The man stood there and begged, "Come across to Macedonia and help us." ¹⁰After Paul had seen the vision, we*a* immediately prepared to leave for Macedonia. We understood that God had called us to tell the Good News to those people.

The Conversion of Lydia

¹¹We left Troas in a ship and sailed to the island of Samothrace. The next day we sailed to the city of Neapolis. ¹²Then we went to Philippi, a Roman colony and the leading city in that part of Macedonia.* We stayed there for a few days.

¹³On the Sabbath* day we went out the city gate to the river. There we thought we might find a special place for prayer. Some women had gathered there, so we sat down and talked with them. ¹⁴There was a woman there named Lydia from the city of Thyatira. Her job was selling purple cloth. She was a worshiper of the true God. Lydia was listening to Paul, and the

*a*16:10 *we* Luke, the writer, apparently went with Paul to Macedonia but did not leave Philippi with him. (See verse 40.) The first person pronoun occurs again in 20:5–21:18 and 27:1–28.

Lord opened her heart to accept what Paul was saying. [15]She and all the people living in her house were baptized.* Then she invited us into her home. She said, "If you think I am a true believer in the Lord Jesus, come stay in my house." She persuaded us to stay with her.

Paul and Silas in Jail

[16]One day we were going to the place for prayer, and a servant girl met us. She had a spirit[a] in her that gave her the power to tell what would happen in the future. By doing this she earned a lot of money for the men who owned her. [17]She started following Paul and the rest of us around. She kept shouting, "These men are servants of the Most High God! They are telling you how you can be saved!" [18]She continued doing this for many days. This bothered Paul, so he turned and said to the spirit, "By the power of Jesus Christ, I command you to come out of her!" Immediately, the spirit came out.

[19]When the men who owned the servant girl saw this, they realized that they could no longer use her to make money. So they grabbed Paul and Silas and dragged them to the public square to meet with the authorities. [20]They brought Paul and Silas before the Roman officials and said, "These men are Jews, and they are making trouble in our city. [21]They are telling people to do things that are not right for us as Romans to do."

[22]The whole crowd turned against Paul and Silas. The officials tore the clothes off of both men and ordered that they be beaten with rods. [23]They were beaten severely and thrown into jail. The officials told the jailer, "Guard them very carefully!" [24]When the jailer heard this special order, he put Paul and Silas far inside the jail and bound their feet between large blocks of wood.

[25]About midnight Paul and Silas were praying and singing songs to God. The other prisoners were listening to them. [26]Suddenly there was an earthquake so strong that it shook the foundation of the jail. All the doors of the jail opened, and the chains on all the prisoners fell off. [27]The jailer woke up and saw that the jail doors were open. He thought that the prisoners had already escaped, so he got his sword and was ready to kill himself.[b] [28]But Paul shouted, "Don't hurt yourself! We are all here!"

[29]The jailer told someone to bring a light. Then he ran inside and, shaking with fear, fell down in front of Paul and Silas. [30]Then he brought them outside and said, "Men, what must I do to be saved?"

[31]They said to him, "Believe in the Lord Jesus and you will be saved—you and all these people from your house." [32]So Paul and Silas told the message* of the Lord to the jailer and all the

---

[a]16:16 *spirit* A spirit from the devil that gave special knowledge.   [b]16:27 *kill himself* He thought the leaders would kill him for letting the prisoners escape.

people who lived in his house. 33It was late at night, but the jailer took Paul and Silas and washed their wounds. Then the jailer and all his people were baptized.* 34After this the jailer took Paul and Silas home and gave them some food. All the people were very happy because they now believed in God.

35The next morning the Roman officials sent some soldiers to tell the jailer, "Let these men go free."

36The jailer said to Paul, "The officials have sent these soldiers to let you go free. You can leave now. Go in peace."

37But Paul said to the soldiers, "Those officials did not prove that we did anything wrong, but they beat us in public and put us in jail. And we are Roman citizens.*a* Now they want us to go away quietly. No, they must come here themselves and lead us out!"

38The soldiers told the officials what Paul said. When they heard that Paul and Silas were Roman citizens, they were afraid. 39So they came and told them they were sorry. They led them out of the jail and asked them to leave the city. 40But when Paul and Silas came out of the jail, they went to Lydia's house. They saw some of the believers* there and encouraged them. Then they left.

Paul and Silas in Thessalonica

17 1Paul and Silas traveled through the cities of Amphipolis and Apollonia. They came to the city of Thessalonica, where there was a Jewish synagogue.* 2Paul went into the synagogue to see the Jews as he always did. The next three weeks, on each Sabbath* day, he discussed the Scriptures* with them. 3He explained the Scriptures to show them that the Christ* had to die and then rise from death. He said, "This Jesus that I am telling you about is the Christ." 4Some of the Jews there believed Paul and Silas and decided to join them. Also, a large number of Greeks who were worshipers of the true God and many important women joined them.

5But the Jews who did not believe became jealous, so they got some bad men from around the city center to make trouble. They formed a mob and caused a riot in the city. They went to Jason's house, looking for Paul and Silas. They wanted to bring them out before the people. 6When they did not find them, they dragged Jason and some of the other believers to the city leaders. The people shouted, "These men have made trouble everywhere in the world, and now they have come here too! 7Jason is keeping them in his house. They all do things against the laws of Caesar.* They say there is another king called Jesus."

8When the city leaders and the other people heard this, they became very upset. 9They made Jason and the other believers

---

*a***16:37** Roman citizens Roman law said that Roman citizens must not be beaten before their trial.

deposit money to guarantee that there would be no more trouble. Then they let them go.

Paul and Silas Go to Berea

¹⁰That same night the believers* sent Paul and Silas to another city named Berea. When they arrived there, they went to the Jewish synagogue.* ¹¹The people in Berea were more open-minded than those in Thessalonica. They were so glad to hear the message Paul told them. They studied the Scriptures* every day to make sure that what they heard was really true. ¹²The result was that many of them believed, including many important Greek women and men.

¹³But when the Jews in Thessalonica learned that Paul was telling people God's message* in Berea, they came there too. They upset the people and made trouble. ¹⁴So the believers immediately sent Paul away to the coast, but Silas and Timothy stayed in Berea. ¹⁵Those who went with Paul took him to the city of Athens. They returned with a message for Silas and Timothy to come and join him as soon as they could.

Paul in Athens

¹⁶While Paul was waiting for Silas and Timothy in Athens, he was upset because he saw that the city was full of idols.* ¹⁷In the synagogue* he talked with the Jews and with the Greeks who were worshipers of the true God. He also went to the public square every day and talked with everyone who came by. ¹⁸Some of the Epicurean and some of the Stoic philosophers* argued with him.

Some of them said, "This man doesn't really know what he is talking about. What is he trying to say?" Paul was telling them the Good News* about Jesus and the resurrection.* So they said, "He seems to be telling us about some other gods."

¹⁹They took Paul to a meeting of the Areopagus council.* They said, "Please explain to us this new idea that you have been teaching. ²⁰The things you are saying are new to us. We have never heard this teaching before, and we want to know what it means." ²¹(The people of Athens and the foreigners who lived there spent all their time either telling or listening to all the latest ideas.)

²²Then Paul stood up before the meeting of the Areopagus council and said, "Men of Athens, everything I see here tells me you are very religious. ²³I was going through your city and I saw the things you worship. I found an altar that had these words written on it: 'TO AN UNKNOWN GOD.' You worship a god that you don't know. This is the God I want to tell you about.

²⁴"He is the God who made the whole world and everything in it. He is the Lord of the land and the sky. He does not live in temples built by human hands. ²⁵He is the one who gives people life, breath, and everything else they need. He does not

need any help from them. He has everything he needs. ²⁶God began by making one man, and from him he made all the different people who live everywhere in the world. He decided exactly when and where they would live.

²⁷"God wanted people to look for him, and perhaps in searching all around for him, they would find him. But he is not far from any of us. ²⁸It is through him that we are able to live, to do what we do, and to be who we are. As your own poets have said, 'We all come from him.'

²⁹"That's right. We all come from God. So you must not think that he is like something people imagine or make. He is not made of gold, silver, or stone. ³⁰In the past people did not understand God, and he overlooked this. But now he is telling everyone in the world to change and turn to him. ³¹He has decided on a day when he will judge all the people in the world in a way that is fair. To do this he will use a man he chose long ago. And he has proved to everyone that this is the man to do it. He proved it by raising him from death!"

³²When the people heard about Jesus being raised from death, some of them laughed. But others said, "We will hear more about this from you later." ³³So Paul left the council meeting. ³⁴But some of the people joined with Paul and became believers. Among these were Dionysius, a member of the Areopagus council, a woman named Damaris, and some others.

Paul in Corinth

18 ¹Later, Paul left Athens and went to the city of Corinth. ²There he met a Jewish man named Aquila, who was born in the country of Pontus. But he and his wife, Priscilla, had recently moved to Corinth from Italy. They left Italy because Claudius* had given an order for all Jews to leave Rome. Paul went to visit Aquila and Priscilla. ³They were tentmakers, the same as Paul, so he stayed with them and worked with them.

⁴Every Sabbath* day Paul went to the synagogue* and talked with both Jews and Greeks, trying to persuade them to believe in Jesus. ⁵But after Silas and Timothy came from Macedonia,* Paul spent all his time telling God's message* to the Jews, trying to convince them that Jesus is the Christ.* ⁶But they disagreed with what Paul was teaching and started insulting him. So Paul shook the dust from his clothes.ᵃ He said to them, "If you are not saved, it will be your own fault! I have done all I can do. After this I will go only to the non-Jewish people."

⁷Paul left the synagogue and moved into the home of Titius Justus, a man who was a worshiper of the true God. His house

---

ᵃ **18:6** *shook the dust from his clothes* A warning. It showed Paul was finished talking to these Jews.

was next to the synagogue. [8]Crispus was the leader of that synagogue. He and all the people living in his house believed in the Lord Jesus. Many other people in Corinth also listened to Paul. They, too, believed and were baptized.*

[9]During the night, Paul had a vision.* The Lord said to him, "Don't be afraid, and don't stop talking to people. [10]I am with you, and no one will be able to hurt you. Many of my people are in this city." [11]Paul stayed there for a year and a half teaching God's message to the people.

Paul Is Brought Before Gallio

[12]During the time that Gallio was the governor of Achaia,* some of the Jews came together against Paul. They took him to court. [13]They said to Gallio, "This man is teaching people to worship God in a way that is against our law!"

[14]Paul was ready to say something, but Gallio spoke to the Jews. He said, "I would listen to you if your complaint was about a crime or other wrong. [15]But it is only about words and names—arguments about your own law. So you must solve this problem yourselves. I don't want to be a judge of these matters." [16]So Gallio made them leave the court.

[17]Then they all grabbed Sosthenes. (Sosthenes was now the leader of the synagogue.*) They beat him before the court. But this did not bother Gallio.

Paul Returns to Antioch

[18]Paul stayed with the believers* for many days. Then he left and sailed for Syria. Priscilla and Aquila were also with him. At Cenchrea Paul cut off his hair,[a] because he had made a promise to God. [19]Then they went to the city of Ephesus, where Paul left Priscilla and Aquila. While Paul was in Ephesus, he went into the synagogue* and talked with the Jews. [20]They asked him to stay longer, but he refused. [21]He left them and said, "I will come back to you again if God wants me to." And so he sailed away from Ephesus.

[22]When Paul arrived at Caesarea, he went to Jerusalem and visited the church* there. After that, he went to Antioch. [23]Paul stayed in Antioch for a while. Then he left there and went through the countries of Galatia and Phrygia. He traveled from town to town in these countries, helping all the followers grow stronger in their faith.

Apollos in Ephesus and Corinth

[24]A Jew named Apollos came to Ephesus. Born in the city of Alexandria, he was an educated man who knew the Scriptures* well. [25]He had been taught about the Lord and was always

---

[a]**18:18** *cut off his hair* This may show that Paul was ending a Nazirite vow, a time of special dedication and service promised to God. See Num. 6:1–21.

excited[a] to talk to people about Jesus. What he taught was right, but the only baptism* he knew about was the baptism that John* taught. 26Apollos began to speak very boldly in the synagogue.* When Priscilla and Aquila heard him speak, they took him to their home and helped him understand the way of God better.

27Apollos wanted to go to Achaia.* So the believers* in Ephesus helped him. They wrote a letter to the Lord's followers in Achaia and asked them to accept Apollos. When he arrived there, he was a great help to those who had believed in Jesus because of God's grace.* 28He argued very strongly against the Jews before all the people. He clearly proved that the Jews were wrong. He used the Scriptures and showed that Jesus is the Christ.*

Paul in Ephesus

19 1While Apollos was in the city of Corinth, Paul was visiting some places on his way to Ephesus. In Ephesus he found some other followers of the Lord. 2He asked them, "Did you receive the Holy Spirit* when you believed?"

These followers said to him, "We have never even heard of a Holy Spirit!"

3Paul asked them, "So what kind of baptism* did you have?"

They said, "It was the baptism that John* taught."

4Paul said, "John told people to be baptized to show they wanted to change their lives. He told people to believe in the one who would come after him, and that one is Jesus."

5When these followers heard this, they were baptized in the name of the Lord Jesus. 6Then Paul laid his hands on them,[b] and the Holy Spirit came on them. They began speaking different languages and prophesying.* 7There were about twelve men in this group.

8Paul went into the synagogue* and spoke very boldly. He continued doing this for three months. He talked with the Jews, trying to persuade them to accept what he was telling them about God's kingdom.* 9But some of them became stubborn and refused to believe. In front of everyone they said bad things about the Way.* So Paul left these Jews and took the Lord's followers with him. He went to a place where a man named Tyrannus had a school. There Paul talked with people every day. 10He did this for two years. Because of this work, everyone in Asia,* Jews and Greeks, heard the word of the Lord.

The Sons of Sceva

11God used Paul to do some very special miracles.* 12Some people carried away handkerchiefs and clothes that Paul had

[a]18:25 excited Or, "on fire with the Spirit." [b]19:6 laid his hands on them This act was a way of asking God to bless people in a special way—here, to give them power through his Spirit.

used and put them on those who were sick. The sick people were healed, and evil spirits left them.

¹³⁻¹⁴Some Jews also were traveling around forcing evil spirits out of people. The seven sons of Sceva were doing this. (Sceva was one of the leading priests.) These Jews tried to use the name of the Lord Jesus to make the evil spirits go out of people. They all said, "By the same that Paul talks about, I order you to come out!"

¹⁵But one time an evil spirit said to these Jews, "I know Jesus, and I know about Paul, but who are you?"

¹⁶Then the man who had the evil spirit inside him jumped on these Jews. He was much stronger than all of them. He beat them up and tore their clothes off. They all ran away from that house.

¹⁷All the people in Ephesus, Jews and Greeks,* learned about this. They were all filled with fear and gave great honor to the Lord Jesus. ¹⁸Many of the believers began to confess, telling about all the evil things they had done. ¹⁹Some of them had used magic. These believers brought their magic books and burned them before everyone. These books were worth about 50,000 silver coins.ᵃ ²⁰This is how the word of the Lord was spreading in a powerful way, causing more and more people to believe.

Paul Plans a Trip

²¹After this, Paul made plans to go to Jerusalem. He planned to go through the regions of Macedonia* and Achaia,* and then go to Jerusalem. He thought, "After I visit Jerusalem, I must also visit Rome." ²²Timothy and Erastus were two of his helpers. Paul sent them ahead to Macedonia. But he stayed in Asia* for a while.

Trouble in Ephesus

²³But during that time there was some trouble in Ephesus about the Way.* This is how it all happened: ²⁴There was a man named Demetrius. He worked with silver. He made little silver models that looked like the temple of the goddess Artemis. The men who did this work made a lot of money. ²⁵Demetrius had a meeting with these men and some others who did the same kind of work. He told them, "Men, you know that we make a lot of money from our business. ²⁶But look at what this man Paul is doing. Listen to what he is saying. He has convinced many people in Ephesus and all over Asia* to change their religion. He says the gods that people make by hand are not real. ²⁷I'm afraid this is going to turn people against our business. But there is also another problem. People will begin to think that the temple of the great goddess Artemis is not important. Her

---

ᵃ**19:19** silver coins Probably drachmas. One coin was enough to pay a man for working one day.

greatness will be destroyed. And Artemis is the goddess that everyone in Asia and the whole world worships."

[28]When the men heard this, they became very angry. They shouted, "Great is Artemis, the goddess of Ephesus!" [29]The whole city was thrown into confusion. The people grabbed Gaius and Aristarchus, men from Macedonia* who were traveling with Paul, and rushed all together into the stadium. [30]Paul wanted to go in and talk to the people, but the Lord's followers did not let him go. [31]Also, some leaders of the country who were friends of Paul sent him a message telling him not to go into the stadium.

[32]Some people were shouting one thing and others were shouting something else. The meeting was very confused. Most of the people did not know why they had come there. [33]Some Jews made a man named Alexander stand before the crowd, and they told him what to say. Alexander waved his hand, trying to explain things to the people. [34]But when the people saw that Alexander was a Jew, they all began shouting the same thing. For two hours they continued shouting, "Great is Artemis of Ephesus! Great is Artemis of Ephesus! Great is Artemis …!"

[35]Then the city clerk persuaded the people to be quiet. He said, "Men of Ephesus, everyone knows that Ephesus is the city that keeps the temple of the great goddess Artemis. Everyone knows that we also keep her holy rock.[a] [36]No one can deny this, so you should be quiet. You must stop and think before you do anything else.

[37]"You brought these men[b] here, but they have not said anything bad against our goddess. They have not stolen anything from her temple. [38]We have courts of law and there are judges. Do Demetrius and those men who work with him have a charge against anyone? They should go to the courts. Let them argue with each other there.

[39]"Is there something else you want to talk about? Then come to the regular town meeting of the people. It can be decided there. [40]I say this because someone might see this trouble today and say we are rioting. We could not explain all this trouble, because there is no real reason for this meeting." [41]After the city clerk said this, he told the people to go home.

Paul Goes to Macedonia and Greece

20 [1]When the trouble stopped, Paul invited the Lord's followers to come visit him. After encouraging them, he told them goodbye and left for Macedonia.* [2]On his way through Macedonia he had many words of encouragement for the followers in various places. Then he went to Greece [3]and stayed there three months.

Paul was ready to sail for Syria, but some Jews were planning something against him. So he decided to go back through

---

[a]19:35 holy rock Probably a meteorite or rock that the people thought looked like Artemis and worshiped. [b]19:37 men Gaius and Aristarchus, the men traveling with Paul.

Macedonia to Syria. ⁴These men were traveling with him: Sopater, the son of Pyrrhus, from the city of Berea Aristarchus and Secundus, from the city of Thessalonica; Gaius, from the city of Derbe; Timothy; and two men from Asia,* Tychicus and Trophimus. ⁵These men went first, ahead of Paul. They waited for us in the city of Troas. ⁶We sailed from the city of Philippi after the Festival of Unleavened Bread.* We met these men in Troas five days later and stayed there seven days.

Paul's Last Visit to Troas

⁷On Sunday*ᵃ* we all met together to eat the Lord's Supper.*ᵇ* Paul talked to the group. Because he was planning to leave the next day, he continued talking until midnight. ⁸We were all together in a room upstairs, and there were many lights in the room. ⁹There was a young man named Eutychus sitting in the window. Paul continued talking, and Eutychus became very, very sleepy. Finally, he went to sleep and fell out of the window. He fell to the ground from the third floor. When the people went down and lifted him up, he was dead.

¹⁰Paul went down to where Eutychus was, knelt down beside him, and put his arms around him. He said to the other believers, "Don't worry. He is alive now." ¹¹Then Paul went upstairs again, broke off some pieces of bread and ate. He spoke to them a long time. It was early morning when he finished, and then he left. ¹²The Lord's followers took Eutychus home alive, and they were all greatly comforted.

The Trip From Troas to Miletus

¹³We went on ahead of Paul and sailed for the city of Assos, planning to meet him there. This is what he told us to do because he wanted to go by land. ¹⁴When he caught up with us at Assos, we took him on board, and we all sailed to Mitylene. ¹⁵The next day, we sailed away from there and came to a place near the island of Chios. Then the next day, we sailed to the island of Samos. A day later, we came to the city of Miletus. ¹⁶Paul had already decided not to stop at Ephesus. He did not want to stay too long in Asia.* He was hurrying because he wanted to be in Jerusalem on the day of Pentecost* if possible.

Paul Speaks to the Elders From Ephesus

¹⁷In Miletus Paul sent a message back to Ephesus. He invited the elders* of the church* in Ephesus to come to him. ¹⁸When they came, Paul said to them, "You know about my life from the first day I came to Asia.* You know the way I lived all the time I was with you. ¹⁹The Jews planned things against

---

*ᵃ***20:7** *Sunday* Literally, "first day of the week," which for the Jews began at sunset on Saturday. But if Luke is using Greek time here, then the meeting was Sunday night. *ᵇ***20:7** *to eat the Lord's Supper* Literally, "to break bread." This may mean a meal or the Lord's Supper, the special meal Jesus told his followers to eat to remember him. See Lk. 22:14–20.

me, and this gave me much trouble. But you know that I always served the Lord, sometimes with tears. I never thought about myself first. ²⁰I always did what was best for you. I told you the Good News* about Jesus in public before the people and also taught in your homes. ²¹I told everyone—Jewish and non-Jewish people—to change and turn to God. I told them all to believe in our Lord Jesus.

²²"But now I must obey the Spirit* and go to Jerusalem. I don't know what will happen to me there. ²³I know only that in every city the Holy Spirit tells me that troubles and even jail wait for me. ²⁴I don't care about my own life. The most important thing is that I finish my work. I want to finish the work that the Lord Jesus gave me to do—to tell people the Good News about God's grace.*

²⁵"And now listen to me. I know that none of you will ever see me again. All the time I was with you, I told you the Good News about God's kingdom.* ²⁶So today I can tell you one thing that I am sure of: God will not blame me if some of you are not saved. ²⁷I can say this because I know that I told you everything that God wants you to know. ²⁸Be careful for yourselves and for all the people God has given you. The Holy Spirit gave you the work of caring for^a this flock.^b You must be like shepherds to the church of God.^c This is the church that God bought with his own blood.^d ²⁹I know that after I leave, some men will come into your group. They will be like wild wolves and will try to destroy the flock. ³⁰Also, men from your own group will begin to teach things that are wrong. They will lead some of the Lord's followers away from the truth to follow them. ³¹So be careful! And always remember what I did during the three years I was with you. I never stopped reminding each one of you how you should live, counseling you day and night and crying over you.

³²"Now I am putting you in God's care. I am depending on the message* about his grace to make you strong. That message is able to give you the blessings that God gives to all his holy people.* ³³When I was with you, I never wanted anyone's money or fine clothes. ³⁴You know that I always worked to take care of my own needs and the needs of the people who were with me. ³⁵I always showed you that you should work just as I did and help people who are weak. I taught you to remember the words of the Lord Jesus: 'You will have a greater blessing when you give than when you receive.'"

³⁶When Paul finished speaking, he knelt down, and they all prayed together. ³⁷⁻³⁸They cried and cried. They were especially sad because Paul had said they would never see him again.

---

^a**20:28** *gave ... caring for* Literally, "made you overseers of." ^b**20:28** *flock* A flock is many sheep. Here, it means a group of God's people who follow their leaders (elders) like sheep following a shepherd. ^c**20:28** *of God* Some Greek copies say, "of the Lord." ^d**20:28** *his own blood* Or, "the blood of his own Son."

They hugged him and kissed him. Then they went with him to the ship to say goodbye.

Paul Goes to Jerusalem

21 [1]After we said goodbye to the elders,* we sailed away straight to Cos island. The next day we went to the island of Rhodes, and from there we went to Patara. [2]There we found a ship that was going to the area of Phoenicia. We got on the ship and sailed away.

[3]We sailed near the island of Cyprus. We could see it on the north side, but we did not stop. We sailed to the country of Syria. We stopped at Tyre because the ship needed to unload its cargo there. [4]We found the Lord's followers there and stayed with them for seven days. They warned Paul not to go to Jerusalem because of what the Spirit* had told them. [5]But when our time there was up, we returned to the ship to continue our trip. All the followers, even the women and children, came with us to the seashore. We all knelt down on the beach, prayed, [6]and said goodbye. Then we got on the ship, and the followers went home.

[7]We continued our trip from Tyre and went to the city of Ptolemais. We greeted our brothers and sisters in God's family there and stayed with them one day. [8]The next day we left Ptolemais and went to the city of Caesarea. We went into the home of Philip and stayed with him. He had the work of telling the Good News.* He was one of the seven helpers.[a] [9]He had four unmarried daughters who had the gift of prophesying.*

[10]After we had been there for many days, a prophet* named Agabus came from Judea. [11]He came to us and borrowed Paul's belt. He used it to tie his own hands and feet. He said, "The Holy Spirit tells me, 'This is how the Jews in Jerusalem will tie up the man who wears this belt.[b] Then they will hand him over to people who don't know God.'"

[12]When we heard this, we and the other followers there begged Paul not to go to Jerusalem. [13]But he said, "Why are you crying and making me feel so sad? I am willing to be put in jail in Jerusalem. I am even ready to die for the name of the Lord Jesus!"

[14]We could not persuade him to stay away from Jerusalem. So we stopped begging him and said, "We pray that what the Lord wants will be done."

[15]After this, we got ready and left for Jerusalem. [16]Some of the followers of Jesus from Caesarea went with us. These followers took us to the home of Mnason, a man from Cyprus, who was one of the first people to be a follower of Jesus. They took us to his home so that we could stay with him.

[a] 21:8 seven helpers Men chosen for a special work. See Acts 6:1–6.   [b] 21:11 belt Paul's belt; so Agabus means that the Jews in Jerusalem will tie Paul up (arrest him).

Paul Visits James

¹⁷The brothers and sisters in Jerusalem were very happy to see us. ¹⁸The next day Paul went with us to visit James, and all the elders* were there. ¹⁹After greeting them, Paul told them point by point all that God had used him to do among the non-Jewish people.

²⁰When the leaders heard this, they praised God. Then they said to Paul, "Brother, you can see that thousands of Jews have become believers, but they think it is very important to obey the law of Moses.* ²¹They have been told that you teach the Jews who live in non-Jewish regions to stop following the law of Moses. They have heard that you tell them not to circumcise* their sons or follow our other customs.

²²"What should we do? The Jewish believers here will learn that you have come. ²³So we will tell you what to do: Four of our men have made a vow*ᵃ* to God. ²⁴Take these men with you and share in their cleansing ceremony.*ᵇ* Pay their expenses so that they can shave their heads.*ᶜ* This will prove to everyone that the things they have heard about you are not true. They will see that you obey the law of Moses in your own life.

²⁵"In regard to the non-Jewish believers, we have already sent a letter to them saying what we think they should do:

'Don't eat food that has been given to idols.*
Don't eat meat from animals that have been strangled
    or any meat that still has the blood in it.
Don't be involved in sexual sin.'"

Paul Is Arrested

²⁶So Paul took the four men with him. The next day he shared in their cleansing ceremony. Then he went to the Temple* area and announced the time when the days of the cleansing ceremony would be finished. On the last day an offering would be given for each of the men.

²⁷When the seven-day period was almost finished, some Jews from Asia* saw Paul in the Temple area. They stirred up everyone into an angry mob. They grabbed Paul ²⁸and shouted, "Men of Israel,* help us! This is the man who is teaching things that are against the law of Moses,* against our people, and against this Temple of ours. This is what he teaches people everywhere. And now he has brought some Greeks* into the Temple area and has made this holy place unclean!" ²⁹(The Jews said this because they had seen Trophimus with Paul in Jerusalem. Trophimus was a man from Ephesus. The Jews thought that Paul had taken him into the holy area of the Temple.)

---

*ᵃ*21:23 *vow* Probably a Nazirite vow, a time of special dedication and service promised to God. See Num. 6:1–21. *ᵇ*21:24 *cleansing ceremony* The special things Jews did to end the Nazirite vow. Also in verse 26. *ᶜ*21:24 *shave their heads* To show that their vow was finished.

³⁰An angry reaction spread throughout the city, and everyone came running to the Temple. They grabbed Paul and dragged him out of the holy area, and the gates were closed immediately. ³¹While they were trying to kill Paul, the commander of the Roman army in Jerusalem got word that the whole city was in a state of riot. ³²Immediately the commander ran to where the crowd had gathered, taking with him some army officers* and soldiers. When the people saw the commander and his soldiers, they stopped beating Paul.

³³The commander went over to Paul and arrested him. He told his soldiers to tie him up with two chains. Then he asked, "Who is this man? What has he done wrong?" ³⁴Some people there were shouting one thing, and others were shouting something else. Because of all this confusion and shouting, the commander could not learn the truth about what had happened. So he told the soldiers to take Paul to the army building. ³⁵⁻³⁶The whole crowd was following them. When the soldiers came to the steps, they had to carry Paul. They did this to protect him, because the people were ready to hurt him. The people were shouting, "Kill him!"

³⁷When the soldiers were ready to take Paul into the army building, he asked the commander, "Can I say something to you?"

The commander said, "Oh, you speak Greek? ³⁸Then you are not the man I thought you were. I thought you were the Egyptian who started some trouble against the government not long ago and led four thousand terrorists out to the desert."

³⁹Paul said, "No, I am a Jew from Tarsus in the country of Cilicia. I am a citizen of that important city. Please, let me speak to the people."

⁴⁰The commander told Paul he could speak. So he stood on the steps and waved his hand so that the people would be quiet. The people became quiet and Paul spoke to them in Aramaic.*

Paul Speaks to the People

22 ¹Paul said, "My brothers and fathers, listen to me! I will make my defense to you."

²When the Jews heard Paul speaking Aramaic,* they became very quiet. Then Paul said,

³"I am a Jew, born in Tarsus in the country of Cilicia. I grew up in this city. I was a student of Gamaliel,ᵃ who carefully taught me everything about the law of our fathers.* I was very serious about serving God, the same as all of you here today. ⁴I persecuted* the people who followed the Way.* Some of them were killed because of me. I arrested men and women and put them in jail.

⁵"The high priest* and the whole council of older Jewish leaders can tell you that this is true. One time these leaders

---

ᵃ**22:3** *Gamaliel* A very important teacher of the Pharisees, a Jewish religious group. See Acts 5:34.

gave me some letters. The letters were to the Jewish brothers in the city of Damascus. I was going there to arrest the followers of Jesus and bring them back to Jerusalem for punishment.

Paul Tells About His Conversion

⁶"But something happened to me on my way to Damascus. It was about noon when I came close to Damascus. Suddenly a bright light from heaven shined all around me. ⁷I fell to the ground and heard a voice saying to me, 'Saul, Saul, why are you persecuting* me?'

⁸"I asked, 'Who are you, Lord?' The voice said, 'I am Jesus from Nazareth, the one you are persecuting.' ⁹The men who were with me did not understand the voice, but they saw the light.

¹⁰"I said, 'What shall I do, Lord?' The Lord answered, 'Get up and go into Damascus. There you will be told all that I have planned for you to do.' ¹¹I could not see, because the bright light had made me blind. So the men led me into Damascus.

¹²"In Damascus a man named Ananias^a came to me. He was a man who was devoted to God and obeyed the law of Moses.* All the Jews who lived there respected him. ¹³He came to me and said, 'Saul, my brother, look up and see again!' Immediately I was able to see him.

¹⁴"Ananias told me, 'The God of our fathers* chose you long ago to know his plan. He chose you to see the Righteous One and to hear words from him. ¹⁵You will be his witness to all people. You will tell them what you have seen and heard. ¹⁶Now, don't wait any longer. Get up, be baptized* and wash your sins away, trusting in Jesus to save you.^b'

¹⁷"Later, I came back to Jerusalem. I was praying in the Temple* area, and I saw a vision.* ¹⁸I saw Jesus, and he said to me, 'Hurry and leave Jerusalem now! The people here will not accept the truth you tell them about me.'

¹⁹"I said, 'But Lord, the people know that I was the one who put the believers in jail and beat them. I went through all the synagogues* to find and arrest the people who believe in you. ²⁰The people also know that I was there when Stephen, your witness, was killed. I stood there and agreed that they should kill him. I even held the coats of the men who were killing him!'

²¹"But Jesus said to me, 'Leave now. I will send you far away to the non-Jewish people.'"

²²The people stopped listening when Paul said this last thing. They all shouted, "Get rid of this man! He doesn't deserve to live." ²³They shouted and threw off their coats.^c They threw

---

^a22:12 Ananias In Acts there are three men with this name. See Acts 5:1 and 23:2 for the other two. ^b22:16 trusting in Jesus … you Literally, "calling on his name," meaning to show faith in Jesus by worshiping him or praying to him for help. ^c22:23 threw off their coats This showed the Jews were very angry with Paul.

dust into the air.^a ²⁴Then the commander told the soldiers to take Paul into the army building and beat him. He wanted to make Paul tell why the people were shouting against him like this. ²⁵So the soldiers were tying Paul, preparing to beat him. But he said to an army officer* there, "Do you have the right to beat a Roman citizen^b who has not been proven guilty?"

²⁶When the officer heard this, he went to the commander and told him about it. The officer said, "Do you know what you are doing? This man is a Roman citizen!"

²⁷The commander came to Paul and said, "Tell me, are you really a Roman citizen?"

He answered, "Yes."

²⁸The commander said, "I paid a lot of money to become a Roman citizen."

But Paul said, "I was born a citizen."

²⁹The men who were preparing to question Paul moved away from him immediately. The commander was afraid because he had already put Paul in chains, and he was a Roman citizen.

Paul Speaks to the Jewish Leaders

³⁰The next day the commander decided to learn why the Jews were accusing Paul. So he ordered the leading priests and the whole high council to meet together. He had Paul's chains taken off and had him brought in to face the council.

23 ¹Paul looked at the council members and said, "Brothers, I have lived my life in a good way before God. I have always done what I thought was right." ²Ananias,^c the high priest,* was there. When he heard this, he told the men who were standing near Paul to hit him in the mouth. ³Paul said to Ananias, "God will hit you too! You are like a dirty wall that has been painted white. You sit there and judge me, using the law of Moses.* But you are telling them to hit me, and that is against the law."

⁴The men standing near Paul said to him, "Are you sure you want to insult God's high priest like that?"

⁵Paul said, "Brothers, I did not know this man was the high priest. The Scriptures* say, 'You must not say bad things about a leader of your people.'^d"

⁶Paul knew that some of the men in the council meeting were Sadducees* and some were Pharisees.* So he shouted, "My brothers, I am a Pharisee and my father was a Pharisee! I am on trial here because I believe that people will rise from death."

⁷When Paul said this, a big argument started between the Pharisees and the Sadducees. The group was divided. ⁸(The Sadducees believe that after people die, they will not live again

^a**22:23** *threw dust into the air* A sign of very strong anger. ^b**22:25** *Roman citizen* Roman law said that Roman citizens must not be beaten before their trial. Also at 23:27. ^c**23:2** *Ananias* Not the same man named Ananias in Acts 22:12. ^d**23:5** Quote from Ex. 22:28.

as an angel or as a spirit. But the Pharisees believe in both.) [9]All these Jews began shouting louder and louder. Some of the teachers of the law, who were Pharisees, stood up and argued, "We find nothing wrong with this man. Maybe an angel or a spirit really did speak to him."

[10]The argument turned into a fight, and the commander was afraid that the Jews would tear Paul to pieces. So he told the soldiers to go down and take Paul away from these Jews and put him in the army building.

[11]The next night the Lord Jesus came and stood by Paul. He said, "Be brave! You have told people in Jerusalem about me. You must do the same in Rome."

Some Jews Plan to Kill Paul

[12]The next morning some of the Jews made a plan to kill Paul. They made a promise to themselves that they would not eat or drink anything until they had killed him. [13]There were more than 40 of them who made this plan. [14]They went and talked to the leading priests and the older Jewish leaders. They said, "We have promised ourselves that we will not eat or drink until we have killed Paul. [15]So this is what we want you to do: Send a message to the commander from you and the high council. Tell him you want him to bring Paul out to you. Say that you want to ask him more questions. We will be waiting to kill him while he is on the way here."

[16]But Paul's nephew heard about this plan. He went to the army building and told Paul. [17]Then Paul called one of the army officers* and said to him, "Take this young man to the commander. He has a message for him." [18]So the army officer brought Paul's nephew to the commander. The officer said, "The prisoner Paul asked me to bring this young man to you. He has something to tell you."

[19]The commander led the young man to a place where they could be alone. The commander asked, "What do you want to tell me?"

[20]The young man said, "Some Jews have decided to ask you to bring Paul down to their council meeting tomorrow. They want you to think that they plan to ask Paul more questions. [21]But don't believe them! More than 40 of them are hiding and waiting to kill him. They have all promised not to eat or drink until they have killed him. Now they are waiting for you to say yes."

[22]The commander sent the young man away, telling him, "Don't tell anyone that you have told me about their plan."

Paul Is Sent to Caesarea

[23]Then the commander called two army officers.* He said to them, "I need some men to go to Caesarea. Get 200 soldiers ready. Also, get 70 soldiers on horses and 200 men to carry spears. Be ready to leave at nine o'clock tonight. [24]Get some

horses for Paul to ride so that he can be taken to Governor Felix safely." [25]The commander wrote a letter that said:

[26]From Claudius Lysias.
To the Most Honorable Governor Felix.

Greetings:
[27]Some Jews had taken this man and planned to kill him. But I learned that he is a Roman citizen, so I went with my soldiers and saved him. [28]I wanted to know why they were accusing him. So I brought him before their council meeting. [29]This is what I learned: The Jews said Paul did some things that were wrong. But these charges were about their own Jewish laws, and there was nothing worthy of jail or death. [30]I was told that some of the Jews were making a plan to kill Paul. So I send him to you. I also told those Jews to tell you what they have against him.

[31]The soldiers did what they were told. They got Paul and took him to the city of Antipatris that night. [32]The next day the soldiers on horses went with Paul to Caesarea, but the other soldiers and the spearmen went back to the army building in Jerusalem. [33]The soldiers on horses entered Caesarea and gave the letter to governor Felix and then turned Paul over to him.

[34]The governor read the letter and asked Paul, "What country are you from?" The governor learned that Paul was from Cilicia. [35]The governor said, "I will hear your case when the Jews who are accusing you come here too." Then the governor gave orders for Paul to be kept in the palace. (This building had been built by Herod.[*])

Some Jews Accuse Paul

24 [1]Five days later Ananias, the high priest,[*] went to the city of Caesarea. He brought with him some of the older Jewish leaders and a lawyer named Tertullus. They went to Caesarea to make charges against Paul before the governor. [2-3]Paul was called into the meeting, and Tertullus began to make his accusations.

Tertullus said, "Most Honorable Felix, our people enjoy much peace because of you, and many wrong things in our country are being made right through your wise help. For this we all continue to be very thankful. [4]But I don't want to take any more of your time. So I will say only a few words. Please be patient. [5]This man is a troublemaker. He causes trouble with the Jews everywhere in the world. He is a leader of the Nazarene group. [6-8]Also, he was trying to make the Temple[*] unclean, but we stopped him.[a] You can decide if all this is true.

[a]**24:6–8** Some Greek copies add 6b-8a: "And we wanted to judge him by our own law. [7]But the officer Lysias came and used great force to take him from us. [8]And Lysias ordered those who wanted to accuse him to come to you."

Ask him some questions yourself." ⁹The other Jews agreed and said it was all true.

Paul Defends Himself Before Felix

¹⁰The governor made a sign for Paul to speak. So Paul answered, "Governor Felix, I know that you have been a judge over this nation for a long time. So I am happy to defend myself before you. ¹¹I went to worship in Jerusalem only twelve days ago. You can learn for yourself that this is true. ¹²These Jews who are accusing me did not find me arguing with anyone at the Temple* or making trouble with the people. And I was not making trouble or arguing in the synagogues* or any other place in the city. ¹³These men cannot prove the things they are saying against me now.

¹⁴But I will tell you this: I worship the God of our fathers* as a follower of the Way* (which these Jews say is not the right way), and I believe everything that is taught in the law of Moses* and all that is written in the books of the prophets.* ¹⁵I have the same hope in God that these Jews have—the hope that all people, good and bad, will be raised from death. ¹⁶This is why I always try to do what I believe is right before God and before everyone.

¹⁷⁻¹⁸I was away from Jerusalem for many years. I went back there to take money to help my people. I also had some gifts to offer at the Temple. I was doing this when some Jews saw me there. I had finished the cleansing ceremony.ᵃ I had not made any trouble, and no one was gathering around me. ¹⁹But some Jews from Asia* were there. They should be here, standing before you. If I have really done anything wrong, they are the ones who should accuse me. They were there! ²⁰Ask these men here if they found any wrong in me when I stood before the high council meeting in Jerusalem. ²¹I did say one thing when I stood before them. I said, 'You are judging me today because I believe that people will rise from death!'"

²²Felix already understood a lot about the Way. He stopped the trial and said, "When commander Lysias comes here, I will decide what to do with you." ²³Felix told the army officer* to keep Paul guarded but to give him some freedom and to let his friends bring whatever he needed.

Paul Speaks to Felix and His Wife

²⁴After a few days Felix came with his wife Drusilla, who was a Jew. Felix asked for Paul to be brought to him. He listened to Paul talk about believing in Christ Jesus. ²⁵But Felix became afraid when Paul spoke about things like doing right, self-control, and the judgment that will come in the future. He said, "Go away now. When I have more time, I will call for

---

ᵃ24:17–18 *cleansing ceremony* The special things Jews did to end the Nazirite vow.

you." [26]But Felix had another reason for talking with Paul. He hoped Paul would pay him a bribe, so he sent for Paul often and talked with him.

[27]But after two years, Porcius Festus became governor. So Felix was no longer governor. But he left Paul in prison to please the Jews.

Paul Asks to See Caesar

25 [1]Festus became governor, and three days later he went from Caesarea to Jerusalem. [2]The leading priests and the important Jewish leaders made charges against Paul before Festus. [3]They asked Festus to do them a favor. They wanted him to send Paul back to Jerusalem because they had a plan to kill Paul on the way. [4]But Festus answered, "No, Paul will be kept in Caesarea. I will be going there soon myself, [5]and your leaders can go with me. If this man has really done anything wrong, they can accuse him there."

[6]Festus stayed in Jerusalem another eight or ten days and then went back to Caesarea. The next day Festus told the soldiers to bring Paul before him. Festus was seated on the judgment seat. [7]Paul came into the room, and the Jews who had come from Jerusalem stood around him. They made many serious charges against him, but they could not prove anything. [8]Paul defended himself, saying, "I have done nothing wrong against the Jewish law, against the Temple,* or against Caesar.*"

[9]But Festus wanted to please the Jews. So he asked Paul, "Do you want to go to Jerusalem for me to judge you there on these charges?"

[10]Paul said, "I am standing at Caesar's judgment seat now. This is where I should be judged. I have done nothing wrong to the Jews, and you know it. [11]If I have done something wrong, and the law says I must die, then I agree that I should die. I don't ask to be saved from death. But if these charges are not true, then no one can hand me over to these people. No, I want Caesar to hear my case!"

[12]Festus talked about this with his advisors. Then he said, "You have asked to see Caesar, so you will go to Caesar!"

Festus Asks King Agrippa About Paul

[13]A few days later King Agrippa* and Bernice* came to Caesarea to visit Festus. [14]They stayed there many days, and Festus told the king about Paul's case. Festus said, "There is a man that Felix left in prison. [15]When I went to Jerusalem, the leading priests and the older Jewish leaders there made charges against him. They wanted me to order his death. [16]But I told them, 'When a man is accused of doing something wrong, Romans don't hand him over for others to judge. First, he must face the people accusing him. And then he must be allowed to defend himself against their charges.'

¹⁷"So when these Jews came here for the trial, I did not waste time. The next day I sat on the judgment seat and ordered Paul to be brought in. ¹⁸The Jews stood up and accused him. But they did not accuse him of the kind of crimes I thought they would. ¹⁹Their charges were all about their own religion and about a man named Jesus. Jesus died, but Paul said that he is still alive. ²⁰I did not have any idea about how to judge these matters. So I asked Paul, 'Do you want to go to Jerusalem and be judged there?' ²¹But Paul asked to be kept in Caesarea. He wants a decision from the emperor.* So I ordered that he be held until I could send him to Caesar* in Rome."

²²Agrippa said to Festus, "I would like to hear this man too." Festus said, "Tomorrow you can hear him."

²³The next day Agrippa and Bernice came to the meeting with great show, acting like very important people. They entered the room with military leaders and important men of the city. Festus ordered the soldiers to bring Paul in.

²⁴Festus said, "King Agrippa and all of you gathered here with us, you see this man. All the Jewish people, here and in Jerusalem, have complained to me about him. When they complain about him, they shout that he should be killed. ²⁵When I judged him, I did not find him guilty of any crime worthy of death. But he asked to be judged by Caesar, so I decided to send him to Rome. ²⁶However, I don't really know what to tell Caesar that this man has done wrong. So I have brought him before all of you—especially you, King Agrippa. I hope that you can question him and give me something to write to Caesar. ²⁷I think it is foolish to send a prisoner to Caesar without making some charges against him."

Paul Before King Agrippa

26 ¹Agrippa* said to Paul, "You may now speak to defend yourself." Paul raised his hand to get their attention and began to speak. ²He said, "King Agrippa, I feel fortunate that I can stand here before you today and answer all the charges these Jews have made against me. ³I am very happy to talk to you, because you know so much about all the Jewish customs and the things the Jews argue about. Please listen to me patiently.

⁴"All the Jews know about my whole life. They know the way I lived from the beginning in my own country and later in Jerusalem. ⁵These Jews have known me for a long time. If they want to, they can tell you that I was a good Pharisee.* And the Pharisees obey the laws of the Jewish religion more carefully than any other group. ⁶Now I am on trial because I hope for the promise that God made to our fathers.* ⁷This is the promise that all the twelve tribes of our people hope to receive. For this hope the Jews serve God day and night. My king, the Jews have accused me because I hope for this same promise. ⁸Why

do you people think it is impossible for God to raise people from death?

9"I used to think that I should do everything I could against Jesus from Nazareth. 10And that's what I did, beginning in Jerusalem. The leading priests gave me the authority to put many of God's people in jail. And when they were being killed, I agreed that it was a good thing. 11I visited all the synagogues* and punished them, trying to make them curse* Jesus. My anger against these people was so strong that I went to other cities to find them and punish them.

Paul Tells About Seeing Jesus

12"One time the leading priests gave me permission and the authority to go to the city of Damascus. 13On the way there, at noon, I saw a light from heaven, brighter than the sun. It shined all around me and those traveling with me. 14We all fell to the ground. Then I heard a voice talking to me in Aramaic.* The voice said, 'Saul, Saul, why are you persecuting* me? You are only hurting yourself by fighting me.'

15"I said, 'Who are you, Lord?'

"The Lord said, 'I am Jesus. I am the one you are persecuting. 16Stand up! I have chosen you to be my servant. You will tell people about me—what you have seen today and what I will show you. This is why I have come to you. 17I will keep you safe from your own people and from the non-Jewish people, the ones I am sending you to. I am sending you to these people. 18You will make them able to understand the truth. They will turn away from darkness to the light. They will turn away from the power of Satan, and they will turn to God. Then their sins can be forgiven, and they can be given a place among God's people—those who have been made holy* by believing in me.'"

Paul Tells About His Work

19Paul continued speaking: "King Agrippa,* after I had this vision* from heaven, I obeyed it. 20I began telling people to change their hearts and lives and turn back to God. And I told them to do what would show that they had really changed. I went first to people in Damascus. Then I went to Jerusalem and to every part of Judea and told the people there. I also went to the non-Jewish people.

21"This is why the Jews grabbed me and were trying to kill me at the Temple.* 22But God helped me, and he is still helping me today. With God's help I am standing here today and telling all people what I have seen. But I am saying nothing new. I am saying only what Moses* and the prophets* said would happen. 23They said that the Christ* would die and

---

*a*26:11 *curse* Literally, "blaspheme," the same as saying they did not believe in Jesus.

be the first to rise from death. They said that he would bring the light of God's saving truth[a] to the Jewish people and to the non-Jewish people."

Paul Tries to Persuade Agrippa

[24]While Paul was still defending himself, Festus shouted, "Paul, you are out of your mind! Too much study has made you crazy."

[25]Paul said, "Most Honorable Festus, I am not crazy. What I am saying is true. It all makes perfect sense. [26]King Agrippa* knows about all this, and I can speak freely to him. I know that he has heard about these things, because they happened where everyone could see them. [27]King Agrippa, do you believe what the prophets* wrote? I know you believe!"

[28]King Agrippa said to Paul, "Do you think you can persuade me to become a Christ follower so easily?"

[29]Paul said, "It is not important if it is easy or if it is hard. I pray to God that not only you but that everyone listening to me today could be saved and be just like me—except for these chains I have!"

[30]King Agrippa, Governor Festus, Bernice,* and all the people sitting with them stood up [31]and left the room. They were talking to each other. They said, "This man has done nothing worthy of being put to death or even put in jail." [32]And Agrippa said to Festus, "We could let him go free, but he has asked to see Caesar.*"

Paul Sails for Rome

27 [1]It was decided that we would sail for Italy. An army officer* named Julius, who served in the emperor's* special army, was put in charge of guarding Paul and some other prisoners on the trip. [2]We got on a ship from the city of Adramyttium that was ready to sail to different places in Asia.* Aristarchus, a man from Thessalonica in Macedonia,* went with us.

[3]The next day we came to the city of Sidon. Julius was very good to Paul and gave him freedom to go visit his friends there, who gave him whatever he needed. [4]We left that city and sailed close to the island of Cyprus because the wind was blowing against us. [5]We went across the sea by Cilicia and Pamphylia. Then we came to the city of Myra in Lycia. [6]There the army officer found a ship from the city of Alexandria that was going to Italy. So he put us on it.

[7]We sailed slowly for many days. It was hard for us to reach the city of Cnidus because the wind was blowing against us. We could not go any farther that way, so we sailed by the south side of the island of Crete near Salmone. [8]We sailed along the

---

[a]26:23 bring . . . truth Literally, "proclaim light."

coast, but the sailing was hard. Then we came to a place called Safe Harbors, near the city of Lasea.

⁹We had lost much time, and it was now dangerous to sail, because it was already after the Jewish day of fasting.ᵃ So Paul warned them, ¹⁰"Men, I can see that there will be a lot of trouble on this trip. The ship, everything in it, and even our lives may be lost!" ¹¹But the captain and the owner of the ship did not agree with Paul. So the army officer accepted what they said instead of believing Paul. ¹²Also, that harbor was not a good place for the ship to stay for the winter, so most of the men decided that we should leave there. They hoped we could reach Phoenix, where the ship could stay for the winter. (Phoenix was a city on the island of Crete. It had a harbor that faced southwest and northwest.)

The Storm

¹³Then a good wind began to blow from the south. The men on the ship thought, "This is the wind we wanted, and now we have it!" So they pulled up the anchor. We sailed very close to the island of Crete. ¹⁴But then a very strong wind called the "Northeaster" came from across the island. ¹⁵This wind took the ship and carried it away. The ship could not sail against the wind, so we stopped trying and let the wind blow us.

¹⁶We went below a small island named Cauda. With the island protecting us from the wind, we were able to bring in the lifeboat, but it was very hard to do. ¹⁷After the men brought the lifeboat in, they tied ropes around the ship to hold it together. The men were afraid that the ship would hit the sandbanks of Syrtis.* So they lowered the sail and let the wind carry the ship.

¹⁸The next day the storm was blowing against us so hard that the men threw some things out of the ship.ᵇ ¹⁹A day later they threw out the ship's equipment. ²⁰For many days we could not see the sun or the stars. The storm was very bad. We lost all hope of staying alive—we thought we would die.

²¹The men did not eat for a long time. Then one day Paul stood up before them and said, "Men, I told you not to leave Crete. You should have listened to me. Then you would not have all this trouble and loss. ²²But now I tell you to be happy. None of you will die; but the ship will be lost. ²³Last night an angel came to me from God—the God I worship and belong to. ²⁴The angel said, 'Paul, don't be afraid! You must stand before Caesar.* And God has given you this promise: He will save the lives of all those sailing with you.' ²⁵So men, there is nothing to worry about. I trust God, and I am sure everything will happen just as his angel told me. ²⁶But we will crash on an island."

ᵃ27:9 day of fasting The Day of Atonement, an important Jewish holy day in the fall of the year. This was the time of year that bad storms happened on the sea.   ᵇ27:18 threw some things ... ship The men did this to make the ship lighter so that it would not sink easily.

27On the fourteenth night we were still being blown around in the Adriatic Sea.* The sailors thought we were close to land. 28They threw a rope into the water with a weight on the end of it. They found that the water was 120 feet deep. They went a little farther and threw the rope in again. It was 90 feet deep. 29The sailors were afraid that we would hit the rocks, so they threw four anchors into the water. Then they prayed for daylight to come. 30Some of the sailors wanted to leave the ship, and they lowered the lifeboat to the water. They wanted the other men to think that they were throwing more anchors from the front of the ship. 31But Paul told the army officer* and the other soldiers, "If these men do not stay in the ship, you will lose all hope of survival." 32So the soldiers cut the ropes and let the lifeboat fall into the water.

33Just before dawn Paul began persuading all the people to eat something. He said, "For the past two weeks you have been waiting and watching. You have not eaten for 14 days. 34Now I beg you to eat something. You need it to stay alive. None of you will lose even one hair off your heads." 35After he said this, Paul took some bread and thanked God for it before all of them. He broke off a piece and began eating. 36All the men felt better and started eating too. 37(There were 276 people on the ship.) 38We ate all we wanted. Then we began making the ship lighter by throwing the grain into the sea.

The Ship Is Destroyed

39When daylight came, the sailors saw land, but they did not know what land it was. They saw a bay with a beach and wanted to sail the ship to the beach if they could. 40So they cut the ropes to the anchors and left the anchors in the sea. At the same time, they untied the ropes that were holding the rudders. Then they raised the front sail into the wind and sailed toward the beach. 41But the ship hit a sandbank. The front of the ship stuck there and could not move. Then the big waves began to break the back of the ship to pieces.

42The soldiers decided to kill the prisoners so that none of the prisoners could swim away and escape. 43But Julius the army officer* wanted to let Paul live. So he did not allow the soldiers to kill the prisoners. He told the people who could swim to jump into the water and swim to land. 44The others used wooden boards or pieces of the ship. And this is how all the people went safely to land.

Paul on the Island of Malta

28 1When we were safe on land, we learned that the island was called Malta. 2The people who lived there were very good to us. It was raining and very cold, so they built a fire and welcomed all of us. 3Paul gathered a pile of sticks for the fire. He was putting the sticks on the fire, and a poisonous snake

came out because of the heat and bit him on the hand. ⁴When the people living on the island saw the snake hanging from his hand, they said, "This man must be a murderer! He did not die in the sea, but Justice*ᵃ* does not want him to live."

⁵But Paul shook the snake off into the fire and was not hurt. ⁶The people thought he would swell up or fall down dead. They waited and watched him for a long time, but nothing bad happened to him. So they changed their opinion. They said, "He is a god!"

⁷There were some fields around that same area. They were owned by a man named Publius, the most important Roman official on the island. He welcomed us into his home and was very good to us. We stayed in his house for three days. ⁸Publius' father was very sick. He had a fever and dysentery,* but Paul went to him and prayed for him. He laid his hands on*ᵇ* the man and healed him. ⁹After this happened, all the other sick people on the island came to Paul, and he healed them too.

¹⁰⁻¹¹The people on the island gave us many honors. And after we had been there three months and were ready to leave, they provided us everything we needed for our trip.

Paul Goes to Rome

We got on a ship from Alexandria that had stayed on the island of Malta during the winter. On the front of the ship was the sign for the twin gods.*ᶜ* ¹²We stopped at the city of Syracuse. We stayed there three days and then left. ¹³We came to the city of Rhegium. The next day a wind began to blow from the southwest, so we were able to leave. A day later we came to the city of Puteoli. ¹⁴We found some believers there, who asked us to stay with them a week. Finally, we came to Rome. ¹⁵The brothers and sisters in Rome heard about us and came out to meet us at the Market of Appius*ᵈ* and at the Three Inns.*ᵉ* When Paul saw these believers, he thanked God and felt encouraged.

Paul in Rome

¹⁶When we came to Rome, Paul was allowed to live alone. But a soldier stayed with him to guard him.

¹⁷Three days later Paul sent for some of the most important Jews. When they came together, he said, "My brothers, I have done nothing against our people or against the customs of our fathers.* But I was arrested in Jerusalem and handed over to the Romans. ¹⁸They asked me many questions, but they could not find any reason why I should be put to death. So they wanted to let me go free. ¹⁹But the Jews there did not want that. So I had

---

*ᵃ*28:4 *Justice* The people thought there was a goddess named Justice who would punish bad people.   *ᵇ*28:8 *laid his hands on* This act was a way of asking God to bless people in a special way—here, to give this man healing.   *ᶜ*28:10–11 *twin gods* Statues of Castor and Pollux, Greek gods.   *ᵈ*28:15 *Market of Appius* A town about 43 miles (69 km) from Rome.   *ᵉ*28:15 *Three Inns* A town about 30 miles (48 km) from Rome.

to ask to come to Rome to have my trial before Caesar.* That doesn't mean I am accusing my people of doing anything wrong. 20That is why I wanted to see you and talk with you. I am bound with this chain because I believe in the hope of Israel.*"

21The Jews answered Paul, "We have received no letters from Judea about you. None of our Jewish brothers who have traveled from there brought news about you or told us anything bad about you. 22We want to hear your ideas. We know that people everywhere are speaking against this new group."

23Paul and the Jews chose a day for a meeting. On that day many more of these Jews met with Paul at his house. He spoke to them all day long, explaining God's kingdom* to them. He used the law of Moses* and the writings of the prophets* to persuade them to believe in Jesus. 24Some of the Jews believed what he said, but others did not believe. 25They had an argument among themselves and were ready to leave. But Paul said one more thing to them: "The Holy Spirit* spoke the truth to your fathers through Isaiah the prophet. He said,

26 'Go to this people and tell them:
   You will listen and you will hear,
      but you will not understand.
   You will look and you will see,
      but you will not understand what you see.
27 Yes, the minds of these people are now closed.
   They have ears, but they don't listen.
   They have eyes, but they refuse to see.
   If their minds were not closed,
      they might see with their eyes;
      they might hear with their ears;
      they might understand with their minds.
   Then they might turn back to me and be healed.'
                                                    Isaiah 6:9-10

28"I want you Jews to know that God has sent his salvation to the non-Jewish people. They will listen!" 29a

30Paul stayed two full years in his own rented house. He welcomed all the people who came and visited him. 31He told them about God's kingdom and taught them about the Lord Jesus Christ. He was very bold, and no one tried to stop him from speaking.

a28:29 Some late copies of Acts add verse 29: "After Paul said this, the Jews left, still having a big argument with each other."

Romans

1 ¹Greetings from Paul, a servant of Christ Jesus. God chose me to be an apostle* and gave me the work of telling his Good News.* ²God promised long ago through his prophets* in the Holy Scriptures* to give this Good News to his people. ³⁻⁴The Good News is about God's Son, Jesus Christ our Lord. As a human, he was born from the family of David,* but through the Holy Spirit*ᵃ* he was shown to be God's powerful Son when he was raised from death.

⁵Through Christ, God gave me the special work of an apostle—to lead people of all nations to believe and obey him. I do all this to honor Christ. ⁶You are some of those who have been chosen to belong to Jesus Christ.

⁷This letter is to all of you in Rome. God loves you and has chosen you to be his holy people.*

Grace* and peace to you from God our Father and from the Lord Jesus Christ.

A Prayer of Thanks

⁸First I want to say that I thank my God through Jesus Christ for all of you. I thank him because people everywhere in the world are talking about your great faith. ⁹⁻¹⁰Every time I pray, I always remember you. God knows this is true. He is the one I serve with all my heart by telling people the Good News* about his Son. I pray that I will be allowed to come to you. It will happen if God wants it. ¹¹I want very much to see you and give you some spiritual gift to make your faith stronger. ¹²I mean that I want us to help each other with the faith that we have. Your faith will help me, and my faith will help you.

¹³Brothers and sisters, I want you to know that I have planned many times to come to you, but something always happens to change my plans. I would like to see the same good result among you that I have had from my work among the other non-Jewish people.

¹⁴I must serve all people—those who share in Greek culture and those who are less civilized,*ᵇ* the educated as well as the ignorant. ¹⁵That is why I want so much to tell the Good News to you there in Rome.

ᵃ **1:3–4** *Holy Spirit* Literally, "spirit of holiness." *ᵇ* **1:14** *those who share ... civilized* Literally, "Greeks and barbarians." See "Greek" in the Word List.

[16]I am proud of the Good News, because it is the power God uses to save everyone who believes—to save the Jews first, and now to save those who are not Jews. [17]The Good News shows how God makes people right with himself. God's way of making people right begins and ends with faith. As the Scriptures* say, "The one who is right with God by faith will live forever."[a]

All People Have Done Wrong

[18]God shows his anger from heaven against all the evil and wrong things that people do. Their evil lives hide the truth they have. [19]This makes God angry because they have been shown what he is like. Yes, God has made it clear to them.

[20]There are things about God that people cannot see—his eternal power and all that makes him God. But since the beginning of the world, those things have been easy for people to understand. They are made clear in what God has made. So people have no excuse for the evil they do.

[21]People knew God, but they did not honor him as God, and they did not thank him. Their ideas were all useless. There was not one good thought left in their foolish minds. [22]They said they were wise, but they became fools. [23]Instead of honoring the divine greatness* of God, who lives forever, they traded it for the worship of idols—things made to look like humans, who get sick and die, or like birds, animals, and snakes.

[24]People wanted only to do evil. So God left them and let them go their sinful way. And so they became completely immoral and used their bodies in shameful ways with each other. [25]They traded the truth of God for a lie. They bowed down and worshiped the things God made instead of worshiping the God who made those things. He is the one who should be praised forever. Amen.*

[26]Because people did those things, God left them and let them do the shameful things they wanted to do. Women stopped having natural sex with men and started having sex with other women. [27]In the same way, men stopped having natural sex with women and began wanting each other all the time. Men did shameful things with other men, and in their bodies they received the punishment for those wrongs.

[28]People did not think it was important to have a true knowledge of God. So God left them and allowed them to have their own worthless thinking. And so they do what they should not do. [29]They are filled with every kind of sin, evil, greed, and hatred. They are full of jealousy, murder, fighting, lying, and thinking the worst things about each other. They gossip [30]and say evil things about each other. They hate God. They are rude, proud, and brag about themselves. They invent ways of doing

[a] 1:17 Quote from Hab. 2:4.

evil. They don't obey their parents, [31]they are foolish, they don't keep their promises, and they show no kindness or mercy to others. [32]They know God's law says that anyone who lives like that should die. But they not only continue to do these things themselves, but they also encourage others who do them.

Let God Be the Judge

2 [1]So do you think that you can judge those other people? You are wrong. You too are guilty of sin. You judge them, but you do the same things they do. So when you judge them, you are really condemning yourself. [2]God judges all who do such things, and we know his judgment is right. [3]And since you do the same things as those people you judge, surely you understand that God will punish you too. How could you think you would be able to escape his judgment? [4]God has been kind to you. He has been very patient, waiting for you to change. But you think nothing of his kindness. Maybe you don't understand that God is kind to you so that you will decide to change your lives.

[5]But you are so stubborn! You refuse to change. So you are making your own punishment greater and greater. You will be punished on the day when God will show his anger. On that day everyone will see how right God is to judge people. [6]He will reward or punish everyone for what they have done. [7]Some people live for God's glory,* for honor, and for life that cannot be destroyed. They live for those things by always continuing to do good. God will give eternal life to them. [8]But others are selfish and refuse to follow truth. They follow evil. God will show his anger and punish them. [9]He will give trouble and suffering to everyone who does evil—to the Jews first and also to those who are not Jews. [10]But he will give glory, honor, and peace to everyone who does good—to the Jews first and also to those who are not Jews. [11]God judges everyone the same. It doesn't matter who they are.

[12]People who have the law* and those who have never heard of the law are all the same when they sin. People who don't have the law and are sinners will be lost. And, in the same way, those who have the law and are sinners will be judged by the law. [13]Hearing the law does not make people right with God. They will be right before him only if they always do what the law says.

[14]Those who are not Jews don't have the law. But when they naturally do what the law commands without even knowing the law, then they are their own law. This is true even though they don't have the written law. [15]They show that in their hearts they know what is right and wrong, the same as the law commands, and their consciences agree. Sometimes their thoughts tell them that they have done wrong, and this makes them guilty. And sometimes their thoughts tell them that they have done right, and this makes them not guilty.

¹⁶All this will happen on the day when God will judge people's secret thoughts through Jesus Christ. This is part of the Good News* that I tell everyone.

The Jews and the Law

¹⁷What about you? You say you are a Jew. You trust in the law and proudly claim to be close to God. ¹⁸You know what God wants you to do. And you know what is important, because you have learned the law. ¹⁹You think you are a guide for people who don't know the right way, a light for those who are in the dark. ²⁰You think you can show foolish people what is right. And you think you are a teacher for those who are just beginning to learn. You have the law, and so you think you know everything and have all truth. ²¹You teach others, so why don't you teach yourself? You tell them not to steal, but you yourself steal. ²²You say they must not commit adultery,* but you yourself are guilty of that sin. You hate idols,* but you steal them from their temples. ²³You are so proud that you have God's law, but you bring shame to God by breaking his law. ²⁴As the Scriptures* say, "People in other nations insult God because of you."ᵃ

²⁵If you follow the law,* then your circumcision* has meaning. But if you break the law, then it is as if you were never circumcised. ²⁶Those who are not Jews are not circumcised. But if they do what the law says, it is as if they were circumcised. ²⁷You have the written law and circumcision, but you break the law. So those who are not circumcised in their bodies, but still obey the law, will show that you are guilty.

²⁸You are not a true Jew if you are only a Jew in your physical body. True circumcisionᵇ is not only on the outside of the body. ²⁹A true Jew is one who is a Jew inside. True circumcision is done in the heart. It is done by the Spirit,* not by the written law. And anyone who is circumcised in the heart by the Spirit gets praise from God, not from people.

3 ¹So, do Jews have anything that others don't have? Do they get any benefit from being circumcised? ²Yes, the Jews have many benefits. The most important one is this: God trusted the Jews with his teachings. ³It is true that some Jews were not faithful to God. But will that stop God from doing what he promised? ⁴No, even if everyone else is a liar, God will always do what he says. As the Scriptures say about him,

> "You will be proved right in what you say,
>   and you will win when people accuse you."   *Psalm 51:4*

⁵When we do wrong, that shows more clearly that God is right. So can we say that God does wrong when he punishes

---

ᵃ2:24 Quote from Isa. 52:5. See also Ezek. 36:20–23. ᵇ2:28 *circumcision* See the Word List. Paul uses it here in a spiritual sense of believers who share in the new agreement God gave his people through Jesus.

us? (That's the way some people think.) ⁶Of course not. If God could not punish us, how could he judge the world?

⁷Someone might say, "When I lie, it really gives God glory,* because my lie makes his truth easier to see. So why am I judged a sinner?" ⁸It would be the same to say, "We should do evil so that good will come." Many people criticize us, saying that's what we teach. They are wrong, and they should be condemned for saying that.

All People Are Guilty

⁹So are we Jews better than other people? No, we have already said that those who are Jews, as well as those who are not Jews, are the same. They are all guilty of sin. ¹⁰As the Scriptures* say,

> "There is no one doing what is right, not even one.
> 11   There is no one who understands.
>   There is no one who is trying to be with God.
> 12   They have all turned away from him,
>   and now they are of no use to anyone.
> There is no one who does good, not even one."

Psalm 14:1–3

¹³"Their words come from mouths that are like open graves." They use their lying tongues to deceive others."   *Psalm 5:9*

"Their words are like the poison of snakes."   *Psalm 140:3*

¹⁴"Their mouths are full of cursing and bitterness."   *Psalm 10:7*

¹⁵"They are always ready to hurt and kill.
16   Everywhere they go they cause ruin and sadness.
17   They don't know the way of peace."   *Isaiah 59:7–8*

¹⁸"They have no fear or respect for God."   *Psalm 36:1*

¹⁹What the law* says is for those who are under the law. It stops anyone from making excuses. And it brings the whole world under God's judgment, ²⁰because no one can be made right with God by following the law. The law only shows us our sin.

How God Makes People Right

²¹But God has a way to make people right, and it has nothing to do with the law. He has now shown us that new way, which the law and the prophets* told us about. ²²God makes people right through their faith inᵃ Jesus Christ. He does this for all who believe in Christ. Everyone is the same. ²³All have sinned and are not good enough to share God's divine greatness.* ²⁴They are made right with God by his grace.* This is a free gift.

ᵃ**3:22** *their faith in* Or, "the faithfulness of."

They are made right with God by being made free from sin through Jesus Christ. ²⁵⁻²⁶God gave Jesus as a way to forgive people's sins through their faith in him. God can forgive them because the blood sacrifice of Jesus pays for their sins. God gave Jesus to show that he always does what is right and fair. He was right in the past when he was patient and did not punish people for their sins. And in our own time he still does what is right. God worked all this out in a way that allows him to be a just judge and still make right any person who has faith in Jesus.

²⁷So do we have any reason to boast about ourselves? No reason at all. And why not? Because we are depending on the way of faith, not on what we have done in following the law. ²⁸I mean we are made right with God through faith, not through what we have done to follow the law. This is what we believe. ²⁹God is not only the God of the Jews. He is also the God of those who are not Jews. ³⁰There is only one God. He will make Jews^a right with him by their faith, and he will also make non-Jews^b right with him through their faith. ³¹So do we destroy the law by following the way of faith? Not at all! In fact, faith causes us to be what the law actually wants.

The Example of Abraham

4 ¹So what can we say about Abraham,* the father of our people? What did he learn about faith? ²If Abraham was made right by the things he did, he had a reason to boast about himself. But God knew different. ³That's why the Scriptures* say, "Abraham believed God, and God accepted his faith. That made him right with God."^c

⁴When people work, their pay is not given to them as a gift. They earn the pay they get. ⁵But people cannot do any work that will make them right with God. So they must trust in him. Then he accepts their faith, and that makes them right with him. He is the one who makes even evil people right. ⁶David* said the same thing when he was talking about the blessing people have when God accepts them as good without looking at what they have done:

⁷"What a blessing it is
  when people are forgiven for the wrongs they have done,
  when their sins are erased!
⁸ What a blessing it is when the Lord accepts people
  as if they are without sin!"   *Psalm 32:1–2*

⁹Is this blessing only for those who are circumcised*? Or is it also for those who are not circumcised? We have already said that God accepted Abraham's faith, and that made him right with God. ¹⁰So how did this happen? Did God accept Abraham

---

^a**3:30** *Jews* Literally, "circumcision." ^b**3:30** *non-Jews* Literally, "uncircumcision."
^c**4:3** Quote from Gen. 15:6.

before or after he was circumcised? God accepted him before his circumcision. [11]Abraham was circumcised later to show that God accepted him. His circumcision was proof that he was right with God through faith before he was circumcised. So Abraham is the father of all those who believe but are not circumcised. They believe and are accepted as people who are right with God. [12]And Abraham is also the father of those who have been circumcised. But it is not their circumcision that makes him their father. He is their father only if they live following the faith that our father Abraham had before he was circumcised.

God's Promise Received Through Faith

[13]Abraham* and his descendants received the promise that they would get the whole world. But Abraham did not receive that promise because he followed the law.* He received that promise because he was right with God through his faith. [14]If people could get God's promise by following the law, then faith is worthless. And God's promise to Abraham is worthless, [15]because the law can only bring God's anger on those who disobey it. But if there is no law, then there is nothing to disobey.

[16]So people get what God promised by having faith. This happens so that the promise can be a free gift. And if the promise is a free gift, then all of Abraham's people will get that promise. The promise is not just for those who live under the law of Moses.* It is for all who live with faith as Abraham did. He is the father of us all. [17]As the Scriptures* say, "I have made you a father of many nations."[a] This is true before God, the one Abraham believed—the God who gives life to the dead and speaks of things that don't yet exist as if they are real.

[18]There was no hope that Abraham would have children, but Abraham believed God and continued to hope. And that is why he became the father of many nations. As God told him, "You will have many descendants."[b] [19]Abraham was almost a hundred years old, so he was past the age for having children. Also, Sarah could not have children. Abraham was well aware of this, but his faith in God never became weak. [20]He never doubted that God would do what he promised. He never stopped believing. In fact, he grew stronger in his faith and just praised God. [21]Abraham felt sure that God was able to do what he promised. [22]So, "God accepted Abraham's faith, and that made him right with God."[c] [23]These words ("God accepted Abraham's faith") were written not only for Abraham. [24]They were also written for us. God will also accept us because we believe. We believe in the one who raised Jesus our Lord from

[a]**4:17** Quote from Gen. 17:5. [b]**4:18** Quote from Gen. 15:5. [c]**4:22** Quote from Gen. 15:6.

death. 25Jesus was handed over to die for our sins, and he was raised from death to make us right with God.

Right With God

5 1We have been made right with God because of our faith. So we have peace with him through our Lord Jesus Christ. 2Through our faith, Christ has brought us into that blessing of God's grace* that we now enjoy. And we are very happy because of the hope we have of sharing God's glory.* 3And we are also happy with the troubles we have. Why are we happy with troubles? Because we know that these troubles make us more patient. 4And this patience is proof that we are strong. And this proof gives us hope. 5And this hope will never disappoint us. We know this because God has poured out his love to fill our hearts through the Holy Spirit* he gave us.

6Christ died for us when we were unable to help ourselves. We were living against God, but at just the right time Christ died for us. 7Very few people will die to save the life of someone else, even if it is for a good person. Someone might be willing to die for an especially good person. 8But Christ died for us while we were still sinners, and in that way God showed how much he loves us.

9We have been made right with God by the blood sacrifice of Christ. So through Christ we will surely be saved from God's anger. 10I mean that while we were God's enemies, he made friends with us through his Son's death. So surely, now that we are God's friends, God will save us through his Son's life. 11And not only will we be saved, but we rejoice right now in what God has done for us through our Lord Jesus Christ. It is because of Jesus that we are now God's friends.

Adam and Christ

12Sin came into the world because of what one man did. And with sin came death. So this is why all people must die— because all people have sinned. 13Sin was in the world before the law of Moses.* But God does not consider people guilty of sin if there is no law. 14But from the time of Adam to the time of Moses, everyone had to die. Adam died because he sinned by not obeying God's command. But even those who did not sin that same way had to die.

That one man, Adam, can be compared to Christ, the one who was coming in the future. 15But God's free gift is not like Adam's sin. Many people died because of the sin of that one man. But the grace* that people received from God was much greater. Many received God's gift of life by the grace of this other man, Jesus Christ. 16After Adam sinned once, he was judged guilty. But the gift of God is different. His free gift came after many sins, and it makes people right with him. 17One man sinned, and so death ruled all people because of that one man.

But now some people accept God's full grace and his great gift of being made right. Surely they will have true life and rule through the one man, Jesus Christ.

¹⁸So that one sin of Adam brought the punishment of death to all people. But in the same way, Christ did something so good that it makes all people right with God. And that brings them true life. ¹⁹One man disobeyed God and many became sinners. But in the same way, one man obeyed God and many will be made right. ²⁰The law was brought in so that more people would sin in the same way Adam did. But where sin increased, there was even more of God's grace. ²¹Sin once used death to rule us. But God gave us more of his grace so that grace could rule by making us right with him. And this brings us eternal life through Jesus Christ our Lord.

Dead to Sin but Alive in Christ

6 ¹So do you think we should continue sinning so that God will give us more and more grace*? ²Of course not! Our old sinful life ended. It's dead. So how can we continue living in sin? ³Did you forget that all of us became part of Christ Jesus when we were baptized*? In our baptism* we shared in his death. ⁴So when we were baptized, we were buried with Christ and took part in his death. We were buried so that we could be raised from death just as Christ was and live a new life. He was raised from death by the wonderful power of the Father.

⁵Christ died, and we have been joined with him by dying too. So we will also be joined with him by rising from death as he did. ⁶We know that our old life was killed on the cross with Christ. This happened so that our sinful selves would have no power over us. Then we would not be slaves to sin. ⁷Anyone who has died is made free from sin's control.

⁸If we died with Christ, we know that we will also live with him. ⁹Christ was raised from death. And we know that he cannot die again. Death has no power over him now. ¹⁰Yes, when Christ died, he died to defeat the power of sin one time— enough for all time. He now has a new life, and his new life is with God. ¹¹In the same way, you should see yourselves as being dead to the power of sin and alive for God through Christ Jesus.

¹²But don't let sin control your life here on earth. You must not be ruled by the things your sinful self makes you want to do. ¹³Don't offer the parts of your body to serve sin. Don't use your bodies to do evil, but offer yourselves to God, as people who have died and now live. Offer the parts of your body to God to be used for doing good. ¹⁴Sin will not be your master, because you are not under law. You now live under God's grace.

Slaves of Goodness

¹⁵So what should we do? Should we sin because we are under grace* and not under law? Certainly not! ¹⁶Surely you

know that you become the slaves of whatever you give yourselves to. Anything or anyone you follow will be your master. You can follow sin, or you can obey God. Following sin brings spiritual death, but obeying God makes you right with him. [17]In the past you were slaves to sin—sin controlled you. But thank God, you fully obeyed what you were taught. [18]You were made free from sin, and now you are slaves to what is right. [19]I use this example from everyday life because you need help in understanding spiritual truths. In the past you offered the parts of your body to be slaves to your immoral and sinful thoughts. The result was that you lived only for sin. In the same way, you must now offer yourselves to be slaves to what is right. Then you will live only for God.

[20]In the past you were slaves to sin, and you did not even think about doing right. [21]You did evil things, and now you are ashamed of what you did. Did those things help you? No, they only brought death. [22]But now you are free from sin. You have become slaves of God, and the result is that you live only for God. This will bring you eternal life. [23]When people sin, they earn what sin pays—death. But God gives his people a free gift—eternal life in Christ Jesus our Lord.

An Example From Marriage

7 [1]Brothers and sisters, you all understand the law of Moses.* So surely you know that the law rules over people only while they are alive. [2]It's like what the law says about marriage: A woman must stay married to her husband as long as he is alive. But if her husband dies, she is made free from the law of marriage. [3]But if she marries another man while her husband is still alive, the law says she is guilty of adultery.* But if her husband dies, she is made free from the law of marriage. So if she marries another man after her husband dies, she is not guilty of adultery.

[4]In the same way, my brothers and sisters, your old selves died and you became free from the law* through the body of Christ. Now you belong to someone else. You belong to the one who was raised from death. We belong to Christ so that we can be used in service to God. [5]In the past we were ruled by our sinful selves. The law made us want to do sinful things. And those sinful desires controlled our bodies, so that what we did only brought us spiritual death. [6]In the past the law held us as prisoners, but our old selves died, and we were made free from the law. So now we serve God in a new way, not in the old way with the written rules. Now we serve God in the new way, with the Spirit.*

Our Fight Against Sin

[7]You might think I am saying that sin and the law* are the same. That is not true. But the law was the only way I could

learn what sin means. I would never have known it is wrong to want something that is not mine. But the law said, "You must not want what belongs to someone else."[a] 8And sin found a way to use that command and make me want all kinds of things that weren't mine. So sin came to me because of the command. But without the law, sin has no power. 9Before I knew the law, I was alive. But when I heard the law's command, sin began to live, 10and I died spiritually. The command was meant to bring life, but for me it brought death. 11Sin found a way to fool me by using the command to make me die.

12Now the law is holy,* and the command is holy and right and good. 13Does this mean that something that is good brought death to me? No, it was sin that used the good command to bring me death. This shows how terrible sin really is. It can use a good command to produce a result that shows sin at its very worst.

The War Inside Us

14We know that the law* is spiritual, but I am not. I am so human. Sin rules me as if I were its slave. 15I don't understand why I act the way I do. I don't do the good I want to do, and I do the evil I hate. 16And if I don't want to do what I do, that means I agree that the law is good. 17But I am not really the one doing the evil. It is sin living in that does it. 18Yes, I know that nothing good lives in me—I mean nothing good lives in the part of me that is not spiritual. I want to do what is good, but I don't do it. 19I don't do the good that I want to do. I do the evil that I don't want to do. 20So if I do what I don't want to do, then I am not really the one doing it. It is the sin living in me that does it.

21So I have learned this rule: When I want to do good, evil is there with me. 22In my mind I am happy with God's law. 23But I see another law working in my body. That law makes war against the law that my mind accepts. That other law working in my body is the law of sin, and that law makes me its prisoner. 24What a miserable person I am! Who will save me from this body that brings me death? 25I thank God for his salvation through Jesus Christ our Lord!

So in my mind I am a slave to God's law, but in my sinful self I am a slave to the law of sin.

Life in the Spirit

8 1So now anyone who is in Christ Jesus is not judged guilty. 2That is because in Christ Jesus the law of the Spirit* that brings life made you[b] free. It made you free from the law that brings sin and death. 3The law* was without power because it was made weak by our sinful selves. But God did what the law

---

[a]7:7 Quote from Ex. 20:17; Deut. 5:21.   [b]8:2 you Some Greek copies have "me." Also in the next sentence.

could not do: He sent his own Son to earth with the same human life that everyone else uses for sin. God sent him to be an offering to pay for sin. So God used a human life to destroy sin. [4]He did this so that we could be right just as the law said we must be. Now we don't live following our sinful selves. We live following the Spirit.

[5]People who live following their sinful selves think only about what they want. But those who live following the Spirit are thinking about what the Spirit wants them to do. [6]If your thinking is controlled by your sinful self, there is spiritual death. But if your thinking is controlled by the Spirit, there is life and peace. [7]Why is this true? Because anyone whose thinking is controlled by their sinful self is against God. They refuse to obey God's law. And really they are not able to obey it. [8]Those who are ruled by their sinful selves cannot please God.

[9]But you are not ruled by your sinful selves. You are ruled by the Spirit, if that Spirit of God really lives in you. But whoever does not have the Spirit of Christ does not belong to Christ. [10]Your body will always be dead because of sin. But if Christ is in you, then the Spirit gives you life, because Christ made you right with God. [11]God raised Jesus from death. And if God's Spirit lives in you, he will also give life to your bodies that die. Yes, God is the one who raised Christ from death, and he will raise you to life through his Spirit living in you.

[12]So, my brothers and sisters, we must not be ruled by our sinful selves. We must not live the way our sinful selves want. [13]If you use your lives to do what your sinful selves want, you will die spiritually. But if you use the Spirit's help to stop doing the wrong things you do with your body, you will have true life.

[14]The true children of God are those who let God's Spirit lead them. [15]The Spirit that we received is not a spirit that makes us slaves again and causes us to fear. The Spirit that we have makes us God's chosen children. And with that Spirit we say, "Abba,[a] Father." [16]And the Spirit himself speaks to our spirits and makes us sure that we are God's children. [17]If we are God's children, we will get the blessings God has for his people. He will give us all that he has given Christ. But we must suffer like Christ suffered. Then we will be able to share his glory.*

We Will Have Glory in the Future

[18]We have sufferings now, but these are nothing compared to the great glory* that will be given to us. [19]Everything that God made is waiting with excitement for the time when he will show the world who his children are. The whole world wants very much for that to happen. [20]Everything God made was allowed to become like something that cannot fulfill its purpose. That was not its choice, but God made it happen with this hope in view: [21]That the creation would be made free from

8:15 *Abba* An Aramaic word that was used by Jewish children as a name for their fathers.

ruin—that everything God made would have the same freedom and glory that belong to God's children.

²²We know that everything God made has been waiting until now in pain like a woman ready to give birth to a child. ²³Not only the world, but we also have been waiting with pain inside us. We have the Spirit* as the first part of God's promise. So we are waiting for God to finish making us his own children. I mean we are waiting for our bodies to be made free. ²⁴We were saved to have this hope. If we can see what we are waiting for, that is not really hope. People don't hope for something they already have. ²⁵But we are hoping for something we don't have yet, and we are waiting for it patiently.

²⁶Also, the Spirit helps us. We are very weak, but the Spirit helps us with our weakness. We don't know how to pray as we should, but the Spirit himself speaks to God for us. He begs God for us, speaking to him with feelings too deep for words. ²⁷God already knows our deepest thoughts. And he understands what the Spirit is saying, because the Spirit speaks for his people in the way that agrees with what God wants.

²⁸We know that in everything God works for the good of those who love him. These are the people God chose, because that was his plan. ²⁹God knew them before he made the world. And he decided that they would be like his Son. Then Jesus would be the firstborn*ᵃ* of many brothers and sisters. ³⁰God planned for them to be like his Son. He chose them and made them right with him. And after he made them right, he gave them his glory.

God's Love in Christ Jesus

³¹So what should we say about this? If God is for us, no one can stand against us. And God is with us. ³²He even let his own Son suffer for us. God gave his Son for all of us. So now with Jesus, God will surely give us all things. ³³Who can accuse the people God has chosen? No one! God is the one who makes them right. ³⁴Who can say that God's people are guilty? No one! Christ Jesus died, but that is not all. He was also raised from death. And now he is at God's right side, speaking to him for us. ³⁵Can anything separate us from Christ's love? Can trouble or problems or persecution* separate us from his love? If we have no food or clothes or face danger or even death, will that separate us from his love? ³⁶As the Scriptures* say,

> "For you we are in danger of death all the time.
>   People think we are worth no more
>   than sheep to be killed." *Psalm 44:22*

³⁷But in all these troubles we have complete victory through God, who has shown his love for us. ³⁸⁻³⁹Yes, I am sure that nothing can separate us from God's love—not death, life, angels,

―――――――――

*ᵃ***8:29** *firstborn* The first male child in a family. Here, it probably means that Christ was the first in God's family to share God's glory.

or ruling spirits. I am sure that nothing now, nothing in the future, no powers, nothing above us or nothing below us—nothing in the whole created world—will ever be able to separate us from the love God has shown us in Christ Jesus our Lord.

God and the Jewish People

9 ¹I am in Christ and I am telling you the truth. I am not lying. And my conscience, ruled by the Holy Spirit,* agrees that what I say now is true. ²I have great sorrow and always feel much sadness ³for my own people. They are my brothers and sisters, my earthly family. I wish I could help them. I would even have a curse on me and cut myself off from Christ if that would help them. ⁴They are the people of Israel,* God's chosen children. They have the glory* of God and the agreements he made between himself and his people. God gave them the law of Moses,* the Temple* worship, and his promises. ⁵They are the descendants of our great fathers,* and they are the earthly family of Christ. And Christ is God over all things. Praise him forever*ᵃ*! Amen.*

⁶I don't mean that God failed to keep his promise to the Jewish people. But only some of the people of Israel are really God's people.*ᵇ* ⁷And only some of Abraham's* descendants are true children of Abraham. This is what God said to Abraham: "Your true descendants will be those who come through Isaac."*ᶜ* ⁸This means that not all of Abraham's descendants are God's true children. Abraham's true children are those who become God's children because of the promise he made to Abraham. ⁹Here is what God said in that promise: "About this time next year I will come back, and Sarah will have a son."*ᵈ*

¹⁰And that is not all. Rebecca also has sons, and they had the same father. He is our father Isaac. ¹¹⁻¹²But before the two sons were born, God told Rebecca, "The older son will serve the younger."*ᵉ* This was before the boys had done anything good or bad. God said this before they were born so that the boy he wanted would be chosen because of God's own plan. He was chosen because he was the one God wanted to call, not because of anything the boys did. ¹³As the Scriptures* say, "I loved Jacob, but I hated Esau."*ᶠ*

¹⁴So what does this mean? That God is not fair? We cannot say that. ¹⁵God said to Moses, "I will show mercy to anyone I want to show mercy to. I will show pity to anyone I choose."*ᵍ* ¹⁶So God will choose anyone he decides to show mercy to, and his choice does not depend on what people want or try to do. ¹⁷In the Scriptures God says to Pharaoh*: "I made you king so

---

*ᵃ***9:5** *And Christ ... forever* This can also mean "May God, who rules over all things, be praised forever!" *ᵇ***9:6** *God's people* Literally, "Israel," the people God chose to bring his blessings to the world. *ᶜ***9:7** Quote from Gen. 21:12. *ᵈ***9:9** Quote from Gen. 18:10, 14. *ᵉ***9:11–12** Quote from Gen. 25:23. *ᶠ***9:13** Quote from Mal. 1:2–3. *ᵍ***9:15** Quote from Ex. 33:19.

that you could do this for me. I wanted to show my power through you. I wanted my name to be announced throughout the world."*ᵃ* ¹⁸So God shows mercy to those he wants to show mercy to and makes stubborn those he wants to make stubborn.

¹⁹So one of you will ask me, "If God controls what we do, why does he blame us for our sins?" ²⁰Don't ask that. You are only human and have no right to question God. A clay jar does not question the one who made it. It does not say, "Why did you make me like this?" ²¹The one who makes the jar can make anything he wants. He uses the same clay to make different things. He might make one thing for special purposes and another for daily use.

²²It is the same way with what God has done. He wanted to show his anger and to let people see his power. But he patiently endured those he was angry with—people who were ready to be destroyed. ²³He waited with patience so that he could make known the riches of his glory* to the people he has chosen to receive his mercy. God has already prepared them to share his glory. ²⁴We are those people, the ones God chose not only from the Jews but also from those who are not Jews. ²⁵As the Scriptures say in the book of Hosea,

> "The people who are not mine—
>   I will say they are my people.
> And the people I did not love—
>   I will say they are the people I love." *Hosea 2:23*

²⁶And,

> "Where God said in the past,
>   'You are not my people'—
> there they will be called children of the living God." *Hosea 1:10*

²⁷And Isaiah cries out about Israel:

> "There are so many people of Israel,
>   they are like the grains of sand by the sea.
> But only a few of them will be saved.
> ²⁸ Yes, the Lord will quickly finish judging the people
>   on the earth." *Isaiah 10:22-23*

²⁹It is just as Isaiah said:

> "The Lord All-Powerful allowed some of our people to live.
> If he had not done that,
>   we would now be like Sodom,*
>   and we would be like Gomorrah.*" *Isaiah 1:9*

³⁰So what does all this mean? It means that people who are not Jews were made right with God because of their faith, even

ᵃ**9:17** Quote from Ex. 9:16.

though they were not trying to make themselves right. ³¹And the people of Israel, who tried to make themselves right with God by following the law, did not succeed. ³²They failed because they tried to make themselves right by the things they did. They did not trust in God to make them right. They fell over the stone that makes people fall. ³³The Scriptures talk about that stone:

"Look, I put in Zion* a stone that will make people stumble.
    It is a rock that will make people fall.
But anyone who trusts in that rock
    will never be disappointed."   *Isaiah 8:14; 28:16*

10 ¹Brothers and sisters, what I want most is for all the people of Israel to be saved. That is my prayer to God. ²I can say this about them: They really try hard to follow God, but they don't know the right way. ³They did not know the way that God makes people right with him. And they tried to make themselves right in their own way. So they did not accept God's way of making people right. ⁴Christ ended the law so that everyone who believes in him is made right with God.

⁵Moses writes about being made right by following the law. He says, "The person who obeys these laws is the one who will have life through them."ᵃ ⁶But this is what the Scriptures say about being made right through faith: "Don't say to yourself, 'Who will go up into heaven?'" (That means "Who will go up to heaven to get Christ and bring him down to earth?") ⁷"And don't say, 'Who will go down into the world below?'" (That means "Who will go down to get Christ and bring him up from death?")

⁸This is what the Scripture says: "God's teaching is near you; it is in your mouth and in your heart."ᵇ It is the teaching of faith that we tell people. ⁹If you openly say, "Jesus is Lord" and believe in your heart that God raised him from death, you will be saved. ¹⁰Yes, we believe in Jesus deep in our hearts, and so we are made right with God. And we openly say that we believe in him, and so we are saved.

¹¹Yes, the Scriptures say, "Whoever believes in him will never be disappointed."ᶜ ¹²It says this because there is no difference between those who are Jews and those who are not. The same Lord is the Lord of all people. And he richly blesses everyone who looks to him for help. ¹³Yes, "everyone who trusts in the Lordᵈ God will be saved."ᵉ

¹⁴But before people can pray to the Lord for help, they must believe in him. And before they can believe in the Lord, they must hear about him. And for anyone to hear about the Lord,

---

ᵃ**10:5** Quote from Lev. 18:5.   ᵇ**10:8** *Verses 6–8* Quotes from Deut. 30:12–14.   ᶜ**10:11** Quote from Isa. 28:16.   ᵈ**10:13** *who trusts in the Lord* Literally, "who calls on the name of the Lord," meaning to show faith in him by worshiping him or praying to him for help.   ᵉ**10:13** Quote from Joel 2:32.

someone must tell them. [15]And before anyone can go and tell them, they must be sent. As the Scriptures say, "How wonderful it is to see someone coming to tell good news."[a]

[16]But not all the people accepted that good news. Isaiah said, "Lord, who believed what we told them?"[b] [17]So faith comes from hearing the Good News.* And people hear the Good News when someone tells them about Christ.

[18]But I ask, "Did people not hear the Good News?" Yes, they heard—as the Scriptures say,

> "Their voices went out all around the world.
> Their words went everywhere in the world." *Psalm 19:4*

[19]Again I ask, "Did the people of Israel not understand?" Yes, they did understand. First, Moses says this for God:

> "I will use those who are not really a nation
>   to make you jealous.
> I will use a nation that does not understand
>   to make you angry." *Deuteronomy 32:21*

[20]Then Isaiah is bold enough to say this for God:

> "The people who were not looking for me—
>   they are the ones who found me.
> I showed myself to those who did not ask for me."
> *Isaiah 65:1*

[21]But about the people of Israel God says,

> "All day long I have waited for those people,
>   but they refuse to obey or to follow me." *Isaiah 65:2*

God Has Not Forgotten His People

11 [1]So I ask, "Did God force his people to leave him?" Of course not. I myself am an Israelite.* I am from the family of Abraham,* from the tribe of Benjamin. [2]God chose the Israelites to be his people before they were born. And he did not force them to leave. Surely you know what the Scriptures* say about Elijah.* The Scriptures tell about Elijah praying to God against the people of Israel.* He said, [3]"Lord, they have killed your prophets* and destroyed your altars.* I am the only prophet still living, and they are trying to kill me now."[c] [4]But what answer did God give to Elijah? God said, "I have kept for myself seven thousand men who have never given worship to Baal.*"[d]

[5]It is the same now. God has chosen a few people by his grace.* [6]And if he chose them by grace, then it is not what they have done that made them his people. If they could be made his people by what they did, his gift of grace would not really be a gift.

---

[a]**10:15** Quote from Isa. 52:7. [b]**10:16** Quote from Isa. 53:1. [c]**11:3** Quote from 1 Kings 19:10, 14. [d]**11:4** Quote from 1 Kings 19:18.

⁷So this is what has happened: The people of Israel wanted God's blessing, but they did not all get it. The people he chose did get his blessing, but the others became hard and refused to listen to him. ⁸As the Scriptures say,

"God caused the people to fall asleep."   *Isaiah 29:10*

"God closed their eyes so that they could not see,
    and he closed their ears so that they could not hear.
This continues until now."   *Deuteronomy 29:4*

⁹And David says,

"Let those people be caught and trapped at their own feasts.
    Let them fall and be punished.
¹⁰ Let their eyes be closed so that they cannot see.
    And let them be troubled forever."   *Psalm 69:22–23*

¹¹So I ask: When the Jews fell, did that fall destroy them? No! But their mistake brought salvation to those who are not Jews. The purpose of this was to make the Jews jealous. ¹²Their mistake brought rich blessings to the world. And what they lost brought rich blessings to the non-Jewish people. So surely the world will get much richer blessings when enough Jews become the kind of people God wants.

¹³Now I am speaking to you people who are not Jews. I am an apostle* to the non-Jewish people. So while I have that work, I will do the best I can. ¹⁴I hope I can make my own people jealous. That way, maybe I can help some of them to be saved. ¹⁵God turned away from the Jews. When that happened, he became friends with the other people in the world. So when he accepts the Jews, it will be like bringing people to life after death. ¹⁶If the first piece of bread is offered to God, then the whole loaf is made holy.* If the roots of a tree are holy, the tree's branches are holy too.

¹⁷It is as if some of the branches from an olive tree have been broken off, and the branch of a wild olive tree has been joined to that first tree. If you are not a Jew, you are the same as that wild branch, and you now share the strength and life of the first tree. ¹⁸But don't act like you are better than those branches that were broken off. You have no reason to be proud of yourself, because you don't give life to the root. The root gives life to you. ¹⁹You might say, "Branches were broken off so that I could be joined to their tree." ²⁰That is true. But those branches were broken off because they did not believe. And you continue to be part of the tree only because you believe. Don't be proud, but be afraid. ²¹If God did not let the natural branches of that tree stay, he will not let you stay if you stop believing.

²²So you see that God is kind, but he can also be very strict. He punishes those who stop following him. But he is kind to you, if you continue trusting in his kindness. If you don't continue depending on him, you will be cut off from the tree.

²³And if the Jews will believe in God again, he will accept them back. He is able to put them back where they were. ²⁴It is not natural for a wild branch to become part of a good tree. But you non-Jewish people are like a branch cut from a wild olive tree. And you were joined to a good olive tree. But those Jews are like a branch that grew from the good tree. So surely they can be joined to their own tree again.

²⁵I want you to understand this secret truth, brothers and sisters. This truth will help you understand that you don't know everything. The truth is this: Part of Israel has been made stubborn, but that will change when enough non-Jewish people have come to God. ²⁶And that is how all Israel will be saved. The Scriptures say,

"The Savior will come from Zion*;
  he will take away all evil from the family of Jacob.*
²⁷ And I will make this agreement with those people
    when I take away their sins." *Isaiah 59:20–21; 27:9*

²⁸The Jews refuse to accept the Good News,* so they are God's enemies. This has happened to help you who are not Jews. But they are still God's chosen people, and he loves them because of the promises he made to their ancestors.* ²⁹God never changes his mind about the people he calls. He never decides to take back the blessings he has given them. ³⁰At one time you refused to obey God. But now you have received mercy, because the Jews refused to obey. ³¹And now they are the ones who refuse to obey, because God showed mercy to you. But this happened so that they can also receive mercy from him. ³²All people have refused to obey God. And he has put them all together as people who don't obey him so that he can show mercy to everyone.

Praise to God

³³Yes, God's riches are very great! His wisdom and knowledge have no end! No one can explain what God decides. No one can understand his ways. ³⁴As the Scriptures* say,

"Who knows the mind of the Lord?
  Who is able to give God advice?" *Isaiah 40:13*

³⁵"Who has ever given God anything?
  God owes nothing to anyone." *Job 41:11*

³⁶Yes, God made all things. And everything continues through him and for him. To God be the glory* forever! Amen.*

Give Your Lives to God

12 ¹So I beg you, brothers and sisters, because of the great mercy God has shown us, offer your lives*ᵃ* as a living

ᵃ 12:1 lives Literally, "bodies." Paul is using the language of Old Testament animal sacrifice to express the idea of a complete giving of oneself to God.

sacrifice* to him—an offering that is only for God and pleasing to him. Considering what he has done, it is only right that you should worship him in this way. ²Don't change yourselves to be like the people of this world, but let God change you inside with a new way of thinking. Then you will be able to decide and accept what God wants for you. You will be able to know what is good and pleasing to him and what is perfect.

³God has given me a special gift, and that is why I have something to say to each one of you. Don't think that you are better than you really are. You must see yourself just as you are. Decide what you are by the faith God has given each of us. ⁴Each one of us has one body, and that body has many parts. These parts don't all do the same thing. ⁵In the same way, we are many people, but in Christ we are all one body. We are the parts of that body, and each part belongs to all the others.

⁶We all have different gifts. Each gift came because of the grace* God gave us. Whoever has the gift of prophecy* should use that gift in a way that fits the kind of faith they have. ⁷Whoever has the gift of serving should serve. Whoever has the gift of teaching should teach. ⁸Whoever has the gift of comforting others should do that. Whoever has the gift of giving to help others should give generously. Whoever has the gift of leading should work hard at it. Whoever has the gift of showing kindness to others should do it gladly.

⁹Your love must be real. Hate what is evil. Do only what is good. ¹⁰Love each other in a way that makes you feel close like brothers and sisters. And give each other more honor than you give yourself. ¹¹As you serve the Lord, work hard and don't be lazy. Be excited about serving him! ¹²Be happy because of the hope you have. Be patient when you have troubles. Pray all the time. ¹³Share with God's people who need help. Look for people who need help and welcome them into your homes.

¹⁴Wish only good for those who treat you badly. Ask God to bless them, not curse them. ¹⁵When others are happy, you should be happy with them. And when others are sad, you should be sad too. ¹⁶Live together in peace with each other. Don't be proud, but be willing to be friends with people who are not important to others. Don't think of yourself as smarter than everyone else.

¹⁷If someone does you wrong, don't try to pay them back by hurting them. Try to do what everyone thinks is right. ¹⁸Do the best you can to live in peace with everyone. ¹⁹My friends, don't try to punish anyone who does wrong to you. Wait for God to punish them with his anger. It is written: "I am the one who punishes; I will pay people back,"ᵃ says the Lord. ²⁰But you should do this:

ᵃ **12:19** Quote from Deut. 32:35.

"If you have enemies who are hungry,
  give them something to eat.
If you have enemies who are thirsty,
  give them something to drink.
In doing this you will make them feel ashamed.[a]"

Proverbs 25:21–22

²¹Don't let evil defeat you, but defeat evil by doing good.

Obey Your Government Rulers

13 ¹All of you must obey the government rulers. Everyone who rules was given the power to rule by God. And all those who rule now were given that power by God. ²So anyone who is against the government is really against something God has commanded. Those who are against the government bring punishment on themselves. ³People who do right don't have to fear the rulers. But those who do wrong must fear them. Do you want to be free from fearing them? Then do only what is right and they will praise you.

⁴Rulers are God's servants to help you. But if you do wrong, you have reason to be afraid. They have the power to punish, and they will use it. They are God's servants to punish those who do wrong. ⁵So you must obey the government, not just because you might be punished, but because you know it is the right thing to do.

⁶And this is why you pay taxes too. Those rulers are working for God and give all their time to the work of ruling. ⁷Give everyone what you owe them. If you owe them any kind of tax, then pay it. Show respect to those you should respect. And show honor to those you should honor.

Loving Others Is the Only Law

⁸You should owe nothing to anyone, except that you will always owe love to each other. The person who loves others has done all that the law* commands. ⁹The law says, "You must not commit adultery,* you must not murder anyone, you must not steal, you must not want what belongs to someone else."[b] All these commands and all other commands are really only one rule: "Love your neighbor[c] the same as you love yourself."[d] ¹⁰Love doesn't hurt others. So loving is the same as obeying all the law.

¹¹I say this because you know that we live in an important time. Yes, it is now time for you to wake up from your sleep. Our salvation is nearer now than when we first believed. ¹²The

---

*a***12:20** *you will make them feel ashamed* Literally, "you will pour burning coals on their head." People in Old Testament times often put ashes on their heads to show that they were sad or sorry. *b***13:9** Quote from Ex. 20:13–15, 17. *c***13:9** *your neighbor* Or, "others." Jesus' teaching in Lk. 10:25–37 makes clear that this includes anyone in need. *d***13:9** Quote from Lev. 19:18.

night* is almost finished. The day* is almost here. So we should stop doing whatever belongs to darkness.* We should prepare ourselves to fight evil with the weapons that belong to the light.* ¹³We should live in a right way, like people who belong to the day. We should not have wild parties or be drunk. We should not be involved in sexual sin or any kind of immoral behavior. We should not cause arguments and trouble or be jealous. ¹⁴But be like the Lord Jesus Christ, so that when people see what you do, they will see Christ. Don't think about how to satisfy your sinful self and the bad things you want to do.

Don't Criticize Others

14 ¹Be willing to accept those who still have doubts about what believers can do. And don't argue with them about their different ideas. ²Some people believe they can eat any kind of food,*ᵃ* but those who have doubts eat only vegetables. ³Those who know they can eat any kind of food must not feel that they are better than those who eat only vegetables. And those who eat only vegetables must not decide that those who eat all foods are wrong. God has accepted them. ⁴You cannot judge the servants of someone else. Their own master decides if they are doing right or wrong. And the Lord's servants will be right, because the Lord is able to make them right.

⁵Some people might believe that one day is more important than another. And others might believe that every day is the same. Everyone should be sure about their beliefs in their own mind. ⁶Those who think one day is more important than other days are doing that for the Lord. And those who eat all kinds of food are doing that for the Lord. Yes, they give thanks to God for that food. And those who refuse to eat some foods do that for the Lord. They also give thanks to God.

⁷We don't live or die just for ourselves. ⁸If we live, we are living for the Lord. And if we die, we are dying for the Lord. So living or dying, we belong to the Lord. ⁹That is why Christ died and rose from death to live again—so that he could be Lord over those who have died and those who are living.

¹⁰So why do you judge your brother or sister in Christ? Or why do you think that you are better than they are? We will all stand before God, and he will judge us all. ¹¹Yes, the Scriptures* say,

"'Everyone will bow before me;
    everyone will say that I am God.
As surely as I live, these things will happen,' says the Lord."

Isaiah 45:23

---

*ᵃ***14:2** *any kind of food* The Jewish law said there were some foods that Jews could not eat. When they became followers of Christ, some of them did not understand that they could now eat all foods.

[12]So each of us will have to explain to God about the things we do.

Don't Cause Others to Sin

[13]So we should stop judging each other. Let's decide not to do anything that will cause a problem for a brother or sister or hurt their faith. [14]I know that there is no food that is wrong to eat. The Lord Jesus is the one who convinced me of that. But if someone believes that something is wrong, then it is wrong for that person.

[15]If you hurt the faith of your brother or sister because of something you eat, you are not really following the way of love. Don't destroy anyone's faith by eating something they think is wrong. Christ died for them. [16]Don't allow what is good for you to become something they say is evil. [17]In God's kingdom,* what we eat and drink is not important. Here is what is important: a right way of life, peace, and joy—all from the Holy Spirit.* [18]Whoever serves Christ by living this way is pleasing God, and they will be accepted by others.

[19]So let's try as hard as we can to do what will bring peace. Let's do whatever will help each other grow stronger in faith. [20]Don't let the eating of food destroy the work of God. All food is right to eat, but it is wrong for anyone to eat something that hurts the faith of another person. [21]It is better not to eat meat or drink wine or do anything else that hurts the faith of your brother or sister.

[22]You should keep your beliefs about these things a secret between yourself and God. It is a blessing to be able to do what you think is right without feeling guilty. [23]But anyone who eats something without being sure it is right is doing wrong. That is because they did not believe it was right. And if you do anything that you believe is not right, it is sin.

15 [1]Some of us have no problem with these things. So we should be patient with those who are not so strong and have doubts. We should not do what pleases us [2]but do what pleases them and is for their good. We should do whatever helps the church* grow stronger in faith. [3]Even Christ did not live trying to please himself. As the Scriptures* say about him, "Those people who insulted you have also insulted me."[a] [4]Everything that was written in the past was written to teach us. Those things were written so that we could have hope. That hope comes from the patience and encouragement that the Scriptures give us. [5]All patience and encouragement come from God. And I pray that God will help you all agree with each other, as Christ Jesus wants. [6]Then you will all be joined together. And all together you will give glory* to God the Father of our Lord Jesus Christ. [7]Christ accepted you, so you

a **15:3** Quote from Ps. 69:9.

should accept each other. This will bring glory to God. ⁸I tell you that Christ became a servant of the Jews to show that God has done what he promised their great ancestors.* ⁹Christ also did this so that the non-Jewish people could praise God for the mercy he gives to them. The Scriptures say,

> "So I will give thanks to you
>   among the people of other nations;
>   I will sing praise to your name."
>
>   *Psalm 18:49*

¹⁰And the Scriptures say,

> "You people of other nations should be happy
>   together with God's people."
>
>   *Deuteronomy 32:43*

¹¹The Scriptures also say,

> "Praise the Lord all you people of other nations;
>   all people should praise the Lord."
>
>   *Psalm 117:1*

¹²And Isaiah says,

> "Someone will come from Jesse's family.ᵃ
>   He will come to rule over the nations,
>   and they will put their hope in him."
>
>   *Isaiah 11:10*

¹³I pray that the God who gives hope will fill you with much joy and peace as you trust in him. Then you will have more and more hope, and it will flow out of you by the power of the Holy Spirit.

Paul Talks About His Work

¹⁴My brothers and sisters, I know without a doubt that you are full of goodness and have all the knowledge you need. So you are certainly able to counsel each other. ¹⁵But I have written to you very openly about some things that I wanted you to remember. I did this because God gave me this special gift: ¹⁶to be a servant of Christ Jesus for those who are not Jews. I serve like a priest whose duty it is to tell God's Good News.* He gave me this work so that you non-Jewish people could be an offering that he will accept—an offering made holy* by the Holy Spirit.*

¹⁷That is why I feel so good about what I have done for God in my service to Christ Jesus. ¹⁸I will not talk about anything I did myself. I will talk only about what Christ has done with me in leading the non-Jewish people to obey God. They have obeyed him because of what I have said and done. ¹⁹And they obeyed him because of the power of the miraculous signs* and wonders* that happened—all because of the power of God's Spirit. I have told people the Good News about Christ in every place from Jerusalem to Illyricum.* And so I have finished that

---

ᵃ**15:12** *Jesse's family* Jesse was the father of David, king of Israel. Jesus was from their family.

part of my work. [20]I always want to tell the Good News in places where people have never heard of Christ. I do this because I don't want to build on the work that someone else has already started. [21]But as the Scriptures* say,

"Those who were not told about him will see,
    and those who have not heard about him will understand."

                                                        Isaiah 52:15

Paul's Plan to Visit Rome

[22]That's what has kept me so busy and prevented my coming to see you even though I have wanted to come many times.

[23]Now I have finished my work in these areas. And for many years I have wanted to visit you. [24]So I will visit you when I go to Spain. Yes, I hope to visit you while I am traveling to Spain, and I will stay and enjoy being with you. Then you can help me continue on my trip.

[25]Now I am going to Jerusalem to help God's people there. [26]Some of them are poor, and the believers in Macedonia* and Achaia* wanted to help them. So they gathered some money to send them. [27]They were happy to do this. And it was like paying something they owed them, because as non-Jews they have been blessed spiritually by the Jews. So now they should use the material blessings they have to help the Jews. [28]I am going because I want to be sure that the poor people in Jerusalem get all this money that has been given for them. After I finish this work, I will leave for Spain. While I am traveling there, I will stop and visit you. [29]And I know that when I visit you, I will bring you Christ's full blessing.

[30]Brothers and sisters, I beg you to help me in my work by praying to God for me. Do this because of our Lord Jesus and the love that the Spirit* gives us. [31]Pray that I will be saved from those in Judea who refuse to accept our message. And pray that this help I am bringing to Jerusalem will please God's people there. [32]Then, if God wants me to, I will come to you. I will come with joy, and together you and I will have a time of rest. [33]The God who gives peace be with you all. Amen.*

Paul Has Some Final Things to Say

16 [1]I want you to know that you can trust our sister in Christ, Phoebe. She is a special servant* of the church* in Cenchrea. [2]I ask you to accept her in the Lord. Accept her the way God's people should. Help her with anything she needs from you. She has helped me very much, and she has helped many others too.

[3]Give my greetings to Priscilla and Aquila, who have worked together with me for Christ Jesus. [4]They risked their own lives to save mine. I am thankful to them, and all the non-Jewish churches are thankful to them. [5]Also, give greetings to the church that meets in their house.

Give greetings to my dear friend Epaenetus. He was the first person to follow Christ in Asia.* [6]Greetings also to Mary. She worked very hard for you. [7]And greet Andronicus and Junia. They are my relatives, and they were in prison with me. They were followers of Christ before I was. And they are some of the most important of the ones Christ sent out to do his work.[a]

[8]Give my greetings to Ampliatus, my dear friend in the Lord, [9]and to Urbanus. He has worked together with me for Christ. Give greetings also to my dear friend Stachys [10]and to Apelles, who has proved himself to be a true follower of Christ. Give greetings to everyone in the family of Aristobulus [11]and to Herodion, my relative. Greetings to all those in the family of Narcissus who belong to the Lord [12]and to Tryphaena and Tryphosa, women who work very hard for the Lord. Greetings to my dear friend Persis. She has also worked very hard for the Lord. [13]Greetings also to Rufus, one of the Lord's chosen people, and to his mother, who has been a mother to me too.

[14]Give my greetings to Asyncritus, Phlegon, Hermes, Patrobas, Hermas, and all the brothers in Christ who are with them. [15]Give greetings to Philologus and Julia, to Nereus and his sister, to Olympas, and to all of God's people with them. [16]Give each other the special greeting of God's people.[b] All the churches that belong to Christ send their greetings to you.

[17]Brothers and sisters, I want you to be very careful of those who cause arguments and hurt people's faith by teaching things that are against what you learned. Stay away from them. [18]People like that are not serving our Lord Christ. They are only pleasing themselves. They use fancy talk and say nice things to fool those who don't know about evil. [19]Everyone has heard that you do what you were taught, and I am very happy about that. But I want you to be wise about what is good and to know nothing about what is evil.

[20]The God who brings peace will soon defeat Satan* and give you power over him.

The grace* of our Lord Jesus be with you.

[21]Timothy, a worker together with me, sends you his greetings. Also Lucius, Jason, and Sosipater (these are my relatives) send their greetings.

[22]I am Tertius, the one writing this letter for Paul. I send you my own greetings as one who belongs to the Lord.

[23]Gaius is letting me and the whole church here use his home. He sends his greetings to you. Erastus and our brother Quartus also send their greetings. Erastus is the city treasurer here. [24][c]

---

[a]16:7 *most important ... work* Literally, "important among (or to) the apostles."
[b]16:16 *the special greeting of God's people* Literally, "a holy kiss." [c]16:24 Some Greek copies add verse 24: "The grace of our Lord Jesus Christ be with you all. Amen."

²⁵Praise God! He is the one who can make you strong in faith. He can use the Good News* that I teach to make you strong. It is the message about Jesus Christ that I tell people. That message is the secret truth that was hidden for ages and ages but has been made known. ²⁶It has now been shown to us. It was made known by what the prophets* wrote, as God commanded. And it has now been made known to all people so that they can believe and obey God, who lives forever. ²⁷Glory* forever to the only wise God through Jesus Christ. Amen.*

1 Corinthians

1 ¹Greetings from Paul. I was chosen to be an apostle* of Christ Jesus. God chose me because that is what he wanted. Greetings also from Sosthenes, our brother in Christ.

²To God's church* in Corinth, you who have been made holy* because you belong to Christ Jesus. You were chosen to be God's holy people* together with all people everywhere who trust in the Lord*a* Jesus Christ—their Lord and ours.

³Grace* and peace to you from God our Father and the Lord Jesus Christ.

Paul Gives Thanks to God

⁴I always thank my God for you because of the grace* that he has given you through Christ Jesus. ⁵In him you have been blessed in every way. You have been blessed in all your speaking and all your knowledge. ⁶This proves that what we told you about Christ is true. ⁷Now you have every gift from God while you wait for our Lord Jesus Christ to come again. ⁸He will keep you strong until the end so that on the day when our Lord Jesus Christ comes again, you will be free from all blame. ⁹God is faithful. He is the one who has chosen you to share life with his Son, Jesus Christ our Lord.

Problems in the Church at Corinth

¹⁰Brothers and sisters, by the authority of our Lord Jesus Christ, I beg all of you to agree with each other. You should not be divided into different groups. Be completely joined together again with the same kind of thinking and the same purpose.

¹¹My brothers and sisters, some members of Chloe's family told me that there are arguments among you. ¹²This is what I mean: One of you says, "I follow Paul," and someone else says, "I follow Apollos." Another says, "I follow Peter,*b*" and someone else says, "I follow Christ." ¹³Christ cannot be divided into different groups. It wasn't Paul who died on the cross for you, was it? Were you baptized* in Paul's name? ¹⁴I am thankful that I did not baptize any of you except Crispus and Gaius. ¹⁵I am thankful because now no one can say that

---

*a***1:2** *who trust in the Lord* Literally, "who call on the name of the Lord," meaning to show faith in him by worshiping or praying to him for help. *b***1:12** *Peter* The text says "Cephas," the Aramaic name for Peter, one of Jesus' twelve apostles.

you were baptized in my name. ¹⁶(I also baptized the family of Stephanas, but I don't remember that I myself baptized any others.) ¹⁷Christ did not give me the work of baptizing people. He gave me the work of telling the Good News.* But he sent me to tell the Good News without using clever speech, which would take away the power that is in the cross*[a] of Christ.

God's Power and Wisdom in Christ

¹⁸The teaching about the cross seems foolish to those who are lost. But to us who are being saved it is the power of God. ¹⁹As the Scriptures* say,

"I will destroy the wisdom of the wise.
   I will confuse the understanding of the intelligent."

Isaiah 29:14

²⁰So what does this say about the philosopher,* the law expert, or anyone in this world who is skilled in making clever arguments? God has made the wisdom of the world look foolish. ²¹This is what God in his wisdom decided: Since the world did not find him through its own wisdom, he used the message* that sounds foolish to save those who believe it.

²²The Jews ask for miraculous signs,* and the Greeks* want wisdom. ²³But this is the message we tell everyone: Christ was killed on a cross. This message is a problem for Jews, and to other people it is nonsense. ²⁴But Christ is God's power and wisdom to the people God has chosen, both Jews and Greeks. ²⁵Even the foolishness of God is wiser than human wisdom. Even the weakness of God is stronger than human strength.

²⁶Brothers and sisters, God chose you to be his. Think about that! Not many of you were wise in the way the world judges wisdom. Not many of you had great influence, and not many of you came from important families. ²⁷But God chose the foolish things of the world to shame the wise. He chose the weak things of the world to shame the strong. ²⁸And God chose what the world thinks is not important—what the world hates and thinks is nothing. He chose these to destroy what the world thinks is important. ²⁹God did this so that no one can stand before him and boast about anything. ³⁰It is God who has made you part of Christ Jesus. And Christ has become for us wisdom from God. He is the reason we are right with God and pure enough to be in his presence. Christ is the one who set us free from sin. ³¹So, as the Scriptures say, "Whoever boasts should boast only about the Lord."[b]

---

[a] 1:17 *cross* Paul uses the cross as a picture of the Good News, the story of Christ's death to pay for people's sins. The cross (Christ's death) was God's way to save people.   [b] 1:31 Quote from Jer. 9:24.

The Message About Christ on the Cross

2 ¹Dear brothers and sisters, when I came to you, I told you the secret truth of God. But I did not use fancy words or great wisdom. ²I decided that while I was with you I would forget about everything except Jesus Christ and his death on the cross. ³When I came to you, I was weak and shook with fear. ⁴My teaching and my speaking were not with wise words that persuade people. But the proof of my teaching was the power that the Spirit* gives. ⁵I did this so that your faith would be in God's power, not in human wisdom.

God's Wisdom

⁶We teach wisdom to people who are mature, but the wisdom we teach is not from this world. It is not the wisdom of the rulers of this world, who are losing their power. ⁷But we speak God's secret wisdom that has been hidden from everyone until now. God planned this wisdom for our glory.* He planned it before the world began. ⁸None of the rulers of this world understood this wisdom. If they had understood it, they would not have killed our great and glorious Lord on a cross. ⁹But as the Scriptures* say,

> "No eye has seen,
>> no ear has heard,
>> no one has imagined
>>> what God has prepared for those who love him."

Isaiah 64:4

¹⁰But God has shown us these things through the Spirit.*

The Spirit knows all things. The Spirit even knows the deep secrets of God. ¹¹It is like this: No one knows the thoughts that another person has. Only the person's spirit that lives inside knows those thoughts. It is the same with God. No one knows God's thoughts except God's Spirit. ¹²We received the Spirit that is from God, not the spirit of the world. We received God's Spirit so that we can know all that God has given us.

¹³When we say this, we don't use words taught to us by human wisdom. We use words taught to us by the Spirit. We use the Spirit's words to explain spiritual truths. ¹⁴People who do not have God's Spirit do not accept the things that come from his Spirit. They think these things are foolish. They cannot understand them, because they can only be understood with the Spirit's help. ¹⁵We who have the Spirit are able to make judgments about all these things. But anyone without the Spirit is not able to make proper judgments about us. ¹⁶As the Scriptures say,

> "Who ever knew what the Lord was thinking?
>> Who could tell the Lord what to do?"

Isaiah 40:13 (Greek version)

But we have been given Christ's way of thinking.

Teachers Are Only God's Servants

3 ¹Brothers and sisters, when I was there, I could not talk to you the way I talk to people who are led by the Spirit. I had to talk to you like ordinary people of the world. You were like babies in Christ. ²And the teaching I gave you was like milk, not solid food. I did this because you were not ready for solid food. And even now you are not ready. ³You are still not following the Spirit. You are jealous of each other, and you are always arguing with each other. This shows that you are still following your own selfish desires. You are acting like ordinary people of the world. ⁴One of you says, "I follow Paul," and someone else says, "I follow Apollos." When you say things like that, you are acting like people of the world.

⁵Is Apollos so important? Is Paul so important? We are only servants of God who helped you believe. Each one of us did the work God gave us to do. ⁶I planted the seed and Apollos watered it. But God is the one who made the seed grow. ⁷So the one who plants is not important, and the one who waters is not important. Only God is important, because he is the one who makes things grow. ⁸The one who plants and the one who waters have the same purpose. And each one will be rewarded for his own work. ⁹We are workers together for God, and you are like a farm that belongs to God.

And you are a house that belongs to God. ¹⁰Like an expert builder I built the foundation of that house. I used the gift that God gave me to do this. Other people are building on that foundation. But everyone should be careful how they build. ¹¹The foundation that has already been built is Jesus Christ, and no one can build any other foundation. ¹²People can build on that foundation using gold, silver, jewels, wood, grass, or straw. ¹³But the work that each person does will be clearly seen, because the Day*ᵃ* will make it plain. That Day will appear with fire, and the fire will test everyone's work. ¹⁴If the building they put on the foundation still stands, they will get their reward. ¹⁵But if their building is burned up, they will suffer loss. They will be saved, but it will be like someone escaping from a fire.

¹⁶You should know that you yourselves are God's temple.*ᵇ* God's Spirit lives in you. ¹⁷If you destroy God's temple, God will destroy you, because God's temple is holy.* You yourselves are God's temple.

¹⁸Don't fool yourselves. Whoever thinks they are wise in this world should become a fool. That's the only way they can be wise. ¹⁹I say this because the wisdom of this world is foolishness to God. As the Scriptures* say, "He catches the wise in their own clever traps."*ᶜ* ²⁰The Scriptures also say, "The Lord knows the thoughts of the wise. He knows that their thoughts

---

ᵃ **3:13 Day** The day Christ will come to judge everyone and take his people to live with him. *ᵇ* **3:16 temple** God's house—the place where God's people worship him. Here, it means that believers are the spiritual temple where God lives.   *ᶜ* **3:19** Quote from Job 5:13.

are worth nothing."*a* 21So there is not a person on earth that any of you should be boasting about. Everything is yours: 22Paul, Apollos, Peter,*b* the world, life, death, the present, and the future—all these are yours. 23And you belong to Christ, and Christ belongs to God.

Apostles of Christ

4 1You should think of us as servants of Christ, the ones God has trusted to do the work of making known his secret truths. 2Those who are trusted with such an important work must show that they are worthy of that trust. 3But I don't consider your judgment on this point to be worth anything. Even an opinion from a court of law would mean nothing. I don't even trust my own judgment. 4I don't know of any wrong I have done, but that does not make me innocent. The Lord is the one who must decide if I have done well or not. 5So don't judge anyone now. The time for judging will be when the Lord comes. He will shine light on everything that is now hidden in darkness. He will make known the secret purposes of our hearts. Then the praise each person should get will come from God.

6Brothers and sisters, I have used Apollos and myself as examples for you. I did this so that you could learn from us the meaning of the words, "Follow what the Scriptures* say." Then you will not brag about one person and criticize another. 7Who do you think you are? Everything you have was given to you. So, if everything you have was given to you, why do you act as if you got it all by your own power?

8You think you have everything you need. You think you are rich. You think you have become kings without us. I wish you really were kings. Then we could rule together with you. 9But it seems to me that God has given me and the other apostles* the last place. We are like prisoners condemned to die, led in a parade for the whole world to see—not just people but angels too. 10We are fools for Christ, but you think you are so wise in Christ. We are weak, but you think you are so strong. People give you honor, but they don't honor us. 11Even now we still don't have enough to eat or drink, and we don't have enough clothes. We often get beatings. We have no homes. 12We work hard with our own hands to feed ourselves. When people insult us, we ask God to bless them. When people treat us badly, we accept it. 13When people say bad things about us, we try to say something that will help them. But people still treat us like the world's garbage—everyone's trash.

14I am not trying to make you feel ashamed, but I am writing this to counsel you as my own dear children. 15You may have ten thousand teachers in Christ, but you don't have many fathers.

---

*a*3:20 Quote from Ps. 94:11. *b*3:22 *Peter* The text says "Cephas," the Aramaic name for Peter, one of Jesus' twelve apostles.

Through the Good News* I became your father in Christ Jesus. [16]So I beg you to be like me. [17]That is why I am sending Timothy to you. He is my son in the Lord. I love him and trust him. He will help you remember the way I live in Christ Jesus—a way of life that I teach in all the churches* everywhere.

[18]Some of you are acting so proud, it seems as though you think I won't be coming there again. [19]But I will come to you very soon, the Lord willing. Then I will see if these proud talkers have the power to do anything more than talk. [20]God's kingdom* is not seen in talk but in power. [21]Which do you want: that I come to you with punishment, or that I come with love and gentleness?

A Moral Problem in the Church

5 [1]I don't want to believe what I am hearing—that there is sexual sin among you. And it is such a bad kind of sexual sin that even those who have never known God don't allow it. People say that a man there has his father's wife. [2]And still you are proud of yourselves! You should have been filled with sadness. And the man who committed that sin should be put out of your group. [3]I cannot be there with you in person, but I am with you in spirit. And I have already judged the man who did this. I judged him the same as I would if I were really there. [4]Come together in the name of our Lord Jesus. I will be with you in spirit, and you will have the power of our Lord Jesus with you. [5]Then turn this man over to Satan.* His sinful self[a] has to be destroyed so that his spirit will be saved on the day when the Lord comes again.

[6]Your proud talk is not good. You know the saying, "Just a little yeast* makes the whole batch of dough rise." [7]Take out all the old yeast, so that you will be a new batch of dough. You really are bread without yeast—Passover bread.[b] Yes, Christ our Passover Lamb[c] has already been killed. [8]So let us eat our Passover meal, but not with the bread that has the old yeast, the yeast of sin and wrong doing. But let us eat the bread that has no yeast. This is the bread of goodness and truth.

[9]I wrote to you in my letter that you should not associate with people who sin sexually. [10]But I did not mean the people of this world. You would have to leave the world to get away from all the people who sin sexually, or who are greedy and cheat each other, or who worship idols. [11]I meant you must not associate with people who claim to be believers* but continue to live in sin. Don't even eat with a brother or sister who sins sexually, is greedy, worships idols, abuses others with insults, gets drunk, or cheats people.

---

[a]**5:5** *sinful self* Or, "body." Literally, "flesh."   [b]**5:7** *Passover bread* The special bread without yeast that the Jews ate at their Passover meal. Paul means that believers are free from sin, just as the Passover bread was free from yeast.   [c]**5:7** *Passover Lamb* Jesus was a sacrifice for his people, like a lamb killed for the Jewish Passover Feast.

¹²⁻¹³It is not my business to judge those who are not part of the group of believers. God will judge them, but you must judge those who are part of your group. The Scriptures* say, "Make the evil person leave your group."ᵃ

Judging Problems Between Believers

6 ¹When one of you has something against someone else in your group, why do you go to the judges in the law courts? The way they think and live is wrong. So why do you let them decide who is right? Why don't you let God's holy people* decide who is right? ²Don't you know that God's people will judge the world? So if you will judge the world, then surely you can judge small disagreements like this. ³You know that in the future we will judge angels. So surely we can judge life's ordinary problems. ⁴So if you have such disagreements to be judged, why do you take them to those who are not part of the church*? They mean nothing to you. ⁵I say this to shame you. Surely there is someone in your group wise enough to judge a complaint between two believers. ⁶But now one believer goes to court against another, and you let people who are not believers judge their case!

⁷The lawsuits that you have against each other show that you are already defeated. It would be better for you to let someone wrong you. It would be better to let someone cheat you. ⁸But you are the ones doing wrong and cheating. And you do this to your own brothers and sisters in Christ!

⁹⁻¹⁰Surely you know that people who do wrong will not get to enjoy God's kingdom.* Don't be fooled. These are the people who will not get to enjoy his kingdom: those who sin sexually, those who worship idols,* those who commit adultery,* men who let other men use them for sex or who have sex with other men, those who steal, those who are greedy, those who drink too much, those who abuse others with insults, and those who cheat. ¹¹In the past some of you were like that. But you were washed clean, you were made holy,* and you were made right with God in the name of the Lord Jesus Christ and by the Spirit of our God.

Use Your Bodies for God's Glory

¹²"I am allowed to do anything," you say. My answer to this is that not all things are good. Even if it is true that "I am allowed to do anything," I will not let anything control me like a slave. ¹³Someone else says, "Food is for the stomach, and the stomach for food." Yes, and God will destroy them both. But the body is not for sexual sin. The body is for the Lord, and the Lord is for the body. ¹⁴And God will raise our bodies from death with the same power he used to raise the Lord Jesus. ¹⁵Surely

ᵃ5:12–13 Quote from Deut. 22:21, 24.

you know that your bodies are parts of Christ himself. So I must never take what is part of Christ and join it to a prostitute! [16]The Scriptures* say, "The two people will become one."[a] So you should know that anyone who is joined with a prostitute becomes one with her in body. [17]But anyone who is joined with the Lord is one with him in spirit.

[18]So run away from sexual sin. It involves the body in a way that no other sin does. So if you commit sexual sin, you are sinning against your own body. [19]You should know that your body is a temple[b] for the Holy Spirit* that you received from God and that lives in you. You don't own yourselves. [20]God paid a very high price to make you his. So honor God with your body.

About Marriage

7 [1]Now I will discuss the things you wrote me about. You asked if it is better for a man not to have any sexual relations at all. [2]But sexual sin is a danger, so each man should enjoy his own wife, and each woman should enjoy her own husband. [3]The husband should give his wife what she deserves as his wife. And the wife should give her husband what he deserves as her husband. [4]The wife does not have power over her own body. Her husband has the power over her body. And the husband does not have power over his own body. His wife has the power over his body. [5]Don't refuse to give your bodies to each other. But you might both agree to stay away from sex for a while so that you can give your time to prayer. Then come together again so that Satan* will not be able to tempt you in your weakness. [6]I say this only to give you permission to be separated for a time. It is not a rule. [7]I wish everyone could be like me. But God has given each person a different ability. He makes some able to live one way, others to live a different way.

[8]Now for those who are not married and for the widows I say this: It is good for you to stay single like me. [9]But if you cannot control your body, then you should marry. It is better to marry than to burn with sexual desire.

[10]Now, I have a command for those who are married. Actually, it is not from me; it is what the Lord commanded. A wife should not leave her husband. [11]But if a wife does leave, she should remain single or get back together with her husband. And a husband should not divorce his wife.

[12]The advice I have for the others is from me. The Lord did not give us any teaching about this. If you have a wife who is not a believer, you should not divorce her if she will continue to live with you. [13]And if you have a husband who is not a believer, you should not divorce him if he will continue to live with you. [14]The husband who is not a believer is set apart for

---

[a]6:16 Quote from Gen. 2:24. [b]6:19 temple God's house—the place where God's people worship him. Here, it means that believers are the spiritual temple where God lives.

God through his believing wife. And the wife who is not a believer is set apart for God through her believing husband. If this were not true, your children would be unfit for God's use. But now they are set apart for him.

[15]But if the husband or wife who is not a believer decides to leave, let them leave. When this happens, the brother or sister in Christ is free. God chose you to have a life of peace. [16]Wives, maybe you will save your husband; and husbands, maybe you will save your wife. You don't know now what will happen later.

Live as God Called You

[17]But each one of you should continue to live the way the Lord God has given you to live—the way you were when God chose you. This is a rule I make for all the churches.* [18]If a man was already circumcised* when he was chosen, he should not change his circumcision. If a man was without circumcision when he was chosen, he should not be circumcised. [19]It is not important if anyone is circumcised or not. What is important is obeying God's commands. [20]Each one of you should stay the way you were when God chose you. [21]If you were a slave when God chose you, don't let that bother you. But if you can be free, then do it. [22]If you were a slave when the Lord chose you, you are now free in the Lord. You belong to the Lord. In the same way, if you were free when you were chosen, you are now Christ's slave. [23]God paid a high price for you, so don't be slaves to anyone else. [24]Brothers and sisters, in your new life with God, each one of you should continue the way you were when God chose you.

Questions About Getting Married

[25]Now I write about people who are not married.[a] I have no command from the Lord about this, but I give my opinion. And I can be trusted, because the Lord has given me mercy. [26]This is a time of trouble. So I think it is good for you to stay the way you are. [27]If you have a wife, don't try to get free from her. If you are not married, don't try to find a wife. [28]But if you decide to marry, that is not a sin. And it is not a sin for a girl who has never married to get married. But those who marry will have trouble in this life, and I want you to be free from this trouble.

[29]Brothers and sisters, this is what I mean: We don't have much time left. So starting now, those who have wives should be the same as those who don't. [30]It should not be important whether you are sad or whether you are happy. If you buy something, it should not matter to you that you own it. [31]You should use the things of the world without letting them become important to you. This is how you should live, because this world, the way it is now, will soon be gone.

---

[a]7:25 people who are not married Literally, "virgins."

³²I want you to be free from worry. A man who is not married is busy with the Lord's work. He is trying to please the Lord. ³³But a man who is married is busy with things of the world. He is trying to please his wife. ³⁴He must think about two things—pleasing his wife and pleasing the Lord. A woman who is not married or a girl who has never married is busy with the Lord's work. She wants to give herself fully—body and spirit—to the Lord. But a married woman is busy with things of the world. She is trying to please her husband. ³⁵I am saying this to help you. I am not trying to limit you, but I want you to live in the right way. And I want you to give yourselves fully to the Lord without giving your time to other things.

³⁶A man might think that he is not doing the right thing with his fiancée. She might be almost past the best age to marry.ᵃ So he might feel that he should marry her. He should do what he wants. It is no sin for them to get married. ³⁷But another man might be more sure in his mind. There may be no need for marriage, so he is free to do what he wants. If he has decided in his own heart not to marry his fiancée, he is doing the right thing. ³⁸So the man who marries his fiancée does right, and the man who does not marry does better.

³⁹A woman should stay with her husband as long as he lives. But if the husband dies, the woman is free to marry any man she wants, but he should belong to the Lord. ⁴⁰The woman is happier if she does not marry again. This is my opinion, and I believe that I have God's Spirit.

About Food Offered to Idols

8 ¹Now I will write about meat that is sacrificedᵇ to idols. We know that "we all have knowledge," as you say. But this knowledge puffs a person up with pride, while love helps the church grow stronger. ²Whoever thinks they know something does not yet know anything as they should. ³But whoever loves God is known by God.

⁴So this is what I say about eating meat: We know that an idol is really nothing in the world, and we know that there is only one God. ⁵It's really not important if there are things called gods in heaven or on earth—and there are many of these "gods" and "lords" out there. ⁶For us there is only one God, and he is our Father. All things came from him, and we live for him. And there is only one Lord, Jesus Christ. All things were made through him, and we also have life through him.

⁷But not all people know this. Some have had the habit of worshiping idols. So now when they eat meat, they still feel as if it belongs to an idol. They are not sure that it is right to eat this meat. So when they eat it, they feel guilty. ⁸But food will

---

ᵃ7:36 *She ... to marry* Or, "He may have trouble controlling his desires."   ᵇ8:1 *sacrificed* Killed and offered as a gift to show worship. Also in verse 10.

not bring us closer to God. Refusing to eat does not make us less pleasing to God, and eating does not make us closer to him.

⁹But be careful with your freedom. Your freedom to eat anything may make those who have doubts about what they can eat fall into sin. ¹⁰You understand that it's all right to eat anything, so you can eat in an idol's temple. But someone who has doubts might see you eating there, and this might encourage them to eat meat sacrificed to idols too. But they really think it is wrong. ¹¹So this weak brother or sister—someone Christ died for—is lost because of your better understanding. ¹²When you sin against your brothers and sisters in Christ in this way and you hurt them by causing them to do things they feel are wrong, you are also sinning against Christ. ¹³So if the food I eat makes another believer fall into sin, I will never eat meat again. I will stop eating meat, so that I will not make my brother or sister sin.

Rights That Paul Has Not Used

9 ¹I am a free man. I am an apostle.* I have seen Jesus our Lord. You people are an example of my work in the Lord. ²Others may not accept me as an apostle, but surely you accept me as an apostle. You are proof that I am an apostle in the Lord.

³Some people want to judge me. So this is the answer I give them: ⁴We have the right to eat and drink, don't we? ⁵We have the right to bring a believing wife with us when we travel, don't we? The other apostles and the Lord's brothers and Peter*ᵃ* all do this. ⁶And are Barnabas and I the only ones who must work to earn our living? ⁷No soldier ever serves in the army and pays his own salary. No one ever plants a vineyard* without eating some of the grapes himself. No one takes care of a flock of sheep without drinking some of the milk himself.

⁸These aren't just my own thoughts. God's law says the same thing. ⁹Yes, it is written in the law of Moses*: "When a work animal is being used to separate grain, don't keep it from eating the grain."*ᵇ* When God said this, was he thinking only about work animals? No. ¹⁰He was really talking about us. Yes, that was written for us. The one who plows and the one who separates the grain should both expect to get some of the grain for their work. ¹¹We planted spiritual seed among you, so we should be able to harvest from you some things for this life. Surely that is not asking too much. ¹²Others have this right to get things from you. So surely we have this right too. But we don't use this right. No, we endure everything ourselves so that we will not stop anyone from obeying the Good News* of Christ. ¹³Surely you know that those who work at the Temple*

---

*ᵃ*9:5 *Peter* The text says "Cephas," the Aramaic name for Peter, one of Jesus' twelve apostles.
*ᵇ*9:9 Quote from Deut. 25:4.

get their food from the Temple. And those who serve at the altar* get part of what is offered at the altar. ¹⁴It is the same with those who have the work of telling the Good News. The Lord has commanded that those who tell the Good News should get their living from this work.

¹⁵But I have not used any of these rights, and I am not trying to get anything from you. That is not my purpose for writing this. I would rather die than to have someone take away what for me is a great source of pride. ¹⁶It's not my work of telling the Good News that gives me any reason to boast. This is my duty—something I must do. If I don't tell people the Good News, I am in real trouble. ¹⁷If I did it because it was my own choice, I would deserve to be paid. But I have no choice. I must tell the Good News. So I am only doing the duty that was given to me. ¹⁸So what do I get for doing it? My reward is that when I tell people the Good News I can offer it to them for free and not use the rights that come with doing this work.

¹⁹I am free. I belong to no other person, but I make myself a slave to everyone. I do this to help save as many people as I can. ²⁰To the Jews I became like a Jew so that I could help save Jews. I myself am not ruled by the law,* but to those who are ruled by the law I became like someone who is ruled by the law. I did this to help save those who are ruled by the law. ²¹To those who are without the law I became like someone who is without the law. I did this to help save those who are without the law. (But really, I am not without God's law—I am ruled by the law of Christ.) ²²To those who are weak, I became weak so that I could help save them. I have become all things to all people. I did this so that I could save people in any way possible. ²³I do all this to make the Good News known. I do it so that I can share in the blessings of the Good News.

²⁴You know that in a race all the runners run, but only one runner gets the prize. So run like that. Run to win! ²⁵All who compete in the games use strict training. They do this so that they can win a prize*—one that doesn't last. But our prize is one that will last forever. ²⁶So I run like someone who has a goal. I fight like a boxer who is hitting something, not just the air. ²⁷It is my own body I fight to make it do what I want. I do this so that I won't miss getting the prize myself after telling others about it.

Warning From History

10 ¹Brothers and sisters, I want you to know what happened to our ancestors* who were with Moses.* They were all under the cloud,*a* and they all walked through the sea. ²They

---

a **10:1** *cloud* The cloud that led and protected the people of Israel on their journey out of Egypt, across the Red Sea, and through the wilderness. See Ex. 13:20–22; 14:19, 20.

were all baptized^a into Moses in the cloud and in the sea. ³They all ate the same spiritual food, ⁴and they all drank the same spiritual drink. They drank from that spiritual rock that was with them, and that rock was Christ. ⁵But God was not pleased with most of those people, so they were killed in the desert.

⁶And these things that happened are examples for us. These examples should stop us from wanting evil things like those people did. ⁷Don't worship idols* as some of them did. As the Scriptures* say, "The people sat down to eat and drink and then got up to have a wild party."^b ⁸We should not commit sexual sins as some of them did. In one day 23,000 of them died because of their sin. ⁹We should not test Christ^c as some of them did. Because of that, they were killed by snakes. ¹⁰And don't complain as some of them did. Because they complained, they were killed by the angel that destroys.

¹¹The things that happened to those people are examples. They were written to be warnings for us. We live in the time that all those past histories were pointing to. ¹²So anyone who thinks they are standing strong should be careful that they don't fall. ¹³The only temptations that you have are the same temptations that all people have. But you can trust God. He will not let you be tempted more than you can bear. But when you are tempted, God will also give you a way to escape that temptation. Then you will be able to endure it.

¹⁴So, my dear friends, stay away from worshiping idols. ¹⁵You are intelligent people. Judge for yourselves the truth of what I say now. ¹⁶The cup of blessing^d that we give thanks for is a sharing in the blood sacrifice of Christ, isn't it? And the bread that we break is a sharing in the body of Christ, isn't it? ¹⁷There is one loaf of bread, so we who are many are one body, because we all share in that one loaf.

¹⁸And think about what the people of Israel* do. When they eat the sacrifices,^e they are united by sharing what was offered on the altar.* ¹⁹So, am I saying that sacrifices to idols are the same as those Jewish sacrifices? No, because an idol is nothing, and the things offered to idols are worth nothing. ²⁰But I am saying that when food is sacrificed to idols, it is an offering to demons,* not to God. And I don't want you to share anything with demons. ²¹You cannot drink the cup of the Lord and then go drink a cup that honors demons. You cannot share a meal at the Lord's table and then go share a meal that honors demons. ²²Doing that would make the Lord jealous.^f Do you really want to do that? Do you think we are stronger than he is?

---

^a10:2 *baptized* See the Word List. Here, Paul seems to mean that what happened to the Jews with Moses can be compared to the baptism of a believer into Christ. ^b10:7 Quote from Ex. 32:6. ^c10:9 *Christ* Some Greek copies say, "the Lord." ^d10:16 *cup of blessing* The cup of wine that believers in Christ thank God for and drink at the Lord's Supper. ^e10:18 *sacrifices* Animals killed and offered as gifts to God. ^f10:22 *make the Lord jealous* See Deut. 32:16, 17.

Use Your Freedom for God's Glory

23"All things are allowed," you say. But not all things are good. "All things are allowed." But some things don't help anyone. 24Try to do what is good for others, not just what is good for yourselves.

25Eat any meat that is sold in the meat market. Don't ask questions about it to see if it is something you think is wrong to eat. 26You can eat it, "because the earth and everything in it belong to the Lord."*a*

27Someone who is not a believer might invite you to eat with them. If you want to go, then eat anything that is put before you. Don't ask questions to see if it is something you think is wrong to eat. 28But if someone tells you, "That food was offered to idols,*" then don't eat it. That's because some people think it is wrong, and it might cause a problem for the person who told you that. 29I don't mean that you think it is wrong. But the other person might think it is wrong. That's the only reason not to eat it. My own freedom should not be judged by what another person thinks. 30I eat the meal with thankfulness. So I don't want to be criticized because of something I thank God for.

31So if you eat or if you drink or if you do anything, do it for the glory* of God. 32Never do anything that might make other people do wrong—Jews, non-Jews, or anyone in God's church.* 33I do the same thing. I try to please everyone in every way. I am not trying to do what is good for me. I am trying to do what is good for the most people so that they can be saved. 11 1Follow my example, just as I follow the example of Christ.

Being Under Authority

2I praise you because you remember me in all things. You follow closely the teachings I gave you. 3But I want you to understand this: The head of every man is Christ. And the head of a woman is the man.*b* And the head of Christ is God.

4Every man who prophesies* or prays with his head covered brings shame to his head. 5But every woman who prays or prophesies should have her head covered. If her head is not covered, she brings shame to her head. Then she is the same as a woman who has her head shaved. 6If a woman does not cover her head, it is the same as cutting off all her hair. But it is shameful for a woman to cut off her hair or to shave her head. So she should cover her head.

7But a man should not cover his head, because he is made like God and is God's glory.* But woman is man's glory. 8Man did not come from woman. Woman came from man. 9And man was not made for woman. Woman was made for man. 10So that

*a***10:26** Quote from Ps. 24:1; 50:12; 89:11. *b***11:3** *the man* This could also mean "her husband."

is why a woman should have her head covered with something that shows she is under authority.[a] Also, she should do this because of the angels.

[11]But in the Lord the woman needs the man, and the man needs the woman. [12]This is true because woman came from man, but also man is born from woman. Really, everything comes from God.

[13]Decide this for yourselves: Is it right for a woman to pray to God without something on her head? [14]Even nature itself teaches you that wearing long hair is shameful for a man. [15]But wearing long hair is a woman's honor. Long hair is given to the woman to cover her head. [16]Some people may still want to argue about this. But we and the churches* of God don't accept what those people are doing.

The Lord's Supper

[17]In the things I tell you now I don't praise you. Your meetings hurt you more than they help you. [18]First, I hear that when you meet together as a church* you are divided. And this is not hard to believe [19]because of your idea that you must have separate groups to show who the real believers are!

[20]When you all come together, it is not really the Lord's Supper[b] you are eating. [21]I say this because when you eat, each one eats without waiting for the others. Some people don't get enough to eat or drink, while others have too much.[c] [22]You can eat and drink in your own homes. It seems that you think God's church is not important. You embarrass those who are poor. What can I say? Should I praise you? No, I cannot praise you for this.

[23]The teaching I gave you is the same that I received from the Lord: On the night when the Lord Jesus was handed over to be killed, he took bread [24]and gave thanks for it. Then he divided the bread and said, "This is my body; it is for you. Eat this to remember me." [25]In the same way, after they ate, Jesus took the cup of wine. He said, "This cup represents the new agreement* from God, which begins with my blood sacrifice. When you drink this, do it to remember me." [26]This means that every time you eat this bread and drink this cup, you are telling others about the Lord's death until he comes again.

[27]So if you eat the bread or drink the cup of the Lord in a way that does not fit its meaning, you are sinning against the body and the blood of the Lord. [28]Before you eat the bread and drink the cup, you should examine your own attitude. [29]If you eat and drink without paying attention to those who are the

---

[a]11:10 *have her head ... authority* Literally, "have authority on her head." This could also be translated, "keep control of her head," meaning, "do what will keep people from misunderstanding her uncovered head." [b]11:20 *Lord's Supper* The special meal Jesus told his followers to eat to remember him. See Lk. 22:14-20. [c]11:21 *have too much* Literally, "get drunk."

Lord's body, your eating and drinking will cause you to be judged guilty. [30]That is why many in your group are sick and weak, and many have died. [31]But if we judged ourselves in the right way, then God would not judge us. [32]But when the Lord judges us, he punishes us to show us the right way. He does this so that we will not be condemned with the world.

[33]So, my brothers and sisters, when you come together to eat, wait for each other. [34]If some are too hungry to wait, they should eat at home. Do this so that your meeting together will not bring God's judgment on you. I will tell you what to do about the other things when I come.

Gifts From the Holy Spirit

12 [1]Now, brothers and sisters, I want you to understand about spiritual gifts. [2]You remember the lives you lived before you were believers. You let yourselves be influenced and led away to worship idols*—things that have no life. [3]So I tell you that no one who is speaking with the help of God's Spirit says, "Jesus be cursed." And no one can say, "Jesus is Lord," without the help of the Holy Spirit.*

[4]There are different kinds of spiritual gifts, but they are all from the same Spirit. [5]There are different ways to serve, but we serve the same Lord. [6]And there are different ways that God works in people, but it is the same God who works in all of us to do everything.

[7]Something from the Spirit can be seen in each person. The Spirit gives this to each one to help others. [8]The Spirit gives one person the ability to speak with wisdom. And the same Spirit gives another person the ability to speak with knowledge. [9]The same Spirit gives faith to one person and to another he gives gifts of healing. [10]The Spirit gives to one person the power to do miracles,* to another the ability to prophesy,* and to another the ability to know the difference between good and evil spirits. The Spirit gives one person the ability to speak in different kinds of languages, and to another the ability to interpret those languages. [11]One Spirit, the same Spirit, does all these things. The Spirit decides what to give each one.

The Body of Christ

[12]A person has only one body, but it has many parts. Yes, there are many parts, but all those parts are still just one body. Christ is like that too. [13]Some of us are Jews and some of us are not; some of us are slaves and some of us are free. But we were all baptized* to become one body through one Spirit.* And we were all given[a] the one Spirit.

[14]And a person's body has more than one part. It has many parts. [15]The foot might say, "I am not a hand, so I don't belong

[a]12:13 given Literally, "given to drink."

to the body." But saying this would not stop the foot from being a part of the body. [16]The ear might say, "I am not an eye, so I don't belong to the body." But saying this would not make the ear stop being a part of the body. [17]If the whole body were an eye, it would not be able to hear. If the whole body were an ear, it would not be able to smell anything. [18–19]If each part of the body were the same part, there would be no body. But as it is, God put the parts in the body as he wanted them. He made a place for each one. [20]So there are many parts, but only one body.

[21]The eye cannot say to the hand, "I don't need you!" And the head cannot say to the foot, "I don't need you!" [22]No, those parts of the body that seem to be weaker are really very important. [23]And the parts that we think are not worth very much are the parts we give the most care to. And we give special care to the parts of the body that we don't want to show. [24]The more beautiful parts don't need this special care. But God put the body together and gave more honor to the parts that need it. [25]God did this so that our body would not be divided. God wanted the different parts to care the same for each other. [26]If one part of the body suffers, then all the other parts suffer with it. Or if one part is honored, then all the other parts share its honor.

[27]All of you together are the body of Christ. Each one of you is a part of that body. [28]And in the church* God has given a place first to apostles,* second to prophets,* and third to teachers. Then God has given a place to those who do miracles,* those who have gifts of healing, those who can help others, those who are able to lead, and those who can speak in different kinds of languages. [29]Not all are apostles. Not all are prophets. Not all are teachers. Not all do miracles. [30]Not all have gifts of healing. Not all speak in different kinds of languages. Not all interpret those languages. [31]Continue to give your attention to the spiritual gifts you consider to be the greatest. But I want to point out a way of life that is even greater.

Let Love Be Your Guide

And now I will show you the best way of all.

13 [1]I may speak in different languages, whether human or even of angels. But if I don't have love, I am only a noisy bell or a ringing cymbal. [2]I may have the gift of prophecy,* I may understand all secrets and know everything there is to know, and I may have faith so great that I can move mountains. But even with all this, if I don't have love, I am nothing. [3]I may give away everything I have to help others. I may even give my body as an offering to be burned. But I gain nothing by doing all this if I don't have love.

[4]Love is patient and kind. Love is not jealous, it does not brag, and it is not proud. [5]Love is not rude, it is not selfish, and

it cannot be made angry easily. Love does not remember wrongs done against it. [6]Love is never happy to see others do wrong, but it is always happy to hear the truth. [7]Love never gives up on people. It never stops trusting, never loses hope, and never quits.

[8]Love will never end. But all those gifts will come to an end—even the gift of prophecy, the gift of speaking in different kinds of languages, and the gift of knowledge. [9]These will all end because this knowledge and these prophecies we have are not complete. [10]But when perfection comes, the things that are not complete will end.

[11]When I was a child, I talked like a child, I thought like a child, and I made plans like a child. When I became a man, I stopped those childish ways. [12]It is the same with us. Now we see God as if we are looking at a reflection in a mirror. But then, in the future, we will see him right before our eyes. Now I know only a part, but at that time I will know fully, as God has known me. [13]So these three things continue: faith, hope, and love. And the greatest of these is love.

Use Spiritual Gifts to Help the Church

14 [1]Love should be the goal of your life, but you should also want to have the gifts that come from the Spirit.* And the gift you should want most is to be able to prophesy.* [2]I will explain why. Those who have the gift of speaking in a different language are not speaking to people. They are speaking to God. No one understands them—they are speaking secret things through the Spirit. [3]But those who prophesy are speaking to people. They help people grow stronger in faith, and they give encouragement and comfort. [4]Those who speak in a different language are helping only themselves. But those who prophesy are helping the whole church.*

[5]I would like all of you to have the gift of speaking in different languages. But what I want more is for you to prophesy. Anyone who prophesies is more important than those who can only speak in different languages. However, if they can also interpret those languages, they are as important as the one who prophesies. If they can interpret, then the church can be helped by what they say.

[6]Brothers and sisters, will it help you if I come to you speaking in different languages? No, it will help you only if I bring you a new truth or some knowledge, prophecy,* or teaching. [7]This is true even with lifeless things that make sounds—like a flute or a harp. If the different musical notes are not made clear, you can't understand what song is being played. Each note must be played clearly for you to be able to understand the tune. [8]And in a war, if the trumpet does not sound clearly, the soldiers will not know it is time to prepare for fighting.

⁹It is the same with you. If you don't speak clearly in a language people know, they cannot understand what you are saying. You will be talking to the air! ¹⁰It is true that there are many different languages in the world, and they all have meaning. ¹¹But if I don't understand the meaning of what someone is saying, it will just be strange sounds to me, and I will sound just as strange to them. ¹²That's why you who want spiritual gifts so much should prefer those gifts that help the church grow stronger.

¹³So those who have the gift of speaking in a different language should pray that they can also interpret what they say. ¹⁴If I pray in a different language, my spirit is praying, but my mind does nothing. ¹⁵So what should I do? I will pray with my spirit, but I will also pray with my mind. I will sing with my spirit, but I will also sing with my mind. ¹⁶You might be praising God with your spirit. But someone there without understanding cannot say "Amen*" to your prayer of thanks, because they don't know what you are saying. ¹⁷You may be thanking God in a good way, but others are not helped.

¹⁸I thank God that my gift of speaking in different kinds of languages is greater than any of yours. ¹⁹But in the church meetings I would rather speak five words that I understand than thousands of words in a different language. I would rather speak with my understanding, so that I can teach others.

²⁰Brothers and sisters, don't think like children. In evil things be like babies, but in your thinking you should be like full-grown adults. ²¹As the Scriptures*a* say,

> "Using those who speak a different language
>   and using the lips of foreigners,
> I will speak to these people.
>   But even then, they will not obey me."   *Isaiah 28:11–12*

This is what the Lord says.

²²And from this we see that the use of different languages shows how God deals with those who don't believe, not with those who believe. And prophecy shows how God works through those who believe, not through unbelievers. ²³Suppose the whole church meets together and you all speak in different languages. If some people come in who are without understanding or don't believe, they will say you are crazy. ²⁴But suppose you are all prophesying and someone comes in who does not believe or who is without understanding. Their sin will be shown to them, and they will be judged by everything you say. ²⁵The secret things in their heart will be made known. So they will bow down and worship God. They will say, "Surely, God is with you."*b*

---

*a*14:21 Scriptures Literally, "law," which sometimes means the Old Testament.
*b*14:25 See Isa. 45:14 and Zech. 8:23.

Your Meetings Should Be Helpful to All

26So, brothers and sisters, what should you do? When you meet together, one person has a song, another has a teaching, and another has a new truth from God. One person speaks in a different language, and another interprets that language. The purpose of whatever you do should be to help everyone grow stronger in faith. 27When you meet together, if anyone speaks to the group in a different language, it should be only two or no more than three people who do this. And they should speak one after the other. And someone else should interpret what they say. 28But if there is no interpreter, then anyone who speaks in a different language should be quiet in the church meeting. They should speak only to themselves and to God.

29And only two or three prophets* should speak. The others should judge what they say. 30And if a message from God comes to someone who is sitting, the first speaker should be quiet. 31You can all prophesy* one after the other. In this way everyone can be taught and encouraged. 32The spirits of prophets are under the control of the prophets themselves. 33God is not a God of confusion but a God of peace. This is the rule for all the meetings of God's people.

34The women should keep quiet in these church* meetings. They are not allowed to speak out but should be under authority, as the law of Moses says. 35If there is something they want to know, they should ask their own husbands at home. It is shameful for a woman to speak up like that in the church meeting.

36God's teaching did not come from you, and you are not the only ones who have received it. 37If you think you are a prophet or that you have a spiritual gift, you should understand that what I am writing to you is the Lord's command. 38If you do not accept this, you will not be accepted.

39So my brothers and sisters, continue to give your attention to prophesying. And don't stop anyone from using the gift of speaking in different languages. 40But everything should be done in a way that is right and orderly.

The Good News About Christ

15 1Now, brothers and sisters, I want you to remember the Good News* I told you about. You received that Good News message, and you continue to base your life on it. 2It is that Good News that saves you, but you must continue believing the message just as I told it to you. If you don't, then you believed for nothing.

3I gave you the message that I received. I told you the most important truths: that Christ died for our sins, as the Scriptures* say; 4that he was buried and was raised to life on the third day, as the Scriptures say; 5and that he showed himself to Peter and then to the twelve apostles.* 6After that, Christ showed himself to more than 500 of the brothers and sisters at the same time. Most of them are still living today, but some have died. [7]Then he showed himself to James and later to all the apostles. [8]Last of all, he showed himself to me. I was different, like a baby born before the normal time.

[9]All the other apostles are greater than I am. I say this because I persecuted* the church* of God. That is why I am not even good enough to be called an apostle. [10]But, because of God's grace,* that is what I am. And his grace that he gave me was not wasted. I worked harder than all the other apostles. (But I was not really the one working. It was God's grace that was with me.) [11]So then it is not important if I told you God's message or if it was the other apostles who told you—we all tell people the same message, and this is what you believed.

We Will Be Raised From Death

[12]We tell everyone that Christ was raised from death. So why do some of you say that people will not be raised from death? [13]If no one will ever be raised from death, then Christ has never been raised. [14]And if Christ has never been raised, then the message we tell is worth nothing. And your faith is worth nothing. [15]And we will also be guilty of lying about God, because we have told people about him, saying that he raised Christ from death. And if no one is raised from death, then God never raised Christ from death. [16]If those who have died are not raised, then Christ has not been raised either. [17]And if Christ has not been raised from death, then your faith is for nothing; you are still guilty of your sins. [18]And those in Christ who have already died are lost. [19]If our hope in Christ is only for this life here on earth, then people should feel more sorry for us than for anyone else.

[20]But Christ really has been raised from death—the first one of all those who will be raised. [21]Death happens to people because of what one man *(Adam)* did. But the rising from death also happens because of one man *(Christ)*. [22]In Adam all of us die. In the same way, in Christ all of us will be made alive again. [23]But everyone will be raised to life in the right order. Christ was first to be raised. Then, when Christ comes again, those who belong to him will be raised to life. [24]Then the end will come. Christ will destroy all rulers, authorities, and powers. Then he will give the kingdom to God the Father.

[25]Christ must rule until God puts all enemies under his control.[a] [26]The last enemy to be destroyed will be death. [27]As the Scriptures* say, "God put everything under his control."[b] When it says that "everything" is put under him, it is clear that this does not include God himself. God is the one putting everything under Christ's control. [28]After everything has been put

[a]**15:25** control Literally, "feet." [b]**15:27** Quote from Ps. 8:6.

under Christ, then the Son himself will be put under God. God is the one who put everything under Christ. And Christ will be put under God so that God will be the complete ruler over everything.

²⁹If no one will ever be raised from death, then what will the people do who are baptized* for those who have died? If the dead are never raised, then why are people baptized for them?

³⁰And what about us? Why do we put ourselves in danger every hour? ³¹I face death every day. That is true, brothers and sisters, just as it is true that I am proud of what you are because of Christ Jesus our Lord. ³²I fought wild animals in Ephesus. If I did that only for human reasons, then I have gained nothing. If we are not raised from death, then "Let us eat and drink, because tomorrow we die."*

³³Don't be fooled: "Bad friends will ruin good habits." ³⁴Come back to your right way of thinking and stop sinning. Some of you don't know God. I say this to shame you.

What Kind of Body Will We Have?

³⁵But someone may ask, "How are the dead raised? What kind of body will they have?" ³⁶These are stupid questions. When you plant something, it must die in the ground before it can live and grow. ³⁷And when you plant something, what you plant does not have the same "body" that it will have later. What you plant is only a seed, maybe wheat or something else. ³⁸But God gives it the body that he has planned for it, and he gives each kind of seed its own body. ³⁹All things made of flesh are not the same: People have one kind of flesh, animals have another, birds have another, and fish have yet another kind. ⁴⁰Also there are heavenly bodies and earthly bodies. But the beauty of the heavenly bodies is one kind, and the beauty of the earthly bodies is another. ⁴¹The sun has one kind of beauty, the moon has another kind, and the stars have another. And each star is different in its beauty.

⁴²It will be the same when those who have died are raised to life. The body that is "planted" in the grave will ruin and decay, but it will be raised to a life that cannot be destroyed. ⁴³When the body is "planted," it is without honor. But when it is raised, it will be great and glorious. When the body is "planted," it is weak. But when it is raised, it will be full of power. ⁴⁴The body that is "planted" is a physical body. When it is raised, it will be a spiritual body.

There is a physical body. So there is also a spiritual body. ⁴⁵As the Scriptures* say, "The first man, Adam, became a living thing."*ᵇˀᶜ But the last Adamᵈ is a life-giving spirit. ⁴⁶The spiritual man did not come first. It was the physical man that came first;

ᵃ**15:32** Quote from Isa. 22:13; 56:12. ᵇ**15:45** *thing* Literally, "soul." ᶜ**15:45** Quote from Gen. 2:7. ᵈ**15:45** *Adam* The name Adam means "man." Here, "the last Adam" refers to Christ, the "man of heaven."

then came the spiritual. [47]The first man came from the dust of the earth. The second man came from heaven. [48]All people belong to the earth. They are like that first man of earth. But those who belong to heaven are like that man of heaven. [49]We were made like that man of earth, so we will also be made like that man of heaven.

[50]I tell you this, brothers and sisters: Our bodies of flesh and blood cannot have a part in God's kingdom.* Something that will ruin cannot have a part in something that never ruins. [51]But listen, I tell you this secret: We will not all die, but we will all be changed. [52]It will only take the time of a second. We will be changed as quickly as an eye blinks. This will happen when the last trumpet blows. The trumpet will blow and those who have died will be raised to live forever. And we will all be changed. [53]This body that ruins must clothe itself with something that will never ruin. And this body that dies must clothe itself with something that will never die. [54]So this body that ruins will clothe itself with that which never ruins. And this body that dies will clothe itself with that which never dies. When this happens, the Scriptures will be made true:

"Death is swallowed in victory."

Isaiah 25:8

[55]"O death, where is your victory?
    Where is your power to hurt?"

Hosea 13:14

[56]Death's power to hurt is sin, and the power of sin is the law. [57]But we thank God who gives us the victory through our Lord Jesus Christ!

[58]So, my dear brothers and sisters, stand strong. Don't let anything change you. Always give yourselves fully to the work of the Lord. You know that your work in the Lord is never wasted.

The Collection for Believers in Judea

16 [1]Now, about the collection of money for God's people: Do the same as I told the Galatian churches* to do. [2]On the first day of every week, each of you should take some of your money and put it in a special place. Save up as much as you can from what you are blessed with. Then you will not have to gather it all after I come. [3]When I arrive, I will send some men to take your gift to Jerusalem. These will be the ones you all agree should go. I will send them with letters of introduction. [4]If it seems good for me to go too, we can all travel together.

Paul's Plans

[5]I plan to go through Macedonia,* so I will come to you after that. [6]Maybe I will stay with you for a time. I might even stay all winter. Then you can help me on my trip, wherever I go. [7]I

don't want to come see you now, because I would have to leave to go to other places. I hope to stay a longer time with you, if the Lord allows it. ⁸But I will stay in Ephesus until Pentecost.* ⁹I will stay here, because a good opportunity for a great and growing work has been given to me now. And there are many people working against it.

¹⁰Timothy might come to you. Try to make him feel comfortable with you. He is working for the Lord the same as I am. ¹¹So none of you should refuse to accept Timothy. Help him continue on his trip in peace so that he can come back to me. I am expecting him to come back with the other brothers.

¹²Now about our brother Apollos: I strongly encouraged him to visit you with the other brothers. But he was sure that he did not want to go now. But when he has the opportunity, he will visit you.

Paul Ends His Letter

¹³Be careful. Hold firmly to your faith. Have courage and be strong. ¹⁴Do everything in love.

¹⁵You know that Stephanas and his family were the first believers in Achaia.* They have given themselves to the service of God's people. I ask you, brothers and sisters, ¹⁶to follow the leading of people like these and others who work hard and serve together with them.

¹⁷I am happy that Stephanas, Fortunatus, and Achaicus have come. You are not here, but they have filled your place. ¹⁸They have been a great encouragement to me and to you as well. You should recognize the value of such people.

¹⁹The churches* in Asia* send you their greetings. Aquila and Priscilla greet you in the Lord. Also the church that meets in their house sends greetings. ²⁰All the brothers and sisters send their greetings. Give each other the special greeting of God's people.ᵃ

²¹Here's my greeting in my own handwriting—PAUL.

²²If anyone does not love the Lord, let that person be separated from God—lost forever!

Come, O Lord!ᵇ

²³The grace* of the Lord Jesus be with you.

²⁴My love be with all of you in Christ Jesus.

ᵃ**16:20** the special greeting of God's people Literally, "a holy kiss."   ᵇ**16:22** Come, O Lord This is a translation of the Aramaic "marana tha."

don't want to come see you now, because I would have to
leave to go to other places. I hope to stay a longer time with
you, if the Lord allows it. ⁸But I will stay in Ephesus until
Pentecost. ⁹I will stay here because a good opportunity for a
great and growing work has been given to me, and there
are many who are against me.

...

2 Corinthians

1

¹Greetings from Paul, an apostle* of Christ Jesus. I am an
apostle because that is what God wanted. Greetings also
from Timothy our brother in Christ.

To God's church* in Corinth and to all of God's holy people*
throughout Achaia.*

²Grace* and peace to you from God our Father and the Lord
Jesus Christ.

Paul Gives Thanks to God

³Praise be to the God and Father of our Lord Jesus Christ.
He is the Father who is full of mercy, the God of all comfort.
⁴He comforts us every time we have trouble so that when
others have trouble, we can comfort them with the same comfort God gives us. ⁵We share in the many sufferings of Christ. In
the same way, much comfort comes to us through Christ. ⁶If
we have troubles, it is for your comfort and salvation. If we are
comforted, it is so that we can comfort you. And this helps you
patiently accept the same sufferings we have. ⁷Our hope for
you is strong. We know that you share in our sufferings. So we
know that you also share in our comfort.

⁸Brothers and sisters, we want you to know about the
trouble we suffered in Asia.* We had great burdens there,
which were greater than our own strength. We even gave up
hope for life. ⁹In fact, it seems like God has been telling us we
are going to die. But this is so that we will not trust in ourselves but in God, who raises people from death. ¹⁰God saved
us from these great dangers of death, and he will continue to
save us. We feel sure he will always save us. ¹¹And you can
help us with your prayers. Then many people will give thanks
for us—that God blessed us because of their many prayers.

The Change in Paul's Plans

¹²This is what we are proud of, and I can say with a clear conscience that it is true: In everything we have done in the world,
we have done it with an honest and pure heart from God. And
this is even truer in what we have done with you. We did this
by God's grace,* not by the kind of wisdom the world has. ¹³We
write to you only what you can read and understand. And I
hope you will fully understand, ¹⁴just as you already understand
many things about us. I hope you will understand that you can

be proud of us, just as we will be proud of you on the day when our Lord Jesus Christ comes again.

[15]I was very sure of all this. That is why I made plans to visit you first. Then you could be blessed twice. [16]I planned to visit you on my way to Macedonia* and again on my way back. I wanted to get help from you for my trip to Judea. [17]Do you think that I made these plans without really thinking? Or maybe you think I make plans as the world does, saying yes and no at the same time.

[18]But if you can believe God, then you can believe that what we tell you is never both yes and no. [19]The Son of God, Jesus Christ, the one that Silas, Timothy, and I told you about was not yes and no. In Christ it has always been yes. [20]The yes to all of God's promises is in Christ. And that is why we say "Amen*" through Christ to the glory* of God. [21]And God is the one who makes you and us strong in Christ. God is also the one who chose us for his work.[a] [22]He put his mark on us to show that we are his. Yes, he put his Spirit* in our hearts as the first payment that guarantees all that he will give us.

[23]I tell you this, and I ask God to be my witness that this is true: The reason I did not come back to Corinth was that I did not want to punish or hurt you. [24]I don't mean that we are trying to control your faith. You are strong in faith. But we are workers with you for your own happiness.

2 [1]So I decided that my next visit to you would not be another visit to make you sad. [2]If I make you sad, then who will make me happy? Only you can make me happy—you, the ones I made sad. [3]I wrote you a letter so that when I came to you I would not be made sad by those who should make me happy. I felt sure that all of you would share my joy. [4]When I wrote to you before, I was very troubled and my heart was full of sadness. I wrote with many tears. I did not write to make you sad, but to let you know how much I love you.

Forgive the Person Who Did Wrong

[5]Someone in your group has caused sadness—not to me, but to all of you. I mean he has caused sadness to all in some way. (I don't want to make it sound worse than it really is.) [6]The punishment that most of your group gave him is enough for him. [7]But now you should forgive him and encourage him. This will keep him from having too much sadness and giving up completely. [8]So I beg you to show him that you love him. [9]This is why I wrote to you. I wanted to test you and see if you obey in everything. [10]If you forgive someone, then I also forgive them. And what I have forgiven—if I had anything to forgive—I forgave it for you, and Christ was with me. [11]I did this so that

---

[a]**1:21** *chose us for his work* Literally, "anointed us." In Greek this word is related to the title "Christ," which means "anointed one." See "anoint" and "Christ" in the Word List.

Satan* would not win anything from us. We know very well what his plans are.

Paul Leaves Troas to Find Titus

12I went to Troas to tell people the Good News* of Christ. The Lord gave me a good opportunity there. 13But I had no peace because I did not find my brother Titus. So I said goodbye and went to Macedonia.*

Victory Through Christ

14But thanks be to God, who always leads us in victory through Christ. God uses us to spread his knowledge everywhere like a sweet-smelling perfume. 15Our offering to God is to be the perfume of Christ that goes out to those who are being saved and to those who are being lost. 16To those who are being lost this perfume smells like death, and it brings them death. But to those who are being saved, it has the sweet smell of life, and it brings them life. So who is good enough to do this work? 17Certainly not those who are out there selling God's message* for a profit! But we don't do that. With Christ's help we speak God's truth honestly, knowing that we must answer to him.

Servants of God's New Agreement

3 1Why are we beginning again to tell you all these good things about ourselves? Do we need letters of introduction to you or from you, like some other people? 2No, you yourselves are our letter, written on our hearts. It is known and read by all people. 3You show that you are a letter from Christ that he sent through us. This letter is not written with ink but with the Spirit* of the living God. It is not written on stone*a* tablets but on human hearts.

4We can say this, because through Christ we feel sure before God. 5I don't mean that we are able to do anything good ourselves. It is God who makes us able to do all that we do. 6He made us able to be servants of a new agreement* from himself to his people. It is not an agreement of written laws, but it is of the Spirit. The written law brings death, but the Spirit gives life.

An Agreement With Greater Glory

7The old agreement*b* that brought death, written with words on stone, came with God's glory.* In fact, the face of Moses* was so bright with glory (a glory that was ending) that the people of Israel* could not continue looking at his face. 8So surely the new agreement that comes from the life-giving Spirit* has even more glory. 9This is what I mean: That old agreement judged people guilty of sin, but it had glory. So surely the new agreement that

*a*3:3 stone Meaning the law that God gave to Moses, which was written on stone tablets. Also in verse 7. See Ex. 24:12; 25:16. *b*3:7 agreement In verses 7–11 literally, "service" or "ministry."

makes people right with God has much greater glory. ¹⁰That old agreement had glory. But it really loses its glory when it is compared to the much greater glory of the new agreement. ¹¹If the agreement that was brought to an end came with glory, then the agreement that never ends has much greater glory.

¹²We are so sure of this hope that we speak very openly. ¹³We are not like Moses, who put a covering over his face. He covered his face so that the people of Israel would not see it. The glory was disappearing, and Moses did not want them to see it end. ¹⁴But their minds were closed. And even today, when those people read the writings of the old agreement,ᵃ that same covering hides the meaning. That covering has not been removed for them. It is taken away only through Christ. ¹⁵Yes, even today, when they read the law of Moses, there is a covering over their minds. ¹⁶But when someone changes and follows the Lord, that covering is taken away. ¹⁷The Lord is the Spirit, and where the Spirit of the Lord is, there is freedom. ¹⁸And our faces are not covered. We all show the Lord's glory. We are being changed to be like him. This change in us brings more and more glory. This glory comes from the Lord, who is the Spirit.

Spiritual Treasure in Clay Jars

4 ¹God, with his mercy, gave us this work to do, so we don't give up. ²But we have turned away from secret and shameful ways. We don't use trickery, and we don't change the teaching of God. We teach the truth plainly. This is how we show people who we are. And this is how they can know in their hearts what kind of people we are before God. ³The Good News* that we tell people may be hidden, but it is hidden only to those who are lost. ⁴The rulerᵇ of this world* has blinded the minds of those who don't believe. They cannot see the light of the Good News—the message about the divine greatness* of Christ. Christ is the one who is exactly like God. ⁵We don't tell people about ourselves. But we tell people that Jesus Christ is Lord, and we tell them that we are your servants for Jesus. ⁶God once said, "Let light shine out of the darkness!"ᶜ And this is the same God who made his light shine in our hearts to let us know that his own divine greatness is seen in the face of Christ.

⁷We have this treasure from God, but we are only like clay jars that hold the treasure. This is to show that the amazing power we have is from God, not from us. ⁸We have troubles all around us, but we are not defeated. We often don't know what to do, but we don't give up. ⁹We are persecuted,* but God does not leave us. We are hurt sometimes, but we are not destroyed. ¹⁰So we constantly experience the death of Jesus in our own bodies, but this is so that the life of Jesus can also be seen in

---

ᵃ3:14 old agreement See the Word List. Here, it is used to mean the law of Moses on which that agreement was based. ᵇ4:4 The ruler Literally, "The god." ᶜ4:6 Let … darkness See Gen. 1:3.

our bodies. [11]We are alive, but for Jesus we are always in danger of death, so that the life of Jesus can be seen in our bodies that die. [12]So death is working in us, but the result is that life is working in you.

[13]The Scriptures* say, "I believed, so I spoke."[a] Our faith is like that too. We believe, and so we speak. [14]God raised the Lord Jesus from death, and we know that he will also raise us with Jesus. God will bring us together with you, and we will stand before him. [15]All these things are for you. And so the grace* of God is being given to more and more people. This will bring more and more thanks to God for his glory.*

Living by Faith

[16]That is why we never give up. Our physical body is becoming older and weaker, but our spirit inside us is made new every day. [17]We have small troubles for a while now, but these troubles are helping us gain an eternal glory.* That eternal glory is much greater than our troubles. [18]So we think about what we cannot see, not what we see. What we see lasts only a short time, and what we cannot see will last forever.

5 [1]We know that our body—the tent we live in here on earth—will be destroyed. But when that happens, God will have a home for us to live in. It will not be the kind of home people build here. It will be a home in heaven that will continue forever. [2]But now we are tired of this body. We want God to give us our heavenly home. [3]It will clothe us and we will not be naked. [4]While we live in this tent, we have burdens and so we complain. I don't mean that we want to remove this tent, but we want to be clothed with our heavenly home. Then this body that dies will be covered with life. [5]This is what God himself made us for. And he has given us the Spirit* as the first payment to guarantee the life to come.

[6]So we always have confidence. We know that while we live in this body, we are away from the Lord. [7]We live by what we believe will happen, not by what we can see. [8]So I say that we have confidence. And we really want to be away from this body and be at home with the Lord. [9]Our only goal is to always please the Lord, whether we are living here in this body or there with him. [10]We must all stand before Christ to be judged. Everyone will get what they should. They will be paid for whatever they did—good or bad—when they lived in this earthly body.

Helping People Become God's Friends

[11]We know what it means to fear the Lord, so we try to help people accept the truth. God knows what we really are, and I hope that in your hearts you know us too. [12]We are not trying to prove ourselves to you again. But we are telling you about

---

[a]**4:13** Quote from Ps. 116:10.

ourselves. We are giving you reasons to be proud of us. Then you will have an answer for those who are proud about what can be seen. They don't care about what is in a person's heart. [13]If we are crazy, it is for God. If we have our right mind, it is for you. [14]The love of Christ controls us, because we know that one person died for everyone. So all have died. [15]He died for all so that those who live would not continue to live for themselves. He died for them and was raised from death so that they would live for him.

[16]From this time on we don't think of anyone as the world thinks of people. It is true that in the past we thought of Christ as the world thinks. But we don't think that way now. [17]When anyone is in Christ, it is a whole new world.[a] The old things are gone; suddenly, everything is new! [18]All this is from God. Through Christ, God made peace between himself and us. And God gave us the work of bringing people into peace with him. [19]I mean that God was in Christ, making peace between the world and himself. In Christ, God did not hold people guilty for their sins. And he gave us this message of peace to tell people. [20]So we have been sent to speak for Christ. It is like God is calling to people through us. We speak for Christ when we beg you to be at peace with God. [21]Christ had no sin, but God made him become sin[b] so that in Christ we could be right with God.

6 [1]We are workers together with God. So we beg you: Don't let the grace* that you received from God be for nothing. [2]God says,

"I heard you at the right time,
    and I gave you help on the day of salvation."   *Isaiah 49:8*

I tell you that the "right time" is now. The "day of salvation" is now.

[3]We don't want people to find anything wrong with our work. So we do nothing that will be a problem to others. [4]But in every way we show that we are servants of God. We never give up, even though we face troubles, difficulties, and problems of every kind. [5]We are beaten and thrown into prison. People get upset at us and fight against us. We work hard, and sometimes we get no sleep or food. [6]We show that we are God's servants by our pure lives, by our understanding, by our patience, and by our kindness. We show it by the Holy Spirit,* by genuine love, [7]by speaking the truth, and by depending on God's power. This right way of living has prepared us to defend ourselves against every kind of attack.

[8]Some people honor us, but others shame us. Some people say good things about us, but others say bad things. Some people say we are liars, but we speak the truth. [9]To some

---

[a]**5:17** *When anyone ... world* Or, "Anyone who is in Christ is a new creation."   [b]**5:21** *sin* Or, "an offering for sin."

people we are not known, but we are well-known. We seem to be dying, but look! We continue to live. We are punished, but we are not killed. [10]We have much sadness, but we are always rejoicing. We are poor, but we are making many people rich in faith. We have nothing, but really we have everything.

[11]We have spoken freely to you people in Corinth. We have opened our hearts to you. [12]Our feelings of love for you have not stopped. It is you who have stopped your feelings of love for us. [13]I speak to you as if you were my children. Do the same as we have done—open your hearts also.

We Are God's Temple

[14]You are not the same as those who don't believe. So don't join yourselves to them. Good and evil don't belong together. Light and darkness cannot share the same room. [15]How can there be any unity between Christ and the devil[a]? What does a believer have in common with an unbeliever? [16]God's temple[b] cannot have anything to do with idols,* and we are the temple of the living God. As God said,

> "I will live with them and walk with them;
> I will be their God, and they will be my people."
>
> *Leviticus 26:11–12*

[17]"So come away from those people
> and separate yourselves from them, says the Lord.
> Touch nothing that is not clean,
> and I will accept you."
>
> *Isaiah 52:11*

[18]"I will be your father,
> and you will be my sons and daughters,
> says the Lord All-Powerful."
>
> *2 Samuel 7:8, 14*

7 [1]Dear friends, we have these promises from God. So we should make ourselves pure—free from anything that makes our body or our soul unclean. Our respect for God should make us try to be completely holy* in the way we live.

Paul's Joy

[2]Open your hearts to us. We have not done wrong to anyone or caused harm to anyone. And we have not cheated anyone. [3]I do not say this to blame you. I told you before that we love you so much we would live or die with you. [4]I feel that I can tell you anything. I am very proud of you. Even with all the troubles we have had, I am greatly encouraged and feel very happy.

[5]When we came into Macedonia,* we had no rest. We found trouble all around us. We had fighting on the outside and

---

[a] **6:15** *the devil* Literally, *"beliar,"* a form of the Hebrew word *"belial,"* which means "worthlessness" and came to be used as another name for Satan. See "Satan" in the Word List. [b] **6:16** *God's temple* God's house—the place where God's people worship him. Here, it means that believers are the spiritual temple where God lives.

fear on the inside. [6]But God encourages those who are troubled, and he certainly encouraged us by bringing Titus to us. [7]It was so good to see him, but we were encouraged even more to hear about the encouragement you gave him. He told us that you really want to see me and that you are very sorry for what you did. And he told us how ready and willing you are to help me. When I heard this, I was so much happier.

[8]Even if the letter I wrote you made you sad, I am not sorry I wrote it. I know that letter made you sad, and I was sorry for that. But it made you sad only for a short time. [9]Now I am happy, not because you were made sad, but because your sorrow made you decide to change. That is what God wanted, so you were not hurt by us in any way. [10]The kind of sorrow God wants makes people decide to change their lives. This leads them to salvation, and we cannot be sorry for that. But the kind of sorrow the world has will bring death. [11]You had the kind of sorrow God wanted you to have. Now see what that sorrow has brought you: It has made you very serious. It made you want to prove that you were not wrong. It made you angry and afraid. It made you want to see me. It made you care. It made you want the right thing to be done. You proved that you were not guilty in any part of that problem. [12]The main reason I wrote that letter was not because of the one who did the wrong or the one who was hurt. I wrote so that you would realize, before God, how very much you care for us. [13]And that is what was so encouraging to us.

We were greatly encouraged, but we were especially pleased to see how happy Titus was. You all made him feel so much better. [14]I had bragged about you to Titus, and you didn't embarrass me. We have always told you the truth, and now what we told Titus about you has been shown to be true. [15]And his love for you is stronger when he remembers that you were all ready to obey. You welcomed him with respect and fear. [16]I am so happy that I can trust you fully.

Giving to Help Others

8 [1]And now, brothers and sisters, we want you to know about the grace* that God gave the churches* in Macedonia.* [2]Those believers have been tested by great troubles, and they are very poor. But they gave much because of their great joy. [3]I can tell you that they gave as much as they were able and even more than they could afford. No one told them to do this. It was their idea. [4]But they asked us again and again—they begged us to let them share in this service for God's people. [5]And they gave in a way that we did not expect: They gave themselves to the Lord and to us before they gave their money. This is what God wants.

[6]So we asked Titus to help you finish this special work of giving. He is the one who started this work. [7]You are rich in everything—in faith, in speaking ability, in knowledge, in the

willingness to help, and in the love you learned from us. And so we want you to also be rich in this work of giving.

[8]I am not ordering you to give, but I want to see how real your love is by comparing you with others who have been so ready and willing to help. [9]You know the grace of our Lord Jesus Christ. You know that he gave up his heavenly riches for you. He gave up everything so that you could be richly blessed.

[10]This is what I think you should do: Last year you were the first to want to give, and you were the first who gave. [11]So now finish the work you started. Then your "doing" will be equal to your "wanting to do." Give from what you have. [12]If you want to give, your gift will be accepted. Your gift will be judged by what you have, not by what you don't have. [13]We don't want you to have troubles while others are comforted. We want everything to be equal. [14]At this time you have plenty and can provide what they need. Then later, when they have plenty, they can provide what you need. Then everyone will have an equal share. [15]As the Scriptures* say,

"Those who gathered much did not have too much,
and those who gathered little did not have too little."

Exodus 16:18

Titus and His Companions

[16]I thank God because he gave Titus the same love for you that I have. [17]Titus agreed to do what we asked. In fact, he himself wanted very much to come see you. [18]We are sending with Titus the brother who is praised by all the churches.* He is praised because of his service to the Good News.* [19]Also, he was chosen by the churches to go with us when we carry this gift. We are doing this service to bring glory* to the Lord and to show that we really want to help.

[20]We are being careful so that no one will criticize us about the way we are caring for this large gift. [21]We are trying to do what is right. We want to do what the Lord accepts as right and also what people think is right.

[22]Also, we are sending with them our brother who is always ready to help. He has proved this to us in many ways. And he wants to help even more now because he has much faith in you.

[23]Now about Titus—he is my partner. He is working together with me to help you. And about the other brothers—they are sent from the churches, and they bring glory to Christ. [24]So show these men that you really have love. Show them why we are proud of you. Then all the churches can see it.

Help for Fellow Believers

9 [1]I really don't need to write to you about this help for God's people. [2]I know that you want to help. I have been bragging about you to the people in Macedonia.* I told them that you people in Achaia* have been ready to give since last year. And your desire to give has made most of the people here ready to give also. ³But I am sending the brothers to you. I don't want our bragging about you in this to be for nothing. I want you to be ready just as I said you would be. ⁴If any of those from Macedonia come with me, and they find that you are not ready, we will be ashamed. We will be ashamed that we were so sure of you. And you will be ashamed too! ⁵So I thought that I should ask these brothers to come there before we do. They will help in getting together the generous gift you promised. Then it will be ready when we come, and it will be seen as a blessing you are giving, not as something you were forced to do.

⁶Remember this: The one who plants few seeds will have a small harvest. But the one who plants a lot will have a big harvest. ⁷Each one of you should give what you have decided in your heart to give. You should not give if it makes you unhappy or if you feel forced to give. God loves those who are happy to give. ⁸And God can give you more blessings than you need, and you will always have plenty of everything. You will have enough to give to every good work. ⁹As the Scriptures* say,

"He gives generously to the poor;
    his goodness will continue forever."
                                        Psalm 112:9

¹⁰God is the one who gives seed to those who plant, and he gives bread for food. And God will give you spiritual seed and make that seed grow. He will produce a great harvest from your goodness. ¹¹God will make you rich in every way so that you can always give freely. And your giving through us will make people give thanks to God.

¹²The service you are offering helps God's people with their needs, but that is not all it does. It is also bringing more and more thanks to God. ¹³This service is a proof of your faith, and people will praise God because of it. They will praise him because you are following the message* about Christ—the message you say you believe. They will praise God because you freely share with them and with all people. ¹⁴And when they pray, they will wish they could be with you. They will feel this way because of the great grace* that God gave you. ¹⁵Thanks be to God for his gift that is too wonderful to describe.

Paul Defends His Ministry

10 ¹I, Paul, am begging you with the gentleness and the kindness of Christ. Some say that I am bold when I am writing you from a distance, but not when I am there with you. ²Some people think that we live on a purely human level. I plan to be very bold against those people when I come. I hope that I will not need to use that same boldness with you. ³We are human, but we don't fight in the same way that humans do. ⁴The weapons we use are not human ones. Our weapons have power from God and can destroy the enemy's strong places. We destroy people's arguments, [5]and we tear down every proud idea that raises itself against the knowledge of God. We also capture every thought and make it give up and obey Christ. [6]We are ready to punish anyone there who does not obey, but first we want you to be fully obedient.

[7]You must look at the facts before you. If you feel sure you belong to Christ, you must remember that we belong to Christ the same as you do. [8]It may seem as though we boast too much about the authority the Lord gave us. But he gave us this authority to strengthen you, not to hurt you. So I will not be ashamed of whatever boasting we do. [9]I don't want you to think that I am trying to scare you with my letters. [10]Some people say, "Paul's letters are powerful and sound important, but when he is with us, he is weak and the worst speaker you have ever heard." [11]Those people should know this: When we are there with you, we will show the same power that we show now in our letters.

[12]We don't dare put ourselves in the same class with those who think they are so important. We don't compare ourselves to them. They use themselves to measure themselves, and they judge themselves by what they themselves are. This shows that they know nothing.

[13]But we will not boast about anything outside the work that was given us to do. We will limit our boasting to the work God gave us, but this work includes our work with you. [14]We would be boasting too much only if we had not already come to you. But we have come to you with the Good News* of Christ. [15]We limit our boasting to the work that is ours. We don't boast about the work other people have done. We hope that your faith will continue to grow. We hope that you will help our work to grow much larger. [16]We want to tell the Good News in the areas beyond your city. We don't want to boast about work that has already been done in someone else's area. [17]"Whoever boasts should boast only about the Lord."[a] [18]What people say about themselves means nothing. What counts is whether or not the Lord says they have done well.

Paul and the False Apostles

11 [1]I wish you would be patient with me even when I am a little foolish. But you are already patient with me. [2]I am jealous for you with a jealousy that comes from God. I promised to give you to Christ. He must be your only husband. I want to give you to Christ to be his pure bride.[b] [3]But I am afraid that your minds will be led away from your true and pure following of Christ. This could happen just like Eve was

[a]**10:17** Quote from Jer. 9:24.　[b]**11:2** *bride* Literally, "virgin."

tricked by that snake with his clever lies. ⁴You seem to be quite patient with anyone who comes to you and tells you about a Jesus that is different from the Jesus we told you about. You seem very willing to accept a spirit or a message that is different from the Spirit* and message* that you received from us.

⁵I don't think that those "super apostles*" are any better than I am. ⁶It is true that I am not a trained speaker, but I do have knowledge. We have shown this to you clearly in every way.

⁷I did the work of telling God's Good News* to you without pay. I humbled myself to make you important. Do you think that was wrong? ⁸I accepted pay from other churches.* I took their money so that I could serve you. ⁹If I needed something when I was with you, I did not trouble any of you. The brothers who came from Macedonia* gave me all that I needed. I did not allow myself to be a burden to you in any way. And I will never be a burden to you. ¹⁰No one in Achaia* will stop me from boasting about that. I say this with the truth of Christ in me. ¹¹And why do I not burden you? Do you think it is because I don't love you? God knows that I love you.

¹²And I will continue doing what I am doing now, because I want to stop those people from having a reason to boast. They would like to say that the work they boast about is the same as ours. ¹³They are false apostles, lying workers. They only pretend to be apostles of Christ. ¹⁴That does not surprise us, because even Satan* changes himself to look like an angel of light.*ᵃ ¹⁵So it does not surprise us if Satan's servants make themselves look like servants who work for what is right. But in the end those people will get the punishment they deserve.

Paul Tells About His Sufferings

¹⁶I tell you again: No one should think that I am a fool. But if you think I am a fool, then accept me as you would accept a fool. Then I can boast a little too. ¹⁷But I am not talking like the Lord would talk. I am boasting like a fool. ¹⁸Others are boasting about their lives in the world. So I will boast too. ¹⁹You are wise, so you will gladly be patient with fools! ²⁰I say this because you are even patient with someone who forces you to do things and uses you. You are patient with those who trick you, or think they are better than you, or hit you in the face! ²¹I am ashamed to say it, but we were too "weak" to do such things to you.

But if anyone dares to boast, I will too. (I am talking like a fool.) ²²Are those people Hebrews? So am I. Are they Israelitesᵇ? So am I. Are they from Abraham's* family? So am I. ²³Are they serving Christ? I am serving him more. (I am crazy to talk like this.) I have worked much harder than they have. I

ᵃ**11:14** *angel of light* Messenger from God. The devil fools people so that they think he is from God.   ᵇ**11:22** *Hebrews … Israelites* Other names for the Jewish people.

have been in prison more often. I have been hurt more in beatings. I have been near death many times.

²⁴Five times the Jews have given me their punishment of 39 lashes with a whip. ²⁵Three different times I was beaten with rods. One time I was almost killed with rocks. Three times I was in ships that were wrecked, and one of those times I spent the night and the next day in the sea. ²⁶In my constant traveling I have been in danger from rivers, from thieves, from my own people, and from people who are not Jews. I have been in danger in cities, in places where no one lives, and on the sea. And I have been in danger from people who pretend to be believers* but are not.

²⁷I have done hard and tiring work, and many times I did not sleep. I have been hungry and thirsty. Many times I have been without food. I have been cold and without clothes. ²⁸And there are many other problems. One of these is the care I have for all the churches.* I worry about them every day. ²⁹I feel weak every time another person is weak. I feel upset inside myself every time another person is led into sin.

³⁰If I must boast, I will boast about the things that show I am weak. ³¹God knows that I am not lying. He is the God and Father of the Lord Jesus, and he is to be praised forever. ³²When I was in Damascus, the governor under King Aretas wanted to arrest me, so he put guards around the city. ³³But some friends put me in a basket. Then they put the basket through a hole in the wall and lowered me down. So I escaped from the governor.

A Special Blessing in Paul's Life

12 ¹There is more that I have to say about myself. It won't help, but I will talk now about visions* and revelations*ᵃ* from the Lord. ²I know a man*ᵇ* in Christ who was taken up to the third heaven. This happened 14 years ago. I don't know if the man was in his body or out of his body, but God knows. ³⁻⁴And I know that this man was taken up to paradise.* I don't know if he was in his body or away from his body, but he heard things that he is not able to explain. He heard things that no one is allowed to tell. ⁵I will boast about a man like that, but I will not boast about myself. I will boast only about my weaknesses.

⁶But if I wanted to say more about myself, I would not be a fool, because I would be telling the truth. But I won't say any more, because I don't want people to think more of me than what they see me do or hear me say.

⁷But I must not be too proud of the wonderful things that were shown to me. So a painful problem*ᶜ* was given to me—an angel from Satan,* sent to make me suffer, so that I would not

---

*ᵃ***12:1** *revelation* An opening up (making known) of truth that was hidden. *ᵇ***12:2** *a man* In 12:2–5 Paul is probably talking about himself. *ᶜ***12:7** *painful problem* Literally, "thorn in the flesh."

think that I am better than anyone else. ⁸I begged the Lord three times to take this problem away from me. ⁹But the Lord said, "My grace* is all you need. Only when you are weak can everything be done completely by my power." So I will gladly boast about my weaknesses. Then Christ's power can stay in me. ¹⁰Yes, I am glad to have weaknesses if they are for Christ. I am glad to be insulted and have hard times. I am glad when I am persecuted* and have problems, because it is when I am weak that I am really strong.

Paul's Love for the Believers in Corinth

¹¹I have been talking like a fool, but you made me do it. You people are the ones who should say good things about me. I am worth nothing, but those "super apostles*" are not worth any more than I am! ¹²When I was with you, I patiently did the things that prove I am an apostle—signs,* wonders,* and miracles.* ¹³So you received everything that the other churches* have received. Only one thing was different: I was not a burden to you. Forgive me for this!

¹⁴I am now ready to visit you for the third time, and I will not be a burden to you. I don't want any of the things you own. I only want you. Children should not have to save things to give to their parents. Parents should save to give to their children. ¹⁵So I am happy to give everything I have for you. I will even give myself for you. If I love you more, will you love me less?

¹⁶It is clear that I was not a burden to you, but you think that I was tricky and used lies to catch you. ¹⁷Did I cheat you by using any of the men I sent to you? You know I didn't. ¹⁸I asked Titus to go to you, and I sent our brother with him. Titus did not cheat you, did he? No, you know that his actions and his attitude were the same as ours.

¹⁹Do you think that we have been defending ourselves to you all this time? No, we say these things in Christ and before God. You are our dear friends, and everything we do is to make you stronger. ²⁰I do this because I am afraid that when I come, you will not be what I want you to be. And I am afraid that I will not be what you want me to be. I am afraid that I will find arguing, jealousy, anger, selfish fighting, evil talk, gossip, pride, and confusion there. ²¹I am afraid that when I come to you again, my God will make me humble before you. I may have to cry over the loss of some who sinned before. Many of them have still not changed their hearts to be sorry for their evil lives, their sexual sins, and the shameful things they have done.

Final Warnings and Greetings

13 ¹This will be my third time to visit to you. And remember, "For every complaint there must be two or three people to say that they know it is true."[a] ²When I was with you the second time, I gave a warning to those who had sinned. I am not there now, but I am giving another warning to them and to anyone else who has sinned: When I come to you again, I will punish you. ³You want proof that Christ is speaking through me. My proof is that he is not weak in dealing with you but is showing his power among you. ⁴It is true that Christ was weak when he was killed on the cross, but he lives now by God's power. It is also true that we share his weakness, but in dealing with you we will be alive in him by God's power.

⁵Look closely at yourselves. Test yourselves to see if you are living in the faith. Don't you realize that Christ Jesus is in you? Of course, if you fail the test, he is not in you. ⁶But I hope you will see that we have not failed the test. ⁷We pray to God that you will not do anything wrong. Our concern here is not for people to see that we have passed the test in our work with you. Our main concern is that you do what is right, even if it looks as if we have failed the test. ⁸We cannot do anything that is against the truth but only what promotes the truth. ⁹We are happy to be weak if you are strong. And this is what we pray—that your lives will be made completely right again. ¹⁰I'm writing this before I come, so that when I am there I will not have to use my authority to punish you. The Lord gave me that authority to make you stronger, not to destroy you.

¹¹Now, brothers and sisters, I say goodbye. Try to make everything right, and do what I have asked you to do. Agree with each other, and live in peace. Then the God of love and peace will be with you.

¹²Give each other the special greeting of God's people.[b] All of God's holy people* here send you their greetings.

¹³I pray that you will enjoy the grace* of the Lord Jesus Christ, the love of God, and the fellowship[c] of the Holy Spirit.*

---

[a] 13:1 Quote from Deut. 19:15.   [b] 13:12 *the special greeting of God's people* Literally, "a holy kiss."   [c] 13:13 *fellowship* This can mean a sharing or participation in the Holy Spirit or the loving association and unity among believers that is created by the Spirit.

Galatians

1 ¹Greetings from Paul, an apostle.* I was chosen to be an apostle, but not by any group or person here on earth. My authority came from none other than Jesus Christ and God the Father, who raised Jesus from death. ²Greetings also from all those in God's family who are with me.

To the churches* in Galatia*:

³I pray that God our Father and the Lord Jesus Christ will be good to you and give you peace. ⁴Jesus gave himself for our sins to free us from this evil world we live in. This is what God our Father wanted. ⁵The glory* belongs to God forever and ever. Amen.*

There Is Only One Good News Message

⁶A short time ago God chose you to follow him. He chose you through his grace* that came through Christ. But now I am amazed that you are already turning away and believing something different from the Good News* we told you. ⁷There is no other message that is good news, but some people are confusing you. They want to change the Good News about Christ. ⁸We told you the true Good News message. So anyone who tells you a different message should be condemned—even if it's one of us or even an angel from heaven! ⁹I said this before. Now I say it again: You have already accepted the Good News. Anyone who tells you another way to be saved should be condemned!

¹⁰Now do you think I am trying to make people accept me? No, God is the one I am trying to please. Am I trying to please people? If I wanted to please people, I would not be a servant of Jesus Christ.

Paul's Authority Is From God

¹¹Brothers and sisters, I want you to know that the Good News* message I told you was not made up by anyone. ¹²I did not get my message from any other human. The Good News is not something I learned from other people. Jesus Christ himself gave it to me. He showed me the Good News that I should tell people.

*a*1:2 *Galatia* Probably the area where Paul began churches on his first missionary trip. See Acts 13 and 14.

¹³You have heard about my past life in the Jewish religion. I persecuted* the church* of God very much. I tried to destroy his people. ¹⁴I was becoming a leader in the Jewish religion. I did better than most other Jews my own age. I tried harder than anyone else to follow the traditions we got from our ancestors.*

¹⁵But God had special plans for me even before I was born. So he chose me through his grace.* He wanted me ¹⁶to tell the Good News about his Son to the non-Jewish people. So God let me see and learn about his Son. When this happened, I did not get advice or help from anyone. ¹⁷I did not go to Jerusalem to see those who were apostles* before I was. But, without waiting, I went away to Arabia. Later, I went back to the city of Damascus.

¹⁸Three years later I went to Jerusalem to meet Peter.ᵃ I stayed with him 15 days. ¹⁹I met no other apostles—only James, the brother of the Lord. ²⁰God knows there is nothing untrue in any of this. ²¹Later, I went to the areas of Syria and Cilicia.

²²The groups of believersᵇ in Judea who belong to Christ had never met me before. ²³They had only heard this about me: "This man was persecuting us. But now he is telling people about the same faith that he once tried to destroy." ²⁴These believers praised God because of me.

The Other Apostles Accepted Paul

2 ¹After 14 years I went back to Jerusalem with Barnabas and took Titus with me. ²I went there because God showed me that I should go. I explained to them the message* that I tell the non-Jewish people. I also met alone with those who were considered to be the leaders. I wanted to be sure we were in agreement so that my past work and the work I do now would not be wasted.

³Titus, who was with me, is a Greek.* But these leaders still did not force him to be circumcised.* ⁴We needed to talk about these problems, because some who pretended to be our brothers had come into our group secretly. They came in like spies to find out about the freedom we have in Christ Jesus. They wanted to make us slaves, ⁵but we did not agree with anything those false brothers wanted. We wanted the truth of the Good News* to continue for you.

⁶Those men who were considered to be important did not change the Good News message I tell people. (It doesn't matter to me if they were "important" or not. To God everyone is the same.) ⁷But these leaders saw that God had given me a special work, the same as Peter. God gave Peter the work of telling the

---

ᵃ1:18 Peter The text says "Cephas," the Aramaic name for Peter, one of Jesus' twelve apostles. Also in 2:7. ᵇ1:22 groups of believers Literally, "churches" or "assemblies." See "church" in the Word List.

Good News to the Jews. But God gave me the work of telling the Good News to the non-Jewish people. [8]God gave Peter the power to work as an apostle* for the Jewish people. God gave me the power to work as an apostle too, but for those who are not Jews. [9]James, Peter, and John seemed to be the leaders. And they saw that God had given me this special gift of ministry, so they accepted Barnabas and me. They said to us, "We agree that you should go to those who are not Jews, and we will go to the Jews." [10]They asked us to do only one thing—to remember to help those who are poor. And this was something that I really wanted to do.

Paul Shows That Peter Was Wrong

[11]When Peter came to Antioch, he did something that was not right. I stood against him, because he was wrong. [12]This is what happened: When Peter first came to Antioch, he ate and associated with the non-Jewish people. But when some Jewish men came from James, Peter separated himself from the non-Jews. He stopped eating with them, because he was afraid of the Jews who believe that all non-Jewish people must be circumcised.* [13]So Peter was a hypocrite.* The other Jewish believers joined with him, so they were hypocrites too. Even Barnabas was influenced by what these Jewish believers did. [14]They were not following the truth of the Good News.* When I saw this, I spoke to Peter in front of everyone. I said, "Peter, you are a Jew, but you don't live like one. You live like someone who is not a Jew. So why are you trying to force those who are not Jewish to live like Jews?"

[15]We are Jews by birth. We were not born "sinners," as we call those who are not Jews. [16]But we know that no one is made right with God by following the law.* It is trusting in[a] Jesus Christ that makes a person right with God. So we have put our faith in Christ Jesus, because we wanted to be made right with God. And we are right with him because we trusted in[b] Christ—not because we followed the law. I can say this because no one can be made right with God by following the law.

[17]We Jews came to Christ to be made right with God, so it is clear that we were sinners too. Does this mean that Christ makes us sinners? Of course not. [18]But I would be wrong to begin teaching again those things that I gave up. [19]It was the law itself that caused me to end my life under the law. I died to the law so that I could live for God. I have been nailed to the cross with Christ. [20]So I am not the one living now—it is Christ living in me. I still live in my body, but I live by faith in[c] the Son of God. He is the one who loved me and gave himself to save me. [21]I am not the one destroying the meaning of God's

---

[a]**2:16** *trusting in* Or, "the faithfulness of."   [b]**2:16** *because we trusted in* Or, "through the faithfulness of."   [c]**2:20** *faith in* Or, "the faithfulness of."

grace.* If following the law is how people are made right with
God, then Christ did not have to die.

God's Blessing Comes Through Faith

3 ¹You people in Galatia are so foolish! Why do I say this?
Because I told you very clearly about the death of Jesus
Christ on the cross. But now it seems as though you have let
someone use their magical powers to make you forget. ²Tell me
this one thing: How did you receive the Spirit*? Did you
receive the Spirit by following the law*? No, you received the
Spirit because you heard the message about Jesus and believed
it. ³You began your life in Christ with the Spirit. Now do you
try to complete it by your own power? That is foolish. ⁴You
have experienced many things. Were all those experiences
wasted? I hope they were not wasted! ⁵Does God give you the
Spirit because you follow the law? Does God work miracles*
among you because you follow the law? No, God gives you his
Spirit and works miracles among you because you heard the
message about Jesus and believed it.

⁶The Scriptures* say the same thing about Abraham.*
"Abraham believed God, and God accepted Abraham's faith.
That made him right with God."ᵃ ⁷So you should know that
the true children of Abraham are those who have faith. ⁸The
Scriptures told what would happen in the future. These writings said that God would make the non-Jewish people right
through their faith. God told this Good News* to Abraham
before it happened. God said to Abraham, "I will use you to
bless all the people on earth."ᵇ ⁹Abraham believed this, and
because he believed, he was blessed. All people who believe
are blessed the same as Abraham was.

¹⁰But people who depend on following the law to make
them right are under a curse. As the Scriptures say, "They must
do everything that is written in the law. If they do not always
obey, they are under a curse."ᶜ ¹¹So it is clear that no one can
be made right with God by the law. The Scriptures say, "The
one who is right with God by faith will live forever."ᵈ

¹²The law does not depend on faith. No, it says that the only
way a person will find life by the law is to obey its commands.ᵉ
¹³The law says we are under a curse for not always obeying it.
But Christ took away that curse. He changed places with us
and put himself under that curse. The Scriptures say, "Anyone
who is hung on a treeᶠ is under a curse."ᵍ ¹⁴Because of what
Jesus Christ did, the blessing God promised to Abraham was

ᵃ3:6 Quote from Gen. 15:6. ᵇ3:8 Quote from Gen. 12:3. ᶜ3:10 Quote from Deut. 27:26.
ᵈ3:11 Quote from Hab. 2:4. ᵉ3:12 *the only way ... commands* See Lev. 18:5. ᶠ3:13 *hung
on a tree* Deut. 21:22–23 says that when a person was killed for doing wrong, his body was
hung on a tree to show shame. Paul means the cross of Jesus was like that. ᵍ3:13 Quote
from Deut. 21:23.

given to all people. Christ died so that by believing in him we could have the Spirit that God promised.

The Law and the Promise

¹⁵Brothers and sisters, let me give you an example from everyday life: Think about an agreement that one person makes with another. After that agreement is made official, no one can stop it or add anything to it, and no one can ignore it. ¹⁶God made promises to Abraham* and his Descendant.ᵃ The Scripture* does not say, "and to your descendants." That would mean many people. But it says, "and to your Descendant." That means only one, and that one is Christ. ¹⁷This is what I mean: The agreement that God gave to Abraham was made official long before the law* came. The law came 430 years later. So the law could not take away the agreement and change God's promise.

¹⁸Can following the law give us the blessing God promised? If we could receive it by following the law, then it would not be God's promise that brings it to us. But God freely gave his blessings to Abraham through the promise God made.

¹⁹So what was the law for? The law was given to show the wrong things people do. The law would continue until the special Descendant of Abraham came. This is the Descendant mentioned in the promise, which came directly from God. But the law was given through angels, and the angels used Moses as a mediator* to give the law to the people. ²⁰But when God gave the promise, there was no mediator, because a mediator is not needed when there is only one side, and God is one.ᵇ

The Purpose of the Law of Moses

²¹Does this mean that the law* works against God's promises? Of course not. The law was never God's way of giving new life to people. If it were, then we could be made right by following the law. ²²But this is not possible. The Scriptures* put the whole world in prison under the control of sin, so that the only way for people to get what God promised would be through faith inᶜ Jesus Christ. It is given to those who believe in him.

²³Before this faith came, the law guarded us as prisoners. We had no freedom until God showed us the way of faith that was coming. ²⁴I mean the law was our guardian until Christ came. After he came, we could be made right with God through faith. ²⁵Now that the way of faith has come, we no longer need the law to be our guardian.

²⁶⁻²⁷You are all baptized* into Christ, and so you were all clothed with Christ. This shows that you are all children of God through faith in Christ Jesus. ²⁸Now, in Christ, it doesn't

---

ᵃ**3:16** *Descendant* Literally, "seed," which could also mean "family." In that case, it would refer to the one family of God in Christ.   ᵇ**3:20** *But … God is one* Literally, "But the mediator is not of one, but God is one."   ᶜ**3:22** *faith in* Or, "the faithfulness of."

matter if you are a Jew or a Greek,* a slave or free, male or female. You are all the same in Christ Jesus. ²⁹You belong to Christ, so you are Abraham's* descendants. You get all of God's blessings because of the promise that God made to Abraham.

4 ¹This is what I am saying: When young children inherit all that their father owned, they are still no different from his slaves. It doesn't matter that they own everything. ²While they are children, they must obey those who are chosen to care for them. But when they reach the age the father set, they are free. ³It is the same for us. We were once like children, slaves to the useless rules*ᵃ* of this world. ⁴But when the right time came, God sent his Son, who was born from a woman and lived under the law. ⁵God did this so that he could buy the freedom of those who were under the law. God's purpose was to make us his children.

⁶Since you are now God's children, he has sent the Spirit of his Son into your hearts. The Spirit* cries out, "*Abba,*ᵇ Father." ⁷Now you are not slaves like before. You are God's children, and you will receive everything he promised his children.

Paul's Love for the Galatian Believers

⁸In the past you did not know God. You were slaves to gods that were not real. ⁹But now you know the true God. Really, though, it is God who knows you. So why do you turn back to the same kind of weak and useless rules you followed before? Do you want to be slaves to those things again? ¹⁰–¹¹It worries me that you follow teachings about special days, months, seasons, and years. I fear that my work for you has been wasted.

¹²Brothers and sisters, I became like you. So please become like me. You were very good to me before. ¹³You know that I came to you the first time because I was sick. That was when I told you the Good News* to you. ¹⁴My sickness was a burden to you, but you did not hate me or make me leave. Instead, you welcomed me as if I were an angel from God. You accepted me as if I were Jesus Christ himself! ¹⁵You were very happy then. Where is that joy now? I can say without a doubt that you would have done anything to help me. If it had been possible, you would have taken out your own eyes and given them to me. ¹⁶Am I now your enemy because I tell you the truth?

¹⁷Those peopleᶜ are working hard to persuade you, but this is not good for you. They want to persuade you to turn against us and work hard for them. ¹⁸It is good for you to work hard, of course, if it is for something good. That's something you should do whether I am there or not. ¹⁹My little children, I am in pain again over you, like a mother giving birth. I will feel this pain until people can look at you and see Christ. ²⁰I wish I could be

---

*ᵃ***4:3** *rules* Or, "powers." Also in verse 9. *ᵇ***4:6** *Abba* An Aramaic word that was used by Jewish children as a name for their fathers. *ᶜ***4:17** *Those people* The false teachers who were bothering the believers in Galatia. See Gal. 1:7.

with you now. Then maybe I could change the way I am talking to you. Now I don't know what to do about you.

The Example of Hagar and Sarah

²¹Some of you people want to be under the law.* Tell me, do you know what the law says? ²²The Scriptures* say that Abraham* had two sons. The mother of one son was a slave woman, and the mother of the other son was a free woman. ²³Abraham's son from the slave woman was born in the normal human way. But the son from the free woman was born because of the promise God made to Abraham.

²⁴This true story makes a picture for us. The two women are like the two agreements between God and his people. One agreement is the law that God made on Mount Sinai.* The people who are under this agreement are like slaves. The mother named Hagar is like that agreement. ²⁵So Hagar is like Mount Sinai in Arabia. She is a picture of the earthly Jewish city of Jerusalem. This city is a slave, and all its people are slaves to the law. ²⁶But the heavenly Jerusalem that is above is like the free woman, who is our mother. ²⁷The Scriptures say,

> "Be happy, woman—you who cannot have children.
> 　Be glad you never gave birth.
> Shout and cry with joy!
> 　You never felt those labor pains.
> The woman who is alone[a] will have more children
> 　than the woman who has a husband."　　*Isaiah 54:1*

²⁸My brothers and sisters, you are children who were born because of God's promise, just as Isaac was. ²⁹But the other son of Abraham, who was born in the normal way, caused trouble for the one who was born by the power of the Spirit.* It is the same today. ³⁰But what do the Scriptures say? "Throw out the slave woman and her son! The son of the free woman will receive everything his father has, but the son of the slave woman will receive nothing."[b] ³¹So, my brothers and sisters, we are not children of the slave woman. We are children of the free woman.

Keep Your Freedom

5 ¹We have freedom now, because Christ made us free. So stand strong in that freedom. Don't go back into slavery again. ²Listen! I, Paul, tell you that if you start following the law by being circumcised,* then Christ cannot help you. ³Again, I warn everyone: If you allow yourselves to be circumcised, then you must follow the whole law.* ⁴If you try to be made right with God through the law, your life with Christ is finished—you have left God's grace.* ⁵I say this because our hope of being right with God comes through faith. And the

---

[a]4:27 *woman . . . alone* This means her husband has left her.　[b]4:30 Quote from Gen. 21:10.

Spirit* helps us feel sure as we wait for that hope. ⁶When someone belongs to Christ Jesus, it is not important if they are circumcised or not. The important thing is faith—the kind of faith that works through love.

⁷You were doing so well. Who caused you to stop following the truth? ⁸It certainly wasn't the one who chose you. ⁹Be careful! "Just a little yeast* makes the whole batch of dough rise."ᵃ ¹⁰I trust in the Lord that you will not believe those different ideas. Someone is trying to confuse you. Whoever it is will be punished.

¹¹My brothers and sisters, I don't teach that a man must be circumcised. If I do teach circumcision, then why am I still being persecuted*? If I still taught circumcision, then my message about the cross would not be a problem. ¹²I wish those people who are bothering you would add castrationᵇ to their circumcision.

¹³My brothers and sisters, God chose you to be free. But don't use your freedom as an excuse to do what pleases your sinful selves. Instead, serve each other with love. ¹⁴The whole law is made complete in this one command: "Love your neighborᶜ the same as you love yourself."ᵈ ¹⁵If you continue hurting each other and tearing each other apart, be careful, or you will completely destroy each other.

The Spirit and Human Nature

¹⁶So I tell you, live the way the Spirit* leads you. Then you will not do the evil things your sinful self wants. ¹⁷The sinful self wants what is against the Spirit, and the Spirit wants what is against the sinful self. They are always fighting against each other, so that you don't do what you really want to do. ¹⁸But if you let the Spirit lead you, you are not under law.ᵉ

¹⁹The wrong things the sinful self does are clear: committing sexual sin, being morally bad, doing all kinds of shameful things, ²⁰worshiping false gods, taking part in witchcraft,* hating people, causing trouble, being jealous, angry or selfish, causing people to argue and divide into separate groups, ²¹being filled with envy, getting drunk, having wild parties, and doing other things like this. I warn you now as I warned you before: The people who do these things will not have a part in God's kingdom.* ²²But the fruit that the Spirit produces in a person's life is love, joy, peace, patience, kindness, goodness,

---

ᵃ5:9 "Just ... rise" A proverb meaning that a small thing (like a little wrong teaching) can make a big problem or that just one person can have a bad influence on the whole group. ᵇ5:12 castration To cut off part of the male sex organs. Paul uses a word that means "to cut off" in place of "circumcision," which means "to cut around," to show how angry he is at the false teachers for forcing non-Jewish men to be circumcised. ᶜ5:14 your neighbor Or, "others." Jesus' teaching in Lk. 10:25–37 makes clear that this includes anyone in need. ᵈ5:14 Quote from Lev. 19:18. ᵉ5:18 law Here, a law system, like the law of Moses.

faithfulness, ²³gentleness, and self-control. There is no law against these kinds of things. ²⁴Those who belong to Christ Jesus have crucified their sinful self. They have given up their old selfish feelings and the evil things they wanted to do. ²⁵We get our new life from the Spirit, so we should follow the Spirit. ²⁶We must not feel proud and boast about ourselves. We must not cause trouble for each other or be jealous of each other.

Help Each Other

6 ¹Brothers and sisters, someone in your group might do something wrong. You who are following the Spirit* should go to the one who is sinning. Help make that person right again, and do it in a gentle way. But be careful, because you might be tempted to sin too. ²Help each other with your troubles. When you do this, you are obeying the law of Christ. ³If you think you are too important to do this, you are only fooling yourself. ⁴Don't compare yourself with others. Just look at your own work to see if you have done anything to be proud of. ⁵You must each accept the responsibilities that are yours.

Never Stop Doing Good

⁶Whoever is being taught God's word should share the good things they have with the one who is teaching them.

⁷Don't be fooled: You cannot cheat God. You will harvest what you plant.*ᵃ* ⁸If you live to satisfy your sinful self, the harvest you will get from that will be eternal death. But if you live to please the Spirit,* your harvest from the Spirit will be eternal life. ⁹We must not get tired of doing good. We will receive our harvest of eternal life at the right time. We must not give up. ¹⁰When we have the opportunity to do good to anyone, we should do it. But we should give special attention to those who are in the family of believers.

Paul Ends His Letter

¹¹This is my own handwriting. You can see how big the letters are. ¹²Those men who are trying to force you to be circumcised* are only doing it so that their people will accept them. They are afraid they will be persecuted* if they follow only the cross*ᵇ* of Christ. ¹³They are circumcised, but they don't obey the law* themselves. They want you to be circumcised so that they can boast about what they did to you.

¹⁴I hope I will never boast about things like that. The cross of our Lord Jesus Christ is my only reason for boasting. Through Jesus' death on the cross the world is dead*ᶜ* to me, and I am dead to the world. ¹⁵It doesn't matter if anyone is circumcised

---

*ᵃ***6:7** *harvest what you plant* This means that life is like farming. Farmers get from their fields only what they plant. *ᵇ***6:12** *cross* Paul uses the cross as a picture of the Good News, the story of Christ's death to pay for people's sins. The cross (Christ's death) was God's way to save people. Also in verse 14. *ᶜ***6:14** *is dead* Literally, "has been crucified."

or not. The only thing that matters is this new life we have from God.[a] [16]Peace and mercy to those who follow this rule—to all of God's people.[b]

[17]So don't give me any more trouble. I have scars on my body that show[c] I belong to Jesus.

[18]My brothers and sisters, I pray that the grace* of our Lord Jesus Christ will be with your spirits. Amen.*

---

[a]**6:15** *this new life ... God* Or, "being the new people God has made."   [b]**6:16** *all of God's people* Literally, "the Israel of God."   [c]**6:17** *scars ... show* Many times Paul was beaten by people who tried to stop him from teaching about Christ. The scars were from these beatings.

Ephesians

1 ¹Greetings from Paul, an apostle* of Christ Jesus. I am an apostle because that is what God wanted.

To God's holy people* living in Ephesus,*ᵃ believers who belong to Christ Jesus.

²Grace* and peace to you from God our Father and the Lord Jesus Christ.

Spiritual Blessings in Christ

³Praise be to the God and Father of our Lord Jesus Christ. In Christ, God has given us every spiritual blessing in heaven. ⁴In Christ, he chose us before the world was made. He chose us in love to be his holy people*—people who could stand before him without any fault. ⁵And before the world was made, God decided to make us his own children through Jesus Christ. This was what God wanted, and it pleased him to do it. ⁶And this brings praise to God because of his wonderful grace.* God gave that grace to us freely. He gave us that grace in Christ, the one he loves.

⁷In Christ we are made free by his blood sacrifice. We have forgiveness of sins because of God's rich grace. ⁸God gave us that grace fully and freely. With full wisdom and understanding, ⁹he let us know his secret plan. This was what God wanted, and he planned to do it through Christ. ¹⁰God's goal was to finish his plan when the right time came. He planned that all things in heaven and on earth be joined together with Christ as the head.

¹¹In Christ we were chosen to be God's people. God had already planned for us to be his people, because that is what he wanted. And he is the one who makes everything agree with what he decides and wants. ¹²We Jews were the first to hope in Christ. And we were chosen so that we would bring praise to God in all his glory.* ¹³It is the same with you. You heard the true message, the Good News* about your salvation. When you heard that Good News, you believed in Christ. And in Christ, God put his special mark on you by giving you the Holy Spirit* that he promised. ¹⁴The Spirit is the first payment that guarantees we will get all that God has for us. Then we will enjoy complete freedom as people who

---

ᵃ**1:1** *in Ephesus* Some Greek copies do not have the words "in Ephesus."

belong to him. The goal for all of us is the praise of God in all his glory.

Paul's Prayer

15–16That is why I always remember you in my prayers and thank God for you. I have done this ever since I heard about your faith in the Lord Jesus and your love for all of God's people. 17I always pray to the great and glorious Father, the God of our Lord Jesus Christ. I pray that he will give you the Spirit,* who will let you know truths about God and help you understand them, so that you will know him better.

18I pray that God will open your minds to see his truth. Then you will know the hope that he has chosen us to have. You will know that the blessings God has promised his holy people* are rich and glorious. 19And you will know that God's power is very great for us who believe. It is the same as the mighty power 20he used to raise Christ from death and put him at his right side in the heavenly places. 21He put Christ over all rulers, authorities, powers, and kings. He gave him authority over everything that has power in this world or in the next world. 22God put everything under Christ's power and made him head over everything for the church.* 23The church is Christ's body. It is filled with him. He makes everything complete in every way.

From Death to Life

2 1In the past you were spiritually dead because of your sins and the things you did against God. 2Yes, in the past your lives were full of those sins. You lived the way the world lives, following the ruler of the evil powers* over the earth. That same spirit is now working in those who refuse to obey God. 3In the past all of us lived like that, trying to please our sinful selves. We did all the things our bodies and minds wanted. Like everyone else in the world, we deserved to suffer God's anger just because of the way we were.

4But God is rich in mercy, and he loved us very much. 5We were spiritually dead because of all we had done against him. But he gave us new life together with Christ. (You have been saved by God's grace.*) 6Yes, it is because we are a part of Christ Jesus that God raised us from death and seated us together with him in the heavenly places. 7God did this so that his kindness to us who belong to Christ Jesus would clearly show for all time to come the amazing richness of his grace.

8I mean that you have been saved by grace because you believed. You did not save yourselves; it was a gift from God. 9You are not saved by the things you have done, so there is nothing to boast about. 10God has made us what we are. In Christ Jesus, God made us new people so that we would spend our lives doing the good things he had already planned for us to do.

One in Christ

[11]You were not born as Jews. You are the people the Jews call "uncircumcised.[a]" Those Jews who call you "uncircumcised" call themselves "circumcised." (Their circumcision* is only something they themselves do to their bodies.) [12]Remember that in the past you were without Christ. You were not citizens of Israel,* and you did know about the agreements[b] with the promises that God made to his people. You had no hope, and you did not know God. [13]Yes, at one time you were far away from God, but now in Christ Jesus, you are brought near to him. You are brought near to God through the blood sacrifice of Christ.

[14]Christ is the reason we are now at peace. He made us Jews and you who are not Jews one people. We were separated by a wall of hate that stood between us, but Christ broke down that wall. By giving his own body, [15]Christ ended the law with its many commands and rules. His purpose was to make the two groups become one in him. By doing this he would make peace. [16]Through the cross Christ ended the hate between the two groups. And after they became one body, he wanted to bring them both back to God. He did this with his death on the cross. [17]Christ came and brought the message of peace to you non-Jews who were far away from God. And he brought that message of peace to those who were near to God. [18]Yes, through Christ we all have the right to come to the Father in one Spirit.*

[19]So now you non-Jewish people are not visitors or strangers, but you are citizens together with God's holy people.* You belong to God's family. [20]You believers are like a building that God owns. That building was built on the foundation that the apostles* and prophets* prepared. Christ Jesus himself is the most important stone[c] in that building. [21]The whole building is joined together in Christ, and he makes it grow and become a holy temple[d] in the Lord. [22]And in Christ you are being built together with his other people. You are being made into a place where God lives through the Spirit.

Paul's Work for the Non-Jewish People

3 [1]So I, Paul, am a prisoner because I serve Christ Jesus for you who are not Jews. [2]Surely you know that God gave me this work through his grace* to help you. [3]God let me know his secret plan by showing it to me. I have already written a little about this. [4]And if you read what I wrote, you can see that I understand the secret truth about the Christ. [5]People who lived in other times were not told that secret truth. But now,

---

[a]**2:11** *uncircumcised* People not having the mark of circumcision like the Jews have.
[b]**2:12** *agreements* The agreements with special promises that God gave at various times to people in the Old Testament. See "agreement" in the Word List. [c]**2:20** *most important stone* Literally, "cornerstone." The first and most important stone in a building. [d]**2:21** *temple* God's house—the place where God's people worship him. Here, it means that believers are the spiritual temple where God lives.

through the Spirit,* God has made it known to his holy apostles* and prophets.* ⁶And this is the secret truth: that by hearing the Good News,* those who are not Jews will share with the Jews in the blessings God has for his people. They are part of the same body, and they share in the promise God made through Christ Jesus.

⁷By God's special gift of grace, I became a servant to tell that Good News. He gave me that grace by using his power. ⁸I am the least important of all God's people. But he gave me this gift—to tell the non-Jewish people the Good News about the riches Christ has. These riches are too great to understand fully. ⁹And God gave me the work of telling all people about the plan for his secret truth. That secret truth has been hidden in him since the beginning of time. He is the one who created everything. ¹⁰His purpose was that all the rulers and powers in the heavenly places will now know the many different ways he shows his wisdom. They will know this because of the church.* ¹¹This agrees with the plan God had since the beginning of time. He did what he planned, and he did it through Christ Jesus our Lord. ¹²In Christ we come before God with freedom and without fear. We can do this because of our faith in Christ. ¹³So I ask you not to be discouraged because of what is happening to me. My sufferings are for your benefit—for your honor and glory.*

The Love of Christ

¹⁴So I bow in prayer before the Father. ¹⁵Every family in heaven and on earth gets its true name from him. ¹⁶I ask the Father with his great glory* to give you the power to be strong in your spirits. He will give you that strength through his Spirit.* ¹⁷I pray that Christ will live in your hearts because of your faith. I pray that your life will be strong in love and be built on love. ¹⁸And I pray that you and all God's holy people* will have the power to understand the greatness of Christ's love—how wide, how long, how high, and how deep that love is. ¹⁹Christ's love is greater than anyone can ever know, but I pray that you will be able to know that love. Then you can be filled with everything God has for you.

²⁰With God's power working in us, he can do much, much more than anything we can ask or think of. ²¹To him be glory in the church* and in Christ Jesus for all time, forever and ever. Amen.*

The Unity of the Body

4 ¹So, as a prisoner for the Lord, I beg you to live the way God's people should live, because he chose you to be his. ²Always be humble and gentle. Be patient and accept each other with love. ³You are joined together with peace through the Spirit.* Do all you can to continue together in this way. Let

peace hold you together. ⁴There is one body and one Spirit, and God chose you to have one hope. ⁵There is one Lord, one faith, and one baptism.* ⁶There is one God and Father of us all, who rules over everyone. He works through all of us and in all of us.

⁷Christ gave each one of us a special gift. Everyone received what he wanted to give them. ⁸That is why the Scriptures* say,

> "He went up high into the sky;
>> he took prisoners with him,
>>> and he gave gifts to people."
>>>
>>> *Psalm 68:18*

⁹When it says, "He went up," what does it mean? It means that he first came down low to earth. ¹⁰So Christ came down, and he is the same one who went up. He went up above the highest heaven in order to fill everything with himself. ¹¹And that same Christ gave gifts to people—he made some to be apostles,* some to be prophets,* some to go and tell the Good News,* and some to care for and teach God's people.ᵃ ¹²Christ gave these gifts to prepare God's holy people* for the work of serving, to make the body of Christ stronger. ¹³This work must continue until we are all joined together in what we believe and in what we know about the Son of God. Our goal is to become like a full-grown man—to look just like Christ and have all his perfection.

¹⁴Then we will no longer be like babies. We will not be people who are always changing like a ship that the waves carry one way and then another. We will not be influenced by every new teaching we hear from people who are trying to deceive us—those who make clever plans and use every kind of trick to fool others into following the wrong way. ¹⁵No, we will speak the truth with love. We will grow to be like Christ in every way. He is the head, ¹⁶and the whole body depends on him. All the parts of the body are joined and held together, with each part doing its own work. This causes the whole body to grow and to be stronger in love.

The Way You Should Live

¹⁷I have something from the Lord to tell you. I warn you: Don't continue living like those who don't believe. Their thoughts are worth nothing. ¹⁸They have no understanding, and they know nothing because they refuse to listen. So they cannot have the life that God gives. ¹⁹They have lost their feeling of shame and use their lives to do what is morally wrong. More and more they want to do all kinds of evil. ²⁰But that way of life is nothing like what you learned when you came to know Christ. ²¹I know that you heard about him, and in him you were taught the truth. Yes, the truth is in Jesus. ²²You were taught to leave your old self. This means that you

---

ᵃ**4:11** *to care for … people* Literally, "to be shepherds and teachers."

must stop living the evil way you lived before. That old self gets worse and worse, because people are fooled by the evil they want to do. [23]You must be made new in your hearts and in your thinking. [24]Be that new person who was made to be like God, truly good and pleasing to him.

[25]So you must stop telling lies. "You must always speak the truth to each other,"[a] because we all belong to each other in the same body. [26]"When you are angry, don't let that anger make you sin,"[b] and don't stay angry all day. [27]Don't give the devil a way to defeat you. [28]Whoever has been stealing must stop it and start working. They must use their hands for doing something good. Then they will have something to share with those who are poor.

[29]When you talk, don't say anything bad. But say the good things that people need—whatever will help them grow stronger. Then what you say will be a blessing to those who hear you. [30]And don't make the Holy Spirit* sad. God gave you his Spirit as proof that you belong to him and that he will keep you safe until the day he makes you free. [31]Never be bitter, angry, or mad. Never shout angrily or say things to hurt others. Never do anything evil. [32]Be kind and loving to each other. Forgive each other the same as God forgave you through Christ.

5 [1]You are God's dear children, so try to be like him. [2]Live a life of love. Love others just as Christ loved us. He gave himself for us—a sweet-smelling offering and sacrifice* to God.

[3]But there must be no sexual sin among you. There must not be any kind of evil or selfishly wanting more and more, because such things are not right for God's holy people.* [4]Also, there must be no evil talk among you. Don't say things that are foolish or filthy. These are not for you. But you should be giving thanks to God. [5]You can be sure of this: No one will have a place in the kingdom of Christ and of God if that person commits sexual sins, or does evil things, or is a person who selfishly wants more and more. A greedy person like that is serving a false god.

[6]Don't let anyone fool you with words they don't really believe. God gets very angry when people who don't obey him talk like that. [7]So don't have anything to do with them. [8]In the past you were full of darkness,* but now you are full of light* in the Lord. So live like children who belong to the light. [9]This light produces every kind of goodness, right living, and truth. [10]Try to learn what pleases the Lord. [11]Have no part in the things that people in darkness do, which produce nothing good. Instead, tell everyone how wrong those things are. [12]It is really very shameful to even talk about the things those people do in secret. [13]But the light makes clear how wrong those

[a]4:25 Quote from Zech. 8:16.   [b]4:26 Quote from Ps. 4:4.

things are. [14]Yes, everything is made clear by the light. This is why we say,

"Wake up, you who are sleeping!
Rise from death, and Christ will shine on you."

[15]So be very careful how you live. Live wisely, not like fools. [16]I mean that you should use every opportunity you have for doing good, because these are evil times. [17]So don't be foolish with your lives, but learn what the Lord wants you to do. [18]Don't be drunk with wine, which will ruin your life, but be filled with the Spirit.* [19]Encourage each other with psalms, hymns, and spiritual songs. Sing and make music in your hearts to the Lord. [20]Always give thanks to God the Father for everything in the name of our Lord Jesus Christ.

Wives and Husbands

[21]Be willing to serve each other out of respect for Christ.

[22]Wives, be willing to serve your husbands the same as the Lord. [23]A husband is the head of his wife, just as Christ is the head of the church.* Christ is the Savior of the church, which is his body. [24]The church serves under Christ, so it is the same with you wives. You should be willing to serve your husbands in everything.

[25]Husbands, love your wives the same as Christ loved the church and gave his life for it. [26]He died to make the church holy.* He used the telling of the Good News* to make the church clean by washing it with water. [27]Christ died so that he could give the church to himself like a bride in all her beauty. He died so that the church could be holy and without fault, with no evil or sin or any other thing wrong in it.

[28]And husbands should love their wives like that. They should love their wives as they love their own bodies. The man who loves his wife loves himself, [29]because no one ever hates his own body, but feeds and takes care of it. And that is what Christ does for the church [30]because we are parts of his body. [31]The Scriptures* say, "That is why a man will leave his father and mother and join his wife, and the two people will become one."[a] [32]That secret truth is very important—I am talking about Christ and the church. [33]But each one of you must love his wife as he loves himself. And a wife must respect her husband.

Children and Parents

6 [1]Children, obey your parents the way the Lord wants, because this is the right thing to do. [2]The command says, "You must respect your father and mother."[b] That is the first command that has a promise with it. [3]That promise is: "Then

---

[a]5:31 Quote from Gen. 2:24.   [b]6:2 Quote from Ex. 20:12; Deut. 5:16.

everything will be fine with you, and you will have a long life on the earth."[a]

[4]Fathers, don't make your children angry, but raise them with the kind of teaching and training you learn from the Lord.

Slaves and Masters

[5]Slaves, obey your masters here on earth with fear and respect. And do that with a heart that is true, the same as you obey Christ. [6]You must do this not just to please your masters while they are watching, but all the time. Since you are really slaves of Christ, you must do with all your heart what God wants. [7]Do your work, and be happy to do it. Work as though it is the Lord you are serving, not just an earthly master. [8]Remember that the Lord will give everyone a reward for doing good. Everyone, slave or free, will get a reward for the good things they do.

[9]Masters, in the same way, be good to your slaves. Don't say things to scare them. You know that the one who is your Master and their Master is in heaven, and he judges everyone the same.

Wear the Full Armor of God

[10]To end my letter I tell you, be strong in the Lord and in his great power. [11]Wear the full armor of God. Wear God's armor so that you can fight against the devil's clever tricks. [12]Our fight is not against people on earth. We are fighting against the rulers and authorities and the powers of this world's darkness. We are fighting against the spiritual powers of evil in the heavenly places. [13]That is why you need to get God's full armor. Then on the day of evil you will be able to stand strong. And when you have finished the whole fight, you will still be standing.

[14]So stand strong with the belt of truth tied around your waist, and on your chest wear the protection of right living. [15]On your feet wear the Good News* of peace to help you stand strong. [16]And also use the shield of faith with which you can stop all the burning arrows that come from the Evil One.* [17]Accept God's salvation as your helmet. And take the sword of the Spirit*—that sword is the teaching of God. [18]Pray in the Spirit at all times. Pray with all kinds of prayers, and ask for everything you need. To do this you must always be ready. Never give up. Always pray for all of God's people.

[19]Also pray for me—that when I speak, God will give me words so that I can tell the secret truth about the Good News without fear. [20]I have the work of speaking for that Good News, and that is what I am doing now, here in prison. Pray that when I tell people the Good News, I will speak without fear as I should.

[a]6:3 Quote from Ex. 20:12; Deut. 5:16.

Final Greetings

²¹I am sending you Tychicus, the brother we love. He is a faithful servant of the Lord's work. He will tell you everything that is happening with me. Then you will know how I am and what I am doing. ²²That's why I am sending him—to let you know how we are and to encourage you.

²³I pray that God the Father and the Lord Jesus Christ will give peace and love with faith to all the brothers and sisters there. ²⁴God's grace* to all of you who love our Lord Jesus Christ with love that never ends.

Final Greeting

²¹I am sending you Tychicus, the brother we love. He is a faithful servant of the Lord's work. He will tell you everything that is happening with me. Then you will know how I am and what I am doing. ²²That's why I am sending him—to let you know how we are and to encourage you.

²³Peace to all the brothers and sisters there. And love with faith to you from God the Father and the Lord Jesus Christ. ²⁴Grace to all of you who love our Lord Jesus.

Philippians

1 ¹Greetings from Paul and Timothy, servants of Jesus Christ. To all of you in Philippi who are God's holy people* in Christ Jesus, including your elders*ᵃ* and special servants.*

²Grace* and peace to you from God our Father and the Lord Jesus Christ.

Paul's Prayer

³I thank God every time I remember you. ⁴And I always pray for all of you with joy. ⁵I thank God for the help you gave me while I told people the Good News.* You helped from the first day you believed until now. ⁶I am sure that the good work God began in you will continue until he completes it on the day when Jesus Christ comes again.

⁷I know I am right to think like this about all of you because you are so close to my heart. This is because you have all played such an important part in God's grace* to me—now, during this time that I am in prison, and whenever I am defending and proving the truth of the Good News. ⁸God knows that I want very much to see you. I love all of you with the love of Christ Jesus.

⁹This is my prayer for you:

that your love will grow more and more;
that you will have knowledge and understanding
    with your love;
¹⁰ that you will see the difference between what is important
    and what is not and choose what is important;
that you will be pure and blameless for the coming of Christ;
¹¹ that your life will be full of the many good works
    that are produced by Jesus Christ to bring glory*
    and praise to God.

Paul's Troubles Help the Lord's Work

¹²Brothers and sisters, I want you to know that all that has happened to me has helped to spread the Good News.* ¹³All the Roman guards and all the others here know that I am in prison for serving Christ. ¹⁴My being in prison has caused most of the believers* to put their trust in the Lord and to show more courage in telling people God's message.*

---

*ᵃ**1:1** *elders* Here, literally, "overseers." See "elders" in the Word List.

¹⁵Some people are telling the message about Christ because they are jealous and bitter. Others do it because they want to help. ¹⁶They are doing it out of love. They know that God gave me the work of defending the Good News. ¹⁷But those others tell about Christ because of their selfish ambition. Their reason for doing it is wrong. They only do it because they think it will make trouble for me in prison. ¹⁸But that doesn't matter. What is important is that they are telling people about Christ, whether they are sincere or not. So I am glad they are doing it.

I will continue to be glad, ¹⁹because I know that your prayers and the help the Spirit* of Jesus Christ gives me will cause this trouble to result in my freedom.ᵃ ²⁰I am full of hope and feel sure I will not have any reason to be ashamed. I am certain I will have now the same boldness to speak freely that I always have. I will let God use my life to bring more honor to Christ. It doesn't matter whether I live or die. ²¹To me, the only important thing about living is Christ. And even death would be for my benefit.ᵇ ²²If I continue living here on earth, I will be able to work for the Lord. But what would I choose—to live or to die? I don't know. ²³It would be a hard choice. Sometimes I want to leave this life and be with Christ. That would be much better for me; ²⁴however, you people need me here alive. ²⁵I am sure of this, so I know that I will stay here and be with you to help you grow and have joy in your faith. ²⁶When I am there with you again, you will be bursting with pride over what Christ Jesus did to help me.

²⁷Just be sure you live as God's people in a way that honors the Good News of Christ. Then if I come and visit you or if I am away from you, I will hear good things about you. I will know that you stand together with the same purpose and that you work together like a team to help others believe the Good News. ²⁸And you will not be afraid of those who are against you. All of this is proof from God that you are being saved and that your enemies will be lost. ²⁹God gave you the honor of believing in Christ. But that is not all. He also gave you the honor of suffering for Christ. Both of these bring glory* to Christ. ³⁰You saw the difficulties I had to face, and you hear that I am still having troubles. Now you must face them too.

Be United and Care for Each Other

2 ¹Think about what we have in Christ: the encouragement he has brought us, the comfort of his love, our sharing in his Spirit,* and the mercy and kindness he has shown us. If you enjoy these blessings, ²then do what will make my joy complete: Agree with each other, and show your love for each other. Be united in your goals and in the way you think. ³In whatever you do, don't let selfishness or pride be your guide. Be humble, and

---

ᵃ **1:19** *freedom* Or, "salvation." ᵇ **1:21** *death … benefit* Paul says that death would be better, because death would bring him nearer to Christ.

honor others more than yourselves. [4]Don't be interested only in your own life, but care about the lives of others too.

Learn From Christ to Be Unselfish

[5]In your life together, think the way Christ Jesus thought. [6]He was like God in every way, but he did not think that his being equal with God was something to use for his own benefit. [7]Instead, he gave up everything, even his place with God. He accepted the role of a servant, appearing in human form. During his life as a man, [8]he humbled himself by being fully obedient to God, even when that caused him to die. And he died on a cross.

[9]So God raised him up to the most important place and gave him the name that is greater than any other name. [10]God did this so that every person will bow down to honor the name of Jesus. Everyone in heaven, on earth, and under the earth will bow. [11]They will all confess, "Jesus Christ is Lord," and this will bring glory* to God the Father.

Be the People God Wants You to Be

[12]My dear friends, you always obeyed what you were taught. Just as you obeyed when I was with you, it is even more important for you to obey now that I am not there. You must continue to live in a way that gives meaning to your salvation. Do this with fear and respect for God. [13]Yes, it is God who is working in you. He helps you want to do what pleases him, and he gives you the power to do it.

[14]Do everything without complaining or arguing [15]so that you will be blameless and pure, children of God without any fault. But you are living with evil people all around you, who have lost their sense of what is right. Among those people you shine like lights in a dark world, [16]and you offer them the teaching that gives life. So I can be proud of you when Christ comes again. You will show that my work was not wasted—that I ran in the race and won.

[17]Your faith makes you give your lives as a sacrifice* in serving God. Maybe I will have to offer my own life with your sacrifice. But if that happens, I will be glad, and I will share my joy with all of you. [18]You also should be glad and share your joy with me.

News About Timothy and Epaphroditus

[19]With the blessing of the Lord Jesus, I hope I will be able to send Timothy to you soon. I will be glad to learn how you are. [20]I have no one else like Timothy, who genuinely cares for you. [21]Others are interested only in their own lives. They don't care about the work of Christ Jesus. [22]You know the kind of person Timothy is. He has served with me in telling the Good News* like a son with his father. [23]I plan to send him to you quickly, as

soon as I know what will happen to me. [24]I am sure the Lord will help me come to you soon.

[25]For now, I think I must send Epaphroditus back to you. He is my brother in God's family, who works and serves with me in the Lord's army. When I needed help, you sent him to me, [26]but now he wants very much to see all of you again. He is worried because you heard that he was sick. [27]He was sick and near death. But God helped him and me too, so that I would not have even more grief. [28]So I want very much to send him to you. When you see him, you can be happy. And I can stop worrying about you. [29]Welcome him in the Lord with much joy. Give honor to people like Epaphroditus. [30]He should be honored because he almost died for the work of Christ. He put his life in danger so that he could help me. This was help that you could not give me.

Christ Is More Important Than Anything

3 [1]And now, my brothers and sisters, be filled with joy in the Lord. It is no trouble for me to write the same things to you again. I want to be sure that you are prepared.

[2]Be careful of the dogs—those people whose work does no one any good. They want to cut off everyone who isn't circumcised.[a] [3]But we are the ones who have the true circumcision[b]— we who worship God through his Spirit.* We don't trust in ourselves or anything we can do. We take pride only in Christ Jesus. [4]Even if I am able to trust in myself, still I don't do it. If anyone else thinks they have a reason to trust in themselves, they should know that I have a greater reason for doing so. [5]I was circumcised on the eighth day after my birth. I am from the people of Israel* and the tribe of Benjamin. I am a true Jew, and so were my parents. The law was very important to me. That is why I became a Pharisee.* [6]I was such a fanatic that I persecuted* the church.* And no one could find fault with how I always obeyed the law.

[7]At one time all these things were important to me. But because of Christ, I decided that they are worth nothing. [8]Not only these things, but now I think that all things are worth nothing compared with the greatness of knowing Christ Jesus my Lord. Because of Christ, I lost all these things, and now I know that they are all worthless trash. All I want now is Christ. [9]I want to belong to him. In Christ I am right with God, but my being right does not come from following the law. It comes from God through faith. God uses my faith in[c] Christ to make

---

[a]**3:2** *want to cut off ... circumcised* There is a play on words here in Greek. The key word is like "circumcision" (see the Word List), but it means "mutilation" or "cutting to pieces." [b]**3:3** *we are ... circumcision* Literally, "we are the circumcision." Paul uses the word "circumcision" (see the Word List) here in a spiritual sense of believers who share in the new agreement that God gave his people through Jesus. [c]**3:9** *my faith in* Or, "the faithfulness of."

me right with him. [10]All I want is to know Christ and the power that raised him from death. I want to share in his sufferings and be like him even in his death. [11]Then there is hope that I myself will somehow be raised from death.

Trying to Reach the Goal

[12]I don't mean that I am exactly what God wants me to be. I have not yet reached that goal. But I continue trying to reach it and make it mine. That's what Christ Jesus wants me to do. It is the reason he made me his. [13]Brothers and sisters, I know that I still have a long way to go. But there is one thing I do: I forget what is in the past and try as hard as I can to reach the goal before me. [14]I keep running hard toward the finish line to get the prize that is mine because God has called me through Christ Jesus to life up there in heaven.

[15]All of us who have grown to be spiritually mature should think this way too. And if there is any of this that you don't agree with, God will make it clear to you. [16]But we should continue following the truth we already have.

[17]Brothers and sisters, join together in following my example. Also, learn by watching those who are living the way we showed you. [18]There are many who live like enemies of the cross of Christ. I have often told you about them. And it makes me cry to tell you about them now. [19]The way they live is leading them to destruction. They have replaced God with their own desires. They do shameful things, and they are proud of what they do. They think only about earthly things. [20]But the government that rules us is in heaven. We are waiting for our Savior, the Lord Jesus Christ, to come from there. [21]He will change our humble bodies and make them like his own glorious body. Christ can do this by his power, with which he is able to rule everything.

Some Things to Do

4 [1]My dear brothers and sisters, I love you and want to see you. You bring me joy and make me proud of you. Continue following the Lord as I have told you.

[2]Euodia and Syntyche, you both belong to the Lord, so please agree with each other. [3]For this I make a special request to my friend who has served with me so faithfully: Help these women. They worked hard with me in telling people the Good News,* together with Clement and others who worked with me. Their names are written in the book of life.[a]

[4]Always be filled with joy in the Lord. I will say it again. Be filled with joy.

[5]Let everyone see that you are gentle and kind. The Lord is coming soon. [6]Don't worry about anything, but pray and ask

---

[a] 4:3 book of life God's book that has the names of all God's chosen people. See Rev. 3:5; 21:27.

God for everything you need, always giving thanks for what you have. [7]And because you belong to Jesus Christ, God's peace will stand guard over all your thoughts and feelings. His peace can do this far better than our human minds.[a]

[8]Brothers and sisters, continue to think about what is good and worthy of praise. Think about what is true and honorable and right and pure and beautiful and respected. [9]And do what you learned and received from me. Do what I told you and what you saw me do. And the God who gives peace will be with you.

Paul Thanks the Philippian Believers

[10]I am so happy, and I thank the Lord that you have again shown your care for me. You continued to care about me, but there was no way for you to show it. [11]I am telling you this, but not because I need something. I have learned to be satisfied with what I have and with whatever happens. [12]I know how to live when I am poor and when I have plenty. I have learned the secret of how to live through any kind of situation—when I have enough to eat or when I am hungry, when I have everything I need or when I have nothing. [13]Christ is the one who gives me the strength I need to do whatever I must do.

[14]But it was good that you helped me when I needed help. [15]You people in Philippi remember when I first told the Good News* there. When I left Macedonia,* you were the only church* that gave me help. [16]Several times you sent me things I needed when I was in Thessalonica. [17]Really, it is not that I want to get gifts from you. But I want you to have the benefit that comes from giving. [18]I have everything I need. I have even more than I need. I have all I need because Epaphroditus brought your gift to me. Your gift is like a sweet-smelling sacrifice* offered to God. God accepts that sacrifice and it pleases him. [19]My God will use his glorious riches to give you everything you need. He will do this through Christ Jesus. [20]Glory* to our God and Father forever and ever. Amen.*

[21]Give our greetings to God's people there—to each one who belongs to Christ Jesus. Those in God's family who are with me send you their greetings. [22]And greetings to you from all of God's people here, including those from Caesar's* palace.

[23]The grace* of the Lord Jesus Christ be with you all.

---

[a]**4:7** *can do this ... minds* Literally, "surpasses (is better than) every mind," which could also have the meaning, "is beyond all understanding."

Colossians

1 ¹Greetings from Paul, an apostle* of Christ Jesus. I am an apostle because that is what God wanted. Greetings also from Timothy, our brother in Christ.

²To the holy* and faithful brothers and sisters in Christ who live in Colossae.

Grace* and peace to you from God our Father.

³In our prayers we always thank God for you. He is the Father of our Lord Jesus Christ. ⁴We thank him because we have heard about the faith you have in Christ Jesus and the love you have for all of God's people. ⁵Your faith and love continue because you know what is waiting for you in heaven— the hope you have had since you first heard the true message, the Good News* ⁶that was told to you. Throughout the world, this Good News is bringing blessings and is spreading. And that's what has been happening among you since the first time you heard it and understood the truth about God's grace. ⁷You heard it from Epaphras, our dear friend and co-worker. He is a faithful servant of Christ for you. ⁸He also told us about the love you have from the Spirit.*

⁹Since the day we heard these things about you, we have continued praying for you. This is what we pray:

that you will know fully what God wants;
that with your knowledge you will also have great wisdom
    and understanding in spiritual things;
¹⁰ that this will help you live in a way that brings honor
    to the Lord and pleases him in every way;
that your life will produce good works of every kind
    and that you will grow in your knowledge of God*;
¹¹ that God will strengthen you with his own great power,
    so that you will be patient and not give up
    when troubles come.

Then you will be happy ¹²and give thanks to the Father. He has made you able to have what he has promised to give all his holy people,* who live in the light.* ¹³God made us free from the power of darkness.* And he brought us into the kingdom of his dear Son. ¹⁴The Son paid the price to make us free. In him we have forgiveness of our sins.

ᵃ1:10 that your life ... God Or, "that your knowledge of God will produce more and more good works of every kind in your life."

Christ Is the Same as God

¹⁵No one can see God, but Jesus is exactly like God. Jesus rules over everything that has been made.ᵃ ¹⁶Through his power all things were made: things in heaven and on earth, seen and not seen—all spiritual rulers, lords, powers, and authorities. Everything was made through Christ and for Christ. ¹⁷He was there before anything was made. And all things continue because of him. ¹⁸Christ is the head of the body, which is the church.* He is the beginning of everything else. And he is the first among all who will be raised from death.ᵇ So in everything he is most important. ¹⁹God was pleased for all of himself to live in Christ. ²⁰And through Christ, God was happy to bring all things back to himself again—things on earth and things in heaven. God made peace by using the blood sacrifice of Christ on the cross.

²¹At one time you were separated from God. You were his enemies in your minds, because the evil you did was against him. ²²But now Christ has made you God's friends again. Christ did this by his death while he was in his body. He did this so that he could bring you before God. He brings you before God as people who are holy,* blameless, and without anything that would make you guilty before God. ²³Christ will do this if you continue to believe in the Good News* you heard. You must remain strong and sure in your faith. You must not let anything cause you to give up the hope that became yours when you heard the Good News. That same Good News has been told to everyone on earth, and that's the work that I, Paul, was given to do.

Paul's Work for the Church

²⁴I am happy in my sufferings for you. There is much that Christ must still suffer through his body, the church.* I am accepting my part of what must be suffered. I accept these sufferings in my body. ²⁵I became a servant of the church because God gave me a special work to do. This work helps you. My work is to tell the complete message of God. ²⁶This message is the secret truth that was hidden since the beginning of time. It was hidden from everyone for ages, but now it has been made known to God's holy people.* ²⁷God decided to let his people know that rich and glorious truth, which is for all people. That truth is Christ himself, who is in you. He is our only hope for glory.* ²⁸So we continue to tell people about Christ. We use all wisdom to counsel every person and teach every person. We are trying to bring everyone before God as people who have grown to be spiritually mature in Christ. ²⁹To do this, I work and struggle using the great strength that Christ gives me. That strength is working in my life.

ᵃ**1:15** *rules … made* Literally, "firstborn of all creation." ᵇ**1:18** *first … death* Literally, "firstborn from the dead."

2 ¹I want you to know that I am trying very hard to help you. And I am trying to help those in Laodicea and others who have never seen me. ²I want them to be strengthened and joined together with love and to have the full confidence that comes from understanding. I want them to know completely the secret truth that God has made known. That truth is Christ himself. ³In him all the treasures of wisdom and knowledge are kept safe.

⁴I tell you this so that no one can fool you by telling you ideas that seem good, but are false. ⁵Even though I am far away, my thoughts are always with you. I am happy to see your good lives and your strong faith in Christ.

Continue to Live in Christ

⁶You received Christ Jesus the Lord, so continue to live following him without changing anything. ⁷You must depend on Christ only. Life and strength come from him. You were taught the truth, and you must continue to be sure of that true teaching. And always be thankful.

⁸Be sure you are not led away by the teaching of those who have nothing worth saying and only plan to deceive you. That teaching is not from Christ. It is only human tradition and comes from the powers that influence*ᵃ* this world. ⁹I say this because all of God lives in Christ fully, even in his life on earth. ¹⁰And because you belong to Christ you are complete, having everything you need. Christ is ruler over every other power and authority.

¹¹In Christ you had a different kind of circumcision,*ᵇ* one that was not done by human hands. That is, you were made free from the power of your sinful self. That is the kind of circumcision Christ does. ¹²When you were baptized,* you were buried with Christ, and you were raised up with him because of your faith in God's power. God's power was shown when he raised Christ from death.

¹³You were spiritually dead because of your sins and because you were not free from the power of your sinful self. But God gave you new life together with Christ. He forgave all our sins. ¹⁴Because we broke God's laws, we owed a debt—a debt that listed all the rules we failed to follow. But God forgave us of that debt. He took it away and nailed it to the cross. ¹⁵He defeated the rulers and powers of the spiritual world. With the cross he won the victory over them and led them away, as defeated and powerless prisoners, for the whole world to see.

Don't Follow Rules That People Make

¹⁶So don't let anyone make rules for you about eating and drinking or about Jewish customs (festivals, New Moon*

---

*ᵃ*2:8 *powers that influence* Or, "elementary rules of." Also in verse 20. *ᵇ*2:11 *circumcision* See the Word List. Paul uses it here in a spiritual sense of believers who share in the new agreement God gave his people through Jesus.

celebrations, or Sabbath* days). [17]In the past these things were like a shadow that showed what was coming. But the new things that were coming are found in Christ. [18]Some people enjoy acting as if they are humble and love to worship angels.[a] They always talk about the visions* they have seen. Don't listen to them when they say you are wrong because you don't do these things. It is so foolish for them to feel such pride, because it is all based on their own human ideas. [19]They don't keep themselves under the control of the head. Christ is the head, and the whole body depends on him. Because of Christ all the parts of the body care for each other and help each other. So the body is made stronger and held together as God causes it to grow.

[20]You died with Christ and were made free from the powers that influence this world. So why do you act as if you still belong to the world? I mean, why do you follow rules like these: [21]"Don't eat this," "Don't taste that," "Don't touch that"? [22]These rules are talking about earthly things that are gone after they are used. They are only human commands and teachings. [23]These rules may seem to be wise as part of a made-up religion in which people pretend to be humble and punish their bodies. But they don't help people stop doing the evil that the sinful self wants to do.

Your New Life in Christ

3 [1]You were raised from death with Christ. So live for what is in heaven, where Christ is sitting at the right hand of God. [2]Think only about what is up there, not what is here on earth. [3]Your old sinful self has died, and your new life is kept with Christ in God. [4]Yes, Christ is now your life, and when he comes again, you will share in his glory.*

[5]So put everything evil out of your life: sexual sin, doing anything immoral, letting sinful thoughts control you, and wanting things that are wrong. And don't keep wanting more and more for yourself, which is the same as worshiping a false god. [6]God will show his anger against those who don't obey him,[b] because they do these evil things. [7]You also did these things in the past, when you lived like them.

[8]But now put these things out of your life: anger, losing your temper, doing or saying things to hurt others, and saying shameful things. [9]Don't lie to each other, because you have left your old sinful life and what you did before. [10]You have begun to live a new life in which you are being made new. You are becoming like the one who made you. This new life brings you the true knowledge of God. [11]In this new life it doesn't matter if you are a Greek* or a Jew, circumcised* or not. It doesn't matter if you speak a different language or even if you are a

---

[a]**2:18** *worship angels* Or, "worship with angels" (that they see in visions). [b]**3:6** *against … him* Some Greek copies do not have these words.

Scythian.[a] It doesn't matter if you are a slave or free. Christ is all that matters, and he is in all of you.

Your New Life With Each Other

[12]God has chosen you and made you his holy people.[*] He loves you. So your new life should be like this: Show mercy to others. Be kind, humble, gentle, and patient. [13]Don't be angry with each other, but forgive each other. If you feel someone has wronged you, forgive them. Forgive others because the Lord forgave you. [14]Together with these things, the most important part of your new life is to love each other. Love is what holds everything together in perfect unity. [15]Let the peace that Christ gives control your thinking. It is for peace that you were chosen to be together in one body.[b] And always be thankful.

[16]Let the teaching of Christ live inside you richly. Use all wisdom to teach and counsel each other. Sing psalms, hymns, and spiritual songs with thankfulness in your hearts to God. [17]Everything you say and everything you do should be done for Jesus your Lord. And in all you do, give thanks to God the Father through Jesus.

Your New Life at Home

[18]Wives, be willing to serve your husbands. This is the right thing to do in following the Lord.

[19]Husbands, love your wives, and be gentle to them.

[20]Children, obey your parents in everything. This pleases the Lord.

[21]Fathers, don't frustrate your children. If you are too hard to please, they might want to quit trying.

[22]Servants, obey your masters in everything. Obey all the time, even when they can't see you. Don't just pretend to work hard so that they will treat you well. No, you must serve your masters honestly because you respect the Lord. [23]In all the work you are given, do the best you can. Work as though you are working for the Lord, not any earthly master. [24]Remember that you will receive your reward from the Lord, who will give you what he promised his people. You are serving the Lord Christ. [25]Remember that anyone who does wrong will be punished for that wrong. And the Lord treats everyone the same.

4 [1]Masters, give what is good and fair to your servants. Remember that you have a Master in heaven.

Some Things to Do

[2]Never stop praying. Be ready for anything by praying and being thankful. [3]Also pray for us. Pray that God will give us an

---

[a]3:11 *Scythians* Known as wild and uncivilized people. [b]3:15 *body* Christ's spiritual body, meaning the church—his people.

opportunity to tell people his message.* I am in prison for doing this. But pray that we can continue to tell people the secret truth that God has made known about Christ. 4Pray that I will say what is necessary to make this truth clear to everyone.

5Be wise in the way you act with those who are not believers. Use your time in the best way you can. 6When you talk, you should always be kind and wise. Then you will be able to answer everyone in the way you should.

News About Those With Paul

7Tychicus is my dear brother in Christ. He is a faithful helper and he serves the Lord with me. He will tell you everything that is happening with me. 8That is why I am sending him. I want you to know how we are, and I am sending him to encourage you. 9I am sending him with Onesimus, the faithful and dear brother from your group. They will tell you everything that has happened here.

10Aristarchus, the one here in prison with me, sends you his greetings. Mark, the cousin of Barnabas, also sends his greetings. (I have already told you what to do about Mark. If he comes, welcome him.) 11And greetings from Jesus, the one who is also called Justus. These are the only Jewish believers who work with me for God's kingdom.* They have been a great comfort to me.

12Epaphras, another servant of Jesus Christ from your group, sends his greetings. He constantly struggles for you in prayer. He prays that you will grow to be spiritually mature and have everything that God wants for you. 13I know that he has worked hard for you and the people in Laodicea and in Hierapolis. 14Greetings also from Demas and our dear friend Luke, the doctor.

15Give our greetings to the brothers and sisters in Laodicea. Greetings also to Nympha and to the church* that meets in her house. 16After this letter is read to you, be sure it is also read to the church in Laodicea. And you read the letter that I wrote to them. 17Tell Archippus, "Be sure to do the work the Lord gave you."

18Here's my greeting in my own handwriting—PAUL. Remember me in prison. God's grace* be with you.

1 Thessalonians

1 ¹Greetings from Paul, Silas, and Timothy.
To the church* of those in Thessalonica, who are in God the Father and the Lord Jesus Christ.

Grace* and peace be yours.

The Life and Faith of the Thessalonians

²We always remember you when we pray, and we thank God for all of you. ³Every time we pray to God our Father we thank him for all that you have done because of your faith. And we thank him for the work you have done because of your love. And we thank him that you continue to be strong because of your hope in our Lord Jesus Christ.

⁴Brothers and sisters, God loves you. And we know that he has chosen you to be his people. ⁵When we brought the Good News* to you, we came with more than words. We brought that Good News with power, with the Holy Spirit,* and with the sure knowledge that it was true. Also you know how we lived when we were with you. We lived that way to help you. ⁶And you became like us and like the Lord. You suffered much, but still you accepted the teaching with joy. The Holy Spirit gave you that joy.

⁷You became an example to all the believers in Macedonia* and Achaia.* ⁸The Lord's teaching has spread from you throughout Greece and beyond. In fact, your faith in God has become known everywhere, so we never have to tell anyone about it. ⁹People everywhere are already telling the story about the good way you accepted us when we were there with you. They tell about how you stopped worshiping idols* and changed to serve the living and true God. ¹⁰And you began waiting for God's Son to come from heaven—the Son God raised from death. He is Jesus, who saves us from God's angry judgment that is coming.

Paul's Work in Thessalonica

2 ¹Brothers and sisters, you know that our visit to you was not a failure. ²Before we came to you, people in Philippi abused us with insults and made us suffer. You know all about that. And then, when we came to you, many people there caused trouble for us. But our God gave us the courage we needed to tell you his Good News.* ³When we encourage people to

believe the Good News, it's not out of wrong motives. We are not trying to trick or fool anyone. ⁴No, it was God who gave us this work, but only after he tested us and saw that we could be trusted to do it. So when we speak, we are not trying to please people. We are only trying to please God. He is the one who can see what is in our hearts.

⁵You know that we never tried to influence you by saying nice things about you. We were not trying to get your money. We had no greed to hide from you. God knows that this is true. ⁶We were not looking for praise from people. We were not looking for praise from you or anyone else.

⁷When we were with you, as apostles* of Christ we could have used our authority to make you help us. But we were very gentle*ᵃ* with you. We were like a mother caring for her little children. ⁸We loved you very much, so we were happy to share God's Good News with you. But not only that—we were also happy to share even our own lives with you. ⁹Brothers and sisters, I know that you remember how hard we worked. We worked night and day to support ourselves, so that we would not be a burden to anyone while we did the work of telling you God's Good News.

¹⁰When we were there with you believers, we were pure, honest, and without fault in the way we lived. You know, just as God does, that this is true. ¹¹You know that we treated each one of you like a father treats his own children. ¹²We encouraged you, we comforted you, and we told you to live good lives for God. He calls you to be part of his glorious kingdom.

¹³Also, we always thank God because of the way you accepted his message.* You heard it and accepted it as God's message, not our own. And it really is God's message. And it works in you who believe. ¹⁴Brothers and sisters, you are like God's churches* in Christ Jesus that are in Judea.*ᵇ* You were treated badly by your own people, just as God's people in Judea were treated badly by the other Jews there. ¹⁵Those Jews killed the Lord Jesus and the prophets.* And they forced us to leave their country. They are not pleasing to God, and they are against everyone else. ¹⁶And they are trying to stop us from teaching those who are not Jews. They don't want them to be saved. But they are just adding more and more sins to the ones they already have. Now the time has come for them to suffer God's anger.

Paul's Desire to Visit Them Again

¹⁷Brothers and sisters, we were separated from you for a short time. But even though we were not there, our thoughts were still with you. We wanted very much to see you, and we tried

*ᵃ***2:7** *But ... gentle* Several Greek copies have "But we became babies." *ᵇ***2:14** *Judea* The Jewish land where Jesus lived and taught and where the church first began.

very hard to do this. ¹⁸Yes, we wanted to come to you. I, Paul, tried more than once to come, but Satan* stopped us. ¹⁹You are our hope, our joy, and the crown* we will be proud of when our Lord Jesus Christ comes. ²⁰You bring us honor and joy.

3 ¹⁻²We couldn't come to you, but it was very hard to wait any longer. So we decided to send Timothy to you and stay in Athens alone. Timothy is our brother. He works with us for God to tell people the Good News* about Christ. We sent Timothy to strengthen and encourage you in your faith. ³We sent him so that none of you would be upset by the troubles we have now. You yourselves know that we must have these troubles. ⁴Even when we were with you, we told you that we would all have to suffer. And you know that it happened just as we said. ⁵This is why I sent Timothy to you, so that I could know about your faith. I sent him when I could not wait anymore. I was afraid that the devil who tempts people might have defeated you with temptations. Then our hard work would have been wasted.

⁶But now Timothy has come back from his visit with you and told us good news about your faith and love. He told us that you always remember us in a good way. He told us that you want very much to see us again. And it is the same with us—we want very much to see you. ⁷So, brothers and sisters, we are encouraged about you because of your faith. We have much trouble and suffering, but still we are encouraged. ⁸Our life is really full if you stand strong in the Lord. ⁹We have so much joy before our God because of you! So we thank God for you. But we cannot thank him enough for all the joy we feel. ¹⁰Night and day we continue praying with all our heart that we can come there and see you again. We want to give you everything you need to make your faith strong.

¹¹We pray that our God and Father and our Lord Jesus will prepare the way for us to come to you. ¹²We pray that the Lord will make your love grow. We pray that he will give you more and more love for each other and for all people. We pray that you will love everyone like we love you. ¹³This will strengthen your desire to do what is right, and you will be holy* and without fault before our God and Father when our Lord Jesus comes with all his holy people.*

A Life That Pleases God

4 ¹Brothers and sisters, now I have some other things to tell you. We taught you how to live in a way that will please God. And you are living that way. Now we ask and encourage you in the Lord Jesus to live that way more and more. ²You know all that we told you to do by the authority of the Lord Jesus. ³God wants you to be holy.* He wants you to stay away from sexual sins. ⁴God wants each one of you to learn to control your own body. Use your body in a way that is holy and that gives honor to God.[a] [5]Don't let your physical desires control you. That's what happens to the people of the world who don't know God. [6]None of you should do wrong to any of your fellow believers* or cheat them in this way. The Lord will punish those who do that. We have already told you this and warned you about it. [7]God chose us to be holy. He does not want us to live in sin. [8]So anyone who refuses to obey this teaching is refusing to obey God, not us. And God is the one who gives you his Holy Spirit.*

[9]We don't need to write to you about having love for your brothers and sisters in Christ. God has already taught you to love each other. [10]In fact, you love the brothers and sisters in all of Macedonia.* We encourage you now, brothers and sisters, to show your love more and more.

[11]Do all you can to live a peaceful life. Mind your own business, and earn your own living, as we told you before. [12]If you do these things, then those who are not believers will respect the way you live. And you will not have to depend on others for what you need.

The Lord's Coming

[13]Brothers and sisters, we want you to know about those who have died. We don't want you to be sad like other people—those who have no hope. [14]We believe that Jesus died, but we also believe that he rose again. So we believe that God will raise to life through Jesus any who have died and bring them together with him when he comes.

[15]What we tell you now is the Lord's own message. Those of us who are still living when the Lord comes again will join him, but not before those who have already died. [16]The Lord himself will come down from heaven with a loud command, with the voice of the archangel,* and with the trumpet call of God. And the people who have died and were in Christ will rise first. [17]After that, we who are still alive at that time will be gathered up with those who have died. We will be taken up in the clouds and meet the Lord in the air. And we will be with the Lord forever. [18]So encourage each other with these words.

Be Ready for the Lord's Coming

5 [1]Now, brothers and sisters, we don't need to write to you about times and dates. [2]You know very well that the day when the Lord comes again will be a surprise, like a thief who comes at night. [3]People will say, "We have peace and we are safe." At that time destruction will come to them quickly, like the pains of a woman who is having a baby. And those people will not escape.

---

[a]**4:4** *God wants . . . honor to God* Or, "God wants each of you to learn to live with your wife in a way that is holy and that gives honor to God."

[4]But you, brothers and sisters, are not living in darkness.* And so that day will not surprise you like a thief. [5]You are all people who belong to the light.* You belong to the day.* We don't belong to the night* or to darkness. [6]So we should not be like other people. We should not be sleeping. We should be awake and have self-control. [7]People who sleep, sleep at night. People who drink too much, drink at night. [8]But we belong to the day, so we should control ourselves. We should wear faith and love to protect us. And the hope of salvation should be our helmet.

[9]God did not choose us to suffer his anger. God chose us to have salvation through our Lord Jesus Christ. [10]Jesus died for us so that we can live together with him. It is not important if we are alive or dead when Jesus comes. [11]So encourage each other and help each other grow stronger in faith, just as you are already doing.

Final Instructions and Greetings

[12]Now brothers and sisters, we ask you to recognize the value of those who work hard among you—those who, as followers of the Lord, care for you and tell you how to live. [13]Show them the highest respect and love because of the work they do.

Live in peace with each other. [14]We ask you, brothers and sisters, to warn those who will not work. Encourage those who are afraid. Help those who are weak. Be patient with everyone. [15]Be sure that no one pays back wrong for wrong. But always try to do what is good for each other and for all people.

[16]Always be full of joy. [17]Never stop praying. [18]Whatever happens, always be thankful. This is how God wants you to live in Christ Jesus.

[19]Don't stop the work of the Holy Spirit.* [20]Don't treat prophecy* like something that is not important. [21]But test everything. Keep what is good, [22]and stay away from everything that is evil.

[23]We pray that God himself, the God of peace, will make you pure—belonging only to him. We pray that your whole self—spirit, soul, and body—will be kept safe and be blameless when our Lord Jesus Christ comes. [24]The one who calls you will do that for you. You can trust him.

[25]Brothers and sisters, please pray for us. [26]Give all the brothers and sisters the special greeting of God's people.[a] [27]I tell you by the authority of the Lord to read this letter to all the brothers and sisters. [28]The grace* of our Lord Jesus Christ be with you.

---

[a] 5:26 the special greeting of God's people Literally, "a holy kiss."

2 Thessalonians

1 ¹Greetings from Paul, Silas, and Timothy.
To the church* of those in Thessalonica, who are in God our Father and the Lord Jesus Christ.

²Grace* and peace to you from God the Father and the Lord Jesus Christ.

³We thank God for you always. And that's what we should do, because you give us good reason to be thankful: Your faith is growing more and more. And the love that every one of you has for each other is also growing. ⁴So we tell the other churches of God how proud we are of you. We tell them how you patiently continue to be strong and have faith, even though you are being persecuted* and are suffering many troubles.

Paul Tells About God's Judgment

⁵This is proof that God is right in his judgment. He wants you to be worthy of his kingdom.* Your suffering is for that kingdom. ⁶God will do what is right. He will punish those who are causing you trouble. ⁷And he will bring relief to you who are troubled. He will bring it to you and to us when the Lord Jesus comes from heaven for all to see, together with his powerful angels. ⁸He will come with burning fire to punish those who don't know God—those who refuse to accept the Good News* about our Lord Jesus Christ. ⁹They will be punished with a destruction that never ends. They will not be allowed to be with the Lord but will be kept away from his great power. ¹⁰This will happen on the day when the Lord Jesus comes to receive honor with his holy people.* He will be admired among all who have believed. And this includes you because you believed what we told you.

¹¹That is why we always pray for you. We ask our God to help you live the good way he wanted when he chose you. The goodness you have makes you want to do good. And the faith you have makes you work. We pray that with his power God will help you do these things more and more. ¹²Then the name of our Lord Jesus will be honored because of you, and you will be honored because of him. This can happen only by the grace* of our God and the Lord Jesus Christ.

Evil Things Will Happen

2 ¹Brothers and sisters, we have something to say about the coming of our Lord Jesus Christ. We want to talk to you

about that time when we will meet together with him. ²Don't let yourselves be easily upset or worried if you hear that the day of the Lord has already come. Someone might say that this idea came from us—in something the Spirit* told us, or in something we said, or in a letter we wrote. ³Don't be fooled by anything they might say. That day of the Lord will not come until the turning away from God happens. And that day will not come until the Man of Evil appears, the one who belongs to hell.*ᵃ ⁴He will stand against and put himself above everything that people worship or think is worthy of worship. He will even go into God's Temple*ᵇ and sit there, claiming that he is God.

⁵I told you before that all these things would happen. Remember? ⁶And you know what is stopping that Man of Evil now. He is being stopped now so that he will appear at the right time. ⁷The secret power of evil is already working in the world now. But there is one who is stopping that secret power of evil. And he will continue to stop it until he is taken out of the way. ⁸Then that Man of Evil will appear. But the Lord Jesus will kill him with the breath that comes from his mouth. The Lord will come in a way that everyone will see, and that will be the end of the Man of Evil.

⁹When that Man of Evil comes, it will be the work of Satan.* He will come with great power, and he will do all kinds of false miracles, signs, and wonders.*ᶜ ¹⁰The Man of Evil will use every kind of evil to fool those who are lost. They are lost because they refused to love the truth and be saved. ¹¹So God will send them something powerful that leads them away from the truth and causes them to believe a lie. ¹²They will all be condemned because they did not believe the truth and because they enjoyed doing evil.

You Are Chosen for Salvation

¹³Brothers and sisters, you are people the Lord loves. And we always thank God for you. That's what we should do, because God chose you to be some of the first people*ᵈ to be saved. You are saved by the Spirit* making you holy* and by your faith in the truth. ¹⁴God chose you to have that salvation. He chose you by using the Good News* that we told us. You were chosen so that you can share in the glory* of our Lord Jesus Christ. ¹⁵So, brothers and sisters, stand strong and continue to believe the teachings we gave you when we were there and by letter.

¹⁶⁻¹⁷We pray that the Lord Jesus Christ himself and God our Father will comfort you and strengthen you in every good thing you do and say. God loved us and gave us through his grace* a wonderful hope and comfort that has no end.

---

*ᵃ***2:3** *belongs to hell* Literally, "is the son of destruction." *ᵇ***2:4** *Temple* Probably the special building in Jerusalem where God commanded the Jews to worship. *ᶜ***2:9** *false miracles, signs, and wonders* Here, amazing acts done by Satan's power. *ᵈ***2:13** *to be … people* Some Greek copies say, "from the beginning."

Pray for Us

3 ¹And now, brothers and sisters, pray for us. Pray that the Lord's teaching will continue to spread quickly. And pray that people will give honor to that teaching, the same as happened with you. ²And pray that we will be protected from crooked and evil people. Not everyone believes in the Lord, you know.

³But the Lord is faithful. He will give you strength and protect you from the Evil One.* ⁴The Lord gives us confidence that you are doing what we told you and that you will continue to do it. ⁵We pray that the Lord will cause you to feel God's love and remember Christ's patient endurance.

The Obligation to Work

⁶Brothers and sisters, by the authority of our Lord Jesus Christ we tell you to stay away from any believer who refuses to work. People who refuse to work are not following the teaching that we gave them. ⁷You yourselves know that you should live like we do. We were not lazy when we were with you. ⁸We never accepted food from anyone without paying for it. We worked and worked so that we would not be a burden to any of you. We worked night and day. ⁹We had the right to ask you to help us. But we worked to take care of ourselves so that we would be an example for you to follow. ¹⁰When we were with you, we gave you this rule: "Whoever will not work should not be allowed to eat."

¹¹We hear that some people in your group refuse to work. They are doing nothing except being busy in the lives of others. ¹²Our instruction to them is to stop bothering others, to start working and earn their own food. It is by the authority of the Lord Jesus Christ that we are urging them to do this. ¹³Brothers and sisters, never get tired of doing good.

¹⁴If there are some there who refuse to do what we tell you in this letter, remember who they are. Don't associate with them. Then maybe they will feel ashamed. ¹⁵But don't treat them as enemies. Counsel them as fellow believers.*

Final Words

¹⁶We pray that the Lord of peace will give you peace at all times and in every way. The Lord be with you all.

¹⁷Here's my greeting in my own handwriting—PAUL. I do this in all my letters to show they are from me. This is the way I write.

¹⁸The grace* of our Lord Jesus Christ be with you all.

1 Timothy

¹Greetings from Paul, an apostle* of Christ Jesus. I am an apostle by the command of God our Savior and Christ Jesus our hope.

²To Timothy, a true son to me in the faith we share.

Grace,* mercy, and peace from God the Father and Christ Jesus our Lord.

Warnings Against False Teachings

³When I went to Macedonia,* I asked you to stay in Ephesus. Some people there are teaching things that are not true, and I want you to tell them to stop. ⁴Tell them not to give their time to meaningless stories and to long lists of names to prove their family histories. Such things only cause arguments. They don't help God's work, which is done only by faith. ⁵My purpose in telling you to do this is to promote love—the kind of love shown by those whose thoughts are pure, who do what they know is right, and whose faith in God is real. ⁶But some have missed this key point in their teaching and have gone off in another direction. Now they talk about things that help no one. ⁷They want to be teachers of the law,ᵃ but they don't know what they are talking about. They don't even understand the things they say they are sure of.

⁸We know that the law is good if someone uses it right. ⁹We also know that the law is not made for those who do what is right. It is made for those who are against the law and refuse to follow it. The law is for sinners who are against God and all that is pleasing to him. It is for those who have no interest in spiritual things and for those who kill their fathers or mothers or anyone else. ¹⁰It is for those who commit sexual sins, homosexuals, those who sell slaves, those who tell lies, those who don't tell the truth under oath, and those who are against the true teaching of God. ¹¹That teaching is part of the Good News* that God gave me to tell. Through that Good News we see the glory* of God, who is the source of all blessings.

Thanks for God's Mercy

¹²I thank Christ Jesus our Lord because he trusted me and gave me this work of serving him. He gives me strength. ¹³In

ᵃ**1:7** law Probably the Jewish law that God gave to Moses on Mount Sinai. See Ex. 19 and 20. Also in verse 8.

the past I insulted Christ. As a proud and violent man, I persecuted his people. But God gave me mercy because I did not
know what I was doing. I did that before I became a believer.
¹⁴But our Lord gave me a full measure of his grace.* And with
that grace came the faith and love that are in Christ Jesus.

¹⁵Here is a true statement that should be accepted without
question: Christ Jesus came into the world to save sinners, and
I am the worst of them. ¹⁶But I was given mercy so that in me
Christ Jesus could show that he has patience without limit.
Christ showed his patience with me, the worst of all sinners.
He wanted me to be an example for those who would believe
in him and have eternal life. ¹⁷Honor and glory* to the King
who rules forever. He cannot be destroyed and cannot be seen.
Honor and glory forever and ever to the only God. Amen.*

¹⁸Timothy, you are like a son to me. What I am telling you to
do agrees with the prophecies*a* that were told about you in the
past. I want you to remember those prophecies and fight the
good fight of faith. ¹⁹Continue to trust in God and do what you
know is right. Some people have not done this, and their faith
is now in ruins. ²⁰Hymenaeus and Alexander are men like that.
I have given them to Satan* so that they will learn not to speak
against God.

God Wants Us to Pray for Everyone

2 ¹First of all, I ask that you pray for all people. Ask God to
bless them and give them what they need. And give thanks.
²You should pray for rulers and for all who have authority. Pray
for these leaders so that we can live quiet and peaceful lives—
lives full of devotion to God and respect for him. ³This is good
and pleases God our Savior.

⁴God wants everyone to be saved and to fully understand
the truth. ⁵There is only one God, and there is only one way
that people can reach God. That way is through Christ Jesus,
who as a man ⁶gave himself to pay for everyone to be free. This
is the message that was given to us at just the right time. ⁷And I
was chosen as an apostle* to tell people that message. (I am
telling the truth. I am not lying.) I was chosen to teach those
who are not Jews to believe and understand the truth.

Special Instructions for Men and Women

⁸I want the men everywhere to pray. Men who lift their
hands in prayer must be devoted to God and pleasing to him.
They must be men who keep themselves from getting angry
and having arguments.

⁹And I want the women to make themselves attractive in the
right way. Their clothes should be sensible and appropriate. They
should not draw attention to themselves with fancy hairstyles or

*a***1:18 prophecies** Things that prophets said about Timothy's life before those things
happened.

gold jewelry or pearls or expensive clothes. ¹⁰But they should make themselves attractive by the good things they do. That is more appropriate for women who say they are devoted to God.

¹¹A woman should learn while listening quietly and being completely willing to obey. ¹²I don't allow a woman to teach a man or tell him what to do. She must listen quietly, ¹³because Adam was made first. Eve was made later. ¹⁴Also, Adam was not the one who was tricked.ᵃ It was the woman who was tricked and became a sinner. ¹⁵But women will be saved in their work of having children. They will be saved if they continue to live in faith, love, and holiness with sensible behavior.

Leaders in the Church

3 ¹It is a true statement that anyone whose goal is to serve as an elderᵇ has his heart set on a good work. ²An elderᶜ must be such a good man that no one can rightly criticize him. He must be faithful to his wife. He must have self-control and be wise. He must be respected by others. He must be ready to help people by welcoming them into his home. He must be a good teacher. ³He must not drink too much, and he must not be someone who likes to fight. He must be gentle and peaceful. He must not be someone who loves money. ⁴He must be a good leader of his own family. This means that his children obey him with full respect. ⁵(If a man does not know how to lead his own family, he will not be able to take care of God's church.*)

⁶An elder must not be a new believer. It might make him too proud of himself. Then he would be condemned for his pride the same as the devil was. ⁷An elder must also have the respect of people who are not part of the church. Then he will not be criticized by others and be caught in the devil's trap.

Special Servants

⁸In the same way, the men who are chosen to be special servants* must have the respect of others. They must not be men who say things they don't mean or who spend their time drinking too much. They must not be men who will do almost anything for money. ⁹They must follow the true faith that God has now made known to us and always do what they know is right. ¹⁰You should test them first. Then, if you find that they have done nothing wrong, they can be special servants.

¹¹In the same way, the womenᵈ must have the respect of others. They must not be women who speak evil about other people. They must have self-control and be women who can be trusted in everything.

ᵃ2:14 Adam was not ... tricked The devil tricked Eve, and Eve caused Adam to sin. See Gen. 3:1–13. ᵇ3:1 whose ... elder Literally, "who aspires to supervision." ᶜ3:2 elder Here, literally, "overseer." See "elders" in the Word List. ᵈ3:11 women Probably the women who serve as special servants (See Rom. 16:1). It could be translated, "their wives," meaning the wives of the special servants, although there is no word for "their" in the Greek text.

¹²The men who are special servants must be faithful in marriage. They must be good leaders of children and their own families. ¹³Those who do well as special servants are making an honorable place for themselves. And they will feel very sure of their faith in Christ Jesus.

The Secret of Our Life

¹⁴I hope I can come to you soon. But I am writing this to you now, ¹⁵so that, even if I cannot come soon, you will know how people should live in the family*a* of God. That family is the church* of the living God. And God's church is the support and foundation of the truth. ¹⁶Without a doubt, the secret of our life of worship is great:

Christ*b* was shown to us in human form;
the Spirit* proved that he was right;
he was seen by angels.
The message* about him was told to the nations;
people in the world believed in him;
he was taken up to heaven in glory.*

A Warning About False Teachers

4 ¹The Spirit* clearly says that in the last times some will turn away from what we believe. They will obey spirits that tell lies. And they will follow the teachings of demons.* ²Those teachings come through people who tell lies and trick others. These evil people cannot see what is right and what is wrong. It is like their conscience has been destroyed with a hot iron. ³They say that it is wrong to marry. And they say that there are some foods that people must not eat. But God made these foods, and those who believe and who understand the truth can eat them with thanks. ⁴Everything that God made is good. Nothing he made should be refused if it is accepted with thanks to him. ⁵Everything he created is made holy* by what he has said and by prayer.

Be a Good Servant of Christ Jesus

⁶Tell this to the brothers and sisters there. This will show that you are a good servant of Christ Jesus. You will show that you are made strong by the words of faith and good teaching you have followed. ⁷People tell silly stories that don't agree with God's truth. Don't follow what these stories teach. But teach yourself to be devoted to God. ⁸Training your body helps you in some ways. But devotion to God helps you in every way. It brings you blessings in this life and in the future life too. ⁹Here is a true statement that should be accepted without

*a*3:15 family Literally, "house." This could mean that God's people are like God's temple.
*b*3:16 Christ Literally, "who." Some Greek copies have "God."

question: [10]We hope in the living God, the Savior of all people. In particular, he is the Savior of all those who believe in him. This is why we work and struggle.

[11]Command and teach these things. [12]You are young, but don't let anyone treat you as if you are not important. Be an example to show the believers how they should live. Show them by what you say, by the way you live, by your love, by your faith, and by your pure life.

[13]Continue to read the Scriptures* to the people, encourage them, and teach them. Do this until I come. [14]Remember to use the gift you have, which was given to you through a prophecy[a] when the group of elders* laid their hands on[b] you. [15]Continue to do these things. Give your life to doing them. Then everyone can see that your work is progressing. [16]Be careful in your life and in your teaching. Continue to live and teach rightly. Then you will save yourself and those who listen to your teaching.

5 [1]Don't speak angrily to an older man. But talk to him like he was your father. Treat the younger men like brothers. [2]Treat the older women like mothers. And treat the younger women with respect like sisters.

Taking Care of Widows

[3]Take care of widows who really need help. [4]But if a widow has children or grandchildren, the first thing they need to learn is this: to show their devotion to God by taking care of their own family. They will be repaying their parents, and this pleases God. [5]A widow who really needs help is one who has been left all alone. She trusts God to take care of her. She prays all the time, night and day, and asks God for help. [6]But the widow who uses her life to please herself is really dead while she is still living. [7]Tell the believers there to take care of their family so that no one can say they are doing wrong. [8]Everyone should take care of all their own people. Most important, they should take care of their own family. If they do not do that, then they do not accept what we believe. They are worse than someone who does not even believe in God.

[9]To be added to your list of widows, a woman must be 60 years old or older. She must have been faithful to her husband. [10]She must be known for the good she has done: raising children, welcoming travelers into her home, serving the needs[c] of God's people, helping those in trouble, and using her life to do all kinds of good.

[11]But don't put younger widows on that list. When their strong physical needs pull them away from their commitment

---

[a]**4:14** *prophecy* Something said about Timothy's life before that thing happened. [b]**4:14** *laid their hands on* This act was a way of asking God to bless people in a special way—here, to give Timothy power for a special work. [c]**5:10** *serving the needs* Literally, "washing the feet," a social custom of the first century, because people wore open sandals on very dusty roads.

to Christ, they will want to marry again. [12]Then they will be guilty of not doing what they first promised to do. [13]Also, these younger widows begin to waste their time going from house to house. They also begin to gossip and try to run other people's lives. They say things they should not say. [14]So I want the younger widows to marry, have children, and take care of their homes. If they do this, our enemy will not have any reason to criticize them. [15]But some of the younger widows have already turned away to follow Satan.*

[16]If any woman who is a believer has widows in her family, she[a] should take care of them herself. Then the church* will not have that burden and will be able to care for the widows who have no one else to help them.

More About Elders and Other Matters

[17]The elders* who lead the church in a good way should receive double honor[b]—in particular, those who do the work of counseling and teaching. [18]As the Scriptures* say, "When a work animal is being used to separate grain, don't keep it from eating the grain."[c] And the Scriptures also say, "A worker should be given his pay."[d]

[19]Don't listen to someone who accuses an elder. You should listen to them only if there are two or three others who can say what the elder did wrong. [20]Tell those who sin that they are wrong. Do this in front of the whole church so that the others will have a warning.

[21]Before God and Jesus Christ and the chosen angels, I tell you to make these judgments without any prejudice. Treat every person the same.

[22]Think carefully before you lay your hands on[e] anyone to make him an elder. Don't share in the sins of others. Keep yourself pure.

[23]Timothy, stop drinking only water, and drink a little wine. This will help your stomach, and you will not be sick so often.

[24]The sins of some people are easy to see. Their sins show that they will be judged. But the sins of some others are seen only later. [25]It is the same with the good things people do. Some are easy to see. But even if they are not obvious now, none of them will stay hidden forever.

Special Instructions for Slaves

6 [1]All those who are slaves should show full respect to their masters. Then God's name and our teaching will not be criticized. [2]Some slaves have masters who are believers, so they

---

[a]5:16 *woman . . . she* Some Greek copies have "man or woman . . . he/she." [b]5:17 *double honor* Or, "double pay." [c]5:18 Quote from Deut. 25:4. [d]5:18 Quote from Lk. 10:7. [e]5:22 *lay your hands on* This act was a way of asking God to bless people in a special way—here, to give them power for a special work.

are brothers. Does this mean they should show their masters any less respect? No, they should serve them even better, because they are helping believers, people they should love.

This is what you must teach and tell everyone to do.

False Teaching and True Riches

³Some people will teach what is false and will not agree with the true teaching of our Lord Jesus Christ. They will not accept the teaching that produces a life of devotion to God. ⁴They are proud of what they know, but they understand nothing. They are sick with a love for arguing and fighting about words. And that brings jealousy, quarrels, insults, and evil mistrust. ⁵They are always making trouble, because they are people whose thinking has been confused. They have lost their understanding of the truth. They think that devotion to God is a way to get rich.

⁶Devotion to God is, in fact, a way for people to be very rich, but only if it makes them satisfied with what they have. ⁷When we came into the world, we brought nothing. And when we die, we can take nothing out. ⁸So, if we have food and clothes, we will be satisfied with that. ⁹People who want to be rich bring temptations to themselves. They are caught in a trap. They begin to want many foolish things that will hurt them. These things ruin and destroy people. ¹⁰The love of money causes all kinds of evil. Some people have turned away from what we believe because they want to get more and more money. But they have caused themselves a lot of pain and sorrow.

Some Things to Remember

¹¹But you belong to God. So you should stay away from all those things. Always try to do what is right, and to be devoted to God, and to have faith, love, patience, and gentleness. ¹²We have to fight to keep our faith. Try as hard as you can to win that fight. Take hold of eternal life. It is the life you were chosen to have when you confessed your faith in Jesus—that wonderful truth that you spoke so openly and that so many people heard. ¹³Before God and Christ Jesus I give you a command. Jesus is the one who confessed that same wonderful truth when he stood before Pontius Pilate.* And God is the one who gives life to everything. Now I tell you: ¹⁴Do what you were commanded to do without fault or blame until the time when our Lord Jesus Christ comes again. ¹⁵God will make that happen at the right time. God is the only Ruler, the source of all blessings. He is the King of all kings and the Lord of all lords. ¹⁶God is the only one who never dies. He lives in light so bright that people cannot go near it. No one has ever seen him; no one is able to see him. All honor and power belong to him forever. Amen.*

¹⁷Give this command to those who are rich with the things of this world. Tell them not to be proud. Tell them to hope in God,

not their money. Money cannot be trusted, but God takes care of us richly. He gives us everything to enjoy. [18]Tell those who are rich to do good—to be rich in good works. And tell them they should be happy to give and ready to share. [19]By doing this, they will be saving up a treasure for themselves. And that treasure will be a strong foundation on which their future life will be built. They will be able to have the life that is true life.

[20]Timothy, God has trusted you with many things. Keep these things safe. Stay away from people who talk about useless things that are not from God and who argue against you with a "knowledge" that is not knowledge at all. [21]Some people who claim to have that "knowledge" have gone completely away from what we believe.

God's grace* be with you all.

2 Timothy

1 ¹Greetings from Paul, an apostle* of Christ Jesus. I am an apostle because God wanted me to be. God sent me to tell people about the promise of life that is in Christ Jesus.

²To Timothy, a dear son to me.

Grace,* mercy, and peace to you from God the Father and from Christ Jesus our Lord.

Thanksgiving and Encouragement

³I always remember you in my prayers day and night. And in these prayers I thank God for you. He is the God my ancestors* served, and I have always served him with a clear conscience. ⁴I remember that you cried for me. I want very much to see you so that I can be filled with joy. ⁵I remember your true faith. That kind of faith first belonged to your grandmother Lois and to your mother Eunice. I know you now have that same faith. ⁶That is why I want you to remember the gift God gave you. God gave you that gift when I laid my hands on*ᵃ* you. Now I want you to use that gift and let it grow more and more, like a small flame grows into a fire. ⁷The Spirit* God gave us does not make us afraid. He is our source of power and love and self-control.

⁸So don't be ashamed to tell people about our Lord Jesus. And don't be ashamed of me—I am in prison for the Lord. But suffer with me for the Good News.* God gives us the strength to do that.

⁹God saved us and chose us to be his holy* people, but not because of anything we ourselves did. God saved us and made us his people because that was what he wanted and because of his grace.* That grace was given to us through Christ Jesus before time began. ¹⁰And now it has been shown to us in the coming of our Savior Christ Jesus. He destroyed death and showed us the way to have life. Yes, through the Good News Jesus showed us the way to have life that cannot be destroyed.

¹¹I was chosen to tell people that message as an apostle* and teacher. ¹²And I suffer now because of that work. But I am not ashamed. I know the one I have believed, and I am sure that he is able to protect what he has trusted me with until that Day.*ᵇ*

---

*ᵃ***1:6** *laid my hands on* This act was a way of asking God to bless people in a special way—here, to give Timothy power for a special work. *ᵇ***1:12** *Day* The day Christ will come to judge everyone and take his people to live with him. Also in verse 18.

[13]What you heard me teach is an example of what you should teach. Follow that model of right teaching with the faith and love we have in Christ Jesus. [14]This teaching is a treasure that you have been trusted with. Protect it with the help of the Holy Spirit, who lives inside us.

[15]You know that everyone in Asia* has left me. Even Phygelus and Hermogenes have left me. [16]I pray that the Lord will show mercy to the family of Onesiphorus. Many times Onesiphorus encouraged me. He was not ashamed that I was in prison. [17]No, he was not ashamed. When he came to Rome, he looked and looked for me until he found me. [18]I pray that the Lord Jesus will make sure Onesiphorus receives mercy from the Lord God on that Day. You know how many ways this brother helped me in Ephesus.

A Loyal Soldier of Christ Jesus

2 [1]Timothy, you are a son to me. Be strong in the grace* that we have because we belong to Christ Jesus. [2]What you have heard me teach publicly you should teach to others. Share these teachings with people you can trust. Then they will be able to teach others these same things. [3]As a good soldier of Christ Jesus, accept your share of the troubles we have. [4]A soldier wants to please his commanding officer, so he does not spend any time on activities that are not a part of his duty. [5]Athletes in a race must obey all the rules to win. [6]It is the farmer who works hard that deserves the first part of the harvest. [7]Think about what I am saying. The Lord will help you understand it all.

[8]Remember Jesus Christ. He is from the family of David.* After Jesus died, he was raised from death. This is the Good News* that I tell people. [9]And because I tell that message, I am suffering. I am even bound with chains like someone who has really done wrong. But God's message is not bound. [10]So I patiently accept all these troubles. I do this to help the people God has chosen so that they can have the salvation that is in Christ Jesus. With this salvation comes glory* that never ends.

[11]Here is a true statement:

If we died with him, we will also live with him.
[12] If we remain faithful even in suffering,
we will also rule with him.
If we refuse to say we know him,
he will refuse to say he knows us.
[13] If we are not faithful, he will still be faithful,
because he cannot be false to himself.

An Approved Worker

[14]Keep on telling everyone these truths. And warn them before God not to argue about words. Such arguments don't

help anyone, and they ruin those who listen to them. ¹⁵Do your best to be the kind of person God will accept, and give yourself to him. Be a worker who has no reason to be ashamed of his work, one who applies the true teaching in the right way.

¹⁶Stay away from people who talk about useless things that are not from God. That kind of talk will lead a person more and more against God. ¹⁷Their evil teaching will spread like a sickness inside the body. Hymenaeus and Philetus are men like that. ¹⁸They have left the true teaching. They say that the day when people will be raised from death has already come and gone. And they are destroying the faith of some people.

¹⁹But God's strong foundation never moves, and these words are written on it: "The Lord knows those who belong to him."*a* Also, these words are written there: "Everyone who says they believe in the Lord must stop doing wrong."

²⁰In a large house there are things made of gold and silver. But there are also things made of wood and clay. Some of these are used for special purposes, others for ordinary jobs. ²¹The Lord wants to use you for special purposes, so make yourself clean from all evil. Then you will be holy,* and the Master can use you. You will be ready for any good work.

²²Stay away from the evil things a young person like you typically wants to do. Do your best to live right and to have faith, love, and peace, together with others who trust in the Lord with pure hearts. ²³Stay away from foolish and stupid arguments. You know that these arguments grow into bigger arguments. ²⁴As a servant of the Lord, you must not argue. You must be kind to everyone. You must be a good teacher, and you must be patient. ²⁵You must gently teach those who don't agree with you. Maybe God will let them change their hearts so that they can accept the truth. ²⁶The devil has trapped them and now makes them do what he wants. But maybe they can wake up to see what is happening and free themselves from the devil's trap.

Many People Will Stop Loving God

3 ¹Remember this: There are some terrible times coming in the last days. ²People will love only themselves and money. They will be proud and boast about themselves. They will abuse others with insults. They will not obey their parents. They will be ungrateful and against all that is pleasing to God. ³They will have no love for others and will refuse to forgive anyone. They will talk about others to hurt them and will have no self-control. They will be cruel and hate what is good. ⁴People will turn against their friends. They will do foolish things without thinking and will be so proud of themselves. Instead of loving God, they will love pleasure. ⁵They will go on pretending to be devoted to God, but they will refuse to let

*a*2:19 Quote from Num. 16:5.

that "devotion" change the way they live. Stay away from these people!

⁶Some of them go into homes and get control over weak women, whose lives are full of sin—women who are led into sin by all the things they want. ⁷These women always want to learn something new, but they are never able to fully understand the truth. ⁸Remember Jannes and Jambres,ᵃ the men who fought against Moses*? In the same way, these people fight against the truth. Their thinking has been confused. They have failed in their faith. ⁹But they will not succeed in what they are trying to do. Everyone will see how foolish they are. That is what happened to Jannes and Jambres.

Last Instructions

¹⁰But you know all about me. You know what I teach and the way I live. You know my goal in life. You know my faith, my patience, and my love. You know that I never stop trying. ¹¹You know about my persecutions* and my sufferings. You know all the things that happened to me in Antioch, Iconium, and Lystra—the persecution I suffered in those places. But the Lord saved me from all of it. ¹²Everyone who wants to live showing true devotion to God in Christ Jesus will be persecuted. ¹³People who are evil and cheat others will become worse and worse. They will fool others, but they will also be fooling themselves.

¹⁴But you should continue following the teaching you learned. You know it is true, because you know you can trust those who taught you. ¹⁵You have known the Holy Scripturesᵇ since you were a child. These Scriptures are able to make you wise. And that wisdom leads to salvation through faith in Christ Jesus. ¹⁶All Scripture is given by God. And all Scripture is useful for teaching and for showing people what is wrong in their lives. It is useful for correcting faults and teaching the right way to live. ¹⁷Using the Scriptures, those who serve God will be prepared and will have everything they need to do every good work.

4 ¹Before God and Jesus Christ I give you a command. Christ Jesus is the one who will judge all people—those who are living and those who have died. He is coming again to rule in his kingdom.* So I give you this command: ²Tell everyone God's message.* Be ready at all times to do whatever is needed. Tell people what they need to do, tell them when they are doing wrong, and encourage them. Do this with great patience and careful teaching.

³The time will come when people will not listen to the true teaching. But people will find more and more teachers who please them. They will find teachers who say what they want to

---

ᵃ3:8 *Jannes and Jambres* Probably the magicians who opposed Moses in Pharaoh's court. See Ex. 7:11–12, 22.   ᵇ3:15 *Holy Scriptures* Writings that Jews and followers of Christ accepted to be from God—the Old Testament.

hear. [4]People will stop listening to the truth. They will begin to follow the teaching in false stories. [5]But you should control yourself at all times. When troubles come, accept them. Do the work of telling the Good News.* Do all the duties of a servant of God.

[6]My life is being given as an offering for God. The time has come for me to leave this life here. [7]I have fought the good fight. I have finished the race. I have served the Lord faithfully. [8]Now, a prize is waiting for me—the crown* that will show I am approved by God. The Lord, the judge who judges rightly, will give it to me on that Day.[a] Yes, he will give it to me and to everyone else who is eagerly looking forward to his coming.

Personal Notes

[9]Do your best to come to me as soon as you can. [10]Demas loved this world too much. That is why he left me. He went to Thessalonica. Crescens went to Galatia. And Titus went to Dalmatia. [11]Luke is the only one still with me. Get Mark and bring him with you when you come. He can help me in my work here. [12]I sent Tychicus to Ephesus.

[13]When I was in Troas, I left my coat there with Carpus. So when you come, bring it to me. Also, bring my books. The books written on parchment* are the ones I need.

[14]Alexander the metalworker caused me so much harm. The Lord will punish him for what he did. [15]He fought against everything we teach. You should be careful that he doesn't hurt you too.

[16]The first time I defended myself, no one helped me. Everyone left me. I pray that God will forgive them. [17]But the Lord stayed with me. The Lord gave me strength so that I could tell the Good News* everywhere. He wanted all those who are not Jews to hear that Good News. So I was saved from the lion's mouth. [18]The Lord will save me when anyone tries to hurt me. He will bring me safely to his heavenly kingdom. Glory* forever and ever be the Lord's. Amen.*

Final Greetings

[19]Give my greetings to Priscilla and Aquila and to the family of Onesiphorus. [20]Erastus stayed in Corinth. And I left Trophimus in Miletus—he was sick. [21]Try as hard as you can to come to me before winter.

Greetings to you from Eubulus, Pudens, Linus, Claudia, and all the brothers and sisters here.

[22]The Lord be with your spirit. Grace* be with you.

---

[a]4:8 **Day** The day Christ will come to judge everyone and take his people to live with him.

Titus

1 ¹Greetings from Paul, a servant of God and an apostle* of Jesus Christ. I was sent to help God's chosen people have faith and understand the truth that produces a life of devotion to God. ²This faith and knowledge make us sure that we have eternal life. God promised that life to us before time began—and God does not lie. ³At the right time, God let the world know about that life. He did this through the telling of the Good News message,* and he trusted me with that work. I told people that message because God our Savior commanded me to.

⁴To Titus, a true son to me in the faith we share together.

Grace* and peace to you from God the Father and Christ Jesus our Savior.

Titus' Work in Crete

⁵I left you in Crete so that you could finish doing what still needed to be done. And I also left you there so that you could choose men to be elders* in every town. ⁶To be an elder, a man must not be guilty of living in a wrong way. He must be faithful to his wife, and his children must be faithful to God.ᵃ They must not be known as children who are wild and don't obey. ⁷An elderᵇ has the job of taking care of God's work. So people should not be able to say that he lives in a wrong way. He must not be someone who is proud and selfish or who gets angry quickly. He must not drink too much, and he must not be someone who likes to fight. He must not be a man who will do almost anything for money. ⁸An elder must be ready to help people by welcoming them into his home. He must love what is good. He must be wise. He must live right. He must be devoted to God and pleasing to him. And he must be able to control himself. ⁹An elder must be faithful to the same true message we teach. Then he will be able to encourage others with teaching that is true and right. And he will be able to show those who are against this teaching that they are wrong.

¹⁰This is important, because there are many people who refuse to obey—people who talk about worthless things and mislead others. I am talking especially about those who say that men who are not Jews must be circumcised* to please God.

ᵃ1:6 *faithful to God* This word can mean "trustworthy" or "believers." Here, both meanings may be included. Compare this verse with 1 Tim. 3:4. ᵇ1:7 *elder* Here, literally, "overseer." See "elders" in the Word List.

11These people must be stopped, because they are destroying whole families by teaching what they should not teach. They teach only to cheat people and make money. 12Even one of their own prophets said, "Cretans are always liars. They are evil animals and lazy people who do nothing but eat." 13The words that prophet said are true. So tell those people that they are wrong. You must be strict with them. Then they will become strong in the faith, 14and they will stop paying attention to the stories told by those Jews. They will stop following the commands of those who have turned away from the truth.

15To people who are pure, everything is pure. But to those who are full of sin and don't believe, nothing is pure. Really, their thinking has become evil and their consciences have been ruined. 16They say they know God, but the evil things they do show that they don't accept him. They are disgusting. They refuse to obey God and are not capable of doing anything good.

Following the True Teaching

2 1You, however, must tell everyone how to live in a way that agrees with the true teaching. 2Teach the older men to have self-control, to be serious, and to be wise. They must be strong in faith, in love, and in patience.

3Also, teach the older women to live the way those who serve the Lord should live. They should not go around saying bad things about others or be in the habit of drinking too much. They should teach what is good. 4In this way they can teach the younger women to love their husbands and children. 5They can teach them to be wise and pure, to take care of their homes, to be kind, and to be willing to serve their husbands. Then no one will be able to criticize the teaching God gave us.

6In the same way, tell the young men to be wise. 7You should be an example for them in every way by the good things you do. When you teach, be honest and serious. 8And your teaching should be clearly right so that you cannot be criticized. Then anyone who is against you will be ashamed. There will not be anything bad they can say about us.

9And tell this to those who are slaves: They should be willing to serve their masters at all times; they should try to please them, not argue with them; 10they should not steal from them; and they should show their masters that they can be trusted. Then, in everything they do, they will show that the teaching of God our Savior is good.

11That is the way we should live, because God's grace* has come. That grace can save everyone. 12It teaches us not to live against God and not to do the bad things the world wants to do. It teaches us to live on earth now in a wise and right way—a way that shows true devotion to God. 13We should live like that while we are waiting for the coming of our great God and Savior Jesus Christ. He is our great hope, and he will come with glory.* 14He gave himself for us. He died to free us from all evil. He died to make us pure—people who belong only to him and who always want to do good.

15These are the things you should tell people. Encourage them, and when they are wrong, correct them. You have full authority to do this, so don't let anyone think they can ignore you.

The Right Way to Live

3 1Remind your people that they should always be under the authority of rulers and government leaders. They should obey these leaders and be ready to do good. 2Tell them not to speak evil of anyone but to live in peace with others. They should be gentle and polite to everyone.

3In the past we were foolish too. We did not obey, we were wrong, and we were slaves to the many things our bodies wanted and enjoyed. We lived doing evil and being jealous. People hated us and we hated each other. 4But then the kindness and love of God our Savior was made known. 5He saved us because of his mercy, not because of any good things we did. He saved us through the washing that made us new people. He saved us by making us new through the Holy Spirit.* 6God poured out to us that Holy Spirit fully through Jesus Christ our Savior. 7We were made right with God by his grace.* God saved us so that we could be his children and look forward to receiving life that never ends. 8This is a true statement.

And I want you to be sure that the people understand these things. Then those who believe in God will be careful to use their lives for doing good. These things are good and will help everyone.

9Stay away from those who have foolish arguments, who talk about useless family histories, or who make trouble and fight about what the law of Moses teaches. These things are useless and will not help anyone. 10Give a warning to all those who cause arguments. If they continue to cause trouble after a second warning, then don't associate with them. 11You know that people like that are evil and sinful. Their sins prove they are wrong.

Final Instructions and Greetings

12I will send Artemas and Tychicus to you. When I send them, try hard to come to me at Nicopolis. I have decided to stay there this winter. 13Zenas the lawyer and Apollos will be traveling from there. Do all that you can to help them prepare for their trip. Be sure that they have everything they need. 14Our people must learn to use their lives for doing good and helping anyone who has a need. Then they will not have empty lives.

15All the people with me here send you their greetings. Give my greetings to those who love us in the faith.

Grace* be with you all.

Philemon

[1]Greetings from Paul, a prisoner for Jesus Christ, and from Timothy, our brother.

To Philemon, our dear friend and worker with us. [2]Also to Apphia, our sister, to Archippus, a worker with us, and to the church* that meets in your home.

[3]Grace* and peace to you from God our Father and the Lord Jesus Christ.

Philemon's Love and Faith

[4]I remember you in my prayers. And I always thank my God for you. [5]I thank God because I hear about the love you have for all of God's holy people* and the faith you have in the Lord Jesus. [6]I pray that the faith you share will make you understand every blessing we have in Christ. [7]My brother, you have shown love to God's people, and your help has greatly encouraged them. What a great joy and encouragement that has been to me.

Accept Onesimus as a Brother

[8]There is something that you should do. And because of the authority I have in Christ, I feel free to command you to do it. [9]But I am not commanding you; I am asking you to do it out of love. I, Paul, am an old man now, and I am a prisoner for Christ Jesus. [10]I am asking you for my son Onesimus. He became my son while I was in prison. [11]In the past he was useless to you. But now he has become useful[a] for both you and me.

[12]I am sending him back to you, but it's as hard as losing part of myself. [13]I would like to keep him here to help me while I am still in prison for telling the Good News.* By helping me here, he would be representing you. [14]But I did not want to do anything without asking you first. Then whatever you do for me will be what you want to do, not what I forced you to do.

[15]Onesimus was separated from you for a short time. Maybe that happened so that you could have him back forever, [16]not to be just a slave, but better than a slave, to be a dear brother. That's what he is to me. So surely, he will be even more so to you, both as your slave and as one who shares your faith in the Lord.

---

[a]11 useless ... useful Paul here makes a play on words with the name Onesimus, which means "useful."

¹⁷If you accept me as your friend, then accept Onesimus back. Welcome him like you would welcome me. ¹⁸If he has done any wrong to you or owes you anything, charge that to me. ¹⁹I, Paul, am writing this in my own handwriting: I will pay back anything Onesimus owes. And I will say nothing about what you owe me for your own life. ²⁰So, my brother, as a follower of the Lord please do this favor[a] for me. It would be such a great encouragement to me as your brother in Christ. ²¹I write this letter knowing that you will do what I ask, and even more than I ask.

²²Also, please prepare a room for me. I hope that God will answer your prayers and that I will be able to come and see you.

Final Greetings

²³Epaphras is a prisoner with me for Christ Jesus. He sends you his greetings. ²⁴Also Mark, Aristarchus, Demas, and Luke send their greetings. They are workers together with me.

²⁵The grace* of our Lord Jesus Christ be with your spirit.

---

[a] **20** *please do this favor* Paul here makes another wordplay on the name Onesimus, using a verb related to it.

Hebrews

God Has Spoken Through His Son

1 ¹In the past God spoke to our people through the prophets.*
He spoke to them many times and in many different ways.
²And now in these last days, God has spoken to us again
through his Son. He made the whole world through his Son.
And he has chosen his Son to have all things. ³The Son shows
the glory* of God. He is a perfect copy of God's nature, and he
holds everything together by his powerful command. The Son
made people clean from their sins. Then he sat down at the
right side*a* of God, the Great One in heaven. ⁴The Son became
much greater than the angels, and God gave him a name that is
much greater than any of their names.

⁵God never said this to any of the angels:

> "You are my Son.
> Today I have become your Father."   *Psalm 2:7*

God also never said about an angel,

> "I will be his Father,
> and he will be my son."   *2 Samuel 7:14*

⁶And then, when God sent his firstborn*b* Son into the world, he
said,

> "Let all God's angels worship the Son."*c*   *Deuteronomy 32:43*

⁷This is what God said about the angels:

> "God changes his angels into winds*d*
> and his servants into flaming fire."   *Psalm 104:4*

⁸But he said this about his Son:

> "Your throne, O God, will continue forever and ever.
> You will rule your kingdom with right judgments.
> ⁹ You love the right, and you hate the wrong.
> So God, your God, has given you a greater joy
> than he gave the people with you."   *Psalm 45:6-7*

---

*a***1:3** *right side* The place of honor and authority (power). *b***1:6** *firstborn* This word means
that Christ was the first and most important of all God's children. *c***1:6** *"Let ... Son"* These
words are found in Deut. 32:43 in the ancient Greek version of the Old Testament and in a
Hebrew copy among the Dead Sea Scrolls. *d***1:7** *winds* This can also mean "spirits."

[10]God also said,

> "O Lord, in the beginning you made the earth,
>   and your hands made the sky.
> [11] These things will disappear, but you will stay.
>   They will all wear out like old clothes.
> [12] You will fold them up like a coat,
>   and they will be changed like clothes.
> But you never change,
>   and your life will never end."   *Psalm 102:25–27*

[13]And God never said this to an angel:

> "Sit at my right side
>   until I put your enemies under your power.[a]"   *Psalm 110:1*

[14]All the angels are spirits who serve God and are sent to help those who will receive salvation.

Our Salvation Is Greater Than the Law

2 [1]So we must be more careful to follow what we were taught. We must be careful so that we will not be pulled away from the true way. [2]The teaching that God spoke through angels was shown to be true. And every time his people did something against that teaching, they were punished for what they did. They were punished when they did not obey that teaching. [3]So surely we also will be punished if we don't pay attention to the salvation we have that is so great. It was the Lord Jesus who first told people about it. And those who heard him proved to us that it is true. [4]God also proved it by using miraculous signs,* wonders,* and all kinds of miracles.* And he proved it by giving people various gifts through the Holy Spirit* in just the way he wanted.

Christ Became Like People to Save Them

[5]God did not choose angels to be the rulers over the new world that was coming. That future world is the world we have been talking about. [6]It is written some place in the Scriptures,*

> "Why are people so important to you?
>   Why do you even think about them?
> Why do you care about the son of man[b]?
>   Is he so important?
> [7] For a short time you made him lower than the angels.
>   You crowned him with glory* and honor.
> [8] You put everything under his control.[c]"   *Psalm 8:4–6*

If God put everything under his control, then there was nothing left that he did not rule. But we don't yet see him

---

[a]**1:13** *until I put ... power* Literally, "until I make your enemies a footstool for your feet."
[b]**2:6** *son of man* This can mean any human, but the name "Son of Man" (see the Word List) is often used to mean Jesus, who showed what God planned for all people to be.   [c]**2:8** *control* Literally, "feet."

ruling over everything. ⁹For a short time Jesus was made lower than the angels, but now we see him wearing a crown of glory and honor because he suffered and died. Because of God's grace,* Jesus died for everyone.

¹⁰God—the one who made all things and for whose glory all things exist—wanted many people to be his children and share his glory. So he did what he needed to do. He made perfect the one who leads those people to salvation. He made Jesus a perfect Savior through his suffering.

¹¹Jesus, the one who makes people holy,* and those who are made holy are from the same family. So he is not ashamed to call them his brothers and sisters. ¹²He says,

"God, I will tell my brothers and sisters about you.
    Before all your people I will sing your praises." *Psalm 22:22*

¹³He also says,

"I will trust in God."   *Isaiah 8:17*

And he says,

"I am here, and with me are the children God has given me."
                                                           Isaiah 8:18

¹⁴These children are people with physical bodies. So Jesus himself became like them and had the same experiences they have. Jesus did this so that, by dying, he could destroy the one who has the power of death—the devil. ¹⁵Jesus became like these people and died so that he could free them. They were like slaves all their lives because of their fear of death. ¹⁶Clearly, it is not angels that Jesus helps. He helps the people who are from Abraham.* ¹⁷For this reason, Jesus had to be made like us, his brothers and sisters, in every way. He became like people so that he could be their merciful and faithful high priest* in service to God. Then he could bring forgiveness for the people's sins. ¹⁸And now he can help those who are tempted. He is able to help because he himself suffered and was tempted.

Jesus Is Greater Than Moses

3 ¹So, my brothers and sisters, those chosen by God to be his holy people,* think about Jesus. He is the one we believe God sent to save us and to be our high priest.* ²God made him our high priest, and he was faithful to God just as Moses* was. He did everything God wanted him to do in God's house. ³When someone builds a house, people will honor the builder more than the house. It is the same with Jesus. He should have more honor than Moses. ⁴Every house is built by someone, but God built everything. ⁵Moses was faithful as a servant in God's whole house. He told people what God would say in the future. ⁶But Christ is faithful in ruling God's house as the Son.

And we are God's house, if we remain confident of the great hope we are glad to say we have.

We Must Continue to Follow God

[7] So it is just as the Holy Spirit* says:

"If you hear God's voice today,
[8]   don't be stubborn as you were in the past,
      when you turned against God.
    That was the day you tested God in the desert.
[9] For 40 years in the desert your people saw what I did.
    But they tested me and my patience.
[10] So I was angry with them.
    I said, 'Their thoughts are always wrong.
    They have never understood my ways.'
[11] So I was angry and made a promise:
    'They will never enter my place of rest.'"   *Psalm 95:7-11*

[12] So, brothers and sisters, be careful that none of you has the evil thoughts that cause so much doubt that you stop following the living God. [13] But encourage each other every day, while you still have something called "today.*" Help each other so that none of you will be fooled by sin and become too hard to change. [14] We have the honor of sharing in all that Christ has if we continue until the end to have the sure faith we had in the beginning. [15] That's why the Spirit said,

"If you hear God's voice today,
    don't be stubborn as in the past
    when you turned against God."   *Psalm 95:7-8*

[16] Who were those who heard God's voice and turned against him? It was all the people Moses* led out of Egypt. [17] And who was God angry with for 40 years? He was angry with those who sinned. And their dead bodies were left in the desert. [18] And which people was God talking to when he promised that they would never enter his place of rest? He was talking to those who did not obey him. [19] So we see that they were not allowed to enter and have God's rest, because they did not believe.

[4] [1] And we still have the promise that God gave those people. That promise is that we can enter his place of rest. So we should be very careful that none of you fails to get that promise. [2] Yes, the good news about it was told to us just as it was to them. But the message they heard did not help them. They heard it but did not accept it with faith. [3] Only we who believe it are able to enter God's place of rest. As God said,

"I was angry and made a promise:
    'They will never enter my place of rest.'"   *Psalm 95:11*

3:13 today This word is taken from verse 7. It means it is important to do this now, while there is still opportunity.

But God's work was finished from the time he made the world. [4]Yes, somewhere in the Scriptures* he talked about the seventh day of the week. He said, "So on the seventh day God rested from all his work."[a] [5]But in the Scripture above God said, "They will never enter my place of rest."

[6]So the opportunity is still there for some to enter and enjoy God's rest. But those who first heard the good news about it did not enter, because they did not obey. [7]So God planned another special day. It is called "today." He spoke about that day through David* a long time later using the words we quoted before:

"If you hear God's voice today,
don't be stubborn as you were in the past."   *Psalm 95:7–8*

[8]We know that Joshua* did not lead the people into the place of rest that God promised. We know this because God spoke later about another day for rest. [9]This shows that the seventh-day rest[b] for God's people is still to come. [10]God rested after he finished his work. So everyone who enters God's place of rest will also have rest from their own work like God did. [11]So let us try as hard as we can to enter God's place of rest. We must try hard so that none of us will be lost by following the example of those who refused to obey God.

[12]God's word[c] is alive and working. It is sharper than the sharpest sword and cuts all the way into us. It cuts deep to the place where the soul and the spirit are joined. God's word cuts to the center of our joints and our bones. It judges the thoughts and feelings in our hearts. [13]Nothing in all the world can be hidden from God. He can clearly see all things. Everything is open before him. And to him we must explain the way we have lived.

Jesus Is the High Priest Who Helps Us

[14]We have a great high priest* who has gone to live with God in heaven. He is Jesus the Son of God. So let us continue to express our faith in him. [15]Jesus, our high priest, is able to understand our weaknesses. When Jesus lived on earth, he was tempted in every way. He was tempted in the same ways we are tempted, but he never sinned. [16]With Jesus as our high priest, we can feel free to come before God's throne where there is grace.* There we receive mercy and kindness to help us when we need it.

5 [1]Every Jewish high priest is chosen from among men. That priest is given the work of helping people with the things they must do for God. He must offer to God gifts and sacrifices* for sins. [2]The high priest has his own weaknesses. So he is able to be gentle with those who do wrong out of ignorance. [3]He

---

[a]**4:4** Quote from Gen. 2:2.   [b]**4:9** *seventh-day rest* Literally, "Sabbath rest," meaning a sharing in the rest God began after he created the world.   [c]**4:12** *God's word* God's teachings and commands.

offers sacrifices for their sins, but he must also offer sacrifices for his own sins.

[4] To be a high priest is an honor. But no one chooses himself for this work. That person must be chosen by God just as Aaron* was. [5] It is the same with Christ. He did not choose himself to have the glory* of becoming a high priest. But God chose him. God said to Christ,

> "You are my Son.
>   Today I have become your Father."
>
> *Psalm 2:7*

[6] And in another part of the Scriptures* God says,

> "You will be a priest forever, just like Melchizedek.*"
>
> *Psalm 110:4*

[7] While Christ lived on earth he prayed to God, asking for help from the one who could save him from death. He prayed to God with loud cries and tears. And his prayers were answered because of his great respect for God. [8] Jesus was the Son of God, but he still suffered, and through his sufferings he learned to obey whatever God says. [9] This made him the perfect high priest, who provides the way for everyone who obeys him to be saved forever. [10] God made him high priest, just like Melchizedek.

Warning Against Falling Away

[11] We have many things to tell you about this. But it is hard to explain because you have stopped trying to understand. [12] You have had enough time that by now you should be teachers. But you need someone to teach you again the first lessons of God's teaching. You still need the teaching that is milk. You are not ready for solid food. [13] Anyone who lives on milk is still a baby and is not able to understand much about living right. [14] But solid food is for people who have grown up. From their experience they have learned to see the difference between good and evil.

[6] [1-2] So we should be finished with the beginning lessons about Christ. We should not have to keep going back to where we started. We began our new life by turning away from the evil we did in the past and by believing in God. That's when we were taught about baptisms,[a] the laying on of hands,[b] the resurrection* of those who have died, and the final judgment. Now we need to go forward to more mature teaching. [3] And that's what we will do if God allows.

[4-6] After people have left the way of Christ, can you make them change their lives again? I am talking about people who once learned the truth, received God's gift, and shared in the Holy Spirit.* They were blessed to hear God's good message*

---

[a] 6:1–2 *baptisms* The word here may mean the baptism (brief 'burial' in water) of believers in Christ, or it may mean Jewish ceremonial washings. [b] 6:1–2 *the laying on of hands* This act was a way of asking God to bless people in a special way. Here, it probably refers to what was done to give people power to begin a new work.

and see the great power of his new world. But then they left it all behind, and it is not possible to make them change again. That's because those who leave Christ are nailing him to the cross again, shaming him before everyone.

⁷These people are like land that gets plenty of rain. A farmer plants and cares for the land so that it will produce food. If it grows plants that help people, then it has God's blessing. ⁸But if it grows thorns and weeds, it is worthless and in danger of being cursed by God. It will be destroyed by fire.

⁹Dear friends, I am not saying this because I think it is happening to you. We really expect that you will do better—that you will do the good things that will result in your salvation. ¹⁰God is fair, and he will remember all the work you have done. He will remember that you showed your love to him by helping his people and that you continue to help them. ¹¹We want each of you to be willing and eager to show your love like that the rest of your life. Then you will be sure to get what you hope for. ¹²We don't want you to be lazy. We want you to be like those who, because of their faith and patience, will get what God has promised.

¹³God made a promise to Abraham.* And there is no one greater than God, so he used himself to make a vow* that he would do what he said. ¹⁴He said, "I will surely bless you. I will give you many descendants."ᵃ ¹⁵Abraham waited patiently for this to happen, and later he received what God promised.

¹⁶People always use the name of someone greater than themselves to make a vow. The vow proves that what they say is true, and there is no more arguing about it. ¹⁷God wanted to prove that his promise was true. He wanted to prove this to those who would get what he promised. He wanted them to understand clearly that his purposes never change. So God said something would happen, and he proved what he said by also making a vow. ¹⁸These two things cannot change. God cannot lie when he says something, and he cannot lie when he makes a vow.

So these two things are a great help to us who have come to God for safety. They encourage us to hold on to the hope that is ours. ¹⁹This hope is like an anchor for us. It is strong and sure and keeps us safe. It goes behind the curtain.ᵇ ²⁰Jesus has already entered there and opened the way for us. He has become the high priest* forever, just like Melchizedek.*

The Priest Melchizedek

7 ¹Melchizedek* was the king of Salem and a priest for God the Most High. He met Abraham* when Abraham was coming

---

ᵃ**6:14** Quote from Gen. 22:17. ᵇ**6:19** *curtain* The spiritual curtain in the heavenly temple, which was symbolized by the physical one that separated the inner sanctuary (and God's presence) from the other room in the Holy Tent and in the Jerusalem Temple. See "curtain" in the Word List.

back after defeating the kings. That day Melchizedek blessed him. ²Then Abraham gave him a tenth of everything he had.

The name Melchizedek, king of Salem, has two meanings. First, Melchizedek means "king of justice." And "king of Salem" means "king of peace." ³No one knows who his father or mother was or where he came from.ᵃ And no one knows when he was born or when he died. Melchizedek is like the Son of God in that he will always be a priest.

⁴You can see that Melchizedek was very great. Abraham, our great ancestor, gave him a tenth of everything that he won in battle. ⁵Now the law says that those from the tribe of Levi who become priests must get a tenth from their own people, even though they and their people are both from the family of Abraham. ⁶Melchizedek was not even from the tribe of Levi, but Abraham gave him a tenth of what he had. And Melchizedek blessed Abraham—the one who had God's promises. ⁷And everyone knows that the more important person always blesses the less important person.

⁸Those priests get a tenth, but they are only men who live and then die. But Melchizedek, who got a tenth from Abraham, continues to live, as the Scriptures* say. ⁹Now those from the family of Levi are the ones who get a tenth from the people. But we can say that when Abraham paid Melchizedek a tenth, then Levi also paid it. ¹⁰Levi was not yet born, but he already existed in his ancestor Abraham when Melchizedek met him.

¹¹The people were given the law* under the system of priests from the tribe of Levi. But no one could be made spiritually perfect through that system of priests. So there was a need for another priest to come. I mean a priest like Melchizedek, not Aaron.* ¹²And when a different kind of priest comes, then the law must be changed too. ¹³⁻¹⁴We are talking about our Lord Christ, who belonged to a different tribe. No one from that tribe ever served as a priest at the altar.* It is clear that Christ came from the tribe of Judah. And Moses* said nothing about priests belonging to that tribe.

Jesus Is a Priest Like Melchizedek

¹⁵And these things become even clearer when we see that another priest has come who is like Melchizedek.* ¹⁶He was made a priest, but not because he met the requirement of being born into the right family. He became a priest by the power of a life that will never end. ¹⁷This is what the Scriptures* say about him: "You are a priest forever—the kind of priest Melchizedek was."ᵇ

¹⁸The old rule is now ended because it was weak and worthless. ¹⁹The law of Moses* could not make anything perfect. But

---

ᵃ**7:3** *No one ... came from* Literally, "Melchizedek was without father, without mother, without genealogy." ᵇ**7:17** Quote from Ps. 110:4.

now a better hope has been given to us. And with that hope we can come near to God.

²⁰Also, it is important that God made a vow* when he made Jesus high priest.* When those other men became priests, there was no vow. ²¹But Christ became a priest with God's vow. God said to him,

> "The Lord has made a vow
>   and will not change his mind:
> 'You are a priest forever.'"
>   *Psalm 110:4*

²²So this means that Jesus is the guarantee of a better agreement* from God to his people.

²³Also, when one of those other priests died, he could not continue being a priest. So there were many of those priests. ²⁴But Jesus lives forever. He will never stop serving as a priest. ²⁵So Christ can save those who come to God through him. Christ can do this forever, because he always lives and is ready to help people when they come before God.

²⁶So Jesus is the kind of high priest we need. He is holy.ᵃ He has no sin in him. He is pure and not influenced by sinners. And he is raised above the heavens. ²⁷He is not like those other priests. They had to offer sacrifices* every day, first for their own sins, and then for the sins of the people. But Jesus doesn't need to do that. He offered only one sacrifice for all time. He offered himself. ²⁸The law chooses high priests who are men and have the same weaknesses that all people have. But after the law, God spoke the vow that made his Son, who had been made perfect through suffering, to be a high priest who will serve forever.

Jesus Our High Priest

8 ¹Here is the point of what we are saying: We have a high priest* like that, who sits on the right sideᵇ of God's throne in heaven. ²Our high priest serves in the Most Holy Place.ᶜ He serves in the true place of worshipᵈ that was made by God, not by anyone here on earth.

³Every high priest has the work of offering gifts and sacrifices* to God. So our high priest must also offer something to God. ⁴If our high priest were now living on earth, he would not be a priest. I say this because there are already priests here who follow the law by offering gifts to God. ⁵The work that these priests do is really only a copy and a shadow of what is in heaven. That is why God warned Moses* when he was ready to build the Holy Tent*: "Be sure to make everything exactly like the pattern I showed you on the mountain."ᵉ ⁶But the work that has been given to Jesus is much greater than the

---

ᵃ**7:26** *holy* Devoted to God and living in a way that honors and pleases him.   ᵇ**8:1** *right side* The place of honor and authority (power).   ᶜ**8:2** *Most Holy Place* Literally, "holies" for "holy of holies," the spiritual place where God lives and is worshiped.   ᵈ**8:2** *place of worship* Literally, "Tabernacle" or "tent."   ᵉ**8:5** Quote from Ex. 25:40.

work that was given to those priests. In the same way, the new agreement* that Jesus brought from God to his people is much greater than the old one. And the new agreement is based on better promises.

⁷If there was nothing wrong with the first agreement,* then there would be no need for a second agreement. ⁸But God found something wrong with the people. He said,

"The time is coming, says the Lord,
> when I will give a new agreement to the people of Israel*
> > and to the people of Judah.*
⁹ It will not be like the agreement that I gave to their fathers.
> That is the agreement I gave when I took them by the hand
> > and led them out of Egypt.
They did not continue following the agreement I gave them,
> and I turned away from them, says the Lord.
¹⁰ This is the new agreement I will give the people of Israel.
> I will give this agreement in the future, says the Lord:
> I will put my laws in their minds,
> > and I will write my laws on their hearts.
> I will be their God,
> > and they will be my people.
¹¹ Never again will anyone have to teach their neighbors
> > or their family to know the Lord.
> All people—the greatest and the least important—
> > will know me.
¹² And I will forgive the wrongs they have done,
> > and I will not remember their sins."   *Jeremiah 31:31-34*

¹³God called this a new agreement, so he has made the first agreement old. And anything that is old and useless is ready to disappear.

Worship Under the Old Agreement

9 ¹The first agreement* had rules for worship and a place for worship here on earth. ²This place was inside a tent. The first area in the tent was called the Holy Place. In the Holy Place were the lamp and the table with the special bread offered to God. ³Behind the second curtain* was a room called the Most Holy Place.* ⁴In the Most Holy Place was a golden altar* for burning incense.* And also there was the Box of the Agreement.* The Box was covered with gold. Inside this Box was a golden jar of manna* and Aaron's rod—the rod that once grew leaves. Also in the Box were the flat stones with the Ten Commandments of the old agreement on them. ⁵Above the Box were the Cherub angels* that showed God's glory.* These

---

a 8:8 Israel First, Israel was the people descended from Jacob (see "Israel" in the Word List), but the name is also used to mean all of God's chosen people. Also in verse 10.

Cherub angels were over the place of mercy.[a] But we cannot say everything about this now.

[6]Everything in the tent was made ready in the way I have explained. Then the priests went into the first room every day to do their worship duties. [7]But only the high priest* could go into the second room, and he went in only once a year. Also, he could never enter that room without taking blood with him. He offered that blood to God for himself and for the sins the people committed without knowing they were sinning.

[8]The Holy Spirit* uses those two separate rooms to teach us that the way into the Most Holy Place[b] was not open while the first room was still there. [9]This is an example for us today. It shows that the gifts and sacrifices* the priests offer to God are not able to make the consciences of the worshipers completely clear. [10]These gifts and sacrifices are only about food and drink and special washings. They are only rules about the body. God gave them for his people to follow until the time of his new way.

Worship Under the New Agreement

[11]But Christ has already come to be the high priest.* He is the high priest of the good things we now have. But Christ does not serve in a place like the tent that those other priests served in. He serves in a place that is better than that tent. It is more perfect, and it is not made by anyone here on earth. It does not belong to this world. [12]Christ entered the Most Holy Place only one time—enough for all time. He entered the Most Holy Place by using his own blood, not the blood of goats or young bulls. He entered there and made us free from sin forever.

[13]The blood of goats and bulls and the ashes of a cow were sprinkled on those who were no longer pure enough to enter the place of worship. The blood and ashes made them pure again—but only their bodies. [14]So surely the blood sacrifice of Christ can do much more. Christ offered himself through the eternal Spirit[c] as a perfect sacrifice* to God. His blood will make us completely clean from the evil we have done. It will give us clear consciences so that we can worship the living God.

[15]So Christ brings a new agreement* from God to his people. He brings this agreement so that those who are chosen by God can have the blessings God promised, blessings that last forever. This can happen only because Christ died to free people from sins committed against the commands of the first agreement.*

[16]When someone dies and leaves a will,* there must be proof that the one who wrote the will is dead. [17]A will means nothing while the one who wrote it is still living. It can be used only

---

[a] **9:5** *place of mercy* Or "mercy seat," a place on top of the "Box of the Agreement," where the high priest put the blood of an animal once a year to pay for the sins of the people.
[b] **9:8** *Most Holy Place* Literally, "holies" for "holy of holies," the spiritual place where God lives and is worshiped. Also in verses 12, 24. [c] **9:14** *Spirit* Probably the Holy Spirit. See "Holy Spirit" in the Word List.

after that person's death. [18]That is why blood was needed to begin the first agreement between God and his people. [19]First, Moses* told the people every command in the law. Then he took the blood of calves and mixed it with water. Then he used red wool and a branch of hyssop* to sprinkle the blood and water on the book of the law and on all the people. [20]Then he said, "This is the blood that makes the agreement good—the agreement that God commanded you to follow."[a] [21]In the same way, Moses sprinkled the blood on the Holy Tent.* He sprinkled the blood over everything used in worship. [22]The law* says that almost everything must be made clean by blood. Sins cannot be forgiven without a blood sacrifice.

Christ's Sacrifice Takes Away Sins

[23]These things are copies of the real things that are in heaven. These copies had to be made clean by animal sacrifices.* But the real things in heaven must have much better sacrifices. [24]Christ went into the Most Holy Place. But it was not the man-made one, which is only a copy of the real one. He went into heaven, and he is there now before God to help us.

[25]The high priest* enters the Most Holy Place* once every year. He takes with him blood to offer. But he does not offer his own blood like Christ did. Christ went into heaven, but not to offer himself many times like the high priest offers blood again and again. [26]If Christ had offered himself many times, he would have needed to suffer many times since the time the world was made. But he came to offer himself only once. And that once is enough for all time. He came at a time when the world is nearing an end. He came to take away all sin by offering himself as a sacrifice.

[27]Everyone must die once. Then they are judged. [28]So Christ was offered as a sacrifice one time to take away the sins of many people. And he will come a second time, but not to offer himself for sin. He will come the second time to bring salvation to those who are waiting for him.

Christ's Sacrifice Makes Us Perfect

10 [1]The law* gave us only an unclear picture of the good things coming in the future. The law is not a perfect picture of the real things. The law tells people to offer the same sacrifices* every year. Those who come to worship God continue to offer those sacrifices. But the law can never make them perfect. [2]If the law could make people perfect, those sacrifices would have already stopped. They would already be clean from their sins, and they would not still feel guilty. [3]But that's not what happens. Their sacrifices make them remember their

[a]9:20 Quote from Ex. 24:8.

sins every year, [4]because it is not possible for the blood of bulls and goats to take away sins.

[5]So when Christ came into the world he said,

"You don't want sacrifices and offerings,
　　but you have prepared a body for me.
[6] You are not pleased with the sacrifices
　　of animals killed and burned
　　or with offerings to take away sins.
[7] Then I said, 'Here I am, God.
　　It is written about me in the book of the law.
　　I have come to do what you want.'"
　　　　　　　　　　　　　　　　　　Psalm 40:6–8

[8]Christ first said, "You don't want sacrifices and offerings. You are not pleased with animals killed and burned or with sacrifices to take away sin." (These are all sacrifices that the law commands.) [9]Then he said, "Here I am, God. I have come to do what you want." So God ends that first system of sacrifices and starts his new way. [10]Jesus Christ did the things God wanted him to do. And because of that, we are made holy* through the sacrifice of Christ's body. Christ made that sacrifice one time—enough for all time.

[11]Every day the priests stand and do their religious service. Again and again they offer the same sacrifices, which can never take away sins. [12]But Christ offered only one sacrifice for sins, and that sacrifice is good for all time. Then he sat down at the right side of God. [13]And now Christ waits there for his enemies to be put under his power.[a] [14]With one sacrifice Christ made his people perfect forever. They are the ones who are being made holy.

[15]The Holy Spirit* also tells us about this. First he says,

[16]"This is the agreement[b] I will make with my people
　　in the future, says the Lord.
I will put my laws in their hearts.
　　I will write my laws in their minds."
　　　　　　　　　　　　　　　　　　Jeremiah 31:33

[17]Then he says,

"I will forgive their sins
　　and never again remember the evil they have done."
　　　　　　　　　　　　　　　　　　Jeremiah 31:34

[18]And after everything is forgiven, there is no more need for a sacrifice to pay for sins.

Come Near to God

[19]And so, brothers and sisters, we are completely free to enter the Most Holy Place.[c] We can do this without fear because of the

---

[a]**10:13** *to be put under his power* Literally, "to be made a footstool for his feet."
[b]**10:16** *agreement* The new and better agreement that God has given to his people through Jesus. See "agreement" in the Word List.　[c]**10:19** *Most Holy Place* Literally, "holies" for "holy of holies," the spiritual place where God lives and is worshiped.

blood sacrifice of Jesus. [20]We enter through a new way that Jesus opened for us. It is a living way that leads through the curtain[a]— Christ's body. [21]And we have a great priest who rules the house of God. [22]Sprinkled with the blood of Christ, our hearts have been made free from a guilty conscience, and our bodies have been washed with pure water. So come near to God with a sincere heart, full of confidence because of our faith in Christ. [23]We must hold on to the hope we have, never hesitating to tell people about it. We can trust God to do what he promised.

Help Each Other Be Strong

[24]We should think about each other to see how we can encourage each other to show love and do good works. [25]We must not quit meeting together, as some are doing. No, we need to keep on encouraging each other. This becomes more and more important as you see the Day[b] getting closer.

Don't Turn Away From Christ

[26]If we decide to continue sinning after we have learned the truth, then there is no other sacrifice* that will take away sins. [27]If we continue sinning, all that is left for us is a fearful time of waiting for the judgment and the angry fire that will destroy those who live against God. [28]Whoever refused to obey the law of Moses* was found guilty from the testimony given by two or three witnesses. Such people were not forgiven. They were killed. [29]So think how much more punishment people deserve who show their hate for the Son of God—people who show they have no respect for the blood sacrifice that began the new agreement* and once made them holy, or who insult the Spirit* of God's grace.* [30]We know that God said, "I will punish people for the wrongs they do; I will repay them."[c] And he also said, "The Lord will judge his people."[d] [31]It is a terrible thing to face punishment from the living God.

Keep the Courage and Patience You Had

[32]Remember the days when you first learned the truth. You had a hard struggle with much suffering, but you continued strong. [33]Sometimes people said hateful things to you and mistreated you in public. And sometimes you helped others who were being treated that same way. [34]Yes, you helped them in prison and shared in their suffering. And you were still happy when everything you owned was taken away from you. You continued to be happy, because you knew that you had something much better—something that would continue forever.

---

[a]**10:20** *curtain* The spiritual curtain in the heavenly temple, which was symbolized by the physical one that separated the inner sanctuary (and God's presence) from the outer room in the Holy Tent and in the Jerusalem Temple. See "curtain" in the Word List. [b]**10:25** *Day* Probably the day Christ will come to judge everyone and take his people to live with him. [c]**10:30** Quote from Deut. 32:35. [d]**10:30** Quote from Deut. 32:36.

³⁵So don't lose the courage that you had in the past. Your courage will be rewarded richly. ³⁶You must be patient. After you have done what God wants, you will get what he promised you. ³⁷He says,

"Very soon now, the one who is coming
    will come and will not be late.
³⁸ The person who is right with me
    will live by trusting in me.
But I will not be pleased with the one
    who turns back in fear."   *Habakkuk 2:3–4 (Greek version)*

³⁹But we are not those who turn back and are lost. No, we are the people who have faith and are saved.

Faith

11 ¹Faith is what makes real the things we hope for. It is proof of what we cannot see. ²God was pleased with the people who lived a long time ago, because they had faith like this.

³Faith helps us understand that God created the whole world by his command. This means that the things we see were made by something that cannot be seen.

⁴Cain* and Abel* both offered sacrifices* to God. But Abel offered a better sacrifice to God because he had faith. God said he was pleased with what Abel offered. And so God called him a good man because he had faith. Abel died, but through his faith he is still speaking.

⁵Enoch was carried away from this earth, so he never died. The Scriptures* tell us that before he was carried off, he was a man who pleased God. Later, no one knew where he was, because God had taken Enoch to be with him. This all happened because he had faith. ⁶Without faith no one can please God. Whoever comes to God must believe that he is real and that he rewards those who sincerely try to find him.

⁷Noah was warned by God about things that he could not yet see. But he had faith and respect for God, so he built a large boat to save his family. With his faith, Noah showed that the world was wrong. And he became one of those who are made right with God through faith.

⁸God called Abraham to travel to another place that he promised to give him. Abraham did not know where that other place was. But he obeyed God and started traveling, because he had faith. ⁹Abraham lived in the country that God promised to give him. He lived there like a visitor who did not belong. He did this because he had faith. He lived in tents with Isaac and Jacob, who also received the same promise from God. ¹⁰Abraham was waiting for the city*ᵃ* that has real foundations. He was waiting for the city that is planned and built by God.

ᵃ11:10 city The spiritual "city" where God's people live with him. Also called "the heavenly Jerusalem." See Heb. 12:22.

¹¹Sarah was not able to have children, and Abraham was too old. But he had faith in God, trusting him to do what he promised. And so God made them able to have children. ¹²Abraham was so old he was almost dead. But from that one man came as many descendants as there are stars in the sky. So many people came from him that they are like grains of sand on the seashore.

¹³All these great people continued living with faith until they died. They did not get the things God promised his people. But they were happy just to see those promises coming far in the future. They accepted the fact that they were like visitors and strangers here on earth. ¹⁴When people accept something like that, they show they are waiting for a country that will be their own. ¹⁵If they were thinking about the country they had left, they could have gone back. ¹⁶But they were waiting for a better country—a heavenly country. So God is not ashamed to be called their God. And he has prepared a city for them.

¹⁷⁻¹⁸God tested Abraham's faith. God told him to offer Isaac as a sacrifice. Abraham obeyed because he had faith. He already had the promises from God. And God had already said to him, "It is through Isaac that your descendants will come."ᵃ But Abraham was ready to offer his only son. He did this because he had faith. ¹⁹He believed that God could raise people from death. And really, when God stopped Abraham from killing Isaac, it was as if he got him back from death.

²⁰Isaac blessed the future of Jacob and Esau. He did that because he had faith. ²¹And Jacob, also because he had faith, blessed each one of Joseph's sons. He did this while he was dying, leaning on his rod and worshiping God.

²²And when Joseph was almost dead, he spoke about the people of Israel* leaving Egypt. And he told them what they should do with his body. He did this because he had faith.

²³And the mother and father of Moses* hid him for three months after he was born. They did this because they had faith. They saw that Moses was a beautiful baby. And they were not afraid to disobey the king's order.

²⁴⁻²⁵Moses grew up and became a man. He refused to be called the son of Pharaoh's daughter. He chose not to enjoy the pleasures of sin that last such a short time. Instead, he chose to suffer with God's people. He did this because he had faith. ²⁶He thought it was better to suffer for the Christ* than to have all the treasures of Egypt. He was waiting for the reward that God would give him.

²⁷Moses left Egypt because he had faith. He was not afraid of the king's anger. He continued strong as if he could see the God no one can see. ²⁸Moses prepared the Passover* and spread the blood on the doorways of the people of Israel, so that the angel

ᵃ**11:17–18** Quote from Gen. 21:12.

of death[a] would not kill their firstborn[b] sons. Moses did this because he had faith.

²⁹And God's people all walked through the Red Sea as if it were dry land. They were able to do this because they had faith. But when the Egyptians tried to follow them, they were drowned.

³⁰And the walls of Jericho fell because of the faith of God's people. They marched around the walls for seven days, and then the walls fell.

³¹And Rahab, the prostitute, welcomed the Israelite* spies like friends. And because of her faith, she was not killed with the ones who refused to obey.

³²Do I need to give you more examples? I don't have enough time to tell you about Gideon, Barak, Samson, Jephthah, David, Samuel, and the prophets.* ³³All of them had great faith. And with that faith they defeated kingdoms. They did what was right, and God helped them in the ways he promised. With their faith some people closed the mouths of lions. ³⁴And some were able to stop blazing fires. Others escaped from being killed with swords. Some who were weak were made strong. They became powerful in battle and defeated other armies. ³⁵There were women who lost loved ones but got them back when they were raised from death. Others were tortured* but refused to accept their freedom. They did this so that they could be raised from death to a better life. ³⁶Some were laughed at and beaten. Others were tied up and put in prison. ³⁷They were killed with stones. They were cut in half. They were killed with swords. The only clothes some of them had were sheep skins or goat skins. They were poor, persecuted,* and treated badly by others. ³⁸The world was not good enough for these great people. They had to wander in deserts and mountains, living in caves and holes in the ground.

³⁹God was pleased with all of them because of their faith. But not one of them received God's great promise. ⁴⁰God planned something better for us. He wanted to make us perfect. Of course, he wanted those great people to be made perfect too, but not before we could all enjoy that blessing together.

We Also Should Follow Jesus' Example

12 ¹We have all these great people around us as examples. Their lives tell us what faith means. So we, too, should run the race that is before us and never quit. We should remove from our lives anything that would slow us down and the sin that so often makes us fall. ²We must never stop looking to Jesus. He is the leader of our faith, and he is the one who makes our faith complete. He suffered death on a cross. But he

---

[a]**11:28** *angel of death* Literally, "the destroyer." To punish the Egyptians, God sent an angel to kill the oldest son in each home. See Ex. 12:29–32. [b]**11:28** *firstborn* The first child born into a family.

accepted the shame of the cross as if it were nothing because of the joy he could see waiting for him. And now he is sitting at the right side of God's throne. ³Think about Jesus. He patiently endured the angry insults that sinful people were shouting at him. Think about him so that you won't get discouraged and stop trying.

God Is Like a Father

⁴You are struggling against sin, but you have not had to give up your life for the cause. ⁵You are children of God, and he speaks words of comfort to you. You have forgotten these words:

"My child, don't think the Lord's discipline is worth nothing,
    and don't stop trying when he corrects you.
⁶ The Lord disciplines everyone he loves;
    and he punishes everyone he accepts as a child."

Proverbs 3:11–12

⁷So accept sufferings like a father's discipline. God does these things to you like a father correcting his children. You know that all children are disciplined by their fathers. ⁸So, if you never receive the discipline that every child must have, you are not true children and don't really belong to God. ⁹We have all had fathers here on earth who corrected us with discipline. And we respected them. So it is even more important that we accept discipline from the Father of our spirits. If we do this, we will have life. ¹⁰Our fathers on earth disciplined us for a short time in the way they thought was best. But God disciplines us to help us so that we can be holy* like him. ¹¹We don't enjoy discipline when we get it. It is painful. But later, after we have learned our lesson from it, we will enjoy the peace that comes from doing what is right.

Be Careful How You Live

¹²You have become weak, so make yourselves strong again. ¹³Live in the right way so that you will be saved and your weakness will not cause you to be lost.

¹⁴Try to live in peace with everyone. And try to keep your lives free from sin. Anyone whose life is not holy* will never see the Lord. ¹⁵Be careful that no one fails to get God's grace.* Be careful that no one loses their faith and becomes like a bitter weed growing among you. Someone like that can ruin your whole group. ¹⁶Be careful that no one commits sexual sin. And be careful that no one is like Esau and never thinks about God. As the oldest son, Esau would have inherited everything from his father. But he sold all that for a single meal. ¹⁷You remember that after Esau did this, he wanted to get his father's blessing. He wanted that blessing so much that he cried. But his father refused to give him the blessing, because Esau could find no way to change what he had done.

[18] You have not come to a place that can be seen and touched, like the mountain the people of Israel* saw, which was burning with fire and covered with darkness, gloom, and storms. [19] There is no sound of a trumpet or a voice speaking words like those they heard. When they heard the voice, they begged never to hear another word. [20] They did not want to hear the command: "If anything, even an animal, touches the mountain, it must be killed with stones."[a] [21] What they saw was so terrible that Moses said, "I am shaking with fear."[bc]

[22] But you have come to Mount Zion,* to the city of the living God, the heavenly Jerusalem.[d] You have come to a place where thousands of angels have gathered to celebrate. [23] You have come to the meeting of God's firstborn[e] children. Their names are written in heaven. You have come to God, the judge of all people. And you have come to the spirits of good people who have been made perfect. [24] You have come to Jesus—the one who brought the new agreement* from God to his people. You have come to the sprinkled blood[f] that tells us about better things than the blood of Abel.*

[25] Be careful and don't refuse to listen when God speaks. Those people refused to listen to him when he warned them on earth. And they did not escape. Now God is speaking from heaven. So now it will be worse for those who refuse to listen to him. [26] When he spoke before, his voice shook the earth. But now he has promised, "Once again I will shake the earth, but I will also shake heaven."[g] [27] The words "once again" clearly show us that everything that was created will be destroyed—that is, the things that can be shaken. And only what cannot be shaken will remain.

[28] So we should be thankful because we have a kingdom that cannot be shaken. And because we are thankful, we should worship God in a way that will please him. We should do this with respect and fear, [29] because our God is like a fire that can destroy us.

Worship That Pleases God

13 [1] Continue loving each other as brothers and sisters in Christ. [2] Always remember to help people by welcoming them into your home. Some people have done that and have helped angels without knowing it. [3] Don't forget those who are in prison. Remember them as though you were in prison with them. And don't forget those who are suffering. Remember them as though you were suffering with them.

[a] **12:20** Quote from Ex. 19:12–13. [b] **12:21** Quote from Deut. 9:19. [c] **12:21** *Verses 18–21* These verses refer to things that happened to the people of Israel in the time of Moses as described in Ex. 19. [d] **12:22** *Jerusalem* Here, the spiritual city of God's people. [e] **12:23** *firstborn* The first son born in a Jewish family had the most important place in the family and received special blessings. All God's children are like that. [f] **12:24** *sprinkled blood* The blood (death) of Jesus. [g] **12:26** Quote from Hag. 2:6.

⁴Marriage should be honored by everyone. And every marriage should be kept pure between husband and wife. God will judge guilty those who commit sexual sins and adultery.* ⁵Keep your lives free from the love of money. And be satisfied with what you have. God has said,

> "I will never leave you;
> I will never run away from you."   *Deuteronomy 31:6*

⁶So we can feel sure and say,

> "The Lord is my helper;
> I will not be afraid.
> People can do nothing to me."   *Psalm 118:6*

⁷Remember your leaders. They taught God's message to you. Remember how they lived and died, and copy their faith. ⁸Jesus Christ is the same yesterday, today, and forever. ⁹Don't let all kinds of strange teachings lead you into the wrong way. Depend only on God's grace* for spiritual strength, not on rules about foods. Obeying those rules doesn't help anyone.

¹⁰We have a sacrifice.*ᵃ And those priests who serve in the Holy Tent* cannot eat from the sacrifice we have. ¹¹The high priest* carries the blood of animals into the Most Holy Place*ᵇ and offers that blood for sins. But the bodies of those animals are burned outside the camp. ¹²So Jesus also suffered outside the city. He died to make his people holy* with his own blood. ¹³So we should go to Jesus outside the camp and accept the same shame that he had. ¹⁴Here on earth we don't have a city that lasts forever. But we are waiting for the city that we will have in the future. ¹⁵So through Jesus we should never stop offering our sacrifice* to God. That sacrifice is our praise, coming from lips that speak his name. ¹⁶And don't forget to do good and to share what you have with others, because sacrifices like these are very pleasing to God.

¹⁷Obey your leaders. Be willing to do what they say. They are responsible for your spiritual welfare, so they are always watching to protect you. Obey them so that their work will give them joy, not grief. It won't help you to make it hard for them.

¹⁸Continue praying for us. We feel right about what we do, because we always try to do what is best. ¹⁹And I beg you to pray that God will send me back to you soon. I want this more than anything else.

²⁰⁻²¹I pray that the God of peace will give you every good thing you need so that you can do what he wants. God is the one who raised from death our Lord Jesus, the Great Shepherd of his sheep. He raised him because Jesus sacrificed his blood to begin the new agreement* that never ends. I pray that God will

---

ᵃ13:10 sacrifice Literally, "altar." Here, it means the sacrifice (offering) of Jesus. He gave his life to pay for people's sins.   *ᵇ13:11* Most Holy Place Literally, "the holies," the place in the Jewish Tabernacle or Temple where God met the high priest.

work through Jesus Christ to do the things in us that please him. To him be glory* forever. Amen.*

²²My brothers and sisters, I beg you to listen patiently to what I have said. I wrote this letter to strengthen you. And it is not very long. ²³I want you to know that our brother Timothy is out of prison. If he comes to me soon, we will both come to see you.

²⁴Give my greetings to all your leaders and to all God's people. All those from Italy send you their greetings.

²⁵God's grace be with you all.

James

1 ¹Greetings from James, a servant of God and of the Lord Jesus Christ.

To God's people*ᵃ* who are scattered all over the world.

Faith and Wisdom

²My brothers and sisters, you will have many kinds of trouble. But this gives you a reason to be very happy. ³You know that when your faith is tested, you learn to be patient in suffering. ⁴If you let that patience work in you, the end result will be good. You will be mature and complete. You will be all that God wants you to be.

⁵Do any of you need wisdom? Ask God for it. He is generous and enjoys giving to everyone. So he will give you wisdom. ⁶But when you ask God, you must believe. Don't doubt him. Whoever doubts is like a wave in the sea that is blown up and down by the wind. ⁷⁻⁸People like that are thinking two different things at the same time. They can never decide what to do. So they should not think they will receive anything from the Lord.

True Riches

⁹Believers who are poor should be glad that God considers them so important. ¹⁰Believers who are rich should be glad when bad things happen that humble them. Their riches won't keep them from disappearing as quickly as wild flowers. ¹¹As the sun rises and gets hotter, its heat dries up the plants, and the flowers fall off. The flowers that were so beautiful are now dead. That's how it is with the rich. While they are still making plans for their business, they will die.

Temptation Does Not Come From God

¹²What great blessings there are for those who are tempted and remain faithful! After they have proved their faith, God will give them the crown* of eternal life. God promised this to all people who love him. ¹³Whenever you feel tempted to do something bad, you should not say, "God is tempting me." Evil cannot tempt God, and God himself does not tempt anyone. ¹⁴You are tempted by the evil things you want. Your own desire leads you away and traps you. ¹⁵Your desire grows inside you

*ᵃ***1:1** *God's people* Literally, "the twelve tribes." Believers in Christ are like the tribes of Israel, God's chosen people in the Old Testament.

until it results in sin. Then the sin grows bigger and bigger and finally ends in death.

¹⁶My dear brothers and sisters, don't be fooled about this. ¹⁷Everything good comes from God. Every perfect gift is from him. These good gifts come down from the Father who made all the lights in the sky. But God never changes like the shadows from those lights. He is always the same. ¹⁸God decided to give us life through the true message* he sent to us. He wanted us to be the most important of all that he created.

Listening and Obeying

¹⁹My dear brothers and sisters, always be more willing to listen than to speak. Keep control of your anger. ²⁰Anger does not help you live the way God wants. ²¹So get rid of everything evil in your lives—every kind of wrong you do. Be humble and accept God's teaching that is planted in your hearts. This teaching can save you.

²²Do what God's teaching says; don't just listen and do nothing. When you only sit and listen, you are fooling yourselves. ²³Hearing God's teaching and doing nothing is like looking at your face in the mirror ²⁴and doing nothing about what you saw. You go away and immediately forget how bad you looked. ²⁵But when you look into God's perfect law that sets people free, pay attention to it. If you do what it says, you will have God's blessing. Never just listen to his teaching and forget what you heard.

The True Way to Worship God

²⁶You might think you are a very religious person. But if your tongue is out of control, you are fooling yourself. Your careless talk makes your offerings to God worthless. ²⁷The worship that God wants is this: caring for orphans or widows who need help and keeping yourself free from the world's evil influence. This is the kind of worship that God accepts as pure and good.

Love All People

2 ¹My dear brothers and sisters, you are believers in our glorious Lord Jesus Christ. So don't treat some people better than others. ²Suppose someone comes into your meeting wearing very nice clothes and a gold ring. At the same time a poor person comes in wearing old, dirty clothes. ³You show special attention to the person wearing nice clothes. You say, "Sit here in this good seat." But you say to the poor person, "Stand there!" or, "Sit on the floor by our feet!" ⁴Doesn't this show that you think some people are more important than others? You set yourselves up as judges—judges who make bad decisions.

⁵Listen, my dear brothers and sisters. God chose the poor people in the world to be rich in faith. He chose them to receive the kingdom* God promised to those who love him.

[6]But you show no respect to those who are poor. And you know that the rich are the ones who always try to control your lives. And they are the ones who take you to court. [7]And the rich are the ones who insult the wonderful name of Christ, the name by which you are known.

[8]One law rules over all other laws. This royal law is found in the Scriptures*: "Love your neighbor[a] the same as you love yourself."[b] If you obey this law, you are doing right. [9]But if you are treating one person as more important than another, you are sinning. You are guilty of breaking God's law.

[10]You might follow all of God's law. But if you fail to obey only one command, you are guilty of breaking all the commands in that law. [11]God said, "Don't commit adultery."[c] The same God also said, "Don't kill."[d] So if you don't commit adultery, but you kill someone, you are guilty of breaking all of God's law.

[12]You will be judged by the law that makes people free. You should remember this in everything you say and do. [13]Yes, you must show mercy to others. If you do not show mercy, then God will not show mercy to you when he judges you. But the one who shows mercy can stand without fear before the Judge.

Faith and Good Works

[14]My brothers and sisters, if someone says they have faith but do nothing, that faith is worth nothing. Faith like that cannot save anyone. [15]Suppose a brother or sister in Christ comes to you in need of clothes or something to eat. [16]And you say to them, "God be with you! I hope you stay warm and get plenty to eat," but you don't give them the things they need. If you don't help them, your words are worthless. [17]It is the same with faith. If it is just faith and nothing more—if it doesn't do anything—it is dead.

[18]But someone might argue, "Some people have faith, and others have good works." My answer would be that you can't show me your faith if you don't do anything. But I will show you my faith by the good I do. [19]You believe there is one God. That's good, but even the demons* believe that! And they shake with fear.

[20]You fool! Faith that does nothing is worth nothing. Do you want me to prove this to you? [21]Our father* Abraham* was made right with God by what he did. He offered his son Isaac to God on the altar.* [22]So you see that Abraham's faith and what he did worked together. His faith was made perfect by what he did. [23]This shows the full meaning of the Scriptures* where they say, "Abraham believed God, and God accepted Abraham's faith. That faith made Abraham right with God."[e]

---

[a]2:8 your neighbor Or, "others." Jesus' teaching in Lk. 10:25–37 makes clear that this includes anyone in need.   [b]2:8 Quote from Lev. 19:18.   [c]2:11 Quote from Ex. 20:14; Deut. 5:18.   [d]2:11 Quote from Ex. 20:13; Deut. 5:17.   [e]2:23 Quote from Gen. 15:6.

Abraham was called "God's friend."[a] [24]So you see that people are made right with God by what they do. They cannot be made right by faith alone.

[25]Another example is Rahab. She was a prostitute, but she was made right with God by something she did. She helped those who were spying for God's people. She welcomed them into her home and helped them escape by a different road.[b]

[26]A person's body that does not have a spirit is dead. It is the same with faith—faith that does nothing is dead!

Controlling the Things We Say

3 [1]My brothers and sisters, not many of you should be teachers. I say this because, as you know, we who teach will be judged more strictly than others.

[2]We all make many mistakes. A person who never said anything wrong would be perfect. Someone like that would be able to control their whole body too. [3]We put bits into the mouths of horses to make them obey us. With these bits we can control their whole body. [4]It is the same with ships. A ship is very big, and it is pushed by strong winds. But a very small rudder controls that big ship. And the one who controls the rudder decides where the ship will go. It goes where he wants it to go. [5]It is the same with our tongue. It is a small part of the body, but it can boast about doing great things.

A big forest fire can be started with only a little flame. [6]The tongue is like a fire. It is a world of evil among the parts of our body. It spreads its evil through our whole body and starts a fire that influences all of life. It gets this fire from hell.

[7]Humans have control over every kind of wild animal, bird, reptile, and fish, and they have controlled all these things. [8]But no one can control the tongue. It is wild and evil, full of deadly poison. [9]We use our tongues to praise our Lord and Father, but then we curse people who were created in God's likeness. [10]These praises and curses come from the same mouth. My brothers and sisters, this should not happen. [11]Do good water and bad water flow from the same spring? Of course not. [12]My brothers and sisters, can a fig tree make olives? Or can a grapevine make figs? No, and a well full of salty water cannot give good water.

True Wisdom

[13]Are there any among you who are really wise and understanding? Then you should show your wisdom by living right. You should do what is good with humility. A wise person does not boast. [14]If you are selfish and have bitter jealousy in your hearts, you have no reason to boast. Your boasting is a lie that

---

[a] **2:23** Quote from 2 Chron. 20:7; Isa. 41:8. [b] **2:25** *She helped ... road* The story about Rahab is found in Josh. 2:1–21.

hides the truth. [15]That kind of "wisdom" does not come from God. That "wisdom" comes from the world. It is not spiritual. It is from the devil. [16]Where there is jealousy and selfishness, there will be confusion and every kind of evil. [17]But the wisdom that comes from God is like this: First, it is pure. It is also peaceful, gentle, and easy to please. This wisdom is always ready to help people who have trouble and to do good for others. This wisdom is always fair and honest. [18]People who work for peace in a peaceful way get the blessings that come from right living.

Give Yourselves to God

4 [1]Do you know where your fights and arguments come from? They come from the selfish desires that make war inside you. [2]You want things, but you don't get them. So you kill and are jealous of others. But you still cannot get what you want. So you argue and fight. You don't get what you want because you don't ask God. [3]Or when you ask, you don't receive anything, because the reason you ask is wrong. You only want to use it for your own pleasure.

[4]You people are not faithful to God! You should know that loving what the world has is the same as hating God. So anyone who wants to be friends with this evil world becomes God's enemy. [5]Do you think the Scriptures* mean nothing? The Scriptures say, "The Spirit* God made to live in us wants us only for himself."[a] [6]But the grace* that God gives is greater. Like the Scripture says, "God is against the proud, but he gives grace to the humble."[b]

[7]So give yourselves to God. Stand against the devil, and he will run away from you. [8]Come near to God and he will come near to you. You are sinners, so clean sin out of your lives.[c] You are trying to follow God and the world at the same time. Make your thinking pure. [9]Be sad, be sorry, and cry! Change your laughter into crying. Change your joy into sadness. [10]Be humble before the Lord, and he will make you great.

You Are Not the Judge

[11]Brothers and sisters, don't say anything against each other. If you criticize your brother or sister in Christ or judge them, you are criticizing and judging the law they follow. And when you are judging the law, you are not a follower of the law. You have become a judge. [12]God is the one who gave us the law, and he is the Judge. He is the only one who can save and destroy. So it is not right for you to judge anyone.

---

[a]**4:5** *"The Spirit … himself"* Other possible translations: "God strongly desires the spirit that he made to live in us." Or, "The spirit that he made to live in us is full of envious desires." See Ex. 20:5. [b]**4:6** Quote from Prov. 3:34. [c]**4:8** *so clean sin out of your lives* Literally, "so wash your hands."

Let God Plan Your Life

¹³Some of you say, "Today or tomorrow we will go to some city. We will stay there a year, do business, and make money." Listen, think about this: ¹⁴You don't know what will happen tomorrow. Your life is like a fog. You can see it for a short time, but then it goes away. ¹⁵So you should say, "If the Lord wants, we will live and do this or that." ¹⁶But now you are proud and boast about yourself. All such boasting is wrong. ¹⁷If you fail to do what you know is right, you are sinning.

A Warning to Rich and Selfish People

5 ¹You rich people, listen! Cry and be very sad because much trouble will come to you. ²Your riches will rot and be worth nothing. Your clothes will be eaten by moths. ³Your gold and silver will rust, and that rust will be a proof that you were wrong. That rust will eat your bodies like fire. You saved your treasure in the last days. ⁴People worked in your fields, but you did not pay them. They are crying out against you. They harvested your crops. Now the Lord All-Powerful has heard their cries.

⁵Your life on earth was full of rich living. You pleased yourselves with everything you wanted. You made yourselves fat, like an animal ready for the day of slaughter.ᵃ ⁶You showed no mercy to good people. They were not against you, but you killed them.

Be Patient

⁷Brothers and sisters, be patient; the Lord will come. So be patient until that time. Look at the farmers. They have to be patient. They have to wait for their valuable crop to grow and produce a harvest. They wait patiently for the first rain and the last rain.ᵇ ⁸You must be patient too. Never stop hoping. The Lord is coming soon. ⁹Brothers and sisters, don't complain against each other. If you don't stop complaining, you will be judged guilty. And the Judge is ready to come!

¹⁰Brothers and sisters, follow the example of the prophets* who spoke for the Lord. They suffered many bad things, but they were patient. ¹¹And we say that those who accepted their troubles with patience now have God's blessing. You have heard about Job's patience.ᶜ You know that after all his troubles, the Lord helped him. This shows that the Lord is full of mercy and is kind.

Be Careful What You Say

¹²My brothers and sisters, it is very important that you not use an oath when you make a promise. Don't use the name of

---

ᵃ**5:5** *You made yourselves fat ... slaughter* Literally, "You fattened your hearts for the day of slaughter." ᵇ**5:7** *first rain ... last rain* The "first rain" came in the fall, and the "last rain" came in the spring. ᶜ**5:11** *Job's patience* See the book of Job in the Old Testament.

heaven, earth, or anything else to prove what you say. When you mean yes, say only "yes." When you mean no, say only "no." Do this so that you will not be judged guilty.

The Power of Prayer

[13] Are you having troubles? You should pray. Are you happy? You should sing. [14] Are you sick? Ask the elders* of the church* to come and rub oil on you[a] in the name of the Lord and pray for you. [15] If such a prayer is offered in faith, it will heal anyone who is sick. The Lord will heal them. And if they have sinned, he will forgive them.

[16] So always tell each other the wrong things you have done. Then pray for each other. Do this so that God can heal you. Anyone who lives the way God wants can pray, and great things will happen. [17] Elijah* was a person just like us. He prayed that it would not rain. And it did not rain on the land for three and a half years! [18] Then Elijah prayed that it would rain. And the rain came down from the sky, and the land grew crops again.

Helping People When They Sin

[19] My brothers and sisters, if anyone wanders away from the truth and someone helps that person come back, [20] remember this: Anyone who brings a sinner back from the wrong way will save that person from eternal death and cause many sins to be forgiven.

---

a 5:14 rub oil on you Oil was used like medicine.

1 Peter

1 ¹Greetings from Peter, an apostle* of Jesus Christ.

To God's chosen people who are away from their homes—people scattered all over the areas of Pontus, Galatia, Cappadocia, Asia, and Bithynia. ²God planned long ago to choose you and to make you his holy people,* which is the Spirit's* work. God wanted you to obey him and to be made clean by the blood sacrifice*a* of Jesus Christ.

I pray that you will enjoy more and more of God's grace* and peace.

A Living Hope

³Praise be to the God and Father of our Lord Jesus Christ. God has great mercy, and because of his mercy he gave us a new life. This new life brings us a living hope through Jesus Christ's resurrection from death. ⁴Now we wait to receive the blessings God has for his children. These blessings are kept for you in heaven. They cannot be ruined or be destroyed or lose their beauty.

⁵God's power protects you through your faith, and it keeps you safe until your salvation comes. That salvation is ready to be given to you at the end of time. ⁶I know the thought of that is exciting, but for a short time now, you are having to suffer through different kinds of troubles. ⁷These troubles test your faith and prove that it is pure. And such faith is worth more than gold. Gold can be proved to be pure by fire, but gold will ruin. When your faith is proven to be pure, the result will be praise and glory* and honor when Jesus Christ comes.

⁸You have not seen Christ, but still you love him. You can't see him now, but you believe in him. You are filled with a wonderful and heavenly joy that cannot be explained. ⁹Your faith has a goal, and you are reaching that goal—your salvation.

¹⁰The prophets* studied carefully and tried to learn about this salvation. They spoke about the grace* that was coming to you. ¹¹The Spirit* of Christ was in those prophets. And the Spirit was telling about the sufferings that would happen to Christ and about the glory that would come after those sufferings. The

---

a **1:2 made clean … sacrifice** Or "sprinkled with the blood," which probably compares the beginning of the new agreement by the blood sacrifice of Christ (Mk. 14:24) with Moses' sprinkling the blood of animal sacrifices on the people of Israel to seal the agreement God made with them (Ex. 24:3–8). See also Heb. 9:15–26.

prophets tried to learn about what the Spirit was showing them—when it would happen and what the world would be like at that time.

12It was made clear to them that their service was not for themselves. They were serving you when they told about the things you have now heard. You heard them from those who told you the Good News,* with the help of the Holy Spirit sent from heaven. Even the angels would like very much to know more about these things you were told.

A Call to Holy Living

13So prepare your minds for service. With complete self-control put all your hope in the grace* that will be yours when Jesus Christ comes. 14In the past you did not have the understanding you have now, so you did the evil things you wanted to do. But now you are children of God, so you should obey him and not live the way you did before. 15Be holy* in everything you do, just as God is holy. He is the one who chose you. 16In the Scriptures* God says, "Be holy, because I am holy."a

17You pray to God and call him Father, but he will judge everyone the same way—by what they do. So while you are visiting here on earth, you should live with respect for God. 18You know that in the past the way you were living was useless. It was a way of life you learned from those who lived before you. But you were saved from that way of living. You were bought, but not with things that ruin like gold or silver. 19You were bought with the precious blood of Christ's death. He was a pure and perfect sacrificial Lamb.* 20Christ was chosen before the world was made, but he was shown to the world in these last times for you. 21You believe in God through Christ. God is the one who raised him from death and gave honor to him. So your faith and your hope are in God.

22You have made yourselves pure by obeying the truth. Now you can have true love for your brothers and sisters. So love each other deeply—with all your heart. 23You have been born again. This new life did not come from something that dies. It came from something that cannot die. You were born again through God's life-giving message* that lasts forever. 24The Scriptures say,

> "Our lives are like the grass of spring,
>   and any glory* we enjoy is like the beauty of a wildflower.
> The grass dries up and dies,
>   and the flower falls to the ground.
> 25 But the word of the Lord lasts forever."   Isaiah 40:6–8

And that word is the Good News* that was told to you.

a1:16 Quote from Lev. 11:44, 45; 19:2; 20:7.

The Living Stone and the Holy Nation

2 ¹So then, stop doing anything to hurt others. Don't lie anymore, and stop trying to fool people. Don't be jealous or say bad things about others. ²Like newborn babies hungry for milk, you should want the pure teaching that feeds your spirit. With it you can grow up and be saved. ³You have already tasted the goodness of the Lord.

⁴The Lord Jesus is the living stone.ᵃ The people of the world decided that they did not want this stone. But he is the one God chose as one of great value. So come to him. ⁵You also are like living stones, and God is using you to build a spiritual house.ᵇ You are to serve God in this house as holy* priests, offering him spiritual sacrifices* that he will accept because of Jesus Christ. ⁶The Scriptures* say,

> "Look, I have chosen a cornerstone* of great value,
>   and I put that stone in Zion*;
> the one who trusts in him will never be disappointed."
>
> Isaiah 28:16

⁷That stone has great value for you who believe. But for those who don't believe he is

> "the stone that the builders refused to accept,
>   which became the most important stone."   Psalm 118:22

⁸For them he is also

> "a stone that makes people stumble,
>   a rock that makes people fall."
>
> Isaiah 8:14

People stumble because they don't obey what God says. This is what God planned to happen to those people.

⁹But you are his chosen people, the King's priests. You are a holy nation, people who belong to God. He chose you to tell about the wonderful things he has done. He brought you out of the darkness of sin into his wonderful light.

¹⁰ In the past you were not a special people,
     but now you are God's people.
Once you had not received mercy,
     but now God has given you his mercy.ᶜ

Live for God

¹¹Dear friends, you are like visitors and strangers in this world. So I beg you to keep your lives free from the evil things you want to do, those desires that fight against your true selves. ¹²People who don't believe are living all around you. They may

---

ᵃ2:4 stone The most important stone in God's spiritual temple or house (his people). ᵇ2:5 house God's house—the place where God's people worship him. Here, it means that believers are the spiritual building where God lives. ᶜ2:10 In the past ... his mercy See Hos. 2:23.

say that you are doing wrong. So live such good lives that they will see the good you do, and they will give glory* to God on the day he comes.

Obey Every Human Authority

¹³Be willing to serve the people who have authority*a* in this world. Do this for the Lord. Obey the king, the highest authority. ¹⁴And obey the leaders who are sent by the king. They are sent to punish those who do wrong and to praise those who do good. ¹⁵When you do good, you stop ignorant people from saying foolish things about you. This is what God wants. ¹⁶Live like free people, but don't use your freedom as an excuse to do evil. Live as those who are serving God. ¹⁷Show respect for all people. Love all the brothers and sisters of God's family. Respect God, and honor the king.

The Example of Christ's Suffering

¹⁸Slaves, be willing to serve your masters. Do this with all respect. You should obey the masters who are good and kind, and you should obey the masters who are bad. ¹⁹One of you might have to suffer even when you have done nothing wrong. If you think of God and bear the pain, this pleases God. ²⁰But if you are punished for doing wrong, there is no reason to praise you for bearing that punishment. But if you suffer for doing good and you are patient, this pleases God. ²¹This is what you were chosen to do. Christ gave you an example to follow. He suffered for you. So you should do the same as he did:

²²"He never sinned, and he never told a lie."   *Isaiah 53:9*

²³People insulted him, but he did not insult them back. He suffered, but he did not threaten anyone. No, he let God take care of him. God is the one who judges rightly. ²⁴Christ carried our sins in his body on the cross. He did this so that we would stop living for sin and live for what is right. By his wounds you were healed. ²⁵You were like sheep that went the wrong way. But now you have come back to the Shepherd and Protector of your lives.

Wives and Husbands

3 ¹In the same way, you wives should be willing to serve your husbands. Then, even those who have refused to accept God's teaching will be persuaded to believe because of the way you live. You will not need to say anything. ²Your husbands will see the pure lives that you live with respect for God. ³It is not fancy hair, gold jewelry, or fine clothes that should make you beautiful. ⁴No, your beauty should come from inside you—the beauty of a gentle and quiet spirit. That beauty will never disappear. It is worth very much to God.

a **2:13** *people ... authority* Literally, "every human creation," meaning rulers, governors, presidents, or other government leaders.

[5]It was the same with the holy* women who lived long ago and followed God. They made themselves beautiful in that same way. They were willing to serve their husbands. [6]I am talking about women like Sarah. She obeyed Abraham,* her husband, and called him her master. And you women are true children of Sarah if you always do what is right and are not afraid.

[7]In the same way, you husbands should live with your wives in an understanding way, since they are weaker than you. You should show them respect, because God gives them the same blessing he gives you—the grace* of true life. Do this so that nothing will stop your prayers from being heard.

Suffering for Doing Right

[8]So all of you should live together in peace. Try to understand each other. Love each other like brothers and sisters. Be kind and humble. [9]Don't do wrong to anyone to pay them back for doing wrong to you. Or don't insult anyone to pay them back for insulting you. But ask God to bless them. Do this because you yourselves were chosen to receive a blessing. [10]The Scriptures* say,

> "If you want to enjoy true life
> and have only good days,
> then avoid saying anything hurtful,
> and never let a lie come out of your mouth.
> [11] Stop doing what is wrong, and do good.
> Look for peace, and do all you can to help people
> live peacefully.
> [12] The Lord watches over those who do what is right
> and he listens to their prayers.
> But he is against those who do evil."   *Psalm 34:12–16*

[13]If you are always trying to do good, no one can really harm you. [14]But you may suffer for doing right. If that happens, you have God's blessing. "Don't be afraid of the people who make you suffer; don't be worried."[a] [15]But keep the Lord Christ holy in your hearts. Always be ready to answer everyone who asks you to explain about the hope you have. [16]But answer them in a gentle way with respect. Keep your conscience clear. Then people will see the good way you live as followers of Christ, and those who say bad things about you will be ashamed of what they said.

[17]It is better to suffer for doing good than for doing wrong. Yes, it is better if that is what God wants. [18]Christ himself suffered when he died for you, and with that one death he paid for your sins. He was not guilty, but he died for people who are guilty. He did this to bring all of you to God. In his physical form he was killed, but he was made alive in the spirit. [19]And in the spirit he went and preached to the spirits in prison.

a3:14 Quote from Isa. 8:12.

²⁰Those were the spirits who refused to obey God long ago in the time of Noah. God was waiting patiently for people while Noah was building the big boat. And only a few—eight in all—were saved in the boat through the floodwater. ²¹And that water is like baptism,* which now saves you. Baptism is not the washing of dirt from the body. It is asking God for a clean conscience. It saves you because Jesus Christ was raised from death. ²²Now he has gone into heaven. He is at God's right side and rules over angels, authorities, and powers.

Changed Lives

4 ¹Christ suffered while he was in his body. So you should strengthen yourselves with the same kind of thinking Christ had. The one who accepts suffering in this life has clearly decided to stop sinning. ²Strengthen yourselves so that you will live your lives here on earth doing what God wants, not the evil things that people want to do. ³In the past you wasted too much time doing what those who don't know God like to do. You were living immoral lives, doing the evil things you wanted to do. You were always getting drunk, having wild drinking parties, and doing shameful things in your worship of idols.

⁴Now those "friends" think it is strange that you no longer join them in all the wild and wasteful things they do. And so they say bad things about you. ⁵But they will have to face God to explain what they have done. He is the one who will soon judge everyone—those who are still living and those who have died. ⁶Some were told the Good News* before they died. They were criticized by others in their life here on earth. But it was God's plan that they hear the Good News so that they could have a new life in the spirit.ᵃ

Be Good Managers of God's Gifts

⁷The time is near when all things will end. So keep your minds clear, and control yourselves. This will help you in your prayers. ⁸Most important of all, love each other deeply, because love makes you willing to forgive many sins. ⁹Open your homes to each other and share your food without complaining. ¹⁰God has shown you his grace* in many different ways. So be good servants and use whatever gift he has given you in a way that will best serve each other. ¹¹If your gift is speaking, your words should be like words from God. If your gift is serving, you should serve with the strength that God gives. Then it is God who will be praised in everything through Jesus Christ. Power and glory* belong to him forever and ever. Amen.*

Suffering as a Follower of Christ

¹²My friends, don't be surprised at the painful things that you are now suffering, which are testing your faith. Don't think

---

ᵃ**4:6** *in the spirit* Or "through the Spirit," meaning by the power of the Holy Spirit.

that something strange is happening to you. [13]But you should be happy that you are sharing in Christ's sufferings. You will be happy and full of joy when Christ shows his glory.* [14]When people say bad things to you because you follow Christ, consider it a blessing. When that happens, it shows that God's Spirit, the Spirit of glory, is with you. [15]You may suffer, but don't let it be because you murder, steal, make trouble, or try to control other people's lives. [16]But if you suffer because you are a "Christ follower," don't be ashamed. You should praise God for that name. [17]It is time for judging to begin. That judging will begin with God's family. If it begins with us, then what will happen to those who don't accept the Good News* of God?

[18]"If it is hard for even a good person to be saved,
     what will happen to the one who is against God
          and full of sin?"   *Proverbs 11:31 (Greek version)*

[19]So if God wants you to suffer, you should trust your lives to him. He is the one who made you, and you can trust him. So continue to do good.

The Flock of God

5 [1]Now I have something to say to the elders* in your group. I am also an elder. I myself have seen Christ's sufferings. And I will share in the glory* that will be shown to us. I beg you to [2]take care of the group of people you are responsible for. They are God's flock.[a] Watch over that flock because you want to, not because you are forced to do it. That is how God wants it. Do it because you are happy to serve, not because you want money. [3]Don't be like a ruler over those you are responsible for. But be good examples to them. [4]Then when Christ the Ruling Shepherd comes, you will get a crown*—one that will be glorious and never lose its beauty.

[5]Young people, I have something to say to you too. You should accept the authority of the elders. You should all have a humble attitude in dealing with each other.

   "God is against the proud,
     but he gives grace* to the humble."   *Proverbs 3:34*

[6]So be humble under God's powerful hand. Then he will lift you up when the right time comes. [7]Give all your worries to him, because he cares for you.

[8]Control yourselves and be careful! The devil is your enemy, and he goes around like a roaring lion looking for someone to attack and eat. [9]Refuse to follow the devil. Stand strong in your faith. You know that your brothers and sisters all over the world are having the same sufferings that you have.

---

[a] **5:2** *God's flock* God's people. They are like a flock (group) of sheep that need to be cared for.

¹⁰Yes, you will suffer for a short time. But after that, God will make everything right. He will make you strong. He will support you and keep you from falling. He is the God who gives all grace. He chose you to share in his glory in Christ. That glory will continue forever. ¹¹All power is his forever. Amen.*

Final Greetings

¹²Silas will bring this letter to you. I know that he is a faithful brother in Christ. I wrote this short letter to encourage you. I wanted to tell you that this is the true grace* of God. Stand strong in that grace.

¹³The church in Babylon*ᵃ* sends you greetings. They were chosen just as you were. Mark, my son in Christ, also sends his greetings. ¹⁴Give each other a special greeting*ᵇ* of love when you meet.

Peace to all of you who are in Christ.

ᵃ5:13 The church in Babylon Literally, "She in Babylon." *ᵇ5:14 special greeting* Literally, "kiss."

Peace to all of you...

2 Peter

1 ¹Greetings from Simon Peter, a servant and apostle* of Jesus Christ.

To all of you who share in the same valuable faith that we have. This faith was given to us because our God and Savior Jesus Christ always does what is good and right.

²Grace* and peace be given to you more and more, because now you know God and Jesus our Lord.

God Has Given Us Everything We Need

³Jesus has the power of God. And his power has given us everything we need to live a life devoted to God. We have these things because we know him. Jesus chose us by his glory* and goodness, ⁴through which he also gave us the very great and rich gifts that he promised us. With these gifts you can share in being like God. And so you will escape the ruin that comes to people in the world because of the evil things they want.

⁵Because you have these blessings, do all you can to add to your life these things: to your faith add goodness; to your goodness add knowledge; ⁶to your knowledge add self-control; to your self-control add patience; to your patience add devotion to God; ⁷to your devotion add kindness toward your brothers and sisters in Christ; and to this kindness add love. ⁸If all these things are in you and growing, you will never fail to be useful to God. You will produce the kind of fruit that should come from your knowledge of our Lord Jesus Christ. ⁹But those who don't grow in these blessings are blind. They cannot see clearly what they have. They have forgotten that they were cleansed from their past sins.

¹⁰My brothers and sisters, God called you and chose you to be his. Do your best to live in a way that shows you really are God's called and chosen people. If you do all this, you will never fall. ¹¹And you will be given a very great welcome into the kingdom* of our Lord and Savior Jesus Christ, a kingdom that never ends.

¹²You already know these things. You are very strong in the truth you have. But I am always going to help you remember them. ¹³While I am still living here on earth, I think it is right for me to remind you of them. ¹⁴I know that I must soon leave this body. Our Lord Jesus Christ has shown me that. ¹⁵I will try my best to make sure you remember these things even after I am gone.

We Saw Christ's Glory

16We told you about the power of our Lord Jesus Christ. We told you about his coming. The things we told you were not just clever stories that people invented. No, we saw the greatness of Jesus with our own eyes. **17**Jesus heard the voice of the great and glorious God. That was when he received honor and glory* from God the Father. The voice said, "This is my Son, the one I love. I am very pleased with him." **18**And we heard that voice. It came from heaven while we were with Jesus on the holy mountain.*^a

19This makes us more sure about what the prophets* said. And it is good for you to follow closely what they said, which is like a light shining in a dark place. You have that light until the day begins and the morning star brings new light to your minds. **20**Most important of all, you must understand this: No prophecy* in the Scriptures* comes from the prophet's own understanding. **21**No prophecy ever came from what some person wanted to say. But people were led by the Holy Spirit* and spoke words from God.

False Teachers

2¹In the past there were false prophets* among God's people. It is the same now. You will have some false teachers in your group. They will teach things that are wrong—ideas that will cause people to be lost. And they will teach in a way that will be hard for you to see that they are wrong. They will even refuse to follow the Master who bought their freedom. And so they will quickly destroy themselves. **2**Many people will follow them in the morally wrong things they do. And because of them, others will say bad things about the way of truth we follow. **3**These false teachers only want your money. So they will use you by telling you things that are not true. But the judgment against these false teachers has been ready for a long time. And they will not escape God who will destroy them.

4When angels sinned, God did not let them go free without punishment. He sent them to hell. He put those angels in caves of darkness, where they are being held until the time when God will judge them.

5And God punished the evil people who lived long ago. He brought a flood to the world that was full of people who were against God. But he saved Noah and seven other people with him. Noah was a man who told people about living right.

6God also punished the evil cities of Sodom and Gomorrah. He burned them until there was nothing left but ashes. He used those cities as an example of what will happen to people who are against God. **7**But he saved Lot, a good man who lived there.

---

^a**1:17–18** *Jesus heard ... holy mountain* This event is described in the gospels. See Mt. 17:1–8; Mk. 9:2–8; Lk. 9:28–36.

Lot was greatly troubled by the morally bad lives of those evil people. [8]This good man lived with those evil people every day, and his good heart was hurt by the evil things he saw and heard.

[9]So you see that the Lord God knows how to save those who are devoted to him. He will save them when troubles come. And the Lord will hold evil people to punish them on the day of judgment. [10]That punishment is for those who are always doing the evil that their sinful selves want to do. It is for those who hate the Lord's authority.

These false teachers do whatever they want, and they are so proud of themselves. They are not afraid even to say bad things against the glorious ones.[a] [11]The angels are much stronger and more powerful than these beings. But even the angels don't accuse them and say bad things about them to the Lord.

[12]But these false teachers speak evil against what they don't understand. They are like animals that do things without really thinking—like wild animals that are born to be caught and killed. And, like wild animals, they will be destroyed. [13]They have made many people suffer. So they themselves will suffer. That is their pay for what they have done.

They think it is fun to do evil where everyone can see them. They enjoy the evil things that please them. So they are like dirty spots and stains among you—they bring shame to you in the meals you eat together. [14]Every time they look at a woman, they want her. They are always sinning this way. And they lead weaker people into the trap of sin. They have taught themselves well to be greedy. They are under a curse.[b]

[15]These false teachers left the right way and went the wrong way. They followed the same way that the prophet Balaam went. He was the son of Beor, who loved being paid for doing wrong. [16]But a donkey told him that he was doing wrong. A donkey cannot talk, of course, but that donkey spoke with a man's voice and stopped the prophet from acting so crazy.

[17]These false teachers are like springs that have no water. They are like clouds that are blown by a storm. A place in the deepest darkness has been kept for them. [18]They boast with words that mean nothing. They lead people into the trap of sin. They find people who have just escaped from a wrong way of life and lead them back into sin. They do this by using the evil things people want to do in their human weakness. [19]These false teachers promise those people freedom, but they themselves are not free. They are slaves to a mind that has been ruined by sin. Yes, people are slaves to anything that controls them.

[20]People can be made free from the evil in the world. They can be made free by knowing our Lord and Savior Jesus Christ. But if they go back into those evil things and are controlled by

---

[a] 2:10 the glorious ones Literally, "the glories." These seem to be some kind of angelic beings.
[b] 2:14 under a curse Literally, "children of a curse," meaning that God will punish them.

them, then it is worse for them than it was before. ²¹Yes, it would be better for them to have never known the right way. That would be better than to know the right way and then to turn away from the holy* teaching that was given to them. ²²What they did is like these true sayings: "A dog vomits and goes back to what it threw up."*ᵃ* And, "After a pig is washed, it goes back and rolls in the mud again."

Jesus Will Come Again

3 ¹My friends, this is the second letter I have written to you. I wrote both letters to you to help your honest minds remember something. ²I want you to remember the words that the holy prophets* spoke in the past. And remember the command that our Lord and Savior gave us. He gave us that command through your apostles.*

³It is important for you to understand what will happen in the last days. People will laugh at you. They will live following the evil they want to do. ⁴They will say, "Jesus promised to come again. Where is he? Our fathers have died, but the world continues the way it has been since it was made."

⁵But these people don't want to remember what happened long ago. The skies were there, and God made the earth from water and with water. All this happened by God's word. ⁶Then the world was flooded and destroyed with water. ⁷And that same word of God is keeping the skies and the earth that we have now. They are being kept to be destroyed by fire. They are kept for the day of judgment and the destruction of all people who are against God.

⁸But don't forget this one thing, dear friends: To the Lord a day is like a thousand years, and a thousand years is like a day. ⁹The Lord is not being slow in doing what he promised—the way some people understand slowness. But God is being patient with you. He doesn't want anyone to be lost. He wants everyone to change their ways and stop sinning.

¹⁰But the day when the Lord comes again will surprise everyone like the coming of a thief. The sky will disappear with a loud noise. Everything in the sky will be destroyed with fire. And the earth and everything in it will be burned up.*ᵇ* ¹¹Everything will be destroyed in this way. So what kind of people should you be? Your lives should be holy* and devoted to God. ¹²You should be looking forward to the day of God, wanting more than anything else for it to come soon. When it comes, the sky will be destroyed with fire, and everything in the sky will melt with heat. ¹³But God made a promise to us. And we are waiting for what he promised—a new sky and a new earth. That will be the place where goodness lives.

---

*ᵃ***2:22** Quote from Prov. 26:11.   *ᵇ***3:10** *will be burned up* Other Greek copies say, "will be found." One copy says, "will disappear."

[14]Dear friends, we are waiting for this to happen. So try as hard as you can to be without sin and without fault. Try to be at peace with God. [15]Remember that we are saved because our Lord is patient. Our dear brother Paul told you that same thing when he wrote to you with the wisdom that God gave him. [16]That's what he says in all his letters when he writes about these things. There are parts of his letters that are hard to understand, and some people give a wrong meaning to them. These people are ignorant and weak in faith. They also give wrong meanings to the other Scriptures.* But they are destroying themselves by doing that.

[17]Dear friends, you already know about this. So be careful. Don't let these evil people lead you away by the wrong they do. Be careful that you do not fall from your strong faith. [18]But grow in the grace* and knowledge of our Lord and Savior Jesus Christ. Glory* be to him now and forever! Amen.*

1 John

1 ¹We want to tell you about the Word*ᵃ* that gives life—the one who existed before the world began. This is the one we have heard and have seen with our own eyes. We saw what he did, and our hands touched him. ²Yes, the one who is life was shown to us. We saw him, and so we can tell others about him. We now tell you about him. He is the eternal life that was with God the Father. And God has shown him to us. ³We are telling you about what we have seen and heard because we want you to have fellowship*ᵇ* with us. The fellowship we share together is with God the Father and his Son Jesus Christ. ⁴We write these things to you so that you can be full of joy with us.

God Forgives Our Sins

⁵We heard the true teaching from God. Now we tell it to you: God is light,*ᶜ* and in him there is no darkness.* ⁶So if we say that we share in life with God, but we continue living in darkness, we are liars, who don't follow the truth. ⁷We should live in the light, where God is. If we live in the light, we have fellowship with each other, and the blood sacrifice of Jesus, God's Son, washes away every sin and makes us clean.

⁸If we say that we have no sin, we are fooling ourselves, and the truth is not in us. ⁹But if we confess our sins, God will forgive us. We can trust God to do this. He always does what is right. He will make us clean from all the wrong things we have done. ¹⁰If we say that we have not sinned, we are saying that God is a liar and that we don't accept his true teaching.

Jesus Is Our Helper

2 ¹My dear children, I write this letter to you so that you will not sin. But if anyone sins, we have Jesus Christ to help us. He always did what was right, so he is able to defend us before God the Father. ²Jesus is the way our sins are taken away. And he is the way all people can have their sins taken away too.

³If we obey what God has told us to do, then we are sure that we know him. ⁴If we say we know God but do not obey

ᵃ **1:1** *Word* The Greek word is *"logos,"* meaning any kind of communication. Here, it means Christ—the way God told people about himself. *ᵇ* **1:3** *fellowship* Associating with people and sharing things together with them. Believers in Christ share love, joy, sorrow, faith, and other things with each other and with God. Also in verse 7. *ᶜ* **1:5** *light* This word is used to show what God is like. It means goodness or truth.

his commands, we are lying. The truth is not in us. ⁵But when we obey God's teaching, his love is truly working in us. This is how we know that we are living in him. ⁶If we say we live in God, we must live like Jesus lived.

Jesus Told Us to Love Others

⁷My dear friends, I am not writing a new command to you. It is the same command you have had since the beginning. This command is the teaching you have already heard. ⁸But what I write is also a new command. It is a true one; you can see its truth in Jesus and in yourselves. The darkness* is passing away, and the true light is already shining.

⁹Someone might say, "I am in the light,*" but if they hate any of their brothers or sisters in God's family, they are still in the darkness. ¹⁰Those who love their brothers and sisters live in the light, and there is nothing in them that will make them do wrong. ¹¹But whoever hates their brother or sister is in darkness. They live in darkness. They don't know where they are going, because the darkness has made them blind.

¹² I write to you, dear children,
   because your sins are forgiven through Christ.
¹³ I write to you, fathers,
   because you know the one who existed from the beginning.
   I write to you, young people,
   because you have defeated the Evil One.*
¹⁴ I write to you, children,
   because you know the Father.
   I write to you, fathers,
   because you know the one who existed from the beginning.
   I write to you, young people,
   because you are strong.
   The word of God lives in you,
   and you have defeated the Evil One.

¹⁵Don't love this evil world or the things in it. Whoever loves the world does not have the love of the Father in them. ¹⁶This is all there is in the world: wanting to please our sinful selves, wanting the sinful things we see, and being too proud of what we have. But none of these comes from the Father. They come from the world. ¹⁷The world is passing away, and all the things that people want in the world are passing away. But whoever does what God wants will live forever.

Don't Follow the Enemies of Christ

¹⁸My dear children, the end is near! You have heard that the enemy of Christ* is coming. And now many enemies of Christ are already here. So we know that the end is near. ¹⁹These enemies were in our group, but they left us. They did not really belong with us. If they were really part of our group, they

would have stayed with us. But they left. This shows that none of them really belonged with us.

²⁰You have the gift*ᵃ* that the Holy One*ᵇ* gave you. So you all know the truth. ²¹Do you think I am writing this letter because you don't know the truth? No, I am writing because you do know the truth. And you know that no lie comes from the truth.

²²So who is the liar? It is the one who says Jesus is not the Christ. Whoever says that is the enemy of Christ—the one who does not believe in the Father or in his Son. ²³Whoever does not believe in the Son does not have the Father, but whoever accepts the Son has the Father too.

²⁴Be sure that you continue to follow the teaching you heard from the beginning. If you do that, you will always be in the Son and in the Father. ²⁵And this is what the Son promised us—eternal life.

²⁶I am writing this letter about those who are trying to lead you into the wrong way. ²⁷Christ gave you a special gift. You still have this gift in you. So you don't need anyone to teach you. The gift he gave you teaches you about everything. It is a true gift, not a false one. So continue to live in Christ, as his gift taught you.

²⁸Yes, my dear children, live in him. If we do this, we can be without fear on the day when Christ comes back. We will not need to hide and be ashamed when he comes. ²⁹You know that Christ always did what was right. So you know that all those who do what is right are God's children.

We Are God's Children

3 ¹The Father has loved us so much! This shows how much he loved us: We are called children of God. And we really are his children. But the people in the world don't understand that we are God's children, because they have not known him. ²Dear friends, now we are children of God. We have not yet been shown what we will be in the future. But we know that when Christ comes again, we will be like him. We will see him just as he is. ³He is pure, and everyone who has this hope in him keeps themselves pure like Christ.

⁴Anyone who sins breaks God's law. Yes, sinning is the same as living against God's law. ⁵You know that Christ came to take away people's sins. There is no sin in Christ. ⁶So whoever lives in Christ does not continue to sin. If they continue to sin, they have never really understood Christ and have never known him.

⁷Dear children, don't let anyone lead you into the wrong way. Christ always did what was right. So to be good like Christ, you must do what is right. ⁸The devil has been sinning since the beginning. Anyone who continues to sin belongs to the devil. The Son of God came for this: to destroy the devil's work.

---

*ᵃ***2:20** *gift* Literally, "anointing." This might mean the Holy Spirit. Or, it might mean teaching or truth as in verse 24. Also in verse 27. *ᵇ***2:20** *Holy One* God or Christ.

⁹Those who are God's children do not continue to sin, because the new life God gave them*a* stays in them. They cannot keep sinning, because they have become children of God. ¹⁰So we can see who God's children are and who the devil's children are. These are the ones who are not God's children: those who don't do what is right and those who do not love their brothers and sisters in God's family.

We Must Love One Another

¹¹This is the teaching you have heard from the beginning: We must love each other. ¹²Don't be like Cain.* He belonged to the Evil One.* Cain killed his brother. But why did he kill him? Because what Cain did was evil, and what his brother did was good.

¹³Brothers and sisters, don't be surprised when the people of this world hate you. ¹⁴We know that we have left death and have come into life. We know this because we love each other as brothers and sisters. Anyone who does not love is still in death. ¹⁵Anyone who hates a fellow believer* is a murderer.*b* And you know that no murderer has eternal life.

¹⁶This is how we know what real love is: Jesus gave his life for us. So we should give our lives for each other as brothers and sisters. ¹⁷Suppose a believer who is rich enough to have all the necessities of life sees a fellow believer who is poor and does not have even basic needs. What if the rich believer does not help the poor one? Then it is clear that God's love is not in that person's heart. ¹⁸My children, our love should not be only words and talk. No, our love must be real. We must show our love by the things we do.

¹⁹⁻²⁰That's how we know that we belong to the way of truth. And when our hearts make us feel guilty, we can still have peace before God, because God is greater than our hearts. He knows everything.

²¹My dear friends, if we don't feel that we are doing wrong, we can be without fear when we come to God. ²²And God gives us what we ask for. We receive it because we obey God's commands and do what pleases him. ²³This is what God commands: that we believe in his Son Jesus Christ, and that we love each other as he commanded. ²⁴Anyone who obeys God's commands lives in God. And God lives in them. How do we know that God lives in us? We know because of the Spirit* he gave us.

John Warns Against False Teachers

4 ¹My dear friends, many false prophets* are in the world now. So don't believe every spirit, but test the spirits to see if they are from God. ²This is how you can recognize God's Spirit.

---

*a*3:9 *the new life God gave them* Literally, "his seed." *b*3:15 *Anyone … murderer* Those who hate someone have in their mind the same motive that causes murder. So, morally, hating is equal to murder. Jesus taught his followers about this sin. See Mt. 5:21–26.

One spirit says, "I believe that Jesus is the Christ* who came to earth and became a man." That Spirit is from God. [3]Another spirit refuses to say this about Jesus. That spirit is not from God. This is the spirit of the enemy of Christ. You have heard that the enemy of Christ is coming, and now he is already in the world.

[4]My dear children, you belong to God, so you have already defeated these false prophets. That's because the one who is in you is greater than the one who is in the world. [5]And they belong to the world, so what they say is from the world too. And the world listens to what they say. [6]But we are from God. So the people who know God listen to us. But the people who are not from God don't listen to us. That is how we know the Spirit that is true and the spirit that is false.

Love Comes From God

[7]Dear friends, we should love each other, because love comes from God. Everyone who loves has become God's child. And so everyone who loves knows God. [8]Anyone who does not love does not know God, because God is love. [9]This is how God showed his love to us: He sent his only Son into the world to give us life through him. [10]True love is God's love for us, not our love for God. He sent his Son as the way to take away our sins.

[11]That is how much God loved us, dear friends! So we also must love each other. [12]No one has ever seen God. But if we love each other, God lives in us. If we love each other, God's love has reached its goal—it is made perfect in us.

[13]We know that we live in God and God lives in us. We know this because he gave us his Spirit.* [14]We have seen that the Father sent his Son to be the Savior of the world, and this is what we tell people now. [15]If someone says, "I believe that Jesus is the Son of God," then God lives in them, and they live in God. [16]So we know the love that God has for us, and we trust that love.

God is love. Everyone who lives in love lives in God, and God lives in them. [17]If God's love is made perfect in us, we can be without fear on the day when God judges the world. We will be without fear, because in this world we are like him.[a] [18]Where God's love is, there is no fear, because God's perfect love takes away fear. It is his punishment that makes a person fear. So his love is not made perfect in the one who has fear.

[19]We love because God first loved us. [20]If we say we love God but hate any of our brothers or sisters in his family, we are liars. If we don't love someone we have seen, how can we love God? We have never even seen him. [21]God gave us this command: If we love God, we must also love each other as brothers and sisters.

[a]**4:17** *him* Christ or God.

God's Children Win Against the World

5 ¹The people who believe that Jesus is the Christ* are God's children. Anyone who loves the Father also loves the Father's children. ²How do we know that we love God's children? We know because we love God and we obey his commands. ³Loving God means obeying his commands. And God's commands are not too hard for us, ⁴because everyone who is a child of God has the power to win against the world. ⁵It is our faith that has won the victory against the world. So who wins against the world? Only those who believe that Jesus is the Son of God.

God Told Us About His Son

⁶Jesus Christ is the one who came. He came with water*a* and with blood.*b* He did not come by water only. No, Jesus came by both water and blood. And the Spirit* tells us that this is true. The Spirit is the truth. ⁷So there are three witnesses that tell us about Jesus: ⁸the Spirit, the water, and the blood. These three witnesses agree.

⁹We believe people when they say something is true. But what God says is more important. And this is what God told us: He told us the truth about his own Son. ¹⁰Whoever believes in the Son of God has the truth that God told us. Whoever does not believe God makes God a liar, because they do not believe what God told us about his Son. ¹¹This is what God told us: God has given us eternal life, and this life is in his Son. ¹²Whoever has the Son has life, but whoever does not have the Son of God does not have life.

We Have Eternal Life Now

¹³I write this letter to you who believe in the Son of God. I write so that you will know that you have eternal life now. ¹⁴We can come to God with no doubts. This means that when we ask God for things (and those things agree with what God wants for us), God cares about what we say. ¹⁵He listens to us every time we ask him. So we know that he gives us whatever we ask from him.

¹⁶Suppose you see your fellow believer* sinning (sin that does not lead to eternal death). You should pray for them. Then God will give them life. I am talking about people whose sin does not lead to eternal death. There is sin that leads to death. I don't mean that you should pray about that kind of sin. ¹⁷Doing wrong is always sin. But there is sin that does not lead to eternal death.

¹⁸We know that those who have been made God's children do not continue to sin. The Son of God keeps them safe.*c* The

---

*a***5:6** *water* This probably means the water of Jesus' baptism. *b***5:6** *blood* This probably means the blood Jesus shed on the cross. *c***5:18** *The Son … safe* Literally, "The one who was born from God keeps him safe" or "… keeps himself safe."

Evil One* cannot hurt them. [19]We know that we belong to God, but the Evil One controls the whole world. [20]And we know that the Son of God has come and has given us understanding. So now we can know the one who is true, and we live in that true God. We are in his Son, Jesus Christ. He is the true God, and he is eternal life. [21]So, dear children, keep yourselves away from false gods.

2 John

¹Greetings from the Elder.ᵃ

To the ladyᵇ chosen by God and to her children.

I truly love all of you. And I am not the only one. All those who know the truthᶜ love you in the same way. ²We love you because of the truth—the truth that lives in us. That truth will be with us forever.

³Grace,* mercy, and peace will be with us from God the Father and from his Son, Jesus Christ as we live in truth and love.

⁴I was very happy to learn about some of your children. I am happy that they are following the way of truth, just as the Father commanded us. ⁵And now, dear lady, I tell you: We should all love each other. This is not a new command. It is the same command we had from the beginning. ⁶And loving means living the way he commanded us to live. And God's command is this: that you live a life of love. You heard this command from the beginning.

⁷Many false teachers are in the world now. They refuse to say that Jesus Christ came to earth and became a man. Anyone who refuses to accept this fact is a false teacher and the enemy of Christ. ⁸Be careful! Don't lose the reward you have worked for. Be careful so that you will receive all of your reward.

⁹Everyone must continue to follow only the teaching about Christ. Whoever changes that teaching does not have God. But whoever continues to follow the teaching about Christ has both the Father and his Son. ¹⁰Don't accept those who come to you but do not bring this teaching. Don't invite them into your house. Don't welcome them in any way. ¹¹If you do, you are helping them with their evil work.

¹²I have much to say to you. But I don't want to use paper and ink. Instead, I hope to come visit you. Then we can be together and talk. That will make us very happy. ¹³The children of your sisterᵈ who was chosen by God send you their love.

ᵃ1 *Elder* This is probably John the apostle. "Elder" means an older man or a special leader in the church (as in Titus 1:5). ᵇ1 *lady* This might mean a woman. Or, in this letter, it might mean a church. If it is a church, then "her children" would be the people of the church. Also in verse 5. ᶜ1 *truth* The truth or "Good News" about Jesus Christ that joins all believers together. ᵈ13 *sister* Sister of the "lady" in verse 1. This might be another woman or another church.

3 John

¹Greetings from the Elder.[a]

To my dear friend Gaius, a person I truly love.

²My dear friend, I know that you are doing well spiritually. So I pray that everything else is going well with you and that you are enjoying good health. ³Some believers* came and told me about the truth[b] in your life. They told me that you continue to follow the way of truth. This made me very happy. ⁴It always gives me the greatest joy when I hear that my children are following the way of truth.

⁵My dear friend, it is good that you continue to help the believers. They are people you don't even know. ⁶They told the church* about the love you have. Please help them to continue their trip. Help them in a way that will please God. ⁷They went on their trip to serve Christ. They did not accept any help from people who are not believers. ⁸So we should help them. When we help them, we share with their work for the truth.

⁹I wrote a letter to the church, but Diotrephes will not listen to what we say. He always wants to be the leader. ¹⁰When I come, I will talk with him about what he is doing. He lies and says evil things about us, but that is not all. He refuses to welcome and help the believers who travel there. And he will not let anyone else help them. If they do, he makes them leave the church.

¹¹My dear friend, don't follow what is bad; follow what is good. Whoever does what is good is from God. But whoever does evil has never known God.

¹²Everyone says good things about Demetrius, and the truth agrees with what they say. Also, we say good about him. And you know that what we say is true.

¹³I have many things I want to tell you. But I don't want to use pen and ink. ¹⁴I hope to visit you soon. Then we can be together and talk. ¹⁵Peace to you. The friends here with me send their love. Please give our love to each one of the friends there.

---

[a]1 *Elder* This is probably John the apostle. "Elder" means an older man or a special leader in the church (as in Titus 1:5). [b]3 *truth* The truth or "Good News" about Jesus Christ that joins all believers together. Also in verses 8, 12.

Jude

¹Greetings from Jude, a servant of Jesus Christ and a brother of James.

To those who have been chosen and are loved by God the Father and have been kept safe in Jesus Christ.

²Mercy, peace, and love be yours more and more.

God Will Punish Those Who Do Wrong

³Dear friends, I wanted very much to write to you about the salvation we all share together. But I felt the need to write to you about something else: I want to encourage you to fight hard for the faith that God gave his holy people.* God gave this faith once, and it is good for all time. ⁴Some people have secretly entered your group. These people have already been judged guilty for what they are doing. Long ago the prophets* wrote about them. They are against God. They have used the grace* of our God in the wrong way—to do sinful things. They refuse to follow Jesus Christ, our only Master and Lord.

⁵I want to help you remember some things you already know: Remember that the Lord saved his people by bringing them out of the land of Egypt. But later he destroyed all those who did not believe. ⁶And remember the angels who lost their authority to rule. They left their proper home. So the Lord has kept them in darkness, bound with everlasting chains, to be judged on the great day. ⁷Also, remember the cities of Sodom* and Gomorrah* and the other towns around them. Like those angels they were full of sexual sin and wrongdoing. And they suffer the punishment of eternal fire, an example for us to see.

⁸It is the same way with these people who have entered your group. They are guided by dreams. They make themselves dirty with sin. They reject God's authority and say bad things against the glorious ones.ᵃ ⁹Not even the archangel* Michael did this. Michael argued with the devil about who would have the body of Moses.* But Michael did not dare to condemn even the devil for his false accusations. Instead, Michael said, "The Lord punish you!"

¹⁰But these people criticize things they don't understand. They do understand some things. But they understand these things not by thinking, but by feeling, the way dumb animals understand things. And these are the things that destroy them.

ᵃ 8 *the glorious ones* Literally, "the glories." These seem to be some kind of angelic beings.

[11] It will be bad for them. They have followed the way that Cain* went. To make money, they have given themselves to following the wrong way that Balaam* went. They have fought against God like Korah[a] did. And like Korah, they will be destroyed.

[12] These people are like dirty spots among you—they bring shame to you in the special meals you share together. They eat with you and have no fear. They take care of only themselves. They are like clouds without rain. The wind blows them around. They are like trees that have no fruit at harvest time and are pulled out of the ground. So they are twice dead. [13] Like the dirty foam on the wild waves in the sea, everyone can see the shameful things they do. They are like stars that wander in the sky. A place in the blackest darkness has been kept for them forever.

[14] Enoch, the seventh descendant from Adam, said this about these people: "Look, the Lord is coming with thousands and thousands of his holy* angels [15] to judge everyone. He will punish all those who are against him for all the evil they have done in their lack of respect for him. Yes, the Lord will punish all these sinners who don't honor him. He will punish them for all the evil things they have said against him."

[16] These people always complain and find wrong in others. They always do the evil things they want to do. They boast about themselves. The only reason they say good things about others is to get what they want.

A Warning and Things to Do

[17] Dear friends, remember what the apostles* of our Lord Jesus Christ said before. [18] The apostles said to you, "In the last times there will be people who laugh about God." They do only what they want to do—things that are against God. [19] These are the people who divide you. They are not spiritual, because they don't have the Spirit.*

[20] But you, dear friends, use your most holy* faith to build yourselves up even stronger. Pray with the help of the Holy Spirit. [21] In this way, keep yourselves safe in God's love, as you wait for the Lord Jesus Christ in his mercy to give you eternal life.

[22] Help those who have doubts. [23] Rescue those who are living in danger of hell's fire. There are others you should treat with mercy, but be very careful that their filthy lives don't rub off on you.[b]

Praise God

[24] God is strong and can keep you from falling. He can bring you before his glory* without any wrong in you and give you great joy. [25] He is the only God, the one who saves us. To him be glory, greatness, power, and authority through Jesus Christ our Lord for all time past, now, and forever. Amen.*

[a] 11 *Korah* He turned against Moses. See Numbers 16:1-40. [b] 23 *that . . . on you* Literally, "hating even their undershirt that is defiled from the flesh."

Revelation

John Tells About This Book

1 ¹This is a revelation[a] from Jesus Christ, which God gave him to show his servants what must happen soon. And Christ sent his angel to show it to his servant John, ²who has told everything he saw. It is the truth that Jesus Christ told him; it is the message from God. ³What a great blessing there is for the person who reads the words of this message from God and for those who hear this message and do what is written in it. There is not much time left.

Jesus' Messages to the Churches

⁴From John,

To the seven churches* in the province of Asia*:

Grace* and peace to you from the one who is, who always was, and who is coming; and from the seven spirits before his throne; ⁵and from Jesus Christ. Jesus is the faithful witness. He is first among all who will be raised from death. He is the ruler of the kings of the earth.

Jesus is the one who loves us and has made us free from our sins with his blood sacrifice. ⁶He made us his kingdom* and priests who serve God his Father. To Jesus be glory* and power forever and ever! Amen.*

⁷Look, Jesus is coming with the clouds! Everyone will see him, even those who pierced[b] him. All peoples of the earth will cry loudly because of him. Yes, this will happen! Amen.

⁸The Lord God says, "I am the Alpha and the Omega.[c] I am the one who is, who always was, and who is coming. I am the All-Powerful."

⁹I am John, your fellow believer.* We are together in Jesus, and we share these things: suffering, the kingdom, and patient endurance. I was on the island of Patmos[d] because I was faithful to God's message* and to the truth of Jesus. ¹⁰On the Lord's Day, the Spirit* took control of me. I heard a loud voice behind me that sounded like a trumpet. ¹¹It said, "Write down in a book what you see, and send it to the seven churches: to

---

a **1:1** *revelation* An opening up (making known) of truth that was hidden. *b* **1:7** *pierced* When Jesus was killed, he was stabbed with a spear in the side. See Jn. 19:34. *c* **1:8** *Alpha ... Omega* The first and last letters in the Greek alphabet, meaning the beginning and the end. *d* **1:9** *Patmos* A small island in the Aegean Sea, near the coast of modern Turkey.

Ephesus, Smyrna, Pergamum, Thyatira, Sardis, Philadelphia, and Laodicea."

¹²I turned to see who was talking to me. When I turned, I saw seven golden lampstands. ¹³I saw someone among the lampstands who looked like the Son of Man.* He was dressed in a long robe, with a golden sash tied around his chest. ¹⁴His head and hair were white like wool—wool that is white as snow. His eyes were like flames of fire. ¹⁵His feet were like brass that glows hot in a furnace. His voice was like the noise of flooding water. ¹⁶He held seven stars in his right hand. A sharp two-edged sword came out of his mouth. He looked like the sun shining at its brightest time.

¹⁷When I saw him, I fell down at his feet like a dead man. He put his right hand on me and said, "Don't be afraid! I am the First and the Last. ¹⁸I am the one who lives. I was dead, but look, I am alive forever and ever! And I hold the keys of death and Hades.* ¹⁹So write what you see. Write the things that happen now and the things that will happen later. ²⁰Here is the hidden meaning of the seven stars that you saw in my right hand and the seven golden lampstands that you saw: The seven lampstands are the seven churches. The seven stars are the angels of the seven churches.

Jesus' Letter to the Church in Ephesus

2 ¹"Write this to the angel of the church* in Ephesus:

"Here is a message from the one who holds the seven stars in his right hand and walks among the seven golden lampstands.

²"I know what you do, how hard you work and never give up. I know that you don't accept evil people. You have tested those who say they are apostles* but are not. You found that they are liars. ³You never stop trying. You have endured troubles for my name and have not given up.

⁴"But I have this against you: You have left the love you had in the beginning. ⁵So remember where you were before you fell. Change your hearts and do what you did at first. If you don't change, I will come to you and remove your lampstand from its place. ⁶But there is something you do that is right—you hate the things that the Nicolaitans*ᵃ* do. I also hate what they do.

⁷"Everyone who hears this should listen to what the Spirit* says to the churches. To those who win the victory, I will give the right to eat the fruit from the tree of life,* which is in God's paradise.*

Jesus' Letter to the Church in Smyrna

⁸"Write this to the angel of the church* in Smyrna:

"Here is a message from the one who is the First and the Last, the one who died and came to life again.

ᵃ **2:6** *Nicolaitans* A religious group that followed wrong ideas. Also in verse 15.

⁹"I know your troubles, and I know that you are poor, but really you are rich! I know the insults you have suffered from people who say they are Jews. But they are not true Jews. They are a group*a* that belongs to Satan.* ¹⁰Don't be afraid of what will happen to you. I tell you, the devil will put some of you in prison. He will do this to test you. You will suffer for ten days, but be faithful, even if you have to die. If you continue to be faithful, I will give you the crown* of life.

¹¹"Everyone who hears this should listen to what the Spirit* says to the churches. Those who win the victory will not be hurt by the second death.

Jesus' Letter to the Church in Pergamum

¹²"Write this to the angel of the church* in Pergamum:

"Here is a message from the one who has the sharp two-edged sword.

¹³"I know where you live. You live where Satan* has his throne, but you are true to me. You did not refuse to tell about your faith in me even during the time of Antipas. Antipas was my faithful witness*b* who was killed in your city, the city where Satan lives.

¹⁴"But I have a few things against you. You have people there who follow the teaching of Balaam.* Balaam taught Balak how to make the people of Israel* sin. They sinned by eating food offered to idols* and by committing sexual sins. ¹⁵It is the same in your group. You have people who follow the teaching of the Nicolaitans. ¹⁶So change your hearts! If you don't change, I will come to you quickly and fight against these people with the sword that comes out of my mouth.

¹⁷"Everyone who hears this should listen to what the Spirit* says to the churches!

"I will give the hidden manna* to everyone who wins the victory. I will also give each one a white stone that has a new name written on it. And no one will know this name except the one who gets the stone.

Jesus' Letter to the Church in Thyatira

¹⁸"Write this to the angel of the church* in Thyatira:

"Here is a message from the Son of God, the one who has eyes that blaze like fire and feet like shining brass.

¹⁹"I know what you do. I know about your love, your faith, your service, and your patience. I know that you are doing more now than you did at first. ²⁰But I have this against you: You let that woman Jezebel do what she wants. She says that she is a prophet,*c* but she is leading my people away with her

---

*a*2:9 group Literally, "synagogue." *b*2:13 faithful witness A person who speaks God's message truthfully, even in times of danger. *c*2:20 prophet Jezebel was a false prophet. She claimed to speak for God, but she didn't really speak God's truth.

teaching. Jezebel leads my people to commit sexual sins and to eat food that is offered to idols.* ²¹I have given her time to change her heart and turn away from her sin, but she does not want to change.

²²"So I will throw her on a bed of suffering. And all those who commit adultery* with her will suffer greatly. I will do this now if they don't turn away from the things she does. ²³I will also kill her followers. Then all the churches will know that I am the one who knows what people feel and think. And I will repay each of you for what you have done.

²⁴"But others of you in Thyatira have not followed her teaching. You have not learned the things they call 'Satan's* deep secrets.' This is what I say to you: I will not put any other burden on you. ²⁵Only hold on to the truth you have until I come.

²⁶"I will give power over the nations to all those who win the victory and continue until the end to do what I want. ²⁷They will rule the nations with an iron rod. They will break them to pieces like clay pots.ᵃ ²⁸They will have the same power I received from my Father, and I will give them the morning star. ²⁹Everyone who hears this should listen to what the Spirit* says to the churches.

Jesus' Letter to the Church in Sardis

3 ¹"Write this to the angel of the church* in Sardis:
"Here is a message from the one who has the seven spirits and the seven stars.

"I know what you do. People say that you are alive, but really you are dead. ²Wake up! Make yourselves stronger before what little strength you have left is completely gone. I find that what you do is not good enough for my God. ³So don't forget what you have received and heard. Obey it. Change your hearts and lives! You must wake up, or I will come to you and surprise you like a thief. You will not know when I will come.

⁴"But you have a few people in your group there in Sardis who have kept themselves clean. They will walk with me. They will wear white clothes, because they are worthy. ⁵Everyone who wins the victory will be dressed in white clothes like them. I will not remove their names from the book of life. I will say that they belong to me before my Father and before his angels. ⁶Everyone who hears this should listen to what the Spirit* says to the churches.

Jesus' Letter to the Church in Philadelphia

⁷"Write this to the angel of the church* in Philadelphia:
"Here is a message from the one who is holy and true, the one who holds the key of David.* When he opens something,

---

ᵃ**2:26–27** These verses are almost the same as Ps. 2:8–9.

it cannot be closed. And when he closes something, it cannot be opened.

⁸"I know what you do. I have put before you an open door that no one can close. I know you are weak, but you have followed my teaching. You were not afraid to speak my name. ⁹Listen! There is a group*ᵃ* that belongs to Satan.* They say they are Jews, but they are liars. They are not true Jews. I will make them come before you and bow at your feet. They will know that you are the people I have loved. ¹⁰You followed my command to endure patiently. So I will keep you from the time of trouble that will come to the world—a time that will test everyone living on earth.

¹¹"I am coming soon. Hold on to the faith you have, so that no one can take away your crown.* ¹²Those who win the victory will be pillars* in the temple of my God. I will make that happen for them. They will never again have to leave God's temple. I will write the name of my God on them and the name of the city of my God on them. That city is the new Jerusalem.*ᵇ* It is coming down out of heaven from my God. I will also write my new name on them. ¹³Everyone who hears this should listen to what the Spirit* says to the churches.

Jesus' Letter to the Church in Laodicea

¹⁴"Write this to the angel of the church* in Laodicea:

"Here is a message from the Amen,*ᶜ* the faithful and true witness, the ruler of all that God has made.

¹⁵"I know what you do. You are not hot or cold. I wish that you were hot or cold! ¹⁶But you are only warm—not hot, not cold. So I am ready to spit you out of my mouth. ¹⁷You say you are rich. You think you have become wealthy and don't need anything. But you don't know that you are really miserable, pitiful, poor, blind, and naked. ¹⁸I advise you to buy gold from me—gold made pure in fire. Then you will be rich. I tell you this: Buy clothes that are white. Then you will be able to cover your shameful nakedness. I also tell you to buy medicine to put on your eyes. Then you will be able to see.

¹⁹"I correct and punish the people I love. So show that nothing is more important to you than living right. Change your hearts and lives. ²⁰Here I am! I stand at the door and knock. If you hear my voice and open the door, I will come in and eat with you. And you will eat with me.

²¹"I will let everyone who wins the victory sit with me on my throne. It was the same with me. I won the victory and sat down with my Father on his throne. ²²Everyone who hears this should listen to what the Spirit* says to the churches."

---

*ᵃ*3:9 *group* Literally, "synagogue." *ᵇ*3:12 *new Jerusalem* The spiritual city where God's people live with him. *ᶜ*3:14 *Amen* Used here, as a name for Jesus, it means to agree strongly that something is true.

John Sees Heaven

4 ¹Then I looked, and there before me was an open door in heaven. And I heard the same voice that spoke to me before. It was the voice that sounded like a trumpet. It said, "Come up here, and I will show you what must happen after this." ²Immediately the Spirit* took control of me, and there in heaven was a throne with someone sitting on it. ³The one sitting there was as beautiful as precious stones, like jasper and carnelian. All around the throne was a rainbow with clear colors like an emerald.

⁴In a circle around the throne were 24 other thrones with 24 elders* sitting on them. The elders were dressed in white, and they had golden crowns on their heads. ⁵Lightning flashes and noises of thunder came from the throne. Before the throne there were seven lamps burning, which are the seven Spirits of God. ⁶Also before the throne there was something that looked like a sea of glass, as clear as crystal.

In front of the throne and on each side of it there were four living beings. They had eyes all over them, in front and in back. ⁷The first living being was like a lion. The second was like a cow. The third had a face like a man. The fourth was like a flying eagle. ⁸Each of these four living beings had six wings. They were covered all over with eyes, inside and out. Day and night they never stopped saying,

"Holy, holy, holy is the Lord God All-Powerful.
    He always was, he is, and he is coming."

⁹These living beings were giving glory* and honor and thanks to the one who sits on the throne, the one who lives forever and ever. And every time they did this, ¹⁰the 24 elders bowed down before the one who sits on the throne. They worshiped him who lives forever and ever. They put their crowns down before the throne and said,

¹¹"Our Lord and God!
    You are worthy to receive glory
        and honor and power.
    You made all things.
    Everything existed and was made
        because you wanted it."

Who Can Open the Scroll?

5 ¹Then I saw a scroll* in the right hand of the one sitting on the throne. The scroll had writing on both sides and was kept closed with seven seals.* ²And I saw a powerful angel, who called in a loud voice, "Who is worthy to break the seals and open the scroll?" ³But there was no one in heaven or on earth or under the earth who could open the scroll or look inside it. ⁴I cried and cried because there was no one who was

worthy to open the scroll or look inside. ⁵But one of the elders* said to me, "Don't cry! The Lion*ᵃ* from the tribe of Judah has won the victory. He is David's* descendant. He is able to open the scroll and its seven seals."

⁶Then I saw a Lamb* standing in the center near the throne with the four living beings around it. The elders were also around the Lamb. The Lamb looked as if it had been killed. It had seven horns and seven eyes, which are the seven spirits of God that were sent into all the world. ⁷The Lamb came and took the scroll from the right hand of the one sitting on the throne. ⁸After the Lamb took the scroll, the four living beings and the 24 elders bowed down before the Lamb. Each one of them had a harp. Also, they were holding golden bowls full of incense,* which are the prayers of God's holy people.* ⁹And they all sang a new song to the Lamb:

"You are worthy to take the scroll
        and to open its seals,
    because you were killed,
        and with your blood sacrifice you bought people for God
            from every tribe, language, race of people, and nation.
¹⁰ You made them to be a kingdom and to be priests
            for our God.
        And they will rule on the earth."

¹¹Then I looked, and I heard the voices of many angels. The angels were around the throne, the four living beings, and the elders. There were thousands and thousands of angels—10,000 times 10,000. ¹²The angels said with a loud voice,

"All power, wealth, wisdom and strength
        belong to the Lamb who was killed.
    He is worthy to receive honor, glory,* and praise!"

¹³Then I heard every created being that is in heaven and on earth and under the earth and in the sea, everything in all these places, saying,

"All praise and honor and glory and power forever and ever
        to the one who sits on the throne and to the Lamb!"

¹⁴The four living beings said, "Amen*!" And the elders bowed down and worshiped.

The Lamb Opens the Scroll

6 ¹Then I watched as the Lamb* opened the first of the seven seals.* Then I heard one of the four living beings speak with a voice like thunder. It said, "Come!" ²I looked, and there before me was a white horse. The rider on the horse held a bow and was given a crown.* He rode out to defeat the enemy and win the victory.

*ᵃ*5:5 *Lion* Used here to refer to Jesus.

³The Lamb opened the second seal. Then I heard the second living being say, "Come!" ⁴Then another horse came out, a red one. The rider on the horse was given power to take away peace from the earth so that people would kill each other. He was given a big sword.

⁵The Lamb opened the third seal. Then I heard the third living being say, "Come!" I looked, and there before me was a black horse. The rider on the horse held a pair of scales in his hand. ⁶Then I heard something that sounded like a voice. The voice came from where the four living beings were. It said, "A quart*ª* of wheat or three quarts of barley will cost a full day's pay. But don't harm the supply of olive oil and wine!"

⁷The Lamb opened the fourth seal. Then I heard the voice of the fourth living being say, "Come!" ⁸I looked, and there before me was a pale-colored horse. The rider on the horse was death, and Hades* was following close behind him. They were given power over a fourth of the earth—power to kill people with the sword, by starving, by disease, and with the wild animals of the earth.

⁹The Lamb opened the fifth seal. Then I saw some souls under the altar.* They were the souls of those who had been killed because they were faithful to God's message* and to the truth they had received. ¹⁰These souls shouted in a loud voice, "Holy and true Lord, how long until you judge the people of the earth and punish them for killing us?" ¹¹Then each one of them was given a white robe. They were told to wait a short time longer. There were still some of their brothers and sisters in the service of Christ who must be killed as they were. These souls were told to wait until all of the killing was finished.

¹²Then I watched while the Lamb opened the sixth seal. There was a great earthquake, and the sun became as black as sackcloth.*ᵇ* The full moon became red like blood. ¹³The stars in the sky fell to the earth like a fig tree drops its figs when the wind blows. ¹⁴The sky was split in the middle and both sides rolled up like a scroll.* And every mountain and island was moved from its place.

¹⁵Then all the people—the kings of the world, the rulers, the army commanders, the rich people, the powerful people, every slave, and every free person—hid themselves in caves and behind the rocks on the mountains. ¹⁶They said to the mountains and the rocks, "Fall on us. Hide us from the face of the one who sits on the throne. Hide us from the anger of the Lamb! ¹⁷The great day for their anger has come. No one can stand against it."

---

*ª*6:6 *quart* Literally, *"choinix,"* the amount of the daily ration of grain for a soldier. Equals about 1 liter. *ᵇ*6:12 *sackcloth* Here, literally "sackcloth of hair." This was a rough, dark cloth made from the hair of goats or camels that people sometimes wore as a symbol of mourning or sadness.

The 144,000 People of Israel

7 ¹After this happened I saw four angels standing at the four corners of the earth. The angels were holding the four winds of the earth. They were stopping the wind from blowing on the land or the sea or on any tree. ²Then I saw another angel coming from the east. This angel had the seal* of the living God. The angel called out with a loud voice to the four angels. These were the four angels that God had given the power to hurt the earth and the sea. The angel said to them, ³"Don't harm the land or the sea or the trees before we mark the foreheads of those who serve our God."

⁴Then I heard how many people had God's mark on their foreheads. There were 144,000. They were from every tribe of the people of Israel*ᵃ*:

⁵	From the tribe of Judah	12,000
	from the tribe of Reuben	12,000
	from the tribe of Gad	12,000
⁶	from the tribe of Asher	12,000
	from the tribe of Naphtali	12,000
	from the tribe of Manasseh	12,000
⁷	from the tribe of Simeon	12,000
	from the tribe of Levi	12,000
	from the tribe of Issachar	12,000
⁸	from the tribe of Zebulun	12,000
	from the tribe of Joseph	12,000
	from the tribe of Benjamin	12,000

The Great Crowd

⁹Then I looked, and there was a large crowd of people. There were so many people that no one could count them all. They were from every nation, tribe, race of people, and language of the earth. They were standing before the throne and before the Lamb.* They all wore white robes and had palm branches in their hands. ¹⁰They shouted with a loud voice, "Victory belongs to our God, who sits on the throne, and to the Lamb."

¹¹The elders* and the four living beings were there. All the angels were standing around them and the throne. The angels bowed down on their faces before the throne and worshiped God. ¹²They said, "Amen*! Praise, glory,* wisdom, thanks, honor, power, and strength belong to our God forever and ever. Amen!"

¹³Then one of the elders asked me, "Who are these people in white robes? Where did they come from?"

¹⁴I answered, "You know who they are, sir."

---

*ᵃ*7:4 *Israel* First, Israel was the people descended from Jacob (see "Israel" in the Word List), but the name is also used to mean all of God's people.

And the elder said, "These are the ones who have come out of the great suffering. They have washed their robes[a] with the blood of the Lamb, and they are clean and white. [15]So now these people are before the throne of God. They worship God day and night in his temple. And the one who sits on the throne will protect them. [16]They will never be hungry again. They will never be thirsty again. The sun will not hurt them. No heat will burn them. [17]The Lamb in front of the throne will be their shepherd. He will lead them to springs of water that give life. And God will wipe away every tear from their eyes."

The Seventh Seal

8 [1]The Lamb* opened the seventh seal.* Then there was silence in heaven for about half an hour. [2]And I saw the seven angels who stand before God. They were given seven trumpets.

[3]Another angel came and stood at the altar.* This angel had a golden holder for incense.* The angel was given much incense to offer with the prayers of all God's holy people.* The angel put this offering on the golden altar before the throne. [4]The smoke from the incense went up from the angel's hand to God. The smoke went up with the prayers of God's people. [5]Then the angel filled the incense holder with fire from the altar and threw it down on the earth. Then there were flashes of lightning, thunder and other noises, and an earthquake.

The First of Seven Trumpet Blasts

[6]Then the seven angels with the seven trumpets prepared to blow their trumpets.

[7]The first angel blew his trumpet. Then hail and fire mixed with blood was poured down on the earth. And a third of the earth and all the green grass and a third of the trees were burned up.

[8]The second angel blew his trumpet. Then something that looked like a big mountain burning with fire was thrown into the sea. And a third of the sea became blood. [9]And a third of the created beings in the sea died, and a third of the ships were destroyed.

[10]The third angel blew his trumpet. Then a large star, burning like a torch, fell from the sky. It fell on a third of the rivers and on the springs of water. [11]The name of the star was Bitterness.[b] And a third of all the water became bitter. Many people died from drinking this bitter water.

[12]The fourth angel blew his trumpet. Then a third of the sun and a third of the moon and a third of the stars were struck. So

---

[a]**7:14** *washed their robes* Meaning that they believed in Jesus so that their sins could be forgiven. [b]**8:11** *Bitterness* Literally, "Wormwood," a very bitter plant; here, it is a symbol of bitter sorrow.

a third of them became dark. A third of the day and night was without light.

[13]While I watched, I heard an eagle that was flying high in the air. The eagle said with a loud voice, "Terrible! Terrible! How terrible for those who live on the earth! The terrible trouble will begin after the sounds of the trumpets that the other three angels will blow."

The Fifth Trumpet Begins the First Terror

9 [1]The fifth angel blew his trumpet. Then I saw a star fall from the sky to the earth. The star was given the key to the deep hole that leads down to the bottomless pit. [2]Then the star opened the hole leading to the pit. Smoke came up from the hole like smoke from a big furnace. The sun and sky became dark because of the smoke from the hole.

[3]Then locusts* came out of the smoke and went down to the earth. They were given the power to sting like scorpions. [4]They were told not to damage the fields of grass or any plant or tree. They were to hurt only those who did not have God's mark on their foreheads. [5]They were not given the power to kill them but only to cause them pain for five months—pain like a person feels when stung by a scorpion. [6]During those days people will look for a way to die, but they will not find it. They will want to die, but death will hide from them.

[7]The locusts looked like horses prepared for battle. On their heads they wore something that looked like a gold crown. Their faces looked like human faces. [8]Their hair was like women's hair. Their teeth were like lions' teeth. [9]Their chests looked like iron breastplates. The sound their wings made was like the noise of many horses and chariots hurrying into battle. [10]The locusts had tails with stingers like scorpions. The power they had to give people pain for five months was in their tails. [11]They had a ruler, who was the angel of the bottomless pit. (His name in Hebrew is Abaddon.[a] In Greek it is Apollyon.[b])

[12](The first terror is now past. There are still two other terrors to come.)

The Sixth Trumpet Blast

[13]The sixth angel blew his trumpet. Then I heard a voice coming from the horns on the four corners of the golden altar* that is before God. [14]It said to the sixth angel who had the trumpet, "Free the four angels who are tied at the great river Euphrates." [15]These four angels had been kept ready for this hour and day and month and year. The angels were set free to kill a third of all the people on the earth. [16]I heard how many troops on horses were in their army. There were 200,000,000.

---

[a]9:11 *Abaddon* In the Old Testament this was a name for the place of death. See Job 26:6 and Ps. 88:11.   [b]9:11 *Apollyon* A name that means "Destroyer."

[17]In my vision,* I saw the horses and the riders on the horses. They looked like this: They had breastplates that were fiery red, dark blue, and yellow like sulfur. The heads of the horses looked like heads of lions. The horses had fire, smoke, and sulfur coming out of their mouths. [18]A third of all the people on earth were killed by these three plagues coming out of the horses' mouths: the fire, the smoke, and the sulfur. [19]The horses' power was in their mouths and also in their tails. Their tails were like snakes that have heads to bite and hurt people.

[20]The other people on earth were not killed by these plagues. But these people still did not change their hearts and turn away from worshiping the things they had made with their own hands. They did not stop worshiping demons* and idols* made of gold, silver, bronze, stone, and wood—things that cannot see or hear or walk. [21]They did not change their hearts and turn away from killing other people or from their evil magic, their sexual sins, and their stealing.

The Angel and the Little Scroll

10 [1]Then I saw another powerful angel coming down from heaven. The angel was dressed in a cloud. He had a rainbow around his head. The angel's face was like the sun, and his legs were like poles of fire. [2]The angel was holding a small scroll.* The scroll was open in his hand. He put his right foot on the sea and his left foot on the land. [3]He shouted loudly like the roaring of a lion. After he shouted, the voices of seven thunders spoke.

[4]The seven thunders spoke, and I started to write. But then I heard a voice from heaven that said, "Don't write what the seven thunders said. Keep those things secret."

[5]Then the angel I saw standing on the sea and on the land raised his right hand to heaven. [6]The angel made a promise by the power of the one who lives forever and ever. He is the one who made the skies and all that is in them. He made the earth and all that is in it, and he made the sea and all that is in it. The angel said, "There will be no more waiting! [7]In the days when the seventh angel is ready to blow his trumpet, God's secret plan will be completed—the Good News* that God told to his servants, the prophets.*"

[8]Then I heard the same voice from heaven again. It said to me, "Go and take the open scroll that is in the angel's hand. This is the angel who is standing on the sea and on the land."

[9]So I went to the angel and asked him to give me the little scroll. He said to me, "Take the scroll and eat it. It will be sour in your stomach, but in your mouth it will be sweet like honey." [10]So I took the little scroll from the angel's hand and ate it. In my mouth it tasted sweet like honey, but after I ate it, it was sour in my stomach. [11]Then I was told, "You must prophesy* again about many races of people, many nations, languages, and rulers."

The Two Witnesses

11 ¹Then I was given a measuring rod as long as a walking stick. I was told, "Go and measure the temple*ᵃ* of God and the altar,* and count the people worshiping there. ²But don't measure the yard outside the temple. Leave it alone. It has been given to those who are not God's people. They will show their power over the holy city for 42 months. ³And I will give power to my two witnesses. And they will prophesy* for 1260 days. They will be dressed in sackcloth.*"

⁴These two witnesses are the two olive trees and the two lampstands that stand before the Lord of the earth. ⁵If anyone tries to hurt the witnesses, fire comes from the mouths of the witnesses and kills their enemies. Anyone who tries to hurt them will die like this. ⁶These witnesses have the power to stop the sky from raining during the time they are prophesying. These witnesses have power to make the water become blood. They have power to send every kind of plague to the earth. They can do this as many times as they want.

⁷When the two witnesses have finished telling their message, the beast will fight against them. This is the beast that comes up from the bottomless pit. It will defeat and kill them. ⁸The bodies of the two witnesses will lie in the street of the great city. This city is named Sodom* and Egypt. These names for the city have a special meaning. This is the city where the Lord was killed. ⁹People from every race of people, tribe, language, and nation will look at the bodies of the two witnesses for three and a half days. The people will refuse to bury them. ¹⁰Everyone on the earth will be happy because these two are dead. They will have parties and send each other gifts. They will do this because these two prophets brought much suffering to the people living on earth.

¹¹But after three and a half days, God let life enter the two prophets again. They stood on their feet. All those who saw them were filled with fear. ¹²Then the two prophets heard a loud voice from heaven say, "Come up here!" And the two prophets went up into heaven in a cloud. Their enemies watched them go.

¹³At that same time there was a great earthquake. A tenth of the city was destroyed. And 7000 people were killed in the earthquake. Those who did not die were very afraid. They gave glory* to the God of heaven.

¹⁴(The second terror is now past. The third terror is coming soon.)

The Seventh Trumpet Blast

¹⁵The seventh angel blew his trumpet. Then there were loud voices in heaven. The voices said,

---

*ᵃ*11:1 **temple** God's house—the place where God's people worship and serve him. Here, John sees it pictured as the special building in Jerusalem for Jewish worship. Also in verse 19.

"The kingdom of the world has now become the kingdom of
   our Lord and of his Christ.*
   And he will rule forever and ever."

[16]Then the 24 elders* bowed down on their faces and worshiped God. These are the elders who sit on their thrones
before God. [17]The elders said,

"We give thanks to you, Lord God All-Powerful.
   You are the one who is and who always was.
   We thank you because you have used your great power
      and have begun to rule.
[18] The people of the world were angry,
   but now is the time for your anger.
   Now is the time for the dead to be judged.
   It is time to reward your servants, the prophets,*
      and to reward your holy people,* the people,
         great and small, who respect you.
   It is time to destroy those people who destroy the earth!"

[19]Then God's temple in heaven was opened. The Box of the
Agreement* that God gave to his people could be seen in his
temple. Then there were flashes of lightning, noises, thunder,
an earthquake, and a great hailstorm.

The Woman Giving Birth and the Dragon

12 [1]And then a great wonder appeared in heaven: There was
a woman who was clothed with the sun, and the moon
was under her feet. She had a crown of twelve stars on her
head. [2]She was pregnant and cried out with pain because she
was about to give birth.

[3]Then another wonder appeared in heaven: There was a
giant red dragon there. The dragon had seven heads with a
crown on each head. It also had ten horns. [4]Its tail swept a third
of the stars out of the sky and threw them down to the earth. It
stood in front of the woman who was ready to give birth to the
baby. It wanted to eat the woman's baby as soon as it was born.

[5]The woman gave birth to a son, who would rule all the
nations with an iron rod. And her child was taken up to God
and to his throne. [6]The woman ran away into the desert to a
place that God had prepared for her. There she would be taken
care of for 1260 days.

[7]Then there was a war in heaven. Michael[a] and his angels
fought against the dragon. The dragon and its angels fought
back, [8]but they were not strong enough. The dragon and its
angels lost their place in heaven. [9]It was thrown down out of
heaven. (This giant dragon is that old snake, the one called the
devil or Satan, who leads the whole world into the wrong
way.) The dragon and its angels were thrown to the earth.

---

[a]**12:7** *Michael* The archangel—leader of God's angels. See Jude 9.

[10]Then I heard a loud voice in heaven say, "The victory and the power and the kingdom of our God and the authority of his Christ* have now come. These things have come, because the accuser of our brothers and sisters has been thrown out. He is the one who accused them day and night before our God. [11]They defeated him by the blood sacrifice of the Lamb* and by the message of God that they told people. They did not love their lives too much. They were not afraid of death. [12]So rejoice you heavens and all who live there! But it will be terrible for the earth and sea, because the devil has gone down to you. He is filled with anger. He knows he doesn't have much time."

[13]The dragon saw that he had been thrown down to the earth. So he chased the woman who had given birth to the child. [14]But the woman was given the two wings of a great eagle. Then she could fly to the place that was prepared for her in the desert. There she would be taken care of for three and a half years. There she would be away from the dragon.[a] [15]Then the dragon poured water out of its mouth like a river. It poured the water toward the woman so that the flood would carry her away. [16]But the earth helped the woman. The earth opened its mouth and swallowed the river that came from the mouth of the dragon. [17]Then the dragon was very angry with the woman. It went away to make war against all her other children. (Her children are those who obey God's commands and have the truth that Jesus taught.)

[18]The dragon stood on the seashore.

The Beast From the Sea

13 [1]Then I saw a beast coming up out of the sea. It had ten horns and seven heads. There was a crown on each of its horns. It had an evil name written on each head. [2]This beast looked like a leopard, with feet like a bear's feet. It had a mouth like a lion's mouth. The dragon gave the beast all of its power and its throne and great authority.

[3]One of the heads of the beast looked as if it had been wounded and killed, but the death wound was healed. All the people in the world were amazed, and they all followed the beast. [4]People worshiped the dragon because it had given its power to the beast, and they also worshiped the beast. They asked, "Who is as powerful as the beast? Who can make war against it?"

[5]The beast was allowed to boast and speak insults against God. It was allowed to use its power for 42 months. [6]The beast opened its mouth to insult God—to insult his name, the place where he lives, and all those who live in heaven. [7]It was given power to make war against God's holy people* and to defeat them. It was given power over every tribe, race of

---

[a] 12:14 *dragon* Here and in verse 15 literally, "snake." See verse 9 above.

people, language, and nation. [8]Everyone living on earth would worship the beast. (These are all the people since the beginning of the world whose names are not written in the Lamb's* book of life. The Lamb is the one who was killed.)

[9]Anyone who hears these things should listen to this:

[10] Whoever is to be a prisoner,
    will be a prisoner.
Whoever is to be killed with a sword,
    will be killed with a sword.

This means that God's holy people must have patience and faith.

The Beast From the Earth

[11]Then I saw another beast coming up out of the earth. He had two horns like a lamb, but he talked like a dragon. [12]This beast stood before the first beast and used the same power the first beast had. He used this power to make everyone living on the earth worship the first beast. The first beast was the one that had the death wound that was healed. [13]The second beast did great miracles.[a] He even made fire come down from heaven to earth while people were watching.

[14]This second beast fooled the people living on earth by using the miracles that he had been given the power to do for the first beast. He ordered people to make an idol* to honor the first beast, the one that was wounded by the sword but did not die. [15]The second beast was given power to give life to the idol of the first beast. Then the idol could speak and order all those who did not worship it to be killed. [16]The second beast also forced all people, small and great, rich and poor, free and slave, to have a mark put on their right hand or on their forehead. [17]No one could buy or sell without this mark. (This mark is the name of the beast or the number of its name.)

[18]Anyone who has understanding can find the meaning of the beast's number. This requires wisdom. This number is the number of a man. It is 666.

God's People Sing a New Song

14 [1]Then I looked, and there before me was the Lamb,* who was standing on Mount Zion.[b] There were 144,000 people with him. They all had his name and his Father's name written on their foreheads.

[2]And I heard a sound from heaven as loud as the crashing of floodwaters or claps of thunder. But it sounded like harpists playing their harps. [3]The people sang a new song before the throne and before the four living beings and the elders.* The

---

[a]13:13 *miracles* False miracles—amazing acts done by the power of the devil.
[b]14:1 *Mount Zion* Another name for Jerusalem, here meaning the spiritual city where God's people live with him.

only ones who could learn the new song were the 144,000 who had been bought from the earth. No one else could learn it.

⁴These are the ones who did not do sinful things with women. They kept themselves pure. Now they follow the Lamb wherever he goes. They were bought from among the people of the earth as the first to be offered to God and the Lamb. ⁵They are not guilty of telling lies; they are without fault.

The Three Angels

⁶Then I saw another angel flying high in the air. The angel had the eternal Good News* to announce to the people living on earth—to every nation, tribe, language, and race of people. ⁷The angel said in a loud voice, "Fear God and give him praise. The time has come for God to judge all people. Worship God. He made the heavens, the earth, the sea, and the springs of water."

⁸Then the second angel followed the first angel and said, "She is destroyed! The great city of Babylon is destroyed! She made all the nations drink the wine of her sexual sin and of God's anger."

⁹A third angel followed the first two angels. This third angel said in a loud voice, "God will punish all those who worship the beast and the beast's idol* and agree to have the beast's mark on their forehead or on their hand. ¹⁰They will drink the wine of God's anger. This wine is prepared with all its strength in the cup of God's anger. They will be tortured* with burning sulfur before the holy angels and the Lamb.* ¹¹And the smoke from their burning pain will rise forever and ever. There will be no rest, day or night, for those who worship the beast and its idol or who wear the mark of its name." ¹²This means that God's holy people* must be patient. They must obey God's commands and keep their faith in Jesus.

¹³Then I heard a voice from heaven. It said, "Write this: What a great blessing there is from now on for those who belong to the Lord when they die."

The Spirit* says, "Yes, that is true. They will rest from their hard work. What they have done will stay with them."

The Earth Is Harvested

¹⁴I looked and there before me, sitting on a white cloud, was one who looked like the Son of Man.* He had a gold crown on his head and a sharp sickle* in his hand. ¹⁵Then another angel came out of the temple. This angel called to the one who was sitting on the cloud, "Take your sickle and gather from the earth. The time to harvest has come, and the fruit on the earth is ripe." ¹⁶So the one who was sitting on the cloud swung his sickle over the earth. And the earth was harvested.

¹⁷Then another angel came out of the temple in heaven. This angel also had a sharp sickle. ¹⁸And then another angel, one with power over the fire, came from the altar.* He called to the angel with the sharp sickle and said, "Take your sharp sickle and

gather the bunches of grapes from the earth's vine. The earth's grapes are ripe." ¹⁹The angel swung his sickle over the earth. He gathered the earth's grapes and threw them into the great winepress of God's anger. ²⁰The grapes were squeezed in the winepress outside the city. Blood flowed out of the winepress. It rose as high as the heads of the horses for a distance of 200 miles.ᵃ

The Angels With the Last Plagues

15 ¹Then I saw another wonder in heaven. It was great and amazing. There were seven angels bringing seven plagues. (These are the last plagues, because after these, God's anger is finished.)

²I saw what looked like a sea of glass mixed with fire. All those who had won the victory over the beast and his idol* and over the number of its name were standing by the sea. These people had harps that God had given them. ³They sang the song of Moses,* the servant of God, and the song of the Lamb*:

> "Great and wonderful are the things you do,
>   Lord God All-Powerful.
> Right and true are your ways,
>   Ruler of the nations.
> ⁴ All people will fear you, O Lord.
> All people will praise your name.
>   Only you are holy.
> All people will come and worship before you,
>   because it is clear that you do what is right."

⁵After this I saw the temple, the holy place of God's presence,ᵇ in heaven. It was opened, ⁶and the seven angels bringing the seven plagues came out. They were dressed in clean, shining linen cloth. They wore golden bands tied around their chests. ⁷Then one of the four living beings gave seven golden bowls to the seven angels. The bowls were filled with the anger of God, who lives forever and ever. ⁸The temple was filled with smoke from the glory* and the power of God. No one could enter the temple until the seven plagues of the seven angels were finished.

The Bowls Filled With God's Anger

16 ¹Then I heard a loud voice from the temple. It said to the seven angels, "Go and pour out the seven bowls of God's anger on the earth."

²The first angel left. He poured out his bowl on the land. Then all those who had the mark of the beast and who worshiped its idol* got sores that were ugly and painful.

ᵃ**14:20** *200 miles* Literally, "1600 *stadia*," a little more than 300 km. ᵇ**15:5** *holy place of God's presence* Literally, "tent of the testimony." In the Old Testament this was a name for the Holy Tent, the portable building where God lived among his people. Inside this tent were the Ten Commandments written on flat stones, which were the "testimony" or "proof" of God's agreement with his people. See Ex. 25:8–22.

³The second angel poured out his bowl on the sea. Then the sea became blood like the blood of someone who has died. And everything living in the sea died.

⁴The third angel poured out his bowl on the rivers and the springs of water. The rivers and the springs of water became blood. ⁵Then I heard the angel of the waters say to God,

"You are the one who is and who always was.
  You are the Holy One.
You are right in these judgments that you have made.
⁶ The people have spilled the blood of your holy people*
    and your prophets.*
Now you have given those people blood to drink.
  This is what they deserve."

⁷And I heard the altar* say,

"Yes, Lord God All-Powerful,
  your judgments are true and right."

⁸The fourth angel poured out his bowl on the sun. The sun was given power to burn the people with fire. ⁹The people were burned by the great heat. They cursed the name of God, who had control over these plagues. But they refused to change their hearts and lives and give glory* to God.

¹⁰The fifth angel poured out his bowl on the throne of the beast. And darkness covered the beast's kingdom. People bit their tongues because of the pain. ¹¹They cursed the God of heaven because of their pain and the sores they had. But they refused to change their hearts and turn away from the evil things they did.

¹²The sixth angel poured out his bowl on the great river Euphrates. The water in the river was dried up. This prepared the way for the rulers from the east to come. ¹³Then I saw three evil spirits that looked like frogs. They came out of the mouth of the dragon, out of the mouth of the beast, and out of the mouth of the false prophet.* ¹⁴(These evil spirits are the spirits of demons.* They have power to do miracles.ᵃ They go out to the rulers of the whole world to gather them for battle on the great day of God All-Powerful.)

¹⁵"Listen! I will come at a time you don't expect, like a thief. What a great blessing there is for those who stay awake and keep their clothes with them. They will not have to go without clothes and be ashamed for people to see them."

¹⁶Then the evil spirits gathered the rulers together to the place that in Hebrew is called Armageddon.

¹⁷The seventh angel poured out his bowl into the air. Then a loud voice came out of the temple from the throne. It said, "It is finished!" ¹⁸Then there were flashes of lightning, noises, thunder, and a big earthquake. This was the worst earthquake

ᵃ16:14 *miracles* False miracles—amazing acts done by the power of the devil.

that has ever happened since people have been on earth. ¹⁹The great city split into three parts. The cities of the nations were destroyed. And God did not forget to punish Babylon the Great. He gave that city the cup filled with the wine of his terrible anger. ²⁰Every island disappeared and there were no more mountains. ²¹Giant hailstones fell on the people from the sky. These hailstones weighed almost 100 pounds*a* each. People cursed God because of this plague of the hail. It was terrible.

The Woman on the Red Beast

17 ¹One of the seven angels came and spoke to me. This was one of the angels that had the seven bowls. The angel said, "Come, and I will show you the punishment that will be given to the famous prostitute. She is the one sitting over many waters. ²The rulers of the earth sinned sexually with her. The people of the earth became drunk from the wine of her sexual sin."

³Then the angel carried me away by the Spirit* to the desert. There I saw a woman sitting on a red beast. The beast was covered with evil names. It had seven heads and ten horns. ⁴The woman was dressed in purple and red. She was shining with the gold, jewels, and pearls that she was wearing. She had a golden cup in her hand. This cup was filled with terribly evil things and the filth of her sexual sin. ⁵She had a title written on her forehead. This title has a hidden meaning. This is what was written:

THE GREAT BABYLON
MOTHER OF PROSTITUTES
AND THE EVIL THINGS OF THE EARTH

⁶I saw that the woman was drunk. She was drunk with the blood of God's holy people.* She was drunk with the blood of those who told about their faith in Jesus.

When I saw the woman, I was fully amazed. ⁷Then the angel said to me, "Why are you amazed? I will tell you the hidden meaning of this woman and the beast she rides—the beast with seven heads and ten horns. ⁸The beast you saw was once alive, but now it is not. However, it will come up out of the bottomless pit and go away to be destroyed. The people who live on the earth will be amazed when they see the beast, because it was once alive, is no longer living, but will come again. These are the people whose names have never been written in the book of life since the beginning of the world.

⁹"You need wisdom to understand this. The seven heads on the beast are the seven hills where the woman sits. They are also seven rulers. ¹⁰Five of the rulers have already died. One of the

a **16:21** *100 pounds* Literally, *"talanton"* or *"talent."* A talent was about 27 to 36 kg (60 to 80 pounds).

rulers lives now, and the last ruler is coming. When he comes, he will stay only a short time. [11]The beast that was once alive but is no longer living is an eighth ruler. This eighth ruler also belongs to the first seven rulers. And he will go away to be destroyed.

[12]"The ten horns you saw are ten rulers. These ten rulers have not yet received their kingdom, but they will receive power to rule with the beast for one hour. [13]All ten of these rulers have the same purpose. And they will give their power and authority to the beast. [14]They will make war against the Lamb.* But the Lamb will defeat them, because he is Lord of lords and King of kings. And with him will be his chosen and faithful followers—the people he has called to be his."

[15]Then the angel said to me, "You saw the waters where the prostitute sits. These waters are the many peoples, the different races, nations, and languages in the world. [16]The beast and the ten horns you saw will hate the prostitute. They will take everything she has and leave her naked. They will eat her body and burn her with fire. [17]God put the idea in their minds to do what would complete his purpose. They agreed to give the beast their power to rule until what God has said is completed. [18]The woman you saw is the great city that rules over the kings of the earth."

Babylon Is Destroyed

18 [1]Then I saw another angel coming down from heaven. This angel had great power. The angel's glory* made the earth bright. [2]The angel shouted with a powerful voice,

"She is destroyed!
　　The great city of Babylon is destroyed!
　She has become a home for demons.*
　　That city has become a place for every unclean spirit to live.
　　She is a city filled with all kinds of unclean birds.
　　She is a place where every unclean and hated animal lives.
[3] All the peoples of the earth have drunk the wine
　　　of her sexual sin and of God's anger.
　The rulers of the earth sinned sexually with her,
　　and the merchants* of the world grew rich
　　　from the great wealth of her luxury."

[4]Then I heard another voice from heaven say,

"Come out of that city, my people,
　　so that you will not share in her sins.
Then you will not suffer any of the terrible punishment
　　she will get.
[5] That city's sins are piled up as high as heaven.
　　God has not forgotten the wrongs she has done.
[6] Give that city the same as she gave to others.
　　Pay her back twice as much as she did.

Prepare wine for her that is twice as strong as the wine
    she prepared for others.
7 She gave herself much glory and rich living.
    Give her that much suffering and sadness.
She says to herself, 'I am a queen sitting on my throne.
    I am not a widow;
    I will never be sad.'
8 So in one day she will suffer
    great hunger, mourning, and death.
She will be destroyed by fire,
    because the Lord God who judges her is powerful.

9 "The rulers of the earth who sinned sexually with her and shared her wealth will see the smoke from her burning. Then they will cry and be sad because of her death. 10 The rulers will be afraid of her suffering and stand far away. They will say,

'Terrible! How terrible, O great city,
    O powerful city of Babylon!
Your punishment came in one hour!'

11 "And the merchants of the earth will cry and be sad for her. They will be sad because now there is no one to buy the things they sell— 12 gold, silver, jewels, pearls, fine linen cloth, purple cloth, silk, and scarlet cloth, all kinds of citron wood, and all kinds of things made from ivory, expensive wood, bronze, iron, and marble. 13 They also sell cinnamon, spice, incense,* frankincense,* myrrh,* wine, olive oil, fine flour, wheat, cattle, sheep, horses, carriages, and slaves—yes, even human lives. The merchants will cry and say,

14 'O Babylon, the good things you wanted have left you.
All your rich and fancy things have disappeared.
    You will never have them again.'

15 "The merchants will be afraid of her suffering and will stand far away from her. They are the ones who became rich from selling those things to her. They will cry and be sad. 16 They will say,

'Terrible! How terrible for the great city!
    She was dressed in fine linen;
    she wore purple and scarlet cloth.
    She was shining with gold, jewels, and pearls!
17 All these riches have been destroyed in one hour!'

"Every sea captain, all those who travel on ships, the sailors, and all those who earn money from the sea stood far away from Babylon. 18 They saw the smoke from her burning. They said loudly, 'There was never a city like this great city!' 19 They threw dust on their heads. They cried and were sad. They said loudly,

'Terrible! How terrible for the great city!
　　All those who had ships on the sea became rich
　　　　because of her wealth!
　　But she has been destroyed in one hour!
20　Be happy because of this, O heaven!
　　Be happy, God's holy people* and apostles* and prophets*!
　　God has punished her because of what she did to you.'"

21Then a powerful angel picked up a large rock. This rock was as big as a large millstone.* The angel threw the rock into the sea and said,

"That is how the great city of Babylon will be thrown down.
　　It will never be found again.
22　O Babylon, the music of people playing harps
　　　　and other instruments, flutes and trumpets,
　　　　will never be heard in you again.
　　No worker doing any job will ever be found in you again.
　　The sound of a millstone will never be heard in you again.
23　The light of a lamp will never shine in you again.
　　The voices of a bridegroom* and bride
　　　　will never be heard in you again.
　　Your merchants were the world's great people.
　　All the nations were tricked by your magic.
24　You are guilty of the death of the prophets,
　　　　of God's holy people,
　　　　and of all those who have been killed on earth."

People in Heaven Praise God

19 1After this I heard what sounded like a large crowd of people in heaven. The people were saying,

"Hallelujah![a]
Victory, glory,* and power belong to our God.
2　His judgments are true and right.
　Our God has punished the prostitute.
　　She is the one who ruined the earth with her sexual sin.
　God has punished the prostitute to pay her back
　　　for the death of his servants."

3These people also said,

"Hallelujah!
She is burning and her smoke will rise forever and ever."

4Then the 24 elders* and the four living beings bowed down. They worshiped God, who sits on the throne. They said,

"Amen*! Hallelujah!"

---

[a] **19:1** *Hallelujah* This means "Praise God!" Also in verses 3, 4, 6.

⁵Then a voice came from the throne and said,

"Praise our God, all you who serve him!
Praise our God, all you small and great who honor him!"

⁶Then I heard something that sounded like a large crowd of people. It was as loud as crashing waves or claps of thunder. The people were saying,

"Hallelujah!
Our Lord God rules.
He is the All-Powerful.
⁷ Let us rejoice and be happy and give God glory!
Give God glory, because the wedding of the Lamb* has come.
And the Lamb's bride has made herself ready.
⁸ Fine linen was given to the bride for her to wear.
The linen was bright and clean."

(The fine linen means the good things that God's holy people* did.)

⁹Then the angel said to me, "Write this: What a great blessing there is for those who are invited to the wedding meal of the Lamb!" Then the angel said, "These are the true words of God." ¹⁰Then I bowed down before the angel's feet to worship him. But the angel said to me, "Don't worship me! I am a servant like you and your brothers and sisters who have the truth of Jesus. So worship God! Because the truth of Jesus is the spirit of prophecy.*"

The Rider on the White Horse

¹¹Then I saw heaven open. There before me was a white horse. The rider on the horse was called Faithful and True, because he is right in his judging and in making war. ¹²His eyes were like burning fire. He had many crowns on his head. A name was written on him, but he was the only one who knew its meaning. ¹³He was dressed in a robe dipped in blood, and he was called the Word of God. ¹⁴The armies of heaven were following the rider on the white horse. They were also riding white horses. They were dressed in fine linen, white and clean. ¹⁵A sharp sword came out of the rider's mouth, a sword that he would use to defeat the nations. And he will rule the nations with a rod of iron. He will crush the grapes in the winepress of the terrible anger of God the All-Powerful. ¹⁶On his robe and on his leg was written this name:

KING OF KINGS AND LORD OF LORDS

¹⁷Then I saw an angel standing in the sun. The angel said with a loud voice to all the birds flying in the sky, "Come together for the great supper of God. ¹⁸Come together so that you can eat the bodies of rulers and army commanders and famous men. Come to eat the bodies of the horses and their

riders and the bodies of all people—free, slave, small, and great."

¹⁹Then I saw the beast and the rulers of the earth. Their armies were gathered together to make war against the rider on the horse and his army. ²⁰But the beast was captured, and the false prophet* was also captured. He was the one who did the miracles[a] for the beast. He had used these miracles to trick those who had the mark of the beast and worshiped its idol.* The false prophet and the beast were thrown alive into the lake of fire that burns with sulfur. ²¹Their armies were killed with the sword that came out of the mouth of the rider on the horse. All the birds ate these bodies until they were full.

The 1000 Years

20 ¹I saw an angel coming down out of heaven. The angel had the key to the bottomless pit. The angel also held a large chain in his hand. ²The angel grabbed the dragon, that old snake, also known as the devil or Satan. The angel tied the dragon with the chain for 1000 years. ³Then the angel threw the dragon into the bottomless pit and closed it. The angel locked it over the dragon. The angel did this so that the dragon could not trick the people of the earth until the 1000 years were ended. (After 1000 years the dragon must be made free for a short time.)

⁴Then I saw some thrones and people sitting on them. These were the ones who had been given the power to judge. And I saw the souls of those who had been killed because they were faithful to the truth of Jesus and the message* from God. They did not worship the beast or its idol.* They did not receive the mark of the beast on their foreheads or on their hands. They came back to life and ruled with Christ for 1000 years. ⁵(The rest of the dead did not live again until the 1000 years were ended.)

This is the first resurrection.* ⁶What a great blessing there is for those who share in this first resurrection. They are God's holy people.* The second death has no power over them. They will be priests for God and for Christ. They will rule with him for 1000 years.

The Defeat of Satan

⁷When the 1000 years are ended, Satan* will be made free from his prison. ⁸He will go out to trick the nations in all the earth, the nations known as Gog and Magog. Satan will gather the people for battle. There will be more people than anyone can count, like sand on the seashore.

⁹I saw Satan's army march across the earth and gather around the camp of God's people and the city that God loves. But fire came down from heaven and destroyed Satan's army.

[a] **19:20 miracles** False miracles—amazing acts done by the power of the devil.

[10]And he (the one who tricked these people) was thrown into the lake of burning sulfur with the beast and the false prophet.* There they would be tortured* day and night forever and ever.

People of the World Are Judged

[11]Then I saw a large white throne. I saw the one who was sitting on the throne. Earth and sky ran away from him and disappeared. [12]And I saw those who had died, great and small, standing before the throne. Some books were opened. And another book was opened—the book of life. The people were judged by what they had done, which is written in the books.

[13]The sea gave up the dead who were in it. Death and Hades* gave up the dead who were in them. Every person was judged by what they had done. [14]And Death and Hades were thrown into the lake of fire. This lake of fire is the second death. [15]And anyone whose name was not found written in the book of life was thrown into the lake of fire.

The New Jerusalem

21 [1]Then I saw a new heaven and a new earth. The first heaven and the first earth had disappeared. Now there was no sea. [2]And I saw the holy city, the new Jerusalem,[a] coming down out of heaven from God. It was prepared like a bride dressed for her husband.

[3]I heard a loud voice from the throne. It said, "Now God's home is with people. He will live with them. They will be his people. God himself will be with them and will be their God. [4]He will wipe away every tear from their eyes. There will be no more death, sadness, crying, or pain. All the old ways are gone."

[5]The one who was sitting on the throne said, "Look, I am making everything new!" Then he said, "Write this, because these words are true and can be trusted."

[6]The one on the throne said to me, "It is finished! I am the Alpha and the Omega,[b] the Beginning and the End. I will give free water from the spring of the water of life to anyone who is thirsty. [7]All those who win the victory will receive all this. And I will be their God, and they will be my children. [8]But those who are cowards, those who refuse to believe, those who do terrible things, those who kill, those who sin sexually, those who do evil magic, those who worship idols,* and those who tell lies—they will all have a place in the lake of burning sulfur. This is the second death."

[9]One of the seven angels came to me. This was one of the angels who had the seven bowls full of the seven last plagues. The angel said, "Come with me. I will show you the bride, the wife of the Lamb.*" [10]The angel carried me away by the Spirit*

---

[a] 21:2 *new Jerusalem* The spiritual city where God's people live with him. [b] 21:6 *Alpha . . . Omega* The first and last letters in the Greek alphabet, meaning the beginning and the end.

to a very large and high mountain. The angel showed me the holy city, Jerusalem. The city was coming down out of heaven from God.

¹¹The city was shining with the glory* of God. It was shining bright like a very expensive jewel, like a jasper. It was clear as crystal. ¹²The city had a large, high wall with twelve gates. There were twelve angels at the gates. On each gate was written the name of one of the twelve tribes of Israel.ᵃ ¹³There were three gates on the east, three gates on the north, three gates on the south, and three gates on the west. ¹⁴The walls of the city were built on twelve foundation stones. On the stones were written the names of the twelve apostles* of the Lamb.

¹⁵The angel who talked with me had a measuring rod made of gold. The angel had this rod to measure the city, its gates, and its wall. ¹⁶The city was built in a square. Its length was equal to its width. The angel measured the city with the rod. The city was 12,000 *stadia*ᵇ long, 12,000 *stadia* wide, and 12,000 *stadia* high. ¹⁷The angel also measured the wall. It was 144 cubitsᶜ high. (The angel was using the same measurement that people use.) ¹⁸The wall was made of jasper. The city was made of pure gold, as pure as glass.

¹⁹The foundation stones of the city walls had every kind of expensive jewels in them. The first foundation stone was jasper, the second was sapphire, the third was chalcedony, the fourth was emerald, ²⁰the fifth was onyx, the sixth was carnelian, the seventh was yellow quartz, the eighth was beryl, the ninth was topaz, the tenth was chrysoprase, the eleventh was jacinth, and the twelfth was amethyst. ²¹The twelve gates were twelve pearls. Each gate was made from one pearl. The street of the city was made of pure gold, as clear as glass.

²²I did not see a temple in the city. The Lord God All-Powerful and the Lamb were the city's temple. ²³The city did not need the sun or the moon to shine on it. The glory of God gave the city light. The Lamb was the city's lamp.

²⁴The peoples of the world will walk by the light given by the Lamb. The rulers of the earth will bring their glory into the city. ²⁵The city's gates will never close on any day, because there is no night there. ²⁶The greatness and the honor of the nations will be brought into the city. ²⁷Nothing unclean will ever enter the city. No one who does shameful things or tells lies will ever enter the city. Only those whose names are written in the Lamb's book of life will enter the city.

22 ¹The angel showed me the river of the water of life, clear as crystal. The river flows from the throne of God and the Lamb. ²It flows down the middle of the street of the city. The

---

ᵃ**21:12** *Israel* First, Israel was the people descended from Jacob (see "Israel" in the Word List), but the name is also used to mean all of God's people. ᵇ**21:16** *stadia* One *stadion* was one-eighth of a Roman mile or 192 meters. ᶜ**21:17** *cubits* A cubit is the length of a man's arm from the elbow to the tip of the little finger, about half a meter.

tree of life* is on each side of the river, and it produces fruit every month, twelve times a year. The leaves of the tree are for healing the nations.

³Nothing that God judges guilty will be there in that city. The throne of God and the Lamb will be in the city. God's servants will worship him. ⁴They will see his face. God's name will be written on their foreheads. ⁵There will never be night again. People will not need the light of a lamp or the light of the sun. The Lord God will give them light. And they will rule like kings forever and ever.

⁶Then the angel said to me, "These words are true and can be trusted. The Lord, the God of the spirits of the prophets,* has sent his angel to show his servants what must happen soon: ⁷'Listen, I am coming soon! What a great blessing there is for the one who obeys the words of prophecy* in this book.'"

⁸I am John. I am the one who heard and saw these things. After I heard and saw them, I bowed down to worship at the feet of the angel who showed them to me. ⁹But the angel said to me, "Don't worship me! I am a servant like you and your brothers the prophets. I am a servant like all those who obey the words in this book. You should worship God!"

¹⁰Then the angel told me, "Don't keep secret the words of prophecy in this book. The time is near for these things to happen. ¹¹Let anyone who is doing wrong continue to do wrong. Let anyone who is unclean continue to be unclean. Let anyone who is doing right continue to do right. Let anyone who is holy* continue to be holy."

¹²"Listen, I am coming soon! I will bring rewards with me. I will repay everyone for what they have done. ¹³I am the Alpha and the Omega,ᵃ the First and the Last, the Beginning and the End.

¹⁴"What a great blessing there is for those who have washed their robes.ᵇ They will have the right to eat the food from the tree of life. They can go through the gates into the city. ¹⁵Outside the city are all those who live like dogs—those who do evil magic, those who sin sexually, those who murder, those who worship idols, and those who love to lie and pretend to be good.

¹⁶"I, Jesus, have sent my angel to tell you these things for the churches.* I am the descendant from the family of David.* I am the bright morning star."

¹⁷The Spirit and the bride say, "Come!" Everyone who hears this should also say, "Come!" If anyone is thirsty, let them come; they can have the water of life as a free gift if they want it.

¹⁸I warn everyone who hears the words of prophecy in this book: If anyone adds anything to these, God will give them the

---

ᵃ**22:13** *Alpha ... Omega* The first and last letters in the Greek alphabet, meaning the beginning and the end. ᵇ**22:14** *washed their robes* Meaning that they believed in Jesus so that their sins could be forgiven.

plagues written about in this book. ¹⁹And if anyone takes away from the words of this book of prophecy, God will take away their share of the tree of life and of the holy city, which are written about in this book.

²⁰Jesus is the one who says that all of this is true. Now he says, "Yes, I am coming soon."

Amen*! Come, Lord Jesus!

²¹The grace* of the Lord Jesus be with all people.

Psalms

BOOK 1 *(Psalms 1–41)*

1 ¹What great blessings there are for those
    who don't listen to evil advice,
    who don't live like sinners
    and don't join those who make fun of God.*ᵃ*
² Instead, they love the Lᴏʀᴅ's teachings
    and think about them day and night.
³ So they grow strong, like a tree planted by a stream—
    a tree that produces fruit when it should
    and has leaves that never fall.
Everything they do is successful.

⁴ But the wicked are not like that.
    They are like chaff* that the wind blows away.
⁵ When the time for judgment comes,
    the wicked will be found guilty.
    Sinners have no place among those who do what is right.*ᵇ*
⁶ The Lᴏʀᴅ protects those who do right,
    but the wicked are on their way to destruction.

2 ¹Why are the nations so angry?
    Why are the people making such foolish plans?
² Their kings and leaders join together
    to fight against the Lᴏʀᴅ and the king he has chosen.*ᶜ*
³ They say, "Let's rebel against them.
    Let's break free from them!"

⁴ But the one who rules in heaven laughs at them.
    The Lord makes fun of them.
⁵ He speaks to them in anger,
    and it fills them with fear.
⁶ He says, "I have chosen this man to be king,
    and he will rule on Zion,* my holy mountain."

⁷ Let me tell you about the Lᴏʀᴅ's agreement:
    He said to me, "Today I have become your father,*ᵈ*
    and you are my son.

*ᵃ***1:1** Or, "The one who does not follow the advice of the wicked or turn onto Sinners Road or stay at Scoffers' House is blessed." *ᵇ***1:5** Or, "The wicked will not be allowed to sit as judges nor sinners in the meeting of good people." *ᶜ***2:2** *the king he chose* Or, "his anointed one." *ᵈ***2:7** *I have become your father* Literally, "I fathered you." Originally, this probably meant God was "adopting" the king as his son.

8 If you ask, I will give you the nations.
   Everyone on earth will be yours.
9 You will rule over them with a power that cannot be broken.
   You will scatter your enemies like broken pieces of pottery!"

10 So, kings and rulers, be smart and learn this lesson.
11 Serve the LORD with fear and trembling.
12 Show that you are loyal to his son,[a]
   or the Lord will be angry and destroy you.
   He is almost angry enough to do that now,
      but those who go to him for protection will be blessed.

3 *This is a song of David* telling about the time he was running
   from his son Absalom.
1 LORD, I have so many enemies.
   So many people have turned against me.
2 They tell themselves, "God will not rescue him!"   *Selah**

3 But you, LORD, protect me.
   You bring me honor; you give me hope.
4 I will pray to the LORD,
   and he will answer me from his holy mountain.   *Selah*

5 I can lie down and rest, and I know I will wake up,
   because the LORD covers and protects me.
6 So I will not be afraid of my enemies,
   even if thousands of them surround me.

7 LORD, get up![b]
   My God, come rescue me!
   If you hit my enemies on the cheek,
      you will break all their teeth.

8 LORD, the victory[c] is yours!
   You are so good to your people.   *Selah*

4 *To the director.** With stringed instruments.
   *A song of David.**
1 God, you showed I was innocent.
   You gave me relief from all my troubles.
   So listen to my prayer again when I call to you for help.
   Be kind to me.

2 Honorable men,[d] how long will you try to dishonor me?
   Do you enjoy wasting your time searching for new lies
      against me?   *Selah**

---

[a]2:12 Show ... his son Literally, "Kiss the son." [b]3:7 *LORD, get up* The people said this
when they lifted the Box of the Agreement and took it into battle with them. This showed
that God was with them. See Num. 10:35–36. [c]3:8 *victory* Or, "salvation."
[d]4:2 *Honorable men* Literally, "Sons of man." This is probably a term of respect spoken to the
leaders who were judging the writer of this psalm.

3 You know the LORD listens to his loyal servant.
    The LORD hears me when I pray to him.

4 If something is bothering you, then be angry,[a] but don't sin.
    Think about it when you go to bed, and then calm down.

                           Selah

5 Give the right sacrifices* to the LORD,
    and put your trust in him!

6 Many people say, "I wish I could enjoy the good life.
    LORD, give us some of those blessings."[b]

7 But you have made me happier than they will ever be
    with all their wine and grain.

8 When I go to bed, I sleep in peace,
    because, LORD, you keep me safe.

5 To the director.* For the flutes.[c]
A song of David.*

1 LORD, listen to me and understand what I am trying to say.

2 My God and King, listen to my prayer.

3 Every morning, LORD, I lay my gifts before you
    and look to you for help.
And every morning you hear my prayers.

4 God, you don't want evil people near you.
    They cannot stay in your presence.[d]

5 Fools[e] cannot come near you.
    You hate those who do evil.

6 You destroy those who tell lies.
    LORD, you hate those who make secret plans to hurt others.

7 But by your great mercy, I can enter your house.
    I can worship in your holy Temple*
    with fear and respect for you.

8 LORD, show me your right way of living,
    and make it easy for me to follow.
People are looking for my weaknesses,
    so show me how you want me to live.

9 My enemies never tell the truth.
    They only want to destroy people.
Their words come from mouths that are like open graves.
    They use their lying tongues to deceive others.[f]

10 Punish them, God!
    Let them be caught in their own traps.
They have turned against you,
    so punish them for their many crimes.

---

[a]4:4 *be angry* Or, "be upset" or "be excited."   [b]4:6 *I wish … blessings* Or, "Who will show us good. Lift up on us the light of your face, LORD."   [c]**Psalm 5** *For the flutes* This might be the name of a tune instead of a type of instrument.   [d]5:4 Or, "You are not a God who likes evil people, and they don't respect you."   [e]5:5 *Fools* Here, this means someone who does not follow God and his wise teachings.   [f]5:9 *They use … others* Or, "They say nice things to others, but only to trap them."

11 But let those who trust in you be happy forever.
    Protect and strengthen those who love your name.
12 LORD, when you bless good people,
    you surround them with your love
        like a large shield that protects them.

6

To the director,* with stringed instruments, on the sheminith.*
A song of David.*

1 LORD, don't punish me.
    Don't correct me when you are so angry.
2 LORD, be kind to me.
    I am sick and weak.
  Heal me, LORD!
    My bones are shaking.
3 I am trembling all over.
  LORD, how long until you heal me?[a]
4 LORD, come back and make me strong again.
    You are so loyal and kind, so save me.
5 If I am dead, I cannot sing about you.
    Those in the grave don't praise you.

6 LORD, I am so weak.
    I cried to you all night.
  My pillow is soaked,
    my bed is dripping wet from my tears.
7 My enemies have caused me such sorrow
    that my eyes are worn out from crying.

8 Go away, you wicked people,
    because the LORD has heard my cries.
9 The LORD has heard my request for mercy.
    The LORD has accepted my prayer.

10 All my enemies will be filled with fear and shame.
    They will be sorry when disgrace suddenly comes
        upon them.

7

A song[b] of David that he sang to the LORD. This song is about Kish[c]
from the tribe of Benjamin.

1 LORD my God, I come to you for protection.
    Save me from those who are chasing me.
2 If you don't help me, I will be torn apart
    like an animal caught by a lion.
  I will be carried away with no one to save me.

3 LORD my God, I have done nothing wrong.
4 I have done nothing to hurt a friend[d] or to help his enemies.

---

[a] **6:3** *LORD ... heal me* Literally, "As for you, LORD, how long?"   [b] **Psalm 7** *song* Literally,
"shiggayon." This probably means a song full of emotion.   [c] **Psalm 7** *Kish* Or, "Cush."
[d] **7:4** *friend* Or, "ally," a person or country that has agreed to help another person or country.

5 If that is not true, then punish me.
  Let my enemies chase me, catch me, and kill me.
  Let them grind me into the dirt and put me in my grave.

  *Selah**

6 Lᴏʀᴅ, get up*ᵃ* and show your anger!
  My enemy is angry, so stand and fight against him.
  Get me the justice that you demand.

7 Gather the nations around you,
  and take your place as judge.

8 Lᴏʀᴅ, judge the people.
  Lᴏʀᴅ, judge me.
  Prove that I am right and that I am innocent.

9 Stop those who do evil.
  Support those who do good.
  God, you are fair.
  You know what people are thinking.

10 God helps good people, so he will protect me.

11 God is a good judge.
  He always condemns evil.

12–13If the wicked will not change,
  then God is ready to punish them.
  He has prepared his deadly weapons.
  His sword is sharp.
  His bow is strung, drawn back, and ready
    to shoot its flaming arrow.

14 The minds of the wicked are full of evil;
  they conceive their wicked plans, which give birth to lies.

15 They dig a pit to trap others,
  but they are the ones who will fall into it.

16 The trouble they cause will come back on themselves.
  They plan harm for others, but they are the ones
    who will get hurt.

17 I praise the Lᴏʀᴅ because he is good.
  I praise the name of the Lᴏʀᴅ Most High.

8

To the director,* on the gittith.*
A song of David.*

1 Lᴏʀᴅ our Lord, your name is the most wonderful
    in all the earth!
  It brings you praise everywhere in heaven.

2 From the mouths of children and babies come songs
    of praise to you.
  They sing of your power to silence your enemies
    who were seeking revenge.

*ᵃ***7:6** *Lᴏʀᴅ, get up* The people said this when they lifted the Box of the Agreement and took it
into battle with them. This showed that God was with them. See Num. 10:35–36.

3 I look at the heavens that you made with your hands.
    I see the moon and stars you created.
4 And I wonder, "Why are people so important to you?
    Why do you even think about them?
Why do you care so much about humans[a]?
    Why do you even notice them?"

5 Yet, you made people[b] almost like gods
    and crowned them with glory and honor.
6 You put them in charge of everything you made.
    You put everything under their[c] control.
7 People rule over the sheep and cattle and all the wild animals.
8 They rule over the birds in the sky
    and over the fish that swim in the ocean currents.
9 LORD our Lord, your name is the most wonderful
    in all the earth!

9

To the director. Alamoth of Ben.[d]
A song of David.

1 I will praise you, LORD, with all my heart.
    I will tell about the wonderful things you have done.
2 You make me happy, so I will rejoice in you.
    God Most High, I praise your name.
3 My enemies turned to run from you,
    but they fell and were destroyed.

4 You listened to me from your throne like a good judge,
    and you decided that I was right.
5 You told the nations how wrong they were.
    You destroyed those evil people.
You erased their names from our memory forever and ever.
6 The enemy is finished!
    You destroyed their cities.
    There is nothing left to remind us of them.

7 The LORD set up his throne to bring justice,
    and he will rule forever.
8 He judges everyone on earth fairly.
    He judges all nations honestly.
9 Many people are suffering—
    crushed by the weight of their troubles.
But the LORD is a refuge for them,
    a safe place they can run to.

---

[a]**8:4** *people … humans* Literally, "man … son of man" or "Enosh … son of Adam." These are Hebrew ways of saying humans—descendants of Adam and Enosh. [b]**8:5** *people* Literally, "him." This is still talking about "man" and "son of man" and can be understood as one person or as all people. [c]**8:6** *their* Literally, "his." [d]**Psalm 9** *Alamoth of Ben* This might be the name of a tune, *On the Death of the Son,* or a song for the ceremony of when a boy becomes a man, or it might refer to one of the orchestral groups in the Temple. See 1 Chron. 15:20.

¹⁰ LORD, those who know your name
   come to you for protection.
And when they come,
   you do not leave them without help.

¹¹ Sing praises to the LORD who sits as King in Zion.ᵃ
   Tell the nations about the great things he has done.
¹² He punishes murderers
   and remembers those who go to him for help.
When those poor people cry for help,
   he does not forget them.

¹³ I said this prayer: "LORD, be kind to me.
   See how my enemies are hurting me?
   Save me from the 'gates of death.'
¹⁴ Then, at the gates of Jerusalem,ᵇ
   I can sing praises to you.
   I will be so happy because you saved me."

¹⁵ Those other nations have fallen into the pit
   they dug to catch others.
They have been caught in their own trap.
¹⁶ The LORD showed that he judges fairly.
   The wicked were caught by what they did.

                    *Higgayonᶜ   Selah**

¹⁷ The wicked will go to the place of death,
   as will all the nations that forget God.
¹⁸ It may seem that those who are poor and needy
   have been forgotten, but God will not forget them.
He will not leave them without hope.

¹⁹ LORD, get upᵈ and judge the nations.
   Don't let anyone think they can win against you.
²⁰ Teach them a lesson.
   Let them know they are only human.   *Selah*

10 ¹ LORD, why do you stay so far away?
       Why do you hide from people in time of trouble?
² The wicked are proud and make evil plans to hurt the poor,
   who are caught and made to suffer.
³ Those greedy people brag about the things they want to get.
   They curse* the LORD and show they hate him.
⁴ The wicked are too proud to ask God for help.
   He does not fit into their plans.

ᵃ**9:11** *Sing . . . Zion* Or, "Inhabitants of Zion, sing praises to the LORD." See "Zion" in the Word
List. ᵇ**9:14** *gates of Jerusalem* Literally, "Gates of Daughter Zion." ᶜ**9:16** *Higgayon* Or,
"Meditation." This may mean a time to think quietly during the song. ᵈ**9:19** *LORD, get up*
The people said this when they lifted the Box of the Agreement and took it into battle with
them. This showed that God was with them. See Num. 10:35–36.

⁵ They succeed in everything they do.
     They don't understand how you can judge them.
     They make fun of their enemies.

⁶ They say to themselves, "Nothing bad will happen to us.
     We will have our fun and never be punished."

⁷ They are always cursing, lying,
     and planning evil things to do.

⁸ They hide just outside the villages,
     waiting to kill innocent people.
     They are always looking for any helpless person they can hurt.

⁹ They are like lions hiding in the bushes
     to catch weak and helpless animals.
     They lay their traps for the poor,
     who are caught in their nets.

¹⁰ Again and again they hurt people
     who are already weak and suffering.

¹¹ So the poor begin to think, "God has forgotten us.
     He has turned away from us forever.
     He does not see what is happening to us."

¹² LORD, get up and do something.
     God, punish those who are wicked.
     Don't forget those who are poor and helpless.

¹³ The wicked turn against God
     because they think he will not punish them.

¹⁴ More than anyone else, God,
     you see the cruel, evil things that bad people do.
     Helpless people were abandoned and left for you to care for.
     After all, you are the one who cares for orphans.
     So help them!

¹⁵ Break the arms of those who are wicked and evil.
     Punish them for the wicked things they have done.
     Stop them from doing any more evil.

¹⁶ LORD, you are King forever and ever,
     so I know you will remove the wicked nations
     from your land.

¹⁷ LORD, you have heard what the poor want.
     Listen to their prayers, and do what they ask.

¹⁸ Protect the orphans and those who have been hurt.
     Don't let powerful people drive us from our land!

11 To the director.*
     David's ⸤song⸥.

¹ I trust in the LORD, so why did you tell me to run and hide?
     Why did you say, "Fly like a bird to your mountain?"

² Like hunters, the wicked hide in the dark.
     They pull back on the bowstring and aim their arrows.
     They shoot straight into the hearts of good, honest people.

3 What would good people do
    if the wicked destroyed all that is good?[a]

4 The Lord is in his holy temple.
    The Lord sits on his throne in heaven.
  He sees everything that happens.
    He watches people closely.

5 The Lord examines those who are good
        and those who are wicked;
    he hates those who enjoy hurting others.

6 He will make hot coals and burning sulfur fall
        like rain on the wicked.
    They will get nothing but a hot, burning wind.[b]

7 The Lord always does what is right,
        and he loves those who do right.
    They will get to meet with him.[c]

12 To the director,* on the sheminith.*
    A song of David.*

1 Save me, Lord!
    We cannot trust anyone anymore!
    All the good, loyal people are gone.

2 People lie to their neighbors.
    They say whatever they think people want to hear.

3 The Lord should cut off their lying lips
    and cut out their bragging tongues.

4 Those people think they can win any argument.
    They say, "We are so good with words,
        no one will be our master."

5 They took advantage of the poor
        and stole what little they had.
  But the Lord knows what they did, and he says,
    "I will rescue those who are poor and helpless,
        and I will punish those who hurt them."[d]

6 The Lord's words are true and pure,
        like silver purified by fire,
    like silver melted seven times to make it perfectly pure.

7 Lord, take care of the helpless.
    Protect them forever from the wicked people in this world.

8 The wicked are all around us,
    and everyone thinks evil is something to be praised!

---

[a]11:3 Or, "What if the foundations of society were really destroyed? [b]11:6 hot, burning
wind This is like the hot fire a worker uses to melt silver and separate it from the worthless
things that are left. [c]11:7 They … him Literally, "They will see his face." [d]12:5 I will
rescue … hurt them Or, "I will rescue poor, helpless people who were hurt and asked me for
help."

13

To the director.*
A song of David.*

1 How long will you forget me, LORD?
  Will you forget me forever?
  How long will you refuse to accept me?[a]

2 How long must I wonder if you have forgotten me?
  How long must I feel this sadness in my heart?
  How long will my enemy win against me?

3 LORD my God, look at me.
  Answer my question.
  Let me know the answer, or I will die.

4 If that happens, my enemy will say, "I beat him!"
  He will be so happy that he won.

5 But, LORD, I trust in your faithful love,
  so let me rejoice because you saved me.

6 Then I will sing to the LORD
  because he was so good to me.

14

To the director.*
David's ₍song₎.

1 Only fools think there is no God.
  People like that are evil and do terrible things.
  They never do what is right.

2 The LORD looks down from heaven
  to see if there is anyone who is wise,
  anyone who looks to him for help.

3 But everyone has turned away from him.
  Everyone has become evil.
  No one does anything good.
  No, not one person!

4 The LORD said, "The wicked don't ask for my advice.
  And they treat my people like bread to be eaten.
  Don't they understand what they are doing?"

5 They will have plenty to fear,
  because God is with those who do what is right.

6 You wicked people want to spoil the hopes of the poor,
  but the LORD will protect them.

7 I wish the one who lives on Mount Zion*
  would bring victory to Israel*!
  Jacob's* people will be very happy
  when the LORD makes Israel prosper again.[b]

---

[a]13:1 refuse to accept me Literally, "hide your face from me." [b]14:7 Jacob's people ... prosper again Or, "The LORD's people were taken away as captives, but he will bring them back. Then Jacob (Israel) will be very happy."

15 *A song of David.*[*]

1 LORD, who can live in your Holy Tent[a]?
　　Who can live on your holy mountain[b]?
2 Only those who live pure lives, do good things,
　　and speak truth from their hearts can live
　　　　on your mountain.
3 Such people don't say bad things about others.
　　They don't do things to hurt their neighbors.
　　They don't tell shameful things about those close to them.
4 They despise those who hate God
　　and honor those who respect the LORD.
　　If they make a promise to their neighbor,
　　　　they do what they promised.[c]
5 If they loan money to someone,
　　they do not charge them interest.
　　And they refuse to testify against an innocent person,
　　　　even if someone offers them money to do it.

　Whoever lives like this will always stand strong.

16 *A miktam[*] of David.*

1 Protect me, God, because I depend on you.
2 I said, "LORD, you are my Lord.
　　You are responsible for every good thing I have."
3 But you also said, "The gods[d] of this world have authority
　　over all that I desire."[e]

4 But those who worship other gods will have many troubles.
　　I will not share in the gifts of blood that they offer
　　　　to their idols.
　　I will not even say their names.
5 LORD, you give me all that I need.
　　You support me.
　　You give me my share.
6 My share[f] is wonderful.
　　My inheritance[g] is very beautiful.
7 I praise the LORD because he taught me well.
　　Even at night he put his instructions deep inside my mind.[h]

---

[a]**15:1** *Holy Tent* The special tent where the people of Israel worshiped God. Here, it is probably the Temple in Jerusalem. [b]**15:1** *holy mountain* Mount Zion, the hill in Jerusalem where the Temple was built. [c]**15:4** *If they ... promised* Or, "They promised not to do bad things, and they do not do bad things." [d]**16:3** *gods* Literally, "holy ones." This can also mean, "angels," or "true followers of God." [e]**16:2–3** Or, "²I said to the LORD, 'LORD, you are my Lord. Every good thing I have comes from you.' ³The LORD does wonderful things for his followers on earth. The LORD shows he really loves them." [f]**16:6** *share* Or, "section of land." [g]**16:6** *inheritance* Here, this probably means the land each Israelite received. [h]**16:7** *mind* Literally, "my kidneys."

8 I always remember the LORD,[a]
   and I will never leave his side.
9 So my heart and soul will be very happy.
   Even my body will live in safety,
10 because you will not leave me in the place of death.
   You will not let your faithful one rot in the grave.[b]
11 You will teach me the right way to live.
   Just being with you will bring complete happiness.
   Being at your right side will bring happiness forever.

17 A prayer of David.[c]

1 LORD, hear my prayer for justice.
   I am calling loudly to you.
   I am being honest in what I say,
     so please listen to my prayer.
2 You will make the right decision
     because you can see the truth.
3 You were with me all night
   and looked deep into my heart.
   You questioned me and found that
     I did not say or do anything wrong.
4 I have done all that is humanly possible
     to obey your commands.
5 I have followed your way.
   My feet never left your path.
6 Every time I call to you, God, you answer me.
   So listen to me now, and hear what I say.
7 Show your amazing kindness
   and rescue those who depend on you.
   Use your great power
   and protect them from their enemies.
8 Protect me like the pupil[d] of your eye.
   Hide me in the shadow of your wings.
9 Save me from the wicked ones who are trying to destroy me.
   Protect me from those who come to hurt me.
10 They think only of themselves
   and brag about what they will do.
11 They have been following me,
   and now they are all around me.
   They watch me, waiting to throw me to the ground.
12 Like hungry lions, they want to kill and eat.
   Like young lions, they hide, ready to attack.

---

a 16:8 Literally, "I set the LORD before me always." b 16:10 rot ... grave Literally, "see decay." c Psalm 17 A prayer of David Or, "A prayer dedicated to David." d 17:8 pupil The center of the eye, which everyone wants to protect.

13 LORD, get up[a] and face the enemy.
   Make them surrender.
   Use your sword and save me from those wicked people.
14 LORD, use your power and remove them from this life.
   But as for the people you treasure, fill them with food.
      Give them plenty for their children
         and their grandchildren.

15 I have done only what is right, so I will see your face.
   And seeing you,[b] I will be fully satisfied.

18 [c]*To the director.* The song of the LORD's servant, David. He sang this song when the LORD saved him from Saul and all his other enemies.

1 I love you, LORD!
   You are my strength.

2 The LORD is my Rock,* my fortress,* my place of safety.
   My God is my Rock; I run to him for protection.
   He is my shield; by his power I am saved.[d]
   He is my hiding place high in the hills.

3 I called to the LORD for help,
   and he saved me from my enemies!
   He is worthy of my praise!
4 Death had its ropes wrapped around me.
   I was caught in a flood carrying me to the place
      of no return.[e]
5 The ropes of the grave wound around me.
   Death set its trap right there in front of me.
6 In my trouble I called to the LORD.
   Yes, I cried out to my God for help.
   There in his temple he heard my voice,
   He heard my cry for help.
7 The earth shook and shivered.
   The foundations of the mountains trembled.
   They shook because God was angry.
8 Smoke came from his nose.
   Burning flames came from his mouth.
   Red-hot coals fell from him.
9 He tore open the sky and came down!
   He stood on a thick, dark cloud.
10 He flew across the sky, riding on the Cherub angels.*
   He was soaring high on the wind.

---

[a]**17:13** *LORD, get up* The people said this when they lifted the Box of the Agreement and took it into battle with them. This showed that God was with them. See Num. 10:35–36. [b]**17:15** *you* Literally, "your likeness." [c]**Psalm 18** This song is also found in 2 Sam. 22. [d]**18:2** *by his power I am saved* Literally, "He is the horn of my salvation." [e]**18:4** *place of no return* That is, "death."

¹¹ He covered himself in dark clouds
            that surrounded him like a tent.
    He was hidden by thick thunderclouds.
¹² Then God's shining brightness broke through the clouds.
    Hail came down with flashes of lightning.
¹³ The LORD thundered from the sky;
        God Most High let his voice be heard.
¹⁴ The LORD shot his arrows and scattered the enemy.
        His lightning bolts threw them into confusion.

¹⁵ LORD, you shouted your command,
            and a powerful wind began to blow.ᵃ
    The water was pushed back,
        and we could see the bottom of the sea;
        the earth's foundations were uncovered.

¹⁶ The Lord reached down from above and grabbed me.
        He pulled me from the deep water of my troubles.
¹⁷ My enemies were powerful, and they hated me.
        They were too strong for me, so he saved me.
¹⁸ In my time of trouble my enemies attacked me,
        but the LORD was there to support me.
¹⁹ He was pleased with me, so he rescued me.
        He took me to a safe place.
²⁰ The LORD rewarded me for doing what is right.
        He was good to me because I am innocent.
²¹ The LORD did that because I have obeyed him.
        I have not turned against my God.
²² I never forget or ignore his laws.
        I never reject his rules.
²³ He knows that I am not guilty of doing wrong.
        I have kept myself from sinning.
²⁴ So the LORD rewarded me for doing right.
        He knows I am innocent.

²⁵ Lord, you are always faithful to those
            who remain faithful to you.
    You are true to those who are true to you.
²⁶ All whose hearts are good and pure can depend on you
            to be good to them.
    But you can outsmart the wicked,
        no matter how clever they are.
²⁷ You help the humble,
        but you humiliate the proud.
²⁸ LORD, you provide the flame for my lamp.
        My God turns the darkness around me into light.
²⁹ With your help I can defeat an army.
        If my God is with me, I can climb over enemy walls.

ᵃ18:15 Or, "and a breath of wind came from your nostrils."

30 God's way is perfect.
   The LORD's promise always proves to be true.
He protects those who trust in him.

31 There is no God except the LORD.
   There is no Rock except our God.

32 God is the one who gives me strength.
   He clears the path I need to take.

33 He makes my feet steady, like the feet of a deer;
   on high mountain paths he keeps me from falling.

34 He trains me for war,
   so that my arms can bend the most powerful bow.

35 God, you have given me your shield to protect me.
   You support me with your right hand.
   Your gentle care for me has made me great.

36 You clear the path for my feet,
   so I can walk without stumbling.

37 I chased my enemies and caught them.
   I did not stop until they were destroyed.

38 I struck down my enemies; they will not get up again.
   They have fallen under my feet.

39 God, you made me strong in battle.
   You made my enemies fall before me.

40 You made my enemies turn and run away.
   I destroyed those who hated me.

41 They cried out for help,
   but there was no one to save them.
   They cried out to the LORD,
   but he did not answer them.

42 I beat them to pieces, like dust blown by the wind.
   I smashed them like mud in the streets.

43 You saved me from those who fought against me.
   You made me the ruler over nations.
   People I never knew now serve me.

44 As soon as they hear about me, they are ready to obey.
   Those foreigners fall down before me.

45 They lose all their courage
   and come out of their hiding places shaking with fear.

46 The LORD lives!
   I praise my Rock, the God who saves me.
   How great he is!

47 You punish my enemies for me.
   You put people under my control.

48 You rescue me from my enemies.
   You help me defeat those who attack me.
   You save me from cruel people.

49 LORD, that is why I praise you among the nations.
   That is why I sing songs of praise to your name.

50 The Lord helps his king win battle after battle.
   He shows his faithful love to the one he has chosen,[a]
   to David* and his descendants forever.

19 *To the director.* *A song of David.*

1 The heavens speak about the glory* of God.
   The skies tell about the good things his hands have made.
2 Each new day tells more of the story,
   and each night reveals more and more about God's power.[b]
3 You cannot hear them say anything.
   They don't make any sound we can hear.
4 But their message goes throughout the world.
   Their teaching reaches the ends of the earth.

   The sun set up his tent among them.
5 It comes out like a happy bridegroom from his bedroom.
   The sun begins its path across the sky
      like an athlete eager to run a race.
6 The sun starts at one end of the sky
   and runs all the way to the other end.
   Nothing can hide from its heat.

7 The Lord's teachings are perfect.
   They give strength to his people.
   The Lord's rules can be trusted.
   They help even the foolish to become wise.
8 The Lord's laws are right.
   They make people happy.
   The Lord's commands are good.
   They show people the right way to live.
9 Respect for the Lord is pure.
   It will continue forever.
   The Lord's judgments are good and fair.
   They are completely right.
10 His teachings are worth more than the best gold.
   They are sweeter than the best honey
      dripping from the honeycomb.
11 His teachings warn his servants,
   and good things come to those who obey them.

12 People cannot see their own mistakes,
   so don't let me do secret sins.
13 Don't let me do what I know is wrong.
   Don't let sin control me.
   If you help me, then I can be pure and free from sin.

---

[a]18:50 *the one he has chosen* Literally, "anointed one." [b]19:2 Or, "Like the changing of the guards, each day passes the news to the next day and each night passes information to the next night."

14 May my words and thoughts please you.
Lord, you are my Rock— the one who rescues me.

20
To the director.*
A song of David.*

1 May the Lord answer you in times of trouble.
May the God of Jacob* protect you.
2 May he send you help from his Holy Place.*
May he support you from Zion.*
3 May he remember all the gifts you have offered.
May he accept all your sacrifices.*   *Selah**
4 May he give you what you really want.
May he make all your plans successful.
5 We will celebrate when he helps you.
We will praise the name of God.
May the Lord give you everything you ask for.

6 Now I know the Lord helps his chosen king.
From his holy heaven he answered.
With his great power he saved him.
7 Some give the credit for victory to their chariots* and soldiers,
but we honor the Lord our God.
8 They fall in battle, totally defeated,
but we survive as the winners!

9 Lord, save the king!
Answer us when we call to you for help.

21
To the director.*
A song of David.*

1 Lord, your strength makes the king happy.
He is so happy when you give him the victory.
2 And you gave him what he wanted.
You gave him what he asked for.   *Selah**
3 What wonderful blessings you gave the king.
You put a golden crown on his head.
4 He asked for life, and you gave it.
You gave him life that goes on forever.
5 You led him to victory that brought him great glory.
You gave him honor and fame.
6 You have given him blessings that will last forever.
You have given him the joy of being near you.
7 The king trusts in the Lord,
and the faithful love of God Most High
will keep him from falling.

8 Lord, you will show all your enemies that you are strong.
Your power will defeat those who hate you.
9 When you appear, you will burn them up
like a blazing furnace.

In his anger the LORD will completely destroy them;
 they will be swallowed by flames of fire.[a]

10 Their families will be destroyed.
 They will be removed from the earth.

11 That is because they made evil plans against you.
 They wanted to do things they couldn't do.

12 You will make them turn and run away
 when you aim your arrows at their faces.

13 LORD, we lift you up with our songs of praise.
 We sing and play songs about your power!

22
To the director.* To the tune of "The Deer of Dawn."[b]
A song of David.*

1 My God, my God, why did you leave me?
 You seem too far away to save me,
 too far to hear my cries for help!

2 My God, I kept calling by day,
 and I was not silent at night.
But you did not answer me.

3 God, you are the Holy One.
 You sit as King upon the praises of Israel.*

4 Our ancestors* trusted you.
 Yes, they trusted you, and you saved them.

5 Our ancestors called to you for help,
 and they escaped their enemies.
They trusted you, and they were not disappointed!

6 But I feel like a worm, less than human!
 People insult me and look down on me.

7 Everyone who sees me makes fun of me.
 They shake their heads and stick out their tongues at me.

8 They say, "Call to the LORD for help.
 Maybe he will save you.
If he likes you so much, then surely he will rescue you!"

9 God, the truth is, you are the one I depend on.
 You have taken care of me since the day I was born.
You made me feel safe while I was still
 at my mother's breasts.

10 You have been my God since the day I was born.
 I was thrown into your arms as I came
 from my mother's womb.

11 So don't leave me!
 Trouble is near, and there is no one to help me.

12 My enemies have surrounded me like angry bulls.

---

a21:9 Or, "You will make your king like a burning oven when you come to help him, LORD.
And in his anger, he will completely destroy them." bPsalm 22 *The Deer of Dawn* This is
probably the name of the tune for this song, but it might refer to a type of instrument.

13 Their mouths are opened wide,
   like a lion roaring and tearing at its prey.

14 My strength is gone,
   like water poured out on the ground.
   My bones have separated.
   My courage is gone.*ᵃ*

15 My mouth*ᵇ* is as dry as a piece of baked pottery.
   My tongue is sticking to the roof of my mouth.
   You have left me dying in the dust.

16 The "dogs" are all around me—
   a pack*ᶜ* of evil people has trapped me.
   They have pierced my hands and my feet.*ᵈ*

17 I can see each one of my bones.
   My enemies are looking at me; they just keep staring.

18 They divide my clothes among them,
   and they throw lots* for what I am wearing.

19 Lᴏʀᴅ, don't leave me!
   You are my strength— hurry and help me!

20 Save me from the sword.
   Save my precious life from these dogs.

21 Rescue me from the lion's mouth.
   Protect me from the horns of the bulls.*ᵉ*

22 I will tell my people about you.
   I will praise you in the great assembly.

23 Praise the Lᴏʀᴅ, all you who worship him!
   Honor him, you descendants of Jacob*!
   Fear and respect him, all you people of Israel.*

24 He does not ignore those who need help.
   He does not hate them.
   He does not turn away from them.
   He listens when they cry for help.

25 Lord, my praise in the great assembly comes from you.
   In front of all these worshipers I will offer the sacrifices
   that I promised.

26 Poor people, come and be satisfied.*ᶠ*
   You who have come looking for the Lᴏʀᴅ, praise him!
   May your hearts be happy*ᵍ* forever.

---

*ᵃ***22:14** *My courage is gone* Literally, "My heart is melted in me like wax." *ᵇ***22:15** *mouth* Or, "strength." *ᶜ***22:16** *pack* A group of dogs. Dogs travel together in packs to hunt and kill other animals for food. *ᵈ***22:16** *They ... feet* Or, "Like a lion, my hands and feet." *ᵉ***22:21** *Protect me ... bulls* Or, "You have answered me and protected me from the horns of the bulls." This could be both a prayer for help (like the first half of the psalm) and also a statement that God had answered this prayer (like the second half of the psalm). *ᶠ***22:26** *come eat ... satisfied* This person was giving a thank offering that would be shared with other people at the Temple. This was how someone shared their happiness when God blessed them. See Lev. 3:1–5 and Deut. 14:22–29. *ᵍ***22:26** *be happy* Literally, "live."

27 May those in faraway countries remember the LORD
    and come back to him.
  May those in distant lands worship him,
28   because the LORD is the King.
    He rules all nations.
29 The people have eaten all they wanted
    and bowed down to worship the Lord.
  Yes, everyone will bow down to him—
    those who are on the way to the grave
    and those who are not yet alive.
30 Our descendants will serve him.
    Those who are not yet born will be told about him.
31 Each generation will tell their children
    about the good things our Lord has done.

23 *A song of David.**

1 The LORD is my shepherd.
    I will always have everything I need.*a*
2 He gives me green pastures to lie in.
    He leads me by calm pools of water.
3 He restores my strength
    and leads me on good paths*b* to show he is good.
4 Even if I walk through a valley as dark as the grave,*c*
    I will not be afraid of any danger, because you are with me.
  Your rod and staff*d* comfort me.
5 You prepared my table in front of my enemies.
    You welcomed me as an honored guest.*e*
  My cup is full and spilling over.
6 Goodness and mercy will be with me the rest of my life,
    and I will live in the LORD's house*f* a long, long time.*g*

24 *A song of David.**

1 The earth and everything on it belong to the LORD.
    The world and all its people belong to him.
2 He built the earth on the water.
    He built it over the rivers.

3 Who can go up the LORD's mountain*h*?
    Who can stand in his holy Temple*?

---

*a***23:1** *I will always have everything I need* Literally, "I will lack nothing." *b***23:3** *good paths*
Or, "paths of goodness." *c***23:4** *valley … grave* Or, "death's dark valley" or "a very dark
valley." *d***23:4** *rod and staff* The club and walking stick a shepherd uses to guide and protect
his sheep. *e***23:5** *You … guest* Literally, "You anointed my head with oil." *f***23:6** *house* Or,
"Temple." See "Temple" in the Word List. *g***23:6** *I … long time* Or, "I will return, again and
again, to the LORD's Temple a long, long time." *h***24:3** *LORD's mountain* Mount Zion, the hill in
Jerusalem where the Temple was built.

4 Only those who have not done evil,
   who have pure hearts,
   who have not used my name[a] to hide their lies,
   and who have not made false promises.

5 Good people ask the LORD to bless others.
   They ask God, their Savior, to do good things.
6 They try to follow God.
   They go to the God of Jacob* for help.   *Selah*

7 Gates, lift up your heads!
   Open, ancient doors, and the glorious King will come in.
8 Who is the glorious King?
   He is the LORD, the powerful soldier.
   He is the LORD, the war hero.

9 Gates, lift up your heads!
   Open, ancient doors, and the glorious King will come in.
10 Who is the glorious King?
   The LORD All-Powerful is the glorious King.

25 [b] *A song of David.*

1 LORD, I put my life in your hands.[c]
2 My God, I trust in you,
   and I will not be disappointed.
   My enemies will not laugh at me.
3 No one who trusts in you will be disappointed.
   But traitors* will be disappointed.
   They will get nothing.

4 LORD, help me learn your ways.
   Show me how you want me to live.
5 Guide me and teach me your truths.
   You are my God, my Savior.
   You are the one I have been waiting for.

6 Remember to be kind to me, LORD.
   Show me the tender love that you have always had.
7 Don't remember the sinful things I did when I was young.
   For your good name, LORD,
   remember me with your faithful love.

8 The LORD is good and does what is right.
   He shows sinners the right way to live.
9 He teaches his ways to humble people.
   He leads them with fairness.
10 The LORD is kind and true to those
   who obey what he said in his agreement.*

---

a **24:4** *my name* Literally, "my soul." b **Psalm 25** In Hebrew, each verse in this psalm begins with the next letter of the alphabet. c **25:1** *I put . . . hands* Literally, "I lift my soul to you."

¹¹ LORD, I have done many things wrong.
    I am guilty, but to show your goodness,
        forgive me for everything I did.

¹² When people choose to follow the LORD,
    he shows them the best way to live.

¹³ They will enjoy good things,
    and their children will keep the land
        God promised to give them.

¹⁴ The LORD tells his secrets to his followers.
    He teaches them about his agreement.

¹⁵ I always look to the LORD for help.
    Only he can free me from my troubles.^a

¹⁶ I am hurt and lonely.
    Turn to me, and show me mercy.

¹⁷ Free me from my troubles.
    Help me solve my problems.

¹⁸ Look at my trials and troubles.
    Forgive me for all the sins I have done.

¹⁹ Look at all the enemies I have.
    They hate me and want to hurt me.

²⁰ Protect me! Save me from them!
    I come to you for protection, so don't disappoint me.

²¹ You are good and do what is right.
    I trust you to protect me.

²² God, save the people of Israel* from all their enemies.

26 A song of David.

¹ LORD, judge me and prove that I have lived a pure life
    and that I have depended on you to keep me from falling.

² LORD, try me and test me.
    Test my deepest thoughts and emotions.

³ I always remember your faithful love.
    I depend on your faithfulness.

⁴ I don't run around with troublemakers.
    I have nothing to do with hypocrites.*

⁵ I hate being around evil people.
    I refuse to join those gangs of crooks.

⁶ LORD, I wash my hands to make myself pure
    so that I can come to your altar.

⁷ I sing a song to give you thanks,
    and I tell about all the wonderful things you have done.

⁸ LORD, I love the house^b where you live,
    the place where your glory* is.

---

^a25:15 he … troubles Literally, "He removes my feet from the net."   ^b26:8 house Or, "Temple." See "Temple" in the Word List.

⁹ Lord, don't group me with those sinners.
　　Don't kill me with those murderers.
¹⁰ They are guilty of cheating people.
　　They take money to do bad things.
¹¹ But I am innocent,
　　so be kind to me and save me.
¹² I am safe from all dangers as I stand here praising you
　　among those who are calling your people to the assembly.ᵃ

27 A song of David.

¹ Lord, you are my Light and my Savior,
　　so why should I be afraid of anyone?
The Lord is where my life is safe,
　　so I will be afraid of no one!
² Evil people might attack me.
　　They might try to destroy my body.
Yes, my enemies might attack me and try to destroy me,
　　but they will stumble and fall.
³ Even if an army surrounds me, I will not be afraid.
　Even if people attack me in war, I will trust in the Lord.

⁴ I ask only one thing from the Lord.
　　This is what I want most:
Let me live in the Lord's house all my life,
　　enjoying the Lord's beauty and spending time
　　　in his palace.ᵇ

⁵ The Lord will protect me when I am in danger.
　　He will hide me in his tent.ᶜ
　　He will take me up to his place of safety.

⁶ If he will help me defeat the enemies around me,
　　I will offer sacrifices* in his tent with shouts of joy.
　　I will sing and play songs to honor the Lord.

⁷ Lord, hear my voice.
　　Be kind and answer me.

⁸ My heart told me to come to you, Lord,
　　so I am coming to ask for your help.

⁹ Don't turn away from me.
　　Don't be angry with your servant.
　　You are the only one who can help me.
My God, don't leave me all alone.
　　You are my Savior.

ᵃ**26:12** *I am safe … assembly* Or, "I stand on level ground, blessing the Lord when your followers come together." This probably carries the double meaning of being safe from danger and being on the platform with the other priests and Levites calling the people to come together and worship God. ᵇ**27:4** *palace* A large house built for a king. Here, it is the Temple. ᶜ**27:5** *tent* The place where God lives among his people. Here, it is the Temple in Jerusalem. Earlier, it was the Holy Tent where the people worshiped God before the Temple was built.

10 Even if my mother and father leave me,
    the LORD will take me in.
11 I have enemies, LORD, so teach me your ways.
    Show me the right way to live.
12 My enemies have attacked me.
    They have told lies about me and have tried to hurt me.
13 But I really believe that I will see the LORD's goodness
    before I die.[a]
14 Wait for the LORD's help.
    Be strong and brave, and wait for the LORD's help.

28 A song of David.*

1 LORD, you are my Rock.*
  I am calling to you for help.
    Don't close your ears to my prayers.
  If you don't answer me,
    then I will be counted among the dead.
2 I lift my hands and pray toward your Most Holy Place.*
    Hear me when I call to you.
    Show mercy to me.
3 Don't treat me like the evil people who do wicked things.
  They greet their neighbors like a friend,
    but they secretly plan to hurt them.
4 They do bad things to others,
    so make bad things happen to them.
    Give them the punishment they deserve.
5 They don't notice what the LORD does.
    They ignore all the good things he has made.
  So instead of building them up, he will destroy them.

6 Praise the LORD!
    He has heard my prayer for mercy.
7 The LORD is my strength and shield.
    I trusted him with all my heart.
  He helped me, so I am happy.
    I sing songs of praise to him.
8 The LORD protects his chosen one.[b]
    He saves him and gives him strength.

9 Save your people.
    Bless those who belong to you.
    Lead them and honor them[c] forever.

---

[a]27:13 before I die Literally, "in the land of the living." [b]28:8 chosen one Or, "anointed one." This might be anyone God has chosen in a special way, but it is usually the king he chose. [c]28:9 honor them Or, "forgive them." Literally, "lift them up."

29 *A song of David.*[*]

1 Praise the LORD, you heavenly angels^a!
    Praise the LORD's glory* and power.
2 Praise the LORD and honor his name!
    Worship the LORD in your special clothes.^b
3 The LORD raises his voice at the sea.
    The voice of our glorious God is like thunder
        over the great ocean.
4 The LORD's voice is powerful.
    It shows the LORD's glory.
5 The LORD's voice shatters great cedar trees.
    He breaks the great cedars of Lebanon.
6 He makes Lebanon shake like a young calf dancing.
    Sirion^c trembles like a young bull jumping up and down.
7 The LORD's voice cuts the air with flashes of lightning.
8 The LORD's voice shakes the desert.
    Kadesh Desert^d trembles at the LORD's voice.
9 The LORD's voice frightens the deer.^e
    He destroys the forests.
    In his temple everyone shouts, "Glory to God!"
10 The LORD ruled as king at the time of the flood,
    and he will rule as king forever.

11 May the LORD make his people strong.
    May the LORD bless his people with peace.

30 *A song of David for the dedication* of the Temple.*^f

1 LORD, you lifted me out of my troubles.
    You did not give my enemies a reason to laugh,
        so I will praise you.
2 LORD my God, I prayed to you, and you healed me.
3 LORD, you lifted me out of the grave.
    I was falling into the place of death, but you saved my life.

4 Praise the LORD, you who are loyal to him!
    Praise his holy name^g!
5 His anger lasts for a little while,
    but then his kindness brings life.
    The night may be filled with tears,
    but in the morning we can sing for joy!

---

^a**29:1** *heavenly angels* Literally, "sons of gods." This probably means God's angels who are pictured here as priests worshiping him in heaven. ^b**29:2** *special clothes* The special clothes people wore when they went to the Temple to worship God. ^c**29:6** *Sirion* Or, "Mount Hermon." ^d**29:8** *Kadesh Desert* A desert in Syria. This might also mean "the holy desert." ^e**29:9** *deer* Or, "oak trees." ^f**Psalm 30** *A song … Temple* Or, "A psalm. The song for the dedication of the house. Dedicated to David." ^g**30:4** *name* Literally, "memory" or "memorial."

6 When I was safe and secure,
    I thought nothing could hurt me.
7 Yes, Lord, while you were kind to me,
    I felt like nothing could defeat me.*a*
  But when you turned away from me,
    I was filled with fear.
8 So Lord, I turned and prayed to you.
    I asked you to show me mercy.
9 I said, "What good is it if I die
    and go down into the grave?
  The dead just lie in the dirt.
    They cannot praise you.
  They cannot tell anyone how faithful you are.
10 Lord, hear my prayer, and be kind to me.
    Lord, help me!"

11 You have changed my crying into dancing.
    You have taken away my clothes of sadness
      and covered me with joy.
12 You wanted me to praise you and not be silent.
    Lord my God, I will praise you forever!

31
To the director.*
A song of David.*

1 Lord, I come to you for protection.
    Don't disappoint me.
  Be kind to me and save me.
2 Listen to me.
    Come quickly and save me.
  Be my Rock,* my place of safety.
    Be my fortress.* Protect me!
3 You are my Rock.
    For the good of your name, lead me and guide me.
4 Save me from the traps my enemy has set.
    You are my place of safety.
5 Lord, you are the God we can trust.
    I put my life*b* in your hands. Save me!
6 I hate those who worship false gods.
    I trust only in the Lord.
7 Your kindness makes me so happy.
    You have seen my suffering.
    You know about the troubles I have.
8 You will not let my enemies take me.
    You will free me from their traps.
9 Lord, I have many troubles, so be kind to me.
    I have cried until my eyes hurt.
    My throat and stomach are aching.

a 30:7 I felt ... defeat me Literally, "You placed me on the strong mountains." *b* 31:5 life Literally, "spirit."

10 Because of my sins, my life is ending in grief;
   my years are passing away in sighs of pain.
   My life is ending in weakness.
   My strength is draining away.

11 My enemies despise me,
   and even my neighbors have turned away.
   When my friends see me in the street,
      they turn the other way.
   They are afraid to be around me.

12 People want to forget me.
   It is as if I am already dead.
   I am like some lost tool.

13 I hear them whispering about me.
   They have turned against me, and they plan to kill me.

14 LORD, I trust in you.
   You are my God.

15 My life is in your hands.
   Save me from those who are persecuting me.

16 Please welcome and accept your servant.[a]
   Be kind to me and save me.

17 LORD, I am praying to you,
   don't let me be disappointed.
   It is the evil people who should be disappointed.
   Let them go to the grave in silence.

18 Those evil people brag
   and tell lies about good people.
   They are so proud now,
   but their lying lips will be silent.

19 Lord, you have hidden away
   many wonderful things for your followers.
   You have done so many good things
   for those who trust in you.
   You have blessed them so that all the world can see.

20 Others make plans to hurt them.
   They say such bad things about them.
   But you hide your people in your shelter and protect them.

21 Praise the LORD because he showed me how wonderful his
      faithful love is
   when the city was surrounded by enemies.

22 I was afraid and said,
   "I am in a place where he cannot see me."
   But I prayed to you, and you heard my loud cries for help.

23 Love the LORD, all of you who are his loyal followers.
   The LORD protects those who are loyal to him.
   But he punishes those who brag about their own power.
   He gives them all that they deserve.

a **31:16** *Please ... servant* Literally, "Let your face shine on your servant."

²⁴ Be strong and brave,
    all of you who are waiting for the LORD's help.

32 A maskil* of David.

¹ What a blessing it is
    when people are forgiven for the wrong they have done,
    when their sins are erased.ᵃ
² What a blessing it is
    when the LORD says they are not guilty,
    when they don't try to hide their sins.

³ Lord, I prayed to you again and again,
    but I did not talk about my secret sins.
    So I only became weaker and more miserable.
⁴ Every day, you made life harder for me.
    I became like a dry land in the hot summertime.   *Selah**

⁵ But then I decided to confess all my sins to the LORD.
    I told you about my sins.
    I did not hide any of my guilt.
    And you forgave me for all my sins!   *Selah*
⁶ That is why your loyal followers
    pray to you when the time comes.
    So when trouble rises like a flood,
    it does not reach them.
⁷ You are a hiding place for me.
    You protect me from my troubles.
    You surround me and protect me,
    so I sing about the way you saved me.   *Selah*
⁸ The Lord says,
    "I will teach you and guide you in the way you should live.
    I will watch over you and be your guide.
⁹ Don't be like a stupid horse or mule that will not come to you
    unless you put a bit in its mouth and pull it with reins."

¹⁰ Many pains will come to bad people,
    but the LORD's faithful love will surround
    those who trust in him.
¹¹ Good people, rejoice and be very happy in the LORD.
    All you people with pure hearts, rejoice!

33 ¹Rejoice in the LORD, good people!
It is only right for good people to praise him.
² Play the lyre* and praise the LORD.
    Play the ten-stringed harp for him.
³ Sing a new songᵇ to him.
    Play it well and sing it loud!

ᵃ32:1 erased Or, "covered over" or "atoned." ᵇ33:3 new song Whenever God did a new
and wonderful thing for his people, they would write a new song about it.

4 The LORD's word is true.
 You can depend on his teachings.
5 He loves goodness and justice.
 The LORD's faithful love fills the earth.
6 The LORD spoke the command, and the world was made.
 The breath from his mouth created everything
  in the heavens.
7 He gathered together the water of the sea.
 He put the ocean in its place.
8 Everyone on earth should fear and respect the LORD.
 All the people in the world should fear him,
9 because when he speaks, things happen.
 And if he says, "Stop!"—then it stops.*a*
10 The LORD can make everyone's advice useless.
 He can ruin all their plans.
11 But the LORD's advice is good forever.
 His plans are good for generation after generation.
12 Those who have the LORD as their God are very fortunate,
 because he chose them to be his own special people.
13 The LORD looked down from heaven
 and saw all the people.
14 From his high throne he looked down
 at all the people living on earth.
15 He created every person's mind.
 He knows what every person is thinking.
16 A king is not saved by his own great power.
 A strong soldier is not saved by his own great strength.
17 Horses don't really bring victory in war.
 Their strength cannot help you escape.
18 The LORD watches over his followers
 who wait for him to show his faithful love.
19 He saves them from death.
 He gives them strength when they are hungry.
20 So we will wait for the LORD.
 He helps us and protects us.
21 He makes us happy.
 We trust his holy name.
22 LORD, we worship you,
 so show your great love for us.

34 *b A song of David* when he pretended to be crazy so Abimelech*
 would send him away, which he did.
1 I will praise the LORD at all times.
 I will never stop singing his praises.

---

a33:9 And if ... stops Or, "He gives the command, and it stands!" The word "stand" can
mean "stand forever" or "stop." *b Psalm 34* In Hebrew, each verse in this psalm begins
with the next letter of the alphabet.

2 Humble people, listen and be happy,
   while I brag about the LORD.
3 Praise the LORD with me.
   Let us honor his name.
4 I went to the LORD for help, and he listened.
   He saved me from all that I fear.
5 Look to the LORD for help.
   You will be accepted.
   Do not be ashamed.[a]
6 This poor man called to the LORD for help, and he heard me.
   He saved me from all my troubles.
7 The LORD's angel builds a camp around his followers
   and protects them.
8 Give the LORD a chance to show you[b] how good he is.
   What blessings there are for those who depend on him!
9 The LORD's holy people should fear and respect him.
   Those who respect him will always have what they need.
10 Even strong lions get weak and hungry,
   but those who go to the LORD for help
   will have every good thing.
11 Children, come and listen to me;
   I will teach you to respect the LORD.
12 Do you want to enjoy life?
   Do you want to have many happy days?
13 Then avoid saying anything hurtful,
   and never let a lie come out of your mouth.
14 Stop doing anything evil, and do good.
   Look for peace, and do all you can to help people
   live peacefully.
15 The LORD watches over those who do what is right,
   and he hears their prayers.
16 But the LORD is against those who do evil,
   so they are forgotten soon after they die.

17 Pray to the LORD, and he will hear you.
   He will save you from all your troubles.
18 The LORD is close to those who have suffered disappointment.
   He saves those who are discouraged.
19 Good people might have many problems,
   but the LORD will take them all away.
20 He will protect them completely.
   Not one of their bones will be broken.
21 But troubles will kill the wicked.
   The enemies of those who live right will all be punished.
22 The LORD saves his servants.
   All who go to him for protection will escape punishment.

---

[a]34:5 You will be accepted … be ashamed Literally, "Look at him and shine. Don't let your face be pale." [b]34:8 Give … show you Literally, "Taste and see."

35 *A song of David.*

1 Lord, oppose those who oppose me.
   Fight those who fight me.
2 Pick up the shield and buckler.*a*
   Get up and help me.
3 Take a spear and javelin
   and fight those who are chasing me.
   Tell my soul, "I will rescue you."
4 Some people are trying to kill me.
   Disappoint them and make them ashamed.
   Make them turn and run away.
   They are planning to hurt me.
   Defeat them and embarrass them.
5 Make them like chaff* blown by the wind.*b*
   Let them be chased by the Lord's angel.
6 Make their road dark and slippery.
   Let the Lord's angel chase them.
7 I did nothing wrong, but they tried to trap me.
   For no reason at all, they tried to trap me.
8 So let them fall into their own traps.
   Let them stumble into their own nets.
   Let some unknown danger catch them.
9 Then I will rejoice in the Lord.
   I will be happy when he saves me.
10 With my whole self I will say, "Lord, there is no one like you.
   You protect the poor from those who are stronger.
   You save the poor and helpless from those
      who try to rob them."
11 A group of witnesses*c* are planning to hurt me.
   They will ask me questions that I know nothing about.
12 For the good I have done, they repay me with evil.
   They make me so very sad.
13 When they were sick, I was sad and wore sackcloth.*
   I went without eating to show my sorrow.
   (May my prayers for them not be answered!)
14 I mourned for them as I would for a friend or a brother.
   I bowed low with sadness, crying as I would
      for my own mother.
15 But when I had troubles, they laughed at me.
   They were not really friends.
   I was surrounded and attacked by people I didn't even know.
16 They made fun of me, using the worst language.
   They ground their teeth to show their anger.

---

*a***35:2** *buckler* A shield large enough to protect the whole body. *b***35:5** *wind* This may be a wordplay, because the Hebrew word also means "spirit." *c***35:11** *witnesses* People who tell what they have seen or heard. Here, these people were probably telling lies.

¹⁷ My Lord, how long will you watch these bad things happen?
  Those people are trying to destroy me.
Lord, save my life.
  Save my dear life from those bad people.
  They are like lions.

¹⁸ I will praise you in the great assembly.
  I will praise you among those many people.
¹⁹ My lying enemies will not keep laughing.
  They hate me without cause.
  Surely they will be punished for their secret plans.^a
²⁰ My enemies are not really making plans for peace.
  They are secretly making plans to do bad things
    to the peaceful people in this country.
²¹ My enemies are lying about me.
  They say, "Aha! We know what you are doing!"
²² Lord, surely you can see what is happening.
  So don't keep quiet.
  Lord, don't leave me.
²³ Wake up! Get up!
  My God and my Lord, fight for me, and bring me justice.
²⁴ Lord my God, judge me with your fairness.
  Don't let those people laugh at me.
²⁵ Don't let them think, "Aha! We got what we wanted!"
  Don't let them say, "We destroyed him!"
²⁶ Let my enemies be ashamed and embarrassed—
    all those who were happy about my troubles.
  Proud of themselves, they treated me as worthless.
  So let them be covered with shame and disgrace.
²⁷ To those who want the best for me,
  I wish them joy and happiness.
  May they always say, "Praise the Lord who wants
    what is best for his servant."

²⁸ So, Lord, I will tell people how good you are.
  I will praise you all day long.

36
To the director.* To the servant of the Lord.
To David.

¹ The wicked do a very bad thing when they say to themselves,
  "I will not fear and respect God."
² They lie to themselves.
  They don't see their own faults,
    so they do not ask for forgiveness.
³ Their words are wicked lies
    that offer no wisdom and do no good.
⁴ They make wicked plans while lying in bed at night.
  When they get up, they go out to do no good
    and to refuse no evil.

^a**35:19** Surely ... plans Literally, "Will the people who hate me freely wink their eyes?"

5 LORD, your faithful love reaches to the sky.
    Your faithfulness is as high as the clouds.
6 Your goodness is higher than the highest mountains.
    Your fairness is deeper than the deepest ocean.
  LORD, you protect people and animals.
7 Nothing is more precious than your loving kindness.
    People and angels[a] come to you for protection.
8 They get strength from all the good things in your house.
    You let them drink from your wonderful river.
9 The fountain of life flows from you.
    Your light lets us see light.
10 Continue to love those who really know you,
    and do good to those who are true to you.[b]
11 Don't let proud people trap me.
    Don't let me be caught by evil people.

12 Put this on their grave markers:
    "Here fell the wicked.
    They were crushed.
    They will never stand up again."

37 [c] A song of David.

1 Don't get upset about evil people.
    Don't be jealous of those who do wrong.
2 They are like grass and other green plants
    that dry up quickly and then die.
3 So trust in the LORD and do good.
    Live on your land and be dependable.[d]
4 Enjoy serving the LORD,
    and he will give you what you ask for.
5 Depend on the LORD.
    Trust in him, and he will make it happen.
6 Let your goodness and fairness shine like the sun at noon.
7 Trust in the LORD and wait quietly for his help.
    Don't be angry when bad people make evil plans
        and succeed.
8 Don't become angry and upset enough that you, too,
        want to do evil.
9 Evil people will be destroyed,
    but those who call to the LORD for help
        will get the land he promised.
10 In a short time there will be no more evil people.
    You can look for them all you want, but they will be gone.
11 Humble people will get the land God promised,
    and they will enjoy peace.

---

[a] **36:7** angels Or, "gods." [b] **36:10** true to you Or, "honest hearted." [c] **Psalm 37** In Hebrew, each verse in this psalm begins with the next letter of the alphabet. [d] **37:3** be dependable Literally, "shepherd faithfulness."

¹² The wicked plan bad things for those who are good.
  They show their teeth in anger at them.

¹³ But our Lord will laugh at them.
  He will make sure they get what they deserve.

¹⁴ The wicked draw their swords to kill
    the poor and the helpless.
  They aim their arrows to murder all who live right.

¹⁵ But their bows will break,
  and their swords will pierce their own hearts.

¹⁶ A few good people are better
  than a large crowd of evil people.

¹⁷ Why? Because evil people will be destroyed,
  but the LORD cares for good people.

¹⁸ The LORD protects pure people all their life.
  Their reward will continue forever.

¹⁹ When trouble comes,
    good people will not be destroyed.
  When times of hunger come,
    good people will have plenty to eat.

²⁰ But evil people are the LORD's enemies,
    and they will be destroyed.
  Their valleys will dry up and burn.
  They will be destroyed completely.

²¹ The wicked borrow money and never pay it back.
  But good people are kind and generous.

²² Everyone the Lord blesses
    will get the land he promised.
  Everyone the Lord curses*
    will be destroyed.

²³ The LORD shows us how we should live,
  and he is pleased when he sees people living that way.

²⁴ If they stumble, they will not fall,
  because the LORD reaches out to steady them.

²⁵ I was young, and now I am old,
    but I have never seen good people left
      with no one to help them;
  I have never seen their children begging for food.

²⁶ They are kind and generous,
  and their children are a blessing.

²⁷ Stop doing anything evil, and do good,
  and you will always have a place to live.

²⁸ The LORD loves what is right,
    and he will never leave his followers without help.
  He will always protect them,
    but he will destroy the families of the wicked.

²⁹ Good people will get the land God promised
  and live on it forever.

³⁰ Those who do what is right give good advice.
  Their decisions are always fair.

31 They have learned God's teachings,
    and they will never stop living right.[a]

32 The wicked are always looking for ways to kill good people.
33 But the LORD will not let the wicked defeat them.
    He will not let good people be judged guilty.
34 Do what the LORD says, and wait for his help.
    He will reward you and give you the land he promised.
    You will see the wicked being forced to leave.

35 I once saw a wicked man who was powerful.
    He was like a strong, healthy tree.
36 But then he was gone.
    I looked for him, but I couldn't find him.
37 Be pure and honest.
    Peace loving people will have many descendants.
38 But those who break the law will be destroyed completely.
    And their descendants will be forced to leave the land.[b]
39 The LORD saves good people.
    When they have troubles, he is their strength.
40 The LORD helps good people and rescues them.
    They depend on him, so he rescues them from bad people.

38 A song of David* for the day of remembrance.[c]

1 LORD, don't criticize me when you are angry.
    Don't discipline me in anger.
2 You have hurt me.
    You punished me and hurt me deeply.
3 You punished me severely; now my whole body is sore.
    I sinned, so all my bones hurt.
4 My guilt is like a heavy burden.
    I am sinking beneath its weight.
5 I did a foolish thing,
    and now I have infected sores that stink.
6 I am bent and bowed down.
    I am depressed all day long.
7 I am burning with fever,
    and my whole body hurts.
8 I hurt so much I cannot feel anything.
    My pounding heart makes me scream!
9 My Lord, you heard my groaning.
    You can hear my sighs.
10 My heart is pounding.
    My strength is gone, and I am going blind.[d]

---

[a]37:31 they ... right Literally, "his steps will not slip." [b]37:38 forced to leave the land Or, "destroyed." Literally, "cut off." [c]Psalm 38 for the day of remembrance The ancient Greek version has "for the Sabbath." [d]38:10 I am going blind Or, "My eyes have lost their sparkle." Literally, "Even the light of my eyes is no longer with me."

11 Because of my sickness,
    my friends and neighbors will not visit me;
    my family will not come near me.
12 My enemies say bad things about me.
    They are spreading lies and rumors.*a*
    They talk about me all the time.
13 But I am like a deaf person who cannot hear.
    I am like a mute person who cannot speak.
14 I am like someone who cannot hear
    what people are saying about them.
    I cannot argue and prove that my enemies are wrong.
15 LORD, you must defend me.
    My Lord and God, you must speak for me.
16 If I say anything, then my enemies will laugh at me.
    They will see I am sick and say that I am being punished
       for doing wrong.
17 I know I am guilty of doing wrong.
    I cannot forget my pain.
18 LORD, I told you about the bad things I did.
    I am worried about my sins.
19 But my enemies are alive and healthy,
    and they have told many lies.
20 I did nothing but good,
    and they paid me back with evil.
    I try to do what is right,
    but that only makes them turn against me.
21 LORD, don't leave me.
    My God, stay close to me.
22 Come quickly and help me.
    My Lord, you are the one who saves me.

39

To the director.* To Jeduthun.*b*
A song of David.*

1 I said, "I will be careful about what I say.
    I will not let my tongue cause me to sin.
    I will keep my mouth closed*c*
       when I am around wicked people."

2 So I didn't say anything.
    I didn't even say anything good,
    but I became even more upset.
3 I was very angry,
    and the more I thought about it, the angrier I became.
    So I said something.

---

*a***38:12** *rumors* Hurtful stories about someone that other people tell without knowing if the stories are true. *b***Psalm 39** *To Jeduthun* Or, "To the director, Jeduthun," one of the three main temple musicians. See 1 Chron. 9:16; 16:38–42. *c***39:1** *will keep … closed* Literally, "guard my mouth with a muzzle."

4 LORD, tell me, what will happen to me now?
   Tell me, how long will I live?
   Let me know how short my life really is.
5 You gave me only a short life.
   Compared to you, my short life is nothing.
   The life of every human is like a cloud
      that quickly disappears.   *Selah**

6 Our life is like an image in a mirror.*a*
   We rush through life collecting things,
      but we don't know who will get them after we die.

7 So, Lord, what hope do I have?
   You are my hope!
8 Save me from the bad things I did.
   Don't let me be treated like a fool.
9 I will not open my mouth.
   I will not say anything.
   You did what should have been done.
10 But please stop punishing me.
   You will destroy me if you do not stop.
11 You punish people for doing wrong
      to teach them the right way to live.
   As a moth destroys cloth, you destroy what people love.
   Yes, our lives are like a small cloud
      that quickly disappears.   *Selah*

12 LORD, hear my prayer!
   Listen to the words I cry to you.
   Look at my tears.
   I am only a traveler passing through this life with you.
   Like all my ancestors, I will live here only a short time.*b*
13 Leave me alone*c* and let me be happy
   before I am dead and gone.

40

*To the director.**
*A song of David.**

1 I called*d* to the LORD, and he heard me.
   He heard my cries.
2 He lifted me out of the grave.*e*
   He lifted me from that muddy place.*f*
   He picked me up, put me on solid ground,
      and kept my feet from slipping.

---

*a***39:6** *Our life ... mirror* Or, "This life is not real—it is only a shadow" or "People wander around in the dark—not knowing what will happen." *b***39:12** *I live ... time* Literally, "I am a settler." *c***39:13** *Leave me alone* Or, "Stop looking at me." *d***40:1** *called* Or, "waited patiently." *e***40:2** *grave* Literally, "pit of destruction." That is, "Sheol," the place of death. *f***40:2** *muddy place* In many ancient stories, Sheol, the place of death, is a dark place with mud all around, like a grave.

3 He put a new song[a] in my mouth,
    a song of praise to our God.
Many will see what he did and worship him.
    They will put their trust in the LORD.

4 What great blessings there are
    for those who trust in the LORD,
    for those who do not turn to demons
        and false gods[b] for help.

5 LORD my God, you have done many amazing things!
    You have made great plans for us—too many to list.
I could talk on and on about them
    because there are too many to count.

6 Lord, you made me understand this:[c]
    You don't really want sacrifices* and grain offerings.
    You don't really want burnt offerings* and sin offerings.*

7 So I said, "Here I am,
    ready to do what was written about me in the book.

8 I am happy to do whatever you want, my God.
    I never stop thinking about your teachings."

9 I told the good news of victory[d]
    to the people in the great assembly.
And LORD, you know that
    I will never stop telling that good news.

10 I told about the good things you did.
    I did not hide these things in my heart.
I spoke of how you can be trusted to save us.
    I did not hide your love and loyalty
    from the people in the great assembly.

11 LORD, do not hide your mercy from me.
    Let your love and loyalty always protect me.

12 Troubles have surrounded me.
    They are too many to count!
My sins have caught me,
    and I cannot escape them.
They are more than the hairs on my head.
    I have lost my courage.

13 Run to me, LORD, and rescue me![e]
    LORD, hurry and help me!

14 People are trying to kill me.
    Please disappoint them.
    Humiliate them!
They wanted to hurt me.
    Make them run away in shame!

---

[a]40:3 new song Whenever God did a new and wonderful thing for his people, they would
write a new song about it.   [b]40:4 demons and false gods Or, "proud and deceptive people."
[c]40:6 you made me understand this Literally, "you have dug my ears." The ancient Greek
version has "you prepared a body for me."   [d]40:9 victory Or, "goodness," or
"righteousness."   [e]40:13 Run . . . me Or, "Please, LORD, rescue me!"

15 May those who make fun of me be too embarrassed to speak!
16 But may those who come to you be happy and rejoice.
    May those who love being saved by you always be able
      to say, "Praise the Lord!"[a]

17 My Lord, I am only a poor, helpless man,
    but please consider my request.
  Help me. Save me.
    My God, don't be too late.

41
To the director.*
A song of David.*

1 Those who help the poor succeed will get many blessings.[b]
    When trouble comes, the Lord will save them.
2 The Lord will protect them and save their lives.
    He will bless them in this land.
    He will not let their enemies harm them.
3 When they are sick in bed,
    the Lord will give them strength and make them well!

4 I say, "Lord, be kind to me.
    I sinned against you, but forgive me and make me well."
5 My enemies say bad things about me.
    They say, "When will he die and be forgotten?"
6 If people do come to see me,
    they don't talk about what's on their mind.
  They come to gather a little gossip
    and then go to spread their rumors.
7 Those who don't like me
    whisper and think the worst about me.
8 They say, "He did something wrong.
    That is why he is sick.
    He will never get well."
9 My best friend, the one I trusted,
    the one who ate with me, even he has turned against me.
10 Lord, please be kind to me.
    Let me get up, and I will pay them back.
11 Don't let my enemy defeat me.
    Then I will know that you care for me.
12 I was innocent and you supported me.
    You let me stand and serve you forever.

13 Praise the Lord, the God of Israel.*
    He always was, and he always will be.

  Amen* and Amen!

---

[a]**40:16** *Praise the Lord* Literally, "The Lord is great" or "May the Lord be magnified."
[b]**41:1** Or, "Those who teach the poor will be very fortunate."

BOOK 2 *(Psalms 42–72)*

42 To the director.*
A maskil* from the Korah family.

1 Like a deer drinking from a stream,
　　I reach out to you, my God.[a]
2 My soul thirsts for the living God.
　　When can I go to meet with him?
3 Instead of food, I have only tears day and night,
　　as my enemies laugh at me and say,
　　　"Where is your God?"

4 My heart breaks as I remember the pleasant times in the past,
　　when I walked with the crowds as I led them
　　　up to God's Temple.*
　I remember the happy songs of praise
　　as they celebrated the festival.

5 Why am I so sad?
　　Why am I so upset?
　I tell myself, "Wait for God's help!
　　You will again have a chance to praise him,
　　　your God, the one who will save you."

6 So I tell myself, "I will remember you from here
　　where I am—on this small hill,[b]
　　　where Mount Hermon and the Jordan River meet."
7 I hear the roar of the water coming from deep
　　within the earth.
　It shouts to the water below as it tumbles down
　　the waterfall.
　LORD, your waves come one after another,
　　crashing all around and over me.[c]

8 By day the LORD shows his faithful love,
　　and at night I have a song for him—
　　　a prayer for the God of my life.[d]
9 I say to God, my Rock,* "Why have you forgotten me?
　　Why must I suffer this sadness that my enemies
　　　have brought me?"
10 Their constant insults are killing me.
　　They never stop asking, "Where is your God?"

11 Why am I so sad?
　　Why am I so upset?
　I tell myself, "Wait for God's help!
　　You will again have a chance to praise him,
　　　your God, the one who will save you."

---

[a]42:1 Or, "As a deer stretches out to drink water from a stream, so my soul thirsts for you,
God." [b]42:6 *small hill* Or, "Mount Mizar." [c]42:7 LORD, *your waves ... over me* These word
pictures describe the psalmist's feelings about the many troubles the Lord has allowed him to
experience." [d]42:8 *the God of my life* Or, "my living God."

43

¹Defend me, God.
Argue my case against those lying foreigners.
Protect me from those wicked people who do not follow you.

² You are my place of safety.
    Why have you turned away from me?
    Why must I suffer this sadness that my enemies
        have brought me?

³ Send your light and your truth to guide me.
    They will lead me to your holy mountain, to your home.

⁴ I want to go to God's altar,
        to the God who makes me so very happy.
    God, my God, I want to play my harp
        and sing praises to you!

⁵ Why am I so sad?
    Why am I so upset?
    I tell myself, "Wait for God's help!
        You will again have a chance to praise him,
        your God, the one who will save you."

44

To the director.*
A maskil* from the Korah family.

¹ God, we have heard about you.
    Our fathers* told us what you did in their lifetime.
    They told us what you did long ago.

² With your great power you took this land from other people,
        and you gave it to us.
    You crushed those foreigners
        and forced them to leave this land.

³ It was not our fathers' swords that took the land.
        It was not their strong arms that brought them the victory.
    It was your power.
        You accepted them and smiled down on them.

⁴ God, you are my king.
    Give the command and lead Jacob's* people to victory.

⁵ We need your help to push our enemies back.
    Only in your name can we walk over those
        who attacked us.

⁶ I don't put my trust in my bow.
    My sword cannot save me.

⁷ You are the one who saved us from our enemies.
    You are the one who put our enemies to shame.

⁸ We have praised you all day long,
    and we will praise your name forever.   Selah*

⁹ But, God, you left us.
    You put us to shame.
    You did not come with us into battle.

¹⁰ You let our enemies push us back.
    You let them take our wealth.

11 You gave us away like sheep to be killed for food.
　　You scattered us among the other nations.
12 You sold your people for nothing.
　　You didn't even argue over the price.
13 You made us a joke to our neighbors.
　　They laugh and make fun of us.
14 You made us one of the stories
　　that people of other nations love to tell.
　People all over the world laugh at us and shake their heads.
15 All I can think about is my shame.
　　Just look at my face, and you will see it.
16 All I can hear are the jokes and insults of my enemies
　　as I watch them take their revenge.
17 We have not forgotten you.
　　Yet you do all those things to us.
　We did not break the agreement you gave us.
18 We did not turn away from you.
　　We did not stop following you.
19 But you crushed us in this home of jackals.*
　　You left us in this place as dark as death.
20 Did we forget the name of our God?
　　Did we pray to foreign gods?
21 If we did, then God knows it,
　　because he knows our deepest secrets.
22 All day long we died for you.
　　We were like sheep led away to be killed.
23 Lord, wake up!
　　Why are you sleeping?
　　Get up! Don't ignore us forever!
24 Why are you hiding from us?
　　Have you forgotten our pain and troubles?
25 We have been pushed down into the dirt.
　　We are lying face down in the dust.*a*
26 Get up and help us!
　　Rescue us because of your faithful love.

45 To the director.* To the tune of "Shoshanim."*b*
　　A maskil* from the Korah family. A love song.
1 Beautiful thoughts fill my mind
　　as I speak these lines for the king.
　These words come from my tongue
　　as from the pen of a skilled writer.

2 You are more handsome than anyone,
　　and you say such pleasant things.
　So God will always bless you.

---

a 44:25 This shows that the people were being treated like slaves who must bow down to their masters. *b* Psalm 45 To the tune of Shoshanim Or, "On the Shoshanim."

3 Put on your sword, mighty warrior,
   so impressive in your splendid uniform.
4 Go out in your greatness to win the victory
      for what is true and right.
   Let us see the amazing things you can do
      with your powerful right arm.*a*
5 Your sharp arrows will go deep into the hearts
      of your enemies,
   who will fall to the ground in front of you.
6 God,*b* your throne will last forever.
   Your justice is a sign of your power to rule.
7 You love what is right and hate what is evil.
   So God, your God, chose you to be king
      and made you happier than any of your friends.*c*
8 From your clothes comes the wonderful smell of myrrh,*
      aloes,* and cassia.*
   Inside palaces decorated with ivory,
      you enjoy the music of stringed instruments.
9 Here are ladies of honor, the daughters of kings.
   Your bride*d* stands at your right side,
      dressed in a gown decorated with the finest gold.

10 My lady,*e* listen to me.
   Listen carefully and understand me.
   Forget your people and your father's family,
11 so that the king will be pleased with your beauty.
   He will be your new husband,*f*
      so you must honor him.
12 People from Tyre will bring you gifts.
   Their richest people will try to win your friendship.

13 In all her glory, the princess in her gown
      is like a pearl set in gold.
14 Draped in beauty, she is led to the king,
      as her bridesmaids follow behind her.
15 Filled with joy and excitement,
      they enter into the king's palace.

16 Your sons will be kings, like their ancestors.*
   You will make them rulers throughout the land.
17 You will be famous for generations.
   People will praise you forever and ever.

---

*a***45:4** *right arm* This pictures God as a warrior-king. The right arm symbolizes his power and authority.   *b***45:6** *God* This might be a song to God as king. Or here, the writer might be using the word "God" as a title for the king.   *c***45:7** *chose ... friends* Literally, "poured the oil of rejoicing on you over your friends." This refers to the special oil kept in the Temple and used in the dedication of kings, priests, and prophets.   *d***45:9** *bride* Or, "queen."   *e***45:10** *My lady* Literally, "Daughter."   *f***45:11** *husband* Or, "master."

46

To the director. A song from the Korah family.
By the alamoth.[a] A song.

[1] God is our storehouse of strength.
We come to him and find help in times of trouble.

[2] So we are not afraid when the earth quakes,
and the mountains fall into the sea.

[3] We are not afraid when the seas become rough and dark,
and the mountains tremble.   *Selah**

[4] There is a river whose streams bring happiness to God's city,
to the holy city of God Most High.

[5] God is in that city, so it will never be destroyed.
He is there to help even before sunrise.

[6] Nations will shake with fear and kingdoms will fall
when God shouts and makes the earth move.

[7] The LORD All-Powerful is with us.
The God of Jacob* is our place of safety.   *Selah*

[8] Look at the powerful things the LORD has done.
See the awesome things he has done on earth.

[9] He stops wars anywhere on earth.
He breaks the soldiers' bows, shatters their spears,
and burns their shields.[b]

[10] God says, "Stop fighting and know that I am God!
I am the one who defeats the nations;
I am the one who controls the world."

[11] The LORD All-Powerful is with us.
The God of Jacob is our place of safety.   *Selah*

47

To the director.*
A song from the Korah family.

[1] Everyone, clap your hands.
Shout with joy to God!

[2] The LORD Most High is awesome.
He is the great King over all the earth.

[3] He helped us defeat other nations.
He put those people under our control.

[4] He chose our land for us.
He chose that wonderful land for Jacob,* the one he loved.   *Selah**

[5] The LORD God goes up to his throne
at the sound of the trumpet and horn.

[6] Sing praises to God. Sing praises.
Sing praises to our King. Sing praises.

---

[a]**Psalm 46** *alamoth* This might be a special instrument, a special way of tuning an instrument, or one of the groups that played harps in the Temple orchestra. See 1 Chron. 15:21.   [b]**46:9** *shields* Or, "chariots."

7 God is the King of the whole world.
  Sing songs of praise.[a]
8 God sits on his holy throne;
  he rules all the nations.
9 The leaders of the nations have come together
  with the people of the God of Abraham.[*]
  All the rulers of the world belong to God.
  He is over them all!

48 A song of praise from the Korah family.

1 The LORD is great!
  He is praised throughout the city of our God,
    on his holy mountain.
2 His city is such a pleasant place.
  It brings joy to people from around the world.
  Mount Zion[*] is the true mountain of God.[b]
  It is the city of the great King.
3 In the palaces of that city,
  God is known as the fortress.[*]
4 Once some kings met together
  and planned an attack against this city.
  They marched toward the city,
5   but when they saw it, they were amazed.
  They all panicked and ran away.
6 Fear grabbed them;
  they trembled like a woman giving birth.
7 God, with a strong east wind,
  you wrecked their big ships.
8 Yes, we heard the stories about your power.
  But we also saw it in the city of our God,
    the city of the LORD All-Powerful.
  God makes that city strong forever.   Selah[*]

9 God, in your Temple[*] we remember your loving kindness.
10 God, you are famous.
  People praise you everywhere on earth.
  Everyone knows how good you are.
11 Mount Zion is happy, and the towns of Judah[*] rejoice
    because of your good decisions.
12 Walk around Zion.
  Look at Jerusalem and count its towers.
13 See the tall walls and admire all the palaces.
  Then you can tell the next generation about them.
14 This God is our God forever and ever.
  He will lead us forever[c]!

---

[a] **47:7** *songs of praise* Literally, "maskil." See the Word List. [b] **48:2** *true mountain of God*
Literally, "the summit of Zaphon." In Canaanite stories, Mt. Zaphon was where the gods lived.
[c] **48:14** *forever* Or, "even through death."

49

*To the director.**
*A song from the Korah family.**

1 Listen to this, all you nations.
  Pay attention, all you people on earth.
2 Everyone, rich and poor, listen to me.
3 I have some very wise words for you.
  My thoughts will give you understanding.
4 I myself listened to these sayings.
  And now, with my harp, I will sing
    and make the hidden meaning clear.

5 Why should I be afraid when trouble comes?
  There is no need to fear when wicked enemies
    surround me.
6 Some people think their wealth
  will protect them, but they are fools.
7 No human friends can save you,
  and they cannot bribe*a* God.
8 No one will ever get enough money
  to buy their own life.
9 No one will ever have enough
  to buy the right to live forever
    and keep their body out of the grave.
10 Look, the wise die the same as fools and stupid people.*b*
   They die and leave their wealth to others.
11 The grave will be their new home forever.
   And how much land they owned
     will not make any difference.
12 People might be wealthy,
   but they cannot stay here forever.
   They will die like the animals.
13 That is what happens to such people.
   That is the fate of those who follow their desires.   *Selah**
14 They are just like sheep, but the grave will be their pen.
   Death will be their shepherd.
   Then on that morning the good people will be the winners.
   The bodies of those proud people will slowly rot
     in the grave, far away from their fancy houses.

15 But God will pay the price and save my life.*c*
   He will save me from the power of the grave
     when he takes me to be with him.   *Selah*

16 Don't be afraid of people
   just because they are rich.
   Don't be afraid of people
     just because they have big, fancy houses.

---

a **49:7 bribe** Here, this means offering a gift or sacrifice so that God will not punish a guilty person.   *b* **49:10 stupid people** Or, "animals."   *c* **49:15 life** Literally, "soul."

17 They will not take anything with them when they die.
   They will not take their wealth with them.

18 A wealthy man might congratulate himself
   on how well he has done in life.
   And other people might praise him.

19 But the time will come for him to die
   and go to his ancestors.
   And he will never again see the light of day.

20 People might be wealthy
   and still not understand that they will die like the animals.

50 *One of Asaph's songs.*

1 The LORD God Most Powerful has spoken.
   He calls to all the people on earth,
   from the rising to the setting of the sun.

2 God appeared from Zion,* the city of perfect beauty.*a*

3 Our God is coming, and he will not keep quiet.
   Fire burns in front of him.
   There is a great storm around him.

4 Our God calls to the earth and sky
   to be witnesses as he judges his people.

5 He says, "My followers, gather around me.
   Come, my worshipers, who made an agreement with me."

6 God is the judge, and the skies tell about his goodness.
                                                    *Selah**

7 God says, "My people, listen to me!
   People of Israel,* I will show my evidence against you.
   I am God, your God.

8 The problem I have with you is not your sacrifices*
   or the burnt offerings* you bring to me everyday.

9 Why would I want more bulls from your barns
   or goats from your pens?

10 I already own all the animals in the forest.
   I own all the animals on a thousand hills.

11 I know every bird in the mountains.
   Everything that moves in the fields is mine.

12 If I were hungry, I would not ask you for food.
   I already own the world and everything in it.

13 I don't eat the meat of bulls or drink the blood of goats."

14 You made promises to God Most High,
   so give him what you promised.
   Bring your sacrifices and thank offerings.*

15 God says, "Call me when trouble comes.
   I will help you, and you will honor me."

---

a **50:2** *God . . . beauty* Or, "God shining from Zion is absolutely beautiful."

16 God says to the wicked, "Stop quoting my laws!
    Stop talking about my agreement*!
17 You hate for me to tell you what to do.
    You ignore what I say.
18 You see a thief, and you run to join him.
    You jump into bed with those who commit adultery.*
19 You say evil things and tell lies.
20 You sit around talking about people
    and finding fault with your own brothers.
21 You did this, and I said nothing.
    So you thought I was just like you.
    But I will not be quiet any longer.
    I will correct you and make it very clear to you.
22 You people who have forgotten God,
    understand what I am telling you,
or I will tear you apart,
    and no one will be able to save you!
23 Whoever gives a thank offering shows me honor.
    And whoever decides to live right will see my power
      to save."

51 *To the director.* A song of David* telling about the time Nathan the prophet came to him after David's sin with Bathsheba.

1 God, be merciful to me
because of your faithful love.
Because of your great compassion,
    erase all the wrongs I have done.
2 Scrub away my guilt.
    Wash me clean from my sin.
3 I know I have done wrong.
    I remember that sin all the time.
4 I did what you said is wrong.
    You are the one I have sinned against.
I say this so that people will know
    that I am wrong, and you are right.
    Your decisions are fair.
5 I was born in sin.
    In sin my mother conceived me.
6 You want me to be truly loyal,
    so put true wisdom deep inside of me.
7 Remove my sin and make me pure.[a]
    Wash me until I am whiter than snow!
8 Let me hear sounds of joy and happiness again.
    Let the bones you crushed be happy again.

---

[a] **51:7 Remove … pure** Literally, "Cleanse me with hyssop." This plant was used to sprinkle blood or water in a purification ceremony after something or someone had been contaminated by sin.

9 Don't look at my sins.
　　Erase them all.
10 God, create a pure heart in me,
　　and make my spirit strong again.
11 Don't push me away
　　or take your Holy Spirit from me.
12 Your help made me so happy.
　　Give me that joy again.
　　Make my spirit strong and ready to obey you.
13 I will teach the guilty how you want them to live,
　　and the sinners will come back to you.
14 God, spare me from the punishment of death.[a]
　　My God, you are the one who saves me!
　　Let me sing about all the good things you do for me!
15 My Lord, I will open my mouth and sing your praises!
16 You don't really want sacrifices,*
　　or else I would give them to you.
17 The sacrifice that God wants is a humble spirit.
　　God, you will not turn away someone who comes
　　　with a humble heart, willing to obey you.[b]

18 God, please be good to Zion.*
　　Rebuild the walls of Jerusalem.
19 Then you can enjoy the kind of sacrifices you want.[c]
　　You will receive whole burnt offerings,*
　　and people will again offer bulls on your altar.

52 To the director.* A maskil* of David when Doeg the Edomite
went to Saul and told him, "David is in Ahimelech's house."
1 Great warrior, why are you bragging about the evil you did?
　　You are a disgrace to God.
2 You are nothing but a hired killer,[d]
　　making plans to hurt people and making up lies!
3 You love evil more than goodness.
　　You love lying more than truth.　　　　　　Selah*

4 You and your lying tongue love to hurt people.
5 So God will ruin you forever!
　　He will grab you and pull you from your home,[e]
　　　like someone pulling a plant out of the ground,
　　　roots and all![f]
6 Good people will see this
　　and learn to fear and respect God.

---

[a]51:14 spare ... death Or, "don't consider me guilty of murder." [b]51:17 someone ... obey
you Literally, "a broken and crushed heart." *51:19 the kind ... you want Or, "the offering
of righteousness." [d]52:2 hired killer Literally, "sharpened razor." [e]52:5 home This means
the body. This is a poetic way of saying God will destroy you forever. [f]52:5 He ... roots and
all Literally, "He will root you up from the land of the living." This also means "He will kill you
and your descendants."

They will laugh at you and say,
7 "Look what happened to the warrior
  who did not depend on God.
That fool thought his wealth and lies would protect him."

8 But I am like a green olive tree growing in God's Temple.*
  I will trust God's faithful love forever and ever.
9 God, I praise you forever for what you have done.
  I will speak your name[a] before your followers
    because it is so good!

53 To the director.* On the mahalath.[b]
A maskil* of David.

1 Only fools think there is no God.
  People like that are evil and do terrible things.
  They never do what is right.

2 God looks down from heaven to see
  if there is anyone who is wise,
  if anyone is looking to him for help.

3 But everyone has turned away from him.
  Everyone has become evil.
No one does anything good.
No, not one person!

4 God says, "The wicked don't ask for my advice.
  And they treat my people like bread to be eaten.
  Don't they understand what they are doing?"

5 But those evil people will be filled with fear—
  a fear like they have never felt before!
Israel,* you will defeat those who attacked you,
  because God has rejected them.
And he will scatter their bones.

6 I wish the one who lives on Mount Zion*
  would bring victory to Israel!
Jacob's people will be very happy
  when God makes Israel prosper again.[c]

54 To the director.* With instruments. A maskil* of David when
the Ziphites went to Saul and told him, "We think David
is hiding among our people."

1 God, use your power and save me.
  Use your great power to set me free.[d]

---

[a]52:9 *speak your name* Or, "I will trust your name." [b]**Psalm 53** *mahalath* This is probably
a musical word. It might be the name of a tune, or it might mean to dance and shout.
[c]**53:6** *Jacob's people … prosper again* Or, "The Lᴏʀᴅ's people were taken away as captives,
but he will bring his people back. Then Jacob (Israel) will be very happy." [d]**54:1** Literally,
"God, save me with your name, judge me with your might."

2 God, listen to my prayer.
  Listen to what I say.
3 Strangers who don't even think about God
      have turned against me.
    Those powerful men are trying to kill me.   Selah*

4 Look, my God will help me.
    My Lord will support me.
5 My God will punish the people who turned against me.
    God, be faithful to me and destroy them.

6 Lord, I will give freewill offerings to you.
    I will praise your good name.
7 You saved me from all my troubles.
    I saw my enemies defeated.

55 To the director.* With instruments.
      A maskil* of David.
1 God, hear my prayer.
    Please don't ignore my prayer for mercy.
2 Please listen to me and answer me.
    Let me speak to you and tell you what upsets me.
3 Like an enemy, they yelled at me and threatened me.
    They were angry and attacked me.
    They brought troubles crashing down on me.
4 My heart is pounding inside me.
    I am scared to death.
5 I am trembling with fear.
    I am terrified!
6 Oh, I wish I had wings like a dove.
    I would fly away and find a place to rest.
7   I would go far into the desert and stay there.   Selah*

8 I would run away.
    I would escape from this storm of trouble.
9 My Lord, stop their lies.
    I see the violence and fighting in this city.
10 Day and night, in every neighborhood,
      the city is filled with crime and trouble.
11 There is so much crime in the streets.
      People are lying and cheating everywhere.

12 If it were an enemy insulting me,
      I could bear it.
    If it were my enemies attacking me,
      I could hide.
13 But it is you, my companion,
      my colleague, my close friend, who does this.
14 We used to share our secrets with one another,
      as we walked through the crowds
        together in God's Temple.*

15 I wish death would take my enemies by surprise!
　　I wish the earth would open up and swallow them alive^a
　　because they plan such terrible things together.

16 I will call to God for help,
　　and the LORD will answer me.
17 I speak to God morning, noon, and night.
　　I tell him what upsets me, and he listens to me!
18 I have fought in many battles,
　　but God has always rescued me
　　and brought me back safely.
19 God, who has always ruled as king,
　　will hear me and punish my enemies.　　　　　　Selah

　　But they will never change.
　　　They don't fear and respect God.
20 This one who was once my friend now attacks his friends.
　　He is breaking every promise he made.
21 His words about peace are as smooth as butter,
　　but he has only war on his mind.
　　His words are as slick as oil,
　　but they cut like a knife.

22 Give your worries to the LORD, and he will care for you.
　　He will never let those who are good be defeated.

23 But, God, you will send those liars and murderers
　　to their grave.
　　They will die before their life is half finished!
　　As for me, I will put my trust in you.

56

To the director.* To the tune "The Dove in the Distant Oak."
A miktam* of David from the time the Philistines captured him
in Gath.

1 God, people have attacked me, so be merciful to me.
　　They have been chasing me constantly,
　　　closing in to attack me.
2 My enemies come at me constantly.
　　There are too many fighters to count.^b
3 When I am afraid, I put my trust in you.
4 I trust God, so I am not afraid of what people can do to me!
　　I praise God for his promise to me.
5 My enemies are always twisting my words.
　　They are always making plans against me.
6 They hide together and watch my every move,
　　hoping for some way to kill me.
7 God, send them away because of the bad things they did.
　　Show your anger and defeat those people.

^a**55:15** Literally, "I wish death would surprise them. I wish they would go down into Sheol alive." This would be like the time Korah, the enemy of Moses, was punished by God. See Num. 16:31–33.　^b**56:2** *There are … count* Or, "There are many attacking me from above."

8 You know I am very upset.
   You know how much I have cried.
 Surely you have kept an account of all my tears.

9 I know that when I call for help,
   my enemies will turn and run.
 I know that because God is with me!

10 I praise God for his promise.
   I praise the LORD for his promise to me.

11 I trust God, so I am not afraid
   of what people can do to me!

12 God, I made special promises to you,
   and I will do what I promised.
 I will give you my thank offering.

13 You saved me from death.
   You kept me from being defeated.
 So I will worship you in the light that only the living can see.

57 To the director.* To the tune "Don't Destroy."
 A miktam* of David when he escaped from Saul and went
 into the cave.

1 God, be merciful to me.
   Be kind because my soul trusts in you.
 I have come to you for protection,
   while the trouble passes.

2 I pray to God Most High for help,
   and he takes care of me completely!

3 From heaven he helps me and saves me.
   He will punish the one who attacks me.   Selah*
 God will remain loyal to me
   and send his love to protect me.

4 My life is in danger.
   My enemies are all around me.
 They are like man-eating lions,
   with teeth like spears or arrows
   and tongues that cut like sharp swords.

5 God, rise above the heavens!
   Let all the world see your glory.*

6 My enemies set a trap for me.
   They were trying to trap me.
 They dug a deep pit for me, but they fell into it.   Selah

7 God, I am ready.
   I am ready to sing songs of praise.

8 Wake up, my soul*a!
   Harps and lyres,* wake up, and let us wake the dawn.

---

a **57:8** *soul* Literally, "my glory."

⁹ My Lord, I praise you to everyone.
    I will sing praises about you to every nation.

¹⁰ Your faithful love is higher than the highest clouds in the sky!

¹¹ God, rise above the heavens.
    Let all the world see your glory.

58

To the director.* To the tune "Don't Destroy."
A miktam* of David.

¹ You judges are not being fair in your decisions.
    You are not judging people fairly.

² No, you only think of evil things to do.
    You do violent crimes in this country.

³ Those wicked people started doing wrong
        as soon as they were born.
    They have been liars from birth.

⁴ Their anger is as dangerous as snake venom.ᵃ
    And, like cobras that cannot hear,
        they refuse to listen to the truth.

⁵ Cobras cannot hear the music or songs of snake charmers,
    and those wicked people are like that
        as they make their evil plans.ᵇ

⁶ God, they are like lions.
    So Lᴏʀᴅ, break their teeth.

⁷ May they disappear like water down a drain.
    May they be crushed like weeds on a path.ᶜ

⁸ May they be like snails melting away as they move.
    May they be like a baby born dead,
        who never saw the light of day.

⁹ May they be destroyed quickly,
    like the thorns that are burned to heat a pot quickly.

¹⁰ Good people will be happy when they see the wicked
        getting the punishment they deserve.
    They will feel like soldiers walking through the blood
        of their enemies!ᵈ

¹¹ Then people will say, "Good people really are rewarded.
    Yes, there is a God judging the world!"ᵉ

59

To the director.* To the tune "Don't Destroy."
A miktam* of David from the time Saul sent people to watch
David's house to try to kill him.

¹ God, save me from my enemies.
    Protect me from those who stand against me.

ᵃ**58:4** *Their anger ... snake venom* A wordplay in Hebrew. The word meaning "anger" sounds like the word "venom" (poison). ᵇ**58:5** *snake charmers ... evil plans* The Hebrew phrase can mean either "snake charmers, who create crafty magic formulas" or "snake charmers. Those wicked people make their sneaky schemes." ᶜ**58:7** Or, "May he shoot his arrows, ⌊cutting them down⌋ as if they were withering ⌊grass⌋." ᵈ**58:10** *They ... enemies* Literally, "They will wash their feet in the blood of the wicked." ᵉ**58:11** *Yes ... world* Or, "There really are judges in this land doing their job."

2 Save me from those who do wrong.
    Save me from those murderers.
3 Look, powerful men are waiting for me.
    They are waiting to kill me, even though I did not sin
       or commit any crime.
4 I have done nothing wrong, but they are rushing
       to attack me.
    Lord, come and see for yourself!
5 You are the LORD God All-Powerful, the God of Israel*!
    Get up and punish them.
    Don't show any mercy to those traitors.   *Selah**

6 Those evil men are like dogs
    that come into town in the evening,
      growling and roaming the streets.
7 Listen to their threats and insults.
    They say such cruel things,
      and they don't care who hears them.

8 LORD, laugh at them.
    Make fun of them all.
9 I will sing my songs of praise to you.*a*
    God, you are my place of safety, high in the mountains.
10 God loves me, and he will help me win.
    He will help me defeat my enemies.
11 Don't just kill them, or my people might forget.
    My Lord and Protector, scatter them and defeat them
      with your strength.
12 Those evil people curse* and tell lies.
    Punish them for what they said.
    Let their pride trap them.
13 Destroy them in your anger.
    Destroy them completely!
    Then people all over the world
      will know that God rules over Jacob's* people.   *Selah*

14 Those evil men are like dogs
    that come into town in the evening,
      growling and roaming the streets.
15 They roam around looking for food,
    but even if they eat their fill,
      they still growl and complain.
16 But I will sing about your strength.
    I will rejoice in your love, because you have been
      my place of safety, high in the mountains.
    And I can run to you when troubles come.
17 I will sing praises to you, my source of strength.
    You, God, are my place of safety.
    You are the God who loves me!

a **59:9** *I will sing . . . to you* Or, "My Strength, I am waiting for you." See Ps. 59:17.

60

To the director.* To the tune "Lily of the Agreement."
A miktam* of David. For teaching. Written during the time
David fought Aram Naharaim[a] and Aram Zobah,[b] and Joab
came back and defeated 12,000 Edomite soldiers at Salt Valley.

1   God, you were angry with us.
    You rejected us and destroyed our defenses.
    Please make us strong again.

2   You shook the earth and split it open.
    It is falling apart like a broken wall.
    Please put it back together again.

3   You have given your people many troubles.
    We are dizzy and falling down like drunks.

4   But then you provided a flag to show your followers
    where to gather to escape the enemy's attack.   Selah*

5   Use your great power and save us!
    Answer my prayer and save the people you love!

6   God has spoken in his Temple:[c]
    "I will win the war and rejoice in victory!
    I will divide this land among my people.
    I will give them Shechem.
    I will give them Succoth Valley.

7   Gilead and Manasseh will be mine.
    Ephraim will be my helmet.
    Judah* will be my royal scepter.*

8   Moab will be the bowl for washing my feet.
    Edom will be the slave who carries my sandals.
    I will defeat the Philistines and shout in victory!"

9–10 But, God, it seems that you have left us!
     You do not go out with our army.
     So who will lead me into the strong, protected city?
     Who will lead me into battle against Edom?

11 God, help us defeat the enemy!
    No one on earth can rescue us.

12 Only God can make us strong.
    Only God can defeat our enemies!

61

To the director.* With stringed instruments.
A song of David.*

1   God, hear my prayer song.
    Listen to my prayer.

2   Wherever I am, however weak,
    I will call to you for help!
    Carry me to the place of safety far above.[d]

---

[a]Psalm 60 *Aram Naharaim* Or, "the Arameans of Mesopotamia." [b]Psalm 60 *Aram Zobah*
Or, "the Arameans of central Syria." [c]60:6 *in his Temple* Or, "in his holiness." [d]61:2 *Carry
... above* Or, "From your fortress high above me, lead me."

3 You are my place of safety!
   You are the strong tower protecting me from my enemies.
4 I want to live in your tent[a] forever.
   I want to hide where you can protect me. *Selah**

5 God, you heard what I promised to give you,
   but everything your worshipers have comes from you.
6 Give the king a long life.
   Let him live forever!
7 Let him rule in your presence forever!
   Protect him with your faithful love.
8 Then I will praise your name forever.
   Every day I will do what I promised.

62 To the director.* To Jeduthun.
A song of David.*

1 I must calm down and turn to God; only he can rescue me.
2 He is my Rock,* the only one who can save me.
   He is my high place of safety, where no army can defeat me.

3 How long will you attack me?
   I am like a leaning wall, a fence ready to fall.
4 In spite of my important position,
   those people are planning to destroy me.
   It makes them happy to tell lies about me.
   In public, they say good things about me,
      but in private, they curse* me. *Selah**

5 I must calm down and turn to God; he is my only hope.
6 He is my Rock, the only one who can save me.
   He is my high place of safety, where no army can defeat me.
7 My victory and honor come from God.
   He is the mighty rock, where I am safe.
8 People, always put your trust in God!
   Tell him all your problems.
   God is our place of safety. *Selah*

9 People cannot really help.
   You cannot depend on them.
   Compared to God, they are nothing—
      a gentle puff of air!
10 Don't trust in your power to take things by force.
   Don't think you will gain anything by stealing.
   And if you become rich, don't trust in your riches
      to help you.
11 God says there is one thing you can really
      depend on, and I believe it:
   "Strength comes from God!"

---

a **61:4 tent** The place where God lives among his people. Here, it is the Temple in Jerusalem.
Earlier, it was the Holy Tent where the people worshiped God before the Temple was built.

¹² My Lord, your love is real.
   You reward or punish people for what they do.

63

A song of David. *from the time he was in the desert of Judah.* *

¹ God, you are my God.
   I am searching so hard to find you.
   Body and soul, I thirst for you
   in this dry and weary land without water.
² Yes, I have seen you in your Temple.*ᵃ*
   I have seen your strength and glory.*
³ Your faithful love is better than life,
   so my lips praise you.
⁴ By my life, I will praise you.
   In your name, I lift my hands in prayer.
⁵ When I sit down to satisfy my hunger,
   my joyful lips hunger to praise you!
⁶ I remember you while lying on my bed.
   I think about you in the middle of the night.
⁷ That is because you are the one who helps me.
   It makes me happy to be under your protection!
⁸ I stay close to you,
   and you hold me with your powerful arm.

⁹ Those who are trying to kill me will be destroyed.
   They will go down to their graves.
¹⁰ They will be killed with swords.
   Wild dogs will eat their dead bodies.
¹¹ But the king will be happy with his God,
   and those who promised to obey him will praise him
      when he defeats those liars.

64

To the director. *
A song of David. *

¹ God, listen to my complaint.
   Save me from the terrible threats of my enemies.
² Protect me from the secret plans of the wicked.
   Hide me from that gang of evil people.
³ They sharpen their tongues to use like swords.
   They aim their poisonous words like arrows.
⁴ Suddenly, from their hiding places, they let their arrows fly
   and shoot to kill innocent people.
⁵ They encourage each other to do wrong.
   They talk about setting their traps, saying,
      "No one will see them here!
⁶ No one will discover our crime; we have the perfect plan!"
   Yes, people can be very tricky and hard to understand.
⁷ But suddenly, God will shoot his arrows,
   and those wicked people will be hit.

ᵃ**63:2** *your Temple* Or, "your holiness."

8 He can use their own words against them
   and teach them a lesson.
Then everyone who sees them
   will shake their heads in amazement.
9 People will see what God has done.
   They will tell other people about him.
Then everyone will learn more about God.
   They will learn to fear and respect him.
10 Good people are happy to serve the LORD.
   They depend on God.
And when other good people see it,
   they praise the LORD!

65
*To the director.**
*A praise song of David.**

1 God on Zion,* we praise you
   and give you what we promised.
2 Anyone can come to you,
   and you will listen to their prayers.
3 When our sins become too heavy for us,
   you wipe them away.
4 Oh, how wonderful it is to be the people
   that you chose to come to your Temple.*
And we are so happy to have the wonderful things
   that are in your Temple, your holy palace.
5 God, you answer our prayers and do what is right.
   You do amazing things to save us.
People all over the world know they can trust in you,
   even those who live across the sea.
6 You made the mountains.
   We see your power all around us.
7 You can calm the roughest seas
   or the nations raging around us.
8 People all around the world are amazed
   at the wonderful things you do.
You make all people, east and west, sing with joy.
9 You take care of the land.
   You water it and make it fertile.
God, you fill the streams with water
   and make the crops grow.
10 You pour rain on the plowed fields;
   you soak the fields with water.
You make the ground soft with rain,
   and you make the young plants grow.
11 You start the new year with a good harvest.
   You end the year with many crops.*a*

*a***65:11** In ancient Israel there were two calendars. The calendar for religious festivals began
in the spring, at barley harvest. The other calendar started in the fall, when they gathered
other crops.

12 The desert and hills are covered with grass.
13 The pastures are covered with sheep.
    The valleys are filled with grain.
    Everyone is singing and shouting with joy.

66
*To the director.**
A song of praise.

1 Everything on earth, shout with joy to God!
2 Praise his glorious name!
    Honor him with songs of praise!
3 Tell God how wonderful his works are!
    God, your power is very great!
    Your enemies bow down before you.
    They are afraid of you!
4 Let the whole world worship you.
    Let everyone sing praises to your name.   *Selah**

5 Look at what God did!
    Those things amaze us.
6 He changed the sea to dry land.*a*
    His people went across the river on foot,*b*
    so let's celebrate him there!
7 He rules the world with his great power.
    He watches people everywhere.
    No one can rebel against him.   *Selah*

8 People, praise our God.
    Sing loud songs of praise to him.
9 He gave us life, and he protects us.
10 God, you tested us, like people test silver with fire.
11 You let us be trapped.
    You put heavy burdens on us.
12 You let our enemies run over us.
    We went through fire and water,
    but you brought us to a safe place.
13–14 So I will bring sacrifices* to your Temple.*
    When I was in trouble,
    I asked you for help and made many promises to you.
    Now, I am giving you what I promised.
15   I am giving you sin offerings.*
    I am giving you incense* with the rams.
    I am giving you bulls and goats.   *Selah*

16 All you people worshiping God,
    come and I will tell you what he has done for me.
17 I cried out to my Lord for help,
    and I praised him.

---

*a*66:6 *changed the sea to dry land* This was with Moses at the Red Sea. See Ex. 14.
*b*66:6 *went across the river on foot* This was with Joshua at the Jordan River. See Josh. 3:14–17.

¹⁸ If I had been hiding sin in my heart,
   he would not have listened to me.

¹⁹ But God did listen to me.
   He heard my prayer.

²⁰ Praise God!
   He did not turn away from me—
      he listened to my prayer.
   He continues to show his love to me!

67

To the director.* With instruments.
A song of praise.

¹ God, show mercy to us and bless us.
   Please accept us!   *Selah**

² Let everyone on earth learn about you.
   Let every nation see how you save people.

³ May people praise you, God!
   May all people praise you.

⁴ May all nations rejoice and be happy
      because you judge people fairly.
   You rule over every nation.

⁵ May the people praise you, God!
   May all people praise you.

⁶ God, our God, bless us.
   Let our land give us a great harvest.

⁷ May God bless us,
   and may all people on earth fear and respect him.

68

To the director.*
A praise song of David.*

¹ God, get up and scatter your enemies.
   May all your enemies run from you.

² May your enemies be scattered
      like smoke blown away by the wind.
   May your enemies be destroyed
      like wax melting in a fire.

³ But let good people be happy.
   Let them gather before God
      and enjoy themselves together.

⁴ Sing to God.
   Sing praises to his name.
Prepare the way for God as he rides his chariot
      over the clouds.
His name is Yah.ᵃ
   Praise his name!

⁵ From the holy place he lives, God is a father to orphans,
      and he takes care of widows.

ᵃ**68:4 Yah** This is a Hebrew name for God. It is like the Hebrew name usually translated
"Lord."

⁶ God provides homes for those who are lonely.
    He frees people from prison and makes them happy.
    But those who turn against him will live in the desert.

⁷ God, you led your people out of Egypt.
    You marched across the desert.   *Selah**

⁸ The ground shook and rain poured from the sky
    when God, the God of Israel,* came to Mount Sinai.*

⁹ God, you sent the rain
    to make a tired, old land strong again.

¹⁰ Your people*a* came back to live there,
    and you provided good things for the poor.

¹¹ My Lord gave the command,
    and many people went to tell the good news:

¹²"The armies of powerful kings ran away!
    At home, the women divide the things the soldiers
        brought from the battle.

¹³ Those who stayed home will share in the wealth.
    They will get the dove wings covered with silver.
    They will get the wings sparkling with gold."

¹⁴ God All-Powerful scattered the enemy kings like snow
    falling on Mount Zalmon.

¹⁵ Mount Bashan is a great mountain with many high peaks.

¹⁶ But, Bashan, why are you jealous of Mount Zion*?
    That is where God has chosen to live.
    The LORD will live there forever.

¹⁷ With his millions of chariots*
    the Lord came from Sinai into the holy place.

¹⁸ You went up to your high place,
    leading a parade of captives.
You received gifts from people,*b*
    even those who turned against you.
The LORD*c* God went up there to live.

¹⁹ Praise the Lord!
    Every day he helps us with the loads we must carry.
    He is the God who saves us.   *Selah*

²⁰ He is our God, the God who saves us.
    My Lord GOD saves us from death.

²¹ God will smash the heads of his enemies.
    He will punish those who fight against him.*d*

²² My Lord said, "Even if they run to the mountains of Bashan
        or to the depths of the sea,
    I will capture them and bring them back.

---

*a*68:10 *people* Or, "animals," or "living things." *b*68:18 *received gifts from people* Or, "took
people as gifts." Or, "gave gifts to people," as in the ancient Syriac and Aramaic versions and
in Eph. 4:8. *c*68:18 *The LORD* Or, "YAH," a Hebrew name for God. *d*68:21 Literally, "God
will smash the heads of his enemies. He will smash the hairy skull walking in guilt."

23 So you will march through pools of their blood,
and there will be plenty left for your dogs."

24 God, everyone can see your victory parade—
the victory march led by my holy God and King!

25 Singers come marching in front, followed by the musicians,
surrounded by young girls playing tambourines.

26 Praise God in the meeting place*a*!
Praise the Lord, people of Israel*!

27 There is the smallest tribe, Benjamin, leading them.
And there comes a large group of leaders from Judah.*
And following them are the leaders of Zebulun and Naphtali.

28 God, show us your power!
Show us the power you used for us in the past.

29 Kings will bring their wealth to you,
to your Temple* in Jerusalem.

30 Punish the people in Egypt.
They are like cattle in the marshes,
like bulls among the calves.
You humiliated them.
You scattered them in war.
Now let them come crawling to you,
bringing their pieces of silver.

31 Messengers from Egypt will come bearing gifts.
Ethiopia will offer God their tribute.*

32 Kings on earth, sing to God!
Sing songs of praise to our Lord!   *Selah*

33 Sing to him who rides his chariot through the ancient skies.
Listen to his powerful voice!

34 Tell everyone how powerful he is!
He rules over Israel.
His power fills the skies.

35 God, you are awesome in your Temple!
The God of Israel is the one who gives strength
and power to his people.
Praise God!

69 To the director.* To the tune "The Lilies."
A song of David.*

1 God, save me from all my troubles!
The rising water has reached my neck.

2 I have nothing to stand on.
I am sinking down, down into the mud.
I am in deep water,
and the waves are crashing around me.
I am about to drown.

---

a **68:26** *in the meeting place* Or, "with the trumpets that announce the assembly!"

3 I am getting weak from calling for help.
  My throat is sore.
I have waited and looked for help from you
  until my eyes are hurting.
4 I have more enemies than the hairs on my head.
  They hate me for no reason.
  They try hard to destroy me.
My enemies tell lies about me.
  They lied and said I stole things.
And then they forced me to pay for things I did not steal.
5 God, you know my faults.
  I cannot hide my sins from you.
6 My Lord GOD All-Powerful, don't let your followers
    be ashamed of me.
God of Israel,* don't let me be an embarrassment to those
    who come to worship you.
7 My face is covered with shame.
  I carry this shame for you.
8 My own brothers treat me like a stranger.
  They act as if I came from a foreign land.
9 My strong devotion to your Temple* is destroying me.
  Those who insult you are also insulting me.
10 When I spend time crying and fasting,*
   they make fun of me.
11 When I wear sackcloth* to show my sorrow,
   they tell jokes about me.
12 They talk about me in public places.
   The beer drinkers make up songs about me.
13 As for me, this is my prayer to you, LORD:
   I want you to accept me!
God, I want you to answer me with love.
   I know I can trust you to save me.
14 Pull me from the mud,
   and don't let me sink down deeper.
Save me from those who hate me.
   Save me from this deep water.
15 Don't let the waves drown me.
   Don't let the deep sea swallow me
   or the grave close its mouth on me.
16 Answer me, LORD, from the goodness of your faithful love.
   Out of your great kindness turn to me and help me!
17 Don't turn away from your servant.
   I am in trouble, so hurry and help me!
18 Come save my soul.
   Rescue me from my enemies.
19 You know my shame.
   You know my enemies humiliated me.
   You saw them do it.

²⁰ I feel the pain of their insults.
   The shame makes me feel like dying!
I wanted some sympathy,
   but there was none.
I waited for someone to comfort me,
   but no one came.
²¹ They gave me poison, not food.
   They gave me vinegar, not wine.
²² Their tables are covered with food.
   They have such big fellowship meals.
   May those meals destroy them.
²³ Let them become blind and their backs become weak.
²⁴ Let them feel all of your anger.
²⁵ Make their homes empty.
   Don't let anyone live there.
²⁶ They try to hurt people you have already punished.
   They tell everyone about the suffering you gave them.
²⁷ Punish them for the bad things they have done.
   Don't show them how good you can be.
²⁸ Erase their names from the book of life.
   Don't let their names appear on the list
      of those who do what is right.
²⁹ I am sad and hurting.
   God, lift me up. Save me!
³⁰ I will praise God's name in song.
   I will write a song that honors him.
³¹ This will make the LORD happy!
   This will be better than killing a bull
      and offering the whole animal as a sacrifice.*
³² Poor people, you came to worship God.
   You will be happy to know these things.
³³ The LORD listens to poor, helpless people.
   He still likes those who are in prison.
³⁴ Praise him, heaven and earth!
   Sea and everything in it, praise him!
³⁵ God will save Zion.*
   He will rebuild the cities of Judah.*
The people will settle there again and own the land.
³⁶ The descendants of his servants will get that land,
   and those who love his name will live there.

70

To the director.
A song of David to help people remember.*

¹ God, rescue me!
   LORD, hurry and help me!
² People are trying to kill me.
   LORD, disappoint them!
Humiliate them!

*70 Praise God literally, "God is great," or "May God be praised," or "praise God," or "praise to you.
Or: "praise you."

They wanted to hurt me.
　　Make them run away in shame!
³ May those who make fun of me
　　be too embarrassed to speak!
⁴ But may those who come to you
　　be happy and rejoice.
　May those who love being saved by you
　　always be able to say, "Praise God!"ᵃ

⁵ I am only a poor, helpless man.
　　God, please hurry to me.
　You are my helper, the one who can save me.
　　LORD, don't be too late!

71

¹ LORD, I trust in you;
　don't let me be disappointed.
² In your goodness, save me.
　　Rescue me.
　　Listen to me and save me.
³ Be my fortress,* the home I can run to for safety.
　　You are my Rock,* my place of safety,
　　so give the command to save me.
⁴ My God, save me from wicked people.
　　Save me from cruel, evil people.
⁵ My Lord GOD, you are my hope.
　　I have trusted you since I was a young boy.
⁶ I depended on you even before I was born.
　　I relied on you even in my mother's womb.
　　I have always prayed to you.ᵇ
⁷ You are my source of strength,
　　so I have been an example to others.
⁸ I am always singing about the wonderful things you do.
⁹ Don't throw me away just because I am old.
　　Don't leave me as I lose my strength.
¹⁰ My enemies have made plans against me.
　　They really did meet together,
　　　and they made plans to kill me.
¹¹ They said, "Go get him!
　　God left him, so there is no one to help him."
¹² God, don't leave me!
　　Hurry, God! Come save me!
¹³ Defeat my enemies!
　　Destroy them completely!
　They are trying to hurt me.
　　Let them feel the shame and disgrace.
¹⁴ Then I will always trust in you
　　and will praise you more and more.

ᵃ70:4 *Praise God* Literally, "God is great" or "May God be magnified."　ᵇ71:6 *prayed to you*
Or, "praised you."

15 I will tell people how good you are.
    I will tell about the times you saved me.
    That has happened too many times to count.
16 I will tell about your greatness, my Lord GOD.
    I will talk only about you and your goodness.
17 God, you have taught me since I was a young boy.
    And to this day I have told people about the wonderful
        things you do!
18 Now I am old and my hair is gray, but don't leave me, God.
    I must tell the next generation about your power
        and greatness.
19 God, your goodness reaches far above the skies.
    God, there is no god like you.
    You have done wonderful things.
20 You have let me see troubles and hard times,
    but you will give me new life;
    you will lift me up from this pit of death!
21 You will help me do even greater things.
    You will comfort me again!
22 And I will play the harp and praise you.
    My God, I will sing about your faithfulness.
    I will play songs on my lyre*for the Holy One of Israel.*
23 I will shout for joy,
    singing songs of praise to you for saving me.
24 My tongue will sing about your goodness all the time,
    because those who wanted to kill me
        have been defeated and disgraced.

72 To Solomon.ᵃ

1 God, help the king be like you and make good decisions.
    Help the king's son know what justice is.
2 Help the king judge your people fairly.
    Help him make wise decisions for your poor people.
3 Let there be peace and justice throughout the land,
    known on every mountain and hill.
4 May the king be fair to the poor.
    May he help the helpless and punish those who hurt them.
5 May people fear and respect the king
    as long as the sun shines and the moon is in the sky.
    May people fear and respect him forever!
6 Help the king be like rain falling on the fields,
    like showers falling on the land.
7 Let goodness blossom while he is king.
    Let peace continue as long as the moon.

ᵃ**Psalm 72** *To Solomon* This might mean this song was written by Solomon or dedicated to him, or that it is from some special collection of songs.

8 Let his kingdom grow from sea to sea,
   from the Euphrates River to the faraway places on earth.[a]
9 May all the people living in the desert bow down to him.
   May all his enemies bow before him with their faces
     in the dirt.
10 May the kings of Tarshish* and all the faraway lands
     by the sea bring gifts to him.
   May the kings of Sheba and Seba bring their tribute[b] to him.
11 May all kings bow down to our king.
   May all nations serve him.
12 Our king helps the poor who cry out to him—
     those in need who have no one to help them.
13 He feels sorry for all who are weak and poor.
   He protects their lives.
14 The king saves them from those who are cruel to them.
   Their lives are very important to him.
15 Long live the king!
   Let him receive gold from Sheba.
   Always pray for the king.
   Bless him every day.
16 May the fields grow plenty of grain
     and the hills be covered with crops.
   May the fields be as fertile as Lebanon
     and the cities be filled with people
     like the fields are covered with grass.
17 May the king be famous forever.
   May people remember his name as long as the sun shines.
   May the people be blessed through him,
     and may they all bless him.

18 Praise the LORD God, the God of Israel*!
   Only God can do such amazing things.
19 Praise his glorious name forever!
   Let his glory* fill the whole world!
   Amen* and Amen!

20 (This ends the prayers of David* son of Jesse.)

BOOK 3 (Psalms 73–89)

73 *Asaph's song of praise.*

1 God is so good to Israel,*
   to those whose hearts are pure.
2 But I almost slipped and lost my balance.
   I almost fell into sin.
3 I saw that wicked people were successful,
   and I became jealous of those proud people.

---

[a] **72:8** *faraway places on earth* This usually means the countries around the Mediterranean Sea.   [b] **72:10** *tribute* The money and gifts a country paid to the country that defeated it.

4 They are healthy.
  They don't have to struggle to survive.*a*

5 They don't suffer like the rest of us.
  They don't have troubles like other people.

6 So they are proud and hateful.
  This is as easy to see as the jewels
    and fancy clothes they wear.

7 If they see something they like, they go and take it.
  They do whatever they want.

8 They make fun of others and say cruel things about them.
  In their pride they make plans to hurt people.

9 They think they are gods!
  They think they are the rulers of earth.

10*b* Even God's people turn to them and do what they say.

11 Those evil people say,
   "God does not know what we are doing!
   God Most High does not know!"

12 Those proud people are wicked,
   but they are rich and getting richer.

13 So why should I make my heart pure?
   Why should I make my hands clean?

14 God, I suffer all day long,
   and you punish me every morning.

15 God, I wanted to talk to others about these things.
   But I knew I would be betraying your people.

16 I tried hard to understand these things,
   but it was all too hard for me,

17 until I went to your Temple.*
   I went to God's Temple, and then I understood.

18 God, you really have put those people
   in a dangerous situation.
   It is so easy for them to fall and be destroyed.

19 Trouble can come suddenly,
   and they will be ruined.
   Terrible things can happen to them,
   and they will be finished.

20 Then they will be like a dream
   that we forget when we wake up.
   You will make them disappear
   like the monsters in our dreams.

21–22 I was so stupid.
   I thought about such people and became upset.
   God, I was upset and angry with you!
   I acted like a senseless animal.

*a***73:4** Literally, "They have no bonds to their death." *b***73:10** This verse is hard to understand in Hebrew.

23 But I am always with you.
    You hold my hand.
24 You lead me and give me good advice,
    and later you will lead me to glory.[a]
25 God, I have you in heaven.
    And if I am with you, what on earth can I want?
26 Maybe my mind[b] and body will be destroyed,
    but I have the Rock* I love.
    I have God forever!
27 God, people who leave you will be lost.
    You will destroy those who are not faithful to you.
28 As for me, I have come to God, and that is good.
    I have made the Lord GOD my place of safety.
    I have come to tell about what you have done.

74 A maskil* of Asaph.

1 God, why have you turned away from us for so long?
    Why are you so angry with us, your own flock?
2 Remember the people you bought so long ago.
    You saved us, and we belong to you.
    Remember Mount Zion,* the place where you lived.
3 God, come walk through these ancient ruins.
    Come back to the Holy Place* that the enemy destroyed.

4 The enemy shouted their war cries in the Temple.*
    They put up their flags there to show
        they had won the war.
5 Their soldiers attacked the doors,
    like workmen chopping down trees.
6 Using axes and hatchets,
    they smashed the carved panels in your Temple.
7 They burned your Holy Place.
    That Temple was built to honor your name,
        but they pulled it down to the ground.
8 The enemy decided to crush us completely.
    They burned every holy place[c] in the country.
9 We do not see any of our signs.[d]
    There are no more prophets.
    No one knows how long this will last.
10 God, how much longer will the enemy make fun of us?
    Will you let them insult your name forever?

[a]73:24 *later … glory* Or, "You take me after honor." [b]73:26 *mind* Literally, "heart." [c]74:8 *holy place* Or, "El meeting place." This means every place where people went to meet with God. [d]74:9 *signs* These were probably signal fires that people burned as a way of passing messages from one town to the next. In war, this was a way people showed other towns that the enemy had not yet destroyed their own town.

11 Why won't you help us?
    Use your power to defeat our enemies!
12 God, you have been our King for a long time.
    You helped us win many battles in this country.
13 You used your great power to split open the sea.
14 You defeated the great sea monsters!
    You smashed the heads of Leviathan[a]
    and left his body for the animals to eat.
15 You make the springs and rivers flow,
    and you make the rivers dry up.
16 You control the day and the night.
    You made the sun and the moon.
17 You set the limits for everything on earth.
    And you created summer and winter.
18 LORD, remember, the enemy insulted you!
    Those foolish people hate your name!
19 Don't let those animals take your dove!
    Don't forget your poor people forever.
20 Remember the agreement you gave us!
    There is violence in every dark place in this land.
21 Your people were treated badly.
    Don't let them be hurt any more.
    Your poor, helpless people praise you.
22 God, get up and defend yourself!
    Remember, those fools challenged you!
23 Don't forget the shouts of your enemies.
    They insulted you again and again.

75 To the director.* To the tune "Don't Destroy."
    One of Asaph's songs of praise.
1 We praise you, God!
    We praise you.
    You[b] are near, and people tell about
        the amazing things you do.

2 God says, "I choose the time for judgment.
    I will judge fairly.
3 The earth with all its people may shake,
    but I make it steady."   Selah*
4-5 Some people are very proud.
    They think they are powerful and important.
    But I tell them, 'Don't brag!
    Don't be so proud!'"

---

[a]74:14 great sea monsters ... Leviathan These were creatures from ancient stories. People believed these creatures kept the world from being a safe, orderly place. So this verse means that God controls every part of the world and everything in it.   [b]75:1 You Literally, "Your name."

6 There is no power on earth
    that can make a person important.[a]
7 God is the judge.
    He decides who will be important.
    He lifts one person up and brings another one down.
8 The LORD has a cup in his hand.
    It is filled with the poisoned wine of his anger.
    He will pour out this wine,
    and the wicked will drink it to the last drop.
9 I will always tell people about this.
    I will sing praise to the God of Israel.*
10 He[b] will take power away from the wicked
    and give it to good people.

76

To the director.* With instruments.
One of Asaph's songs of praise.

1 People in Judah* know God.
    People in Israel* respect his name.
2 His Temple* is in Salem.[c]
    His house is on Mount Zion.*
3 There he shattered the bows and arrows,
    the shields, swords, and other weapons of war.   Selah*

4 God, you are glorious coming back
    from the hills where you defeated your enemies.
5 Those soldiers thought they were strong,
    but now they lie dead in the fields.
    Their bodies are stripped of all they owned.
    None of them could defend themselves.[d]
6 The God of Jacob* shouted at those soldiers,
    and that army of chariots* and horses fell dead.
7 God, you are awesome!
    No one can stand against you when you are angry.
8-9 You stood as judge and announced your decision.
    You saved the humble people of the land.
    From heaven you gave the decision.
    The whole earth was silent and afraid.
10 Even human anger can honor you
    when you use it to punish your enemies.[e]

11 People, you made promises to the LORD your God.
    Now, give him what you promised.
    People everywhere fear and respect God,
    and they will bring gifts to him.
12 God defeats great leaders;
    all the kings on earth fear him.

---

[a] 75:6 Literally, "Not from the east or the west and not from the desert mountains."
[b] 75:10 He Or, "I." [c] 76:2 Salem Another name for Jerusalem. This name means "Peace."
[d] 76:5 None ... themselves Literally, "The warriors could not find their hands."
[e] 76:7–10 The Hebrew here is very hard to understand.

77 To the director.* To Jeduthun.
One of Asaph's songs.

1 I cry out to God for help.
I cry out to you, God; listen to me!

2 My Lord, in my time of trouble I came to you.
I reached out for you all night long.
My soul refused to be comforted.

3 I thought about you, God,
and tried to tell you how I felt, but I could not.

4 You would not let me sleep.
I tried to say something, but I was too upset.

5 I kept thinking about the past,
about things that happened long ago.

6 During the night, I tried to think about my songs.
I talked with myself and tried to understand.

7 I wondered, "Has our Lord rejected us forever?
Will he ever accept us again?

8 Is God's love gone forever?
Will he never again speak to us?

9 Has God forgotten what mercy is?
Has his compassion changed to anger?"   *Selah**

10 Then I said to myself,
"What bothers me most is the thought
that God Most High has lost his power."

11 LORD, I remember what you have done;
I remember the amazing things you did long ago.

12 I think about those things.
I think about them all the time.

13 God, your ways are holy.
No god is as great as you are.

14 You are the God who does amazing things.
You showed the nations your great power.

15 By your power you saved your people,
the descendants of Jacob* and Joseph.   *Selah*

16 God, the water saw you and became afraid.
The deep water shook with fear.

17 The thick clouds dropped their water.
People heard loud thunder in the high clouds.
Then your arrows of lightning flashed
through the clouds.

18 There were loud claps of thunder.
Lightning lit up the world.
The earth shook and trembled.

19 You walked through the water and crossed the deep sea,
but you left no footprints.

20 You used Moses* and Aaron* to lead your people
like sheep.

78

*One of Asaph's maskils.**

1 My people, listen to my teachings.
  Listen to what I say.
2 I will tell you a story.
  I will tell you about things from the past
    that are hard to understand.
3 We heard the story, and we know it well.
  Our fathers told this story.
4 And we will not forget it.
  Our people will be telling this story to the last generation.
  We will all praise the LORD
    and tell about the amazing things he did.
5 The Lord made an agreement with Jacob.*
  He gave the law to Israel.*
  He gave the commands to our ancestors.*
  He told our ancestors to teach the law to their children.
6 Then as new children are born and grow to become adults,
    they would tell the stories to their children.
  Then people would know the law,
    even to the last generation.
7 Then they would all trust in God,
    never forgetting what he has done
    and always obeying his commands.
8 Then they would not be like their ancestors,
    who were stubborn and refused to obey God.
  They were people who were not devoted to him.
  Their hearts were not faithful to him.

9 The men from Ephraim had their weapons,
    but they ran from the battle.
10 They didn't keep their agreement with God.
   They refused to obey his teachings.
11 They forgot the great things God did
   and the amazing things he showed them.
12 God showed their fathers his great power at Zoan in Egypt.
13 He split the Red Sea and led the people across.
   The water stood like a solid wall on both sides of them.
14 Each day God led them with the tall cloud,
   and each night he led them with the light
     from the column of fire.
15 He split the rocks in the desert
   and gave them an ocean of fresh water.
16 He brought the water
   streaming from the rock like a river!
17 But they continued sinning against him.
   They rebelled against God Most High in the desert.
18 Then they decided to test God.
   They asked him for food, just to satisfy their appetites.

19 They complained about him,
"Can God give us food in the desert?

20 He hit the rock and a flood of water came out.
But can he give us bread and meat?"

21 The LORD heard what they said
and became angry with Jacob's people.
He was angry with Israel,

22 because the people did not trust in him.
They did not believe God could save them.

23-24 But then God opened the clouds above,
and manna* rained down on them for food.
It was as if doors in the sky opened,
and grain poured down from a storehouse in the sky.

25 People ate the food of angels.
God sent plenty of food to satisfy them.

26-27 He sent a strong wind from the east,
and quail fell on them like rain.
God made the wind blow from Teman.
There were so many birds that they were like sand
on the seashore.

28 The birds fell in the middle of the camp,
all around their tents.

29 They ate until they were full.
God had given them what they wanted.

30 But before they were completely satisfied,
while the food was still in their mouths,

31 God became angry with them
and killed even the strongest of them.
He brought down Israel's best young men.

32 But the people continued to sin!
They didn't trust in the amazing things God could do.

33 So God ended their worthless lives;
he brought their years to a close with disaster.

34 Whenever he killed some of them,
the others would turn back to him.
They would come running back to God.

35 They would remember that God was their Rock.*
They would remember that God Most High
had saved them.

36 But they tried to fool him with their words;
they told him lies.

37 Their hearts were not really with God.
They were not faithful to the agreement he gave them.

38 But God was merciful.
He forgave them for their sins, and he did not destroy them!
Many times God controlled his anger.
He didn't let himself get too angry.

39 He remembered that they were only people,
like a wind that blows and then is gone.

⁴⁰ Oh, those people caused him so much trouble in the desert!
  They made him so sad!
⁴¹ Again and again they tested his patience.
  They really hurt the Holy One of Israel.
⁴² They forgot about his power.
  They forgot the many times that he saved them
    from the enemy.
⁴³ They forgot the miracles in Egypt,
  the miracles in the fields of Zoan.
⁴⁴ God turned the rivers to blood!
  The Egyptians could not drink the water.
⁴⁵ He sent swarms of flies that bit the people of Egypt.
  He sent the frogs that ruined the Egyptians' lives.
⁴⁶ He gave their crops to the grasshoppers
  and their other plants to the locusts.
⁴⁷ He used hail to destroy their vines,
  and he used sleet to destroy their trees.
⁴⁸ He killed their animals with hail
  and their cattle with lightning.
⁴⁹ He showed the Egyptians his anger.
  He sent his destroying angels against them.
⁵⁰ He found a way to show his anger.
  He did not spare their lives.
  He let them die with a deadly disease.
⁵¹ He killed all the firstborn* sons in Egypt.
  He killed every firstborn in Ham's*ᵃ* family.
⁵² Then he led Israel like a shepherd.
  He led his people like sheep into the desert.
⁵³ He guided his people safely,
  so they had nothing to be afraid of.
  He drowned their enemies in the Red Sea.
⁵⁴ He led his people to his holy land,
  to the mountain he took with his power.
⁵⁵ He forced the other nations to leave the land,
  and he gave each family its share.
  He gave each tribe of Israel its home to live in.
⁵⁶ But they tested God Most High and made him very sad.
  They didn't obey his commands.
⁵⁷ They turned away from God.
  They turned against him, as their fathers did.
  They changed directions like a boomerang.*
⁵⁸ They built high places* and made God angry.
  They built statues of false gods and made God very jealous.
⁵⁹ When God heard this, he became very angry,
  and he rejected Israel completely!
⁶⁰ He abandoned the Holy Tent at Shilohᵇ
  where he lived among the people.

ᵃ**78:51** *Ham* The Egyptians were Ham's descendants. See Gen. 10:6–10.   ᵇ**78:60** *Holy Tent at Shiloh* See 1 Sam. 4:10–11; Jer. 7:17.

61 He let foreigners capture his "Power."
    Enemies took God's "beautiful jewel."[a]
62 He showed his anger
    and let them be killed in war.
63 The young men were burned to death,
    and the girls they were to marry sang no wedding songs.
64 The priests were killed,
    but the widows did not cry for them.
65 Finally, our Lord got up
    like a man waking from his sleep,
    like a soldier after drinking too much wine.
66 He forced his enemies to turn back defeated.
    He brought them shame that will last forever.
67 Then the Lord rejected Joseph's family.
    He did not accept Ephraim's family.
68 No, he chose the tribe of Judah*
    and Zion,* the mountain he loves.
69 He built his holy Temple* high on that mountain.
    Like the earth, God built his Temple to last forever.
70 He chose David* to be his special servant.
    He took him away from the sheep pens.
71 He took him away from the job of caring for sheep
    and gave him the job of caring for the descendants
      of Jacob—Israel, his chosen people.
72 And David led them with a pure heart
    and guided them very wisely.

79 *One of Asaph's songs of praise.*

1 God, some people from other nations came
    to fight your people.
    They ruined your holy Temple.*
    They left Jerusalem in ruins.
2 The enemy left the bodies of your servants
    for the wild birds to eat.
    They left the bodies of your followers
    for wild animals to eat.
3 God, the enemy killed your people
    until the blood flowed like water.
    No one is left to bury the dead bodies.
4 The countries around us insult us.
    The people around us laugh at us and make fun of us.
5 Lord, will you be angry with us forever?
    Will your strong feelings[b] continue to burn like a fire?
6 Turn your anger against the nations that do not know you,
    that do not honor you as God.

---

[a]**78:61** *Power ... beautiful jewel* These terms probably refer to the Box of the Agreement. See 1 Sam. 4:1–18. [b]**79:5** *strong feelings* The Hebrew word can mean any strong feelings such as zeal, jealousy, or love.

7 Those nations killed Jacob's* family and destroyed their land.
8 Please don't punish us for the sins of our ancestors.*
  Hurry, show us your mercy!
  We need you so much!
9 Our God and Savior, help us!
  Help us! Save us!
  That will bring glory to your name.
  Erase our sins for the good of your name.
10 Don't let other nations say to us,
   "Where is your God? Can't he help you?"
   Punish those people so we can see it.
   Punish them for killing your servants.
11 Listen to the sad moans of the prisoners!
   Use your great power to free those
     who are sentenced to die.
12 Punish the nations around us!
   Pay them back seven times for what they did to us.
   Punish them for insulting us.
13 We are your people, the sheep of your flock.
   We will praise you forever.
   We will praise you forever and ever!

80 To the director.* To the tune "Lilies of the Agreement."
   One of Asaph's songs of praise.
1 Shepherd of Israel,* listen to us.
  You lead your people, Joseph's descendants, like sheep.
  You sit on your throne above the Cherub angels.*
  Let us see you.
2 Shepherd of Israel, show your greatness
    to the tribes of Ephraim, Benjamin, and Manasseh.
  Come and save your people.
3 God, accept us again.
  Smile down on us and save us!
4 LORD God All-Powerful,
    when will you listen to our prayers?
  How long will you be angry with us?
5 Instead of bread and water,
    you gave your people tears.
6 You made us the target of everyone's hatred.
  Our enemies make fun of us.
7 God All-Powerful, accept us again.
  Smile down on us and save us!

8 When you brought us out of Egypt,
    we were like your special vine.
  You forced other people to leave this land,
    and you planted that vine here.
9 You prepared the ground for it,
    and it sent its roots down deep
    and spread throughout the land.

10 It covered the mountains,
   and its leaves shaded even the giant cedar trees.
11 Its branches spread to the Mediterranean Sea,
   its shoots to the Euphrates River.
12 God, why did you pull down the walls that protect your vine?
   Now everyone who passes by picks its grapes.
13 Wild pigs come and ruin it.
   Wild animals eat the leaves.
14 God All-Powerful, come back.
   Look down from heaven at your vine and protect it.
15 Look at the vine you planted with your own hands.
   Look at the young plant*a* you raised.
16 Our enemies have cut it down and burned it up.
   Show them how angry you are and destroy them.

17 Reach out and help your chosen one.*b*
   Reach out to the people*c* you raised up.
18 Then we will never leave you.
   Let us live, and we will worship you.
19 Lord God All-Powerful, accept us again.
   Smile down on us and save us!

81

To the director,* on the gittith.*
One of Asaph's songs.

1 Be happy and sing to God, our strength.
   Shout with joy to the God of Jacob.*
2 Begin the music.
   Play the tambourines.
   Play the pleasant harps and lyres.*
3 Blow the ram's horn at the time of the new moon.*d*
   Blow the ram's horn at the time of the full moon,*e*
   when our festival begins.
4 This is the law for the people of Israel.*
   The God of Jacob gave the command.
5 God made this agreement with Joseph's people,
   when he led them out of Egypt.
   In a language we didn't understand, God said,
6 "I took the load from your shoulder.
   I let you drop the worker's basket.
7 When you people were in trouble, you called for help
   and I set you free.
   I was hidden in the storm clouds, and I answered you.
   I tested you by the water at Meribah.*f*"   Selah*

---

a80:15 young plant Literally, "son." *b80:17 chosen one* Literally, "the man of your right
hand." *c80:17 people* Literally, "son of man." *d81:3 new moon* The first day of the
Jewish month. There were special meetings on these days when the people shared fellowship
offerings as part of their worship to God. *e81:3 full moon* The middle of the Hebrew month.
Many of the special meetings and festivals started at the time of a full moon. *f81:7 Meribah*
See Ex. 17:1–7.

8 "My people, I am warning you.
Israel, listen to me!

9 Don't worship any of the false gods
that the foreigners worship.

10 I, the LORD, am your God.
I brought you out of Egypt.
Israel, open your mouth, and I will feed you.

11 "But my people did not listen to me.
Israel did not obey me.

12 So I let them go their own stubborn way
and do whatever they wanted.

13 If my people would listen to me
and would live the way I want,

14 then I would defeat their enemies.
I would punish those who cause them trouble.

15 The LORD's enemies would shake with fear.
They would be punished forever.

16 God would give the best wheat to his people.
He would give them the purest honey,
until they were satisfied."[a]

82   One of Asaph's songs of praise.

1 God stands in the assembly of the gods.[b]
He stands as judge among the judges.

2 He says, "How long will you judge unfairly
and show special favors to the wicked?"   *Selah*[*]

3 "Defend the poor and orphans.
Protect the rights of the poor.

4 Help those who are poor and helpless.
Save them from those who are evil.

5 "They[c] don't know what is happening.
They don't understand!
They don't know what they are doing.
Their world is falling down around them!"

6 I, God Most High, say,
"You are gods,[d] my own sons.

7 But you will die like all people must die.
You will die like all other leaders."

---

[a]81:16 Or, "God would give them mounds of wheat and honey from the rock."
[b]82:1 *assembly of the gods* Other nations taught that El (God) and the other gods met together to decide what to do with the gods on earth. But many times kings and leaders were also called "gods." So this psalm may be God's warning to the leaders of Israel.
[c]82:5 *They* This might mean the poor don't know what is happening. Or, it might mean that the "gods" don't understand they are ruining the world by not being fair and by not doing what is right. [d]82:6 *gods* Or, "judges."

8 Get up, God!
  You be the judge!
  You be the leader over all the nations!

83 One of Asaph's songs of praise.

1 God, don't keep quiet!
  Don't close your ears!
  Please say something, God.

2 God, your enemies are getting ready to do something.
  Those who hate you will soon attack.

3 They are making secret plans against your people.
  Your enemies are discussing plans against the people
    you love.

4 They say, "Come, let us destroy them completely.
  Then no one will ever again remember the name Israel.*"

5 God, all those people have joined together.
  They have united against you.

6–7 Their army includes the Edomites, the Ishmaelites,
  the Moabites and Hagar's descendants,
  people from Byblos, Ammon, and Amalek,
  the Philistines, and the people living in Tyre.

8 Even the Assyrians have joined them.
  They have made Lot's descendants very powerful.   Selah*

9 God, defeat them just as you defeated Midian.
  Do what you did to Sisera and Jabin at the Kishon River.

10 You destroyed the enemy at Endor,
  and their bodies rotted on the ground.

11 Punish their leaders as you did Oreb and Zeeb.
  Do what you did to Zebah and Zalmunna.

12 They said, "Let's make this land our own—
  these fields of grass that belong to God!"

13 Make them like tumbleweeds* blown by the wind.
  Scatter them like the wind scatters straw.

14 Be like a fire that destroys a forest
  or like a flame that sets the hills on fire.

15 Chase them away with your blasts of wind;
  frighten them with your storms.

16 LORD, cover them with shame
  until they come to you for help.

17 May they be forever ashamed and afraid.
  Disgrace and defeat them.

18 Then they will know that your name is YAHWEH*—
  that you alone are the LORD.
  They will know that you are God Most High,
  ruler over all the earth!

*83:18 YAHWEH A Hebrew name for God that is usually translated "Lord." It is like the Hebrew
word meaning "He is" or "He makes things exist."

84

To the director, *on the gittith.* *
A song of praise from the Korah family.

1 LORD All-Powerful, your Temple[a] is really lovely!

2 LORD, I cannot wait to enter your Temple.*
  I am so excited!
  Every part of me cries out to be with the Living God.

3 LORD All-Powerful, my King, my God,
  even the birds have found a home in your Temple.
  They make their nests near your altar,
  and there they have their babies.

4 People living at your Temple are very fortunate.
  They continue to praise you.   *Selah**

5 People coming to the Temple with songs in their heart
  are very happy!
  They know where they are going.

6 They travel through Baca Valley,
  which God has made like a spring.
  Autumn rains form pools of water.[b]

7 The people travel from town to town[c]
  on their way to Zion,* where they will meet with God.

8 LORD God All-Powerful, listen to my prayer.
  God of Jacob,* listen to me.   *Selah*

9 God, protect our protector.[d]
  Be kind to your chosen king.[e]

10 One day in your Temple is better
  than a thousand days in any other place.
  Serving as a guard at the gate of my God's house
  is better than living in the homes of the wicked.

11 The LORD is our protector and glorious king.[f]
  God blesses us with kindness and glory.
  The LORD gives every good thing
  to those who follow and obey him.

12 LORD All-Powerful, those who trust in you are really blessed!

85

To the director. *
A song of praise from the Korah family.

1 LORD, you have been so kind to your land.
  You have brought success again to the people of Jacob.*

2 You have forgiven the bad things your people did;
  you have taken away the guilt of their sins!   *Selah**

---

a **84:1** *Temple* Or, "dwellings."   *b* **84:6** *Autumn rains ... water* Or, "The Teacher gives blessings." This might be a different way to say that God is our teacher and that he gives us many blessings.   *c* **84:7** *town to town* Or, "wall to wall."   *d* **84:9** *protector* Literally, "shield." This probably means the king. This might also be "God, our Shield, look!"   *e* **84:9** *chosen king* Literally, "anointed person."   *f* **84:11** *protector and glorious king* Literally, "sun and shield."

3 You stopped being angry with them.
   Your terrible anger has gone away.
4 Our God and Savior, accept us again.
   Don't be angry with us anymore.
5 Will you be angry with us forever?
   Will your anger reach to our children
     and to their children?
6 Please, give us new life!
   Make your people happy to be yours.

7 LORD, save us and show us your love.
8 I heard what the LORD God said.
   He said there would be peace for his people
     and his loyal followers.
   So they must not go back
     to their foolish way of living.
9 God will soon save his followers.
   We will soon live with honor on our land.[a]
10 God's faithful love will meet his followers.
   Goodness and peace will greet them with a kiss.
11 People on earth will be loyal to God,
   and God in heaven will be good to them.[b]
12 The LORD will give us many good things.
   The ground will grow many good crops.
13 Goodness will go in front of God
   and prepare the way for him.

86 *A prayer of David.*

1 I am a poor, helpless man.
   LORD, please listen to me and answer my prayer.
2 I am your follower, please protect me!
   I am your servant, and you are my God.
   I trust in you, so save me.
3 My Lord, be kind to me.
   I have been praying to you all day.
4 My Lord, I put my life in your hands.
   I am your servant, so make me happy.
5 My Lord, you are good and merciful.
   You love all those who call to you for help.
6 LORD, hear my prayer.
   Listen to my cry for mercy.
7 I am praying to you in my time of trouble.
   I know you will answer me!
8 My Lord, there is no God like you.
   No one can do what you have done.

---

[a]85:9 *We ... land* Or, "His glory will live in our land." [b]85:11 Literally, "Loyalty will sprout from the ground. And goodness will look down from the sky."

9 My Lord, you made everyone.
     I wish they all would come worship you
         and honor your name.
10 You are great and do amazing things!
     You and you alone are God!
11 LORD, teach me your ways,
     and I will live and obey your truths.
     Help me make worshiping your name
         the most important thing in my life.
12 My Lord God, I praise you with all my heart.
     I will honor your name forever!
13 You have such great love for me.
     You save me from the place of death.
14 Proud people are attacking me, God.
     A gang of cruel men is trying to kill me.
     They don't respect you.
15 My Lord, you are a kind and merciful God.
     You are patient, loyal, and full of love.
16 Show that you hear me and be kind to me.
     I am your servant. Give me strength.
     I am your servant. Save me!
17 LORD, give me a sign to show
     that you will help me.
My enemies will see the sign,
     and they will be disappointed.
This will show that you heard my prayer
     and that you will help me.

87 *A song of praise from the Korah family.*

1 The LORD built his city on the holy hills.
2   He loves the gates of Zion*
         more than any other place in Israel.*
3 Wonderful things are said about you, City of God.   *Selah**

4 God says, "Some of my people live in Egypt*a* and Babylon.
     Some of them were born in Philistia, Tyre,
         and even Ethiopia."
5 But about Zion, he says,
     "I know each and every person who was born there."
God Most High is the one who built that city.
6 The LORD keeps a list of all his people,
     and he knows where each of them was born.   *Selah*

7 At the festivals, people will dance and sing,
     "All good things come from Jerusalem."

*a***87:4** *Egypt* Literally, "Rahab." This names means the "Dragon." It became a popular name for Egypt.

88 *A song from the Korah family. To the director.*
About a painful sickness. A maskil from Heman the Ezrahite.*

1 LORD God, you are my Savior.
    I have been praying to you day and night.

2 Please pay attention to my prayers.
    Listen to my prayers for mercy.

3 My soul has had enough of this pain!
    I am ready to die.

4 People already treat me like a dead man,
    like someone too weak to live.

5 Look for me among the dead,
    like a body in the grave.
  I am one of those you have forgotten,
    cut off from you and your care.

6 You put me in that hole in the ground.
    Yes, you put me in that dark place.

7 You were angry with me, and you punished me.

                                        *Selah**

8 You made my friends leave me.
    They all avoid me like someone
      no one wants to touch.
  Like a prisoner in my house, I cannot go out.

9 My eyes hurt from crying about all my suffering.
  LORD, I pray to you constantly!
    I lift my arms in prayer to you.

10 Do you do miracles for the dead?
    Do ghosts rise up and praise you? No!   *Selah*

11 The dead in their graves
      cannot talk about your faithful love.
  People in the world of the dead
      cannot talk about your faithfulness.

12 The dead who lie in darkness cannot see
      the amazing things you do.
    Those in the world of the forgotten cannot talk
      about your goodness.

13 LORD, I am asking you to help me!
    Early each morning I pray to you.

14 LORD, why have you abandoned me?
    Why do you refuse to listen to me?

15 I have been sick and weak since I was young.
    I have suffered your anger; I am helpless.

16 You have been angry with me,
      and your anger is killing me.

17 The aches and pains are always with me.
    I feel like I am drowning in them.

18 You caused my friends and loved ones to leave me.
    Now darkness is my closest friend.

89 A maskil* from Ethan the Ezrahite.

¹ I will sing forever about the LORD's love.
   I will sing about his faithfulness forever and ever!

² I will say, "Your love continues forever.
   Your loyalty is like the sky—there is no end to it!"

³ You said, "I made an agreement with my chosen king.
   I made this promise to my servant David*:

⁴ 'There will always be someone from your family to rule.
   I will make your kingdom continue forever and ever.'"

*Selah**

⁵ LORD, the heavens praise you for the amazing things you do.
   The assembly of holy ones sings about your loyalty.

⁶ No one in heaven is equal to the LORD.
   None of the "gods" can compare to the LORD.

⁷ When God's holy ones meet together—
      those angels who surround his throne—
   they fear and respect God; they stand in awe of him.

⁸ LORD God All-Powerful, there is no one like you.
   You are strong, LORD, and always faithful.

⁹ You rule the stormy sea.
   You can calm its angry waves.

¹⁰ God, you defeated Rahab.*
   You scattered your enemies with your own powerful arm.

¹¹ Everything in heaven and earth belongs to you, God.
   You made the world and everything in it.

¹² You created everything north and south.
      Mount Tabor and Mount Hermon sing praises
         to your name.

¹³ You have the power!
   Your power is great!
   The victory is yours!

¹⁴ Your kingdom is built on truth and justice.
   Love and faithfulness are servants before your throne.

¹⁵ LORD, your loyal followers are happy.
   They live in the light of your kindness.

¹⁶ Your name always makes them happy.
   They praise your goodness.

¹⁷ You are their amazing strength.
   Their power comes from you.

¹⁸ The king, our protector, belongs to the LORD,
   who is the Holy One of Israel.*

¹⁹ Lord, you once spoke in a vision to your followers:
   "I have chosen a young man from the crowd
      and have made him important.
   I made that young soldier strong.

²⁰ I have found my servant David
   and anointed* him as king with my special oil.

²¹ I will support him with my right hand,
   and my arm will make him strong.
²² So no enemy will ever control him.
   The wicked will never defeat him.
²³ I will destroy his enemies before his eyes.
   I will defeat those who hate him.
²⁴ I will always love and support him.
   I will always make him strong.
²⁵ I will put him in charge of the sea.
   He will control the rivers.
²⁶ He will say to me, 'You are my father.
   You are my God, my Rock,* my Savior.'
²⁷ And I will make him my firstborn* son.
   He will be the great king on earth.
²⁸ My love will protect him forever.
   My agreement with him will never end.
²⁹ I will make his family continue forever.
   His kingdom will continue as long as the skies.
³⁰ If his descendants stop following my law
   and stop obeying my commands, then I will punish them.
³¹ If his descendants break my laws and ignore my commands,
³² then I will punish them severely for their sins and wrongs.
³³ But I will never take my love from him.
   I will never stop being loyal to him.
³⁴ I will not break my agreement with David.*
   I will never change what I said.
³⁵ By my holiness, I made a promise to him,
   and I would not lie to David!
³⁶ His family will continue forever.
   His kingdom will last as long as the sun.
³⁷ It will continue forever, like the moon.
   The sky is a witness to the agreement that can be trusted."
                                                          Selah

³⁸ But, God, you became angry with your chosen king,ᵃ
   and you left him all alone.
³⁹ You rejected your agreement.
   You threw the king's crown into the dirt.
⁴⁰ You pulled down the walls of the king's city.
   You destroyed all his fortresses.*
⁴¹ Everyone passing by steals from him.
   His neighbors laugh at him.
⁴² You made all the king's enemies happy
   and let his enemies win the war.
⁴³ You helped them defend themselves.
   You did not help your king win the battle.

ᵃ **89:38 chosen king** Literally, "anointed one."

44 You did not let him win.
   You threw his throne to the ground.
45 You cut his life short.
   You shamed him.   *Selah*

46 LORD, how long will this continue?
   Will you ignore us forever?
   Will your anger burn like a fire forever?
47 Remember how short my life is.
   You created us to live a short life and then die.
48 Is there anyone alive who will never die?
   Will anyone escape the grave?   *Selah*

49 God, where is the love you showed in the past?
   You promised David that you would be loyal to his family.
50–51 My Lord, please remember how people
       insulted your servant.
   LORD, I had to listen to all the insults from your enemies.
   They insulted your chosen king wherever he went.

52 Praise the LORD forever!
   Amen* and Amen!

BOOK 4 *(Psalms 90–106)*

90 The prayer of Moses,* the man of God.*

1 My Lord, you have been our home forever and ever.
2 You were God before the mountains were born
   and the earth and the world were made.
   God, you have always been and will always be God!

3 You bring people into this world,
   and you change them into dust again.
4 To you, a thousand years is like yesterday,
   like a few hours in the night that passed by in your sleep.
5 Our life is like a dream that ends when morning comes.
   We are like grass
6   that grows and looks so fresh in the morning,
        but in the evening it is dry and dying.
7 Your anger could destroy us.
   Your anger scares us!
8 You know about all our sins.
   You see every one of our secret sins.
9 Your anger can end our life.
   Our lives fade away like a whisper.
10 We live about 70 years, or if we are strong, maybe 80 years.
   But most of them are filled with hard work and pain.
   Then, suddenly, the years are gone, and we fly away.
11 No one really knows the full power of your anger,
   but our fear and respect for you is as great as your anger.

¹² Teach us how short our lives are
   so that we can become wise.
¹³ LORD, come back to us.
   Be kind to your servants.
¹⁴ Fill us with your love every morning.
   Let us be happy and enjoy our lives.
¹⁵ For years you have made life hard for us
   and have given us many troubles.
   Now make us happy for just as long.
¹⁶ Let your servants see the wonderful things
       you can do for them.
   And let their children see your glory.*
¹⁷ Lord, our God, be kind to us.
   Make everything we do successful.
   Yes, make it all successful.

91 ¹You can go to God Most High to hide.
       You can go to God All-Powerful for protection.
² I say to the LORD,
   "You are my place of safety, my fortress.*
   My God, I trust in you."
³ God will save you from hidden dangers
   and dangerous diseases.
⁴ You can go to God for protection.
   He will cover you like a bird spreading its wings
       over its babies.
   You can trust him to surround and protect you
       like a shield.
⁵ You will have nothing to fear at night
   and no need to be afraid of enemy arrows during the day.
⁶ You will have no fear of diseases that come in the dark
   or terrible suffering that comes at noon.
⁷ A thousand people may fall dead at your side
   or ten thousand right beside you,
   but nothing bad will happen to you!
⁸ All you will have to do is watch,
   and you will see that the wicked are punished!
⁹ You trust in the LORD for protection.
   You have made God Most High your place of safety.
¹⁰ So nothing bad will happen to you.
   No diseases will come near your home.
¹¹ God will command his angels to protect you
   wherever you go.
¹² Their hands will catch you
   so that you will not hit your foot on a rock.
¹³ You will have power to trample on lions
   and poisonous snakes.
¹⁴ The LORD says, "If someone trusts me, I will save them.
   I will protect my followers who call to me for help.

15 When my followers call to me, I will answer them.
   I will be with them when they have trouble.
   I will rescue them and honor them.
16 I will give my followers a long life
   and show them my power to save."

92 A song of praise for the Sabbath.*

1 It is good to praise the LORD.
   God Most High, it is good to praise your name.
2 It is good to sing about your love in the morning
   and about your faithfulness at night.
3 God, it is good to play music for you
   on ten-stringed instruments, harps, and lyres.*
4 LORD, you make us very happy because of what you did.
   I gladly sing about it.
5 LORD, you did such great things.
   Your thoughts are too hard for us to understand.
6 Stupid people don't know this.
   Fools don't understand.
7 The wicked may sprout like grass,
   and those who do evil may blossom like flowers,
   but they will be destroyed, never to be seen again.
8 But, LORD, you will be honored forever.
9 LORD, all your enemies will be destroyed,
   and all who do evil will be scattered.
10 But you have made me strong, like the horns of an ox.
   You have poured your fresh oil over me.
11 But still, I see my enemies around me, ready to attack.
   Yes, I hear them.

12 Good people are like budding palm trees.
   They grow strong like the cedar trees of Lebanon.
13 They are planted in the LORD's house.^{a}
   They grow strong there in the courtyards of our God.
14 Even when they are old,
   they will continue producing fruit like young, healthy trees.
15 They are there to show everyone that the LORD is good.^{b}
   He is my Rock,* and he does nothing wrong.^{c}

93 1The LORD is King.
   The LORD wears majesty and strength like clothes.
   He is ready, so the whole world is safe.
   It will not be shaken.
2 Your kingdom has continued forever.
   You have lived forever!

---

^{a}92:13 house Or, "Temple." See "Temple" in the Word List. ^{b}92:15 good This is a
wordplay. The Hebrew word means "straight" (like the trees) and "good," or "honest."
^{c}92:15 he … wrong Or, "there is no crookedness in him."

3 LORD, the sound of the rivers is very loud.
    The crashing waves are very loud.
4 The crashing waves of the sea are loud and powerful,
    but the LORD above is even more powerful.
5 LORD, your laws will continue forever.[a]
    Your holy Temple* will stand for a long time.

94

1 The LORD is a God who punishes people.
    God, come punish them.
2 You are the judge of the whole earth.
    Give proud people the punishment they deserve.
3 LORD, how long will the wicked have their fun?
    How much longer?
4 How much longer will those criminals
    brag about the evil they did?
5 LORD, they hurt your people and make them suffer.
6 They kill widows and foreigners living in our country.
    They murder orphans.
7 And they say the LORD does not see them
    doing those evil things!
    They say the God of Israel*
    does not know what is happening.

8 You evil people are foolish.
    When will you learn your lesson?
    You are so stupid!
    You must try to understand.
9 God made our ears,
    so surely he can hear what is happening!
    He made our eyes,
    so surely he can see what is happening!
10 God disciplines nations, so surely he will correct people.
    He is the one who teaches us everything.
11 He knows what people are thinking.
    He knows that their thoughts are like a puff of wind.
12 Whoever the LORD disciplines will receive many blessings.
    He will teach them the right way of living.
13 God, you will help them stay calm when trouble comes.
    You will help them stay calm until evil people
    are put in their grave.
14 The LORD will not leave his people.
    He will not leave them without help.
15 Justice will return, and it will bring fairness.
    And then there will be good, honest people.

16 No one helped me fight against the evil people.
    No one stood with me to fight against those
    who do bad things.

---

a 93:5 *your laws will continue forever* Or, "your agreement can really be trusted."

¹⁷ And if the Lord had not helped me,
    I would have been silenced by death.
¹⁸ I know I was ready to fall,
    but the Lord's faithful love supported me.
¹⁹ I was very worried and upset,
    but you comforted me and made me happy!

²⁰ God, you don't help crooked judges.
    They use the law to make life hard for the people.
²¹ They attack good people.
    They say that innocent people are guilty
    and put them to death.
²² But the Lord is my place of safety,
    high on the mountain.
    God, my Rock,* is my safe place!
²³ He will punish those evil judges for the bad things they did.
    He will destroy them because they sinned.
    The Lord our God will destroy them.

95

¹ Come, let us praise the Lord!
    Let us shout praises to the Rock,* who saves us.
² Let us go to worship the Lord.
    Let us approach him with songs of thanks.^a
    Let us sing happy songs of praise to him.
³ For the Lord is a great God,
    the great King ruling over all the other "gods."
⁴ The deepest caves and the highest mountains belong to him.
⁵ The ocean is his—he created it.
    He made the dry land with his own hands.
⁶ Come, let us bow down and worship him!
    Let us praise the God who made us!
⁷ He is our God, and we are his people.
    We are his sheep—those who walk by his side—
    if we listen to his voice today.

⁸ God says, "Don't be stubborn, as you were at Meribah,
    as you were at Massah^b in the desert.
⁹ Your ancestors* tested me.
    They tested me, but then they saw what I could do!
¹⁰ I was patient with them for 40 years,
    and I know that they are not faithful.
    They refused to follow my teachings.
¹¹ So I was angry, and I swore that
    they would not enter my land of rest."

96

¹ Sing a new song about the new things the Lord
    has done!
    Let the whole world sing to the Lord.

^a**95:2** *songs of thanks* Or, "thank offerings."   ^b**95:8** *Meribah … Massah* See Ex. 17:1–7.

2 Sing to the Lord and bless his name!
    Tell the good news!
    Tell about him saving us every day!
3 Tell people that God is wonderful!
    Tell people everywhere about the amazing things God does.
4 The Lord is great and worthy of praise.
    He is more awesome than any of the "gods."
5 All the "gods" in other nations are nothing but statues,
    but the Lord made the heavens.
6 There is a beautiful glory* shining in front of him.
    There is strength and beauty in God's holy Temple.*
7 Families and nations, sing songs of praise and glory
        to the Lord.
8 Praise the Lord's name.
    Get your offerings, and bring them into his courtyard.
9 Worship the Lord in his beautiful Temple.
    Worship him, every person on earth.
10 Announce to the nations that the Lord is King!
    The world stands firm and will not be destroyed.
    He will rule the people fairly.
11 Be happy, heavens! Rejoice, earth!
    Sea and everything in it, shout with joy!
12 Fields and everything growing in them, be happy!
    Trees in the forest, sing and be happy!
13 Be happy because the Lord is coming!
    He is coming to rule[a] the world.
    He will rule the world with justice and fairness.

97 1 The Lord rules, and the earth is happy.
        All the faraway lands are happy.
2 Thick, dark clouds surround the Lord.
    Goodness and justice make his kingdom strong.
3 A fire goes in front of the Lord
    and destroys his enemies.
4 His lightning flashes in the sky.
    The people see it and are afraid.
5 The mountains melt like wax before the Lord,
    before the Lord of the earth.
6 The skies tell about his goodness,
    and the people see God's glory.*
7 People worship their idols.
    They brag about their "gods."
    But they will be embarrassed.
    And all their "gods" will bow down before the Lord.
8 Zion,* listen and be happy!
    Cities of Judah,* be happy!
    Why? Because the Lord makes wise decisions.

a **96:13** *rule* Or, "judge." Also in 98:9.

9 Lord Most High, you really are the ruler of the earth.
   You are much better than the "gods."
10 Hate evil, you who love the Lord.
   He protects his followers and saves them from evil people.
11 Light and happiness shine on those who are good.
12 Good people, be happy in the Lord!
   Praise his holy name!

98

A song of praise.

1 Sing a new song to the Lord,
   because he has done amazing things!
   His powerful and holy right arm[a]
   has brought him another victory.
2 The Lord showed the nations his power to save.
   He showed them his goodness.
3 God's loyal follower told the people of Israel*
   about God's loyalty.
   The people in faraway lands saw
   our God's power to save.
4 Everyone on earth, shout with joy to the Lord.
   Start singing happy songs of praise!
5 Harps, praise the Lord.
   Music from the harps, praise him.
6 Blow the pipes and horns,
   and shout for joy to the Lord our King!
7 Let the sea and the earth
   and everything in them shout his praise!
8 Rivers, clap your hands!
   All together now, mountains sing out!
9 Sing before the Lord
   because he is coming to rule the world.
   He will rule the world fairly.
   He will rule the people with goodness.

99

1 The Lord is King,
   so let the nations shake with fear.
   God sits as King above the Cherub angels,*
   so let the world shake with fear.
2 The Lord in Zion* is great!
   He is the great leader over all people.
3 Let all the nations praise your name.
   Your name is great and awesome.
   Your name is holy.

---

[a]98:1 **holy right arm** This pictures God as a warrior-king. The right arm symbolizes his power and authority. "Holy" may refer to the special cleansing and dedication that Israelites performed before going into battle.

4 The powerful King loves justice.
    God, you made goodness.
    You brought goodness and fairness to Jacob.*

5 Praise the LORD our God,
    and bow down before his footstool,*ᵃ for he is holy.

6 Moses* and Aaron* were some of his priests,
    and Samuel was one of the men who called on his name.
They prayed to the LORD,
    and he answered them.

7 God spoke from the tall cloud,
    and they obeyed his commands and the law he gave them.

8 LORD our God, you answered their prayers.
    You showed them that you are a forgiving God
    and that you punish people for the evil they do.

9 Praise the LORD our God.
    Bow down toward his holy mountain and worship him.
    The LORD our God is holy!

100 *A song of thanks.*

1 Earth, sing to the LORD!

2 Be happy as you serve the LORD!
    Come before him with happy songs!

3 Know that the LORD is God.
    He made us, and we belong to him.
    We are his people; we are the sheep he takes care of.

4 Come through the gates with songs of thanks.
    Come into his temple with songs of praise.
    Honor him and bless his name.

5 The LORD is good!
    There is no end to his faithful love.
    We can trust him forever and ever!

101 *A song of David.**

1 I will sing about love and justice.
    LORD, I will sing to you.

2 I will be careful to live a pure life.
    I will live in my house with complete honesty.
    When will you come to me?

3 I will not even look at anything shameful.*ᵇ
    I hate all wrongdoing.
    I want no part of it!

4 I will not be involved in anything dishonest.
    I will have nothing to do with evil.

---

*ᵃ***99:5** *footstool* This probably means the Temple.   *ᵇ***101:3** *anything shameful* Or, "an idol."

5 I will stop anyone who secretly
    says bad things about a neighbor.
  I will not allow people to be proud
    and think they are better than others.

6 I will look throughout the land for those who can be trusted.
    Only such people can live with me.
    Only those who live pure lives can be my servants.
7 I will not let a dishonest person live in my house.
    I will not let liars stay near me.
8 I will always destroy bad people living in this country.
    I will force those who are evil to leave the LORD's city.

102

A prayer for a time of suffering, when anyone feels weak and wants to tell their complaints to the LORD.

1 LORD, hear my prayer.
    Listen to my cry for help.
2 Don't turn away from me when I have troubles.
    Listen to me, and answer me quickly
      when I cry for help.
3 My life is passing away like smoke.
    My life is like a fire slowly burning out.
4 My strength is gone—
    I am like dry, dying grass.
    I even forget to eat.
5 Because of my sadness, I am losing so much weight
    that my skin hangs from my bones.
6 I am lonely, like an owl living in the desert.
    I am alone, like an owl living among old ruined buildings.
7 I cannot sleep.
    I am like a lonely bird on the roof.
8 My enemies insult me all the time.
    They make fun of me and use me as an example
      in their curses.*
9 My great sadness is my only food.
    My tears fall into my drink.
10 You were angry with me,
    so you picked me up and threw me away.

11 My life is almost finished,
    like the long shadows at the end of the day.
  I am like dry and dying grass.
12 But you, LORD, will rule as king forever!
    Your name will continue forever and ever!
13 You will rise up and comfort Zion.*
    The time has come for you to be kind to Zion.
14 Your servants love her stones.
    They love even the dust of that city!
15 The nations will worship the LORD's name.
    All the kings on earth will honor you.

16 The LORD will rebuild Zion,
     and people will again see her glory.*

17 He will listen to the prayers of those in poverty.
     He will not ignore them.

18 Write these things for future generations,
     so that they will praise the LORD.

19 The LORD will look down from his Holy Place* above.
     He will look down at the earth from heaven.

20 And he will hear the prisoner's prayers.
     He will free those who were condemned to die.

21 Then people in Zion will tell about the LORD.
     They will praise his name in Jerusalem

22 when nations gather together,
     and kingdoms come to serve the LORD.

23 My strength failed me.
     My life is cut short.

24 So I said, "Don't let me die while I am still young.
     God, you will live forever and ever!

25 Long ago, you made the world.
     You made the sky with your own hands!

26 The earth and sky will end,
     but you will live forever!
   They will wear out like clothes,
     and like clothes, you will change them.
   They will all be changed,

27 but you never change.
   You will live forever!

28 We are your servants today.
   Our children will live here,
     and their descendants will come here to worship you."

103 *A song of David.**

1 My soul, praise the LORD!
     Every part of me, praise his holy name!

2 My soul, praise the LORD
     and never forget how kind he is!

3 He forgives all our sins
     and heals all our sicknesses.

4 He saves us from the grave,
     and he gives us love and compassion.

5 He gives us plenty of good things.
     He makes us young again,
       like an eagle that grows new feathers.

6 The LORD is fair.
     He brings justice to those who have been hurt by others.

7 He taught his laws to Moses.*
     He let Israel* see the powerful things he can do.

⁸ The Lᴏʀᴅ is kind and merciful.
    He is patient and full of love.
⁹ He does not always criticize.
    He does not stay angry with us forever.
¹⁰ We sinned against him,
    but he didn't give us the punishment we deserved.
¹¹ His love for his followers is as high above us
    as heaven is above the earth.
¹² And he has taken our sins as far away from us
    as the east is from the west.
¹³ The Lᴏʀᴅ is as kind to his followers
    as a father is to his children.
¹⁴ He knows all about us.
    He knows we are made from dust.
¹⁵ He knows our lives are short.
    He knows our lives are like grass.
    He knows we are like a little wildflower
        that grows so quickly,
¹⁶ but when the hot wind blows, the flower dies.
    Soon, you cannot even see where the flower was.
¹⁷ But the Lᴏʀᴅ has always loved his followers,
    and he will continue to love them forever and ever!
    He will be good to their children
    and to their children's children.
¹⁸ God is good to those who obey his agreement.
    He is good to those who obey his commands.
¹⁹ The Lᴏʀᴅ set his throne up in heaven,
    and he rules over everything.
²⁰ Angels, praise the Lᴏʀᴅ!
    You angels are the powerful soldiers
        who obey his commands.
    You listen to him and obey his commands.
²¹ Praise the Lᴏʀᴅ, all his armies.*ᵃ*
    You are his servants, and you do what he wants.
²² Everything in every place was made and governed by him.
    Let everything praise the Lᴏʀᴅ!
    My soul, praise the Lᴏʀᴅ!

104

¹ My soul, praise the Lᴏʀᴅ!
Lᴏʀᴅ my God, you are very great!
You are clothed with glory* and honor.
² You wear light like a person wears a robe.
    You spread the skies like a curtain.

---

*ᵃ*103:21 *armies* This word can mean "armies," "angels," or the "stars and planets." This word is part of the name translated "Lᴏʀᴅ All-Powerful." It shows that God is in control of all the powers in the universe.

3 You built your home above them.*a*
    You use the thick clouds like a chariot*
    and ride across the sky on the wings of the wind.
4 You make the winds your messengers
    and flames of fire your servants.*b*
5 You built the earth on its foundations,
    so it can never be moved.
6 You covered it with water like a blanket.
    The water covered even the mountains.
7 But you gave the command, and the water turned back.
    You shouted at the water, and it rushed away.
8 The water flowed down from the mountains into the valleys,
    to the places that you made for it.
9 You set the limits for the seas,
    and the water will never again rise to cover the earth.

10 Lord, you cause water to flow from springs into streams
    that flow down between the mountains.
11 The streams provide water for all the wild animals.
    Even the wild donkeys come there to drink.
12 Wild birds come to live by the pools;
    they sing in the branches of nearby trees.
13 God sends rain down onto the mountains.
    The earth gets everything it needs from what he has made.
14 He makes the grass grow to feed the animals.
    He provides the plants for us to grow—
        the plants that give us food from the earth.
15 He gives us the wine that makes us happy,
    the oil that makes our skin soft,*c*
    and the food that makes us strong.
16 The great cedar trees of Lebanon belong to the LORD.
    He planted them and gives them the water they need.
17 That's where the birds make their nests.
    And storks live in the fir trees.
18 The high mountains are a home for wild goats.
    The large rocks are hiding places for rock badgers.

19 God, you made the moon to show us
        when the festivals begin.
    And the sun always knows when to set.
20 You made darkness to be the night—
    the time when wild animals come out and roam around.
21 Lions roar as they attack,
    as if they are asking God for the food he gives them.

---

*a***104:3** *above them* Literally, "on the water above." This is like the picture of the world in Gen.
1. There the sky was like a bowl turned upside down on the earth. There was water below the
bowl and water above it.   *b***104:4** Or, "You make your angels spirits and your servants flames
of fire." This may be a wordplay referring to the Cherub and Seraph angels.   *c***104:15** *makes
our skin soft* Literally, "makes our face shine." This can also mean "makes us happy."

²² Then the sun rises, and the animals leave.
    They go back to their homes and rest.
²³ Then people go out to do their work,
    and they work until evening.

²⁴ LORD, you created many wonderful things.
    You used wisdom to make them all.
    The earth is filled with things you made.
²⁵ Look at the ocean. It is so big!
    So many things live there!
    There are creatures large and small—too many to count!
²⁶ Ships travel over the ocean
    while Leviathan,^a the sea creature you made,
      plays there in the sea.

²⁷ God, all these things depend on you.
    You give them food at the right time.
²⁸ You give all the living things
    the food they eat.
You open your hands that are filled with good food,
    and they eat until they are full.
²⁹ When you turn away from them,
    they become frightened.
When you take away their breath,^b
    they die, and their bodies return to the dust.
³⁰ But when you send out your life-giving breath,^c
    things come alive, and the world is like new again!

³¹ May the LORD's glory continue forever!
    May the LORD enjoy what he made.
³² He can just look at the earth,
    and it will tremble.
He can just touch the mountains,
    and smoke will rise from them.

³³ I will sing to the LORD for the rest of my life.
    I will sing praises to my God as long as I live.
³⁴ May my words make him happy.
    I am happy with the LORD.
³⁵ I wish sinners would disappear from the earth.
    I wish the wicked would be gone forever.
My soul, praise the LORD!

Praise the LORD!

105 ¹Thank the LORD.
    Call out his name.
    Tell the nations what he has done.

---

^a**104:26** *Leviathan* This might mean any large sea animal, like a whale. But it probably means "the sea monster," the "Dragon," or "Rahab." This creature represents the great power of the ocean, the power that God controls. ^b**104:29** *breath* Or, "spirit." ^c**104:30** *life-giving breath* Or, "Spirit."

2 Sing to the Lord; sing praises to him.
   Tell about the amazing things he has done.
3 Be proud of his holy name.
   You people who came looking for the Lord, be happy!
4 Go to the Lord for strength.
   Always go to him for help.
5 Remember the amazing things he does.
   Remember his miracles and wise decisions.
6 You are descendants of his servant Abraham.*
   You are descendants of Jacob,* the one God chose.*a*
7 The Lord is our God.
   He rules the whole world.*b*
8 He will remember his agreement forever.
   He will keep his word to his people
      for a thousand generations!
9 He will keep the agreement he made with Abraham,
   the promise he made to Isaac.*
10 He gave it as a law to Jacob.
   He gave it to Israel* as an agreement that will last forever!
11 He said, "I will give you the land of Canaan.
   That land will belong to you."
12 He made that promise when Abraham's family was small.
   They were only strangers there.
13 They traveled from nation to nation,
   from one kingdom to another.
14 But the Lord did not let people mistreat them.
   He warned kings not to hurt them.
15 He said, "Don't hurt my chosen people.
   Don't harm my prophets.*"
16 He caused a famine* in that country.
   People did not have enough food to eat.
17 But he sent a man named Joseph to go ahead of them.
   Joseph was sold like a slave.
18 They tied a rope around Joseph's feet
   and put an iron ring around his neck.
19 Joseph was a slave until what he said really happened.
   The Lord's message proved that Joseph was right.
20 So the king of Egypt set him free.
   That nation's leader let him out of jail.
21 He put Joseph in charge of his house.
   Joseph took care of everything he owned.
22 Joseph gave instructions to the other leaders.
   He taught the older men.
23 Then Israel came to Egypt.
   Jacob lived in Ham's country.*c*

a105:6 *the one God chose* Or, "the people God chose." *b105:7* *The Lord rules the whole world* Literally, "The Lord's commands are in the whole earth." *c105:23* *Ham's country* Or, "Egypt." The Bible teaches that the Egyptians were descendants of Ham. See Gen. 10:6–20. Also in verse 27.

24 Jacob's family became very large
    and more powerful than their enemies.
25 So the Egyptians began to hate his people.
    They made plans against his servants.
26 So the Lord sent Moses,* his servant,
    and Aaron,* his chosen priest.
27 He used Moses and Aaron
    to do many miracles in Ham's country.
28 He sent deep darkness,
    but the Egyptians did not listen to him.
29 So he changed the water into blood,
    and all their fish died.
30 Their country was filled with frogs.
    Frogs were even in the king's bedroom.
31 The Lord gave the command,
    and the flies and gnats came.
    They were everywhere!
32 He made the rain become hail.
    Lightning struck throughout their country.
33 He destroyed their vines and fig trees.
    He destroyed every tree in their country.
34 He gave the command,
    and the locusts and grasshoppers came.
    There were too many to count!
35 They ate all the plants in the country
    and all the crops in the fields.
36 Then the Lord killed every firstborn* in their country.
    He killed their oldest sons.
37 He led his people out of Egypt,
    carrying all their gold and silver.
    None of his people stumbled and fell.
38 Egypt was happy to see his people go,
    because they were afraid of them.
39 The Lord spread out his cloud like a blanket.
    He used his column of fire to give his people light at night.
40 They asked for food, and he sent them quail.
    He also gave them plenty of bread from heaven.
41 He split the rock, and water came bubbling out.
    A river began flowing in the desert!

42 The Lord remembered his holy promise
    that he had made to his servant Abraham.
43 He brought his people out of Egypt.
    They came out rejoicing and singing their happy songs!
44 Then he gave his people the lands of other nations.
    His people got what others had worked for.
45 He did this so that his people would obey his laws
    and follow his teachings.

    Praise the LORD!

106 ¹Praise the LORD!

Thank the LORD because he is good!
His love is forever!

² No one can describe how great the LORD really is.
No one can praise him enough.

³ Those who obey his commands are happy.
They do good things all the time.

⁴ LORD, remember me when you show kindness
to your people.
Remember to save me too!

⁵ Let me share in the good things
that you do for your chosen people.
Let me rejoice with your nation.
Let me join with your people in praise.

⁶ We sinned just as our ancestors* did.
We were wrong; we did bad things!

⁷ Lord, our ancestors learned nothing
from the miracles you did in Egypt.
They forgot your kindness at the Red Sea
and rebelled against you.

⁸ But the Lord saved our ancestors for his own name's sake.
He saved them to show his great power.

⁹ He gave the command, and the Red Sea became dry.
He led our ancestors through the deep sea,
on land as dry as the desert.

¹⁰ He saved our ancestors
and rescued them from their enemies.

¹¹ He covered their enemies with the sea.
Not one of them escaped!

¹² Then our ancestors believed the Lord.
They sang praises to him.

¹³ But our ancestors quickly forgot about what he did.
They did not listen to his advice.

¹⁴ Our ancestors became hungry in the desert,
and they tested him in the wilderness.

¹⁵ He gave them what they asked for,
but he also gave them a terrible disease.

¹⁶ The people became jealous of Moses.*
They became jealous of Aaron,* the LORD's holy priest.

¹⁷ So the Lord punished those jealous people.
The ground opened up and swallowed Dathan.
Then the ground closed up and covered Abiram's group.

¹⁸ Then a fire burned that mob of people.
It burned those wicked people.

¹⁹ The people made a golden calf at Mount Horeb.
They worshiped a statue!

20 They traded their glorious God,
    for a statue of a grass-eating bull!
21 He saved our ancestors, but they forgot all about him.
    They forgot the God who did the miracles in Egypt.
22 He did amazing things in Ham's country[a]!
    He did awesome things at the Red Sea!

23 God wanted to destroy those people,
    but Moses, the man he chose, stopped him.
    He was very angry, but Moses blocked the way,
        so God did not destroy the people.[b]

24 But then those people refused to go
    into the wonderful land of Canaan.
    They did not believe that God would help them
    defeat the people living in that land.
25 Our ancestors complained in their tents
    and refused to obey the LORD.
26 So he swore that they would die in the desert.
27 He promised to scatter them among the nations
    and to let other people defeat their descendants.

28 At Baal Peor, God's people joined in worshiping Baal
    and ate sacrifices to honor the dead.[c]
29 The LORD became very angry with his people
    and made them sick.
30 But Phinehas prayed[d] to God,
    and God stopped the sickness.
31 He considered what Phinehas did a good work,
    and it will be remembered forever and ever.

32 At Meribah, the people made God angry
    and created trouble for Moses.
33 They upset Moses,
    and he spoke without stopping to think.

34 The LORD told the people to destroy
    the other nations living in Canaan.
    But the Israelites did not obey him.
35 They mixed with the other people
    and did what those people were doing.
36 God's people began worshiping the gods
        those other people worshiped.
    And those idols became a trap.

---

[a] **106:22** *Ham's country* Or, "Egypt." The Bible teaches that the Egyptians were descendants of Ham. See Gen. 10:6–20. [b] **106:23** Or, "God said he would destroy them. But Moses, his chosen one, stood in the breach and repelled his anger from destroying." This compares Moses to a soldier standing at a break in a wall defending the city (Israel) against enemy soldiers (God's anger). [c] **106:28** *the dead* This might refer to "dead statues" or "lifeless gods," or it might refer to meals eaten at graves to honor dead friends or relatives. [d] **106:30** *prayed* Or, "intervened," or "judged." Phinehas not only prayed to God, but he also did something to stop the people from doing these sins. See Num. 25:1–16.

37 They even killed their own children
   and offered them to those devils.
38 They killed their own innocent children
   and offered them to those false gods.
   So the land was polluted with the sin of murder.
39 They were unfaithful to him,
   and they became dirty with the sins of other nations.
40 So God became angry with his people.
   He rejected those who belonged to him!
41 He gave his people to other nations
   and let their enemies rule over them.
42 Their enemies controlled them
   and made life hard for them.
43 God saved his people many times,
   but they turned against him
   and did what they wanted to do.
   His people did many bad things.
44 But whenever they were in trouble,
   he listened to their prayers.
45 He always remembered his agreement,
   and because of his faithful love, he comforted them.
46 Other nations took them as prisoners,
   but God made them be kind to his people.
47 LORD our God, save us!
   Bring us back from those nations,
   so that we may give thanks
   and sing praises to your holy name.
48 Praise the LORD, the God of Israel.
   He has always lived, and he will live forever.
   Let all the people say, "Amen*!"

   Praise the LORD!

BOOK 5 *(Psalms 107–150)*

107 1 Praise the LORD, because he is good!
       His faithful love is forever!
2 Everyone the LORD has saved and rescued from their enemy
   should repeat that word of thanks.
3 He gathered his people together
   from many different countries.
   He brought them from east and west, north and south.*a*

4 Some of them wandered in the dry desert.
   They were looking for a place to live,
   but they could not find a city.
5 They were hungry and thirsty and growing weak.

---

a **107:3** *south* Or, "the Sea." This is west of Israel and would refer to all the coastal areas
around the Mediterranean Sea.

6 Then they called to the LORD for help,
    and he saved them from their troubles.
7 He led them straight to the city where they would live.
8 Thank the LORD for his faithful love
    and for the amazing things he does for people.
9 He satisfies the thirsty soul.
    He fills the hungry soul with good things.

10 Some of God's people were prisoners,
    locked behind bars in dark prisons.
11 That was because they had fought against what God said.
    They refused to listen to the advice of God Most High.
12 God made life hard for those people
    because of what they did.
They stumbled and fell,
    and there was no one to help them.
13 They were in trouble, so they called to the LORD for help,
    and he saved them from their troubles.
14 He took them out of their dark prisons.
    He broke the ropes that held them.
15 Thank the LORD for his faithful love
    and for the amazing things he does for people.
16 He breaks down their bronze gates.
    He shatters their iron bars.

17 Some people let their sins turn them into fools,
    and they suffered for what they did.
18 They were so sick that they refused to eat
    and almost died.
19 They were in trouble, so they called to the LORD for help,
    and he saved them from their troubles.
20 He gave the command and healed them,
    so they were saved from the grave.
21 Thank the LORD for his faithful love
    and for the amazing things he does for people.
22 Offer sacrifices* to thank him for all he has done.
    Gladly tell what he has done.

23 Some people sailed in boats across the sea.
    Their work carried them across the great sea.
24 They saw what the LORD can do.
    They saw the amazing things he did at sea.
25 God gave the command,
    and a strong wind began to blow.
The waves became higher and higher.
26 The waves lifted them high into the sky
    and dropped them into the deep sea.
The storm was so dangerous the men lost their courage.
27 They were stumbling and falling like someone who is drunk.
    Their skill as sailors was useless.

28 They were in trouble, so they called to the LORD for help,
   and he saved them from their troubles.
29 He stopped the storm and calmed the waves.
30 The sailors were happy that the sea was calm,
   and God led them safely to the place they wanted to go.
31 Thank the LORD for his faithful love
   and for the amazing things he does for people.
32 Praise God in the great assembly.
   Praise him when the older leaders meet together.

33 He changed rivers into a desert.
   He stopped springs from flowing.
34 He changed the fertile land,
   and it became worthless salty land.
   He did it because of the bad people who were living there.
35 God changed the desert,
   and it became a land with pools of water.
   He caused springs of water to flow from dry ground.
36 He led the hungry to that good land,
   and they built a city to live in.
37 They planted seeds in their fields and grapes in their vineyards,*
   and they had a good harvest.
38 God blessed them.
   Their families grew.
   They had many animals.
39 But because of disaster and troubles,
   their families became small and weak.
40 God shamed their leaders.
   He let them wander through the desert
      where there are no roads.
41 But then he rescued those poor people from their misery,
   and now their families are large, like flocks of sheep.
42 Good people see this, and they are happy.
   But the wicked see this, and they don't know what to say.
43 Whoever is wise enough to remember this will begin
   to understand the LORD's faithful love.

108 *A praise song of David.*

1 God, I am ready, heart and soul,
   to sing songs of praise.
2 Harps and lyres,* wake up,
   and let's wake the dawn!
3 LORD, I praise you to everyone.
   I will sing praises about you to every nation.
4 Your faithful love is higher
   than the highest clouds in the sky!
5 Rise above the heavens, God.
   Let all the world see your glory.*

6 Use your great power and save me!
     Answer my prayer and save the people you love!

7 God spoke in his Temple:[a]
     "I will win the war and be happy about the victory!
     I will divide this land among my people.
     I will give them Shechem.
     I will give them Succoth Valley.

8 Gilead and Manasseh will be mine.
     Ephraim will be my helmet.
     Judah* will be my royal scepter.*

9 Moab will be the bowl for washing my feet.
     Edom will be the slave who carries my sandals.
     I will defeat the Philistines and shout about the victory!"

10–11 But, God, you rejected us!
     You did not go with our army.
     So who will lead me into the strong, protected city?
     Who will lead me to fight against Edom?

12 God, help us defeat our enemy!
     People cannot help us!

13 Only God can make us strong.
     He can defeat our enemies!

109

To the director.*
A praise song of David.*

1 God, don't close your ears to my prayer!

2 Wicked people are telling lies about me.
     They are saying things that are not true.

3 People are saying hateful things about me.
     They are attacking me for no reason.

4 I loved them, but they were against me.
     So I said a prayer.

5 I did good things to them,
     but they are doing bad things to me.
     I loved them,
     but they hated me.

6 They said, "Appoint someone evil to judge him.
     Find someone to prove he is wrong.

7 When he is judged, let him be found guilty.
     Let his prayers be used to show how wrong he is.

8 Let his life be cut short,
     and let someone else take over his work.

9 Make his children orphans and his wife a widow.

10 Let them lose their home and become beggars.

11 He owes money to people.
     Let them take everything he owns.
     Let strangers take everything he worked for.

a 108:7 in his Temple Or, "in his holiness."

12 Let no one be kind to him.
    Let no one show mercy to his children.
13 May his name be removed from the list of the citizens of Israel*
    so that his descendants will all lose their land.
14 May the LORD remember the sins of his father,
    and may his mother's sins never be erased.
15 May the LORD remember their sins forever,
    and may he force people to forget him completely.
16 Why? Because that evil man never did anything good.
    He never loved anyone.
    He made life hard for poor, helpless people.
17 He loved to curse* others,
    so let those bad things happen to him.
    He never blessed other people,
    so don't let good things happen to him.
18 Let curses be the clothes he wears,
    the water he drinks, and the oil he puts on his body.
19 Let curses be the robe he wraps around his body
    and the belt around his waist."

20 That is what my enemies said about me.
    They said they spoke for the LORD,
    but they said evil things about me.
21 My Lord GOD, treat me in a way that brings honor
    to your name.
    Save me because of your faithful love.
22 I am only a poor, helpless man.
    I am so sad; my heart is broken.
23 I feel like my life is over, like the long shadows
    at the end of the day.
    I feel like a bug someone brushed away.
24 My knees are weak from fasting.*
    I am losing weight and becoming thin.
25 My enemies insult me.
    They look at me and shake their heads.
26 LORD my God, help me!
    Show your faithful love and save me!
27 Then they will know that you helped me.
    They will know that it was your power, LORD,
    that helped me.
28 They curse me, but you can bless me.
    They attacked me, so defeat them.
    Then I, your servant, will be happy.
29 Humiliate my enemies!
    Let them wear their shame like a coat.
30 I thank the LORD.
    I praise him in front of many people.
31 He stands by the helpless
    and saves them from those who try to put them to death.

110 *A praise song of David.**

[1] The LORD said to my lord,[a]
   "Sit at my right side, while I put your enemies
     under your control.[b]"

[2] The LORD will help your kingdom grow.
   Your kingdom will start at Zion,* and it will grow until
     you rule your enemies in their own countries!

[3] Your people will volunteer
   when you gather your army together.
They will wear their special clothes
   and meet together early in the morning.
Those young men will be all around you,
   like dew on the ground.[c]

[4] The LORD made a promise,
   and he will not change his mind:
"You are a priest forever—
   the kind of priest Melchizedek was."

[5] My Lord is at your right side.
   He will defeat the other kings when he becomes angry.

[6] God will judge the nations.
   The ground will be covered with dead bodies.
He will punish the leaders of powerful nations all around
   the world.

[7] The king will drink from a stream on the way.
   Then he will lift his head and become strong![d]

111 [e] [1]Praise the LORD!

I thank the LORD with all my heart
   in the assembly where good people meet together.

[2] The LORD does wonderful things,
   more than anyone could ask for.[f]

[3] He does glorious and wonderful things!
   His goodness continues forever.

[4] He does amazing things so that we will remember
   that the LORD is kind and merciful.

[5] The Lord gives food to his followers.
   He remembers his agreement forever.

---

[a]**110:1** *lord* That is, the king. [b]**110:1** *while I ... control* Or, "until I make your enemies a footstool for your feet." [c]**110:3** This verse is hard to understand in Hebrew. Literally, "Your people will be freewill offerings on your day of power. In holy splendor from the womb of dawn your dew of youth will be yours." [d]**110:7** *lift his head and become strong* Literally, "lift his head." Here, the poet probably means two things: "he will raise his head after drinking the water," and "he will become strong or important." [e]**Psalm 111** In Hebrew, each line of this psalm begins with the next letter in the alphabet. [f]**111:2** *more ... for* Literally, "They are requested for all their desires."

6 The powerful things he did
    showed his people that he was giving their land to them.
7 Everything the Lord does is good and fair.
    All his commands can be trusted.
8 His commands will continue forever.
    They must be done with truth and honesty.
9 He rescued his people and made his agreement
      with them forever.
    His name is awesome and holy.
10 Wisdom begins with fear and respect for the Lord.
    Those who obey him are very wise.
    Praises will be sung to him forever.

112 *a* 1Praise the Lord!

The Lord blesses those who fear and respect him
    and love his commands.
2 Their descendants will be great on earth.
    They will be really blessed.
3 Their family will be very rich,
    and their goodness will continue forever.
4 A light shines in the dark for those who are good,
    for those who are merciful, kind, and fair.
5 It is good for people to be kind and generous
    and to be fair in business.
6 Such good people will never fall.
    They will always be remembered.
7 They will not be afraid of bad news.
    They are confident because they trust in the Lord.
8 They remain confident and without fear,
    so they defeat their enemies.
9 They freely give to the poor.
    Their goodness will continue forever.
    They will be honored with victory.
10 The wicked become angry when they see this.
    They grind their teeth in anger but then disappear.
    They will never get what they want most.

113 1Praise the Lord!

Servants of the Lord, praise him!
    Praise the Lord's name.
2 May the Lord's name be praised now and forever.
3 May the Lord's name be praised from the rising sun
    in the east to the place where it goes down.
4 The Lord is higher than all nations.
    His glory* rises to the skies.

a **Psalm 112** In Hebrew, each line of this psalm begins with the next letter in the alphabet.

5 There is no one like the LORD our God.
  He sits on his throne high in heaven.
6 He is so high above us
  that he must look down to see the sky and the earth.
7 He lifts the poor out of the dirt
  and takes beggars from the garbage dump.
8 He makes them important.
  He gives them a place among the great leaders
    of his people.
9 He gives children to the woman whose home is empty.
  He makes her a happy mother.

Praise the LORD!

114 ¹The people of Israel* escaped from Egypt.
    Yes, Jacob's* descendants left that foreign country.
2 Then Judah* became God's special people,
  and Israel became his kingdom.
3 The Red Sea saw this and ran away.
  The Jordan River turned and ran.
4 The mountains danced like rams.
  The hills danced like lambs.

5 Red Sea, why did you run away?
  Jordan River, why did you turn and run away?
6 Mountains, why did you dance like rams?
  Hills, why did you dance like lambs?

7 The earth shook in front of the Lord, the God of Jacob.
8 He is the one who caused water to flow from a rock.
  He made a spring of water flow from that hard rock.

115 ¹LORD, you should receive the honor, not us.
    The honor belongs to you
    because of your faithful love and loyalty.
2 Why should the nations wonder where our God is?
3 God is in heaven, and he does whatever he wants.
4 The "gods" of those nations are only statues
  that some human made from gold and silver.
5 Those statues have mouths but cannot talk.
  They have eyes but cannot see.
6 They have ears but cannot hear.
  They have noses but cannot smell.
7 They have hands but cannot feel.
  They have feet but cannot walk.
  No sounds come from their throats.
8 The people who make and trust those statues will become
    like them!

9 People of Israel,* trust in the LORD!
  "He is their strength and shield."

10 Aaron's* family, trust in the LORD!
   "He is their strength and shield."

11 Followers of the LORD, trust in the LORD!
   "He is their strength and shield."

12 The LORD remembers us.
   He will bless us.
   He will bless Israel.
   He will bless Aaron's family.

13 The LORD will bless his followers, great and small.

14 May the LORD give more and more to you
   and to your children.

15 He made heaven and earth,
   and the LORD welcomes you*!

16 Heaven belongs to the LORD,
   but he gave the earth to people.

17 The dead don't praise him.
   Those in the grave don't praise the LORD.

18 But we will praise the LORD now and forever!

   Praise the LORD!

116 1 I love the LORD for hearing me,
   for listening to my prayers.

2 Yes, he paid attention to me,
   so I will always call to him whenever I need help.

3 Death's ropes were around me.
   The grave was closing in on me.
   I was worried and afraid.

4 Then I called on the LORD's name.
   I said: "LORD, save me!"

5 The LORD is good and merciful;
   our God is so kind.

6 The LORD takes care of helpless people.
   I was without help, and he saved me.

7 My soul, relax!
   The LORD is caring for you.

8 Lord, you saved my soul from death.
   You stopped my tears.
   You kept me from falling.

9 I will continue to serve the LORD in the land of the living.

10 I continued believing even when I said,
   "I am ruined!"

11 Yes, even when I was afraid and said,
   "All men are liars!"

115:15 *the LORD welcomes you* Literally, "you are blessed to the LORD." This can mean that people ask God to do good things for these people or that God welcomes the people with a blessing.

¹² What can I give to the LORD?
     He gave me everything I have!
¹³ He saved me,
     so I will give him a drink offering,
     and I will call on the LORD's name.
¹⁴ I will give the LORD what I promised.
     I will go in front of all his people now.
¹⁵ The death of one of his followers is very important to him.
¹⁶ LORD, I am one of your servants!
     I am your servant, a child of one of your slave women.
     You set me free from the chains of death.
¹⁷ I will give you a thank offering.
     I will call on the LORD's name.
¹⁸ I will stand before the gathering of his people
     and give the LORD what I promised.
¹⁹ I will do this in Jerusalem,
     in the courtyards of the LORD's Temple.*

Praise the LORD!

117

¹ Praise the LORD, all you nations.
     Praise him, all you people.
² He loves us very much!
     The LORD will be faithful to us forever!

Praise the LORD!

118

¹ Praise the LORD because he is good!
     His faithful love will last forever!
² Israel,* say it:
     "His faithful love will last forever!"
³ Aaron's family,^a say it:
     "His faithful love will last forever!"
⁴ You people worshiping the LORD, say it:
     "His faithful love will last forever!"

⁵ I was in trouble, so I called to the LORD for help.
     The LORD answered me and made me free.
⁶ The LORD is with me, so I will not be afraid.
     People cannot do anything to hurt me.
⁷ The LORD is my helper.
     I will see my enemies defeated.
⁸ It is better to trust in the LORD
     than to trust in people.
⁹ It is better to trust in the LORD
     than to trust in your leaders.

---

a **118:3** *Aaron's family* That is, the priests.

10 Many enemies surrounded me,
   but with the LORD's power I defeated my enemies.
11 They surrounded me again and again,
   but I defeated them with the LORD's power.
12 They surrounded me like a swarm of bees,
   but they were quickly destroyed like a fast burning bush.
   I defeated them with the LORD's power.

13 My enemy attacked me and almost destroyed me,
   but the LORD helped me.
14 The LORD is my strength and my reason for singing.[a]
   He saved me!

15 You can hear the victory celebration in the homes
   of those who live right.
   The LORD has shown his great power again!
16 The LORD's arm is raised in victory.
   The LORD showed his great power again.

17 I will live and not die,
   and I will tell what the LORD has done.
18 The LORD punished me,
   but he did not let me die.
19 Gates of goodness, open for me,
   and I will come in and worship the LORD.
20 Those are the LORD's gates,
   and only good people can go through them.
21 Lord, I thank you for answering my prayer.
   I thank you for saving me.

22 The stone that the builders rejected became the cornerstone.*
23 The LORD made this happen,
   and we think it is wonderful!
24 Today is the day the LORD has made.
   Let us rejoice and be happy today!

25 ⌊The people say,⌋ "Praise the LORD!
   The LORD saved us![b]
26 Welcome the one who comes in the name of the LORD."

   ⌊The priests answer,⌋ "We welcome you to the LORD's house!
27 The LORD is God, and he accepts us.
   Tie up the lamb for the sacrifice*
   and carry it to the horns of the altar."[c]

28 LORD, you are my God, and I thank you.
   My God, I praise you!
29 Praise the LORD because he is good.
   His faithful love will last forever.

---

[a]118:14 my reason for singing Or, "my protection." [b]118:25 Literally, "LORD, please save us. LORD, please make us successful." This was a shout of victory to honor the king who was coming back from winning a war. [c]118:27 horns of the altar The corners of the altar were shaped like horns and were an important part of the altar.

Aleph[a]

119

¹What blessings there are for those who live pure lives!
They follow the LORD's teachings.

² What blessings there are for those who follow his rules!
They seek him with all their heart.

³ They don't do wrong.
They follow his ways.

⁴ Lord, you gave us your instructions
and told us to always obey them.

⁵ How I wish I could be more faithful
in obeying your laws!

⁶ Then I would never feel ashamed
when I look closely at your commands.

⁷ I will praise you sincerely
when I see the good decisions you have made.

⁸ I will obey your laws,
so please don't leave me!

Beth

⁹ How can a young person live a pure life?
By obeying your word.

¹⁰ I try with all my heart to serve you.
Help me obey your commands.

¹¹ I study your teachings very carefully
so that I will not sin against you.

¹² LORD, you are worthy of praise!
Teach me your laws.

¹³ I will talk about all your wise decisions.

¹⁴ I enjoy following your rules
as much as others enjoy great riches.

¹⁵ I will study your instructions.
I will give thought to your way of life.

¹⁶ I enjoy your laws.
I will not forget your word.

Gimel

¹⁷ Be good to me, your servant,
so that I may live to obey your word.

¹⁸ Open my eyes so that I can see
all the wonderful things in your teachings.

¹⁹ I feel like a stranger visiting here on earth.
I need to know your commands;
don't keep them hidden from me.

²⁰ I always feel a strong hunger
to understand your decisions.

---

[a]**Psalm 119** *Aleph* The first letter of the Hebrew alphabet. This psalm has a section for each letter of the Hebrew alphabet, and each of the eight verses in each section begins with the Hebrew letter for its section.

21 You tell the proud how angry you are with them.
　　All those who refuse to obey your word are cursed.*

22 Don't let me be ashamed and embarrassed.
　　I have obeyed your rules.

23 Even if rulers say bad things about me,
　　I am your servant,
　　and I continue to study your laws.

24 Your rules make me happy.
　　They give me good advice.

Daleth

25 I lie here like a dying man.
　　Say the word, and I will live again.[a]

26 I told you about my life, and you answered me.
　　Now, teach me your laws.

27 Help me understand your instructions,
　　and I will think about your wonderful teachings.[b]

28 I am sad and tired.
　　Say the word, and make me strong again.

29 Don't let me live a lie.
　　Guide me with your teachings.

30 I have chosen to be loyal to you.
　　I respect your wise decisions.

31 I follow your rules closely, Lord.
　　Don't let me be put to shame.

32 I do my best to follow your commands,
　　because you are the one who gives me the desire.

He

33 Lord, teach me your laws,
　　and I will always follow them.

34 Help me understand your teachings,
　　and I will follow them.
　　Obeying them will be my greatest desire.

35 Help me follow your commandments,
　　because that makes me happy.

36 Give me the desire to follow your rules,
　　not the desire to get rich.

37 Don't let me look at worthless things.
　　Help me live your way.

38 Do what you promised me, your servant,
　　so that people will respect you.

39 Take away the shame I fear.
　　Your decisions are good.

40 See how much I want to obey your instructions!
　　Be good to me, and let me live.

---

[a]**119:25** *Say ... again* Or, "Give me life according to your word."　　[b]**119:27** *teachings* Or, "deeds."

Waw

⁴¹ LORD, show me your faithful love.
   Save me, as you promised.

⁴² Then I will have an answer for those who make fun of me
   for trusting what you say.

⁴³ Let me always say what is true.
   I depend on your wise decisions.

⁴⁴ I will follow your teachings forever and ever.

⁴⁵ So I will live in freedom,
   because I do my best to know your instructions.

⁴⁶ I will discuss your rules with kings,
   and no one will embarrass me.

⁴⁷ What joy your commands give me!
   How I love them!

⁴⁸ Not only do I love your commands, but I also honor them.
   I will study your laws.

Zain

⁴⁹ Remember your promise to me, your servant.
   It gives me hope.

⁵⁰ You comfort me in my suffering,
   because your promise gives me new life.

⁵¹ People full of pride are always making fun of me,
   but I have not stopped following your teachings.

⁵² I remember the wise decisions you have made, LORD,
   and that brings me comfort.

⁵³ I am overcome with anger when I see wicked people
   who have stopped following your teachings.

⁵⁴ Your laws are the songs I sing wherever I am living.

⁵⁵ LORD, in the night I remembered your name,
   and I obeyed your teachings.

⁵⁶ This happened because I carefully obey your instructions.

Heth

⁵⁷ LORD, I decided my duty is to obey your commandments.

⁵⁸ I beg you with all my heart,
   be kind to me, as you promised.

⁵⁹ I thought very carefully about my life,
   and I decided to follow your rules.

⁶⁰ Without wasting any time, I hurried back
   to obey your commands.

⁶¹ The wicked tried to trap me,
   but I have not forgotten your teachings.

⁶² In the middle of the night I get up
   to thank you for your good decisions.

⁶³ I am a friend to everyone who worships you.
   I am a friend to everyone who obeys your instructions.

⁶⁴ LORD, your faithful love fills the earth.
   Teach me your laws.

Teth

65 LORD, you did good things for me, your servant.
   You did what you promised to do.
66 Give me the knowledge to make wise decisions.
   I trust your commands.
67 Before I suffered, I did many wrong things.
   But now I carefully obey everything you say.
68 You are good, and you do good things.
   Teach me your laws.
69 People full of pride made up lies about me.
   But I keep obeying your instructions with all my heart.
70 Those people are so stupid that they care for nothing,
   but I enjoy studying your teachings.
71 Suffering was good for me.
   I learned your laws.
72 Your teachings are worth more to me
   than a thousand pieces of silver and gold.

Yod

73 With your hands you made me
      and helped me become what I am.
   Now help me learn and understand your commands.
74 Your followers will see me and be happy,
   because I trust in your word.
75 LORD, I know that your decisions are good,
   and it was right for you to punish me.
76 Now comfort me with your faithful love,
   as you promised.
77 Comfort me and let me live.
   I enjoy your teachings.
78 Bring shame on those proud people who lied about me.
   I just want to study your instructions.
79 Let your followers come back to me
   so that they may learn your rules.
80 Let me obey your laws perfectly
   so that I will not be ashamed.

Kaph

81 I feel weaker and weaker as I wait for you to save me.
   But I put my trust in your word.
82 I keep looking for what you promised,
   but my eyes are feeling tired.
   When will you comfort me?
83 Even when I am like a dried wineskin on the trash pile,
   I will not forget your laws.
84 How long must I wait for you
   to punish those who persecuted me?
85 Some proud people tried to trap me
   and convince me to disobey your teachings.

86 Your commands can be trusted.
    They are wrong to persecute me. Help me!
87 They almost destroyed me,
    but I did not stop obeying your instructions.
88 Show me your faithful love and let me live.
    I will do whatever you say.

Lamedh

89 LORD, your word continues forever in heaven.
90 You are loyal forever and ever.
    You made the earth, and it still stands.
91 All things continue today because of your laws.
    Like slaves, they all obey you.
92 If I had not found joy in your teachings,
    my suffering would have destroyed me.
93 I will never forget your commands,
    because through them you gave me new life.
94 I am yours, so save me!
    I have done my best to know your instructions.
95 The wicked tried to destroy me,
    but your rules made me wise.
96 Everything has its limits, except your commands.

Mem

97 Oh, how I love your teachings!
    I talk about them all the time.
98 Your commands are always with me,
    and they make me wiser than my enemies.
99 I am wiser than all my teachers,
    because I study your rules.
100 I understand more than those who are older,
    because I obey your instructions.
101 I have avoided every path that leads to evil,
    so that I could obey your word.
102 You are my teacher,
    so I will always do whatever you decide.
103 Your words are so sweet to me,
    like the taste of honey!
104 I gain understanding from your instructions,
    so I hate anything that leads people the wrong way.

Nun

105 Your word is like a lamp that guides my steps,
    a light that shows the path I should take.
106 Your laws are good and fair.
    I have promised to obey them, and I will keep my promise.
107 LORD, I have suffered for a long time.
    Say the word, and I will live again*[a]*!

[a] 119:107 Say ... again Or, "Give me life according to your word."

108 LORD, accept the praise I want to give you,
   and teach me your laws.
109 My life is always in danger,
   but I have not forgotten your teachings.
110 The wicked try to trap me,
   but I have not disobeyed your instructions.
111 The rules you have given me to follow will be mine forever.
   They give me great joy.
112 More than anything else, I want to obey your laws,
   every one of them, until the end of my life.

Samekh

113 Lord, I hate those who are not completely loyal to you,
   but I love your teachings.
114 Hide me, and protect me.
   I trust what you say.
115 You who are evil, don't come near me,
   so that I can obey my God's commands.
116 Support me, as you promised, and I will live.
   I trust in you, so don't disappoint me.
117 Help me, and I will be saved.
   And I will always give attention to your laws.
118 You reject all who don't obey your laws,
   because they are liars and did not do what they said.
119 You throw away the wicked of this world like trash.
   So I love your rules.
120 I am shaking with fear before you.
   I fear and respect your decisions.

Ain

121 I have done what is right and good.
   Don't let me fall into the hands of those
      who want to hurt me.
122 Promise to be good to me, your servant.
   Don't let those proud people do harm to me.
123 I have worn out my eyes looking for your help,
   waiting for you to save me, as you promised.
124 Show your faithful love to me, your servant.
   Teach me your laws.
125 I am your servant.
   Give me wisdom to understand your rules.
126 LORD, it is time for you to do something.
   The people do what is against your teachings.
127 I love your commands more than gold,
   more than the purest gold.
128 I carefully obey all your commands.[a]
   So I hate anything that leads people the wrong way.

---

[a] **119:128** The first line of the Hebrew is unclear.

Pe

129 Lord, your rules are wonderful.
         That is why I follow them.
130 As people understand your word, it brings light to their lives.
         Your word makes even simple people wise.
131 My desire to hear your commands is so strong
         that I wait with open mouth, gasping for breath.
132 Look at me, and be kind to me,
         just as you always are to those who love your name.
133 Guide me, as you promised.
         Don't let evil rule over me.
134 Save me from those who want to hurt me,
         and I will obey your instructions.
135 Accept your servant,
         and teach me your laws.
136 I have cried a river of tears
         because people don't obey your teachings.

Tsadhe

137 LORD, you are good,
         and you make good decisions.
138 The rules you have given us are right.
         We can trust them completely.
139 Something that really upsets me is the thought
         that my enemies ignore your commands.
140 I love your word.
         Time and again it has been proven true.
141 I am young, and people don't respect me.
         But I have not forgotten your instructions.
142 Your goodness is forever,
         and your teachings can be trusted.
143 Even though I have troubles and hard times,
         your commands give me joy.
144 Your rules are always right.
         Help me understand them so that I can live.

Qoph

145 LORD, I call to you with all my heart.
         Answer me, and I will obey your laws.
146 I call to you. Save me,
         and I will obey your rules.
147 I get up early in the morning to pray to you.
         I trust what you say.
148 Late into the night I stay awake to think about your word.
149 I know your love is true, so listen to me.
         LORD, you always do what is right, so let me live.
150 Here come those who have evil plans to hurt me.
         They live far away from your teachings.

151 But you are near me, LORD,
   and all your commands can be trusted.
152 Long ago I learned from studying your rules
   that you made them to last forever.

Resh

153 Look at my suffering, and rescue me.
   I have not forgotten your teachings.
154 Argue my case, and set me free.
   Let me live, as you promised.
155 The wicked have no hope of being saved,
   because they don't follow your laws.
156 LORD, you are very kind.
   You always do what is right, so let me live.
157 I have many enemies trying to hurt me,
   but I have not stopped following your rules.
158 I look at those traitors* and hate what I see,
   because they refuse to do what you say.
159 See how much I love your instructions!
   LORD, I know your love is true, so let me live.
160 Every word you say can be trusted,
   and the good decisions you have made will last forever.

Shin

161 Powerful leaders attack me for no reason,
   but the only thing I fear is your command.
162 Your word makes me happy,
   like someone who has found a great treasure.
163 I hate lies; they make me sick!
   But I love your teachings.
164 Seven times a day I praise you
   for the good decisions you have made.
165 Those who love your teachings will find true peace.
   Nothing can make them fall.
166 LORD, I am waiting for you to save me.
   I obey your commands.
167 I follow your rules.
   I love them very much.
168 I obey all your instructions and rules,
   because you know everything I do.

Taw

169 LORD, listen to my cry for help.
   Make me wise, as you promised.
170 Listen to my prayer.
   Save me, as you promised.
171 Let me burst into songs of praise,
   because you have taught me your laws.

172 Let my voice sing about your word,
   because all your commands are good.
173 I have chosen to follow your instructions,
   so reach out and help me!
174 LORD, I want you to save me.
   Your teachings make me happy.
175 Let me live to praise you.
   Let me find the help I need in your laws.
176 I have wandered away like a lost sheep.
   Come and find me.
   I am your servant,
   and I have not forgotten your commands.

120 A song for going up to the Temple.*

1 I was in trouble.
   I called to the LORD for help,
   and he answered me!
2 I said, "LORD, save me from liars,
   from those who say things that are not true."

3 Liars, do you know what God has for you?
   Do you know what you will get?
4 You will get a soldier's sharp arrow and hot coals
   to punish you.

5 How I hate living here among these people!
   It's like living in Meshech or in tents in Kedar.*
6 I have lived too long with those who hate peace.
7 I ask for peace, but they want war.

121 A song for going up to the Temple.*

1 I look up to the hills,
   but where will my help really come from?
2 My help will come from the LORD,
   the Creator of heaven and earth.
3 God will not let you fall.
   Your Protector will not fall asleep.
4 Israel's* Protector does not get drowsy.
   He never sleeps.
5 The LORD is your Protector.
   The LORD stands by your side,
   shading and protecting you.
6 The sun cannot hurt you during the day,
   and the moon cannot hurt you at night.
7 The LORD will protect you from every danger.
   The LORD will protect your soul.

---

*120:5 Meshech ... Kedar Places where the people were known as wild and savage fighters.

8 The LORD will protect you as you come and go.[a]
  He will protect both now and forever!

122 *A song of David* for going up to the Temple.**

1 I was very happy when people said,
  "Let us go to the LORD's Temple."
2 Here we are, standing at the gates of Jerusalem.
3 This is New Jerusalem!
  The city has been rebuilt as one united city.
4 This is where the tribes go.
  The people of Israel* come here to praise the LORD's name.
  They are the tribes who belong to the LORD.
5 The kings from David's family put their thrones here.
  They set up their thrones here to judge the people.

6 Pray for peace in Jerusalem:
  "May those who love you find peace.
7 May there be peace within your walls.
  May there be safety in your great buildings."

8 For the good of my family and neighbors,
  I pray that there will be peace here.
9 For the good of the Temple* of the LORD our God,
  I pray that good things will happen to this city.

123 *A song for going up to the Temple.**

1 God, I look up and pray to you.
  You sit as King in heaven.
2 Slaves depend on their masters for what they need.
  In the same way, we depend on the LORD our God.
  We wait for him to show mercy to us.
3 LORD, be merciful to us,
  because we have been insulted much too long.
4 We have had enough of the hateful words and insults
  of those proud, arrogant people.

124 *A song of David* for going up to the Temple.**

1 What would have happened to us
  if the LORD had not been on our side?
  Tell us about it, Israel.*
2 What would have happened to us
  if the LORD had not been on our side
  when people attacked us?
3 They would have swallowed us alive
  whenever they became angry with us.

---

[a]**121:8** *come and go* This may refer to going to war.

⁴ Their armies would have been
    like a flood washing over us,
    like a river drowning us.
⁵ Those proud people would have been
    like water rising up to our mouth and drowning us.

⁶ Praise the LORD!
    The LORD did not let our enemies
    catch us and kill us like prey in the teeth of a predator.

⁷ We are like a bird that was trapped in a net and then escaped.
    The net broke, and we escaped!
⁸ But our help came from the LORD,
    the one who made heaven and earth!

125 *A song for going up to the Temple.*

¹ Those who trust in the LORD are like Mount Zion.*
    They will never be shaken.
    They will continue forever.
² Mountains are all around Jerusalem,
    and the LORD is around his people.
    He will protect his people now and forever.
³ The wicked will not always control the land
    of those who do right.
If that happened, even those who do right might start doing
    what is wrong.

⁴ LORD, be good to those who are good,
    to those who have pure hearts.
⁵ But, LORD, when you punish those who do evil,
    also punish those who have stopped following your way.

Let Israel* always enjoy peace!

126 *A song for going up to the Temple.*

¹ It will be like a dream
    when the LORD comes back with the captives of Zion.ᵃ
² We will laugh and sing happy songs!
    Then people in other nations will say,
    "The LORD did a great thing for Zion*!"
³ Yes, the LORD will have done a great thing for us,
    and we will be happy.

⁴ So LORD, bring back the good times,
    like a desert stream filled again with flowing water.
⁵ Then those who were sad while planting seeds
    will be happy when they gather the crops!

ᵃ126:1 when ... Zion Or, "when the LORD restores Zion." See "Zion" in the Word List.

6 Those who cried while carrying the seeds*a*
   will be happy when they bring in the crops!

127 *A song from Solomon for going up to the Temple.**

1 If it is not the LORD who builds a house,
   the builders are wasting their time.
   If it is not the LORD who watches over the city,
   the guards are wasting their time.

2 It is a waste of time to get up early and stay up late,
   trying to make a living.
   The Lord provides for the people he loves,
   even while they are sleeping.

3 Children are a gift*b* from the LORD,
   a reward from a mother's womb.

4 A young man's sons are like the arrows
   in a soldier's hand.

5 The man who fills his quiver* with sons
   will be very blessed.
   They will never be defeated
   when they oppose the enemy at the city gates.*c*

128 *A song for going up to the Temple.**

1 Those who fear and respect the LORD
   and live the way he wants will enjoy his blessings.

2 You will get what you work for.
   You will enjoy God's blessings, and all will go well for you.

3 At home, your wife will be like a vine full of grapes;
   she will have many children.
   Around the table, you will have many children
   like an orchard full of olive trees.

4 Yes, the LORD will really bless those who respect him.

5 May the LORD bless you from Mount Zion.*
   May you enjoy the blessings of Jerusalem all your life.

6 And may you live to see your grandchildren.

   Let Israel* always enjoy peace!

129 *A song for going up to the Temple.**

1 All my life many enemies have attacked me.
   Say it again, Israel.*

---

*a***126:6** *carrying the seeds* Or, "carrying all their possessions." *b***127:3** *gift* Literally,
"inheritance." Usually, this means the land God gave to each family in Israel. *c***127:5** *city
gates* This can refer to either a battle to protect the city or to a court case held at this public
place.

2 All my life many enemies have attacked me,
   but they have never defeated me.
3 They beat me until I had deep cuts.
   My back looked like a freshly plowed field.
4 But the LORD does what is right;
   he cut the ropes and set me free
      from those wicked people.
5 May those who hate Zion* be put to shame.
   May they be stopped and chased away.
6 They will be like grass on a flat roof
   that dies before it has time to grow.
7 The one who goes to harvest it
   will not find enough to cut and stack.
8 May no one walking by those wicked people ever say,
   "May the LORD bless you."
   Or, "We bless you in the name of the LORD."

130 *A song for going up to the Temple.*

1 LORD, I am in deep trouble,
   so I am calling to you for help.
2 My Lord, listen to me.
   Listen to my cry for help.
3 LORD, if you punished people for all their sins,
   no one would be left alive.
4 But you forgive people,
   so they fear and respect you.

5 I am waiting for the LORD to help me.
   My soul waits for him.
   I trust what he says.
6 I am waiting for my Lord,
   like a guard waiting and waiting for the morning to come.
7 Israel,* trust in the LORD.
   The LORD is the one who is faithful and true.
   He saves us again and again,
8 and he is the one who will save Israel from all their sins.

131 *A song of David* for going up to the Temple.*

1 LORD, I am not proud.
   I don't try to act important.
   I am not interested in doing great things
      or trying to reach impossible goals.
2 But I am calm and quiet,
   like a child content in its mother's arms.
3 Israel,* trust in the LORD.
   Trust in him now and forever!

132

*A song for going up to the Temple.**

¹ LORD, remember how David* suffered.

² He made a promise to you, LORD,
     an oath to the Mighty God of Jacob.*

³ He said, "I will not go into my house
     or lie down on my bed.

⁴ I will not sleep
     or let my eyes rest,

⁵ until I find a home for the LORD,
     a tent for the Mighty God of Jacob!"

⁶ We heard about this in Ephrathah.*ᵃ*
     We found the Box of the Agreement* at Kiriath Jearim.*ᵇ*

⁷ Now, let's go to the Lord's house.
     Let's worship at his throne.*ᶜ*

⁸ LORD, get up*ᵈ* and go to your resting place;
     go with the Box that shows your power.

⁹ May your priests be clothed in victory,
     and your loyal followers be filled with joy.

¹⁰ For the sake of your servant David,*
     don't reject your chosen king.*ᵉ*

¹¹ The LORD made a promise to David,
     an oath of loyalty to him:
"I will always put one of your descendants on your throne.

¹² David, if your descendants obey my agreement
       and the laws that I teach them,
     then someone from your family will always be the king."

¹³ The LORD has chosen Zion* to be the place for his Temple,*
     the place he wanted for his home.

¹⁴ He said, "This will always be my place of rest.
     This is where I want to sit on my throne.

¹⁵ I will bless this city with plenty of food.
     Even the poor will have enough to eat.

¹⁶ I will clothe the priests with salvation,
     and my followers will be filled with joy.

¹⁷ This is where I will make David's family strong.
     I will never let the lamp of my chosen king stop burning.

¹⁸ I will cover his enemies with shame,
     and on his head will be a shining crown."

---

*ᵃ***132:6** *Ephrathah* Bethlehem, the town where David was born.   *ᵇ***132:6** *Kiriath Jearim* Literally, "fields of the forest." The Hebrew word meaning "forest" is like the name of this city. *ᶜ***132:7** *at his throne* Literally, "at his footstool." This can mean the Box of the Agreement, the Holy Tent, or the Temple. God is like a king sitting on his throne and resting his feet on the place where people worship him.   *ᵈ***132:8** *LORD, get up* The people said this when they lifted the Box of the Agreement and took it into battle with them. This showed that God was with them. See Num. 10:35–36.   *ᵉ***132:10** *chosen king* Literally, "anointed one."

133 *A song of David* for going up to the Temple.**

1 Oh, how wonderful it is
    when God's people sit together united!

2 It is like sweet-smelling oil poured over the high priest's[a] head,
    running down into his beard,
    which flows down over his robes.

3 It is like a gentle rain[b] from Mount Hermon falling
    on Mount Zion.[c]
  It was there at Zion that the LORD gave the blessing
    of eternal life.

134 *A song for going up to the Temple.**

1 Praise the LORD, all his servants who serve
    in the Temple* at night.

2 Lift your hands toward the Temple, and praise the LORD.

3 May the LORD, who made heaven and earth,
    bless you from Zion.*

135 1 Praise the LORD!

  Praise the name of the LORD!
    Praise him, you servants of the LORD,

2 you who serve in the LORD's Temple,*
    in the courtyard of the Temple of our God.

3 Praise the LORD, because he is good.
    Praise his name, because it brings such joy!

4 The LORD chose Jacob,*
    he chose Israel* to be his own people.

5 I know the LORD is great!
    Our Lord is greater than all the gods!

6 The LORD does whatever he wants,
    in heaven and earth, in the seas and deep oceans.

7 He spreads the clouds over all the earth.
  He sends the lightning and rain,
    and he opens the doors to release the winds.

8 He destroyed all the firstborn* males in Egypt,
    both men and animals.

9 He did great wonders and miracles in Egypt.
  He used them against Pharaoh and his officials.

10 He defeated many nations and killed powerful kings.

11 He defeated Sihon, king of the Amorites,
    Og, king of Bashan, and all the kingdoms in Canaan.

12 Then he gave their land to Israel, his people.

---

[a]**133:2** *high priest's* Literally, "Aaron's."   [b]**133:3** *gentle rain* Or, "mist," or "snow." The Hebrew can mean either "the oil is like the mist . . ." or "Aaron's beard is like the snow . . . ." [c]**133:3** *Mount Zion* Or, "the mountain range of Zion" or possibly, "the dry mountains." See "Zion" in the Word List.

[13] LORD, your name will be famous forever!
   LORD, people will remember you forever and ever.

[14] The LORD defends his people;
   he is kind to his servants.

[15] The gods of other nations are only gold and silver idols
   that people have made.

[16] They have mouths but cannot speak.
   They have eyes but cannot see.

[17] They have ears but cannot hear.
   They have mouths but no breath.

[18] Whoever makes idols and puts their trust in them
      will become like them.

[19] Family of Israel, praise the LORD!
   Aaron's* family, praise the LORD!

[20] Levi's family, praise the LORD!
   All you who worship the LORD, praise the LORD!

[21] The LORD should be praised from Zion,*
      from Jerusalem, his home.

Praise the LORD!

136 [1] Praise the LORD because he is good.
   His faithful love will last forever.

[2] Praise the God of gods!
   His faithful love will last forever.

[3] Praise the Lord of Lords!
   His faithful love will last forever.

[4] Praise God, who alone does wonderful miracles!
   His faithful love will last forever.

[5] Praise God, the one who used wisdom to make the skies!
   His faithful love will last forever.

[6] He spread the land over the sea.
   His faithful love will last forever.

[7] He made the great lights.
   His faithful love will last forever.

[8] He made the sun to rule the day.
   His faithful love will last forever.

[9] He made the moon and stars to rule the night.
   His faithful love will last forever.

[10] He killed the firstborn* males in Egypt, both men and animals.
   His faithful love will last forever.

[11] He took Israel* out of Egypt.
   His faithful love will last forever.

[12] He used his powerful arms and strong hands.
   His faithful love will last forever.

[13] He split the Red Sea into two parts.
   His faithful love will last forever.

[14] He led Israel through the sea.
   His faithful love will last forever.

15 He drowned Pharaoh and his army in the Red Sea.
   His faithful love will last forever.
16 He led his people through the desert.
   His faithful love will last forever.
17 He defeated powerful kings.
   His faithful love will last forever.
18 He defeated strong kings.
   His faithful love will last forever.
19 He defeated Sihon, king of the Amorites.
   His faithful love will last forever.
20 He defeated Og, king of Bashan.
   His faithful love will last forever.
21 He gave their land to Israel.
   His faithful love will last forever.
22 He gave it as a gift to Israel, his servant.
   His faithful love will last forever.
23 He remembered us when we were defeated.
   His faithful love will last forever.
24 He saved us from our enemies.
   His faithful love will last forever.
25 He provides food for all living things.
   His faithful love will last forever.
26 Praise the God of heaven!
   His faithful love will last forever.

137

1 We sat by the rivers in Babylon
   and cried as we remembered Zion.*
2 We hung our harps nearby, there on the willow trees.ᵃ
3 There in Babylon, those who captured us told us to sing.
   Our enemies told us to entertain them:
   "Sing us one of your songs about Zion.*"
4 But we cannot sing the LORD's songs in a foreign country!
5 Jerusalem, if I ever forget you,
   may I never play a song again.
6 If I fail to remember you,
   may I never sing again.
   I will never forget you.
   Jerusalem will always be my greatest joy!

7 LORD, remember the Edomites
   and punish them for what they did
      when Jerusalem was captured.
   They shouted, "Destroy its buildings!
   Pull them down to the ground!"
8 Babylon, you will be destroyed!
   Bless the one who pays you back for what you did to us.
9 Bless the one who grabs your babies
   and smashes them against a rock.

ᵃ137:2 These instruments were used to praise God in the Temple in Jerusalem. Since the Temple was destroyed, these people had no reason to play the songs.

138 *A song of David.**

1 LORD, I praise you with all my heart.
   I sing songs of praise to you before the gods.

2 I bow down toward your holy Temple,*
   and I praise your name for your love and loyalty.
   You are famous, and what you promised to do
      will make you even more famous!

3 When I called to you for help,
   you answered me and gave me strength.

4 LORD, all the kings on earth will praise you
   when they hear what you say.

5 They will sing about what the LORD has done,
   because the glory* of the LORD is very great.

6 The LORD has the highest place above all others,
   but he still cares for the humble.
   Even from there, so high above,
      he knows what the proud do.

7 If I am in trouble, you keep me alive.
   If my enemies are angry with me, you save me from them.

8 LORD, I know that you will do what you have promised.
   LORD, your faithful love will last forever.
   You are the one who made us, so don't leave us!

139 *To the director.*
*A praise song of David.**

1 LORD, you have tested me so you know all about me.

2 You know when I sit down and when I get up.
   You know my thoughts from far away.

3 You know where I go and where I lie down.
   You know everything I do.

4 LORD, you know what I want to say,
   even before the words leave my mouth.

5 You are all around me—in front and behind me.
   I feel your hand on my shoulder.

6 I am amazed at what you know;
   it is too much for me to understand.

7 Your Spirit is everywhere I go.
   I cannot escape your presence.

8 If I go up to heaven, there you are.
   If I go down to the place of death, there you are.

9 If I go east where the sun rises
   or go to live in the west beyond the sea,

10 even there you will take my hand and lead me.
   Your strong right hand will protect me.

11 Suppose I wanted to hide from you and said,
   "Surely the darkness will hide me.
   The day will change to night and cover me."

¹² Even the darkness is not dark to you;
        the night is as bright as day.
    Darkness and light are the same to you.

¹³ You made every part of me.*a*
    You put me together in my mother's womb.

¹⁴ I praise you because you made me in such a wonderful way.
    I know how amazing that was!

¹⁵ You could see my bones grow while my body took shape,
        hidden in my mother's womb.*b*

¹⁶ You could see my body grow each passing day.*c*
    You listed all my parts, and not one of them was missing.

¹⁷ Your thoughts are priceless*d* to me.
    They cannot be counted!

¹⁸ If I could count them,
        they would be more than all the grains of sand.
    But when I finished, I would have just begun.*e*

¹⁹ You murderers, get away from me!
    God, kill those wicked people—

²⁰   those who say bad things about you.
    Your enemies use your name falsely.*f*

²¹ LORD, I hate those who hate you.
    I hate those who are against you.

²² I hate them completely!
    Your enemies are also my enemies.

²³ God, examine me and know my mind.
    Test me and know my anxious thoughts.

²⁴ Make sure that I am not going the wrong way.*g*
    Lead me on the path that has always been right.*h*

140

To the director.*
A praise song of David.*

¹ LORD, save me from people who are evil.
    Protect me from those who are cruel,

²   from those who plan to do evil and always cause trouble.

³ Their words are as harmful as the fangs of a snake,
        as deadly as its venom.   *Selah**

⁴ LORD, save me from the wicked!
    Protect me from these cruel people who plan to hurt me.

⁵ These proud people are trying to trap me.
    They spread nets to catch me;
        they set traps in my path.   *Selah*

---

a **139:13** *every part of me* Literally, "kidneys." The ancient Israelites also thought the
emotions were centered in the kidneys. So this probably also means God knew how this
person felt, even before he was born. *b* **139:15** *mother's womb* Literally, "deepest parts of
the earth." *c* **139:16** *each passing
day* Or, "You watched me every day." *d* **139:17** *priceless* Or, "beyond understanding."
e **139:18** *I ... begun* Or, "I would still be with you." *f* **139:20** *Your enemies ... falsely* Here,
the meaning of the Hebrew is not clear. *g* **139:24** *Make sure ... way* Or, "See that I don't
worship idols." *h* **139:24** *Lead me ... right* Or, "Guide me on the ancient path."

6 LORD, you are my God.
    LORD, listen to my prayer.
7 My Lord GOD, you are the powerful one who saves me.
    You protect my head in battle.
8 LORD, don't let the wicked have what they want.
    Don't let their plans succeed.   *Selah*

9 Lord, don't let my enemies win.
    They are planning trouble, but make trouble fall on them.
10 Pour burning coals on their heads.
    Throw my enemies into the fire.
    Throw them into the pit they can never escape.
11 Don't let those cruel liars prosper.
    Let disaster hunt them down.
12 I know the LORD will provide justice for the poor
    and defend the helpless.
13 Those who are right will praise your name;
    those who are honest will live in your presence.

141 *A praise song of David.**

1 LORD, I call to you for help.
    Listen to me as I pray.
    Please hurry and help me!
2 Accept my prayer like a gift of burning incense,
    the words I lift up like an evening sacrifice.*
3 LORD, help me control what I say.
    Don't let me say anything bad.
4 Take away any desire to do evil.
    Keep me from joining the wicked in doing wrong.
    Help me stay away from their feasts.
5 If good people correct me,
    I will consider it a good thing.
    If they criticize me,
    I will accept it like a warm welcome.*a*
    But my prayer will always be
    against the wicked people and the evil they do.
6 Let their judges be put to death.*b*
    Then everyone will know that I told the truth.

7 Like rocks in a field that a farmer has plowed,
    so will our bones be scattered in the grave.
8 My Lord GOD, I look to you for help.
    I look to you for protection; don't let me die.
9 Those evil people are trying to trap me.
    Don't let me fall into their traps.
10 Let the wicked fall into their own traps,
    while I walk away unharmed.

---

*a***141:5** *a warm welcome* Or, "like oil poured over my head."   *b***141:6** *Let their judges . . . to death* Or, "Let their judges be thrown from the cliffs."

142

A maskil* of David. This is a prayer from the time he was in the cave.

1 I cry out to the LORD.
   I beg the LORD to help me.

2 I tell him my problems;
   I tell him about my troubles.

3 I am ready to give up.
   But you, LORD, know the path I am on,
      and you know that my enemies have set a trap for me.

4 I look around,
      and I don't see anyone I know.
   I have no place to run.
      There is no one to save me.

5 LORD, I cry out to you for help:
   "You are my place of safety.
      You are all I need in life."

6 Listen to my prayer.
      I am so weak.
   Save me from those who are chasing me.
      They are stronger than I am.

7 Help me escape this trap*a*
      so that I can praise your name.
   Then good people will celebrate with me,
      because you took care of me.

143

A praise song of David.*

1 LORD, hear my prayer.
      Listen to my call for help and answer my prayer.
   Show me how good and loyal you are.

2 Don't judge me, your servant.
      No one alive could be judged innocent by your standards.

3 My enemies are chasing me.
      They have crushed me into the dirt.
   They are pushing me into the dark grave,
      like people who died long ago.

4 I am ready to give up.
      I am losing my courage.

5 But I remember what happened long ago.
      I am thinking about all you have done.
   I am talking about what you made with your hands!

6 I lift my hands in prayer to you.
      I am waiting for your help, like a dry land waiting for rain.

Selah*

---

*a*142:7 *trap* Literally, "frame around my soul."

7 Hurry, answer me, LORD!
　　I have lost my courage.
　Don't turn away from me.
　　Don't let me die and become like the people lying
　　　in the grave.
8 Show me your faithful love this morning.
　　I trust in you.
　Show me what I should do.
　　I put my life in your hands!
9 LORD, I come to you for protection.
　　Save me from my enemies.
10 Show me what you want me to do.
　　You are my God.
　Let your good Spirit lead me over level ground.
11 LORD, let me live
　　so people will praise your name.
　Show me how good you are,
　　and save me from my trouble.
12 Show me your love,
　　and defeat my enemies.
　Destroy those who are trying to kill me
　　because I am your servant.

144 *A song of David.**

1 The LORD is my Rock.*
　　Praise the LORD!
　He prepares me for war.
　　He trains me for battle.
2 He loves me and protects me.
　　He is my safe place, high on the mountain.
　He rescues me.
　　He is my shield.
　I trust in him.
　　He helps me rule my people.
3 LORD, why are people important to you?
　　Why do you even notice us?
4 Our life is like a puff of air.
　　It is like a passing shadow.
5 LORD, tear open the skies and come down.
　　Touch the mountains and smoke will rise from them.
6 Send the lightning and make my enemies run away.
　　Shoot your "arrows" and make them run away.
7 Reach down from heaven and save me!
　　Don't let me drown in this sea of enemies.
　　Save me from these foreigners.
8 These enemies are liars,
　　even when they swear to tell the truth.

9 God, I will sing a new song about the wonderful things you do.
    I will praise you with a ten-stringed harp.

10 You help kings win their wars.
    You saved your servant David* from his enemy's sword.

11 Save me from these foreigners.
        These enemies are liars,
            even when they swear to tell the truth.

12 Save us so that our sons will be as strong as trees,
    and our daughters like the decorations in the palace.

13 Save us so that our barns will be filled with crops,
    and there will be thousands of sheep in our fields.

14 Then our soldiers will be safe,
    and no enemy will try to break in.
    Then we will not go to war,
    and people will not be screaming in our streets.

15 At times like this, people are very happy.
    They are very happy if the LORD is their God.

145 *A psalm of David.**

1 I will tell of your greatness, my God and King.
    I will praise your name forever and ever.

2 I will praise you every day.
    I will praise your name forever and ever.

3 The LORD is great and deserves all our praise!
    No one can fully understand his greatness.

4 Each generation will praise you
    and tell the next generation about the great things you do.

5 Your majesty and glory* are wonderful.
    I will tell about your miracles.

6 People will tell about the amazing things you do.
    I will tell about the great things you do.

7 They will tell about the good things you do.
    They will sing about your goodness.

8 The LORD is kind and merciful, patient and full of love.

9 The LORD is good to everyone.
    He shows his mercy to everything he made.

10 LORD, all you have made will give thanks to you.
    Your loyal followers will praise you.

11 They will tell how great your kingdom is.
    They will tell how great you are.

12 So others will learn about the mighty things you do,
    about the glory of your kingdom—how marvelous it is!

13 Your kingdom will never end, and you will rule forever.
    The LORD can be trusted in all that he says.
    He is loyal in all that he does.*

*145:13 The LORD ... he does This is not in the standard Hebrew text, but is in a Hebrew text
from Qumran and is in the ancient Greek and Syriac versions.

¹⁴ The Lord lifts up people who have fallen.
    He helps those who are in trouble.
¹⁵ All living things look to you for their food,
    and you give them their food at the right time.
¹⁶ You open your hands
    and give every living thing all that it needs.
¹⁷ Everything the Lord does is good.
    Everything he does shows how loyal he is.
¹⁸ The Lord is near to everyone
    who sincerely calls to him for help.
¹⁹ He listens to his followers,
    and he does what they want.
    He answers their prayers and saves them.
²⁰ The Lord protects everyone who loves him,
    but he destroys all who do evil.
²¹ I will praise the Lord!
    Let everyone praise his holy name forever and ever!

146

¹Praise the Lord!

    My soul, praise the Lord!
² I will praise the Lord all my life.
    I will sing praises to him as long as I live.
³ Don't depend on your leaders for help.
    Don't depend on people because they cannot save you.
⁴ People die and are buried.
    Then all their plans to help are gone.
⁵ But those who ask God for help will be blessed.
    They depend on the Lord their God.
⁶ He made heaven and earth.
    He made the sea and everything in it.
    He can be trusted to do what he says.
⁷ He does what is right for those who have been hurt.
    He gives food to the hungry.
The Lord frees people locked up in prison.
⁸   The Lord makes the blind see again.
The Lord helps those who are in trouble.
    The Lord loves those who do right.
⁹ The Lord protects strangers in our country.
    He cares for widows and orphans,
    but he destroys the wicked.
¹⁰ The Lord will rule forever!
    Zion,* your God will rule forever and ever!

Praise the Lord!

147

¹Praise the Lord because he is good.
    Sing praises to our God.
It is good and pleasant to praise him.

² The LORD rebuilds Jerusalem.
    He brings back the Israelites
        who were taken as prisoners.

³ He heals their broken hearts
    and bandages their wounds.

⁴ He counts the stars
    and knows each of them by name.

⁵ Our Lord is very great.
    He is very powerful.
    There is no limit to what he knows.

⁶ The LORD supports the humble,
    but he shames the wicked.

⁷ Thank the LORD.
    Praise our God with harps.

⁸ He fills the sky with clouds.
    He sends rain to the earth.
    He makes the grass grow on the mountains.

⁹ He gives food to the animals.
    He feeds the young birds.

¹⁰ War horses and powerful soldiers don't make him happy.

¹¹ The LORD is happy with people
    who worship him and trust in his faithful love.

¹² Jerusalem, praise the LORD!
    Zion,* praise your God!

¹³ Jerusalem, God makes your gates strong,
    and he blesses the people in your city.

¹⁴ He brought peace to your country,
    so you have plenty of grain for food.

¹⁵ He gives a command to the earth,
    and it quickly obeys.

¹⁶ He makes the snow fall
    until the ground is white like wool.
    He makes sleet blow through the air like dust.

¹⁷ He makes hail fall like rocks from the sky.
    No one can stand the cold he sends.

¹⁸ Then he gives another command,
    and the warm air blows again.
    The ice melts, and water begins to flow.

¹⁹ He gave his commands to Jacob.*
    He gave his laws and rules to Israel.*

²⁰ He did not do this for any other nation.
    He did not teach his laws to other people.

Praise the LORD!

148

¹Praise the LORD!
Angels above, praise the LORD from heaven!

2 Praise him, all you angels!
   Praise him, all his army[a]!
3 Sun and moon, praise him!
   Stars and lights in the sky, praise him!
4 Praise the LORD, highest heaven!
   Waters above the sky, praise him!
5 They should praise the LORD's name,
   because he gave the command and created them all!
6 He made all these continue forever.
   He made the laws that will never end.
7 Everything on earth, praise him!
   Great sea animals and the oceans, praise the LORD!
8 Praise him, fire and hail, snow and clouds,
   and the stormy winds that obey him.
9 Praise him, mountains and hills,
   fruit trees and cedar trees.
10 Praise him, wild animals and cattle, reptiles and birds.
11 Praise him, kings of the earth and all nations,
   princes and all rulers on earth.
12 Praise him, young men and women,
   old people and children.
13 Praise the LORD's name!
   Honor his name forever!
   His name is greater than any other.
   He is more glorious than heaven and earth.
14 He made his people strong.
   His loyal followers praise him.
   Israel,* his precious people, praise the LORD!

149

1 Praise the LORD.

Sing a new song about the new things
       the LORD has done!
   Sing his praise in the assembly
       where his followers meet together.
2 Let Israel* be happy with their Maker.
   Let the people on Zion* rejoice with their King.
3 Let them praise him by dancing
   and playing their tambourines and harps.
4 The LORD is happy with his people.
   He did a wonderful thing for his humble people.
   He saved them!
5 Let his followers rejoice in their victory!
   Let them be happy, even after going to bed!

6 Let the people shout praise to God
   and take their swords in their hands.

---

a **148:2 his army** This can mean "angels," "stars and planets," or "soldiers in an army."

⁷ Let them go punish the other nations.
   Let them go punish those people.
⁸ God's people will put chains
   on those kings and important people.
⁹ His people will punish them like God commanded.
   All his followers honor him.

Praise the LORD!

150 ¹Praise the LORD!

Praise God in his Temple*!
   Praise him in heaven, his strong fortress*!
² Praise him for the great things he does!
   Praise him for all his greatness!
³ Praise him with trumpets and horns!
   Praise him with harps and lyres*!
⁴ Praise him with tambourines and dancing!
   Praise him with stringed instruments and flutes!
⁵ Praise him with loud cymbals!
   Praise him with crashing cymbals!

⁶ Everything that breathes, praise the LORD!

Praise the LORD!

Proverbs

Introduction

1 ¹These are the proverbs* of Solomon, the son of David* and king of Israel.* ²They will help you learn to be wise, to accept correction, and to understand wise sayings. ³They will teach you to develop your mind in the right way. You will learn to do what is right and to be honest and fair. ⁴These proverbs will make even those without education smart. They will teach young people what they need to know and how to use what they have learned. ⁵Even the wise could become wiser by listening to these proverbs. They will gain understanding and learn to solve difficult problems. ⁶These sayings will help you understand proverbs, stories with hidden meanings, words of the wise, and other difficult sayings.

⁷Knowledge begins with fear and respect for the LORD, but stubborn fools hate wisdom and refuse to learn.

Advice to a Son

⁸My son,ᵃ listen to your father when he corrects you, and don't ignore what your mother teaches you. ⁹What you learn from your parents will bring you honor and respect, like a crown or a gold medal.ᵇ

¹⁰My son, those who love to do wrong will try to trick you. Don't listen to them. ¹¹They will say, "Come with us. Let's hide and beat to death anyone who happens to walk by. ¹²We will swallow them whole, as the grave swallows the dying. ¹³We will take everything they have and fill our houses with stolen goods. ¹⁴So join us, and you can share everything we get."

¹⁵My son, don't follow them. Don't even take the first step along that path. ¹⁶They run to do something evil, and they cannot wait to kill someone.

¹⁷You cannot trap birds with a net if they see you spreading it out. ¹⁸But evil people cannot see the trap they set for themselves. ¹⁹This is what happens to those who are greedy. Whatever they get destroys them.

ᵃ**1:8** *My son* The proverbs in this section may have been directed originally to a teenage boy, perhaps a prince, who was becoming a young man. They are intended to teach him how to be a responsible person and leader who loves and respects God. ᵇ**1:9** Literally, "They are like a wreath of favor to your head and a necklace around your neck."

The Good Woman—Wisdom

²⁰Listen! Wisdom[a] is shouting in the streets. She is crying out in the marketplace. ²¹She is calling out where the noisy crowd gathers:

²²"Fools, how long will you love being ignorant? How long will you make fun of wisdom? How long will you hate knowledge? ²³I wanted to tell you everything I knew and give you all my knowledge, but you didn't listen to my advice and teaching.

²⁴"I tried to help, but you refused to listen. I offered my hand, but you turned away from me. ²⁵You ignored my advice and refused to be corrected. ²⁶So I will laugh at your troubles and make fun of you when what you fear happens. ²⁷Disasters will strike you like a storm. Problems will pound you like a strong wind. Trouble and misery will weigh you down.

²⁸"Fools will call for me, but I will not answer. They will look for me, but they will not find me. ²⁹That is because they hated knowledge. They refused to fear and respect the LORD. ³⁰They ignored my advice and refused to be corrected. ³¹They filled their lives with what they wanted. They went their own way, so they will get what they deserve.

³²"Fools die because they refuse to follow wisdom. They are content to follow their foolish ways, and that will destroy them. ³³But those who listen to me will live in safety and comfort. They will have nothing to fear."

Listen to Wisdom

2 ¹My son, pay attention to what I say. Remember my commands. ²Listen to wisdom, and do your best to understand. ³Ask for good judgment. Cry out for understanding. ⁴Look for wisdom like silver. Search for it like hidden treasure. ⁵If you do this, you will understand what it means to respect the LORD, and you will come to know God.

⁶The LORD is the source of wisdom; knowledge and understanding come from his mouth. ⁷He gives good advice to honest people and shields those who do what is right. ⁸He makes sure that people are treated fairly. He watches over his loyal followers.

⁹If you listen to him, you will understand what is just and fair and how to do what is right. ¹⁰You will gain wisdom, and knowledge will bring you joy.

¹¹Planning ahead will protect you, and understanding will guard you. ¹²These will keep you from following the wrong path and will protect you from those who have evil plans. ¹³Such people have left the straight path and now walk in darkness.* ¹⁴They enjoy doing evil and are happy with the confusion it brings. ¹⁵Their ways are crooked; they lie and cheat.

---

[a]**1:20** *Wisdom* Wisdom is pictured here as a good woman trying to get the attention of this young man, calling him to be wise and obey God. In a later passage (9:13–18) Foolishness is represented as another woman who is urging him toward a life of sin.

[16]Wisdom will save you from that other woman, another man's wife, who tempts you with sweet words. [17]She married when she was young, but then she left her husband. She forgot the marriage vows she made before God. [18]Going into her house leads to death. She will lead you to the grave. [19]All who enter lose their life and never return.

[20]Wisdom will help you follow the example of good people and stay on the right path. [21]Honest people will live in the land, and those who do right will remain there. [22]But the wicked will be forced to leave. Those who lie and cheat will be thrown out of the land.

The Blessing of Wisdom

3 [1]My son, don't forget my teaching. Remember what I tell you to do. [2]What I teach will give you a good, long life, and all will go well for you.

[3]Don't ever let love and loyalty leave you. Tie them around your neck, and write them on your heart. [4]Then God will be pleased and think well of you, and so will everyone else.

[5]Trust the LORD completely, and don't depend on your own knowledge. [6]With every step you take, think about what the Lord wants, and he will help you go the right way. [7]Don't trust in your own wisdom, but fear and respect the LORD and stay away from evil. [8]If you do this, it will be like a refreshing drink and medicine for your body.

[9]Honor the LORD with your wealth and the first part of your harvest. [10]Then your barns will be full of grain, and your barrels will be overflowing with wine.

[11]My son, don't reject the LORD's discipline, and don't be angry when he corrects you. [12]The LORD corrects the one he loves, just as a father corrects a child he cares about.

[13]Those who find wisdom are fortunate; they will be blessed when they gain understanding. [14]Profit that comes from wisdom is better than silver and even the finest gold. [15]Wisdom is worth more than fine jewels. Nothing you desire has more value.

[16]With her right hand, Wisdom offers long life—with the other hand, riches and honor. [17]Wisdom will lead you to a life of joy and peace. [18]Wisdom is like a life-giving tree to those who hold on to her; she is a blessing to those who keep her close.

[19]With wisdom and understanding, the LORD created the earth and sky. [20]With his knowledge, he made the oceans and the clouds that produce rain.

[21]My son, don't ever let wisdom out of your sight. Hold on to wisdom and careful planning. [22]They will bring you a long life filled with honor. [23]As you go through life, you will always be safe and never fall. [24]When you lie down, you will not be afraid. When you rest, your sleep will be peaceful. [25-26]You have no reason to fear some sudden disaster. The LORD will be your

strength. Never fear the destruction that comes to the wicked. The LORD will protect you from that trap.

²⁷Do everything you possibly can for those who need help. ²⁸If your neighbor needs something you have, don't say, "Come back tomorrow." Give it to him immediately.

²⁹Don't make plans to harm your neighbor, who lives near you and trusts you.ᵃ

³⁰Don't take people to court without good reason, especially when they have done nothing to harm you.

³¹Don't envy those who are violent. Never choose to be like them. ³²Such crooked people are disgusting to the LORD. But he is a friend to those who are good and honest.

³³The LORD curses* a wicked family, but he blesses the homes of those who live right.

³⁴He will humiliate those who make fun of others, but he is kind to those who are humble.

³⁵The way the wise live will bring them honor, but the way fools live will bring them shame.

A Father's Advice About Wisdom

4 ¹Children, listen to your father's teaching. Pay attention and you will learn how to learn. ²The advice I give is good, so don't ever forget what I teach you.

³When I was my father's little boy and my mother's dear son,ᵇ ⁴my father taught me this: "Pay attention to what I say. Obey my commands and you will have a good life. ⁵Try to get wisdom and understanding. Don't forget my teaching or ignore what I say. ⁶Don't turn away from wisdom, and she will protect you. Love her, and she will keep you safe.

⁷"The first step to becoming wise is to look for wisdom, so use everything you have to get understanding. ⁸Love wisdom, and she will make you great. Hold on to wisdom, and she will bring you honor. ⁹Wisdom will reward you with a crown of honor and glory."

¹⁰Son, listen to me. Do what I say, and you will live a long time. ¹¹I am teaching you about wisdom and guiding you on the right path. ¹²As you walk on it, you will not step into a trap. Even if you run, you will not trip and fall. ¹³Always remember this teaching. Don't forget it. It is the key to life, so guard it well.

¹⁴Don't take the path of the wicked; don't follow those who do evil. ¹⁵Stay away from that path; don't even go near it. Turn around and go another way. ¹⁶The wicked cannot sleep until they have done something evil. They will not rest until they bring someone down. ¹⁷Evil and violence are their food and drink.

¹⁸The path of those who live right is like the early morning light. It gets brighter and brighter until the full light of day.

ᵃ3:29 who ... trusts you Or, "After all, you live near one another for protection." ᵇ4:3 dear son Or, "only son."

¹⁹But the path of the wicked is like a dark night. They trip and fall over what they cannot see.

²⁰My son, pay attention to what I say. Listen closely to my words. ²¹Don't let them out of your sight. Never stop thinking about them. ²²These words are the secret of life and health to all who discover them. ²³Above all, be careful what you think because your thoughts control your life.

²⁴Don't bend the truth or say things that you know are not right. ²⁵Keep your eyes on the path, and look straight ahead. ²⁶Make sure you are going the right way, and nothing will make you fall. ²⁷Don't go to the right or to the left, and you will stay away from evil.

The Wisdom of Avoiding Adultery

5 ¹Son, listen to this piece of wisdom from me. Pay attention to what I know to be true. ²Remember to live wisely, and what you learn will keep your lips from saying the wrong thing. ³Now, another man's wife might be very charming, and the words from her lips so sweet and inviting. ⁴But in the end, she will bring only bitterness and pain. It will be like bitter poison and a sharp sword. ⁵She is on a path leading to death, and she will lead you straight to the grave. ⁶Don't follow her. She has lost her way and does not even know it. Be careful. Stay on the road that leads to life.

⁷Now, my sons, listen to me. Don't forget the words I say. ⁸Stay away from the woman who commits adultery.* Don't even go near her house. ⁹If you do, others will get the honor you should have had. Some stranger will get everything you worked years to get. ¹⁰People you don't know will take all your wealth. Others will get what you worked for. ¹¹At the end of your life, you will be sad that you ruined your health and lost everything you had. ^{12–13}Then you will say, "Why didn't I listen to my parents? Why didn't I pay attention to my teachers? I didn't want to be disciplined. I refused to be corrected. ¹⁴So now I have suffered through just about every kind of trouble anyone can have, and everyone knows it."

¹⁵Now, about sex and marriage: Drink only the water that comes from your own well, ¹⁶and don't let your water flow out into the streets. ¹⁷Keep it for yourself, and don't share it with strangers. ¹⁸Be happy with your own wife. Enjoy the woman you married while you were young. ¹⁹She is like a beautiful deer, a lovely fawn.* Let her love satisfy you completely. Stay drunk on her love, ²⁰and don't go stumbling into the arms of another woman.

²¹The LORD clearly sees everything you do. He watches where you go. ²²The sins of the wicked will trap them. Those sins will be like ropes holding them back. ²³Evil people will die because they refuse to be disciplined. They will be trapped by their own desires.

Dangers of Debt

6 ¹My son, don't make yourself responsible for the debts of others. Don't make such deals with friends or strangers. ²If you do, your words will trap you. ³You will be under the power of other people, so you must go and free yourself. Beg them to free you from that debt. ⁴Don't wait to rest or sleep. ⁵Escape from that trap like a deer running from a hunter. Free yourself like a bird flying from a trap.

The Dangers of Being Lazy

⁶You lazy people, you should watch what the ants do and learn from them. ⁷Ants have no ruler, no boss, and no leader. ⁸But in the summer, ants gather all of their food and save it. So when winter comes, there is plenty to eat.

⁹You lazy people, how long are you going to lie there? When will you get up? ¹⁰You say, "I need a rest. I think I'll take a short nap." ¹¹But then you sleep and sleep and become poorer and poorer. Soon you will have nothing. It will be as if a thief came and stole everything you owned.

Troublemakers

¹²Some people are just troublemakers. They are always thinking up some crooked plan and telling lies. ¹³They use secret signals to cheat people; they wink their eyes, shuffle their feet, and point a finger. ¹⁴They are always planning to do something bad. ¹⁵But they will be punished. Disaster will strike, and they will be destroyed. There will be no one to help them.

What the Lord Hates

¹⁶ The LORD hates these seven things:
¹⁷ eyes that show pride,
tongues that tell lies,
hands that kill innocent people,
¹⁸ hearts that plan evil things to do,
feet that run to do evil,
¹⁹ witnesses in court who tell lies,
and anyone who causes family members to fight.

Warning Against Adultery

²⁰My son, remember your father's command, and don't forget your mother's teaching. ²¹Remember their words always. Tie them around your neck and keep them over your heart. ²²Let this teaching lead you wherever you go. It will watch over you while you sleep. And when you wake up, it will give you good advice.

²³Your parents give you commands and teachings that are like lights to show you the right way. This teaching corrects you and trains you to follow the path to life. ²⁴It stops you from going to an evil woman, and it protects you from the smooth

talk of another man's wife. ²⁵Such a woman might be beautiful, but don't let that beauty tempt you. Don't let her eyes capture you. ²⁶A prostitute might cost a loaf of bread, but the wife of another man could cost you your life. ²⁷If you drop a hot coal in your lap, your clothes will be burned. ²⁸If you step on one, your feet will be burned. ²⁹If you sleep with another man's wife, you will be punished.

³⁰⁻³¹A hungry man might steal to fill his stomach. If he is caught, he must pay seven times more than he stole. It might cost him everything he owns, but other people understand. They don't lose all their respect for him. ³²But a man who commits adultery* is a fool. He brings about his own destruction. ³³He will suffer disease and disgrace and never be free from the shame. ³⁴The woman's husband will be jealous and angry and do everything he can to get revenge. ³⁵No payment—no amount of money—will stop him.

Wisdom Will Keep You From Adultery

7 ¹My son, remember my words. Don't forget what I have told you. ²Consider my teaching as precious as your own eyes. Obey my commands, and you will have a good life. ³Tie them around your finger. Write them on your heart. ⁴Treat wisdom like the woman you love and knowledge like the one dearest to you. ⁵Wisdom will save you from that other woman, the other man's wife, who tempts you with such sweet words.

⁶One day I was looking out my window ⁷at some foolish teenagers and noticed one who had no sense at all. ⁸He was walking through the marketplace and came to the corner where a certain woman lived. He then turned up the road that goes by her house. ⁹The day was ending. The sun had set, and it was almost dark. ¹⁰Suddenly, there she was in front of him, dressed like a prostitute. She had plans for him. ¹¹She was a wild and rebellious woman who would not stay at home. ¹²She walked the streets, always looking for someone to trap. ¹³She grabbed the young man and kissed him. Without shame, she looked him in the eye and said, ¹⁴"I offered a fellowship offering* today. I gave what I promised to give, ¹⁵and I still have plenty of food left. So I came out to find you, and here you are! ¹⁶I have clean sheets on my bed—special ones from Egypt. ¹⁷My bed smells wonderful with myrrh,* aloes,* and cinnamon. ¹⁸Come, let's enjoy ourselves all night. We can make love until dawn. ¹⁹My husband has gone on a business trip. ²⁰He took enough money for a long trip and won't be home for two weeks.ᵃ"

²¹This is what the woman said to tempt the young man, and her smooth words tricked him. ²²He followed her, like a bull

---

ᵃ**7:20** *won't be … weeks* Literally, "will not come home until the full moon." The fellowship meal shows that this happened at the time of the new moon, the first day of the Hebrew month.

being led to the slaughter. He was like a deer walking into a
trap, ²³where a hunter waits to shoot an arrow through its
heart. The boy was like a bird flying into a net, never seeing
the danger he was in.

²⁴Now, sons, listen to me. Pay attention to what I say.
²⁵Don't let your heart lead you to an evil woman like that.
Don't go where she wants to lead you. ²⁶She has brought down
some of the most powerful men; she has left many dead bodies
in her path. ²⁷Her house is the place of death. The road to it
leads straight to the grave.

Wisdom—the Good Woman

8 ¹Listen, Wisdom is calling.
Yes, Understanding is shouting for us.
² Wisdom stands at the top of the hill,
by the road where the paths meet.
³ She is near the entrance to the city,
calling from the open gates.

⁴"I am calling out to all of you.
I am speaking to everyone.
⁵ You who are ignorant, learn to be wise.
You who are foolish, get some common sense.
⁶ Listen, I have something important to say,
and I am telling you what is right.
⁷ My words are true,
and I will not say anything that is wrong.
⁸ Everything I say is right;
there is nothing false or crooked about it.
⁹ These things are clear
to any intelligent person.
They are right
to anyone with knowledge.
¹⁰ Choose discipline over silver
and knowledge over the finest gold.
¹¹ Wisdom is better than pearls,
and nothing you desire compares with her.

The Value of Wisdom

¹²"I am Wisdom.
I live with Good Judgment.
I am at home with Knowledge and Planning.
¹³ To respect the LORD means to hate evil.
I hate pride and boasting,
evil lives and hurtful words.
¹⁴ I have good advice and common sense to offer.
I have understanding and power.
¹⁵ With my help kings rule,
and governors make good laws.

16 With my help leaders govern,
   and important officials make good decisions.[a]

17 I love those who love me,
   and those who look for me will find me.

18 With me there are riches and honor.
   I have lasting wealth to give to you.

19 What I give is better than fine gold.
   What I produce is better than pure silver.

20 I lead people the right way—
   along the paths of justice.

21 I give riches to those who love me,
   and I fill their houses with treasures.

22 "The LORD made me in the beginning,
   long before he did anything else.

23 I was formed a long time ago,
   before the world was made.

24 I was born before there was an ocean,
   before the springs began to flow.

25 I was born before the mountains and hills were set into place,

26 before the earth and fields were made,
   before the dust of this world was formed.

27 I was there when the Lord set up the skies,
   when he drew a circle in the ocean
      to make a place for the land.

28 I was there when he put the clouds in the sky
   and made the deep springs flow.

29 I was there when he set the limits on the sea
   to make it stop where he said.
   I was there when he laid the foundations of the earth.

30 I grew up as a child by his side,[b]
   laughing and playing all the time.

31 I played in the world he made
   and enjoyed the people he put there.

32 "Now, children, listen to me.
   If you follow my ways,
      you will be happy too.

33 Listen to my teaching and be wise;
   don't ignore what I say.

34 Whoever waits at my door
   and listens for me will be blessed.

35 Those who find me find life,
   and the LORD will reward them.

36 But those who do not find me
   put their lives in danger.
   Whoever hates me loves death."

---

[a] **8:16** *and important … decisions* Or, "as well as important officials, all the judges on earth."
[b] **8:30** *I grew … his side* Or, "I was beside him like a skilled worker."

Wisdom's Invitation

9 ¹Wisdom has built her house; she has made it strong with seven columns.*ᵃ* ²She has cooked meat, mixed wine, and put food on the table. ³She has sent her servant girls to announce from the highest hill in the city,*ᵇ* ⁴"Whoever needs instruction, come." She invites all the simple people and says, ⁵"Come, eat my food and drink the wine I have prepared. ⁶Leave your old, foolish ways and live! Advance along the path of understanding."

⁷Criticize a person who is rude and shows no respect, and you will only get insults. Correct the wicked, and you will only get hurt. ⁸Don't correct such people, or they will hate you. But correct those who are wise, and they will love you. ⁹Teach the wise, and they will become wiser. Instruct those who live right, and they will gain more knowledge.

¹⁰Wisdom begins with fear and respect for the LORD. Knowledge of the Holy One leads to understanding. ¹¹Wisdom will help you live longer; she will add years to your life. ¹²If you become wise, it will be for your own good. If you are rude and show no respect, you are the one who will suffer.

Foolishness—the Other Woman

¹³Foolishness is that other woman, who is loud, stupid, and knows nothing. ¹⁴She sits on her chair at the door of her house, up on the highest hill of the city. ¹⁵When people walk by, she calls out to them. They show no interest in her, but still she says, ¹⁶"Whoever needs instruction, come." She invites all the simple people and says, ¹⁷"Stolen water is sweet. Stolen bread tastes good." ¹⁸Those simple people don't realize that her house is full of ghosts and that her guests have entered the world of the dead.

Solomon's Proverbs

10 ¹These are the proverbs* of Solomon:

A wise son makes his father happy; a foolish one makes his mother sad.

²Wealth gained by doing wrong will not really help you, but doing right will save you from death.

³The LORD takes care of good people and gives them the food they need, but he keeps the wicked from getting what they want.

⁴Lazy hands will make you poor; hard-working hands will make you rich.

⁵A son who works hard while it is harvest time will be successful, but one who sleeps through the harvest is worthless.

⁶People say good things about those who live right, but the words of the wicked only hide their violent plans.

---

*ᵃ*9:1 *seven columns* In ancient Israel, a good house was one that had four main rooms with seven columns to support the roof.   *ᵇ*9:3 Or, "She has sent out her servant girls and invited people to come to the highest hill in the city to eat with her."

[7]Good people leave memories that bless us, but the wicked are soon forgotten.

[8]The wise accept instruction, but fools argue and bring trouble on themselves.

[9]Honest people can always feel secure, but lying cheaters will be caught.

[10]If you fail to speak the truth, trouble will follow. If you speak openly, peace will come.[a]

[11]The words of good people are like a spring of fresh water,[b] but the words of the wicked only hide their violent plans.

[12]Hatred causes arguments, but love overlooks all wrongs.

[13]Intelligent people speak words of wisdom, but fools must be punished before they learn their lesson.[c]

[14]Wise people are quiet and learn new things, but fools talk and bring trouble on themselves.

[15]Wealth protects the rich, but poverty destroys the poor.

[16]What good people do brings life, but wicked people produce only sin.

[17]Those who accept correction show others how to live. Those who reject correction lead others the wrong way.

[18]You might have to lie to hide your hatred, but saying something hurtful could be even more foolish.[d]

[19]A person who talks too much gets into trouble. A wise person learns to be quiet.

[20]Words from good people are like pure silver, but thoughts from the wicked are worthless.

[21]Good people say things that help others, but the wicked die from a lack of understanding.

[22]It is the LORD's blessing that brings wealth, and no hard work can add to it.[e]

[23]Fools enjoy doing wrong, but the wise enjoy wisdom.

[24]The wicked will be defeated by what they fear, but good people will get what they want.

[25]The wicked are destroyed when trouble comes, but good people stand strong forever.

[26]Sending a lazy person to do anything is as irritating as vinegar on your teeth or smoke in your eyes.

[27]Respect for the LORD will add years to your life, but the wicked will have their lives cut short.

[28]What good people hope for brings happiness,[f] but what the wicked hope for brings destruction.

---

[a]**10:10** This is from the ancient Greek version. The Hebrew repeats the second half of verse 8. [b]**10:11** *spring of fresh water* Or, "the source of life." [c]**10:13** Literally, "Wisdom can be found on the lips of the intelligent, but a rod on the back of the senseless." This is a wordplay. In Hebrew, "lip" sounds like "rod." [d]**10:18** Or, "Sometimes it would be foolish to say something negative, but the only way to hide your opposition would be to lie." [e]**10:22** Or, "A blessing from the LORD will bring you true wealth—wealth without troubles." [f]**10:28** *good people … happiness* Or, "Good people can look forward to happiness."

²⁹The LORD protects those who do right, but he destroys those who do wrong.

³⁰Good people will always be safe, but the wicked will be forced out of the land.

³¹Those who live right say wise things, but people stop listening to troublemakers.[a]

³²Good people know the right things to say, but the wicked say things to make trouble.

11 ¹The LORD hates false scales, but he loves accurate weights.

²Proud and boastful people will be shamed, but wisdom stays with those who are modest and humble.

³Good people are guided by their honesty, but crooks who lie and cheat will ruin themselves.

⁴Money is worthless when you face God's punishment, but living right will save you from death.

⁵Doing right makes life better for those who are good, but the wicked are destroyed by their own wicked ways.

⁶Doing right sets honest people free, but people who can't be trusted are trapped by their greed.

⁷When the wicked die, all their hopes are lost; everything they thought they could do comes to nothing.

⁸Good people escape from trouble, but the wicked come along and are trapped by it.

⁹With their words hypocrites* can destroy their neighbors. But with what they know, good people can escape.

¹⁰When good people are successful, the whole city is happy, and they all shout with joy when evil people are destroyed.

¹¹Blessings from the honest people living in a city will make it great, but the things evil people say can destroy it.

¹²Stupid people say bad things about their neighbors.[b] Wise people know to be quiet.

¹³People who tell secrets about others cannot be trusted. Those who can be trusted keep quiet.

¹⁴A nation without wise leaders will fall. Many good advisors make a nation safe.

¹⁵You will be sorry if you promise to pay a stranger's debt. Refuse to make such promises and you will be safe.

¹⁶A kind and gentle woman gains respect, but violent men gain only wealth.

¹⁷People who are kind will be rewarded for their kindness, but cruel people will be rewarded with trouble.

¹⁸The work of evil people is all lies, but those who do right will receive a good reward.[c]

¹⁹People who do what is right are on their way to life, but those who always want to do wrong are on their way to death.

---

[a] 10:31 Or, "The mouth of a good man speaks wisdom, but the tongue of a troublemaker will be cut off."   [b] 11:12 *Stupid people … neighbors* Or, "The neighbors hate a stupid person."   [c] 11:18 This is a wordplay in Hebrew. The word "lies" sounds like the word "reward."

²⁰The LORD hates those who love to do evil, but he is pleased with those who try to do right.

²¹The truth is, evil people will be punished, and good people will be set free.

²²A beautiful woman without good sense is like a gold ring in a pig's nose.

²³What good people want brings more good. What evil people want brings more trouble.

²⁴Some people give freely and gain more; others refuse to give and end up with less.

²⁵Give freely, and you will profit. Help others, and you will gain more for yourself.

²⁶People curse* a greedy man who refuses to sell his grain, but they bless a man who sells his grain to feed others.

²⁷People are pleased with those who try to do good. Those who look for trouble will find it.

²⁸Those who trust in their riches will fall like dead leaves, but good people will blossom.

²⁹Those who cause trouble for their families will inherit nothing but the wind. A foolish person will end up as a servant to one who is wise.

³⁰What good people produce is like a life-giving tree. Those who are wise give new life to others.ᵃ

³¹If good people are rewarded here on earth, then surely those who do evil will also get what they deserve.

12 ¹Whoever loves discipline loves to learn; whoever hates to be corrected is stupid.

²It is good to learn what pleases the LORD, because he condemns those who plan to do wrong.

³Evil people are never safe, but good people remain safe and secure.

⁴A good wife is like a crown to her husband, but a shameful wife is like a cancer.

⁵Good people are honest and fair in all they do, but those who are evil lie and cannot be trusted.

⁶Evil people use their words to hurt others, but the words from good people can save others from danger.

⁷When evil people are destroyed, they are gone and forgotten, but good people are remembered long after they are gone.

⁸You praise people for their intelligence, but no one respects those who are stupid.

⁹It is better to appear unimportant and have a servant than to pretend to be important and have no food.

¹⁰Good people take good care of their animals, but the wicked know only how to be cruel.ᵇ

¹¹Farmers who work their land have plenty of food, but those who waste their time on worthless projects are foolish.

ᵃ**11:30** Or, according to one ancient version, "The fruit of a good man is a tree of life, but a violent man takes lives." ᵇ**12:10** Or, "even the 'kindness' of the wicked is still cruelty."

¹²The wicked want a share of what an evil man might catch. But like a plant with deep roots, a good man is the one who produces the most.ᵃ

¹³The wicked are trapped by their foolish words, but good people escape from such trouble.

¹⁴People get good things for the words they say, and they are rewarded for the work they do.

¹⁵Fools always think their own way is best, but wise people listen to what others tell them.

¹⁶Fools are easily upset, but wise people avoid insulting others.

¹⁷Good people speak the truth and can be trusted in court, but liars make bad witnesses.

¹⁸Speak without thinking, and your words can cut like a knife. Be wise, and your words can heal.

¹⁹Lies last only a moment, but the truth lasts forever.

²⁰People who work for evil make trouble, but those who plan for peace bring happiness.

²¹The Lord will keep good people safe, but evil people will have many troubles.

²²The LORD hates people who tell lies, but he is pleased with those who tell the truth.

²³Smart people don't tell everything they know, but fools tell everything and show they are fools.

²⁴Those who work hard will be put in charge of others, but lazy people will have to work like slaves.

²⁵Worry takes away your joy, but a kind word makes you happy.

²⁶Good people are careful about choosing their friends, but evil people always choose the wrong ones.

²⁷Lazy people don't get what they want, but riches come to those who work hard.

²⁸Along the path of goodness there is life; that is the way to live forever.ᵇ

13 ¹A wise son listens to his father's advice, but a proud son will not listen to correction.

²People get good things for the words they say, but those who cannot be trusted say only bad things.

³People who are careful about what they say will save their lives, but those who speak without thinking will be destroyed.

⁴Lazy people always want things but never get them. Those who work hard get plenty.

⁵Good people hate lies, but the wicked do evil, shameful things.

⁶Goodness protects honest people, but evil destroys those who love to sin.

⁷Some people act like they are rich, but they have nothing. Others act like they are poor, but they are really rich.

ᵃ**12:12** The Hebrew here is hard to understand.   ᵇ**12:28** *that is ... forever* Or, "but there is a path that leads to death."

⁸The rich might have to pay a ransom to save their lives, but the poor never receive such threats.

⁹The light of those who do right shines brighter and brighter, but the lamp of the wicked becomes darker and darker.*ᵃ*

¹⁰Pride causes arguments, but those who listen to others are wise.

¹¹Money gained by cheating others will soon be gone. Money earned through hard work will grow and grow.

¹²Hope that is delayed makes you sad, but a wish that comes true fills you with joy.

¹³Those who reject a command hurt themselves; those who respect a command will be rewarded.

¹⁴The teaching of the wise is a source of life; their words will save you from deadly traps.

¹⁵People like a person with good sense, but life is hard for someone who cannot be trusted.

¹⁶Wise people always think before they do anything, but fools show how stupid they are by what they do.

¹⁷Disaster will catch up to the wicked messenger, but a runner who can be trusted will bring peace.

¹⁸If you refuse to learn from your mistakes, you will be poor, and no one will respect you. If you listen when you are criticized, you will be honored.

¹⁹People are happy when they get what they want. But stupid people want nothing but evil, and they refuse to change.

²⁰Be friends with those who are wise, and you will become wise. Choose fools to be your friends, and you will have trouble.

²¹Trouble chases sinners wherever they go, but good things happen to good people.

²²It is good to have something to pass down to your grandchildren. But wealth hidden away by sinners will be given to those who live right.

²³The poor might have good land that produces plenty of food, but bad decisions can take it away.*ᵇ*

²⁴If you don't correct your children, you don't love them. If you love them, you will be quick to discipline them.

²⁵Good people will have plenty to eat, but the wicked will go hungry.

14 ¹A wise woman makes her home what it should be, but the home of a foolish woman is destroyed by her own actions.*ᶜ*

²Those who live right respect the LORD, but dishonest people hate him.

³Foolish words cause you trouble; wise words protect you.

⁴A barn with no cattle might be clean, but strong bulls are needed for a good harvest.

---

*ᵃ***13:9** Or, "The light of those who do right is happy; the lamp of the wicked goes out."
*ᵇ***13:23** Or, "The fields of the poor might produce plenty of food, but the unjust often take it away." *ᶜ***14:1** Or, "Wisdom builds her house, but Foolishness tears hers down with her own hands."

⁵A good witness is one who does not lie. A bad witness is a liar who cannot be trusted.

⁶Anyone who makes fun of wisdom will never find it, but knowledge comes easily to those who understand its value.

⁷Stay away from fools, there is nothing they can teach you.

⁸Wisdom lets smart people know what they are doing, but stupid people only think they know.

⁹Fines are needed to make fools obey the law, but good people are happy to obey it.

¹⁰When you are sad, no one else feels the pain; and when you are happy, no one else can really feel the joy.

¹¹An evil person's house will be destroyed, but a good person's family will do well.

¹²There is a way that people think is right, but it leads only to death.

¹³Laughter might hide your sadness. But when the laughter is gone, the sadness remains.

¹⁴Evil people will be paid back for the wrong they do, and good people will be rewarded for the good they do.

¹⁵Fools believe every word they hear, but wise people think carefully about everything.

¹⁶Wise people are cautious and avoid trouble; fools are too confident and careless.

¹⁷A quick-tempered person does stupid things, but it is also true that people don't like anyone who quietly plans evil.

¹⁸Fools are rewarded with more foolishness. Smart people are rewarded with knowledge.

¹⁹Good people will defeat those who are evil, and the wicked will be forced to show respect to those who live right.

²⁰The poor have no friends, not even their neighbors, but the rich have many friends.

²¹It is wrong to say bad things about your neighbors. Be kind to the poor, and you will be blessed.

²²Whoever works to do good will find love and loyalty. It is a mistake to work at doing evil.

²³If you work hard, you will have plenty. If you do nothing but talk, you will not have enough.

²⁴A wise person's reward is wealth, but a fool's reward is foolishness.

²⁵A witness who tells the truth saves lives, but one who tells lies hurts others.

²⁶People who respect the LORD will be safe, and they will make their children feel secure.

²⁷Respect for the LORD gives true life and will save you from death's trap.

²⁸Kings of large nations have great honor. Rulers without a country have nothing.

²⁹A patient person is very smart. A quick-tempered person makes stupid mistakes.

³⁰Peace of mind makes the body healthy, but jealousy is like a cancer.

³¹Whoever takes advantage of the poor insults their Maker, but whoever is kind to them honors him.

³²The wicked will be defeated by their evil, but good people are protected by their honesty.ᵃ

³³A wise person is always thinking wise thoughts, but a fool knows nothing about wisdom.

³⁴Goodness makes a nation great, but sin is a shame to any people.

³⁵Kings are pleased with intelligent officials, but they will punish shameful ones.

15 ¹A gentle answer makes anger disappear, but a rough answer makes it grow.

²Listening to wise people increases your knowledge, but only nonsense comes from the mouths of fools.

³The LORD sees what happens everywhere. He watches everyone, good and evil.

⁴Kind words are like a life-giving tree, but lying words will crush your spirit.

⁵Fools refuse to listen to their father's advice, but those who accept discipline are smart.

⁶Good people are rich in many ways, but those who are evil get nothing but trouble.

⁷Wise people say things that give you new knowledge, but fools say nothing worth hearing.

⁸The LORD hates the offerings of the wicked, but he is happy to hear the prayers of those who live right.

⁹The LORD hates the way evil people live, but he loves those who try to do good.

¹⁰Whoever stops living right will be punished. Whoever hates to be corrected will be destroyed.

¹¹The LORD knows everything, even what happens in the place of death. So surely he knows what people are thinking.

¹²Fools hate to be told they are wrong, so they refuse to ask wise people for advice.

¹³If you are happy, your face shows it. If you are sad, your spirit feels defeated.

¹⁴Intelligent people want more knowledge, but fools only want more nonsense.

¹⁵Life is always hard for the poor, but the right attitude can turn it into a party.

¹⁶It is better to be poor and respect the LORD than to be rich and have many troubles.

¹⁷It is better to eat a little where there is love than to eat a lot where there is hate.

ᵃ**14:32** Or, "The wicked will be crushed by their evil, and those who hope for their destruction are right to do so."

¹⁸A quick temper causes fights, but patience brings peace and calm.

¹⁹For lazy people, life is a path overgrown with thorns and thistles. For those who do what is right, it is a smooth highway.

²⁰Wise children make their parents happy. Foolish children bring them shame.

²¹Doing foolish things makes a fool happy, but a wise person is careful to do what is right.

²²If you don't ask for advice, your plans will fail. With many advisors, they will succeed.

²³People are happy when they give a good answer. And there is nothing better than the right word at the right time.

²⁴What wise people do leads to life here on earth*a* and stops them from going down to the place of death.

²⁵The Lord destroys a proud man's house but protects a widow's property.

²⁶The Lord hates evil thoughts, but he is pleased with kind words.

²⁷Whoever takes money to do wrong invites disaster. Refuse such gifts, and you will live.

²⁸Good people think before they answer, but the wicked do not, and what they say causes trouble.

²⁹The Lord is far away from the wicked, but he always hears the prayers of those who do what is right.

³⁰A smile*b* makes people happy. Good news makes them feel better.

³¹To be counted among the wise, you must learn to accept helpful criticism.

³²If you refuse to be corrected, you are only hurting yourself. Listen to criticism, and you will gain understanding.

³³Wisdom teaches you to respect the Lord. You must be humbled before you can be honored.

16 ¹People might plan what they want to say, but it is the Lord who gives them the right words.

²People think that whatever they do is right, but the Lord judges their reason for doing it.

³Turn to the Lord for help in everything you do, and you will be successful.

⁴The Lord has a plan for everything. In his plan, the wicked will be destroyed.

⁵The Lord hates those who are proud. You can be sure he will punish them all.

⁶Faithful love and loyalty will remove your guilt.*c* Respect the Lord, and you will stay far away from evil.

⁷When people live to please the Lord, even their enemies will be at peace with them.

---

a 15:24 *here on earth* Literally, "above," that is, "above the ground." *b* 15:30 *smile* Literally, "a sparkle in the eyes." *c* 16:6 *remove your guilt* Or, "make atonement." The Hebrew word means "to cover or erase a person's sins."

[8]It is better to be poor and do right than to be rich and do wrong.

[9]People can plan what they want to do, but it is the LORD who guides their steps.

[10]When a king speaks, his words are law. So when he makes a decision, it is never a mistake.

[11]The LORD wants all scales and balances to be right; he wants all business agreements to be fair.

[12]Kings hate anyone doing wrong,[a] because kingdoms grow strong only when everyone is honest and fair.

[13]Kings want to hear the truth. They like those who are honest.

[14]When a king gets angry, he can put someone to death. So it is wise to keep the king happy.

[15]When the king is happy, life is better for everyone. When he is pleased, it is like a refreshing spring rain.

[16]Wisdom is worth much more than gold. Understanding is worth much more than silver.

[17]Good people try to avoid evil. They watch what they do and protect themselves.

[18]Pride is the first step toward destruction. Proud thoughts will lead you to defeat.

[19]It is better to be a humble person living among the poor than to share the wealth among the proud.

[20]Good things happen to those who learn from their experiences, and the LORD blesses those who trust him.

[21]People will know if someone is wise. Those who choose their words carefully can be very convincing.

[22]Good sense is a spring of fresh water to those who have it, but fools can offer only foolishness.

[23]Wise people always think before they speak, so what they say is worth listening to.

[24]Kind words are like honey; they are easy to accept and good for your health.

[25]There is a way that seems right to people, but that way leads only to death.

[26]The thought of hunger keeps the workers working so that they can eat.

[27]Troublemakers create disasters. Their advice destroys like a wildfire.

[28]Troublemakers are always causing problems. Their gossip breaks up the closest of friends.

[29]Cruel people trick their neighbors and make them do wrong. [30]With a wink of the eye they plan to trick someone. With a grin they make plans to hurt their friends.

[31]Gray hair is a crown of glory on people who have lived good lives. It is earned by living right.

[a]**16:12** *Kings … wrong* Or, "It is disgusting when kings do wrong,"

³²It is better to be patient than to be a strong soldier. It is better to control your anger than to capture a city.

³³People might throw lots* to make a decision, but the answer always come from the LORD.

17 ¹It is better to have nothing but a dry piece of bread to eat in peace than a whole house full of food with everyone arguing.

²A smart servant will gain control over his master's foolish son. He will be treated like a son and get a share of the inheritance.

³Fire is used to make gold and silver pure, but a person's heart is made pure by the LORD.

⁴People who do evil listen to evil ideas. Liars listen to liars.

⁵Whoever makes fun of beggars insults their Maker. Whoever laughs at someone else's trouble will be punished.

⁶Grandchildren are the pride and joy of old age, and children take great pride in their parents.

⁷You wouldn't expect to hear a fine speech from a fool, and you shouldn't expect lies from a ruler.

⁸Some people think a bribe is like a lucky charm—it seems to work wherever they go.

⁹Forgive someone, and you will strengthen your friendship. Keep reminding them, and you will destroy it.

¹⁰Smart people learn more from a single correction than fools learn from a hundred beatings.

¹¹Those who are evil only want to cause trouble. In the end, punishment without mercy will be sent to them.

¹²It is better to meet a bear robbed of her cubs than a fool who is busy doing foolish things.

¹³If you do wrong to those who were good to you, you will have trouble the rest of your life.

¹⁴The start of an argument is like a small leak in a dam. Stop it before a big fight breaks out.

¹⁵The LORD hates these two things: punishing the innocent and letting the guilty go free.

¹⁶Money is wasted on fools. They cannot buy wisdom when they have no sense.

¹⁷A friend loves you all the time, but a brother was born to help in times of trouble.

¹⁸Only a fool would promise to pay for someone else's debts.

¹⁹A troublemaker loves to start arguments. Anyone who likes to brag is asking for trouble.

²⁰Crooks will not profit from their crimes, and those who plan to cause trouble will be trapped when it comes.

²¹A man who has a fool for a son will be disappointed. A fool brings no joy to his father.

²²Happiness is good medicine, but sorrow is a disease.

²³A wicked judge will accept a bribe, and that keeps justice from being done.

²⁴Intelligent people think about what needs to be done here and now. Fools are always dreaming about faraway places.

²⁵Foolish children upset their parents and make them sad.

²⁶It is wrong to punish an innocent person or attack leaders for doing what is right.

²⁷Intelligent people choose their words carefully. Those who know what they are doing remain calm.*a*

²⁸Silent fools seem wise. They say nothing and appear to be smart.

18 ¹Some people like to do things their own way, and they get upset when people give them advice.

²Fools don't want to learn from others. They only want to tell their own ideas.

³Do something evil, and people will hate you. Do something shameful, and they will have no respect for you.

⁴Words from wise people are like water bubbling up from a deep well—the well of wisdom.

⁵You must be fair in judging others. It is wrong to favor the guilty and rob the innocent of justice.

⁶Fools say things to start arguments. They are just asking for a beating.

⁷Fools hurt themselves when they speak. Their own words trap them.

⁸People love to hear gossip. It is like tasty food on its way to the stomach.

⁹Someone who does careless work is as bad as someone who destroys things.

¹⁰The name of the LORD is like a strong tower. Those who do what is right can run to him for protection.

¹¹The rich think their wealth will protect them. They think it is a strong fortress.

¹²A proud person will soon be ruined, but a humble person will be honored.

¹³Let people finish speaking before you try to answer them. That way you will not embarrass yourself and look foolish.

¹⁴A good attitude will support you when you are sick, but if you give up, nothing can help.*b*

¹⁵Wise people want to learn more, so they listen closely to gain knowledge.

¹⁶Gifts can open many doors and help you meet important people.

¹⁷The first person to speak always seems right until someone comes and asks the right questions.

¹⁸The best way to settle an argument between two powerful people may be to use lots.*

---

*a*17:27 *remain calm* Literally, "have a cool spirit."   *b*18:14 *help* Literally, "lift up" or "heal."

¹⁹An insulted brother is harder to win back than a city with strong walls. Arguments separate people like the strong bars of a palace gate.

²⁰Your words can be as satisfying as fruit, as pleasing as the food that fills your stomach.

²¹The tongue can speak words that bring life or death. Those who love to talk must be ready to accept what it brings.

²²If you find a wife, you have found something good. She shows that the LORD is happy with you.

²³The poor are polite when they beg for help. The rich are rude with their answer.

²⁴Some friends are fun to be with,ᵃ but a true friend can be better than a brother.

19 ¹It is better to be poor and honest than to be a liar and a fool.

²Being excited about something is not enough. You must also know what you are doing. Don't rush into something, or you might do it wrong.

³People ruin their lives with the foolish things they do, and then they blame the LORD for it.

⁴Wealth will bring you many friends, but become poor and your friends will leave you.

⁵A witness who lies will be punished; that liar will not escape.

⁶Many people are nice to a generous person. Everyone wants to be friends with someone who gives gifts.

⁷If you are poor, your family will turn against you, and your friends will avoid you even more. You might beg them for help, but no one will come to help you.

⁸Be a friend to yourself; do all you can to be wise. Try hard to understand, and you will be rewarded.

⁹A witness who lies will be punished. That liar will be destroyed.

¹⁰A fool should not be rich, and a slave should not rule over princes.

¹¹Experience makes you more patient, and you are most patient when you ignore insults.

¹²The shouts of an angry king are like a roaring lion, but his kind words are like a gentle rain falling softly on the grass.

¹³A foolish son brings a flood of troubles to his father, and a complaining wife is like the constant dripping of water.

¹⁴People receive houses and money from their parents, but a good wife is a gift from the LORD.

¹⁵Laziness brings on sleep, and an appetite for rest brings on hunger.

¹⁶Obey the law and live; ignore it and die.

¹⁷Giving help to the poor is like loaning money to the LORD. He will pay you back for your kindness.

ᵃ**18:24** *Some friends … with* Or, "Some friends can bring disaster."

¹⁸Discipline your children while there is still hope. Avoiding it can be deadly.

¹⁹People who are quick to become angry must pay the price. Protect them from punishment, and they become worse.

²⁰Listen to advice and accept discipline; then you, too, will become wise.

²¹People might make many plans, but what the LORD says is what will happen.

²²People want a friend they can trust. It is better to be poor than to be a liar.

²³Respect the LORD and you will have a good life, one that is satisfying and free from trouble.

²⁴Some people are too lazy to take care of themselves. They will not even lift the food from their plate to their mouth.

²⁵Punish a rude, arrogant person, and even slow learners will become wiser. But just a little correction is enough to teach a person who has understanding.

²⁶Those who would steal from their father and chase away their mother are disgusting, shameful people.

²⁷My son, if you stop listening to instructions, you will keep making stupid mistakes.

²⁸Using a criminal as a witness makes a joke of justice. People like that only want to do wrong.

²⁹People who show no respect for anything must be brought to justice. You must punish such fools.

20 ¹Wine and beer make people lose control; they get loud and stumble around. And that is foolish.

²An angry king is like a roaring lion. Make him angry and you could lose your life.

³People who refuse to argue deserve respect. Any fool can start an argument.

⁴Some people are too lazy to plant seeds. So at harvest time, they look for food and find nothing.

⁵Getting information from someone can be like getting water from a deep well. If you are smart, you will draw it out.

⁶You might call many people your "friends," but it is hard to find someone who can really be trusted.

⁷When people live good, honest lives, their children are blessed.

⁸When the king sits and judges people, he must look carefully to separate the evil from the good.

⁹Can anyone say their heart is pure? Who can say, "I am free from sin"?

¹⁰The LORD hates for people to use the wrong weights and measures to cheat others.

¹¹Even children show what they are like by the things they do. You can see if their actions are pure and right.

¹²It was the LORD who gave us eyes for seeing and ears for hearing.

¹³If you love to sleep, you will become poor. Use your time working and you will have plenty to eat.

¹⁴When buying something, people always say, "It's no good. It costs too much." Then they go away and tell others what a good deal they got.

¹⁵The right knowledge can bring you gold, pearls, and other expensive things.

¹⁶If someone promises to pay the debt of a stranger, get a coat or something from him to keep until the debt is paid.

¹⁷It may seem to be a good thing to get something by cheating, but in the end, it will be worth nothing.

¹⁸Get good advice when you make your plans. Before you start a war, find good advisors.

¹⁹You cannot trust someone who would talk about things told in private. So don't be friends with someone who talks too much.

²⁰Those who would curse* their father or mother are like a lamp that goes out on the darkest night.

²¹If your wealth was easy to get, it will not be worth much to you.*a*

²²Don't ever say, "I'll pay them back for what they did to me!" Wait for the LORD. He will make things right.

²³The LORD hates for people to use the wrong weights to cheat others. It is wrong to use scales that are not accurate.

²⁴The LORD guides our steps, and we never know where he will lead us.*b*

²⁵Think carefully before you promise to give something to God. Later, you might wish you had not made that promise.

²⁶Like a farmer who separates wheat from the chaff,* a wise king will decide who is wrong and crush them.

²⁷Your spirit is like a lamp to the LORD. He is able to see into your deepest parts.*c*

²⁸A king who is loyal and true will keep his power. Loyalty will keep his kingdom strong.

²⁹We admire a young man for his strength, but we respect an old man for his gray hair.

³⁰A beating can remove evil and make you completely clean.*d*

21 ¹To the LORD, a king's mind is like a ditch used to water the fields. He can lead the king wherever he wants him to go.

²People think that whatever they do is right, but the LORD judges the reasons for everything they do.

³Do what is right and fair. The LORD loves that more than sacrifices.

⁴Proud looks and proud thoughts are sins. They show a person is evil.

*a***20:21** Or, "An inheritance greedily guarded in the beginning will not be blessed in the end."   *b***20:24** Or, "A man's steps are from the LORD, and people don't understand his way."   *c***20:27** Or, "The LORD examines your breath and searches your deepest thoughts."   *d***20:30** The Hebrew here is hard to understand.

⁵Careful planning leads to profit. Acting too quickly leads to poverty.

⁶Wealth that comes from telling lies disappears quickly and leads to death.

⁷The bad things that evil people do will destroy them, because they refuse to do what is right.

⁸Criminals cause trouble wherever they go, but good people are honest and fair.

⁹It is better to live in a small corner on the roof than to share the house with a woman who is always arguing.

¹⁰Evil people always want to do more evil, and they show no mercy to people around them.

¹¹When you punish a proud person who laughs at what is right, even fools will learn something.[a] But a little instruction is enough for the wise to learn what they should.

¹²God is good. He knows what the wicked are doing, and he will punish them.

¹³Those who refuse to help the poor will not receive help when they need it themselves.

¹⁴If anyone is angry with you, give them a gift in private. A gift given in secret will calm even the strongest anger.

¹⁵A decision that is fair makes good people happy, but it makes those who are evil very afraid.

¹⁶Whoever leaves the path of wisdom will be on their way to an early death.

¹⁷Loving pleasure leads to poverty. Wine and luxury will never make you wealthy.

¹⁸The wicked must pay for what happens to good people—the cheaters will be taken in exchange for the honest.

¹⁹It is better to live alone in the desert than with a short-tempered wife who loves to argue.

²⁰Wise people save the nice things they have. Fools use up everything as soon as they get it.

²¹People who try hard to do good and be faithful will find life, goodness, and honor.

²²A wise person can defeat a city full of warriors and tear down the defenses they trust in.

²³People who are careful about what they say will save themselves from trouble.

²⁴Proud people think they are better than others. They show they are evil by what they do.

²⁵Lazy people will cause their own destruction because they refuse to work.

²⁶Some people are greedy and never have enough. Good people are generous and have plenty.

²⁷The LORD hates sacrifices from the wicked because they offer them for some evil purpose.

---

[a]21:11 Or, "Punish a rude, arrogant person and the others will become wise."

²⁸Witnesses who lie will be caught and punished. A careful listener will always be there to speak up.

²⁹Good people know they are right, but the wicked have to pretend.

³⁰There is no one wise enough to make a plan that can succeed if the Lord is against it.

³¹You can prepare your horses for battle, but only the Lord can give you the victory.

22 ¹It is better to be respected than to be rich. A good name is worth more than silver or gold.

²The rich and the poor are the same. The Lord made them all.

³Wise people see trouble coming and get out of its way, but fools go straight to it and suffer for it.

⁴Respect the Lord and be humble. Then you will have wealth, honor, and true life.

⁵Evil people are trapped by many troubles, but those who want to live avoid them.

⁶Teach children in a way that fits their needs, and even when they are old, they will not leave the right path.

⁷The rich rule over the poor. The one who borrows is a slave to the one who lends.

⁸Those who spread trouble will harvest trouble. In the end, they will be destroyed for the trouble they caused.

⁹Generous people will be blessed, because they share their food with the poor.

¹⁰Get rid of the proud who laugh at what is right, and trouble will leave with them. All arguments and insults will end.

¹¹Love a pure heart and kind words, and the king will be your friend.

¹²The Lord watches over true knowledge, and he opposes those who try to deceive others.

¹³A person who is lazy and wants to stay home says, "There is a lion outside, and I might be killed in the streets!"

¹⁴The sin of adultery* is a trap, and the Lord gets very angry with those who fall into it.

¹⁵Children do foolish things, but if you punish them, they will learn not to do them.

¹⁶These two things will make you poor: hurting the poor to make yourself rich and giving gifts to the rich.

Thirty Wise Sayings

¹⁷Listen carefully to these words from the wise. Pay attention to what I have learned. ¹⁸It will be good for you to remember these words and have them ready when they are needed. ¹⁹I will teach you these things now. I want you to trust the Lord. ²⁰I have written 30 sayings for you.ᵃ These are words of advice

---

ᵃ**22:20** *I have . . . for you* Or, "I wrote this for you earlier."

and wisdom. ²¹They will teach you things that you can know for sure to be true. Then you can give good answers to the one who sent you.

— 1 —

²²It is easy to steal from the poor, but don't do it. And don't take advantage of them in court. ²³The LORD is on their side. He supports the poor, and he will take from those who take from them.

— 2 —

²⁴Don't be friends with people who become angry easily. Don't stay around short-tempered people. ²⁵If you do, you may learn to be like them. Then you will have the same problems they do.

— 3 —

²⁶Don't promise to pay someone else's debt. ²⁷If you cannot pay, you will lose everything you have. So why should you lose the bed you sleep on?

— 4 —

²⁸Never move an old property line that was marked long ago by your ancestors.*

— 5 —

²⁹Skilled workers will always serve kings. They will never have to work for less important people.

— 6 —

23 ¹When you sit and eat with an important person, remember who you are with. ²Never eat too much, even if you are very hungry. ³Don't eat too much of his fine food. It might be a trick.

— 7 —

⁴Don't ruin your health trying to get rich. If you are smart, you will give it up. ⁵In the blink of an eye, money can disappear, as if it grew wings and flew away like a bird.

— 8 —

⁶Don't eat with selfish people. Control any desire you have for their finest foods. ⁷They might tell you to eat and drink all you want, but they don't really mean it. They are the kind of people who are only thinking about the cost. ⁸And if you eat their food, you will get sick and be embarrassed.

— 9 —

⁹Don't try to teach fools. They will make fun of your wise words.

— 10 —

¹⁰Never move an old property line, and don't take land that belongs to orphans. ¹¹The Lord will be against you. He is powerful and protects orphans.

— 11 —

¹²Listen to your teacher and learn all you can.

— 12 —

¹³Always correct children when they need it. If you spank them, it will not kill them. ¹⁴In fact, you might save their lives.

— 13 —

¹⁵My son, it makes me happy when you make a wise decision. ¹⁶It makes me feel good inside when you say the right things.

— 14 —

¹⁷Never envy evil people, but always respect the LORD. ¹⁸This will give you something to hope for that will not disappoint you.

— 15 —

¹⁹So listen, my son, and be wise. Always be careful to follow the right path. ²⁰Don't make friends with people who drink too much wine and eat too much food. ²¹Those who eat and drink too much become poor. They sleep too much and end up wearing rags.

— 16 —

²²Listen to your father. Without him, you would never have been born. Respect your mother, even when she is old. ²³Truth, wisdom, learning, and understanding are worth paying money for. They are worth far too much to ever sell. ²⁴The father of a good person is very happy. A wise child brings him joy. ²⁵Make both of your parents happy. Give your mother that same joy.

— 17 —

²⁶My son, listen closely to what I am saying. Let my life be your example. ²⁷Prostitutes and bad women are a trap. They are like a deep well that you cannot escape. ²⁸A bad woman waits for you like a thief, and she causes many men to be unfaithful to their wives.

— 18 —

²⁹⁻³⁰Who gets into fights and arguments? Who gets hurt for no reason and has red, bloodshot eyes? People who stay out too late drinking wine, staring into their strong drinks. ³¹So be careful with wine. It is pretty and red as it sparkles in the cup. And it goes down so smoothly when you drink it. ³²But in the end, it will bite like a snake.

³³Wine will cause you to see strange things and to say things that make no sense. ³⁴When you lie down, you will think you are on a rough sea and feel like you are at the top of the mast.* ³⁵You will say, "They hit me, but I never felt it. They beat me, but I don't remember it. Now I can't wake up. I need another drink."

— 19 —

24
¹Don't be jealous of evil people. Have no desire to be around them. ²In their hearts they plan to do evil. All they talk about is making trouble.

— 20 —

³Good homes are built on wisdom and understanding. ⁴Knowledge fills the rooms with rare and beautiful treasures.

— 21 —

⁵Wisdom makes a man more powerful. Knowledge gives a man strength. ⁶Get good advice before you start a war. To win, you must have many good advisors.

— 22 —

⁷Fools cannot understand wisdom. They have nothing to say when people are discussing important things.

— 23 —

⁸If you start planning ways to do wrong, people will learn that you are a troublemaker. ⁹Such foolish plans are wrong, and people have no respect for someone who laughs at what is right.

— 24 —

¹⁰If you are weak in times of trouble, that is real weakness.

— 25 —

¹¹If you see someone on their way to death or in danger of being killed, you must do something to save them. ¹²You cannot say, "It's none of my business." The Lord knows everything, and he knows why you do things. He watches you, and he will pay you back for what you do.

— 26 —

¹³My son, eat honey; it is good. Honey straight from the honeycomb is the sweetest. ¹⁴In the same way, know that wisdom is good for you. Wisdom will give you something to hope for that will not disappoint you.

— 27 —

¹⁵Don't be like a criminal who makes plans to rob those who are good or take away their homes. ¹⁶Good people might fall again and again, but they always get up. It is the wicked who are defeated by their troubles.

— 28 —

¹⁷Don't be happy when your enemy has troubles. Don't be glad when they fall. ¹⁸The Lord will see this, and he might be upset with you and decide not to punish your enemy.

— 29 —

¹⁹Don't let those who are evil upset you, and don't be jealous of them. ²⁰They have no hope. Their light will burn out.

— 30 —

²¹Son, respect the LORD and the king, and don't join with those who are against them, ²²because people like that can quickly be destroyed. You have no idea how much trouble God and the king can make for their enemies.

More Wise Sayings

²³These are also words from the wise:

A judge must be fair. He must not support some people simply because he knows them. ²⁴The people will turn against a judge who lets the guilty go free. Even the people of other nations will curse* him. ²⁵But if a judge punishes the guilty, then people will be happy with him, and he will be a blessing to them.

²⁶An honest answer is as pleasing as a kiss on the lips.

²⁷First get your fields ready, next plant your crops, and then build your house.

²⁸Don't speak against someone without a good reason, or you will appear foolish.

²⁹Don't say, "You hurt me, so I will do the same to you. I will punish you for what you did to me."

³⁰I walked past a field that belonged to a lazy man. It was a vineyard that belonged to someone who understood nothing. ³¹Weeds were growing everywhere! Wild vines covered the ground, and the wall around the vineyard was broken and falling down. ³²I looked at this and thought about it. This is what I learned: ³³a little sleep, a little rest, folding your arms, and taking a nap— ³⁴these things will make you poor very quickly. Soon you will have nothing, as if a thief broke in and took everything away.

More Wise Sayings From Solomon

25 ¹These are some more wise sayings from Solomon. These proverbs* were copied by servants of Hezekiah, the king of Judah.

²We honor God for the things he keeps secret. But we honor kings for the things they can discover.

³We cannot discover how high the sky is above us or how deep the earth is below. The same is true with the minds of kings. We cannot understand them.

⁴Remove the worthless things from silver to make it pure, and a worker can make something beautiful. ⁵Take the evil advisors away from a king, and goodness will make his kingdom strong.

⁶Don't brag about yourself before the king and act like you are someone important. ⁷It is much better for the king to invite you to take a more important position than to embarrass you in front of his officials.

⁸Don't be too quick to tell a judge about something you saw. You will be embarrassed if someone else proves you wrong.

⁹If you want to tell your friends about your own problems, tell them. But don't discuss what someone told you in private.

[10]Whoever hears it will lose their respect for you and will never trust you again.

[11]Saying the right thing at the right time is like a golden apple in a silver setting. [12]Wise advice to a listening ear is like gold earrings or fine jewelry.

[13]To his master who sent him, a messenger who can be trusted is as refreshing as a drink of cold water on a hot summer day.[a]

[14]People who promise to give gifts but never give them are like clouds and wind that bring no rain.

[15]With patience, you can make anyone change their thinking, even a ruler. Gentle speech is very powerful.

[16]Honey is good, but don't eat too much of it, or you will be sick. [17]And don't visit your neighbors' homes too often, or they will begin to hate you.

[18]A person who gives false testimony against a neighbor is as deadly as a club, a sword, or a very sharp arrow. [19]Never depend on a liar in times of trouble. It's like chewing with a bad tooth or walking with a crippled foot.

[20]Singing happy songs to a sad person is as foolish as taking a coat off on a cold day or mixing soda and vinegar.

[21]If your enemies are hungry, give them something to eat. If they are thirsty, give them some water. [22]This will make them feel the burning pain of shame,[b] and the LORD will reward you for being good to them.

[23]Just as wind blowing from the north brings rain, telling secrets brings anger.

[24]It is better to live in a small corner of the roof than to share the house with a woman who is always arguing.

[25]Good news from a faraway place is like a cool drink of water when you are hot and thirsty.

[26]Good people who don't stand strong against evil are like springs that have been polluted or pools that have turned dirty and muddy.

[27]Just as eating too much honey is not good, it is not good for people to always be looking for honor.

[28]People who cannot control themselves are like cities without walls to protect them.

Wise Sayings About Fools

26 [1]Just as snow should not fall in summer, nor rain at harvest time, so people should not honor a fool.

[2]Don't worry when someone curses* you for no reason. Nothing bad will happen. Such words are like birds that fly past and never stop.

[3]You have to whip a horse, you have to put a bridle on a mule, and you have to beat a fool.

---

[a]**25:13** *drink ... day* Literally, "as the cold snow at harvest time." This probably refers to snow or ice brought down from Mt. Hermon in Lebanon. [b]**25:22** *This ... shame* Literally, "for you will heap coals of fire on his head."

⁴⁻⁵There is no good way to answer fools when they say something stupid. If you answer them, then you, too, will look like a fool. If you don't answer them, they will think they are smart.

⁶Never let a fool carry your message. If you do, it will be like cutting off your own feet. You are only asking for trouble.

⁷A fool trying to say something wise is like a crippled person trying to walk.

⁸Showing honor to a fool is as bad as tying a rock in a sling.*

⁹A fool trying to say something wise is like a drunk trying to pick a thorn out of his hand.

¹⁰Hiring a fool or a stranger who is just passing by is dangerous—you don't know who might get hurt.

¹¹Like a dog that returns to its vomit, a fool does the same foolish things again and again.

¹²People who think they are wise when they are not are worse than fools.

¹³A person who is lazy and wants to stay home says, "What if there is a lion out there? Really, there might be a lion in the street!"

¹⁴Like a door on its hinges, a lazy man turns back and forth on his bed.

¹⁵Lazy people are too lazy to lift the food from their plate to their mouth.

¹⁶Lazy people think they are seven times smarter than the people who really have good sense.

¹⁷To step between two people arguing is as foolish as going out into the street and grabbing a stray dog by the ears.

¹⁸⁻¹⁹Anyone who would trick someone and then say, "I was only joking" is like a fool who shoots flaming arrows into the air and accidentally kills someone.

²⁰Without wood, a fire goes out. Without gossip, arguments stop.

²¹Charcoal keeps the coals glowing, wood keeps the fire burning, and troublemakers keep arguments alive.

²²People love to hear gossip. It is like tasty food on its way to the stomach.

²³Good words that hide an evil heart are like silver paint over a cheap, clay pot. ²⁴Evil people say things to make themselves look good, but they keep their evil plans a secret. ²⁵What they say sounds good, but don't trust them. They are full of evil ideas. ²⁶They hide their evil plans with nice words, but in the end, everyone will see the evil they do.

²⁷Whoever digs a pit can fall into it. Whoever rolls a large stone can be crushed by it.

²⁸Liars hate the people they hurt, and false praise can hurt people.

27 ¹Never brag about what you will do in the future; you have no idea what tomorrow will bring.

²Never praise yourself. Let others do it.

³A stone is heavy, and sand is hard to carry, but the irritation caused by a fool is much harder to bear.

⁴Anger is cruel and can destroy like a flood, but jealousy is much worse.

⁵Open criticism is better than hidden love.

⁶You can trust what your friend says, even when it hurts. But your enemies want to hurt you, even when they act nice.

⁷When you are full, you will not even eat honey. When you are hungry, even something bitter tastes sweet.

⁸A man away from home is like a bird away from its nest.

⁹Perfume and incense make you feel good, and so does good advice from a friend.

¹⁰Don't forget your own friends or your father's friends. If you have a problem, go to your neighbor for help. It is better to ask a neighbor who is near than a brother who is far away.

¹¹My son, be wise. This will make me happy. Then I will be able to answer those who criticize me.

¹²Wise people see trouble coming and get out of its way, but fools go straight to the trouble and suffer for it.

¹³When you make a deal with a stranger, get something from him and any other foreigners with him to make sure he will pay you.

¹⁴Don't wake up your neighbors early in the morning with a shout of "Good morning!" They will treat it like a curse,* not a blessing.

¹⁵A complaining wife is like water that never stops dripping on a rainy day. ¹⁶Stopping her is like trying to stop the wind or trying to hold oil in your hand.

¹⁷As one piece of iron sharpens another, so friends keep each other sharp.

¹⁸People who take care of fig trees are allowed to eat the fruit. In the same way, people who take care of their masters will be rewarded.

¹⁹Just as you can see your own face reflected in water, so your heart reflects the kind of person you are.

²⁰Just as the place of death and destruction is never full, people always want more and more.

²¹People use fire to purify gold and silver. In the same way, you are tested by the praise people give you.

²²Even if you pound fools to powder like grain in a bowl, you will never force the foolishness out of them.

²³Learn all you can about your sheep. Take care of your goats the best you can. ²⁴Neither wealth nor nations last forever. ²⁵Cut the hay, and new grass will grow. Then gather the new plants that grow on the hills. ²⁶Cut the wool from your lambs, and make your clothes. Sell some of your goats, and buy some land. ²⁷Then there will be plenty of goat's milk for you and your family, with enough to keep the servants healthy.

28 ¹The wicked are afraid of everything, but those who live right are as brave as lions.

²A lawless nation will have many bad leaders. But a smart leader will rule for a long time in a land where people obey the law.

³A leader who takes advantage of the poor is like a hard rain that destroys the crops.[a]

⁴Those who refuse to obey the law promote evil. Those who obey the law oppose evil.

⁵The wicked don't understand justice, but those who love the LORD understand it completely.

⁶It is better to be poor and honest than rich and evil.

⁷A smart son obeys the laws, but a son who spends time with worthless people brings shame to his father.

⁸If you get rich by charging high interest rates, your wealth will go to someone who is kind to the poor.

⁹When people do not listen to God's teachings, he does not listen to their prayers.

¹⁰Those who plan to hurt good people will fall into their own traps, but good things will happen to those who are good.

¹¹The rich always think they are wise, but a poor person who is wise can see the truth.

¹²Everything is great when good people become leaders, but when the wicked rise to power, everyone hides.

¹³Whoever hides their sins will not be successful, but whoever confesses their sins and stops doing wrong will receive mercy.

¹⁴People who respect others will be blessed, but stubborn people will have plenty of troubles.

¹⁵An evil ruler over those who are helpless is like an angry lion or a charging bear.

¹⁶A foolish ruler hurts the people under him, but a ruler who hates wrong will rule for a long time.

¹⁷A murderer will never have peace. Don't support such a person.

¹⁸Honest people will be safe, but dishonest people will be ruined.

¹⁹Whoever works hard will have plenty to eat, but whoever wastes their time with dreams will always be poor.

²⁰People who can be trusted will have many blessings, but those who are just trying to get rich in a hurry will be punished.

²¹It is wrong for a judge to support someone simply because he knows them. But some judges will change their decisions for the price of a loaf of bread.

²²Selfish people only want to get rich. They do not realize that they are very close to being poor.

²³Correct someone, and later they will thank you. That is much better than just saying something to be nice.

---

a **28:3** Or, "A poor person who takes advantage of beggars is like a hard rain and no food."

²⁴Someone might steal from their parents and say, "I did nothing wrong." But that person is as bad as an enemy who smashes everything in the house.

²⁵Greedy people might sue you in court, but those who trust the LORD are rewarded.

²⁶It is foolish to be too confident. Those who ask for advice are wise and will escape disaster.

²⁷Whoever gives to the poor will have plenty. Whoever refuses to help them will get nothing but curses.*

²⁸When the wicked rise to power, everyone hides. When they are defeated, good people multiply.

29 ¹Some people refuse to bend when someone corrects them. Eventually they will break, and there will be no one to repair the damage.

²When the rulers are good, the people are happy. When the rulers are evil, the people complain.

³A son who loves wisdom makes his father happy. One who wastes his money on prostitutes will lose his wealth.

⁴A nation will be strong when it has a fair and just king. A nation will be weak when it has a king who is selfish and demands gifts.

⁵If you give false praise to others in order to get what you want, you are only setting a trap for yourself.

⁶Evil people are defeated by their sin, but good people will sing and be happy.

⁷Good people want to do what is right for the poor, but the wicked don't care.

⁸Proud people who laugh at what is right cause problems that divide whole cities, but people who are wise are able to calm those who are angry.

⁹If someone who is wise tries to settle a problem with a fool, the fool will argue and say stupid things, and they will never agree.

¹⁰If you always try to be honest, murderers will hate you, but those who do what is right will want to be their friend.

¹¹Fools are quick to express their anger, but wise people are patient and control themselves.

¹²If a ruler listens to lies, all his officials will be evil.

¹³In one way the poor and those who steal from them are the same—the LORD made them both.

¹⁴If a king judges the poor fairly, he will rule for a long time.

¹⁵Punishment and discipline can make children wise, but children who are never corrected will bring shame to their mother.

¹⁶If the wicked are ruling the nation, sin will be everywhere, but those who live right will win in the end.

¹⁷Correct your children whenever they are wrong, then you will always be proud of them. They will never make you ashamed.

[18]If a nation is not guided by God, the people will lose self-control, but the nation that obeys God's law will be happy.

[19]Servants will not learn a lesson if you only talk to them. They might understand you, but they will not respond.

[20]There is more hope for a fool than for someone who speaks without thinking.

[21]Give your servants everything they want, and they will learn to be wasteful.

[22]An angry person causes arguments, and someone who is quick-tempered is guilty of many sins.

[23]Your pride can bring you down. Humility will bring you honor.

[24]You are your own worst enemy if you take part in a crime. You will not be able to tell the truth even when people threaten you.

[25]Fear can be a trap, but if you trust in the LORD, you will be safe.

[26]Many people want the friendship of a ruler, but the LORD is the only one who judges people fairly.

[27]Good people think the wicked are disgusting, and the wicked feel disgust for those who are honest.

Wise Sayings of Agur Son of Jakeh

30 [1]These are the wise sayings of Agur son of Jakeh from Massa. He says, "God, I am tired, so tired. How can I keep going?"[a]

[2]I am stupid. I am not as smart as other people are. [3]I have not learned to be wise. I know nothing about the Holy One.[b]
[4]Who has ever gone up to heaven and come back down? Who gathered the winds in his hand? Who can gather up all the water in his lap? Who set the limits for the world? What is his name, and what is his son's name? Do you know?

[5]You can trust this: Every word that God speaks is true. God is a safe place for those who go to him. [6]So don't try to change what God says. If you do, he will punish you and prove that you are a liar.

[7]LORD, I ask you to do two things for me before I die. [8]Don't let me tell lies. And don't make me too rich or too poor—give me only enough food for each day. [9]If I have too much, I might deny that I need you, LORD. But if I am too poor, I might steal and bring shame to the name of my God.

[10]Never say bad things about a slave to his master. If you do, he will curse* you, and you will suffer for it.

[11]Some people curse their fathers and refuse to bless their mothers.

[12]Some people think they are pure, but they have done nothing to remove the filth of their sin.

---

[a]**30:1** He says, "God, ... keep going?" Or, "This is his message to Ithiel and Ucal."
[b]**30:3** Holy One Literally, "the holy ones."

¹³Some people are so proud of themselves, and they look down on everyone else.

¹⁴There are people whose teeth are like swords and their jaws like knives. They take everything they can from the poor.

¹⁵Greedy people know only two things*: "Give me," and "Give me." There are three other things that are never satisfied—really, four things that never have enough: ¹⁶the place of death, a woman with no children, dry ground that needs rain, and a fire that will never stop by itself.

¹⁷People who make fun of their father or refuse to obey their mother should have their eyes plucked out by wild birds and be eaten by vultures.*

¹⁸There are three things that are hard for me to understand—really, four things that I don't understand: ¹⁹an eagle flying in the sky, a snake moving on a rock, a ship moving across the ocean, and a man in love with a woman.

²⁰A woman who is not faithful to her husband acts innocent. She eats, wipes her mouth, and says she has done nothing wrong.

²¹There are three things that make trouble on the earth—really, four that the earth cannot bear: ²²a slave who becomes a king, fools who have everything they need, ²³a woman whose husband hated her but still married her, and a servant girl who becomes ruler over the woman she serves.

²⁴There are four things on the earth that are small but very wise:

25 Ants are small and weak, but they save their food all summer;
26 badgers are small animals, but they make their homes
        in the rocks;
27 locusts have no king, but they are able to work together;
28 lizards are small enough to catch with your hands,
        but you can find them living in kings' palaces.

²⁹There are three things that act important when they walk—really, there are four:

30 a lion—he is the warrior of the animals
        and runs from nothing,
31 a rooster walking proudly,*
    a goat,
    and a king among his people.

³²If you have been foolish enough to become proud and make plans against other people, stop and think about what you are doing.

³³Stirring milk causes butter to form. Hitting someone's nose causes blood to flow. And making people angry causes trouble.

30:15 Literally, "A leech has two daughters." *30:31 a rooster walking proudly* Or possibly, "a greyhound" or "a warhorse."

Wise Words for a King

31 ¹These are the wise sayings that King Lemuel's mother taught him:

²I prayed for a son, and you are the son I gave birth to. ³Don't waste your strength on women. Women destroy kings, so don't waste yourself on them. ⁴Lemuel, it is not wise for kings to drink wine. It is not wise for rulers to want beer. ⁵They may drink too much and forget what the law says. Then they might take away the rights of the poor. ⁶Give beer to people without hope. Give wine to those who are in trouble. ⁷Let them drink to forget their troubles. Let them forget they are poor.

⁸Speak up for people who cannot speak for themselves. Help people who are in trouble. ⁹Stand up for what you know is right, and judge all people fairly. Protect the rights of the poor and those who need help.

The Perfect Wife

¹⁰ ª How hard it is to find the perfect wife ᵇ
   She is worth far more than jewels.
¹¹ Her husband depends on her.
   He will never be poor.
¹² She does good for her husband all her life.
   She never causes him trouble.
¹³ She is always gathering wool and flax ᶜ
   and enjoys making things with her hands.
¹⁴ She is like a ship from a faraway place.
   She brings home food from everywhere.
¹⁵ She wakes up early in the morning,
   cooks food for her family, and gives the servants their share.
¹⁶ She looks at land and buys it.
   She uses the money she has earned and plants a vineyard.
¹⁷ She works very hard.
   She is strong and able to do all her work.
¹⁸ She works late into the night
   to make sure her business earns a profit.
¹⁹ She makes her own thread
   and weaves her own cloth.
²⁰ She always gives to the poor
   and helps those who need it.
²¹ She does not worry about her family when it snows.
   She has given them all good, warm clothes.
²² She makes sheets and spreads for the beds,
   and she wears clothes of fine linen.

ª**31:10** *Verses 10–31* In Hebrew, each verse of this poem starts with the next letter of the alphabet, so this poem shows all the good qualities of a woman, "from A to Z." ᵇ**31:10** *the perfect wife* Or, "a noble woman." ᶜ**31:13** *flax* A plant used to make linen cloth.

²³ Her husband is a respected member of the city council,
  where he meets with the other leaders.
²⁴ She makes clothes and belts
  and sells them to the merchants.*
²⁵ She is a strong person,ᵃ and people respect her.
  She looks to the future with confidence.
²⁶ She speaks with wisdom
  and teaches others to be loving and kind.
²⁷ She oversees the care of her house.
  She is never lazy.
²⁸ Her children say good things about her.
  Her husband brags about her and says,
²⁹"There are many good women,
  but you are the best."
³⁰ Grace and beauty can fool you,
  but a woman who respects the LORD should be praised.
³¹ Give her the reward she deserves.
  Praise her in public for what she has done.

ᵃ**31:25** *She is a strong person* Or, "She is praised."

Word List

Aaron Moses' brother, who was chosen as the first high priest of Israel.

Abel The son of Adam and Eve who was killed by his brother Cain. Read Gen. 4:1–16.

Abraham The most respected ancestor of the Jewish people. Through him God promised to make a great nation and bless all the people of the earth. Read Gen. 12:1–3.

Achaia The region in the southern part of Greece where the ancient cities of Athens and Corinth were located.

Adriatic Sea The sea between Greece and Italy, including the central part of the Mediterranean Sea.

adultery Breaking a marriage promise by committing sexual sin.

agreement A contract or agreement from God to his people. The agreement that God gave his people at Mount Sinai was based on the law of Moses and became the most important for the Israelites or Jews. It replaced or incorporated all other agreements, such as that given earlier to Abraham. In the New Testament it is referred to as the "old" or "first" agreement. After Jesus Christ came and offered his life as payment for the sins of all people, God was able to offer a "new" and "better" agreement based on Christ's sacrifice.

Agrippa Herod Agrippa II, great-grandson of Herod the Great.

alabaster A beautiful kind of stone that can be carved.

aloes The oil from a sweet-smelling wood that was used to make perfume (Ps. 45:8; Prov. 7:17) or the bitter juice from a cactus-like plant that was used to prepare bodies for burial (Jn. 19:39).

altar A raised area, pile of stones, or table where sacrifices were offered as gifts to God. An important altar was the one in front of the Temple in Jerusalem.

Amen A Hebrew word meaning "That's right," "True," or "Yes." It is used to express strong agreement with what has been said.

ancestors Literally, "fathers," meaning a person's parents, grandparents, and all the other people that person is descended from. In the New Testament it usually refers to people who lived during Old Testament times.

anoint To pour a special oil on people or things to show that they have been chosen by God and set apart for a special work or purpose.

apostle A follower of Jesus chosen to represent him in a special way. During his earthly ministry, Jesus named twelve men as apostles. They had the specific responsibility and authority to represent him and proclaim his message throughout the world. Later, he appeared to Paul and gave him a similar commission, especially to non-Jewish people. Barnabas, Paul's missionary companion, and James, the brother of Jesus, are also called apostles, as well as several others in the New Testament. Some of these occurrences of the word, however, have the more general sense of "messenger" or "representative."

Aramaic The official language of the ancient Persian empire. Similar to Hebrew, it later became the common language of many Jews and is the spoken "Hebrew" referred to in the New Testament.

archangel The leader among God's angels.

Areopagus council A group of important leaders in Athens who served like judges.

army officer A centurion, a Roman army officer who had authority over 100 soldiers.

Asia The geographical area, sometimes called Asia Minor, that is now the western part of modern Turkey.

Baal A false god worshiped by the Canaanites. They believed he brought rain and storms and made the land produce good crops.

Balaam A non-Israelite prophet in the Old Testament who was hired by Balak, king of Moab, to curse his enemy Israel. Read Num. 22–24.

baptism A Greek word usually referring to the act of dipping or "burying" a person briefly in water, connected with their decision to change their life and turn to God, trusting him to forgive their sins. For people coming to faith in Jesus Christ it was an expression of their trust in his death as the sacrifice God accepted to pay for their sins. Described as a sharing in the death, burial, and resurrection of Christ, it marked the beginning of their new life in Christ as part of God's people. See Acts 2:38; Rom. 6:3, 4; Gal. 3:26–28; Col. 2:12, 13.

baptize To perform the act of baptism. See "baptism."

believer Where this word is marked, it is literally "brother," a term used by followers of Jesus Christ to refer to fellow members of God's family.

Bernice King Agrippa's sister, the oldest daughter of Herod Agrippa I.

Bethsaida A town by Lake Galilee that Jesus visited during his teaching ministry and where he performed many miracles.

boomerang A curved stick used in hunting birds. When thrown properly, it flies low to the ground and suddenly curves upward, often returning to the thrower. Literally, "a bow of throwing" or "a bow of deception."

Box of the Agreement Or, traditionally, "Ark of the Covenant." The special box kept in the Most Holy Place of the Israelite Holy Tent and, later, the Jerusalem Temple. It contained the stone tablets with the Ten Commandments written on them, which were evidence or "proof" of the agreement between God and his people. In some passages it is literally, "Box of the Testimony" or simply "Testimony." See Ex. 25:10–22; 1 Kings 8:1–9.

bridegroom A man who is getting married.

burnt offering A gift to God. Usually these were animals that were killed and completely burned on the altar.

Caesar The name or title given to the emperor (ruler) of Rome.

Cain The son of Adam and Eve who killed his brother Abel. Read Gen. 4:1–16.

Capernaum A town on the northern shore of Lake Galilee where Jesus often spent time and taught.

cassia The fragrant dried flowers of the ancient cinnamon tree that were used in anointing oil and as perfume.

chaff The seed coverings and stems separated from the seeds of plants like wheat or barley. Farmers saved the seeds but let the wind blow the useless chaff away.

chariot A small, two-wheeled cart pulled by horses and used in war.

Cherub angels Winged beings like angels that serve God, usually as guards around his throne or other holy places. Two statues of these beings were on the cover of the Box of the Agreement that represented God's presence. See Ex. 25:10–22.

Chorazin A town by Lake Galilee that Jesus visited during his teaching ministry and where he performed many miracles.

Christ Literally, "Anointed," a title that comes from the Old Testament ceremony in which perfumed oil was poured or rubbed on someone being appointed to a high office, especially that of prophet, priest, or king, to show that this person was chosen by God for that role. The Hebrew word is "Messiah," a title used for Old Testament kings and for the one God would send as prophet, priest, and king to bring people back to a good relationship with him.

church Literally, "assembly" or "community," the people who have been brought together as God's family through their common faith in Jesus Christ. The word often refers to a group of believers who meet together or who live in the same area, but it is also used to mean the worldwide community of all believers in Christ.

circumcise, circumcision Cutting off the foreskin of the male sex organ, which was done to every Jewish baby boy. It was a mark of the agreement God made with Abraham. Read Gen. 17:9–14.

Claudius The emperor (ruler) of Rome, 41–54 A.D.

cornerstone The first and most important stone of a building.

cross The wooden post that Romans used to execute criminals. It is a symbol of shame, suffering and death. Just as Jesus was willing to suffer death on a cross for all people, so he asks his followers to be willing to give up their lives for him.

crown Literally, "wreath," a ring of leaves or branches that was placed on the head of the winners of athletic contests to honor them. It is a symbol of victory and reward.

curse To ask for bad things to happen to a person or thing. As a noun it is a request for or warning about bad things to come.

curtain The curtain that separated the inner sanctuary (Most Holy Place) from the front room in the Tabernacle (See "Holy Tent") and in the Jerusalem Temple. It represented the spiritual barrier that kept people from entering God's presence. When Jesus died, the curtain was torn open (Mt. 27:51), which was a symbol to show that in the heavenly temple the way into God's presence had been opened. See Heb. 10:19, 20.

darkness A symbol of sin and evil, which characterize Satan's kingdom.

David Israel's greatest king, who ruled about 1000 years before Christ. Besides being a great military and political leader, he was a deeply spiritual man and a gifted musician, who wrote many of the Psalms. He made plans and arrangements for the building of the first Temple in Jerusalem ("the city of David"), which was actually completed by his son Solomon. The Scriptures said that a descendant of David would be God's chosen messiah (king), who would establish an eternal kingdom. For that reason, Jesus is sometimes called "the Son of David."

day A symbol of goodness and truth, which characterize God's kingdom.

dedication The act of offering something to God with a promise that it will be used only for him, or of setting apart something for a special purpose, which means it can then be used only for that purpose.

demon An evil spirit from the devil.

director This title is part of a phrase found at the beginning of many of the Psalms. It could also mean "performer."

divine greatness Literally, "glory," a word that refers to the special qualities of God. See "glory."

dysentery A very bad intestinal sickness that causes pain and diarrhea.

elders (in Revelation) The 24 elders in Revelation could be the great leaders of God's people under both the Old Testament and New Testament periods, combining the leaders of the twelve tribes of Israel and Jesus' twelve apostles. Or, they could be angels as leaders of heavenly worship, corresponding to the 24 groups of priests in charge of worship in the Old Testament.

elders (New Testament) A group of men chosen to lead a church. Also called "overseers" and "pastors" (shepherds), they have the work of caring for God's people. See Acts 14:23; 20:17, 28; Eph. 4:11; Php. 1:1; 1 Tim. 3:1–7; Tit. 1:5–9; 1 Pet. 5:1–3.

Elijah A very important Israelite leader and prophet who spoke for God during a 25-year period ending about 850 B.C. In the time of Jesus, the Jews were expecting Elijah to come again before the Messiah. See Mal. 4:5–6.

Elisha A prophet who served as an assistant to the prophet Elijah and carried on Elijah's ministry after about 850 B.C.

emperor The ruler (leader) of the Roman empire.

eunuch A public official or a servant in charge of the women in a ruler's household. Originally, a man who had been castrated so that he could not have sex.

Evil One The devil or Satan, the ruler of demons and enemy of God.

false prophet A person who claims to speak for God but does not really speak God's truth.

famine A time when there is not enough rain for crops to grow, causing people and animals to die without enough food or water.

fast To live without food for a time of prayer or mourning.

fathers Important ancestors of the Jewish people, especially the leaders of the tribes of Israel.

fawn A baby deer.

fellowship offering An offering to God that was also eaten by the person giving the sacrifice and shared with others, especially during New Moon celebrations.

Festival of Shelters A special week each year when the Israelites, and later the Jews, lived in tents to remember that their people wandered in the desert for 40 years during the time of Moses.

Festival of Unleavened Bread An important and holy week for the people of Israel and their descendants. In the time of the Old Testament it began the day after Passover, but by New Testament times the two festivals had become one. To prepare for it, the people threw out all their yeast and ate only bread without yeast for seven days."

first agreement The contract God gave to the Israelites when he gave them the law of Moses. See "agreement."

firstborn The first child born into a family. The first son was very important in ancient times and became the head of the family at the father's death. It can also mean a person of special importance.

fortress A building or city with tall, strong walls for protection.

frankincense Special dried tree sap that was burned to make a sweet-smelling smoke and offered as a gift to God. See "incense."

Free Men Jews who had been slaves or whose fathers had been slaves, but were now free.

gittith This might be a type of instrument, a tune, or a performer in the Temple orchestra such as Obed Edom from Gath (the Gittite). See I Chron. 15:21; 16:4–7.

glory A word that refers to the special qualities of God. Often it means brightness, referring to the way he appears to people. Sometimes it means majesty or power, referring to a kind of greatness that cannot be compared to anything in human experience. It can also include the ideas of honor, fame or respect, especially in expressions of praise.

God's kingdom The "reign" or "rule" of God over all humanity—a time of great blessing for those who submit to him by accepting Jesus as the Christ (appointed king), who represents God's kingdom on earth and was the perfect example of submission to the will of God. When people give control of their lives to Jesus, they become a part of God's kingdom and begin to enjoy the blessings he has promised his people from the beginning. (Note that in Matthew this term also translates the Greek phrase, "the kingdom of the heavens," which was used by Jews as a way to avoid saying the divine name.)

Gomorrah A city that God destroyed, together with the city of Sodom, because the people living there were so evil. See Gen. 19.

Good News In the Gospels this is usually the news about the coming of God's kingdom (see above) or its representative Jesus Christ. In other places it is, more specifically, the news or message of God's grace—that he has made a way through Jesus Christ for people to be made right with him and enjoy his blessings now and forever.

grace The love and kindness that God shows in his complete willingness to give people favors he does not owe them and blessings they don't deserve.

Greek A non-Jewish person anywhere throughout the first century world who was influenced by Greek language and culture.

Hades The Greek word for "Sheol," the home of the dead. It is often used as a metaphor for death.

Hermes A Greek god. The Greeks believed he was a messenger for the other gods.

Herod (1) Herod I (the Great), king of Judea and all of Palestine (40 B.C.–4 B.C.), Mt. 2:1–22; Lk. 1:5; Acts 23:35. (2) Herod Antipas, son of Herod the Great, tetrarch (ruler) of Galilee and Perea (4 B.C.–39 A.D.), Mt. 14:1–6; Mk. 6:14–22; 8:15; Lk. 3:1, 19; 8:3; 9:7, 9; 13:31; 23:7–15; Acts 4:27; 13:1. (3) Herod Agrippa I, grandson of Herod the Great, king of Palestine (37 A.D.–44 A.D.), Acts 12:1, 6–21.

Herodians Members of a Jewish political group who were supporters of Herod and cooperated with the Pharisees in finding a way to stop Jesus from teaching.

high place A place of worship usually on top of a hill, a mountain, or a man-made platform. Although high places were sometimes used for the worship of Yahweh, they are most often associated with pagan worship of false gods.

high priest The most important priest and leader of the Israelites or the Jews, God's people under the "old agreement." Under the "new agreement" the high priest for God's people is Jesus Christ. Read Heb. 7:11–8:13.

holy Set apart or chosen for a special use; especially, belonging to God or used only for him. Also, pure or perfect, worthy of God and fit for his service. In the New Testament God's people are holy because they have been made pure through Christ and, with the help of the Holy Spirit, keep themselves from sin and live only for God.

holy people Literally, "saints" or "holy ones," a term used in the New Testament to describe followers of Jesus Christ as God's special people. They are holy because they have been made pure through Christ and belong only to God. See "holy."

Holy Place The room in the Holy Tent (Tabernacle) and in the Temple that was used by the Israelite priests to do their daily service for God.

Holy Spirit Also called the Spirit of God, the Spirit of Christ, and the Comforter. In union with God and Christ, he does God's work among people in the world.

Holy Tent Or "Tabernacle," the special tent described in the law of Moses, where God lived among his people and where the Israelite priests performed their worship duties. It was often called the "Meeting Tent" because it was where the Israelites went to meet with God. It was used until Solomon built the Temple in Jerusalem.

hypocrisy Pretending to be good while hiding wrong motives.

hypocrite A person with wrong motives who pretends to be good.

hyssop A plant with fine branches and leaves used for sprinkling blood or water in cleansing ceremonies.

idol A statue of a false god that people worship. It can also mean anything that is more important to a person than God.

Illyricum A Roman province north and west of Greece.

incense Special dried tree sap that was burned to make a sweet-smelling smoke and offered as a gift to God.

Isaac The son of Abraham and one of the most important ancestors of the Israelites or Jews.

Israel Another name for Jacob (see Gen. 32:24–28) and for the nation God chose to accomplish his plan of blessing the world through the Messiah (see "Messiah"). The people of Israel were the descendants of Jacob's twelve sons.

Israelite Belonging to the nation of Israel (see "Israel").

jackal A kind of wild dog that stays where there are no people. Jackals usually hunt together in a pack.

Jacob Another name for Israel (see Gen. 32:24–28), ancestor of the people of Israel (also called Israelites and, later, Jews). He was the father of twelve sons from whom the twelve tribes of Israel descended.

Jeremiah A man who spoke for God about 600 B.C.

John the Baptizer The man God chose to tell people about Christ's coming and to prepare them by warning them to change their lives and by baptizing them (see "baptize") as a sign of their decision to change. Read Mt. 3; Mk. 1:1–11; Lk. 1:5–25, 57–80; 3:1–18.

John See "John the Baptizer."

Joshua The Israelite military captain who, after Moses died, took his place as the leader of the Israelites and led them into the land that God had promised them.

Judah One of the 12 sons of Jacob (Israel); also the tribe and, later, the nation named after him. Described as the "southern kingdom," it was made up of the Israelite tribes that occupied the southern part of Palestine, while the northern tribes were united into a "northern kingdom" known as Israel.

kingdom See "God's kingdom."

Lamb A symbolic name for Jesus Christ. It means that he was an offering for sin like the lambs that were offered as a sacrifice to God in the Old Testament.

law This usually refers to God's law as it is represented in the Mosaic Law, the rules he gave to the Israelites through Moses (See Ex. 34:29–32). Sometimes it may mean the principle of law rather than a specific law or set of laws.

leatherworker Or "tanner," a person who makes leather from animal skins.

leper A person who has leprosy. See "leprosy."

leprosy A very bad skin disease. The word in the text has a broad sense, which may include many different types of skin disease.

Levite Any of the men from the tribe of Levi, who helped the Israelite priests in the Holy Tent (Tabernacle) and Temple. In later periods some Levites worked for the civil government.

light A symbol of goodness and truth, which characterize God's kingdom.

locusts Insects like grasshoppers that could destroy a large crop very quickly. See Ex. 10. The law of Moses said that locusts could be eaten. See Lev. 11:21–22.

lots Stones, sticks, or bones used like dice for making decisions. See Prov. 16:33.

lyre A musical instrument with strings, like a harp.

Macedonia The northern part of Greece, where Thessalonica and Philippi were.

man of God Another title for a prophet. See "prophet."

manna The special food provided by God that the Israelites gathered daily from the ground during the 40 years they wandered through the desert. See Ex. 16:4–36.

maskil The exact meaning of this word is not known. It might mean "a poem of meditation," "a poem of instruction," or "a skillfully written poem."

mast The tall pole to which the sail is tied on a sailboat.

mediator A person who helps one person talk to or give something to another person.

Melchizedek A priest and king who lived in the time of Abraham. See Gen. 14:17–24.

merchant A person who earns a living by buying and selling things.

message See "Good News."

miktam The exact meaning of this word is not known. It might mean "a well-arranged song."

mill Two large, flat rocks used for grinding grain to make flour.

millstone A large, round stone used for grinding grain.

miracle An amazing act done by the power of God.

miraculous sign An amazing act that demonstrates the power of God.

Moses One of the most important leaders of the Israelites during the time of the Old Testament. God used him to give the people his law, which is often called "the law of Moses."

Most Holy Place Literally, "holy of holies," the most important room in the Holy Tent or the Temple, where the Box of the Agreement was kept. It was like a throne room where God sat as king of Israel and where the high priest entered into his presence on the Day of Atonement.

Mount of Olives A hill east of the city of Jerusalem from which a person could see the Temple area.

Mount Sinai The mountain located somewhere on the Sinai Peninsula (the eastern part of modern-day Egypt) where God gave his laws to Moses and the Israelites. Also called Mount Horeb. See Ex. 19 and 20.

Mount Zion See "Zion."

mustard A plant that has a very small seed but grows taller than a man.

myrrh Sweet-smelling sap from the bark of trees or other plants that was used for perfume and also to prepare bodies for burial. Mixed with wine, it was probably used to relieve pain (Mk. 15:23).

nard Very expensive oil from the root of the nard plant. It was used as a perfume.

new agreement The "better agreement" that God has given to his people through Jesus Christ. See "agreement."

New Moon The first day of the month for Israelites or Jews, which they celebrated as a special day of rest and worship. The people met together and shared in the fellowship offerings like those described in Lev. 7:16–21.

night A symbol of sin and evil, which characterize Satan's kingdom.

paradise A wonderful place of blessing, where God's people go when they die.

parchment Something like paper made from the skins of sheep and used for writing on.

Passover A very important holy day for the people of Israel and their descendants. They ate a special meal on this day every year to remember that God made them free from slavery in Egypt in the time of Moses. The name may come from the word in Ex. 12:13, 23, 27 that means "to pass over" or "to protect."

Pentecost An Israelite or Jewish festival celebrating the wheat harvest fifty days after Passover.

persecute To hurt, cause trouble for, or do bad things to someone, especially because of their beliefs.

persecution The act of persecuting or being persecuted. See "persecute."

Pharaoh A title for the king of Egypt.

Pharisee A person who belonged to a Jewish religious group that claimed to follow carefully all Jewish laws and customs.

philosopher A person who spends much time studying, thinking, talking, or writing about different ideas and trying to gain wisdom.

Pilate See "Pontius Pilate."

pillar One of the tall, carved stones used to hold up the roof of a building.

Pontius Pilate The Roman governor of Judea from 26 A.D. to 36 A.D. Read Lk. 23:1–3.

Preparation day Friday, the day before the Sabbath day.

prize See "crown."

prophecy A message or teaching from God. Also, the ability and authority from God to speak for him.

prophesy To speak or teach things from God.

prophet A person who speaks a message from God. Many of the books in the Old Testament are messages spoken or written by "the prophets," who were some of those God chose to speak for him. God often used dreams or visions to tell or show his prophets what they should say.

prophetess A woman prophet.

proverb A wise saying or short story that teaches a lesson.

quiver A bag or container for carrying arrows.

Rahab A dragon or sea monster that people thought controlled the sea. Rahab is often a symbol for God's enemies or for anything evil.

resurrection Being raised from death to live again.

Rock A name for God that means he is a place where people can find safety, like a high mountain or the strong wall of a fortress.

ruler of the evil powers See "Satan."

ruler of this world See "Satan."

Sabbath Saturday, the seventh day of the week and a special day for Israelites or Jews. By God's command it was set aside as a time for the people to rest and honor God.

sackcloth A rough cloth made from animal hair that people sometimes wore to show sadness.

sacrifice To offer a gift to God as an expression of worship, thanksgiving, or payment for sin. Also, the gift that is offered. In the Old Testament it was usually a special animal that was killed and burned on an altar. The Old Testament sacrifices offered for sins were symbolic of the perfect sacrifice that God himself would provide through Jesus Christ. Jesus gave his own life as a sacrifice to pay for the sins of all people. See Heb. 10:1–14.

Sadducees A leading Jewish religious group. They accepted only the first five books of the Old Testament and believed that people will not live again after death.

Samaritans During New Testament times, the people who lived in Samaria, the region north of Judea. They were part Jewish and followed the law of Moses, but the Jews of Judea did not accept them as pure descendants of Israel.

Samuel The last judge (leader) and first prophet of Israel.

Satan A name for the devil meaning "the enemy," or "the accuser."

scepter A special stick carried by kings to show their authority.

Scripture Part of the Scriptures or "Holy Writings"—the Old Testament.

scroll A long roll of paper or leather used for writing on.

seal A small stone or ring with a picture carved in it that was pressed into wet clay or hot wax to hold down the loose end of a scroll. It left a special mark, also called a seal, that was like a signature to keep anyone from opening the scroll except the right person.

Selah A word in the Psalms that was apparently for the singers or musicians, instructing them, perhaps, to pause or to get louder.

sheminith This might be a special instrument, a special way of tuning an instrument, or one of the groups that played harps in the Temple orchestra. See 1 Chron. 15:21.

sickle A tool with a curved blade for harvesting grain and other crops.

Sidon A non-Jewish city on the coast of Phoenicia (modern Lebanon).

sign See "miraculous sign."

silver coin Or *denarius*, a Roman coin that was the average pay for one day's work.

sin offering Or "purification offering," a sacrifice that was offered to God to remove impurities from sin and make a person fit to worship God.

sling A strip of leather used for throwing rocks.

Sodom A city that God destroyed, together with the city of Gomorrah, because the people living there were so evil. See Gen. 19.

Solomon's Porch An area on the east side of the Temple, covered by a roof.

Son of David A name for the Christ (Messiah) because it was prophesied that he would come from the family of David. See "David."

son of David Any person from the family of David. See "David."

Son of Man The name that Jesus most often used for himself. The phrase in Hebrew or Aramaic means "human being" or "mankind," but in Dan. 7:13–14 it is used of a future savior and king, and this was later understood to be the Messiah, the one God would send to save his people.

song of David This phrase (or a variation of it) is found at the beginning of many of the Psalms. It could also mean "a song dedicated to David."

special servant The Greek word is *diakonos*, which is usually translated "servant." However, in three places (Rom. 16:1; Php. 1:2; 1 Tim. 3:8–13) the service of those so described is associated with a local church, indicating that they were chosen to serve in some special way. Cf. Acts 6:1–6.

Spirit See "Holy Spirit."

synagogue A place in many cities where Jews gathered for prayer, study of the Scriptures, and other public meetings.

Syrtis A shallow area in the sea near the Libyan coast.

Tarshish A city far away from Israel, probably in Spain, famous for its large ships that sailed the Mediterranean Sea.

tax collector A Jew hired by the Romans to collect taxes. Tax collectors often cheated, and the other Jews hated them.

Temple The permanent building in Jerusalem that replaced the portable "Holy Tent" that was used by the Israelites from the time of their wandering in the desert to the reign of king Solomon, when the first Temple was built. Like the Holy Tent, the Temple was the center of Israelite worship, although provision was made for it to be "a house of prayer for all nations" (Isa. 56:7).

Ten Towns Greek, "Decapolis," an area on the east side of Lake Galilee that once had ten main towns.

thank offering A special fellowship offering that people gave to praise God and thank him for doing good things for them. A part of the animal being offered was burned on the altar, but the people ate most of it in a fellowship meal at the Temple. See Lev. 7:11–26.

the Way A symbolic name used by followers of Jesus Christ to describe their faith as "the way" to God through Jesus.

tomb A grave dug in a wall of rock or a building where a dead body is buried. It can also be a small building made to show respect for important people who had died.

torture To hurt or cause someone pain, often to force them to say something against their will.

traitor A person who turns against his or her own country, friends, or family and does anything to help their enemy.

tree of life The tree whose fruit gives people the power to live forever. See Gen. 2:9; 3:22 and Rev. 22:1–2.

tumbleweed A large weed that grows in a round shape and has short roots. When a strong wind blows, the dry weed is pulled loose and blown away.

tunic A piece of clothing like a long undershirt.

Tyre A non-Jewish city on the coast of Phoenicia (modern Lebanon).

vineyard A garden or farm where grapes are grown.

virgin A woman, especially a young woman, who is not married and has never had sexual relations.

vision Something like a dream used by God to speak to people.

vow A very strong promise that a person makes, sometimes to God and often using the name of God or something else known to be real or important.

vulture Or "eagle," a bird of prey that eats dead animals.

will The legal paper that people sign to give instructions about what should be done with their possessions after they die.

winepress A place dug in rock used to mash grapes and collect the juice for making wine.

wineskin A bag made from the skin of an animal and used for storing wine.

wise men Greek "*magi*," probably meaning pagan religious scholars who studied the stars to predict future events.

witchcraft Using magic or the power of Satan.

wonders Miracles that cause people to react with amazement and fear of God.

yeast The part of bread dough that makes it rise. Sometimes it is used as a symbol of bad influence.

Zealot A term used to describe Jews who had an enthusiastic desire or "zeal" to maintain the purity of Judaism—the land, the Temple, observance of the law and the traditions. This desire included a willingness to do whatever necessary to protect this purity against any outside threat, such as Roman control. This kind of spirit eventually brought about the formation of a group of Jewish patriots known as the Zealots.

Zeus The most important of the gods in which the ancient Greeks believed.

Zion The southeastern part of the mountain that Jerusalem is built on. Sometimes it means the city of Jerusalem, the people of God living there, or the Temple.

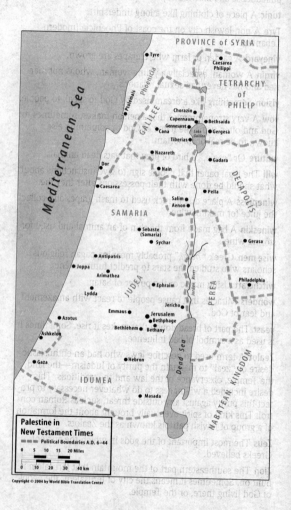

Mediterranean Sea

PROVINCE of SYRIA

Tyre

Caesarea Philippi

Phoenicia

TETRARCHY of PHILIP

Ptolemais

GALILEE

Chorazin

Capernaum
Bethsaida
Gennesaret
Cana
Tiberias
Lake Galilee
Gergesa

Nazareth

Gadara

DECAPOLIS

Dor

Nain

Caesarea

Salim
Aenon

Pella

SAMARIA

Sebaste (Samaria)
Sychar

Gerasa

Antipatris

Joppa

Arimathea

JUDEA

Ephraim

Jordan River

PEREA

Philadelphia

Lydda

Emmaus

Jericho

Jerusalem
Bethphage
Bethlehem   Bethany

Azotus

Ashkelon

Hebron

Dead Sea

NABATEAN KINGDOM

Gaza

Masada

IDUMEA

Palestine in New Testament Times

▬ ▬ ▬ Political Boundaries A.D. 6–44

0   5   10   15   20 Miles

0   10   20   30   40 Km

Copyright © 2004 by World Bible Translation Center